FIFTEEN
GREEK PLAYS

➤➤➤◄◄◄

THE THEATRE AT EPIDAURUS

FIFTEEN
GREEK
PLAYS

TRANSLATED INTO ENGLISH BY
GILBERT MURRAY, BENJAMIN BICKLEY ROGERS, AND OTHERS

WITH AN INTRODUCTION, AND A SUPPLEMENT
FROM THE 'POETICS' OF ARISTOTLE, BY

LANE COOPER

NEW YORK
OXFORD UNIVERSITY PRESS
1943

PREFACE

THE volume entitled *Ten Greek Plays* first appeared in the year 1929, and since then has been six times reprinted. Its success, and the demand for a slightly altered and substantially larger list of masterpieces, have led to an issue of the present book, *Fifteen Greek Plays*, where the new choice has in effect been determined by the votes of teachers who have used the original volume with classes. The Introduction to *Ten Greek Plays* has been retained without significant alteration. The list of useful books at the back has been increased by a few titles.

What it is hoped will be a novel and welcome addition is the Supplement drawn from the *Poetics* of Aristotle and from the De Coislin tract on Comedy, which 'Tractate' doubtless represents to some extent a lost section of Aristotle's treatment of the drama. At the outset, the Supplement is rather a comment on the earlier chapters of the *Poetics,* or a paraphrase of them. As I proceeded with the chapters, I found myself more and more dependent on my earlier expanded version (1913) of Aristotle's famous work; but the reader is to understand that the Supplement does not replace that earlier book. Yet it has, I trust, one merit in giving the less mature student an interpretation of the *Poetics* that for him is more in keeping now than any other with the fruit of recent studies of Aristotle's text.

The attempt made by the Supplement to draw these fifteen plays and the *Poetics* into mutual illustration of each other is no easy thing, and could not be made systematic without unduly swelling the present volume. The student of Greek drama should at all times keep in mind the principles of Aristotle, who was closer to that drama, and understood it better, than any extant critic since his time. If my interlarded illustrations from the plays serve to stimulate the classes who may use this volume to find illustrations of their own, my effort will be well rewarded.

For those who may employ this volume with small classes, and have access to translations other than those here presented, I should like to suggest an order of studying the plays that is different from the chronological sequence which large classes are likely to follow. First read in some good book like that of Haigh, *The Attic Theatre,* or Flickinger's well-known volume; then go through Aristotle, *On the Art of Poetry* (the *Poetics*); and then take up Greek dramas in the following order: *The Bacchae* of Euripides; the Orestean trilogy of Aeschylus; Euripides' *Electra;* then Sophocles'; Euripides' *Iphigenia in Tauris;* Sophocles' *Oedipus Rex;* the *Frogs* of Aristophanes; and, last of all, his *Plutus.* It has been no favorite with German scholars or American classes in 'English.' Yet if we keep returning to it, as did Ruskin, we shall find that both the central thought of *Plutus* and its elaboration by the poet offer much that will throw light on problems of our day. Thereafter I can see no reason why one should not read the plays in any order, or in a chronological sequence where this can be determined.

LANE COOPER

Ithaca, New York
   January 15, 1943

CONTENTS

[vii]

INTRODUCTION

THE air is pure and cool; it is a sunbright morning near the end of March, at Athens, and the year, let us say, 429 B.C. Three days ago began the great annual feast of the City Dionysia, most impressive of the festivals of Bacchus; an ancient image of the god, patron of the tragic and comic drama, was taken from his shrine, escorted in a grand and radiant procession to a grove in the country, and, after a day of feasting and merriment for young and old, brought back by torch-light to Athens to be set up in the orchestra of his theatre, there to witness the dithyrambic choral contests which ended yesterday, and the dramatic contests of to-day, tomorrow, and the day thereafter. Over one hundred years ago (535 B.C.) Thespis took part in the earliest competition of tragic poets that was authorized by the State. Seventy years ago (499) Aeschylus began competing; fifty-five years ago (484), at the age of forty-one, he first won the coveted prize, an honor that fell to him thirteen times, all told, before he died. In 484 Sophocles was thirteen years old, Euripides an infant of one year; when he was a child of four, the Greeks overthrew the Persians in the sea-fight at Salamis. Thirty-nine years ago (468) Aeschylus lost the prize to Sophocles, who then began to compete. Ten years later (458) Aeschylus, on his last appearance, won with the Orestean trilogy; he died in 456, the year before Euripides first had plays accepted for presentation. In the year 429, therefore, Euripides and Sophocles have been rival tragic poets for a quarter of a century. They will be rivals for a quarter of a century more with the watchful eye of Aristophanes upon them; we may suppose that he is in the audience to-day, a stripling sixteen years of age. Sophocles is now sixty-eight years old, still at the height of his powers; and this morning we may imagine that among the four plays he will present will be *Oedipus the King*. As a rule, on each of three successive mornings there are a satyr-drama and three tragedies; on the first two afternoons corresponding there will be two comedies, on the third, but one. In the days of Aeschylus, a group of three plays, a trilogy, might deal with phases of the same tragic story, and if the fourth play, the satyr-drama which then followed, dealt with that theme in a humorous way, we should have a tetralogy proper. Sophocles does not thus link his plays together; at times, following ancient custom, he does act in them, though taking but some minor part. In the dramatic competitions, then, three tragic poets have been, and are, engaged, as authors, trainers, and actors; and, similarly, five comic poets, each presenting one comedy. This will not, we predict, be one of the twenty occasions on which Sophocles is victor in tragedy, for the group of plays including *Oedipus the King* will be adjudged second to the group exhibited by Philocles, nephew of Aeschylus. Two years ago the *Medea* of Euripides fared even worse. There may be five judges for tragedy, as there are five for comedy; the selection of them is an elaborate affair, partly by lot.

Open to the sky, the great theatre of Dionysus lies in his precinct and near his shrine, on the southern slope of the Acropolis, below the Parthenon. The wooden seats, arranged as a vast amphitheatre, will accommodate thousands of spectators, or a good share of the voting population of the city, with a number of boys, probably some women, some of the better-educated slaves, and many of the visitors who throng to Athens at this season. At the winter festival of the Lenaea, when the seas are inclement, fewer alien faces would be seen, and a comic poet would feel freer than he will to-day to ridicule the foibles of the city. The audience is brilliant and lively, and critical; it will audibly reveal its pleasure or displeasure in the action or the actors. It is equally sensitive to false cadence and to expressions of impiety, and is suspicious of improbabilities in the sequence of incident. Though capable of mis-judging a play, and of attributing to an author the sentiment he utters as an actor in the imagined scene, it is the most intelligent audience a poet could hope for; or it will be such after Aristophanes and his fellows have shown on the comic stage what is out of proportion in Greek tragedy. For three generations this audience has been tutored by Aeschylus, Soph-ocles, Euripides, and their rivals. Many of the spectators have sung in a dithyrambic contest; many, in fact, have been mem-bers of a dramatic chorus, so that some actually have been trained by Aeschylus and Sophocles in the recitation and music of their plays. The influence of music and the drama has permeated the domestic and communal life of Athens.

Far beneath the topmost row of seats lies the orchestra, a circle 88 feet in diameter, where the actors and chorus jointly perform the play. Nearest to this circle, and to the statue of Dionysus, is the seat of his priest; in neighboring seats are the judges, other civic worthies, and notable visitors from other city-states. In the middle of the orchestra is an altar; at the rear, a long, low, wooden structure which serves for back-ground, for entrance and exit, and for other ends of stage-presentation.

A Greek tragedy or comedy, we perceive, is in the nature of a civic religious rite, celebrated in a building that is devoted to a god. True, if the impulse from Dionysiac worship was strong in the beginnings of the drama, the natural human im-pulse to imitate was stronger in the end. Yet the choral Attic drama seems never wholly to have lost its original character; herein, therefore, it differs from the modern secular drama, which soon enough forgot its mediaeval origins in the Mass, in the service for Easter. Aeschylus took tragedy from the market-place to the precinct and theatre of Dionysus, and comedy later followed thither. The modern drama left the cathedral for the market-place; ultimately, it found abode in a type of building that descended through Rome from the Greek theatre. Greek tragedy took origin, it seems, from the im-provising leaders of the early Bacchic dithyramb; it seems that the leader split off from the chorus to become an actor, the protagonist. In the chorus he was replaced by a new leader, who in turn was withdrawn by Aeschylus, and converted into a second actor. In various ways Aeschylus diminished the part taken by the chorus. The dithyrambic chorus was large, later numbering fifty; his dramatic chorus numbered twelve. And he drew plots not only from the tales of Dionysus, the satyrs, and Thebes, but from the entire epic cycle, taking 'slices,' as he said, 'from the great banquet of Homer.' Sophocles added a third to the complement of actors, an innovation that was adopted by Aeschylus, as in his *Agamemnon*, where indeed, for the last episode, one of the chorus may be temporarily a fourth actor; ordinarily three actors could fill a half-dozen or more parts. Sophocles, then, has subtracted a third person from the chorus, but, by a kind of restoration, has increased the tragic chorus from twelve to fifteen members. Moreover, in the time of Aeschylus, he developed scene-painting, and Aeschylus seems to have learned to do something for himself with that, too. Both these masters of a very complex art have taught the age much even about the affair of spectacle and outward presentation. Sophocles' weak voice will not let him take a leading part, as did Aeschylus at first, in his own plays; but, like Shakespeare and Molière of later days, he is his own stage-manager. He has trained his chorus and actors, and, with the help of a costumer, attended to their garb, masks, padding, and foot-wear. In the great theatre, his persons must be of heroic mould and stature. They have been carefully drilled in declamation, for they must be heard by an immense, and some-times noisy, audience. Apart, however, from the noise and bustle in the seats, the acoustic function of this outdoor theatre is well-nigh perfect. Careful modulation of spoken words and choral song need not be lost. The note of tragedy is not too often strident; more often its voices are tense, its tones are dreary. When the audience is quiet with pity and fear, a sigh in the orchestra may be heard in the topmost seats.

The meaning of the words will not be concealed by the music, for, in this art, poetry, music, and rhythmical action unite to assist the understanding, as they combine to produce one emotional effect. If the dithyramb proper, as it developed side by side with tragedy, came to be something like a modern oratorio, then tragedy itself, say *Oedipus the King,* has its nearest counterpart in the best modern opera. There is this difference, however, that in Greek tragedy music in the stricter sense was intermittent, being supplied by the chorus and one flutist. The actors spoke most of their lines, yet delivered some others in an intoned chant, and sang the more lyrical passages as solos, or in duet or trios; or, again, they joined with the chorus in a song, for example, of lamentation. Since we know very little about Greek music, we can only infer its beauty in the drama from the verbal and metrical beauty of the choral odes and other songs in the extant works of the tragic poets and Aristophanes; these dramatists were, in truth, the greatest of the ancient lyrical poets. And we can but partly conceive the effect of a play in which the chorus was a group of finished dancers. Their statuesque poses and measured evolutions had the greatest share in producing the whole amazing spectacle of an Attic drama. The orchestra, or place of dancing, was the centre of the entire wheel.

The dramatist, then, had to be poet, musician, and expert in pantomimic dancing as well, a Molière and a Mozart in one. Sophocles was all these things, and more; we have seen that he was also a painter. He and Aeschylus were the chief developers of this inclusive poetic art from a choral dance into a form more comprehensive than is drama or opera in our modern sense; in modern opera the poetic art is feeble. And in modern times this art receives virtually no support from the State. In the age of Pericles all the arts received public encouragement. Painting, sculpture, architecture, music, flourished with all the rest, but drama above all others. The efforts of the poets were directly favored by the government, and by wealthy citizens. In particular, the cost of staging the play, and of supplying and training the chorus, was borne by a private citizen who, unless he volunteered for the service, was chosen by lot, and obliged to serve as 'choregus.' Perhaps the choregus for *Oedipus the King* was unwilling, and a niggard, and the group of plays failed through his parsimony. The rich choregus Antisthenes, who knew nothing about the arts, was always successful in his contests because he never shirked any expense in the preparations.

A poet is often thought to be a man with a singular gift of diction, with a flow of metaphor, and with a knack of composing in metre. The diction and metres of the Greek drama need not be discussed at length in a volume of translations. Aeschylus, apparently more than any one else, elevated the style of tragedy above the level of the old dithyrambic plays. The language of Sophocles is clearer than his, with no loss of dignity or beauty; witness the ode on mankind sung by the Theban Elders in *Antigone*. The diction of Euripides is closer to the language of conversation. But perhaps most natural and beautiful of all is the utterance, clear and bright, of Aristophanes, when he is not distorting his medium for comic ends; he was also the most versatile metrist of antiquity.

But a poet is more than an adept in figures of speech and metrical composition. In a drama, from beginning to end he is framing speeches, which must be suited to the persons of his story, and must fit and promote the march of the action. The Greek dramatists learned much about the art of eloquence and dialogue, and of characterization, from the narrative poems of Homer with their speakers impassioned or subtle. Further, if Aeschylus did not know the Sicilian art of rhetoric at first hand, Sophocles would know it when it came to Athens. As for Athenian eloquence, all four of the great dramatists could have heard Pericles; and all but Aeschylus could have talked with Socrates as a man; all must have known some of the leading Sophists. All seem expert, too, in forensic speaking; Euripides certainly had to defend himself in court, and Sophocles and Aeschylus are said to have done the like. The great trial-scene in the *Eumenides* may have started the tradition about Aeschylus. But of course the dramatic contests themselves fostered the rhetoric of poetry. Actor-managers learned how to weave speeches through declamation, through training their players, and, as did Aeschylus and Sophocles, from each other. Euripides was self-centred, but could deliberately adapt and improve a line from Aeschylus; he was also infected with sophistical rhetoric. It is easy to find fault with him, yet it has always been hard to escape his hold upon our emotions. Aristotle praised his tragic quality, referring, however, not to the speeches, but to the unhappy ending of plays like *Medea*. The same critic thinks extremely well of *Iphigenia in Tauris* for its construction and emotional effect, and withal because the deed of horror is avoided.

It is Euripides rather than Aeschylus who should pass for the type of enthusiastic poet, giving utterance to his own thoughts and emotions. Aeschylus, according to Sophocles, did right as an artist without knowing why; but Aeschylus, after forty years of practice on the stage, is, in *Agamemnon*, for example, more adroit than is Euripides in *Medea*. With Greek reticence, he yet depicts the cold, hard, verbal sparring between unfaithful husband and faithless, murderous wife when they meet after a long separation. In this scene there is an element of that dramatic irony of which Sophocles is thought to be the first and great master, and Euripides master at times. Aeschylus is adroit also in making Clytemnestra a wily deceiver; a difficulty in the play is solved if we interpret her account of the fire-signals as a calculated lie. Euripides is the framer of poignant speeches, and of tragic fantasy; his own personality is not unified, and hence, though it intrudes itself into his plays, it is baffling to study. Sophocles, in devising speeches, as in other points of art, did right, knowing why. Although antiquity found some of his plays to be very inferior, to us his art at its best seems infallible. His heart and head operated in conjunction. The result has the outward finish of sculpture in marble; within, it lives and moves and glows. He seems to have had from nature what Aeschylus must labor for, the plastic ability to enter into one personality after another—an Oedipus, an Ajax, Creon, Antigone—for the ends of artistic representation. Aeschylus gave us men and women of colossal stature. Euripides depicted human nature as it is?

So said Sophocles, while affirming that he himself drew men as they should be drawn in tragedy. With acts of will that are distinct and intelligible, the characters of Sophocles are true to type, true to life, and self-consistent; whoever thinks him inferior to Shakespeare in the life-like delineation of personality should read both poets in the original or both in translation. In spite of the flaws which his personages must reveal if there is to be tragedy, we are struck with their nobility and their desire for justice. Antigone appeals to the higher law; Oedipus and Creon speak like statesmen. Low, petty, and ridiculous motives, bare egoism, pure malignity, are banished from the Sophoclean stage; thus the poet hits the mark at which his two great rivals generally aimed, and is typical of his age and race. The debasement of humanity, noticeable in recent American novels and dramas, will not be learned from Attic tragedy or comedy. Of course we have to reckon with comic foible as well as tragic error. But there is nothing painful or corrupting about the ludicrous characters in the *Frogs;* while the errors of Antigone and Oedipus are often to the modern reader concealed by their virtues. Note, however, that Antigone perishes, not because she buries her brother the first time, or even the second; she taunts her uncle who has power of life and death over her, and finally she is a suicide. Meanwhile, if the virtues of Creon are often overlooked, so also is the fact that his errors are tragic. Oedipus, again, is often considered the generous victim of fate. There is not a word about fate in Aristotle's remarks on tragedy, and hardly as much fatalism in Euripides as in Shakespeare. The characters of Aeschylus will and perform acts which they attribute to ancestral curses. It is Roman tragedy, with its modern offspring, that is fatalistic. In Sophocles' work, one should examine, at each point, which moves first, the hero or his fate. Young Oedipus kills an old man, whom he should have revered, in a dispute over the right of way, and thus unknowingly slays his own father. Unpremeditated murder, under provocation, was done in hot blood. Upon this act, which is anterior to the play, more light is thrown by the repeated bursts of anger from Oedipus in the play, and particularly by his violence to old men, of whom this tragedy has a large share.

Out of the choices of the agents grow dramatic actions. Creon decides that his nephew Polynices, dead foe of the State, shall lie unburied; Antigone, self-appointed instrument of the 'higher law,' resolves to bury the corpse of her brother. The situation is the more piteous because the clash of wills is between members of a family; and the results are deeds of horror. Of seven tragedies by Sophocles, four begin with words like, 'Sister, mine own dear sister!' and, 'Son of him who led our hosts at Troy!' In *Agamemnon* the husband with great effrontery brings home as concubine Cassandra, poor fatalist, now in love with him; here is the ultimate exasperation to guilty Clytemnestra, who would justify her slaughter of Agamemnon by dwelling on his part, ten years before, in the death of their child Iphigenia, at Aulis. By keeping the hateful paramour Aegisthus in the background, Aeschylus makes an ugly domestic situation, of four persons, less ugly. Scholars who do not observe these facts of life, idealized, miss the pity of it, and wonder why the dramatist brings in Cassandra at all. Some think that love has small place in Greek tragedy; oddly enough, they mean the wholesome romantic love that belongs to comedy, and forget the tragic love awry in Clytemnestra and Medea.

That the families concerned are of high estate, while a matter of less importance than is inward nobility, was important enough to the democratic Athenian audience. The stories are about ancient houses, the members of which associate with the gods, and have birth, wealth, power, and physical excellences, so that their tragic humiliation is impressive. In general they have imagination and eloquence with which to signify their glory and bewail its loss; how many of the tragic heroes seem like poets who have gone to wreck! The ever happy and fortunate Sophocles had a genius for representing this type of hero, winning prizes with his ruin.

One may divide the stories into those which deal with

Dionysus and those which do not. Perhaps the essential first step in Greek tragedy was taken when its themes widened out from Dionysiac associations with goat-like and equine satyrs so as to include all the story of Thebes and the whole body of Greek myth. At an early date, says Aristotle, the tragic poets took any subjects that came to hand. If so, they had an ample range of selection in the richest mythology any race has possessed. Later, he says, they narrowed down to the legends of a few houses. And that is the effect the surviving tragedies have upon us; the themes seem limited. We have seven plays of Aeschylus, out of ninety; seven of Sophocles, out of one hundred and twenty; eighteen or nineteen of Euripides, out of ninety-two. Of these surviving thirty-three plays, sixteen deal with aspects of the Trojan cycle, and six with the story of Thebes. But this preponderance is accidental; the choice of plays from Sophocles, for example, three on Thebes, three from the Trojan cycle, and one about Heracles, was made by grammarians at Alexandria for study in the schools. The fragments and titles of lost plays indicate a wider range than that of Elizabethan and classical French tragedy. There were themes from the other two great centres of Grecian story, the Calydonian Hunt and the tale of the Argonauts. To this last cycle belongs the *Medea* of Euripides. If other poets were as prolific and varied as he and Aeschylus, the tragedies of the great age must have numbered perhaps fifteen hundred or two thousand, drawn from many sources besides the four main ones we have noted. The comedies were not quite equally numerous. The eleven we have from Aristophanes, added to thirty-two tragedies plus Euripides' satyric *Cyclops*, give us forty-four surviving plays in all, or, with the fragments from Sophocles' *Trackers*, another satyr-drama, say forty-five that can be studied in some detail. The fifteen in this volume will fairly introduce the reader to the rest.

Turning to the comedies here included, we see that they throw light upon tragedy, which influenced them, and can be studied in that influence. Of primitive comedy we know little. The comic drama had developed far in Sicily before it made much progress at Athens. Here it first received support from the State in the year 486 B.C. The 'Old Comedy' began to flourish about the year 450, reached maturity with Aristophanes, and in his hands was turning into something else when he closed his career. Aristophanes, born about 444, first exhibited, at the Lenaea, in 427; produced the *Frogs* in 405 soon after the death of Sophocles, hardly a year after that of Euripides; and himself died some time after the *Plutus* was exhibited in 388, perhaps after 375. Before he was born, the use of three comic actors had been taken over from tragedy, possibly by Cratinus from Sophocles; and Crates had improved and universalized comic plots. But Aristophanes was the great developer of the Old Comedy, in the *Clouds* (423), *Birds* (414), and *Frogs* (405); his *Women in Council* (392) and *Plutus* (388) set a standard for the Middle Comedy; thereafter, in two plays now lost, or in the last of them, he struck out the type which ultimately matured in the New Comedy of Philemon and Menander. The variety and opulence of Aristophanes, his deep intuitions, and the strange, vivid beauty with which he invests comic ideas, make it difficult to speak of him in brief. Some knowledge of external nature belonged to the Old Comedy in relation to the Dionysiac cult of fertility, but in his amazing knowledge of it Aristophanes doubtless surpassed his rivals. The *Birds* gathers up all the poetry of its subject, and more than we have on birds from Chaucer, Shakespeare, and Wordsworth conjoined. Plays like the *Birds* and the *Frogs*, again, gave rare opportunities for elaborate and fantastic spectacle; an imperfect notion of the feathered Chorus may be had from certain remains of vase-painting. But doubtless what we chiefly now miss in the plays of Aristophanes is the music—in the *Frogs*, the music of both flute and harp. All told, the poet had many means of embellishment, and a genius not only for comic distortion. Moreover, an orderly element in the composition of his dramas atones for any seeming lawlessness in them. The metrical scheme, and the elaboration of parts like the *parabasis* and *agon*, offered special difficulties to the poets of the Old Comedy. These and other difficulties the good sense and good taste of Aristophanes turned to the advantage of his art. He takes credit to himself for diminishing the traditional element of phallic worship in comedy, and for limiting the indecency of the comic dance. In *Plutus*, jokes at the expense of well-known individuals have virtually disappeared. Indeed, in the *Frogs* the poet attacks no one; in a literary comedy he makes two great tragic poets attack each other. His choice of contestants for this *agon* marks his good sense. Even in more improbable situations he has an eye to probability. He laughingly draws attention to what is important and real. Like Molière, once having attained artistic maturity, Aristophanes virtually never makes a mistake in the comic art. His sure skill may be noted in his avoidance of actual pain as a comic motive, and in his way of leading us from familiar circumstance into the world of imagination.

His hold upon reality and his power of imagination make Aristophanes a great political economist and a great literary critic. Ruskin admits a heavy debt in his concepts of poverty and wealth to the *Plutus;* and the other comedies likewise have their subject-matter in the realm of political ideas. It is this, as much as anything else, that distinguishes even the *Plutus* from the later domestic comedy of Greece and Rome. And these political concepts are sound; by skilfully throwing things out of proportion Aristophanes reveals their true proportions. The *Birds* is his comic Utopia, the State as a whole. In the *Frogs* he anticipates a problem of the Platonic Utopia, the function of the poet in the State; this problem he displays in an action that travesties an entire Dionysiac festival.

In the *Persians* (472 B.C.) Aeschylus had celebrated the crushing defeat (480) by the Greeks of their Asiatic foe. The *Frogs* appeared when Athens was exhausted by her last effort in the Peloponnesian war, a few months before her overthrow at Aegospotami; within a year starvation forced the surrender of the city (404), and ended the war. The comedy, however, looks like an expensive one to produce; at all events the poet had an elaborate object to travesty if he was minded at the Lenaea to offer a mock City Dionysia. The parts of the festival are present, adapted to the scheme of a comedy. The wanderer Dionysus becomes the wanderer Heracles for a new harrowing of hell; his labor is to bring back a tragic poet to Athens, for the great age of tragedy has ended. On the way he first has a dithyrambic contest with the Frogs. Then comes the procession, by torch-light, of the initiated, and then the contest of tragic poets, duly closed by an official decision. With unerring intuition Aristophanes anticipates the judgment of all time respecting the three leaders. The *agon* of a comedy, however, is a contest between two opponents; for this he chooses Aeschylus and Euripides. They are extremes in a proportion, where Sophocles doubtless is the golden mean. The comic contrasts between Aeschylus and Euripides betray a profound literary criticism in which Aristophanes is a worthy precursor of Aristotle.

Plutus (388) is (save perhaps the undatable *Rhesus*) the latest extant play of the great Greek drama. In it the difficult features of the Old Comedy are hardly discernible. The structure is simplified, political satire is absent, local allusions are few, and the theme, completely generalized, is intelligible to all. *Plutus* was long the most popular of Aristophanes' works in England. This comedy of Wealth was given after Athens was poor, and depends less than the *Frogs* upon spectacular effect. In time, however, State and theatre recovered their well-being. In the latter half of the fourth century the old theatre was rebuilt, with Peiraic limestone. In this theatre, before an audience of perhaps 17,000 persons, the successors of Euripides and Aristophanes exhibited their tragedies and comedies; in it Aristotle (died 322 B.C.) doubtless studied the emotions of pity and fear, and mirth, in the spectators; and here the comedies of Menander (342-291) and his fellows were presented. Meanwhile theatres of the Attic type had begun to spread; the Romans built the like, even an additional one in Athens; and first and last such buildings have been erected in various parts of the world from the shores of the Black Sea to a sunlit spot in Berkeley, California. They are monuments to the effect of the Attic drama upon the mind of the civilized world.

LANE COOPER

AESCHYLUS
PROMETHEUS BOUND

⇛⇚

TRANSLATED
by
ROBERT WHITELAW

CHARACTERS IN THE PLAY

PROMETHEUS, *son of the Titan Iapetus and the Goddess Themis.*
The God HEPHAESTUS.
STRENGTH
FORCE } *ministers of the wrath of Zeus.*
The God OCEANUS.
Io, *daughter of Inachus, King of Argos; turned into a heifer by Hera.*
The God HERMES, *messenger of Zeus.*
CHORUS *of Oceanides or Sea-Nymphs.*

The scene is a mountain in Scythia.

ARGUMENT

After Zeus with the aid of Prometheus had established his supremacy among the Gods and the Titans, he became proud and cruel; he determined to destroy mankind, and to replace them with a better race. Prometheus alone withstood him, and aided mortal men by bringing fire to them from heaven, and teaching them numerous arts and crafts.

Zeus sent the god Hephaestus, and Strength and Force, to punish the crafty Prometheus for his disobedience, and for his presumption in thwarting the ruler's will. At this point the play begins.

PROMETHEUS BOUND

Strength. So to this world's-end region are we come,
This Scythian tract, this trackless wilderness:
Heed then, Hephaestus, thou, what charge thy Sire
On thee enjoined, to these precipitous cliffs
To bind fast with indissoluble bands
Of adamantine chains the caitiff there—
Who Fire, thy flower, wherefrom all arts have birth,
Stole, and conveyed to mortals; such the sin
That to the gods in heaven he must atone,
That he may learn the sovereignty of Zeus
To bear, and leave his man-befriending mood.
    Hephaestus. What Zeus hath spoken, Strength and Force,
      with you
Hath swift fulfilment, and its course is free:
But I—no heart have I, to chain a god,
My kinsman, in this storm-swept mountain-gorge.
Yet must I surely find the heart to do it;
My Sire's behest not lightly is contemned.
Of righteous Themis lofty-purposed son,
Reluctant, by reluctant hands of mine,
Thou must be riveted firmly past escape
To this lone peak aloof, by no voice cheered,
No form of man; scorched by the sun's bright flame,
Changed shall thy fair skin be; and thou'lt be glad,
When starry-kirtled night shuts out the day
And when the new sun melts the morning rime,
For still the burden of the present pain
Shall vex thee; who shall ease thee, lives not yet.
Friend of mankind, such recompense is thine,
For that, thyself a god, not reverencing
The anger of the gods, thou didst endow
With honors not their due the race of men.

[3]

So shalt thou sentinel this joyless rock—
Here standing, never rest, nor sleep, nor sit—
And many an outcry loud and vain lament
Shalt utter, moving not the mind of Zeus:—
Are not all rulers harsh, that newly reign?
    Strength. Enough: what boots this lingering fond lament?
The god whom gods abhor dost thou not hate,
Who trucked to mortals thy prerogative?
    Hephaestus. The bonds of kin and kindness fear to break!
    Strength. Well spoken: but to brave thy Father's will
What power is thine? Dost not thou fear this more?
    Hephaestus. Unfeeling ever and unmerciful!
    Strength. A soft heart helps not him: I counsel thee,
Spend not for nought thy barren sympathy.
    Hephaestus. O deep-detested handicraft of mine!
    Strength. Why shouldst thou hate it? If plain truth be
      spoken,
For what he bears, thy craft is not to blame.
    Hephaestus. Yet would that to some other it belonged!
    Strength. Nought is that irks not, save to rule the gods.
No one who lives is free, but Zeus alone.
    Hephaestus. I'll not gainsay thee, and the proof is here.
    Strength. Clap then the fetters on this fellow straight,
Nor let thy Father find thee loitering.
    Hephaestus. The arm-rings, lo, are ready, in thy sight.
    Strength. Take them, and round his arms with might and
      main
Strike with thy hammer, rivet to the rocks.
    Hephaestus. Apace, and not in vain, the work proceeds.
    Strength. Smite harder, clinch them fast, leave nothing
      slack:
A chink will serve him, though all doors be barred.
    Hephaestus. One arm at least inextricably is fixed.
    Strength. Clasp now the other safely: let him learn
His wisdom is but dullness, matched with Zeus.
    Hephaestus. Except of him, I shall not merit blame.
    Strength. Now, stubborn-fanged, an adamantine wedge
Drive through his breast and rivet with thy might.
    Hephaestus. Ah, I am grieved, Prometheus, for thy pain.
    Strength. Lingering again, and for the foes of Zeus

[4]

Grieved? Have a care, or soon thyself thou'lt pity.

Hephaestus. Thou seest an evil sight for eyes to see.

Strength. I see this fellow punished as befits.
Come, round his sides lash now the belly-girths.

Hephaestus. It must be done, thy needless chiding spare.

Strength. Chide thee I shall—yea, hound thee to thy work.
Down, and with gyves perforce enring his legs.

Hephaestus. Lo, how with no long toil the work is done.

Strength. Now with thy might smite home the linkèd fetters:
Thou hast no easy taskmaster to please.

Hephaestus. Too well thy accents and thy form accord.

Strength. Be tender-hearted thou, but blame not me,
That I am stubborn and implacable.

Hephaestus. The chains are round his limbs; let us be gone.

Strength. Here, if thou canst, insult; and short-lived men
Grace with the stolen honors of the gods.
Can mortals ease thee of thy load of pain?
Prometheus falsely art thou named in heaven,
Who rather of a counselor hast need,
How to unlock this cunning handiwork.

Prometheus. Bright empyrean, and ye wingèd winds,
Fountains of rivers, and the uncounted smile
Of the ocean-waves, and Earth, Mother of all,
And the Sun's orb, all-seeing, I invoke—
See me tormented by the gods, a god!

Behold me, what agony
Through the measureless course of the ages
Racked, I shall suffer;
I by the upstart Ruler in heaven
To captivity doomed and outrage.
Woe, woe is me!
On pain that is present, and pain to come,
Musing I moan—ah where,
Faint as a star that rises afar,
Shall an end of my anguish dawn?

Nay, but what words are these? All that shall be
Surely I know: no unfamiliar face
To me can sorrow wear, and I must bear
My destined lot composedly as I may,
Nor with Necessity wage feeble strife.

[5]

Yet how to bear in silence, how to speak
My griefs, I know not. Blessings, that on man
I lavished, have involved me in this fate,
And for that in a hollow fennel-stalk
I sought and stored and stole the fount of flame,
Whence men all arts have learned, a potent help.
So well my punishment befits my crime—
Pilloried in these chains—my roof the sky.
Ah! ah!
What sound and what fragrance float round me,
But sight there is none?
Sky-wafted, or of mortals, or of both?
Comes there indeed to this far mountain-top
One to behold my woes, or what desiring?
Ye see me here, a captive god, ill-starred;
Hateful to Zeus and banned by all
The race of the gods, as many as go
In and out of the doors of the palace of Zeus—
Hated and banned for my love of men.
What stir of wingèd creatures, hark!
Anear, around me hovers again,
Filling the air with a gentle sound,
Soft vibrations of pinions light?
How at a whisper I shrink afraid!
   Chorus. Fear not, friend, for a friendly band
With racing pinions swift
To this mountain-height we come—
Our father scarce consenting—
Downward wafted by rushing winds:
For a sound of smiting of iron pierced
To our inmost caves, and scared away
My virgin modesty of downdropt eyes:
So that my wingèd car I yoked,
And in unsandaled haste sped hither.
   Prometheus. Ah me, alas,
Daughters of Tethys, the teeming mother,
Children of Ocean, ye whose sire
The whole round earth
Enwinds with the coil of his sleepless flood,
Behold and see,

[6]

In what chains, rock-riveted,
On this sheer chasm's utmost crags,
A sentinel, whose post
None envies, I shall stand.
    Chorus. I see, Prometheus, and on my sight
A mist of horror fell,
With blinding tears surcharged,
Beholding thus thy body
Shriveling on these rocks, and bound
With chains of iron and cruel wrong.
For at the helm of Olympus now
New rulers sit; and old laws yield to laws
Newfangled, and the will of Zeus.
How is the might of the mighty fallen!
    Prometheus. O that under the earth he had hurled me,
Lower than Hades, the abode of the dead,
Down to the fathomless gloom of Tartarus,
There to endure fierce chains, indissoluble:
So neither a god nor any other
Should have mocked at my grief.
Now by the winds as a plaything buffeted
I suffer, and foes deride me.
    Chorus. Is there a god of heart so hard,
Who in thy sufferings exults?
Who rather aches not with thy pain,
Save Zeus alone? And he, resentful still,
Stiffening his stubborn heart,
Plagues evermore the children of the sky,
Nor will forbear, till that his rage
Be surfeit-sick, or one with stratagem
Surprise the guarded fortress of his power.
    Prometheus. Yet shall the day come, when even to me,
Me, fast bound in chains and misery,
Heaven's monarch shall cry for succor,
Who alone can discover the plot new-hatched,
That of scepter and empire strips him.
But with no honeyed spells of persuasion
Shall he bewitch me,
Nor by his harshest threats affrighted
Will I reveal it, till from fierce chains at last

[7]

He releases me, and for this cruel outrage
Consents to endure correction.
   Chorus. Thou dost defy thy doom indeed;
No throb of anguish bends thy will,
And overbold thou art of speech.
But through my heart a pang of horror thrilled,
And for thy fate I fear—
Where looms for thee across this sea of woe
Land thou shalt touch, and find relief?
A temper not entreated has the son
Of Cronos, and his heart no pity melts.
   Prometheus. Stubborn I know him—
Justice apart in his own thoughts harboring,
Humbled, submissive, yet shall his pride be—
So will I crumble it:
So will I bend him, wrathful, unpardoning—
Eagerly he with my eagerness vying,
Shall seek friendship with me and alliance.
   Chorus. Speak now, and keep back nought, but show us all:
What charge had Zeus against thee? What's the cause
With ignominy and pain he plagues thee thus?
This tell us, if it hurts thee not to tell.
   Prometheus. These things to me 'tis grief indeed to speak,
And grief to hide; do what I will, 'tis hard.
Among the gods when first dissension grew,
And mutual anger quickened into strife,
And some would fain hurl Cronos from his throne,
To wit, that Zeus might rule—the other part
Insisting, Zeus should never reign in heaven—
Then I to wisest counsels sought to win
The Titan-brood of Uranus and Gê,
Vainly; all prudent stratagems they scorned,
And fondly trusted in their pride of strength,
A forceful toilless victory to win.
Me had my mother Themis, mother Earth,
(One nature, but by many names addressed,)
Once and again forewarned, what end should be,
That not by deeds of prowess, nor with might,
The conquerors should triumph, but by guile.
And I these warnings sounded in their ears,

Does aesch mean to condemn From? (handwritten marginal note)

But they disdained, nor heeded what they heard.
Best then I deemed of courses that remained,
To range myself, with free consent of both—
I with my mother—on the side of Zeus,
And by my counsels in the black abyss
Of Tartarus, with all his following,
Lies the primeval Cronos. So have I
Served at his need the monarch of the gods—
Base ingrate, who my service thus requites,
For this is ever, as it seems, the vice
Of tyrants, to distrust the faithful friend.
Now to your question: on what pretext Zeus
Pursues me with his tortures, ye shall hear.
When the usurper on his father's throne
Was seated, to the gods forthwith he dealt
Honors, to each his own, and meted out
Empire, but took of hapless men no count,
Being minded to extirpate all the race,
And to create another in their room.
And none withstood his will, but I alone.
I ventured this; I saved them, I alone,
From sheer annihilation. Therefore now
My head is bowed beneath his chastisements—
Grievous to suffer, piteous to behold.
Who in my heart of pity gave first place
To men, myself found none: a ruthless hand
Corrects me so—for Zeus a shameful sight.
  Chorus. More hard than iron or the senseless flint
His heart must be, Prometheus, who beholds
Unmoved thy pain: I would that I this sight
Had never seen, and seeing my heart is grieved.
  Prometheus. It well may move compassion—of my friends.
  Chorus. Didst thou perchance transgress in aught beside?
  Prometheus. From thoughts of death I freed the minds of
    men.
  Chorus. What medicine finding for this malady?
  Prometheus. Blind hopes I gave them, in their breasts to
    dwell.
  Chorus. A priceless boon they have received from thee.
  Prometheus. Besides, with fire I have enriched their life.

[9]

Chorus. Have short-lived mortals now the flame-eyed fire?
Prometheus. Fire, that shall teach them many a helpful art.
Chorus. And is it for such crimes as these that Zeus
Gives thee no respite from thy cruel pain?
And has thy suffering no foredestined end?
Prometheus. No end at all, except when he shall please.
Chorus. How shall he please? What hope? Dost thou not
    see
Thine is the fault? But of the fault to speak
I loathe, and thee it grieves; talk we no more
Of this, but of thy pain oh seek release.
Prometheus. 'Tis easy, when our own foot 'scapes the slough,
To prate and lecture to one floundering there,
Neck-deep: but all of this I knew before:
With wide, wide-open eyes I sinned, I own,
And helping mortals to myself gat sorrow.
Yet did I never deem with pangs like these
On these aërial cliffs my flesh should waste,
Chained to this lone unneighbored mountain-top:
And now my present griefs weep ye no more,
But here alight, and hearken to my tale
Of coming woe, for I will tell you all.
Grant me, yea grant me, this: suffer with me,
Whose turn 'tis now to suffer. Vagrant still,
The wingèd sorrow flits from life to life.
Chorus. Not upon ears unwilling, Prometheus,
Falls thy petition:
Down from my air-borne chariot lighting,
And heaven, of birds the stainless highway,
Light I plant foot on this ragged rock-ledge:
All thy sad story
I fain would hear told to its ending.
Oceanus. Long is the road, to its end I have traversed,
Journeying hither to thee, Prometheus:
Well have the wings of my bird-beast borne me, *the machine*
Tamed by no bit, to my will submissive:
Doubt not but my heart feels for thy trouble.
So not only, methinks, as a kinsman
Duty constrains me;
Kinsman or other, I know not any

end of parados

1st episode.

[10]

Whom for his worth I should rate more highly.
Prove me and know, from my heart 'tis spoken;
Fair false words are not mine to utter.
Only withhold not, how I should serve thee;
Faster friend, I wot, in adversity
None than Oceanus thou shalt prove.
    Prometheus. Ha, what is this? And art thou come to view
My plight indeed? How didst thou venture, thou,
Leaving the Ocean-stream that bears thy name,
And rock-roofed caves self-built, a land to visit,
Whose stones are iron? Comest thou here to gaze
On my affliction, and deplore my wrongs?
See me, the friend of Zeus—a sight indeed—
Me that have helped the despot to his throne,
How by his plagues he bends me to his will.
    Oceanus. I see, Prometheus, and though thou art wise
I yet am fain to advise thee for the best.
Know thyself better, and amend thy ways;
A new behavior the new reign exacts.
But, if such angry and such bitter words
Thou'lt fling, perchance, though Zeus sits far aloof,
He yet may hear, and all thy trouble now
Shall seem but playing at sorrow to thee then.
Enough of pain: get thee a saner mind,
And seek deliverance from thy misery.
Old-fashioned seem perhaps these words of mine:
But in thy plight, Prometheus, all too well
Are seen the wages of a boastful tongue.
Unhumbled yet thou art, untaught to bend,
Of pain unsated, asking still for more;
Wilt thou be ruled by me, thou wilt not kick
Against the goad so hotly, seeing how harsh, *implies he doesn't approve of Zeus & but he bows to necessity.*
How absolute a monarch rules the sky.
And now I will go hence, and do for thee
All that I can to rid thee of these bonds.
Meanwhile from braggart speech keep silence thou.
So passing wise, dost thou not surely know,
That fraught with sorrow is an idle tongue?
    Prometheus. Lucky thou art to have escaped all blame,
Who shared, it seems, and dared all things with me.

And now let be, concern thyself no further:
For, do thine utmost, him thou'lt not persuade:
He's not persuaded:—nay, peer well and look,
Lest by thine errand thou thyself get harm.
   Oceanus. Thy friends how much more wisely than thyself
Thou dost advise, not words attest, but facts.
But do not from my purpose hold me back.
I promise, promise thee—that Zeus to me
Will grant this boon, to free thee from thy bonds.
   Prometheus. Indeed, I thank thee, and shall never cease;
Thy kindness is unbounded. But, I pray,
Take not such pains for me; thou'lt toil in vain,
Nor shall I fare the better for thy toil.
Make not nor meddle: keep thyself from harm.
I should not wish, being myself distressed,
To see misfortune light on all my friends.
Nay, for my brother's fate afflicts my soul—
Atlas, who at the confines of the west
Stands, and the pillar parting earth and heaven
On shoulders bowed, no dandled burthen, bears.
Yea and the dweller in Cilician caves,
Typhon, the earth-born, hundred-headed, fierce,
I pitying saw, quelled by resistless might,
Fell monster, who defied the banded gods,
And hissed forth slaughter from terrific jaws,
And from his baleful eyes grim lightnings blazed,
Portending ruin to Heaven's high-seated king:
But Zeus against him launched a sleepless bolt
Of headlong thunder, breathing fiery breath,
That spoiled his vauntings and his braggart threats,
And struck them dumb. For cloven to the heart,
Charred by the lightning, by the thunder dazed,
Marred of his strength, a maimed and outstretched form,
Hard by the strait sea-channel, caught and crushed
Beneath incumbent Aetna's roots he lies,
While stroke on stroke Hephaestus at his forge
Toils on the mountain's brow. Wherefrom shall break
Torrents of fire devouring with fierce jaws
The level tilths of fertile Sicily—
Such pelting fiery tempest unappeased

[12]

From Typhon's raging breast shall hotly surge,
Though scorched and calcined by the fire of Zeus.
But thou art warned, and needest not that I
Should teach thee; save thyself, that way thou knowest,
And leave me here tormented to endure,
Until the tyrant's anger be assuaged.

    Oceanus. Knowest thou not, Prometheus, that a mind
By rage distempered may with words be healed?

    Prometheus. Yea, if with timely soothing and with skill
The swelling grief be eased, not rudely pressed.

    Oceanus. What findest thou that is so much amiss
In prudence blent with boldness? tell me that.

    Prometheus. Superfluous toil and vain simplicity.

    Oceanus. So be it: such a fault I would not change:
To wear one's wisdom with a cloak is best.

    Prometheus. I shall be thought to have forgot myself.

    Oceanus. So am I plainly sent about my business.

    Prometheus. Pity of *me* might get thee in disfavor.

    Oceanus. What, with this youthful lord omnipotent?

    Prometheus. Ay, have a care that thou displease not him.

    Oceanus. Thy fate indeed, Prometheus, teaches this.

    Prometheus. Haste thee, depart, change not thy present
      mood.

    Oceanus. Thine exhortation spurs a willing mind.
My four-foot wingèd steed with eager plumes
Flaps at the level pathway of the air:
Gladly at home, safe-stabled, would he rest.

    Chorus. Thy cruel fate, Prometheus, I deplore:
My cheeks run down
Drenched with a dew of dripping tears
Poured from the fountain of my tender eyes:
In such unenvied plight
The elder gods endure
The overbearing will of Zeus
And self-made laws supreme.
A voice of mourning peals from every land:
The reign of thee
And of thy kindred they lament,
Its mighty fashions and its antique pomp:
And for thy bitter grief

All hearts of mortals bleed,
Who in the sacred neighbor fields
Of Asia have their home:
And dwellers by the Colchian shore, *geographical names*
Maidens, of battle unafraid,
And Scythian hordes that range
At earth's remotest verge
Round the Maeotic pool:
And Aria's warlike flower of men,
All they, whose fortress-city frowns
Near Caucasus, high-perched;
Wild host, whose battle-cry
Shrills 'mid the charging spears.
One other only have I seen,
Enduring, bound, such fate as thine
In misery and iron,
A Titan and a God—
Atlas, who bears
On straining shoulders evermore
Earth's huge unconquered strength
And the revolving sky:
And, timing with his groans, the waves o' the sea
Roar, and the deep moans under, and the black
Abyss of Hades mutters to its depths,
And founts of stainless rivers mourn his piteous plight.
   Prometheus. Deem not that I of stubbornness and pride
Am silent: with my thoughts my heart is wrung,
Seeing myself with insult overborne.
Yet to these upstart gods who if not I
Made absolute partition of their sway?
No more of that: it were a twice-told tale
To you who know. The miseries of men *exposition*
I will recount you, how, mere babes before,
With reason I endowed them and with mind;
And not in their disparagement I speak,
But of my gifts to memorize the love:
Who, firstly, seeing, knew not what they saw,
And hearing did not hear; confusedly passed
Their life-days, lingeringly, like shapes in dreams,
Without an aim; and neither sunward homes,

Brick-woven, nor skill of carpentry, they knew;
But lived, like small ants shaken with a breath,
In sunless caves a burrowing buried life:
Of winter's coming no sure sign had they,
Nor of the advent of the flowery spring,
Of fruitful summer none: so fared through each,
And took no thought, till that the hidden lore
Of rising stars and setting I unveiled.
I taught them Number, first of sciences;
I framed the written symbols into speech,
Art all-recording, mother of the Muse:
I first put harness on dumb patient beasts,
Obedient to the yoke; and, with their bodies
That they might lighten men of heavy toil,
I taught to draw the car and love the rein
Horses, crown of the luxury of wealth.
And who but I invented the white-winged   *good metaphor*
Sea-roving chariot of the mariner?   *long words, adjectival forms*
For mortals such contrivances I found,
But for myself alas no wit have I,
Whereby to rid me of my present pain.
    Chorus. Shame with thy pain is blent: forlorn of wisdom,
So do thy counsels err, like some false leech,
Who sickening straight despairs, of all his drugs
Finding not which has power to heal himself.
    Prometheus. More is behind, more wonderful to hear:
Skill and resource, contrived by me for men.
This first and foremost: did a man fall sick,
Deliverance was there none, or 'twixt the teeth,
Or smeared, or drunken; but for very lack
Of healing drugs they wasted, till that I
Showed them to mix each virtuous remedy,
Wherewith they shield them now from all disease.
The manifold art prophetic I traced out:
I first discerned what sort of dreams should grow
To waking truth; and made them understand
All doubtful sounds: what meets the traveler,
And what to flight of fierce-clawed birds pertains,
I sharply severed, these portending good,
And those for ill: habits beside of these,

Loves, hatreds, and companionships of each;
Plump organs of the victim, and what hues
In each express the favor of the god,
Fair-dappled shapeliness of gall and lobe;
Thigh-bones in fat enfolded and long chine
Burning, I to a scarce-conjectured art
Conducted men; and signs of darting flame,
Obscure before, I made bright-eyed with meaning.
These things are so: and 'neath the earth beside
The hidden treasure for the use of man,
Of brass and iron, silver and precious gold,
What one can boast he found ere I could find?
No one, I wis, who would not idly babble.
Nay, take the whole truth briefly, in a word,
All skill that mortals have, Prometheus gave.

    Chorus. Shower not on mortals blessings ill-advised,
Thine own plight not regarding. Hope is mine,
One day to see thee from thy bonds released,
Wielding an equal power with Zeus himself.

    Prometheus. Not these things thus is all-fulfilling Fate
Charged to accomplish yet: me myriad pangs,
Unnumbered woes, must bend, ere I be free:
So mightier far is Destiny than skill.

    Chorus. Who then of Destiny directs the helm?

    Prometheus. Mindful Erinyes and three sister-Fates.

    Chorus. And must all-puissant Zeus submit to these?

    Prometheus. He from their stern decree may not escape.

    Chorus. What is decreed him save to reign for ever?

    Prometheus. I may not tell thee this; seek not to know.

    Chorus. Methinks some awful secret thou dost hide.

    Prometheus. Of other themes bethink ye; 'tis no time
To utter this: but closely in my breast
It must be locked: this knowledge guarding well,
From bonds and cruel anguish I escape.

    Chorus. Never against my will be matched
The might of Zeus who governs all:
Nor let me blench from service of the gods,
With holy hecatombs outspread
Beside the quenchless Ocean-stream:
Nor let my tongue offend,

But in my inmost soul
Deep-graven let this thought abide—
How good to knit my life-days each to each
With hopes untroubled by a doubt,
While in such joyance clear my spirit basks:
But thee, Prometheus, racked
With anguish infinite,
I shudder to behold:
For Zeus thou dost defy—self-willed—
Revering overmuch the sons of men.
For tell me, O my friend,
How, rendering unto them
This thankless service, art thou helped?   *chorus unable to*
Can short-lived mortals mend thy plight?   *see lofty ethical*
Seëst thou not the feeble helpless state,   *of Prom.*
Shadowy as a dream, whereto are bound
The purblind race of men?
No human counsels shall avail
To pass the bounds of that great harmony
Which Zeus ordains.
So am I taught, Prometheus, by the sight
Of this thy ruined state.
So all unlike the strain
I now am moved to sing,
From that which erst I sang
About the nuptial-bath and nuptial-bed,
That chant of Hymen for thy marriage day,
What time thy gifts had won
My sister to thy side,
Thy bride Hesione.

2nd
Episode

    Io. What land, what people is here?
Whom shall I say that I see,
Rock-pinioned yonder,
Storm-buffeted?
To penance of a living death
What crime hath doomed thee?
Tell me, thou luckless one,
Where have I wandered?
Ah me, alas, unhappy!
Frenzied again as by the gadfly's sting,

[17]

The fatal herdsman with the myriad eyes,
The giant Argos, I behold—
The phantom of himself—
O earth, that didst receive him, hold him off!
See where with furtive gaze he stalks—
Whom even in death the earth contains not,
But from the shades returning
Me he pursues, the unhappy,
Over sandy leagues of the waste seashore,
Still famished, wandering still;
With his wax-plight scrannel pipe
Droning ever a drowsy strain.
Whither, alas, ah woe is me
Wandering whither afar—
When shall my wandering end?
What, O what was the sin in me,
O son of Cronos, that thou didst find?
Why hast thou doomed me thus to suffer
By the gadfly's goad still onward driven,
Weary of fleeing, distraught with dread?
Burn me with fire, or in earth entomb me,
Or fling me for food to the sea-beasts' jaws!
King, grant me my prayer, and grudge me not!
Enough I have wandered—
Wandered afar till my strength is spent;
And still from my doom escape is none.
Dost thou mark my speech—
The hornèd maiden hearest thou?

Prometheus. Surely I hear the maiden—Inachus'
Daughter—to frenzy by the gadfly stung;
Whose love makes glow the heart of Zeus, and her
The jealousy of Hera dooms perforce
World-wide to wander on her endless way.

    Io. Who told thee of my sire?
Tell me, the sufferer—who art thou,
That thou hast named aright
One wretched as thyself?
Nor is to thee unknown
The malady sent from heaven,
That me with goads of madness, woe is me,

[18]

Stings, and lays waste my life;
And hither with wild leaps,
Urged by sharp pangs of hunger, see me come:
So have the wiles of Hera and her spite
Constrained me—suffering like to mine,
Alas! what sufferers have borne?
But let me clearly know
What is in store for me to bear;
And, if thou canst, disclose
What remedy, what medicine, has my pain?
Speak, let the wanderer hear her fate!

Prometheus. All that thou askest, clearly I shall speak,
Weaving no riddles to enwrap the truth,
But plainly, as a friend should deal with friends:
This is Prometheus, who gave fire to men.

Io. Of all our human kind proved helper thou,
Ill-starred Prometheus—what hath earned thee this?

Prometheus. From telling of my griefs I scarce have ceased.

Io. And wilt thou not to me vouchsafe this boon?

Prometheus. What wilt thou have? I will hide nought from
thee.

Io. Say, who within this rock-rift pinioned thee!

Prometheus. By Zeus 'twas purposed, by Hephaestus
wrought.

Io. For what transgression dost thou thus atone?   *dramatic*

Prometheus. So much let it suffice thee to have learnt. *economy*

Io. Yet of my wanderings and my grievous ills
What time shall make an end, I fain would hear.

Prometheus. Not to know this were better than to know.

Io. What yet I must endure, spare not to tell.

Prometheus. Think me not jealous of this goodly gift.

Io. Why then dost thou refrain to tell me all?

Prometheus. I grudge thee not, but fear to vex thy soul.

Io. Take not more care for me than I desire.

Prometheus. Have thou thy will; and, what I speak, attend.

Chorus. Tarry awhile; let me have pleasure too.
To us, inquiring of her malady,
Her woeful wanderings shall she recount—
Then hear from thee what troubles are to come.

Prometheus. Thou art their brother's child; for this—for all—
Io, 'tis thine to grant them their desire:
For to lament and to bewail thy fate,
When from kind hearts that hear thee it may win
A pitying tear, is time not all ill-spent.
    Io. Your will is law to me; I must obey.
All that ye crave to hear, I shall relate
Not doubtfully; albeit I blush to tell
Whence on my luckless head the heaven-sent storm
Descended, that has left me thus misshaped.
Haunting my virgin chamber, night by night,
Came visions to beguile me while I slept
With fair smooth words: 'O maiden highly blest,
Be maiden now no more; to whom 'tis given
To mate thee with the Highest: thy beauty's shaft
Glows in the heart of Zeus, and for his bride
He claims thee. Child, despise not thou his wooing:
But to thy father's ox-stalls and his sheep,
To the deep mead of Lerna, get thee forth,
To ease the love-pain in the eyes of Zeus.'
All night and every night by haunting dreams
So was my sleep beset, till I took heart
To tell these nightly visions to my sire;
And he to Pytho and Dodona sent
His messengers inquiring many a time
How he might please the gods by word or deed;
Who brought back oracles of doubtful phrase,
Glancing from sense to sense and tied to none;
But at the last to Inachus there came
A peremptory word, with mandate clear,
To cast me from my country and my home,
At the world's end a wanderer far from men:
And, if he would not, swift from Zeus should come
A fiery bolt that should consume his race.
Not disobedient to Apollo's voice,
He drove me from his doors and banished me,
Not less against his will than mine: but so,
The bit of Zeus constraining him, he did.
Then was my feature changed, my reason fled:

[20]

Wearing these horns ye see, with frenzied bounds,
Pricked and tormented by the gadfly's sting,
To fair Kerchneia's stream and Lerna's shore
I hasted; and upon my traces still,
Of rage unslaked, with myriad eyes agaze,
The earth-born herdsman, Argus, followed hard.
Him unawares a sudden death o'ertook,
And reft him of his life. From land to land
Heaven's scourge, the unsleeping gadfly, drives me still.
My tale is told. What time has yet in store
For me to suffer, tell me if thou canst:
Nor pitying think with lies to comfort me:
False words I count of maladies the worst.
   Chorus. Ah keep her, keep her off!
I never, never deemed
That such strange words should wound my ears,
Nor that, with stab two-edged,
Such evil and intolerable sight,
Such woful sight of horror and of dread,
Should chill me to the heart!
O fate, O cruel fate!
The plight of Io shuddering I behold!
   Prometheus. Faint-hearted, full of fear, thou dost cry out
Too soon: be patient till the rest is told.
   Chorus. Ev'n speak, and tell the worst: for prescience clear
Of coming pain is solace to the sick.
   Prometheus. From me your former asking did ye win
Full lightly, when from her at first ye craved
The self-recital of her grief to hear.
Learn now, what suffering more is yet to be
By Hera's hate upon this maiden laid:
And, child of Inachus, if thou wouldst know
Thy journey's ending, to my words attend.
First from this place unto the rising sun
Turn thou thy face, and fare through lands untilled:
The wandering Scythians thou shalt find, who dwell
'Neath wicker roofs, high-set, on wains well-wheeled,
With bows equipped, death-dealing from afar:
Whom come not near; but, skirting with thy feet
The main sea's sounding surf, so pass their land:

[handwritten margin note:] Aesch. does not mention that Hera sent the gadfly.

Upon thy left hand dwell the Chalybes,
A people skilled in smith-craft; these avoid;
No gentle race, to strangers most unkind.
A violent river, next, and rightly named,
Seek not to cross, for crossing is there none,
Till ev'n to Caucasus' high mountain-ridge
Thou comest, whence the river spouts its might,
Ev'n from the mountain's brow. So shalt thou climb
Its heaven-kissing summit, and descend
Into a southward road, where thou shalt see
The Amazon host man-hating, who shall dwell
At Themiscyra by Thermodon's stream
Hereafter, near the Salmydessian jaws
Of that fierce sea, whose rugged portals gape,
Inhospitable to seamen, and to ships
A stern stepdame: these gladly will conduct thee,
Even to the neck of that Cimmerian shore,
Whose foreland well nigh shuts the strait sea-gates
Of the Maeotic pool: thence boldly strike
O'er the Maeotic channel; after-times
The memory of thy crossing shall not lose,
But name that strait the Ox-ford evermore:
And so to Europe bid farewell—henceforth
'Tis Asia's soil thou treadest. Deem ye not
That this proud lord of heaven on great and small
Tramples alike? For this poor mortal maid,
Enamored of her love, his godhead dooms
To wander thus. Thy most imperious wooer,
Maiden, thou well mayst rue. What I have told,
Deem that the prelude hardly hast thou heard.
    Io. Woe's me, alas, alas!
    Prometheus. Dost thou cry out at this, and make thy moan?
What wilt thou do, when thou shalt hear the rest?
    Chorus. And is there more indeed that thou wilt tell?
    Prometheus. Of mortal anguish a tempestuous sea.
    Io. What boots it then to live? Were it not better
From this hard rock to fling myself outright,
That dashed to earth I might of all my toil
Have riddance? Better surely once to die
Than all my days to be afflicted thus.

Prometheus. How hardly wouldst thou bear what I endure,
For whom it is appointed not to die!
For death had been release from misery:
But now to me of suffering is ordained
No end, till from his empire Zeus be hurled.
    Io. Shall Zeus indeed be downcast from his throne? *Zeus Salonius*
    Prometheus. To see that day methinks thou wouldst rejoice.
    Io. How could I but rejoice, whom he has wronged!
    Prometheus. Content thee then to know that so it is.
    Io. And who shall strip him of his sovereignty?
    Prometheus. By his own foolish counsels he shall fall.
    Io. Say, if it harms not, how shall these things be?
    Prometheus. A marriage he will make that he shall rue. *Thetis*
    Io. With goddess or with mortal—canst thou tell?
    Prometheus. What skills with whom? This may not be divulged.
    Io. Is it his wife who hurls him from his throne?
    Prometheus. Her child shall be one mightier than his sire.
    Io. Has he no means that shall avert this fate?
    Prometheus. None, but an if I from these chains be loosed.
    Io. Who then shall loose thee in despite of Zeus?
    Prometheus. One of thine own descendants he shall be.
    Io. How? shall a child of mine deliver thee?
    Prometheus. Ten generations hence, and three beside.
    Io. Now hard to read the prophecy becomes.
    Prometheus. And of thine own fate ask not thou to know.
    Io. Deny me not, I pray, this promised boon.
    Prometheus. Of two disclosures I will grant thee one.
    Io. Say, what are they? Name them, and let me choose.
    Prometheus. And so thou shalt. Choose then, wilt thou be told
Thy woes to come, or my deliverer?
    Chorus. One of these boons to her, and one to me,
Be pleased to grant: withhold not thou thy speech,
But of her future wanderings let her hear;
By whom thou'rt freed, tell *me*—for this I crave.
    Prometheus. What ye so much desire, I'll not gainsay,
But tell you all your asking. First to thee,
Io, thy hunted course will I unfold:
Grave it on mindful tablets of thy heart.

Once past the stream that parts the continents,
To the sun's fiery rising bend thy steps,
Beyond the booming sea, until thou comest
Unto Kisthene's plains, the Gorgons' home,
Where Phorcys' daughters dwell, gray maidens three,
Swan-plumed with eld, and share among themselves
One eye, one tooth for all, whom with his rays
The sun beholds not nor the moon by night;
And hard by these their sisters, other three,
With snaky locks, winged Gorgons, loathed by men,
Whom none of mortal race shall see and live.
Grim guardians of the place, of these beware:
Nor these alone; another monstrous sight,
Griffins, the fierce unbarking hounds of Zeus,
Sharp-beaked, avoid; and thou shalt see—beside
The river of Pluto named, whose sands are gold—
The one-eyed Arimaspian horseman-host;
These come not near. Thence to a dusky race,
By the sun's fount, in that remotest land,
Where flows the Aethiop river, thou shalt fare.
Follow its course along, until thou comest
Unto the sheer descent, where Nilus pours
Fresh from the Bybline mount his sacred stream,
And follow still his leading to the end:
In that three-cornered land his mouths enclose
'Tis destined for thy children and for thee,
Far from thy country's soil, new homes to plant.
But, if my words sound stammering and obscure,
Ask me again, until the whole is clear:
Leisure is mine, far more than I could wish.
    Chorus. If of her troublous wandering aught to her,
Forgotten or untold, thou still wouldst tell,
Speak; but, if this is all, the boon we crave
(Methinks thou dost remember) grant to us.
    Prometheus. Her journey to its ending she has heard:
Yet, to assure her that my words are sooth,
Her toil I will recount, ere she came hither:
This shall attest that what I speak I know.
To tell the whole were tedious: this I spare,
And of thy wanderings hasten to the end.

To the Molossian plains when thou hadst come,
And to Dodona's rock-ridge, to the seat
And sacred oracle of Thesprotian Zeus,
Famed for its marvel of the talking oaks,
That with clear voice and nowise doubtfully
Hailed thee (sounds this familiar to thine ears?)
The glorious bride of Zeus in days to come,
Thence in thy frenzied course beside the waves
To the great gulf of Rhea thou didst haste:
Wherefrom, poor storm-vexed wanderer, now thou'rt driven.
But through all coming time, of this be sure—
Thy name shall cleave to that Ionian bay,
And of thy journeying keep the world in mind.
Let this convince thee that my thoughts indeed
More than to sight is palpable can see.
Now will I, for her sake, and yours no less,
Re-seek the footprints of my former speech.
Upon a mudbank in the mouths of Nile,
Last of the land, a town, Canopus, lies:
There shall the hand of Zeus, with soft caress
Upon thee laid, restore thee to thy mind:
And thou shalt bear, named of his fruitful touch,
A son, swart Epaphus, whom all that land,
By the broad Nile-stream watered, shall enrich:
But his descendants in the fifth degree,
A band of fifty maidens, shall return
Unwillingly to Argos, loath to wed
With kinsmen and with cousins; who, as hawks
That hold in chase a flight of timorous doves,
Pursuing marriage that they most should shun,
Winged with desire, shall follow; but the god
Allows them not their brides: slain by the swords
Of women boldened to the midnight crime—
On Argive soil such welcome shall they find,
And in each wifely hand the two-edged steel
Shall reek empurpled with a husband's blood:
May to my foes befall such nuptial rites!
One maid alone, by softer passion swayed,
Steels not her purpose to the fell exploit,
But lets her lover live, and makes her choice,

A weakling, not a murderess, to be called.
The royal line of Argos springs from her.
Time fails to tell the story to its close:
But of her strain one valiant shall be born,
Hercules And famous with the bow; he from these ills
Shall loose me. Thus the Titaness, my mother,
Primeval Themis, prophesied to me,
But of the ways and means too long it were
To tell thee, and it profits not to know.

    Io. Alas! woe worth the day!
Again a thrill, a spasm of frenzy
Shoots through me, soul-distracting:
The unforged goad of the gadfly
Stings me afresh; and my seated heart
Knocks at my ribs for fear,
My sight swims, and my senses reel;
And a frantic gust of madness sweeps me
Wide of the course, of my tongue no mistress:
My words in a turbid stream beat idly
Against a resistless tide of ruin—

Io exit The waves of a doom my soul abhors.

2nd Stasimon   *Chorus.* Wise of a truth, most wise was he,
Who first conceived in his mind, and spake with his tongue
    this word,
That to mate with equals is best by far,
And neither with those whom wealth has spoiled,

Io's fate suggests idea that one should not marry above one's station. Nor yet with those whom their birth elates,
Should the mean and humble aspire to wed.
Never, O never, ye puissant Fates,
In the arms of Zeus may ye see me couched:
Nor to any one of the gods in heaven
May I as a bride be brought.

For Io's maiden state,
Unblest with a mortal's love,
I tremble when I see,
Blighted and banned with Hera's curse,
And the homeless pain of a hunted life.
The thought of marriage with my peers
Is the safe thought for me:
On me may no high god

Bend his inevitable gaze;
The unequal war that none can wage
Let me not wage;
The hope that issues in despair.
Let me not know:
What should I do, the helpless that I am?
How from the will of Zeus I should escape
I cannot see.

    Prometheus. Yet Zeus, methinks, for all his stubborn pride,
Shall be abased: such marriage he intends—
A marriage that shall hurl him from his power
To nothingness for ever: and then at last
Shall be fulfilled in full the curse of Cronos,
His sire, when from his ancient throne he fell:
And none of all the gods but I alone
Can teach him how this ruin to avert:
To me the way is known. Now, if he can,
To heaven's high noises trusting, let him sit,
And shake his fiery bolt, and feel no fear.
His weapons shall not save him, not to fall
A shameful and intolerable fall,
So fierce a champion now against himself,
Prodigious, irresistible, he arms;
Who with strange fire his lightnings shall outblaze,
And drown his thunder with a mightier din,
Yea, shatter in Poseidon's hand the spear,
His trident, the earth-shaking ocean-bane.
So stumbling on disaster he shall find
How far beneath the tyrant sits the slave.
    Chorus. Thy wish is father to thy bitter speech.
    Prometheus. What I *shall* see, and *would* see, that I speak.
    Chorus. Must we believe that one shall master Zeus?
    Prometheus. A heavier yoke than this his neck shall bear.
    Chorus. Dost thou not fear to utter words so bold?
    Prometheus. What should I fear, whose fate is not to die?
    Chorus. Ev'n fiercer pains than these he may inflict.
    Prometheus. So let him: for the worst I am prepared.
    Chorus. To bow to the inevitable is best.
    Prometheus. Worship and crouch and flatter those in power!
Not at a pin's fee do I value Zeus.

Let him this brief while overbear, and work
His sovereign will: not long he rules the sky.
But yonder see his lackey, who performs
Nimbly the errands of the upstart god:
Doubtless he comes fresh mischief to announce.

Hermes. Wise of thy wit, and bitter of thy tongue,
Thou biter that art bit, who short-lived men
Didst grace with honors of the slighted gods—
Thou pilferer of fire—I speak to thee:
My sire will have thee say, what marriage 'tis,
Whereof thou bragg'st, that ousts him from his sway;
And see thou tell me not a riddling tale.
Speak out, and nothing hide: I have no mind,
Prometheus, to come hither twice: and Zeus
Will not be trifled with, thou art advised.

Prometheus. Great swelling words thou speakest, and thy
  pride
Soars, for a servant, to no vulgar pitch.
New powers ye wield but newly, and ye deem
Your fencèd towers no sorrow can surprise.
Have I not seen two rulers fall from heaven?
And shall see fall a third, who now bears sway,
Most shamefully and swiftly. Do I seem
To cower and crouch before your upstart gods?
Far—further than most far—am I from that.
Go, get thee back with haste the way thou camest;
For nought of all thou askest shalt thou hear.

Hermes. Yet even by such stubbornness before
To this ill haven were thy fortunes steered.

Prometheus. But for thy servitude my evil plight—
Of this be well assured—I would not change.
Better, methinks, to serve this rock, than be
Of father Zeus the faithful messenger.
By taunts provoked, with taunts I answer thee.

Hermes. It seems thy present state has made thee proud.

Prometheus. Am I so proud? Proud with a pride like mine
Fain would I see my foes—of whom art thou.

Hermes. And have thy sufferings then been caused by me?

Prometheus. All gods, both great and small, I hate alike;
For all have wronged me, who did good to all.

Hermes. As one whose wits are dazed I hear thee rave.
Prometheus. Mad let me be, if to hate foes is madness.
Hermes. If thou shouldst prosper, who could then endure
    thee?
Prometheus. Alas!
Hermes.   Thou speak'st a word unknown to Zeus.
Prometheus. Nothing can time not teach as it grows old.
Hermes. And yet discretion thou hast never learnt.
Prometheus. True; or I had not parleyed with a slave.
Hermes. It seems thou wilt not speak what Zeus requires.
Prometheus. For so much grace methinks I am his debtor!
Hermes. I have been mocked and flouted like a child.
Prometheus. And art thou not more foolish than a child,
If aught thou thinkest to be told by me?
Zeus has no torture-engine, no not any,   *forecast*
Wherewith from me this secret shall be wrung,
Until that first these cruel chains be loosed.
So let him launch his lightning's murky flame,
And with his white-winged snow-storm's blinding whirl,
And din of subterraneous thunder, whelm
All nature and confound; he bends not me,
To speak the name that hurls him from his place.
    Hermes. How thou art helped by this, bethink thee well.
    Prometheus. Long since I have considered and bethought.
    Hermes. Endure, rash boaster, even yet endure,
To suit thy spirit to thy woful plight.
    Prometheus. Thou chidest the waves; forbear, and vex no
    more.
Deem not the pride of Zeus shall make me cower
And tremble like a woman; or that I
To my much-hated enemy shall upturn
The supplication of effeminate hands
To loose me from these chains; 'tis not in me.
    Hermes. More words methinks should be but wasted breath.
Thou'rt nothing moved nor softened in thy heart
By prayers; but headstrong as a new-yoked colt
Dost gnaw the bit and struggle with the rein.
Yet in thy stiffnecked wisdom strength is none,
For obstinacy, alone and void of sense,
Is weakest far of all things that are weak.

[29]

Bethink thee, if to counsel thou art deaf,
How shalt thou 'scape the tempest that shall break,
Disaster's crowning wave. With thunder first
And with his lightning's flame the Almighty Sire
Will rend this rugged gorge, and tomb thee there,
And fold thee in the rock's encircling arms.
Long years shall pass, uncounted: then shalt thou
Back to the light return; and the winged hound
Of Zeus, his ravening eagle, with fierce beak
Shall rend the tatters of thy mighty frame,
A daylong guest unbidden to the feast,
And on thy blackening liver gorge his fill.
And hope not any ending of thy pain,
Until some god to suffer in thy stead
Himself shall offer, and to the sunless gloom
And dark abyss of Tartarus descend.
Therefore consider well; no vain ostent
Of boasting this, but sentenced past recall.
The lips of Zeus speak sooth and cannot lie,
But will accomplish every word. Be it thine
To peer and ponder well, and never prize
A stubborn will more than a prudent mind.
    Chorus. No ill-timed word, methinks, hath Hermes spoken,
Who bids thee to renounce thy stubborn mood,
And in wise paths of prudence set thy feet.
Consent: 'tis shameful for the wise to err.
    Prometheus. Nought this imperious message hath
Of news to me; and for foe from foe
To suffer ill hath no disgrace.
So let him launch at me
The wreathèd curl of his two-edged flame;
Rack with his thunder the vaulted sky,
Rend it with spasm of angry storms,
Foundations firm of the rooted earth
Convulse with struggling wind;
And the stars in their courses, the lamps of heaven,
Confound and blend
With uproar fierce of the heaving sea;
Then to blackness of Tartarus lift and hurl me,
By the eddying torrent snatched and swept

Of his resistless might.
Me he may plague, but cannot slay.
    Hermes. Such thoughts and words of stubborn pride
Sound as the ravings of one distraught;
This rebel's state comes nothing short
Of frenzy, and abates not aught
Of furious madness unconfined:
But ye at least, whose tender hearts
Compassionate his pangs, be warned,
And get you quickly gone from hence
Ere the unpitying thunder-peal
Hath dazed your senses with its roar.
    Chorus. Some other exhortation choose,
Some more persuasive speech than this:
This word of import undisclosed
Is counsel that we loathe.
How dost thou bid me to be base?
I rather choose with him
To suffer what I must:
All traitors I have learned to hate.
Of all diseases that are named
This do I most abhor.
    Hermes. But yet remember: ye are warned,
Nor, when by ruin ye are seized,
Accuse your fate, nor then complain
That Zeus hath cast you in the toils
Of trouble unforeseen:
Not so, but ye have cast yourselves—
For, knowing what ye do,
Not suddenly nor unaware,
By your own senseless deed
Will ye be tangled in a net
Of ruin without end.
    Prometheus. Lo, the solid earth
Now not in word, but in deed is shaken:
Now from the depth anear me
The voice of the thunder roars:
The forked and fiery tongues
Leap forth and light the sky:
A hurricane rolls the pillared dust.

All winds that blow from all the heaven,
Blast against blast careering,
Mix in mid-air their elemental strife:
And sky with sea is blent.
From Zeus upon my fated head
So fraught with fear his vengeance swoops
Already in my sight.
O venerable Mother mine,
And ye revolving skies,
Whose light embraceth all,
How I am wronged, ye see!

AESCHYLUS
AGAMEMNON

TRANSLATED
by
GILBERT MURRAY

CHARACTERS IN THE PLAY

AGAMEMNON, *son of Atreus and King of Argos and Mycenae; Commander-in-Chief of the Greek armies in the War against Troy.*

CLYTEMNESTRA, *daughter of Tyndareus, sister of Helen; wife to Agamemnon.*

AEGISTHUS, *son of Thyestes, cousin and blood-enemy to Agamemnon, lover to Clytemnestra.*

CASSANDRA, *daughter of Priam, King of Troy, a prophetess; now slave to Agamemnon.*

A WATCHMAN.

A HERALD.

CHORUS of Argive Elders, faithful to Agamemnon.

The play was produced in the archonship of Philocles (458 B.C.). *The first prize was won by Aeschylus with the* Agamemnon, Choëphoroe, Eumenides, *and the Satyr-play* Proteus.

ARGUMENT

At the opening of the *Agamemnon* we find Clytemnestra alienated from her husband and secretly befriended by his ancestral enemy, Aegisthus. The air is heavy and throbbing with hate; hate which is evil but has its due cause. Agamemnon, obeying the prophet Calchas, when the fleet lay storm-bound at Aulis, had given his own daughter, Iphigenia, as a human sacrifice.

AGAMEMNON

---

*The scene represents a space in front of the Palace of Agamem-
non in Argos, with an Altar of Zeus in the center and many
other altars at the sides. On a high terrace of the roof stands
a* Watchman. *It is night.*

Watchman. This waste of year-long vigil I have prayed
God for some respite, watching elbow-stayed,
As sleuthhounds watch, above the Atreidae's hall,
Till well I know yon midnight festival
Of swarming stars, and them that lonely go,   *Prologue*
Bearers to man of summer and of snow,
Great lords and shining, throned in heavenly fire.
    And still I await the sign, the beacon pyre
That bears Troy's capture on a voice of flame *fig. lang.*
Shouting o'erseas. So surely to her aim
Cleaveth a woman's heart, man-passionèd! *will of a man*
And when I turn me to my bed—my bed
Dew-drenched and dark and stumbling, to which near
Cometh no dream nor sleep, but alway Fear
Breathes round it, warning, lest an eye once fain
To close may close too well to wake again;
Think I perchance to sing or troll a tune
For medicine against sleep, the music soon
Changes to sighing for the tale untold *builds up*
Of this house, not well mastered as of old. *atmosphere of foreboding*
   Howbeit, may God yet send us rest, and light
The flame of good news flashed across the night.
      [*He is silent, watching. Suddenly at a distance in
        the night there is a glimmer of fire, increasing
        presently to a blaze.* *—Could have started
        play a little before dawn!*
Ha!
O kindler of the dark, O daylight birth
Of dawn and dancing upon Argive earth

[35]

For this great end! All hail!—What ho, within!
What ho! Bear word to Agamemnon's queen
To rise, like dawn, and lift in answer strong
To this glad lamp her women's triumph-song,
If verily, verily, Ilion's citadel
Is fallen, as yon beacons flaming tell.
    And I myself will tread the dance before
All others; for my master's dice I score
Good, and mine own to-night three sixes plain.

                    [*Lights begin to show in the Palace.*
Oh, good or ill, my hand shall clasp again
My dear lord's hand, returning! Beyond that
I speak not. A great ox hath laid his weight
Across my tongue. But these stone walls know well,
If stones had speech, what tale were theirs to tell.
For me, to him that knoweth I can yet
Speak; if another questions I forget.

                    [*Exit into the Palace. The woman's 'Ololûgê,'
                    or triumph-cry, is heard within and then re-
                    peated again and again farther off in the City.
                    Handmaids and Attendants come from the
                    Palace, bearing torches, with which they
                    kindle incense on the altars. Among them
                    comes* CLYTEMNESTRA, *who throws herself on
                    her knees at the central Altar in an agony of
                    prayer.*

                        *Presently from the further side of the open
                    space appear the* CHORUS *of* ELDERS *and move
                    gradually into position in front of the Palace.
                    The day begins to dawn.*

Chorus. Ten years since Ilion's righteous foes,
        The Atreidae strong
    Menelaus and eke Agamemnon arose,
    Two thrones, two scepters, yokèd of God;
    And a thousand galleys of Argos trod
        The seas for the righting of wrong;
    And wrath of battle about them cried,
        As vultures cry,
    Whose nest is plundered, and up they fly

[36]

In anguish lonely, eddying wide,
Great wings like oars in the waste of sky,
Their task gone from them, no more to keep
Watch o'er the vulture babes asleep.
But One there is who heareth on high
Some Pan or Zeus, some lost Apollo—
That keen bird-throated suffering cry
Of the stranger wronged in God's own sky;
And sendeth down, for the law transgressed,
   The Wrath of the Feet that follow.

So Zeus the Watcher of Friend and Friend,
Zeus who Prevaileth, in after quest
For One Belovèd by Many Men
On Paris sent the Atreidae twain;
Yea, sent him dances before the end
      For his bridal cheer,
Wrestlings heavy and limbs forespent
For Greek and Trojan, the knee earth-bent,
The bloody dust and the broken spear.
He knoweth, that which is here is here,
And that which Shall Be followeth near;
He seeketh God with a great desire,
He heaps his gifts, he essays his pyre
With torch below and with oil above,
With tears, but never the wrath shall move
Of the Altar cold that rejects his fire.

We saw the Avengers go that day,
And they left us here; for our flesh is old
And serveth not; and these staves uphold
A strength like the strength of a child at play.
For the sap that springs in the young man's hand
And the valor of age, they have left the land.
And the passing old, while the dead leaf blows
And the old staff gropeth his three-foot way,
Weak as a babe and alone he goes,
A dream left wandering in the day.

   [*Coming near the Central Altar they see* CLY-
TEMNESTRA, *who is still rapt in prayer.*

But thou, O daughter of Tyndareus, *K of Sparta*
Queen Clytemnestra, what need? What news?
What tale or tiding hath stirred thy mood
To send forth word upon all our ways
For incensed worship? Of every god
That guards the city, the deep, the high,
Gods of the mart, gods of the sky,
    The altars blaze.
    One here, one there,

note unnecessarily enigmatic long.

To the skyey night the firebrands flare,
Drunk with the soft and guileless spell
Of balm of kings from the inmost cell.
Tell, O Queen, and reject us not,
All that can or that may be told,
And healer be to this aching thought,
Which one time hovereth, evil-cold,
And then from the fires thou kindlest
Will Hope be kindled, and hungry Care
Fall back for a little while, nor tear
The heart that beateth below my breast.

    [CLYTEMNESTRA *rises silently, as though uncon-*
        scious of their presence, and goes into the
        House. The CHORUS *take position and begin*
        their first Stasimon, or Standing-song.

Chorus.

1st Stasimon

(*The sign seen on the way; Eagles tearing a hare*
    with young.)
It is ours to tell of the Sign of the War-way given,
    To men more strong,
(For a life that is kin unto ours yet breathes from heaven
    A spell, a Strength of Song:)
How the twin-throned Might of Achaia, one Crown divided
    Above all Greeks that are,

Strophe

With avenging hand and spear upon Troy was guided
    By the Bird of War.
'Twas a King among birds to each of the Kings of the Sea,
One Eagle black, one black but of fire-white tail,
By the House, on the Spear-hand, in station that all might see;
And they tore a hare, and the life in her womb that grew,

[38]

Yea, the life unlived and the races unrun they slew.
Sorrow, sing sorrow: but good prevail, prevail!

(*How Calchas read the sign; his Vision of the
    Future.*)
And the War-seer wise, as he looked on the Atreïd Yoke
    Twain-tempered, knew
Those fierce hare-renders the lords of his host; and spoke,
    Reading the omen true.
'At the last, the last, this Hunt hunteth Ilion down,
    Yea, and before the wall
Violent division the fullness of land and town
    Shall waste withal;
If only God's eye gloom not against our gates,
    And the great War-curb of Troy, fore-smitten, fail.
For Pity lives, and those wingèd Hounds she hates,
    Which tore in the Trembler's body the unborn beast.
And Artemis abhorreth the eagles' feast.'
    Sorrow, sing sorrow: but good prevail, prevail!

(*He prays to Artemis to grant the fulfilment of the
Sign, but, as his vision increases, he is afraid and
calls on Paian, the Healer, to hold her back.*)
    'Thou beautiful One, thou tender lover
        Of the dewy breath of the Lion's child;
    Thou the delight, through den and cover,
        Of the young life at the breast of the wild,
Yet, oh, fulfil, fulfil the Sign of the Eagles' Kill!
Be the vision accepted, albeit horrible. . . .
But I-ê, I-ê! Stay her, O Paian, stay!
For lo, upon other evil her heart she setteth,
    Long wastes of wind, held ship and unventured sea,
On, on, till another Shedding of Blood be wrought:—
They kill but feast not; they pray not; the law is broken;
Strife in the flesh, and the bride she obeyeth not,
And beyond, beyond, there abideth in wrath re-awoken—
It plotteth, it haunteth the house, yea, it never forgetteth—
    Wrath for a child to be.' —
So Calchas, reading the wayside eagles' sign,

Spake to the Kings, blessings and words of bale;
   And like his song be thine,
Sorrow, sing sorrow: but good prevail, prevail!

    (*Such religion belongs to old and barbarous gods,
    and brings no peace. I turn to Zeus, who has shown
    man how to Learn by Suffering.*)
        Zeus! Zeus, whate'er He be,
        If this name He love to hear
        This He shall be called of me.
        Searching earth and sea and air
        Refuge nowhere can I find
        Save Him only, if my mind
        Will cast off before it die
        The burden of this vanity.

        One there was who reigned of old,
        Big with wrath to brave and blast,
        Lo, his name is no more told!
        And who followed met at last
        His Third-thrower, and is gone.
        Only they whose hearts have known
        Zeus, the Conqueror and the Friend,
        They shall win their vision's end;

        Zeus the Guide, who made man turn
        Thought-ward, Zeus, who did ordain
        Man by Suffering shall Learn.
        So the heart of him, again
        Aching with remembered pain,
        Bleeds and sleepeth not, until
        Wisdom comes against his will.
        'Tis the gift of One by strife
        Lifted to the throne of life.

    (AGAMEMNON *accepted the sign. Then came long de-
    lays and storm while the fleet lay at Aulis.*)
        So that day the Elder Lord,
        Marshal of the Achaian ships,
        Strove not with the prophet's word,

Bowed him to his fate's eclipse,
When with empty jars and lips
Parched and seas impassable
Fate on that Greek army fell,
Fronting Chalcis as it lay,
By Aulis in the swirling bay.

(*Till at last Calchas answered that Artemis was wroth
and demanded the death of* AGAMEMNON's *daughter. The King's doubt and grief.*)

And winds, winds   blew from Strymon River,
Unharbored, starving,   winds of waste endeavor,
Man-blinding, pitiless   to cord and bulwark,
   And the waste of days   was made long, more long,
Till the flower of Argos   was aghast and withered;
   Then through the storm   rose the War-seer's song,
And told of medicine   that should tame the tempest,
   But bow the Princes   to a direr wrong.
Then 'Artemis' he whispered, he named the name;
And the brother Kings they shook in the hearts of them,
And smote on the earth their staves, and the tears came.

But the King, the elder,   hath found voice and spoken:
'A heavy doom, sure,   If God's will were broken;
But to slay mine own child,   who my house delighteth,
   Is that not heavy?   That her blood should flow
On her father's hand,   hard beside an altar?
   My path is sorrow   wheresoe'er I go.
Shall Agamemnon   fail his ships and people
   And the hosts of Hellas   melt as melts the snow?
They cry, they thirst, for a death that shall break the spell,
For a Virgin's blood: 'tis a rite of old, men tell.
And they burn with longing.—O God may the end be well!'

(*But ambition drove him, till he consented to the sin
of slaying his daughter, Iphigenia, as a sacrifice.*)

To the yoke of Must-Be   he bowed him slowly,
   And a strange wind   within his bosom tossed,
A wind of dark thought,   unclean, unholy;
   And he rose up, daring   to the uttermost.

For men are boldened   by a Blindness, straying
   Toward base desire,   which brings grief hereafter,
      Yea, and itself is grief;
So this man hardened   to his own child's slaying,
   As help to avenge him   for a woman's laughter
      And bring his ships relief!

Her 'Father, Father,'   her sad cry that lingered,
   Her virgin heart's breath   they held all as naught,
Those bronze-clad witnesses   and battle-hungered;
   And there they prayed, and   when the prayer was wrought
He charged the young men   to uplift and bind her,
   As ye lift a wild kid,   high above the altar,
      Fierce-huddling forward,   fallen, clinging sore
To the robe that wrapt her; yea, he bids them hinder
   The sweet mouth's utterance,   the cries that falter,
      —His curse for evermore!—

With violence and a curb's voiceless wrath.
   Her stole of saffron then to the ground she threw,
And her eye with an arrow of pity found its path
      To each man's heart that slew:
A face in a picture, striving amazedly;
   The little maid who danced at her father's board,
The innocent voice man's love came never nigh,
   Who joined to his her little paean-cry
      When the third cup was poured. . . .

What came thereafter I saw not neither tell.
   But the craft of Calchas failed not.—'Tis written, He
Who Suffereth Shall Learn; the law holdeth well.
      And that which is to be,
Ye will know at last; why weep before the hour?
   For come it shall, as out of darkness dawn.
Only may good from all this evil flower;
So prays this Heart of Argos, this frail tower
      Guarding the land alone.

                [*As they cease,* CLYTEMNESTRA *comes from the
                Palace with Attendants. She has finished her*

1st episode

> *prayer and sacrifice, and is now wrought up*
> *to face the meeting with her husband. The*
> *Leader approaches her.*

Leader. Before thy state, O Queen, I bow mine eyes.
'Tis written, when the man's throne empty lies,
The woman shall be honored.—Hast thou heard
Some tiding sure? Or is it Hope, that stirred
To fire these altars? Dearly though we seek
To learn, 'tis thine to speak or not to speak.

Clytemnestra. Glad-voiced, the old saw telleth, comes this morn,
The Star-child of a dancing midnight born,
And beareth to thine ear a word of joy
Beyond all hope: the Greek hath taken Troy.

Leader. How?
Thy word flies past me, being incredible.

Clytemnestra. Ilion is ours. No riddling tale I tell.

Leader. Such joy comes knocking at the gate of tears.

Clytemnestra. Aye, 'tis a faithful heart that eye declares.

Leader. What warrant hast thou? Is there proof of this?

Clytemnestra. There is; unless a God hath lied there is.

Leader. Some dream-shape came to thee in speaking guise?

Clytemnestra. Who deemeth me a dupe of drowsing eyes?

Leader. Some word within that hovereth without wings?

Clytemnestra. Am I a child to hearken to such things?

Leader. Troy fallen?—But how long? When fell she, say?

Clytemnestra. The very night that mothered this new day.

Leader. And who of heralds with such fury came?

Clytemnestra. A Fire-god, from Mount Ida scattering flame.
Whence starting, beacon after beacon burst
In flaming message hitherward. Ida first
Told Hermes' Lemnian Rock, whose answering sign
Was caught by towering Athos, the divine,
With pines immense—yea, fishes of the night
Swam skyward, drunken with that leaping light,
Which swelled like some strange sun, till dim and far
Makistos' watchman marked a glimmering star;
They, nowise loath nor idly slumber-won,
Spring up to hurl the fiery message on,
And a far light beyond the Eurîpus tells

How message came fr. Troy

That word hath reached Messapion's sentinels.
They beaconed back, then onward with a high
Heap of dead heather flaming to the sky.
And onward still, not failing nor aswoon,
Across the Asopus like a beaming moon
The great word leapt, and on Kithairon's height
Uproused a new relay of racing light.
His watchers knew the wandering flame, nor hid
Their welcome, burning higher than was bid.
Out over Lake Gorgopis then it floats,
To Aigiplanctos, waking the wild goats,
Crying for 'Fire, more Fire!' And fire was reared,
Stintless and high, a stormy streaming beard,
That waved in flame beyond the promontory
Rock-ridged, that watches the Saronian sea,
Kindling the night: then one short swoop to catch
The Spider's Crag, our city's tower of watch;
Whence hither to the Atreidae's roof it came,
A light true-fathered of Idaean flame.
Torch-bearer after torch-bearer, behold
The tale thereof in stations manifold,
Each one by each made perfect ere it passed,
And Victory in the first as in the last.
These be my proofs and tokens that my lord
From Troy hath spoke to me a burning word.

    Leader. Woman, speak on. Hereafter shall my prayer
Be raised to God; now let me only hear,
Again and full, the marvel and the joy.

    Clytemnestra. Now, even now, the Achaian holdeth Troy!
Methinks there is a crying in her streets
That makes no concord. When sweet unguent meets
With vinegar in one phial, I warrant none
Shall lay those wranglers lovingly at one.
So conquerors and conquered shalt thou hear,
Two sundered tones, two lives of joy or fear.

    Here women in the dust about their slain,
Husbands or brethren, and by dead old men
Pale children who shall never more be free,
For all they loved on earth cry desolately.

[44]

And hard beside them war-stained Greeks, whom stark
Battle and then long searching through the dark
Hath gathered, ravenous, in the dawn, to feast
At last on all the plenty Troy possessed,
No portion in that feast nor ordinance,
But each man clutching at the prize of chance.
Aye, there at last under good roofs they lie
Of men spear-quelled, no frosts beneath the sky,
No watches more, no bitter moony dew. . . .
How blessèd they will sleep the whole night through!
Oh, if these days they keep them free from sin
Toward Ilion's conquered shrines and Them within
Who watch unconquered, maybe not again
The smiter shall be smit, the taker ta'en.
May God but grant there fall not on that host
The greed of gold that maddeneth and the lust
To spoil inviolate things! But half the race
Is run which windeth back to home and peace.
Yea, though of God they pass unchallengèd,
Methinks the wound of all those desolate dead
Might waken, groping for its will. . . .
                                                    Ye hear
A woman's word, belike a woman's fear.
May good but conquer in the last incline
Of the balance! Of all prayers that prayer is mine.
     Leader. O Woman, like a man faithful and wise
Thou speakest. I accept thy testimonies
And turn to God with praising, for a gain
Is won this day that pays for all our pain.
               [CLYTEMNESTRA *returns to the Palace. The* CHORUS
                    take up their position for the Second Stasimon.

     An Elder. O Zeus, All-ruler, and Night the Aid,
               Gainer of glories, and hast thou thrown
               Over the towers of Ilion
                    Thy net close-laid,
               That none so nimble and none so tall
               Shall escape withal
               The snare of the slaver that claspeth all?

Another. And Zeus the Watcher of Friend and Friend
    I also praise, who hath wrought this end.
    Long since on Paris his shaft he drew,
        And hath aimèd true,
    Not too soon falling nor yet too far,
    The fire of the avenging star.

Chorus. (*This is God's judgment upon Troy. May it not
    be too fierce! Gold cannot save one who spurneth
    Justice.*)
The stroke of Zeus hath found them! Clear this day
    The tale, and plain to trace.
He judged, and Troy hath fallen.—And have men said
That God not deigns to mark man's hardihead,
    Trampling to earth the grace
Of holy and delicate things?—Sin lies that way.
For visibly Pride doth breed its own return
    On prideful men, who, when their houses swell
    With happy wealth, breathe ever wrath and blood.
Yet not too fierce let the due vengeance burn;
    Only as deemeth well
        One wise of mood.

        Never shall state nor gold
            Shelter his heart from aching
        Whoso the Altar of Justice old
            Spurneth to Night unwaking.

(*The Sinner suffers in his longing till at last Tempta-
    tion overcomes him; as longing for Helen over-
    came Paris.*)
The tempting of misery forceth him, the dread
        Child of fore-scheming Woe!
And help is vain; the fell desire within
Is veilèd not, but shineth bright like Sin:
        And as false gold will show
Black where the touchstone trieth, so doth fade
His honor in God's ordeal. Like a child,
    Forgetting all, he hath chased his wingèd bird,
        And planted amid his people a sharp thorn.

And no God hears his prayer, or, have they heard,
   The man so base-beguiled
   They cast to scorn.

   Paris to Argos came;
     Love of a woman led him;
     So God's altar he brought to shame,
     Robbing the hand that fed him.

(Helen's flight; the visions seen by the King's seers;
the phantom of Helen and the King's grief.)
She hath left among her people   a noise of shield and sword,
  A tramp of men armèd   where the long ships are moored;
She hath ta'en in her goings   Desolation as a dower;
She hath stept, stept quickly,   through the great gated Tower,
  And the thing that could not be,   it hath been!
And the Seers they saw visions,   and they spoke of strange ill:
'A Palace, a Palace;   and a great King thereof:
A bed, a bed empty,   that was once pressed in love:
And thou, thou, what art thou?   Let us be, thou so still,
  Beyond wrath, beyond beseeching,   to the lips reft of thee!'
 For she whom he desireth   is beyond the deep sea,
 And a ghost in his castle   shall be queen.

    Images in sweet guise
     Carven shall move him never,
    Where is Love amid empty eyes?
    Gone, gone for ever!

(His dreams and his suffering; but the War that he
made caused greater and wider suffering.)
But a shape that is a dream, 'mid the breathings of the night,
Cometh near, full of tears, bringing vain vain delight:
For in vain when, desiring, he can feel the joy's breath
—Nevermore! Nevermore!—from his arms it vanisheth,
  As a bird along the wind-ways of sleep.
In the mid castle hall, on the hearthstone of the Kings,
These griefs there be, and griefs passing these,
But in each man's dwelling of the host that sailed the seas,
A sad woman waits; she has thoughts of many things,
  And patience in her heart lieth deep.

Knoweth she them she sent,
Knoweth she? Lo, returning,
Comes in stead of the man that went
Armor and dust of burning.

(*The return of the funeral urns; the murmurs of the
People.*) *more*
And the gold-changer, Ares, who changeth quick for dead,
Who poiseth his scale   in the striving of the spears,
Back from Troy sendeth dust,   heavy dust, wet with tears,
Sendeth ashes with men's names   in his urns neatly spread.
And they weep over the men,   and they praise them one by one,
How this was a wise fighter,   and this nobly slain—
    'Fighting to win back another's wife!'
Till a murmur is begun,
    And there steals an angry pain
    Against Kings too forward in the strife.

There by Ilion's gate
Many a soldier sleepeth,
Young men beautiful; fast in hate
Troy her conqueror keepeth.

(*For the Shedder of Blood is in great peril, and not
unmarked by God. May I never be a Sacker of
Cities!*)

foreboding But the rumor of the People,   it is heavy, it is chill;
And tho' no curse be spoken,   like a curse doth it brood;
And my heart waits some tiding   which the dark holdeth still,
For of God not unmarked   is the shedder of much blood.
And who conquers beyond right . . . Lo, the life of man
    decays;
    There be Watchers dim his light in the wasting of the years;
    He falls, he is forgotten, and hope dies.
There is peril in the praise
    Over-praisèd that he hears;
    For the thunder it is hurled from God's eyes.

Glory that breedeth strife,
Pride of the Sacker of Cities;

> Yea, and the conquered captive's life,
> Spare me, O God of Pities!

Divers Elders. The fire of good tiding it hath sped the city
  through,
But who knows if a god mocketh? Or who knows if all be
  true?

> 'Twere the fashion of a child,
> Or a brain dream-beguiled,
> To be kindled by the first
> Torch's message as it burst,

And thereafter, as it dies, to die too.
'Tis like a woman's scepter, to ordain
Welcome to joy before the end is plain!

Too lightly opened are a woman's ears;
Her fence downtrod by many trespassers,
  And quickly crossed; but quickly lost
The burden of a woman's hopes or fears.

left chyt.

> *Here a break occurs in the action, like the descent of
> the curtain in a modern theater. A space of some
> days is assumed to have passed and we find the
> Elders again assembled.*

Leader. Soon surely shall we read the message right;
Where fire and beacon-call and lamps of light
True speakers, or but happy things that seem
And are not, like sweet voices in a dream.
I see a Herald yonder by the shore.   *identifies next character*
Shadowed with olive sprays. And from his sore
Rent raiment cries a witness from afar,   *figure elab.*
Dry Dust, born brother to the Mire of war,
That mute he comes not, neither through the smoke
Of mountain forests shall his tale be spoke;
But either shouting for a joyful day,
Or else. . . . But other thoughts I cast away.
As good hath dawned, may good shine on, we pray!
  And whoso for this City prayeth aught
  Else, let him reap the harvest of his thought!

[49]

[*Enter the* HERALD, *running. His garments are torn and war-stained. He falls upon his knees and kisses the Earth, and salutes each Altar in turn.*

2nd actor
episode

Herald. Land of my fathers! Argos! Am I here . . .
Home, home at this tenth shining of the year,
And all Hope's anchors broken save this one!
For scarcely dared I dream, here in mine own
Argos at last to fold me to my rest. . . .
But now—All Hail, O Earth! O Sunlight blest!
And Zeus Most High!

[*Checking himself as he sees the altar of Apollo.*
                    And thou, O Pythian Lord;
No more on us be thy swift arrows poured!
Beside Scamander well we learned how true
Thy hate is. Oh, as thou art Healer too,
Heal us! As thou art Saviour of the Lost,
Save also us, Apollo, being so tossed
With tempest! . . . All ye Daemons of the Pale!
And Hermes! Hermes, mine own guardian, hail!
Herald beloved, to whom all heralds bow. . . .
Ye Blessèd Dead that sent us, receive now
In love your children whom the spear hath spared.
    O House of Kings, O roof-tree thrice-endeared,
O solemn thrones! O gods that face the sun!
Now, now, if ever in the days foregone,
After these many years, with eyes that burn,
Give hail and glory to your King's return!
For Agamemnon cometh! A great light
Cometh to men and gods out of the night.
    Grand greeting give him—aye, it need be grand—
Who, God's avenging mattock in his hand,
Hath wrecked Troy's towers and digged her soil beneath,
Till her gods' houses, they are things of death;
Her altars waste, and blasted every seed
Whence life might rise! So perfect is his deed,
So dire the yoke on Ilion he hath cast,
The first Atreides, King of Kings at last,
And happy among men! To whom we give
Honor most high above all things that live.

For Paris nor his guilty land can score
The deed they wrought above the pain they bore.
'Spoiler and thief,' he heard God's judgment pass;
Whereby he lost his plunder, and like grass
Mowed down his father's house and all his land;
And Troy pays twofold for the sin she planned.

Leader. Be glad, thou Herald of the Greek from Troy!
Herald. So glad, I am ready, if God will, to die!
Leader. Did love of this land work thee such distress?
Herald. The tears stand in mine eyes for happiness.
Leader. Sweet sorrow was it, then, that on you fell.
Herald. How sweet? I cannot read thy parable.
Leader. To pine again for them that loved you true.
Herald. Did ye then pine for us, as we for you?
Leader. The whole land's heart was dark, and groaned for thee.
Herald. Dark? For what cause? Why should such darkness be?
Leader. Silence in wrong is our best medicine here.
Herald. Your kings were gone. What others need you fear?
Leader. 'Tis past! Like thee now, I could gladly die.
Herald. Even so! 'Tis past, and all is victory.
And, for our life in those long years, there were
Doubtless some grievous days, and some were fair.
Who but a god goes woundless all his way? . . .
  Oh, could I tell the sick toil of the day,
The evil nights, scant decks ill-blanketed;
The rage and cursing when our daily bread
Came not! And then on land 'twas worse than all.
Our quarters close beneath the enemy's wall;
And rain—and from the ground the river dew—
Wet, always wet! Into our clothes it grew,
Plague-like, and bred foul beasts in every hair.
  Would I could tell how ghastly midwinter
Stole down from Ida till the birds dropped dead!
Or the still heat, when on his noonday bed
The breathless blue sea sank without a wave! . . .
  Why think of it? They are past and in the grave,
All those long troubles. For I think the slain
Care little if they sleep or rise again;

[51]

And we, the living, wherefore should we ache
With counting all our lost ones, till we wake
The old malignant fortunes? If Good-bye
Comes from their side, Why, let them go, say I.
Surely for us, who live, good doth prevail
Unchallenged, with no wavering of the scale;
Wherefore we vaunt unto these shining skies,
As wide o'er sea and land our glory flies:
'By men of Argolis who conquered Troy,
These spoils, a memory and an ancient joy,
Are nailed in the gods' houses throughout Greece.'
Which whoso readeth shall with praise increase
Our land, our kings, and God's grace manifold
Which made these marvels be.—My tale is told.

    Leader. Indeed thou conquerest me. Men say, the light
In old men's eyes yet serves to learn aright.
But Clytemnestra and the House should hear
These tidings first, though I their health may share.
              [*During the last words* CLYTEMNESTRA *has en-
              tered from the Palace.*

    Clytemnestra. Long since I lifted up my voice in joy,
When the first messenger from flaming Troy
Spake through the dark of sack and overthrow.
And mockers chid me: 'Because beacons show
On the hills, must Troy be fallen? Quickly born
Are women's hopes!' Aye, many did me scorn;
Yet gave I sacrifice; and by my word
Through all the city our woman's cry was heard,
Lifted in blessing round the seats of God,
And slumbrous incense o'er the altars glowed
In fragrance.
             And for thee, what need to tell
Thy further tale? My lord himself shall well
Instruct me. Yet, to give my lord and king
All reverent greeting at his homecoming—
What dearer dawn on woman's eyes can flame
Than this, which casteth wide her gate to acclaim
The husband whom God leadeth safe from war?—
Go, bear my lord his prayer: That fast and far
He haste him to this town which loves his name;

[52]

And in his castle may he find the same *dramatic irony*
Wife that he left, a watchdog of the hall, *d. m. r.,* ————,
True to one voice and fierce to others all;
A body and soul unchanged, no seal of his
Broke in the waiting years.—No thought of ease
Nor joy from other men hath touched my soul,
Nor shall touch, until bronze be dyed like wool. *of her sword*
                                                                w/ his blood
  A boast so faithful and so plain, I wot,
Spoke by a royal Queen doth shame her not.
                                         [*Exit* CLYTEMNESTRA.

  Leader. Let thine ear mark her message. 'Tis of fair
Seeming, and craves a clear interpreter. . . .
But, Herald, I would ask thee; tell me true
Of Menelaus. Shall he come with you,
Our land's belovèd crown, untouched of ill?
  Herald. I know not how to speak false words of weal
For friends to reap thereof a harvest true.
  Leader. Canst speak of truth with comfort joined? Those two
Once parted, 'tis a gulf not lightly crossed.
  Herald. Your king is vanished from the Achaian host,
He and his ship! Such comfort have I brought.
  Leader. Sailed he alone from Troy? Or was he caught
By storms in the midst of you, and swept away?
  Herald. Thou hast hit the truth; good marksman, as men say!
And long to suffer is but brief to tell.
  Leader. How ran the sailors' talk? Did there prevail
One rumor, showing him alive or dead?
  Herald. None knoweth, none hath tiding, save the head
Of Helios, ward and watcher of the world.
  Leader. Then tell us of the storm. How, when God hurled
His anger, did it rise? How did it die?
  Herald. It likes me not, a day of presage high
With dolorous tongue to stain. Those twain, I vow,
Stand best apart. When one with shuddering brow, *storm speech*
From armies lost, back beareth to his home
Word that the terror of her prayers is come;
One wound in her great heart, and many a fate
For many a home of men cast out to sate
The twofold scourge that worketh Ares' lust,

[53]

Spear crossed with spear, dust wed with bloody dust;
Who walketh laden with such weight of wrong,
Why, let him, if he will, uplift the song
That is Hell's triumph. But to come as I
Am now come, laden with deliverance high,
Home to a land of peace and laughing eyes,
And mar all with that fury of the skies
Which made our Greeks curse God—how should this be?
   Two enemies most ancient, Fire and Sea,
A sudden friendship swore, and proved their plight
By war on us poor sailors through that night
Of misery, when the horror of the wave
Towered over us, and winds from Strymon drave
Hull against hull, till good ships, by the horn
Of the mad whirlwind gored and overborne,
One here, one there, 'mid rain and blinding spray,
Like sheep by a devil herded, passed away.
And when the blessèd Sun upraised his head,
We saw the Aegean waste a-foam with dead,
Dead men, dead ships, and spars disasterful.
Howbeit for us, our one unwounded hull
Out of that wrath was stolen or begged free
By some good spirit—sure no man was he!—
Who guided clear our helm; and on till now
Hath Saviour Fortune throned her on the prow,
No surge to mar our moorings, and no floor
Of rock to tear us when we made for shore.
Till, fled from that sea-hell, with the clear sun
Above us and all trust in fortune gone,
We drove like sheep the thoughts about our brain
Of that lost army, broken and scourged amain
With evil. And, methinks, if there is breath
In them, they talk of us as gone to death—
How else?—and so say we of them! For thee,
Since Menelaus thy first care must be,
If by some word of Zeus, who wills not yet
To leave the old house for ever desolate,
Some ray of sunlight on a far-off sea
Lights him, yet green and living . . . we may see

[54]

His ship some day in the harbor!—'Twas the word
Of truth ye asked me for, and truth ye have heard!

> [*Exit* HERALD. *The* CHORUS *take position for the
> Third Stasimon.*

3rd Stasimon

marked time
lapse between
herald + coming
of ag.

*Chorus. (Surely there was mystic meaning in the name
HELENA, meaning which was fulfilled when she fled
to Troy.)*

Who was He who found for thee
That name, truthful utterly—
Was it One beyond our vision
Moving sure in pre-decision
Of man's doom his mystic lips?—
Calling thee, the Battle-wed,
Thee, the Strife-encompassèd,
HELEN? Yea, in fate's derision,   *the Helen chorus*
Hell in cities, Hell in ships,
Hell in hearts of men they knew her,
When the dim and delicate fold
Of her curtains backward rolled,
And to sea, to sea, she threw her
In the West Wind's giant hold;
And with spear and sword behind her
Came the hunters in a flood,
Down the oarblade's viewless trail
Tracking, till in Simoïs' vale
Through the leaves they crept to find her,
A Wrath, a seed of blood.

*(The Trojans welcomed her with triumph and praised
Alexander, till at last their song changed and they
saw another meaning in Alexander's name also.)*

So the Name to Ilion came
On God's thought-fulfilling flame,
She a vengeance and a token
Of the unfaith to bread broken,
Of the hearth of God betrayed,
Against them whose voices swelled
Glorying in the prize they held
And the Spoiler's vaunt outspoken
And the song his brethren made

'Mid the bridal torches burning;
   Till, behold, the ancient City
Of King Priam turned, and turning
Took a new song for her learning,
A song changed and full of pity,
With the cry of a lost nation;
   And she changed the bridegroom's name:
Called him Paris Ghastly-wed;
For her sons were with the dead,
And her life one lamentation,
   'Mid blood and burning flame.

(Like a lion's whelp reared as a pet and turning after-
   wards to a great beast of prey.)
     Lo, once there was a herdsman reared
       In his own house, so stories tell,
     A lion's whelp, a milk-fed thing
     And soft in life's first opening
     Among the sucklings of the herd;
       The happy children loved him well,
     And old men smiled, and oft, they say,
     In men's arms, like a babe, he lay,
Bright-eyed, and toward the hand that teased him
     Eagerly fawning for food or play.

     Then on a day outflashed the sudden
       Rage of the lion brood of yore;
     He paid his debt to them that fed
     With wrack of herds and carnage red,
     Yea, wrought him a great feast unbidden,
       Till all the house-ways ran with gore;
     A sight the thralls fled weeping from,
       A great red slayer, beard a-foam,
High-priest of some blood-cursèd altar
     God had uplifted against that home.

     (So was it with Helen in Troy.)
     And how shall I call the thing that came
       At the first hour to Ilion city?
     Call it a dream of peace untold,

A secret joy in a mist of gold,
A woman's eye that was soft, like flame,
A flower which ate a man's heart with pity.

But she swerved aside and wrought to her kiss a bitter ending,
And a wrath was on her harboring, a wrath upon her friend-
ing,
When to Priam and his sons she fled quickly o'er the deep,
With the god to whom she sinned for her watcher on the wind,
A death-bride, whom brides long shall weep.

(*Men say that Good Fortune wakes the envy of God;
not so; Good Fortune may be innocent, and then
there is no vengeance.*)
A gray word liveth, from the morn
Of old time among mortals spoken,
That man's Wealth waxen full shall fall
Not childless, but get sons withal;
And ever of great bliss is born
A tear unstanched and a heart broken.

But I hold my thought alone and by others unbeguiled;
'Tis the deed that is unholy shall have issue, child on child,
Sin on sin, like his begetters; and they shall be as they were.
But the man who walketh straight, and the house thereof, tho'
Fate
Exalt him, the children shall be fair.

(*It is Sin, it is Pride and Ruthlessness, that beget
children like themselves till Justice is fulfilled
upon them.*)
But Old Sin loves, when comes the hour again,
To bring forth New,
Which laugheth lusty amid the tears of men;
Yea, and Unruth, his comrade, wherewith none
May plead nor strive, which dareth on and on,
Knowing not fear nor any holy thing;
Two fires of darkness in a house, born true,
Like to their ancient spring.

But Justice shineth in a house low-wrought
   With smoke-stained wall,
And honoreth him who filleth his own lot;
But the unclean hand upon the golden stair
With eyes averse she flieth, seeking where
   Things innocent are; and, recking not the power
Of wealth by man misgloried, guideth all
     To her own destined hour.

> [*Here amid a great procession enter* AGAMEMNON
> *on a Chariot. Behind him on another Chariot
> is* CASSANDRA. *The* CHORUS *approach and make
> obeisance. Some of* AGAMEMNON's *men have on
> their shields a White Horse, some a Lion. Their
> arms are rich and partly barbaric.*

Leader. All hail, O King! Hail, Atreus' Son!
Sacker of Cities! Ilion's bane!
With what high word shall I greet thee again,
How give thee worship, and neither outrun
The point of pleasure, nor stint too soon?
For many will cling to fair seeming
The faster because they have sinned erewhile;
And a man may sigh with never a sting
Of grief in his heart, and a man may smile
With eyes unlit and a lip that strains.
But the wise Shepherd knoweth his sheep,
   And his eyes pierce deep
The faith like water that fawns and feigns.

But I hide nothing, O King. That day
When in quest of Helen our battle array
Hurled forth, thy name upon my heart's scroll
Was deep in letters of discord writ;
   And the ship of thy soul,
Ill-helmed and blindly steered was it,
Pursuing ever, through men that die,
One wild heart that was fain to fly.
   But on this new day,
From the deep of my thought and in love, I say
   'Sweet is a grief well-ended';

[58]

And in time's flow Thou wilt learn and know
   The true from the false,
Of them that were left to guard the walls
   Of thine empty Hall unfriended.

they try to warn him

      [*During the above* CLYTEMNESTRA *has appeared
      on the Palace steps, with a train of Attend-
      ants, to receive her Husband.*

   Agamemnon. To Argos and the gods of Argolis
All hail, who share with me the glory of this
Home-coming and the vengeance I did wreak
On Priam's City! Yea, though none should speak,
The great gods heard our cause, and in one mood
Uprising, in the urn of bitter blood,
That men should shriek and die and towers should burn,
Cast their great vote; while over Mercy's urn
Hope waved her empty hands and nothing fell.
   Even now in smoke that City tells her tale;
The wrack-wind liveth, and where Ilion died
The reek of the old fatness of her pride
From hot and writhing ashes rolls afar.
    For which let thanks, wide as our glories are,
Be uplifted; seeing the Beast of Argos hath
Round Ilion's towers piled high his fence of wrath
And, for one woman ravished, wrecked by force
A City. Lo, the leap of the wild Horse
In darkness when the Pleiades were dead;
A mailèd multitude, a Lion unfed,
Which leapt the tower and lapt the blood of Kings!

   Lo, to the Gods I make these thanksgivings.
But for thy words: I marked them, and I mind
Their meaning, and my voice shall be behind
Thine. For not many men, the proverb saith,
Can love a friend whom fortune prospereth
Unenvying; and about the envious brain
Cold poison clings, and doubles all the pain
Life brings him. His own woundings he must nurse,
And feels another's gladness like a curse.
   Well can I speak. I know the mirrored glass
Called friendship, and the shadow shapes that pass

— or his character

his arrival speech?

misinterprets warning of Chorus?

And feign them a King's friends. I have known but one—
Odysseus, him we trapped against his own
Will!—who once harnessed bore his yoke right well . . .
Be he alive or dead of whom I tell
The tale. And for the rest, touching our state
And gods, we will assemble in debate
A concourse of all Argos, taking sure
Counsel, that what is well now may endure
Well, and if aught needs healing medicine, still
By cutting and by fire, with all good will,
I will essay to avert the after-wrack
Such sickness breeds.
          Aye, Heaven hath led me back;
And on this hearth where still my fire doth burn
I will go pay to heaven my due return,
Which guides me here, which saved me far away.
   O Victory, now mine own, be mine alway!

   [CLYTEMNESTRA, *at the head of her retinue, steps
      forward. She controls her suspense with diffi-
      culty but gradually gains courage as she pro-
      ceeds.*

   Clytemnestra. Ye Elders, Council of the Argive name
Here present, I will no more hold it shame
To lay my passion bare before men's eyes.
There comes a time to a woman when fear dies
For ever. None hath taught me. None could tell,
Save me, the weight of years intolerable
I lived while this man lay at Ilion.
That any woman thus should sit alone
In a half-empty house, with no man near,
Makes her half-blind with dread! And in her ear
Alway some voice of wrath; now messengers
Of evil; now not so; then others worse,
Crying calamity against mine and me.
   Oh, had he half the wounds that variously
Came rumored home, his flesh must be a net,
All holes from heel to crown! And if he met
As many deaths as I met tales thereon,
Is he some monstrous thing, some Geryon

Three-souled, that will not die, till o'er his head,
Three robes of earth be piled, to hold him dead?
　Aye, many a time my heart broke, and the noose
Of death had got me; but they cut me loose.
It was those voices alway in mine ear.

　For that, too, young Orestes is not here
Beside me, as were meet, seeing he above
All else doth hold the surety of our love;
Let not thy heart be troubled. It fell thus:
Our loving spear-friend took him, Strophios
The Phocian, who forewarned me of annoy
Two-fronted, thine own peril under Troy,
And ours here, if the rebel multitude
Should cast the Council down. It is men's mood
Alway, to spurn the fallen. So spake he,
And sure no guile was in him.
　　　　　　　　But for me,
The old stormy rivers of my grief are dead
Now at the spring; not one tear left unshed.
Mine eyes are sick with vigil, endlessly
Weeping the beacon-piles that watched for thee
For ever answerless. And did I dream,
A gnat's thin whirr would start me, like a scream
Of battle, and show me thee by terrors swept,
Crowding, too many for the time I slept.

　From all which stress delivered and free-souled,
I greet my lord: O watchdog of the fold,
O forestay sure that fails not in the squall,
O strong-based pillar of a towering hall;
O single son to a father age-ridden;
O land unhoped for seen by shipwrecked men;
Sunshine more beautiful when storms are fled;
Spring of quick water in a desert dead. . . .
How sweet to be set free from any chain!

　These be my words to greet him home again.
No god shall grudge them. Surely I and thou
Have suffered in time past enough! And now

Dismount, O head with love and glory crowned,
From this high car; yet plant not on bare ground
Thy foot, great King, the foot that trampled Troy.
  Ho, bondmaids, up! Forget not your employ,
A floor of crimson broideries to spread
For the King's path. Let all the ground be red
Where those feet pass; and Justice, dark of yore,
Home light him to the hearth he looks not for!
  What followeth next, our sleepless care shall see
Ordered as God's good pleasure may decree.

        [*The attendants spread tapestries of crimson and
          gold from the Chariot to the Door of the Palace.*
        AGAMEMNON *does not move.*

  Agamemnon. Daughter of Leda, watcher of my fold,
In sooth thy welcome, grave and amply told,
Fitteth mine absent years. Though it had been
Seemlier, methinks, some other, not my Queen,
Had spoke these honors. For the rest, I say,
Seek not to make me soft in woman's way;
Cry not thy praise to me wide-mouthed, nor fling
Thy body down, as to some barbarous king.
Nor yet with broidered hangings strew my path,
To awake the unseen ire. 'Tis God that hath
Such worship; and for mortal man to press
Rude feet upon this broidered loveliness . . .
I vow there is danger in it. Let my road
Be honored, surely; but as man, not god.
Rugs for the feet and yonder broidered pall . . .
The names ring diverse! . . . Aye, and not to fall
Suddenly blind is of all gifts the best
God giveth, for I reckon no man blest
Ere to the utmost goal his race be run.
  So be it; and if, as this day I have done,
I shall do always, then I fear no ill.
  Clytemnestra. Tell me but this, nowise against thy will . . .
  Agamemnon. My will, be sure, shall falter not nor fade.
  Clytemnestra. Was this a vow in some great peril made?
  Agamemnon. Enough! I have spoke my purpose, fixed and
    plain.

Clytemnestra. Were Priam the conquerer . . . Think, would
  he refrain?
Agamemnon. Oh, stores of broideries would be trampled
  then!
Clytemnestra. Lord, care not for the cavillings of men!
Agamemnon. The murmur of a people hath strange weight.
Clytemnestra. Who feareth envy, feareth to be great.
Agamemnon. 'Tis graceless when a woman strives to lead.
Clytemnestra. When a great conqueror yields, 'tis grace in-
  deed.
Agamemnon. So in this war thou must my conqueror be?
Clytemnestra. Yield! With good will to yield is victory!
Agamemnon. Well, if I needs must . . . Be it as thou hast
  said!
Quick! Loose me these bound slaves on which I tread,
And while I walk yon wonders of the sea
God grant no eye of wrath be cast on me
From far!

                  [*The Attendants untie his shoes.*
        For even now it likes me not
To waste mine house, thus marring underfoot
The pride thereof, and wondrous broideries
Bought in far seas with silver. But of these
Enough.—And mark, I charge thee, this princess
Of Ilion; tend her with all gentleness.
God's eye doth see, and loveth from afar,
The merciful conqueror. For no slave of war
Is slave by his own will. She is the prize
And chosen flower of Ilion's treasuries,
Set by the soldiers' gift to follow me.
   Now therefore, seeing I am constrained by thee
And do thy will, I walk in conqueror's guise
Beneath my Gate, trampling sea-crimson dyes.

      [*As he dismounts and sets foot on the Tapestries*
       Clytemnestra's *women utter again their Cry*
       of Triumph. The people bow or kneel as he
       passes.
Clytemnestra. There is the sea—its caverns who shall drain?
Breeding of many a purple-fish the stain
Surpassing silver, ever fresh renewed,

For robes of kings. And we, by right indued,
Possess our fill thereof. Thy house, O King,
Knoweth no stint, nor lack of anything.
  What trampling of rich raiment, had the cry
So sounded in the domes of prophesy,
Would I have vowed these years, as price to pay
For this dear life in peril far away!
Where the root is, the leafage cometh soon
To clothe an house, and spread its leafy boon
Against the burning star; and, thou being come,
Thou, on the midmost hearthstone of thy home,
Oh, warmth in winter leapeth to thy sign.
And when God's summer melteth into wine
The green grape, on that house shall coolness fall
Where the true man, the master, walks his hall.

Zeus, Zeus! True Master, let my prayers be true!
And, oh, forget not that thou art willed to do!

> [*She follows* AGAMEMNON *into the Palace. The
> retinues of both King and Queen go in after
> them.* CASSANDRA *remains.*

[*Strophe.*

Chorus. What is this that evermore,
        A cold terror at the door
    Of this bosom presage-haunted,
    Pale as death hovereth?
    While a song unhired, unwanted,
    By some inward prophet chanted,
        Speaks the secret at its core;
        And to cast it from my blood
        Like a dream not understood
        No sweet-spoken Courage now
        Sitteth at my heart's dear prow.

        Yet I know that manifold
        Days, like sand, have waxen old
    Since the day those shoreward-thrown
    Cables flapped and line on line

Standing forth for Ilion
   The long galleys took the brine.

[Antistrophe.

   And in harbor—mine own eye
   Hath beheld—again they lie;
Yet that lyreless music hidden
   Whispers still words of ill,
'Tis the Soul of me unbidden,
Like some Fury sorrow-ridden,
   Weeping over things that die.
   Neither waketh in my sense
   Ever Hope's dear confidence;
   For this flesh that groans within,
   And these bones that know of Sin,
   This tossed heart upon the spate
   Of a whirlpool that is Fate,
   Surely these lie not. Yet deep
      Beneath hope my prayer doth run,
   All will die like dreams, and creep
      To the unthought of and undone.

[Strophe.

Surely of great Weal at the end of all
Comes not Content; so near doth Fever crawl,
Close neighbor, pressing hard the narrow wall.
Woe to him who fears not fate!
'Tis the ship that forward straight
Sweepeth, strikes the reef below;
He who fears and lightens weight,
Casting forth, in measured throw
From the wealth his hand hath got
His whole ship shall founder not,
With abundance overfraught.
Nor deep seas above him flow.
Lo, when famine stalketh near,
One good gift of Zeus again
From the furrows of one year
Endeth quick the starving pain.

[Antistrophe.

[65]

But once the blood of death is fallen, black
And oozing at a slain man's feet, alack!
By spell or singing who shall charm it back?

One there was of old who showed
    Man the path from death to day;
But Zeus, lifting up his rod,
    Spared not, when he charged him stay.

Save that every doom of God
    Hath by other dooms its way
Crossed, that none may rule alone,
In one speech-outstripping flood
Forth had all this passion flown,
    Which now murmuring hides away,
Full of pain, and hoping not
Ever one clear thread to unknot
From the tangle of my soul,
From a heart of burning coal.
        [*Suddenly* CLYTEMNESTRA *appears standing in the*
            Doorway.

Clytemnestra. Thou likewise, come within! I speak thy
    name,
Cassandra;
        [CASSANDRA *trembles, but continues to stare in*
            front of her, as though not hearing CLYTEM-
            NESTRA.
        seeing the Gods—why chafe at them?—
Have placed thee here, to share within these walls
Our lustral waters, 'mid a crowd of thralls
Who stand obedient round the altar-stone
Of our Possession. Therefore come thou down,
And be not over-proud. The tale is told
How once Alcmena's son himself, being sold,
Was patient, though he liked not the slaves' mess.
    And more, if Fate must bring thee to this stress,
Praise God thou art come to a House of high report
And wealth from long ago. The baser sort,
Who have reaped some sudden harvest unforeseen,

Are ever cruel to their slaves, and mean
In the measure. We shall give whate'er is due.

> [CASSANDRA *is silent*.

Leader. To thee she speaks, and waits . . . clear words and
true!
Oh, doom is all around thee like a net;
Yield, if thou canst. . . . Belike thou canst not yet.
Clytemnestra. Methinks, unless this wandering maid is one
Voiced like a swallow-bird, with tongue unknown
And barbarous, she can read my plain intent.
I use but words, and ask for her consent.
Leader. Ah, come! 'Tis best, as the world lies to-day.
Leave this high-thronèd chariot, and obey!
Clytemnestra. How long must I stand dallying at the Gate?
Even now the beasts to Hestia consecrate *Goddess of the Hearth (Vesta)*
Wait by the midmost fire, since there is wrought
This high fulfilment for which no man thought.
Wherefore, if 'tis thy pleasure to obey
Aught of my will, prithee, no more delay!
If, deaf to sense, thou wilt not understand . . .
Thou show her, not with speech but with brute hand!

> [*To the Leader of the* CHORUS.

Leader. The strange maid needs a rare interpreter.
She is trembling like a wild beast in a snare.
Clytemnestra. 'Fore God, she is mad, and heareth but her
own
Folly! A slave, her city all o'erthrown,
She needs must chafe her bridle, till this fret
Be foamed away in blood and bitter sweat.
I waste no more speech, thus to be defied.

> [*She goes back inside the Palace*.

Leader. I pity thee so sore, no wrath nor pride
Is in me.—Come, dismount! Bend to the stroke
Fate lays on thee, and learn to feel thy yoke.

> [*He lays his hand softly on* CASSANDRA'S *shoulder*.

Cassandra (*moaning to herself*). Otototoi . . . Dreams.
Dreams.

Apollo. O Apollo!

Second Elder. Why sob'st thou for Apollo? It is writ,
He loves not grief nor lendeth ear to it.

Cassandra. Otototoi . . . Dreams. Dreams.
Apollo. O Apollo!
Leader. Still to that god she makes her sobbing cry
  Who hath no place where men are sad, or die.
Cassandra. Apollo, Apollo! Light of the Ways of Men!
Mine enemy!
  Hast lighted me to darkness yet again?
Second Elder. How? Will she prophesy about her own
  Sorrows? That power abides when all is gone!
Cassandra. Apollo, Apollo! Light of all that is!
Mine enemy!
Where hast thou led me? . . . Ha! What house is this?
Leader. The Atreidae's castle. If thou knowest not, I
  Am here to help thee, and help faithfully.
Cassandra (whispering). Nay, nay. This is the house that
  God hateth.
There be many things that know its secret; sore
And evil things; murders and strangling death.
  'Tis here they slaughter men . . . A splashing floor.
Second Elder. Keen-sensed the strange maid seemeth, like
  a hound
For blood.—And what she seeks can sure be found!
Cassandra. The witnesses . . . I follow where they lead.
  That weeping: here quite close: children are there,
    Weeping: and wounds that bleed.
The smell of the baked meats their father tare.
Second Elder (recognizing her vision, and repelled). Word
  of thy mystic power had reached our ear
Long since. Howbeit we need no prophets here.
Cassandra. Ah, ah! What would they? A new dreadful thing.
  A great great sin plots in the house this day;
  Too strong for the faithful, beyond medicining . . .
    And help stands far away.
Leader. This warning I can read not, though I knew
  That other tale. It rings the city through.
Cassandra. O Woman, thou! The lord who lay with thee!
  Wilt lave with water, and then . . . How speak the end?
  It comes so quick, A hand . . . Another hand . . .
    That reach, reach gropingly . . .
Leader. I see not yet. These riddles, pierced with blind

[68]

Gleams of foreboding but bemuse my mind.
Cassandra. Ah, ah! What is it? There; it is coming clear.
  A net . . . some net of Hell.
  Nay, she that lies with him . . . is she the snare?
  And half of his blood upon it. It holds well . . .
  O Crowd of ravening Voices, be glad, yea, shout
  And cry for the stoning, cry for the casting out!
Second Elder. What Fury Voices call'st thou to be hot
  Against this castle? Such words like me not. .
  And deep within my breast I feel that sick
    And saffron drop, which creepeth to the heart
  To die as the last rays of life depart.
      Misfortune comes so quick.
Cassandra. Ah, look! Look! Keep his mate from the Wild
  Bull!
      A tangle of raiment, see;
  A black horn, and a blow, and he falleth, full
    In the marble amid the water. I counsel ye.
  I speak plain. . . . Blood in the bath and treachery!
Leader. No great interpreter of oracles
  Am I; but this, I think, some mischief spells.
    What spring of good hath seercraft ever made
        Up from the dark to flow?
      'Tis but a weaving of words, a craft of woe,
        To make mankind afraid.
Cassandra. Poor woman! Poor dead woman! . . . Yea, it is I,
  Poured out like water among them. Weep for me. . . .
  Ah! What is this place? Why must I come with thee . . .
        To die, only to die?
Leader. Thou art borne on the breath of God, thou spirit
  wild,
      For thine own weird to wail,
    Like to that winged voice, that heart so sore
    Which, crying alway, hungereth to cry more,
    'Itylus, Itylus,' till it sing her child
    · Back to the nightingale.
Cassandra. Oh, happy Singing Bird, so sweet, so clear!
      Soft wings for her God made,
    And an easy passing, without pain or tear . . .
    For me 'twill be torn flesh and rending blade.

Second Elder. Whence is it sprung, whence wafted on God's
   breath,
          This anguish reasonless?
     This throbbing of terror shaped to melody,
     Moaning of evil blent with music high?
     Who hath marked out for thee that mystic path
         Through thy woe's wilderness?
Cassandra. Alas for the kiss, the kiss of Paris, his people's
   bane!
     Alas for Scamander Water, the water my fathers drank!
       Long, long ago, I played about thy bank,
         And was cherished and grew strong;
     Now by a River of Wailing, by shores of Pain,
       Soon shall I make my song.
Leader. How sayst thou? All too clear,
     This ill word thou hast laid upon thy mouth!
       A babe could read thee plain.
     It stabs within me like a serpent's tooth,
     The bitter thrilling music of her pain:
       I marvel as I hear.
Cassandra. Alas for the toil, the toil of a City, worn unto
   death!
     Alas for my father's worship before the citadel,
     The flocks that bled and the tumult of their breath!
       But no help from them came
     To save Troy Towers from falling as they fell! . . .
     And I on the earth shall writhe, my heart aflame.
Second Elder. Dark upon dark, new ominous words of ill!
     Sure there hath swept on thee some Evil Thing.
       Crushing, which makes thee bleed
       And in the torment of thy vision sing
     These plaining death-fraught oracles . . . Yet still, still,
     Their end I cannot read!
Cassandra. (*By an effort she regains mastery of herself,
     and speaks directly to the Leader.*)
'Fore God, mine oracles shall no more hide
With veils his visage, like a new-wed bride!
A shining wind out of this dark shall blow,
Piercing the dawn, growing as great waves grow,
To burst in the heart of sunrise . . . stronger far

[70]

Than this poor pain of mine. I will not mar
With mists my wisdom.
                              Be near me as I go,
Tracking the evil things of long ago,
And bear me witness. For this roof, there clings
Music about it, like a choir which sings
One-voiced, but not well-sounding, for not good
The words are. Drunken, drunken, and with blood,
To make them dare the more, a revelling rout
Is in the rooms, which no man shall cast out,
Of sister Furies. And they weave to song,
Haunting the House, its first blind deed of wrong,
Spurning in turn that King's bed desecrate,
Defiled, which paid a brother's sin with hate. . . *At. & thy. pray*
    Hath it missed or struck, mine arrow? Am I a poor
Dreamer, that begs and babbles at the door?
Give first thine oath in witness, that I know
Of this great dome the sins wrought long ago.
    Elder. And how should oath of mine, though bravely sworn,
Appease thee? Yet I marvel that one born
Far over seas, of alien speech, should fall
So apt, as though she had lived here and seen all.
    Cassandra. The Seer Apollo made me too to see.
    Elder (*in a low voice*). Was the God's heart pierced with
        desire for thee?
    Cassandra. Time was, I held it shame hereof to speak.
    Elder. Ah, shame is for the mighty, not the weak.
    Cassandra. We wrestled, and his breath to me was sweet.
    Elder. Ye came to the getting of children, as is meet?
    Cassandra. I swore to Loxias, and I swore a lie. *Apollo.*
    Elder. Already thine the gift of prophecy?
    Cassandra. Already I showed my people all their path.
    Elder. And Loxias did not smite thee in his wrath?
    Cassandra. After that sin . . . no man believed me more.
    Elder. Nay, then, to us thy wisdom seemeth sure.
    Cassandra. Oh, oh! Agony, agony!
Again the awful pains of prophecy
Are on me, maddening as they fall. . . .
Ye see them there . . . beating against the wall?
So young . . . like shapes that gather in a dream . . .

[71]

Slain by a hand they loved. Children they seem,
Murdered . . . and in their hands they bear baked meat:
I think it is themselves. Yea, flesh; I see it;
And inward parts. . . . Oh, what a horrible load
To carry! And their father drank their blood.
    From these, I warn ye, vengeance broodeth still,
A lion's rage, which goes not forth to kill
But lurketh in his lair, watching the high
Hall of my war-gone master . . . Master? Aye;
Mine, mine! The yoke is nailed about my neck. . . .
Oh, lord of ships and trampler on the wreck
Of Ilion, knows he not this she-wolf's tongue,
Which licks and fawns, and laughs with ear up-sprung.
To bite in the end like a secret death?—And can
The woman? Slay a strong and armèd man? . . .
    What fangèd reptile like to her doth creep?
Some serpent amphisbene, some Skylla, deep
Housed in the rock, where sailors shriek and die,
Mother of Hell blood-raging, which doth cry
On her own flesh war, war without alloy . . .
God! And she shouted in his face her joy,
Like men in battle when the foe doth break.
And feigns thanksgiving for his safety's sake!
    What if no man believe me? 'Tis all one.
The thing which must be shall be; aye, and soon
Thou too shalt sorrow for these things, and here
Standing confess me all too true a seer.
    Leader. The Thyestean feast of children slain
I understood, and tremble. Aye, my brain
Reels at these visions, beyond guesswork true.
But after, though I heard, I had lost the clue.
    Cassandra. Man, thou shalt look on Agamemnon dead.
    Leader. Peace, Mouth of Evil! Be those words unsaid!
    Cassandra. No god of peace hath watch upon that hour.
    Leader. If it must come. Forefend it, Heavenly Power!
    Cassandra. They do not think of prayer; they think of
      death.
    Leader. They? Say, what man this foul deed compasseth?
    Cassandra. Alas, thou art indeed fallen far astray!
    Leader. How could such deed be done? I see no way.

[72]

Cassandra. Yet know I not the Greek tongue all too well?
Leader. Greek are the Delphic dooms, but hard to spell.
Cassandra. Ah! Ah! There!
What a strange fire! It moves . . . It comes at me.
O Wolf Apollo, mercy! O agony! . . .
Why lies she with a wolf, this lioness lone,
Two-handed, when the royal lion is gone?
God, she will kill me! Like to them that brew
Poison, I see her mingle for me too
A separate vial in her wrath, and swear,
Whetting her blade for him, that I must share
His death . . . because, because he hath dragged me here!
  Oh, why these mockers at my throat? This gear
Of wreathèd bands, this staff of prophecy?
I mean to kill you first, before I die.
Begone!

> [*She tears off her prophetic habiliments; and pres-
> ently throws them on the ground, and stamps
> on them.*

        Down to perdition! . . . Lie ye so?
So I requite you! Now make rich in woe
Some other Bird of Evil, me no more!

> [*Coming to herself.*

Ah, see! It is Apollo's self, hath tore
His crown from me! Who watched me long ago
In this same prophet's robe, by friend, by foe,
All with one voice, all blinded, rocked to scorn:
'A thing of dreams' 'a beggar-maid outworn,'
Poor, starving and reviled, I endured all;
And now the Seer, who called me till my call
Was perfect, leads me to this last dismay. . . .
'Tis not the altar-stone where men did slay
My father; 'tis a block, a block with gore
Yet hot, that waits me, of one slain before.
  Yet not of God unheeded shall we lie.   *Orestes*
There cometh after, one who lifteth high
The downfallen; a branch where blossometh
A sire's avenging and a mother's death.
Exiled and wandering, from this land outcast,
One day He shall return, and set the last

[73]

Crown on these sins that have his house downtrod.
For, lo, there is a great oath sworn of God,
His father's upturned face shall guide him home.
  Why should I grieve? Why pity these men's doom?
I who have seen the City of Ilion
Pass as she passed; and they who cast her down
Have thus their end, as God gives judgment sure. . . .
  I go to drink my cup. I will endure
To die. O Gates, Death-Gates, all hail to you!
Only, pray God the blow be stricken true!
Pray God, unagonized, with blood that flows
Quick unto friendly death, these eyes may close!
  Leader. O full of sorrows, full of wisdom great,
Woman, thy speech is a long anguish; yet,
Knowing thy doom, why walkst thou with clear eyes,
Like some god-blinded beast, to sacrifice?
  Cassandra. There is no escape, friends; only vain delay.
  Leader. Is not the later still the sweeter day?
  Cassandra. The day is come. Small profit now to fly.
  Leader. Through all thy griefs, Woman, thy heart is high.
  Cassandra. Alas! None that is happy hears that praise.
  Leader. Are not the brave dead blest in after days?
  Cassandra. O Father! O my brethren brave, I come!
    [*She moves towards the House, but recoils shud-
        dering.*
  Leader. What frights thee? What is that thou startest from?
  Cassandra. Ah, faugh! Faugh!
  Leader.   What turns thee in that blind
Horror? Unless some loathing of the mind . . .
  Cassandra. Death drifting from the doors, and blood like
    rain!
  Leader. 'Tis but the dumb beasts at the altar slain.
  Cassandra. And vapors from a charnel-house . . . See
    there!
  Leader. 'Tis Tyrian incense clouding in the air.
  Cassandra (*recovering herself again*). So be it!—I will go,
    in yonder room
To weep mine own and Agamemnon's doom.
May death be all! Strangers, I am no bird
That pipeth trembling at a thicket stirred

By the empty wind. Bear witness on that day
When woman for this woman's life shall pay,
And man for man ill-mated low shall lie:
I ask this boon, as being about to die.

    Leader. Alas, I pity thee thy mystic fate!

    Cassandra. One word, one dirge-song would I utter yet
O'er mine own corpse. To this last shining Sun
I pray that, when the Avenger's work is done,
His enemies may remember this thing too,
This little thing, the woman slave they slew!
   O world of men, farewell! A painted show
Is all thy glory; and when life is low
The touch of a wet sponge out-blotteth all.
Oh, sadder this than any proud man's fall!

                    [*She goes into the House.*

    Chorus. Great Fortune is an hungry thing,
      And filleth no heart anywhere,
    Though men with fingers menacing
      Point at the great house, none will dare,
    When Fortune knocks, to bar the door
    Proclaiming: 'Come thou here no more!'
    Lo, to this man the Gods have given
      Great Ilion in the dust to tread
    And home return, emblazed of heaven;
    If it is writ, he too shall go
    Through blood for blood spilt long ago;
    If he too, dying for the dead,
      Should crown the deaths of alien years,
      What mortal afar off, who hears,
    Shall boast him Fortune's Child, and led
      Above the eternal tide of tears?

               [*A sudden Cry from within.*

    Voice. Ho! Treason in the house! I am wounded: slain.

    Leader. Hush! In the castle! 'Twas a cry
      Of some man wounded mortally.

    Voice. Ah God, another! I am stricken again.

    Leader. I think the deed is done. It was the King
Who groaned. . . Stand close, and think of any thing . . .

       [*The Old Men gather together under the shock,
       and debate confusedly.*

Elder B. I give you straight my judgment. Summon all
The citizens to rescue. Sound a call!

Elder C. No, no! Burst in at once without a word!
In, and convict them by their dripping sword!

Elder D. Yes; that or something like it. Quick, I say,
Be doing! 'Tis a time for no delay.

Elder E. We have time to think. This opening . . . They
      have planned
Some scheme to make enslavement of the land.

Elder F. Yes, while we linger here! They take no thought
Of lingering, and their sword-arm sleepeth not!

Elder G. I have no counsel. I can speak not. Oh,
Let him give counsel who can strike a blow!

Elder H. I say as this man says. I have no trust
In words to raise a dead man from the dust.

Elder I. How mean you? Drag out our poor lives, and
      stand
Cowering to these defilers of the land?

Elder J. Nay, 'tis too much! Better to strive and die!
Death is an easier doom than slavery.

Elder K. We heard a sound of groaning, nothing plain,
How know we—are we seers?—that one is slain?

Elder L. Oh, let us find the truth out, ere we grow
Thus passionate! To surmise is not to know.

Leader. Break in, then! 'Tis the council ye all bring,
And learn for sure, how is it with the King.

> [*They cluster up toward the Palace Door, as
> though to force an entrance, when the great
> Door swings open, revealing* CLYTEMNESTRA,
> *who stands, axe in hand, over the dead bodies
> of* AGAMEMNON *and* CASSANDRA. *The body of*
> AGAMEMNON *is wrapped in a rich crimson
> web. There is blood on* CLYTEMNESTRA'S *brow,
> and she speaks in wild triumph.*

Clytemnestra. Oh, lies enough and more have I this day
Spoken, which now I shame not to unsay.
How should a woman work, to the utter end,
Hate on a damnèd hater, feigned a friend;
How pile perdition round him, hunter-wise,
Too high for overleaping, save by lies?

[76]

To me this hour was dreamed of long ago;
A thing of ancient hate. 'Twas very slow
In coming, but it came. And here I stand
Even where I struck, with all the deed I planned
Done! 'Twas so wrought—what boots it to deny?—
The man could neither guard himself nor fly.
An endless web, as by some fisher strung,
A deadly plenteousness of robe, I flung
All round him, and struck twice; and with two cries
His limbs turned water and broke; and as he lies
I cast my third stroke in, a prayer well-sped
To Zeus of Hell, who guardeth safe his dead!
So there he gasped his life out as he lay;
And, gasping, the blood spouted . . . Like dark spray
That splashed, it came, a salt and deathly dew;
Sweet, sweet as God's dear rain-drops ever blew
O'er parched field, the day the buds are born! . . .

　　Which things being so, ye Councillors high-born,
Depart in joy, if joy ye will. For me,
I glory. Oh, if such a thing might be
As o'er the dead thank-offering to outpour,
On this dead it were just, aye, just and more,
Who filled the cup of the House with treacheries
Curse-fraught, and here hath drunk it to the lees!

　　Leader. We are astonished at thy speech. To fling,
Wild mouth! such vaunt over thy murdered King!

　　Clytemnestra. Wouldst frighten me, like a witless woman?
　　Lo,
This bosom shakes not. And, though well ye know,
I tell you . . . Curse me as ye will, or bless,
'Tis all one . . . This is Agamemnon; this,
My husband, dead by my right hand, a blow
Struck by a righteous craftsman. Aye, 'tis so.

　　Chorus. Woman, what evil tree,
　　　　What poison grown of the ground
　　　Or draught of the drifting sea
　　　　Way to thy lips hath found,
　　　Making thee clothe thy heart
　　　　In rage, yea, in curses burning
　　　When thine own people pray?

Thou hast hewn, thou hast cast away;
And a thing cast away thou art,
A thing of hate and a spurning!
Clytemnestra. Aye, now, for me, thou hast thy words of fate;
Exile from Argos and the people's hate
For ever! Against him no word was cried,
When, recking not, as 'twere a beast that died,
With flocks abounding o'er his wide domain,
He slew his child, my love, my flower of pain.
Great God, as magic for the winds of Thrace!
Why was not he man-hunted from his place,
To purge the blood that stained him? . . . When the deed
Is mine, oh, then thou art a judge indeed!
But threat thy fill. I am ready, and I stand
Content; if thy hand beateth down my hand,
Thou rulest. If aught else be God's decree,
Thy lesson shall be learned, though late it be.
   Chorus. Thy thought, it is very proud;
       Thy breath is the scorner's breath;
      Is not the madness loud
        In thy heart, being drunk with death?
      Yea, and above thy brow
       A star of the wet blood burneth!
      Oh, doom shall have yet her day,
      The last friend cast away,
      When lie doth answer lie
       And a stab for a stab returneth!
   Clytemnestra. And hark what Oath-gods gather to my side!
By my dead child's Revenge, now satisfied,
By Mortal Blindness, by all Powers of Hell
Which Hate, to whom in sacrifice he fell,
My Hope shall walk not in the house of Fear,
While on my hearth one fire yet burneth clear,
One lover, one Aegisthus, as of old!
What should I fear, when fallen here I hold
This foe, this scorner of his wife, this toy
And fool of each Chryseïs under Troy;
And there withal his soothsayer and slave,
His chanting bed-fellow, his leman brave,
Who rubbed the galleys' benches at his side?

[78]

But, oh, they had their guerdon as they died!
For he lies thus, and she, the wild swan's way,
Hath trod her last long weeping roundelay,
And lies, his lover, ravisht o'er the main
For his bed's comfort and my deep disdain.

    Chorus. (*Some Elders.*)
        Would God that suddenly
        With no great agony,
          No long sick-watch to keep,
        My hour would come to me,
        My hour, and presently
        Bring the eternal, the
          Unwaking sleep,
        Now that my Shepherd, he
        Whose love watched over me,
          Lies in the deep!

    Another. For woman's sake he endured and battled well,
      And by a woman's hand he fell.

    Others. What has thou done, O Helen blind of brain,
O face that slew the souls on Ilion's plain,
One face, one face, and many a thousand slain?
    The hate of old that on this castle lay,
Builded in lust, a husband's evil day,
Hath bloomed for thee a perfect flower again
      And unforgotten, an old and burning stain
        Never to pass away.

    Clytemnestra. Nay, pray not for the hour of death, being
    tried
      Too sore beneath these blows,
    Neither on Helen turn my wrath aside,
    The Slayer of Men, the face which hath destroyed
    Its thousand Danaan souls, and wrought a wide
      Wound that no leech can close.

    Chorus. Daemon, whose heel is set
      On the House and the twofold kin
        Of the high Tantalidae,
    A power, heavy as fate,
      Thou wieldest through woman's sin,
        Piercing the heart of me!
    Like a raven swoln with hate

[79]

He hath set on the dead his claw,
He croaketh a song to sate
His fury, and calls it Law!

Clytemnestra. Ah, call upon Him! Yea, call—
And thy thought hath found its path—
The Daemon who haunts this hall,
The thrice-engorgèd Wrath;
From him is the ache of the flesh
For blood born and increased;
Ere the old sore hath ceased
It oozeth afresh.

Chorus. Indeed He is very great,
And heavy his anger, He,
The Daemon who guides the fate
Of the old Tantalidae:
Alas, alas, an evil tale ye tell
Of desolate angers and insatiable!
Ah me,
And yet 'tis all as Zeus hath willed,
Doer of all and Cause of all;
By His Word every chance doth fall,
No end without Him is fulfilled;
What of these things
But cometh by high Heaven's counselings?

[*A band of Mourners has gathered within the House.*

Mourners. Ah, sorrow, sorrow! My King, my King!
How shall I weep, what word shall I say?
Caught in the web of this spider thing,
In foul death gasping thy life away!
Woe's me, woe's me, for this slavish lying,
The doom of craft and the lonely dying,
The iron two-edged and the hands that slay!

Clytemnestra. And criest thou still this deed hath been
My work? Nay, gaze, and have no thought
That this is Agamemnon's Queen.
'Tis He, 'tis He, hath round him wrought
This phantom of the dead man's wife;
He, the old Wrath, the Driver of Men astray,
Pursuer of Atreus for the feast defiled;

To assoil an ancient debt he hath paid this life;
A warrior and a crownèd King this day
    Atones for a slain child.
Chorus. That thou art innocent herein   *Chorus does not accept.*
  What tongue dare boast? It cannot be,
Yet from the deeps of ancient sin
    The Avenger may have wrought with thee.
On the red Slayer crasheth, groping wild
  For blood, more blood, to build his peace again,
And wash like water the old frozen stain
    Of the torn child.
Mourners. Ah, sorrow, sorrow! My King, my King!
    How shall I weep, what words shall I say?
  Caught in the web of this spider thing,
    In foul death gasping thy life away.
Woe's me, woe's me, for this slavish lying,
The doom of craft and the lonely dying,
    The iron two-edged and the hands that slay!
Clytemnestra. And what of the doom of craft that first
    He planted, making the House accurst?
    What of the blossom from this root riven,
    Iphigenia, the unforgiven?
    Even as the wrong was, so is the pain:
    He shall not laugh in the House of the slain,
      When the count is scored;
    He hath but spoilèd and paid again
      The due of the sword.
Chorus.   I am lost; my mind dull-eyed
      Knows not nor feels
    Whither to fly nor hide
      While the House reels.
    The noise of rain that falls
      On the roof affrighteth me,
    Washing away the walls;
      Rain that falls bloodily.
    Doth ever the sound abate?
    Lo, the next Hour of Fate
    Whetting her vengeance due
    On new whet-stones, for new
      Workings of hate.

Mourners. Would thou hadst covered me, Earth, O Earth,
  Or e'er I had looked on my lord thus low,
In the pallèd marble of silvern girth!
  What hands may shroud him, what tears may flow?
Not thine, O Woman who dared to slay him,
Thou durst not weep to him now, nor pray him,
Nor pay to his soul the deep unworth
Of gift or prayer to forget thy blow.
        Oh, who with heart sincere
          Shall bring praise or grief
        To lay on the sepulchre
          Of the great chief?
Clytemnestra. His burial is not thine to array.
        By me he fell, by me he died,
        I watch him to the grave, not cried
      By mourners of his housefolk; nay,
      His own child for a day like this
        Waits, as is seemly, and shall run
        By the white waves of Acheron,
      To fold him in her arms and kiss!
Chorus.   Lo, she who was erst reviled
        Revileth: and what is true?
      Spoil taken from them that spoiled,
        Life-blood from them that slew!
      Surely while God ensueth
        His laws, while Time doth run
      'Tis written: On him that doeth
        It shall be done.
      This is God's law and grace,
      Who then shall hunt the race
      Of curses from out this hall?
      The House is sealed withal
        To dreadfulness.
Clytemnestra. Aye, thou hast found the Law, and stept
      In Truth's way.—Yet even now I call
      The Living Wrath which haunts this hall
    To truce and compact. I accept
    All the affliction he doth heap
      Upon me, and I charge him go
      Far off with his self-murdering woe

[82]

To strange men's houses. I will keep
Some little dower, and leave behind
   All else, contented utterly.
   I have swept the madness from the sky
Wherein these brethren slew their kind.

[*As she ceases, exhausted and with the fire gone
   out of her,* AEGISTHUS, *with Attendants, bursts
   triumphantly in.*

   Aegisthus. O shining day, O dawn of righteousness
Fulfilled! Now, now indeed will I confess
That divine watchers o'er man's death and birth
Look down on all the anguish of the earth,
Now that I see him lying, as I love
To see him, in this net the Furies wove,
To atone the old craft of his father's hand.

   For Atreus, this man's father, in this land
Reigning, and by Thyestes in his throne
Challenged—he was his brother and mine own
Father—from home and city cast him out;
And he, after long exile, turned about
And threw him suppliant on the hearth, and won
Promise of so much mercy, that his own
Life-blood should reek not in his father's hall.
Then did that godless brother, Atreus, call,
To greet my sire—More eagerness, O God,
Was there than love!—a feast of brotherhood.
And, feigning joyous banquet, laid as meat
Before him his dead children. The white feet
And finger-fringèd hands apart he set,
Veiled from all seeing, and made separate
The tables. And he straightway, knowing naught,
Took of those bodies, eating that which wrought
No health for all his race. And when he knew
The unnatural deed, back from the board he threw,
Spewing that murderous gorge, and spurning brake
The table, to make strong the curse he spake:
'Thus perish all of Pleisthenês begot!'

   For that lies this man here; and all the plot
Is mine, most righteously. For me, the third,
When butchering my two brethren, Atreus spared

[83]

And cast me with my broken sire that day,
A little thing in swaddling clothes, away
To exile; where I grew, and at the last
Justice hath brought me home! Yea, though outcast
In a far land, mine arm hath reached this king;
My brain, my hate, wrought all the counseling;
And all is well. I have seen mine enemy
Dead in the snare, and care not if I die!

    Leader. Aegisthus, to insult over the dead
I like not. All the counsel, thou has said,
Was thine alone; and thine the will that spilled
This piteous blood. As justice is fulfilled,
Thou shalt not 'scape—so my heart presageth—
The day of cursing and the hurlèd death.

    Aegisthus. How, thou poor oarsman of the nether row,
When the main deck is master? Sayst thou so? . . .
To such old heads the lesson may prove hard,
I fear me, when Obedience is the word.
But hunger, and bonds, and cold, help men to find
Their wits.—They are wondrous healers of the mind!
Hast eyes and seest not this?—Against a spike
Kick not, for fear it pain thee if thou strike.

    Leader (*turning from him to Clytemnestra*). Woman! A
        soldier fresh from war! To keep
Watch o'er his house and shame him in his sleep . . .
To plot this craft against a lord of spears . . .

            [CLYTEMNESTRA, *as though in a dream, pays no
            heed.* AEGISTHUS *interrupts.*

    Aegisthus. These be the words, old man, that lead to tears!
Thou hast an opposite to Orpheus' tongue,
Who chained all things with his enchanting song,
For thy mad noise will put the chains on thee.
Enough! Once mastered thou shalt tamer be.

    Leader. Thou master? Is old Argos so accurst?
Thou plotter afar off, who never durst
Raise thine own hand to affront and strike him down . . .

    Aegisthus. To entice him was the wife's work. I was known
By all men here, his old confessed blood-foe.
Howbeit, with his possessions I will know
How to be King. And who obeys not me

[84]

Shall be yoked hard, no easy trace-horse he,
Corn-flushed. Hunger, and hunger's prison mate,
The clammy murk, shall see his rage abate.

    Leader. Thou craven soul! Why not in open strife
Slay him? Why lay the blood-sin on his wife,
Staining the Gods of Argos, making ill
The soil thereof? . . . But young Orestes still
Liveth. Oh, Fate will guide him home again,
Avenging, conquering, home to kill these twain!

    Aegisthus. 'Fore God, if 'tis your pleasure thus to speak and
do, ye soon shall hear!

Ho there, my trusty pikes, advance! There cometh business
    for the spear.

> [*A body of Spearmen, from concealment outside,
> rush in and dominate the stage.*

    Leader. Ho there, ye Men of Argos! Up! Stand and be
ready, sword from sheath!

    Aegisthus. By Heaven, I also, sword in hand, am ready, and
refuse not death!

    Leader. Come, find it! We accept thy word. Thou offerest
what we hunger for.

> [*Some of the Elders draw swords with the Leader;
> others have collapsed with weakness. Men from
> AGAMEMNON's retinue have gathered and pre-
> pare for battle, when, before they can come to
> blows, CLYTEMNESTRA breaks from her ex-
> hausted silence.*

    Clytemnestra. Nay, peace, O best-belovèd! Peace! And let
us work no evil more.

Surely the reaping of the past is a full harvest, and not good,
And wounds enough are everywhere.—Let us not stain our-
    selves with blood.

Ye reverend Elders, go your ways, to his own dwelling every
    one,
Ere things be wrought for which men suffer.—What we did
    must needs be done.

And if of all these strifes we now may have no more, oh, I
    will kneel
And praise God, bruisèd though we be beneath the Daemon's
    heavy heel.

This is the word a woman speaks, to hear if any man will
deign.

Aegisthus. And who are these to burst in flower of folly thus
of tongue and brain,

And utter words of empty sound and perilous, tempting Fortune's frown,

And leave wise counsel all forgot, and gird at him who wears
the crown?

Leader. To cringe before a caitiff's crown, it squareth not
with Argive ways.

Aegisthus (*sheathing his sword and turning from them*).

Bah, I will be a hand of wrath to fall on thee in after days.

Leader. Not so, if God in after days shall guide Orestes
home again!

Aegisthus. I know how men in exile feed on dreams . . .
and know such food is vain.

Leader. Go forward and wax fat! Defile the right for this
thy little hour!

Aegisthus. I spare thee now. Know well for all this folly
thou shalt feel my power.

Leader. Aye, vaunt thy greatness, as a bird beside his mate
doth vaunt and swell.

Clytemnestra. Vain hounds are baying round thee; oh, forget them! Thou and I shall dwell

As Kings in this great House. We two at last will order all
things well.

> [*The* ELDERS *and the remains of* AGAMEMNON'S
> *retinue retire sullenly, leaving the Spearmen in
> possession.* CLYTEMNESTRA *and* AEGISTHUS *turn
> and enter the Palace.*

AESCHYLUS
CHOËPHOROE

≫≫ ≪≪

TRANSLATED
by
GILBERT MURRAY

CHARACTERS IN THE PLAY

ORESTES, *son of Agamemnon and Clytemnestra.*
ELECTRA, *daughter of Agamemnon and Clytemnestra.*
CLYTEMNESTRA, *formerly wife to Agamemnon, now wedded to Aegisthus.*
AEGISTHUS, *son of Thyestês, blood-foe to Agamemnon, and now Tyrant of Argos.*
PYLADES, *son of Strophios, King of Phokis, friend to Orestes.*
THE OLD NURSE *of Orestes.*
A SLAVE *of Aegisthus.*
CHORUS *of Bondmaids in the House of Clytemnestra and Aegisthus.*

The play was first in the archonship of Philocles (458 B.C.). *The First Prize was won by Aeschylus with* Agamemnon, Choëphoroe, Eumenides, *and the Satyr-play* Proteus.

ARGUMENT

In the preceding play, *Agamemnon,* we witnessed the murder of Agamemnon by his wife Clytemnestra and her lover Aegisthus. Orestes was absent from Mycenae when the murder took place, having been rescued as a child from the hands of Clytemnestra, who desired to kill him. With the help of Electra he was conveyed to Mount Parnassus where King Strophios took charge of him. Seven years later, at the age of twenty, he is commanded by the Delphic oracle to return and avenge his father's death.

CHOËPHOROE

The scene represents the Grave of Agamemnon, a mound of earth in a desolate expanse. The time is afternoon. ORESTES *and* PYLADES *in the garb of travelers, with swords at their sides, are discovered.* ORESTES' *hair is cut short, that of* PYLADES *streams down his back. Both look grim and travel-stained.* ORESTES *holds a long tress of hair in his hand.*

Orestes. O Warder Hermes of the world beneath,
Son of the Father who is Lord of Death;
Saviour, be thou my saviour; Help in War,
Help me! I am returned from lands afar
To claim mine own. And on this headland steep
Of death, I call my Father o'er the deep
To hearken, to give ear.—Behold, I bring
Out of my poverty one little thing,
To adorn thy grave, though who can touch the dead
Or wake from sleep that unuplifted head?
Yet long ago in Phokis, where I lay
With Strophios in the hills, being cast away
In childhood, plundered by mine enemies,
And friendless, save for this man, Pylades,
I sware an oath which should for ever set
In memory those they taught me to forget:
If once I came to manhood, so I sware,
In tresses twain I would divide mine hair,
One tress for Inachos river, by whose grace
I live, and one for mourning at this place.
Which oath I here fulfil.
                    [*He lays the tress of hair upon the upper part of
                        the grave mound.*
                        O Herald, lay
Before his sight the gift I bring this day,

Who stood not by to mourn him as he fell,
Nor reached mine arms to bid the dead farewell.

> [*As he turns, he sees the* LIBATION-BEARERS *approaching.*

Ha!
What sight is this? What stricken multitude
Of women here in raiment sable-hued
Far-gleameth? How shall I interpret it?
Hath some new death upon my lineage lit?
Or is it to my father's grave they go
With offerings, to appease the wrath below?
It must be. Surely 'tis Electra there,
My sister, moves alone, none like to her
In sorrow. Zeus, Oh, grant to me this day
My vengeance, and be near me in the fray!
Come, Pylades, stand further, till we know
More sure, what means this embassy of woe.

> [ORESTES *and* PYLADES *withdraw, as* ELECTRA *with the* CHORUS *of women bearing offerings for the Grave enters from the other side.*

> [*Strophe.*

Chorus. Driven, yea, driven
  I come: I bear Peace-offering to the dead,
  Mine hands as blades that tear, my tresses riven,
    And cheek plowed red.
  But all my years, before this day as after,
    Have been fed full with weeping as with bread.
    And this dumb cry of linen, as in pain,
    Deep rent about my bosom, speaketh plain
  Of a life long since wounded, where no laughter
    Sounds nor shall sound again.

> [*Antistrophe.*

    Dread, very dread,
  And hair upstarting and the wrath that streams
  From the heart of sleep, have first interpreted
    What manner of dreams
This house hath dreamed; a voice of terror, blasting
  The midnight, up from the inmost place it grew,
  Shaking the women's chambers; and the Seer,
  Being sworn of God, made answer, there is here

Anger of dead men wronged, and hate outlasting
    Death, against them that slew.

    Craving to fly that curse
With graceless gift hither she urgeth me
    —O Earth, Mother and Nurse!—
She whom God hateth. But my spirit fears
    To speak the word it bears.
When blood is spilt, how shall a gift set free?
    O hearthstone wet with tears!
O pillars of a house broken in twain!
    Without sun, without love,
Murk in the heart thereof and mist above,
    For a lord slain!

    The reverence of old years
Is gone, which not by battle nor by strife,
    Stealing through charmèd ears,
Lifted the people's hearts to love their King;
    Gone, yet the land still fears.
For Fortune is a god and rules men's life.
    Who knows the great Wheel's swing,
How one is smitten swift in the eyes of light;
    For one affliction cries
Slow from the border of sunset; and one lies
    In deedless night?

    Has Earth once drunk withal
The blood of her child, Man, the avenging stain
    Hardens, nor flows again.
A blind pain draweth the slayer, draweth him,
On, on, till he is filled even to the brim
With sickness of the soul to atone for all.

    The shrine of maidenhood
Once broken ne'er may be unbroke again.
    And where man's life hath flowed
All the world's rivers in their multitude
    Rolling shall strive in vain
To clean from a brother's hand that ancient blood.

For me, God in far days
Laid hand upon my city, and herded me
From my old home to the House of Slavery,
Where all is violence, and I needs must praise,
        Just or unjust,
The pleasure of them that rule, and speechless hold
The ache of a heart that rageth in the dust.
        Only behind the fold
Of this still veil for a little I hide my face
And weep for the blind doings of this race,
And secret tears are in my heart, ice-cold.

Electra. Ye thrallèd women, tirers of the bower,
Since ye are with me in this suppliant hour,
Your escort giving, give your counsel too.
What speech have I for utterance, when I sue
With offerings to the dead? What word of love
What prayer to reach my father from above?
'To dear Lord,' shall I say, 'due gifts I bear
From loving mistress' . . . when they come from her?
I dare not. And I cannot find the word
To speak, when offerings like these are poured. . . .
Or shall I pray him, as men's custom is,
To send to them who pay these offices
Requital due . . . for murder and for pride?
Or, as in silence and in shame he died,
In shame and silence shall I pour this urn
Of offering to the dust, and pouring turn,
As men cast out some foulness they abhor,
And fling the cup, and fly, and look no more?

    Share with me, Friends, this burden of strange thought.
One hate doth make us one. Oh, hide not aught
For fear of what may fall us! Destiny
Waiteth alike for them that men call free,
And them by others mastered. At thine ease.
Speak, if thou knowest of wiser words than these.

    Leader. As at God's altar, since so fain thou art,
Before this Tomb I will unveil my heart.
    Electra. Speak, by his grave and in the fear thereof.
    Leader. Pray as thou pourest: To all hearts of love . . .
    Electra. And who is such of all around us, who?

Leader. Thyself, and whoso hates Aegisthus true.

Electra. For thee and me alone am I to pray?

Leader. Ask thine own understanding. It will say.

Electra. Who else? What heart that with our sorrow grieves?

Leader. Forget not that—far off—Orestes lives.

Electra. Oh, bravely spoke! Thou counselest not in vain.

Leader. Next; on the sinners pray, their sin made plain. . . .

Electra. Pray what? I know not. Oh, make clear my road!

Leader. Pray that there come to them or man or god. . . .

Electra. A judge? Or an avenger? Speak thy prayer.

Leader. Plain be thy word: one who shall slay the slayer.

Electra. But dare I? Is it no sin thus to pray?

Leader. How else? With hate thine hater to repay.

> [ELECTRA *mounts upon the Grave Mound and
> makes sacrifice.*

Electra. Herald most high of living and of dead,
Thou midnight Hermes, hear; and call the dread
Spirits who dwell below the Earth, my vows
To hearken and to watch my father's house;
And Earth our Mother, who doth all things breed
And nurse, and takes again to her their seed.
And I too with thee, as I pour these streams
To wash dead hands, will call him in his dreams:
O Father, pity me; pity thine own
Orestes, and restore us to thy throne;
We are lost, we are sold like slaves: and in our stead
Lo, she hath brought thy murderer to her bed,
Aegisthus. I am like one chained alway;
Orestes wandering without house or stay;
But they are full of pride, and make turmoil
And banquet of the treasures of thy toil.
Guide thou Orestes homeward, let there be
Some chance to aid him:—Father, hark to me!
And, oh, give me a heart to understand
More than my mother, and a cleaner hand!
These prayers for us; but for our enemies
This also I speak: O Father, let there rise
Against them thine Avenger, and again
The slayer in just recompense be slain.—
  Behold, I pray great evil, and I lay

These tokens down; yea, midmost as I pray
Against thine enemies I lay them—so.
Do thou to us send blessing from below
With Zeus, and Earth, and Right which conquereth all.
  These be the prayers on which mine offerings fall.
Do ye set lamentation like a wreath
Round them, and cry the triumph-song of death.

> [*She proceeds with the pouring of offerings and
> presently finds on the tomb the Lock of Hair.
> The* CHORUS *makes lamentation before the grave.*

Chorus. Let fall the tear that plashes as it dies,
        Where the dead lies,
        Fall on this barrèd door,
  Where Good nor Evil entereth any more,
        This holy, abhorrèd thing,
  We turn from, praying—Lo, the milk and wine
        Are poured. Awake and hear, thou awful King;
  Hear in thy darkened soul, O Master mine!

    Oh, for some man of might
    To aid this land, some high and visible lord
    Of battle, shining bright
    Against Death; the great lance
    Bearing deliverance,
    The back-bent Scythian bow, the hilted sword
    Close-held to smite and smite!

Electra (*excitedly returning from the Grave*).
Behold,
The offerings of the dust are ministered:
But counsel me. I bear another word.
    Leader. Speak on. My spirit leaps for eagerness.
    Electra. Cast on the tomb I found this shaven tress.
    Leader. Who cast it there? What man or zonèd maid?
    Electra. Methinks that is a riddle quickly read!
    Leader. Thy thought is swift; and may thine elder know?
    Electra. What head save mine would blazon thus its woe?
    Leader. She that should mourn him is his enemy.
    Electra (*musing, to herself*). Strange bird, but of one feather
        to mine eye. . . .
    Leader. With what? Oh, speak. Make thy comparison.

[94]

Electra. Look; think ye not 'tis wondrous like mine own?
Leader. Thy brother's! . . . Sent in secret! Can it be?
Electra. 'Tis like his long locks in my memory.
Leader. Orestes! Would he dare to walk this land?
Electra. Belike he sent it by another's hand!
Leader. That calls for tears no less, if never more
His footstep may be set on Argos shore.

Electra. At my heart also bitterer than gall
A great wave beats. The iron hath passed thro' all
My being; and the stormy drops that rise
Fall unforbidden from these starvèd eyes,
Gazing upon this hair. 'Tis past belief
That any Argive tree hath shed this leaf.
And sure she shore it not who wrought his death,
My mother, godless, with no mother's faith
Or kindness for her child.—And yet to swear
Outright that this glad laughter is the hair
Of my beloved Orestes. . . . Oh, I am weak
With dreaming! Had it but a voice to speak
Like some kind messenger, I had not been
This phantom tossing in the wind between
Two fancies. Either quick it would proclaim
Its hate, if from some hater's head it came;
Or, if it were our own, with me 'twould shed
Tears for this tomb and our great father dead. . . .
Surely they know, these gods to whom we pray,
Through what wild seas our vessel beats her way,
And, if to save us is their will, may breed
A mighty oak-trunk from a little seed. . . .
                    [*She goes back to the Tomb, searching.*
  Ah see, the print of feet, a second sign!
The same feet: surely they are shaped like mine.
Surely! Two separate trails of feet are there:
He and perchance some fellow traveler.
The heels; the mark of the long muscle thrown
Athwart them on the sand—just like mine own
In shape and measure. What? . . . Oh, all is vain;
Torment of heart and blinding of the brain!
            [*She buries her face in her hands.* ORESTES *rises
              from his hiding-place and stands before her.*

[95]

Orestes. Thy prayer hath borne its fruit. Hereafter tell
The gods thy thanks, and may the end be well!
    Electra. What meanest thou? What hath God done for me?
    Orestes. Shown thee a face which thou hast longed to see.
    Electra. What face? What know'st thou of my secret heart?
    Orestes. Orestes'. For that name all fire thou art.
    Electra. If that be so, how am I near mine end?
    Orestes. Here am I, Sister. Seek no closer friend.
    Electra. Stranger! It is a plot thou lay'st for me!
    Orestes. Against mine own dear life that plot would be.
    Electra. Thou mock'st me! Thou would'st laugh to hear me
    moan!
    Orestes. Who mocks thy tribulation mocks mine own.
    Electra. My heart half dares foretell that thou art he . . .
    Orestes. Nay, when I face thee plain thou wilt not see!
Oh, seeing but that shorn tress of funeral hair
Thy soul took wings and seemed to hold me there;
Then peering in my steps . . . thou knew'st them mine,
Thy brother's, moulded feet and head like thine.
Set the lock here, where it was cut. Behold
This cloak I wear, thy woven work of old,
The battened ridges and the broidered braid
Of lions . . .
                [ELECTRA *throws herself into his arms.*
        Hold! Ah, be not all dismayed
With joy! Our nearest is our deadliest foe.
    Electra. O best beloved, O dreamed of long ago,
Seed of deliverance washed with tears as rain,
By thine own valor thou shalt build again
Our father's House! O lightener of mine eyes,
Four places in my heart, four sanctities,
Are thine. My father in thy face and mien
Yet living: thine the love that might have been
My mother's—whom I hate, most righteously—
And my poor sister's, fiercely doomed to die,
And thou my faithful brother, who alone
Hast cared for me. . . . O Victory, be our own
This day, with Justice who doth hold us fast,
And Zeus most high, who saveth at the last!
    Orestes. O Zeus, O Zeus, look down on our estate!

Hast seen thine eagle's brood left desolate,
The father in the fell toils overborne
Of some foul serpent, and the young forlorn
And starved with famine, still too weak of wing
To bear to the nest their father's harvesting?
Even so am I, O Zeus, and even so
This woman, both disfathered long ago,
Both to one exile cast, both desolate.
He was thy worshipper, thy giver great
Of sacrifice. If thou tear down his nest,
What hand like his shall glorify thy feast?
Blot out the eagle's brood, and where again
Hast thou thy messenger to speak to men?
Blast this most royal oak, what shade shall cool
Thine altars on the death-day of the Bull?
But cherish us, and from a little seed
Thou shalt make great a House now fallen indeed.

 Leader. O Children, Saviours of your father's House,
Be silent! Children, all is perilous;
And whoso hears may idly speak of ye
To our masters; whom may I yet live to see
Dead where the pine logs ooze in fragrant fire!

 Orestes. (*He speaks with increasing horror as he proceeds.*)
Oh, Loxias shall not mock my great desire,
Who spoke his divine promise, charging me
To thread this peril to the extremity:
Yea, raised his awful voice and surging told
To my hot heart of horrors stormy-cold
Till I seek out those murderers, by the road
Themselves have shown—so spake he—blood for blood,
In gold-rejecting rage, the wild bull's way!
If not, for their offending I must pay
With mine own life, in torment manifold.
Of many things that rise from earth he told,
To appease the angry dead: yea, and strange forms,
On thee and me, of savage-fangèd worms,
Climbing the flesh; lichens, which eat away
Even unto nothingness our natural clay.
And when they leave him, a man's hair is white.
For him that disobeys, he said, the night

[97]

Hath Furies, shapen of his father's blood;
Clear-seen, with eyeball straining through the hood
Of darkness. The blind arrows of dead men
Who cried their kin for mercy and were slain,
And madness, and wild fear out of the night,
Shall spur him, rack him, till from all men's sight
Alone he goes, out to the desert dim,
And that bronze horror clanging after him!
    For such as he there is no mixing bowl,
No dear libation that binds soul to soul:
From every altar fire the unseen rage
Outbars him: none shall give him harborage,
Nor rest beneath one roof with such an one;
Till, without worship, without love, alone
He crawls to his death, a carcase to the core
Through-rotted, and embalmed to suffer more.

                              [Collecting himself.

    So spake he . . . God, and is one to believe
Such oracles as these? Nay, though I give
No credence, the deed now must needs be done.
So many things of power work here as one:
The God's command; grief for my father slain;
And mine own beggary urgeth me amain,
That never shall these Argives, famed afar,
High conquerors of Troy in joyous war
Cower to . . . two women. For he bears, I know,
A woman's heart. . . . If not, this day will show.

      [He kneels at the Grave: ELECTRA *kneels opposite*
        him and the CHORUS *gather behind.*

Chorus. Ye great Apportionments of God,
      The road of Righteousness make straight:
        'For tongue of hate be tongue of hate
    Made perfect': thus, as falls her rod,
    God's justice crieth: 'For the blow
      Of death the blow of death atone'
      'On him that doeth shall be done':
    Speaks a gray word of long ago.

                             [Strophe 1

Orestes. O Father, Father of Doom,
      What word, what deed from me,

Can waft afar to the silent room
Where thy sleep holdeth thee
A light that shall rend thy gloom?
Yet surely, the tale is told,
That tears are comfort beneath the tomb
To the great Kings of old.

[*Strophe 2.*

Leader. No fire ravening red,
O Son, subdueth quite
The deep life of the dead;
His wrath breaks from the night.
When they weep for one who dies
His Avenger doth arise,
Yea, for father and life-giver
There is Justice, when the cries
And the tears run as a river.

[*Antistrophe 1.*

Electra. O Father, hearken and save,
For my sore sorrow's sake!
Children twain are above thy grave
Seeking for thee: Oh, Wake!
Thy grave is their only home,
The beggared and out-cast.
What here is well? What is saved from doom?
O Atê strong to the last!

Chorus. Yet still it may be—God is strong—
A changèd music shall be born
To sound above this dirge forlorn,
And the King's House with Triumph-song
Lead home a Friend in love new-sworn.

[*Strophe 3.*

Orestes. Would that in ancient days,
Father, some Lycian lance
Had slain thee by Ilion's wall;
Then hadst thou left great praise
In thy House, and thy children's glance
In the streets were marked of all:
Men had upreared for thee
A high-piled burial hill

In a land beyond the sea;
And the House could have borne its ill.

[Antistrophe 2.

Leader. And all they who nobly died
Would have loved him in that place,
And observed him in his pride
As he passed with royal pace
To a throne at the right hand
Of the Kings of the Dark Land:
For a king he was when living,
Above all who crownèd stand
With the sceptre of lawgiving.

[Antistrophe 3.

Electra. Nay, would thou hadst died not ever!
Not by the Ilion Gate,
Not when the others fell
Spear-broken beside the river!
If they who wrought thee hate
Had died, it had all been well:
A strange death, full of fear,
That the folk beyond far seas
Should enquire thereof, and hear;
Not of our miseries!

Chorus. My daughter, rare as gold is rare,
And blither than the skies behind
The raging of the northern wind
Are these thy prayers: for what is prayer?
Yet, be thou sure, this twofold scourge
Is heard: it pierceth to the verge
Of darkness, and your helpers now
Are wakening. These encharioted
Above us, lo, their hand is red!
Abhorrèd are they by the dead;
But none so hates as he and thou!

[Strophe 4.

Orestes. Ah me, that word, that word
Stabbeth my heart, as a sword!
God, God, who sendest from below
Blind vengeance in the wake

[100]

Of sin, what deed have I to do,
With hand most weak and full of woe?
'Tis for my father's sake!

[*Strophe* 5.

Leader. May it be mine, may it be mine,
To dance about the blazing pine
    Crying, crying,
'A man is slain, a woman dying!'
It hideth in my bosom's core,
    It beats its wings for death, for death,
A bitter wind that blows before
    The prow, a hate that festereth,
A thing of horror, yet divine!

[*Antistrophe* 4.

Electra. Zeus of the orphan, when
    Wilt lift thy hand among men?
Let the land have a sign. Be strong,
    And smite the neck from the head.
I ask for right after much wrong.
Hear me, O God! Hark to my song,
    Ye Princedoms of the Dead!

Chorus. 'Tis written: the shed drop doth crave
    For new blood. Yea, the murdered cry
Of dead men shrieketh from the grave
    To Her who out of sins gone by
Makes new sin, that the old may die.

[*Strophe* 6.

Orestes. How? Are ye dumb, Ye Princedoms of the Dead?
    O Curses of Them that perish, come hither, hither!
Look on this wreck of kings, the beaten head,
Bowed in despair, roofless, disherited!
    Whither to turn, O Lord Zeus? Whither, whither?

[*Antistrophe* 5.

Leader. My heart, my heart is tossed again
    To see thee yielded up to pain,
        Failing, failing;
    Then mist is on my eyes and wailing
About mine ears, and tears as rain.
But when once more I look on thee

With power exalted, sudden-swift
A hope doth all my burden lift,
And light, and signs of things to be.
[Antistrophe 6.

Electra. What best shall pierce thine ear; the wrongs she
wrought,
Wrought upon us, upon us, she and none other?
Oh, fawn and smile: but the wrongs shall soften not,
Wrongs with a wolfish heart, by a wolf begot:
They see no smile, they reck not the name of Mother!
[Strophe 7.

Chorus. With the dirge of Agbatana I beat my breast:
Like the Keeners of Kissia, I make songs of pain.
Lo, yearning of arms abundant, east and west:
Tearing they smite, again and yet again,
From above, from high; yea, God hath smitten red
This bitter bleeding bosom, this bended head.
[Strophe 8.

Electra. Ho, Mother! Ho, thou, Mother,
Mine enemy, daring all!
What burial made ye here?
His people followed not,
Mourned him not, knew him not:
Enemies bare his pall:
His wife shed no tear!
[Strophe 9.

Orestes. All, all dishonor, so thy story telleth it!
And for that dishonor shall the woman pay,
As the gods have willed it, as my right hand willeth it!
Then Death may take me, let me only slay!
[Antistrophe 9.

Leader. His hands and feet, they were hacked away from
him!
Yea, she that buried him, she wrought it so.
To make thy life blasted, without help or stay from him.
Thou hast it all, the defiling and shame and woe!
[ORESTES *breaks down in speechless tears.*
[Antistrophe 7.

Electra. Thou tellest the doom he died, but I saw him not;
I was far off, dishonored and nothing worth.

Like a dog they drove me back, and the door was shut,
  And alone I poured my tears to him through the earth.
I laughed not, yet rejoiced that none saw me weep.
Write this in thine heart, O Father; grave it deep.

[Antistrophe 8.

Leader. Write! Yea, and draw the word
    Deep unto that still land
      Where thy soul dwells in peace.
    What is, thou hast this day heard;
      What shall be, reach forth thine hand
      And take it! Be hard, be hard
        To smite and not cease!
(ORESTES, ELECTRA, *and the* LEADER.)

[*Strophe* 10.

Orestes. Thee, thee I call. Father, be near thine own.
Electra. I also cry thee, choked with the tears that flow.
Leader. Yea, all this band, it crieth to thee as one.
All. O great King, hear us. Awake thee to the sun.
      Be with us against thy foe!

[*Antistrophe* 10.

Orestes. The slayer shall meet the slayer, wrong smite with
  wrong.
Electra. O Zeus, bless thou the murder to be this day.
Leader. (Dost hear? Oh, fear is upon me and trembling
  strong.)
All. The day of Fate is old, it hath lingered long,
      It cometh to them that pray.

[*Strophe* 11.

Divers Women.
Alas, alas, for the travail born in the race,
  Alas for the harp of Atê, whose strings run blood,
    The beaten bosom, the grief too wild to bear.
      The pain that gnaweth, and will not sink to sleep.

[*Antistrophe* 11.

The House hath healing for its own bitterness;
  It is here within. None other can stay the flood;
    Through bitter striving, through hate and old despair.
      Behold the Song of the Daemons of the deep!
Orestes. O Father mine, O most unkingly slain,
Grant me the lordship of thy House again.

[103]

Electra. A boon for me likewise, O Father, give;
To lay Aegisthus in his blood and live.
Orestes. So men shall honor thee with wassail high;
Else without meat or incense shalt thou lie,
Unhonored when the dead their banquets call.
Electra. And I will pour thee offerings wondrous fair
From my stored riches for a marriage-prayer,
And this thy grave will honor more than all.
Orestes. Send back, O Earth, my sire to comfort me.
Electra. In power, in beauty, Great Persephone!
Orestes. Remember, Father, how they laved thee there!
Electra. Remember the strange weaving thou didst wear!
Orestes. A snarèd beast in chains no anvil wrought!
Electra. In coilèd webs of shame and evil thought!
Orestes. Scorn upon scorn! Oh, art thou wakenèd?
Electra. Dost rear to sunlight that belovèd head?
Orestes. Or send thine helping Vengeance to the light
To aid the faithful: or let even fight
Be joined in the same grapple as of yore,
If, conquered, thou wouldst quell thy conqueror.
Electra. Yet one last cry: O Father, hear and save!
Pity thy children cast upon thy grave:
The woman pity, and the weeping man.
Orestes. And blot not out the old race that began
With Pelops: and though slain thou art not dead!
Electra. Children are living voices for a head
Long silent, floats which hold the net and keep
The twisted line unfoundered in the deep.
Orestes. Listen: 'tis thou we weep for, none but thou:
Thyself are saved if thou save us now.
Leader. Behold, ye have made a long and yearning praise,
This sepulchre for unlamented days
Requiting to the full. And for the rest,
Seeing now thine heart is lifted on the crest
Of courage, get thee to the deed, and see
What power the Daemon hath which guardeth thee.
Orestes. So be it. Yet methinks to know one thing
Were well. Why sent she this drink-offering?
Hoped she by late atonement to undo
That wrong eternal? A vain comfort, too,

Sent to one dead, and feeling not! My mind
Stumbles to understand what lies behind
These gifts, so puny for the deed she hath done.
Yea, though man offer all he hath to atone
For one life's blood, 'tis written, he hath lost
That labor.—But enough. Say all thou know'st.
    Leader. Son, I was near her, and could mark aright.
A dream, a terror wandering in the night,
Shook her dark spirit till she spoke that word.
    Orestes. What was the dream she dreamed? Speak, if ye
      heard.
    Leader. She bore to life, she said, a Serpent Thing.
    Orestes. And after? To its head thy story bring.
    Leader. In swathing clothes she lapt it like a child.
    Orestes. It craved for meat, that dragon of the wild?
    Leader. Yes; in the dream she gave it her own breast.
    Orestes. And took no scathing from the evil beast?
    Leader. The milk ran into blood. So deep it bit.
    Orestes. The dream is come. The man shall follow it.
    Leader. And she, appalled, came shrieking out of sleep;
And many a torch, long blinded in the deep
Of darkness, in our chambers burst afire
To cheer the Queen. Then spake she her desire,
To send, as a swift medicine for the dread
That held her, these peace offerings to the dead.
    Orestes. Behold, I pray this everlasting Earth,
I pray my father's grave, they bring to birth
In fullness all this dream. And here am I
To read its heart and message flawlessly.
Seeing that this serpent, born whence I was born,
Wore the same swathing-bands these limbs had worn,
Fanged the same breast that suckled me of yore,
And through the sweet milk drew that gout of gore,
And seeing she understood, and sore afeared
Shrieked: therefore it must be that, having reared
A birth most ghastly, she in wrath shall die:
And I, the beast, the serpent, even I
Shall slay her! Be it so. The dream speaks clear.
    Leader. I take thyself for mine interpreter,
And pray that this may be. But speak thy will;

[105]

Who shall be doing, say, and who be still?

Orestes. 'Tis simply told. This woman makes her way
Within, and ye my charges shall obey,
That they who slew by guile a man most rare,
By guile, and snarèd in the self-same snare,
May die, as Lord Apollo hath foretold,
Loxias the Seer, who never failed of old.

First, I array me in a stranger's guise,
With all the gear of travel, and likewise
This man—their guest and battle-guest of yore!
Then hither shall we come, and stand before
The courtyard gate, and call. Aye, we will teach
Our tongues an accent of Parnassian speech,
Like men in Phokis born. And say, perchance
None of the warders with glad countenance
Will ope to us, the House being so beset
With evil: aye, what then? Then obdurate
We shall wait on, till all who pass that way
Shall make surmise against the House, and say
'What ails Aegisthus? Wherefore doth he close
His door against the traveler, if he knows
And is within?' So comes it, soon or late,
I cross the threshold of the courtyard gate;
And entering find him on my father's throne. . . .
Or, say he is abroad and comes anon,
And hears, and calls for me—and there am I
Before him, face to face and eye to eye;
'Whence comes the traveler?' ere he speaks it, dead
I lay him, huddled round this leaping blade!
Then shall the Curse have drunken of our gore
Her third, last, burning cup, and thirst no more.

Therefore go thou within, and watch withal
That all this chance may well and aptly fall.
For you, I charge ye of your lips take heed:
Good words or silence, as the hour may need.
While One Below his counsel shall afford
And ope to me the strait way of the sword.

[ORESTES *and* PYLADES *depart,* ELECTRA *goes into
the House.*

[*Strophe* 1.

Chorus. Host on host, breedeth Earth
    Things of fear and ghastly birth;
    Arm on arm spreads the Sea
    That full of coilèd horrors be;
    And fires the sky doth multiply;
    And things that crawl, and things that fly,
And they that are born in the wind can tell of the perils
    Of tempest and the Wrath on high.

[*Antistrophe* 1.

    But, ah, the surge over-bold
    Of man's passion who hath told?
    Who the Love, wild as hate,
    In woman's bosom desperate,
    Which feedeth in the fields of Woe?
    Where lives of mortals linkèd go
The heart of a woman is perilous past all perils
    Of stars above or deeps below.

[*Strophe* 2.

Wist ye not, O light of mind,
    Her who slew her son with hate,
    Thestios' daughter desolate,
How she wrought All her thought
    To one counsel, fiery-blind,
      When she burned the brand of fate,
      That was twin to him and brother
      From the hour of that first cry
    When the babe came from the mother
      Till the strong man turned to die?

[*Antistrophe* 2

    Wist ye not one loathed of old,
      Who to win a foe did sell,
      Cruel, him who loved her well;
Skylla, dyed with blood and pride,
      Who craved the rings of Cretan gold
      That Minos gave, too rich to tell;
    Like a wolf at night she came
      Where he lay with tranquil breath,
    And she cut the Crest of Flame:
      And, a-sudden, all was death.

[107]

But o'er all terrors on man's tongue
　The woman's deed of Lemnos lies;
It echoes, like an evil song,
　Far off, and whensoe'er there rise
　New and strange sins, in dire surmise,
Men mind them of the Lemnian wrong.
Yet surely by the Sin God's eye
Abhorreth, mortal man shall die,
　And all the glory that was his.
For who shall lift that thing on high
　Which God abaseth? Not amiss
I garner to my crown of woe
These sins of Woman long ago.

O lust so old, so hard of heart!
　I lose me in the stories told,
Untimely. Have these walls no part
　In ravening of desire, as bold
　And evil as those deeds of old?
The House with dread thereof doth start
　From dreaming. On, through woe or weal
A woman brooding planned her path,
　Against a warrior robed in steel,
And armies trembled at his wrath.
　And he is gone; and we must kneel
On a cold hearth and bow in fear
Before a woman's trembling spear.

Lo, the sword hovereth at the throat
For Justice' sake. It scorneth not
　What the proud man to earth has trod.
Its edge is bitter to the bone;
It stabbeth on, thro' iron, thro' stone,
Till it reach him who hath forgot
　That Ruth which is the law of God.

For Justice is an oak that yet
Standeth; and Doom the Smith doth whet
　His blade in the dark. But what is this?

A child led to the House from lands
Far off, and blood upon his hands!
The great Erinys wreaks her debt,
   Whose thought is as the vast abyss.

The scene now represents the front of the Palace of the Atridae,
   with one door leading to the main palace, another to the
   Women's House. Dusk is approaching. Enter ORESTES *and*
   PYLADES, *disguised as merchants from Phokis, with At-*
   tendants.   *Action begins*

   Orestes. Ho, Warder! Hear! One knocketh at your gate! . . . .
Ho, Warder, yet again! I knock and wait. . . .
A third time, ye within! I call ye forth;
Or counts your lord the stranger nothing worth?
   A Porter (within, opening the main door).
Enough! I hear. What stranger and wherefrom?
   Orestes. Go, rouse your masters. 'Tis to them I come,
Bearing great news. And haste, for even now
Night's darkling chariot presseth to the brow
Of heaven, and wayfarers like us must find
Quick anchorage in some resthouse for our kind.
Let one come forth who bears authority;
A woman, if God will; but if it be
A man, 'twere seemlier. With a woman, speech
Trembles and words are blinded. Man can teach
Man all his purpose and make clear his thought.
                    [*Enter* CLYTEMNESTRA *from the House.*
   Clytemnestra. Strangers, your pleasure? If ye have need
      of aught
All that beseems this House is yours to-day,
Warm bathing and the couch that soothes away
Toil, and the tendering of righteous eyes.
Else, if ye come on some grave enterprise,
That is man's work; and I will find the man.
   Orestes. I come from Phokis, of the Daulian clan,
And, traveling hither, bearing mine own load
Of merchandise, toward Argos, as the road
Branched, there was one who met me, both of us
Strangers to one another: Strophios,
A Phocian prince, men called him. On we strode

Together, till he asked me of my road
And prayed me thus: 'Stranger, since other care
Takes thee to Argos, prithee find me there
The kin of one Orestes. . . . Plainly said
Is best remembered: tell them he is dead.
Forget not. And howe'er their choice may run,
To bear his ashes home, or leave their son
In a strange grave, in death an exile still,
Discover, and bring back to me their will.
Tell them his ashes lie with me, inurned
In a great jar of bronze, and richly mourned.'
So much I tell you straight, being all I heard.
Howbeit, I know not if I speak my word
To the right hearers, princess of this old
Castle. Methinks his father should be told.
   Clytemnestra. Ah, me,
So cometh the last wreck in spite of all!
Curse of this House, thou foe that fear'st no fall,
How dost thou spy my hidden things and mar
Their peace with keen-eyed arrows from afar,
Till all who might have loved me, all, are gone!
And now Orestes; whom I had thought upon
So wisely, walking in free ways, his gait
Unsnarèd in this poison-marsh of hate!
The one last hope, the healing and the prayer
Of this old House, 'twas writ on empty air!
   Orestes. For me, in a great House and favored thus
By fortune, 'tis by tidings prosperous
I fain were known and welcomed. Pleasantest
Of all ties is the tie of host and guest.
But my heart told me 'twere a faithless thing
To fail a comrade in accomplishing
His charge, when I had pledged both word and hand.
   Clytemnestra. Not for our sorrow shall thy portion stand
The lowlier, nor thyself be less our friend.
Another would have told us; and the end
Is all one. But 'tis time that strangers who
Have spent long hours in travel should have due
Refreshment. Ho, there! Lead him to our broad
Guest-chambers, and these comrades of his road

Who follow. See they find all comfort there
To assuage their way-worn bodies. And have care
That in their tendance naught be found amiss.
   Ourselves shall with our Lord consult of this
Distress, and, having yet good friends, who know
My heart, take counsel how to affront the blow.

> [CLYTEMNESTRA *goes back into the Women's*
> *House; Attendants lead* ORESTES *and his fol-*
> *lowers through the main door.*

Leader. Ye handmaidens, arise, be bold:
   See if our moving lips have power
   To aid Orestes in his hour;
For sure ye loved this House of old.

Chorus. Thou holy Earth, thou holy shore
   Beyond the grave, where rests his head
   The Lord of Ships, the King, the Dead,
Now list, now aid, or never more!
The hour is full. The Guileful Word
   Descends to wrestle for the right,
   And Hermes guards the hour of night
For him that smiteth with the sword.

> [*The* NURSE *enters · from the Women's House,*
> *weeping.*

Leader. The stranger works some mischief, it would seem!
Yonder I see Orestes' Nurse, a-stream
With tears.—How now, Kilissa, whither bound,
And Grief the unbidden partner of thy round?
   Nurse. The mistress bids me call Aegisthus here
Quickly, to see these two, and learn more clear,
As man from man, the truth of what they tell.
Oh, to us slaves she makes it pitiable
And grievous, and keeps hid behind her eyes
The leaping laughter. Aye, 'tis a rich prize
For her, and for the House stark misery,
This news the travelers tell so trippingly.
And, Oh, Aegisthus, he, you may be sure,
Will laugh to hear it! . . . Ah, I am a poor
Old woman! Such a tangle as they were,
The troubles in this House, and hard to bear,

Long years back, and all aching in my breast!
But none that hurt like this! Through all the rest . . .
Well, I was sore, but lived them down and smiled.
But little Orestes, my heart's care, the child
I took straight from his mother; and save me
He had no other nurse! And, Oh, but he
Could scream and order me to tramp the dark!
Aye, times enough, and trouble enough, and stark
Wasted at that! A small thing at the breast,
That has no sense, you tend it like a beast,
By guesswork. For he never speaks, not he,
A babe in swaddling clothes, if thirst maybe
Or hunger comes, or any natural need.
The little belly takes its way. Indeed,
'Twas oft a prophet he wanted, not a nurse;
And often enough my prophecies, of course,
Came late, and then 'twas clothes to wash and dry,
And fuller's work as much as nurse's. Aye,
I followed both trades, from the day when first
His father gave me Orestes to be nursed. . . .
And now he is dead; and strangers come and tell
The news to me. And this poor miserable
Old woman must go tell the plunderer
Who shames this house! Oh, glad he will be to hear!
    Leader. How doth she bid him come? In what array?
    Nurse. I take thee not. . . . What is it ye would say?
    Leader. Comes he with spears to guard him or alone?
    Nurse. She bids him bring the spearmen of the throne.
    Leader. Speak not that bidding to our loathèd Lord!
'Alone, quick, fearing nothing' is the word.
So speak, and in thy heart let joy prevail!
The teller straighteneth many a crookèd tale.
    Nurse. What ails thee? Are these tidings to thy mind?
    Leader. The wind is cold, but Zeus may change the wind.
    Nurse. How, when Orestes, our one hope, is dead?
    Leader. Not yet! So much the dullest seer can read.
    Nurse. What mean'st thou? There is something ye have
        heard!
    Leader. Go, tell thy tale. Obey thy mistress' word!

God, where He guardeth, guardeth faithfully.

Nurse. I go.—May all be well, God helping me!

[*The* NURSE *goes out.*

Chorus. Lo, I pray God, this day: [*Strophe.*
    Father of Olympus, hear!
Grant thy fortunes healingly
Fall for them who crave to see
    In this House of lust and fear,
      Purity, purity.
I have sinned not, I have spoken
In the name of Law unbroken;
Zeus, as thou art just, we pray thee
    Be his guard!

(margin, handwritten) Chorus interrupts plot.

All. There is One within the Gate
    Of his foemen, where they wait;
Oh, prefer him, Zeus, before them
    And exalt and make him great:
Two- and threefold shall he pay thee
    Love's reward.

[*Antistrophe.*

Seest thou one lost, alone,
    Child of him who loved thee well?
As a young steed he doth go,
Maddened, in the yoke of woe:
Oh, set measure on the swell,
    Forth and fro, forth and fro,
Of the beating hoofs that bear him
Through this bitter course. Oh, spare him!
    By his innocence we pray thee
    Be his guard!

All. There is One within the Gate
    Of his foemen, where they wait;
Oh, prefer him, Zeus, before them
    And exalt and make him great:
Two- and threefold shall he pay thee
    Love's reward.

(margin, handwritten) He is to come w/o bodyguard

[Strophe.

Gods of the treasure-house within,
　　One-hearted, where the bronzen door
On darkness gloateth and on gold:
With present cleansing wash the old
Blight of this house: and aged Sin
　　Amid the gloom shall breed no more!

All. And, O Light of the Great Cavern, let it be
That this Man's house look up again, and see,
　Till the dead veil of scorn
　And long darkness shall be torn,
And the kind faces shine and old Argolis be free!

[Antistrophe.

And, Oh, let Hermes, Maia-born,
　　Be near, who moveth in his kind,
As the wind blows, to help at need:
The word he speaketh none may read:
Before his eyes the Day is torn
　　With darkness and the Night is blind.

All. And, O Light of the Great Cavern, let it be
That this Man's house look up again, and see,
　Till the dead veil of scorn
　And long darkness shall be torn,
And the kind faces shine and old Argolis be free!

[Strophe.

Then, then the prison shall unclose:
　　A wind of Freedom stream above:
A flood which faileth not, a voice
Telling of women that rejoice,
One harp in many souls, one spell
Enchanted. Ho, the ship goes well!
For me, for me, this glory grows.
　　And Evil flies from those I love.

All. Oh, in courage and in power,
　　When the deed comes and the hour,
　　As she crieth to thee 'Son'
　　Let thy 'Father' quell her breath!

But a stroke and it is done,
  The unblamèd deed of death.

                          [Antistrophe.

The heart of Perseus, darkly strong,
  Be lifted in thy breast to-day:
For them thou lovest in the grave,
For them on Earth, be blind, be brave:
Uphold the cloak before thine eyes
And see not while thy Gorgon dies;
But him who sowed the seed of wrong,
Go, look him in the face and slay!

All. Oh, in courage and in power,
  When the deed comes and the hour,
  As she crieth to thee 'Son,'
    Let thy 'Father' quell her breath!
But a stroke and it is done,
  The unblamèd deed of death.

            [Enter from the country AEGISTHUS.
Aegisthus. A message called me; else I scarce had thought
To have come so quick. 'Tis a strange rumor, brought,
They tell me, by some Phocian wayfarers
In passing: strange, nor grateful to our ears.
Orestes dead! A galling load it were
And dripping blood for this poor House to bear,
Still scored and festerous with its ancient wound.
How shall I deem it? Living truth and sound?
Or tales of women, born to terrify,
That wildly leap, and up in mid-air die?
What know ye further? I would have this clear.
  Leader. We heard the tale; but go within and hear
With thine own ears. A rumored word hath weak
Force, when the man himself is there to speak.
  Aegisthus. Hear him I will, and question him beside.
Was this man with Orestes when he died,
Or speaks he too from rumor? If he lies . . .
He cannot cheat a mind that is all eyes.
                    [He enters the House.
  Chorus. Zeus, Zeus, how shall I speak, and how
    Begin to pray thee and beseech?

How shall I ever mate with speech
This longing, and obtain my vow?
The edges of the blades that slay
   Creep forth to battle: shall it be
   Death, death for all eternity,
On Agamemnon's House this day;
Or sudden a new light of morn,
   A beacon fire for freedom won,
   The old sweet rule from sire to son,
And golden Argolis reborn?
Against two conquerors all alone,
   His last death-grapple, deep in blood,
   Orestes joineth. . . . O great God,
Give victory!

       [*Death-cry of* AEGISTHUS *within.*
      Ha! The deed is done!

Leader. How? What is wrought? Stand further from the door
Till all is over. Move apart before
Men mark, and deem us sharers in the strife.
For after this 'tis war, for death or life.

      [*The Women stand back almost unseen. A House-
        hold* SLAVE *rushes out from the main Door,
        and beats at the door of the Women's House.*

  Slave. Ho!
Treason! Our master! Treason! Haste amain!
Treason within. Aegisthus lieth slain.
Unbar, unbar, with all the speed ye may
The women's gates! Oh, tear the bolts away! . . .
God, but it needs a man, a lusty one,
To help us, when all time for help is gone!
What ho!
I babble to deaf men, and laboring cry,
To ears sleep-charmèd, words that fail and die.
Where art thou, Clytemnestra? What dost thou? . . .
'Fore God, 'tis like to be her own neck now,
In time's revenge, that shivers to its fate.

             [*Enter* CLYTEMNESTRA.

  Clytemnestra. What wouldst thou? Why this clamor at our
    gate?
  Slave. The dead are risen, and he that liveth slain.

Clytemnestra. Woe's me! The riddle of thy speech is plain.
By treason we shall die, even as we slew. . . .
Ho, there, mine axe of battle! Let us try
Who conquereth and who falleth, he or I . . .   *climax*
To that meseemeth we are come, we two.

         [*Enter from the House* ORESTES *with drawn sword.*
Orestes. 'Tis thou I seek. With him my work is done.
Clytemnestra (*suddenly failing*). Woe's me!
Aegisthus, my beloved, my gallant one!
Orestes. Thou lovest him! Go then and lay thine head
Beside him. Thou shalt not betray the dead.

         [*Makes as if to stab her.*
Clytemnestra. Hold, O my son! My child, dost thou not fear
To strike this breast? Hast thou not slumbered here,
Thy gums draining the milk that I did give?
Orestes (*lowering his sword*). Pylades!   *He falters*
What can I? Dare I let my mother live?   *Apollo is responsible*
His only speech *Pylades.* Where is God's voice from out the golden cloud
At Pytho? Where the plighted troth we vowed?
Count all the world thy foe, save God on high.
Orestes. I will obey. Thou counselest righteously.
Follow! Upon his breast thou shalt expire
Whom, living, thou didst hold above my sire.
Go, lie in his dead arms! . . . This was the thing
Thou lovedst, loathing thine anointed King.
Clytemnestra. I nursed thee. I would fain grow old with
    thee.
Orestes. Shall one who slew my father house with me?
Fate drove *Clytemnestra.* Child, if I sinned, Fate had her part therein.
her to it *Orestes.* Then Fate is here, with the reward of sin.
Clytemnestra. Thou reck'st not of a Mother's Curse, my
    child?
Orestes. Not hers who cast me out into the wild.
Clytemnestra. Cast out? I sent thee to a war-friend's Hall.
Orestes. A free man's heir, ye sold me like a thrall.
Clytemnestra. If thou wast sold, where is the price I got?
Orestes. The price! . . . For very shame I speak it not.
Clytemnestra. Speak. But tell, too, thy father's harlotries.
Orestes. Judge not the toiler, thou who sitt'st at ease!
Clytemnestra. A woman starves with no man near, my son.

[117]

Orestes. Her man's toil wins her bread when he is gone.
Clytemnestra. To kill thy mother, Child: is that thy will?
Orestes. I kill thee not: thyself it is doth kill.
Clytemnestra. A mother hath her Watchers: think and quail!
Orestes. How shall I 'scape my Father's if I fail?
Clytemnestra (*to herself*). Living, I cry for mercy to a tomb!
Orestes. Yea, from the grave my father speaks thy doom.
Clytemnestra. Ah God! The serpent that I bare and fed!
Orestes. Surely of truth prophetic is the dread
That walketh among dreams. Most sinfully
Thou slewest: now hath Sin her will of thee.

[*He drives* CLYTEMNESTRA *before him into the
palace. The* CHORUS *come forward again.*

Leader. For these twain also in their fall I weep.
Yet, seeing Orestes now through mire so deep
Hath climbed the crest, I can but pray this eye
Of the Great House be not made blind and die.

[*Strophe.*

Chorus.   Judgment came in the end
        To Troy and the Trojans' lord,
    (O Vengeance, heavy to fall!)
    There came upon Atreus' Hall
    Lion and lion friend,
        A sword came and a sword.
    A walker in Pytho's way
        On the neck of her kings hath trod,
    A beggar and outcast, yea,
        But led by God.

[*Antistrophe.*

    Came He of the laughing lure,
        The guile and the secret blow,
    (O Vengeance, subtle to slay!)
    But there held his hand that day
    The Daughter of Zeus, the pure,
        Justice yclept below.
    Justice they called her name,
        For where is a goodlier?
    And her breath is a sword of flame
        On the foes of her.

[118]

All.   Cry, Ho for the perils fled,
    For the end of the long dismay!
Cry, Ho for peace and bread;
For the Castle's lifted head,
For the two defilers dead,
    And the winding of Fortune's way!

                              [Strophe.

Even as Apollo gave
    His charge on the Mountain, He
Who holdeth the Earth-heart Cave,
    Hast thou wrought innocently
Great evil, hindered long,
    Tracking thy mother's sin . . .
Is the power of God hemmed in
So strangely to work with wrong?
    Howbeit, let praise be given
    To that which is throned in Heaven:
        The Gods are strong.

                            [Antistrophe.

And soon shall the Perfect Hour
    O'er the castle's threshold stone
Pass with his foot of power,
    When out to the dark is thrown
The sin thereof and the stain
    By waters that purify.
    Now, now with a laughing eye
God's fortune lieth plain;
    And a cry on the wind is loud:
    'The stranger that held us bowed
        Is fallen again!'

All.   O light of the dawn to be!
    The curb is broken in twain,
And the mouth of the House set free.
Up, O thou House, and see!
Too long on the face of thee
    The dust hath lain!

    [The doors are thrown open, and ORESTES *dis-
    covered standing over the dead bodies of*

Aegisthus and Clytemnestra. *The Household
is grouped about him and Attendants hold the
great red robe in which Agamemnon was murdered.*

Orestes. (He speaks with ever-increasing excitement).
Behold your linkèd conquerors! Behold
My Father's foes, the spoilers of the fold!
Oh, lordly were these twain, when thronèd high,
And lovely now, as he who sees them lie
Can read, two lovers faithful to their troth!
They vowed to slay my father, or that both
As one should die, and both the vows were true!
And mark, all ye who hear this tale of rue,
This robe, this trap that did my father greet,
Irons of the hand and shackling of the feet!
Outstretch it north and south: cast wide for me
This man-entangler, that our Sire may see—
Not mine, but He who watcheth all deeds done,
Yea, all my mother's wickedness, the Sun—
And bear me witness, when they seek some day
To judge me, that in justice I did slay
This woman: for of him I take no heed.
He hath the adulterer's doom, by law decreed.
But she who planned this treason 'gainst her own
Husband, whose child had lived beneath her zone—
Oh, child of love, now changed to hate and blood!—
What is she? Asp or lamprey of the mud,
That, fangless, rotteth with her touch, so dire
That heart's corruption and that lust like fire?
Woman? Not woman, though I speak right fair.
                    [*His eyes are caught by the great red robe.*
A dead man's winding-sheet? A hunter's snare?
A trap, a toil, a tangling of the feet. . . .
I think a thief would get him this, a cheat
That robs the stranger. He would snare them so,
And kill them, kill them, and his heart would glow. . . .
Not in my flesh, not in my house, O God,
May this thing live! Ere that, Oh, lift thy rod
And smiting blast me, dead without a child!
                              [*He stops exhausted.*

Chorus. O deeds of anger and of pain!
　　　　O woman miserably slain!
　　　　Alas, Alas!
　　　　And he who lives shall grieve again.

Orestes. Did she the deed or no? This robe defiled
Doth bear me witness, where its web is gored,
How deep the dye was of Aegisthus' sword;
And blood hath joined with the old years, to spoil
The many tinctures of the broidered coil.
Oh, now I weep, now praise him where he died,
And calling on this web that pierced his side. . . .
Pain, pain is all my doing, all my fate,
My race, and my begetting: and I hate
This victory that sears me like a brand. . . .

Chorus. No mortal thro' this life shall go
　　　　For ever portionless of woe.
　　　　Alas! Alas!
　　　　It comes to all, or swift or slow.

Orestes. Yet wait: for I would have you understand.
The end I know not. But methinks I steer
Unseeing, like some broken charioteer,
By curbless visions borne. And at my heart
A thing of terror knocketh, that will start
Sudden a-song, and she must dance to hear.
But while I am still not mad, I here declare
To all who love me, and confess, that I
Have slain my mother, not unrighteously;
Who with my father's blood hath stained the sod
Of Argos and drawn down the wrath of God.
And the chief spell that wrought me to the deed
Is Loxias, Lord of Pytho, who decreed
His high commandment: if this thing I dare,
He lays on me no sin; if I forbear . . .
I cannot speak his judgment: none can know
The deeps thereof, no arrow from the bow
Out-top it. Therefore here ye see me, how
I go prepared, with wreaths and olive bough,

To kneel in supplication on the floor
Of Loxias, touch the fire that evermore
Men call the undying, and the midmost stone
Of earth, flying this blood which is mine own.
And how these evil things were wrought, I pray
All men of Argos on an after day
Remember, and bear witness faithfully
When Menelaus comes. . . . And take from me,
Living or dead, a wanderer and outcast
For ever, this one word, my last, my last. . . .

Leader. Nay, all is well. Leave no ill omen here,
Nor bind upon thy lips the yoke of fear.
All Argos thou hast freed, and with one sweep
Two serpents' heads hurled reeking to the deep.

Orestes (*overcome with sudden terror*). Ah! Ah!
Ye bondmaids! They are here: like Gorgons, gowned
In darkness; all bewreathed and interwound
With serpents! . . . I shall never rest again.

Leader. What fantasies, most father-loved of men,
Haunt thee? Be strong, thou conqueror! Have no fear!

Orestes. These are no fantasies. They are here; they are here,
The Hounds of my dead Mother, hot to kill.

Leader. The blood upon thine hand is reeking still:
For that the turmoil in thy heart is loud.

Orestes. O Lord Apollo! More and more they crowd
Close, and their eyes drip blood, most horrible!

Leader. One cleansing hast thou. Loxias can quell
Thy tempest with his touch, and set thee free.

Orestes. You cannot see them. I alone can see.
I am hunted. . . . I shall never rest again.

[*Exit* ORESTES.

Chorus. Farewell. May blessing guide thee among men.
May God with love watch over thee, and heed
Thy goings and be near thee at thy need.

All. Behold a third great storm made wild
By winds of wrath within the race,
Hath shook this castle from its place.
The ravin of the murdered child
First broke Thyestes in his pride:

[122]

Second, a warrior and a King,
   Chief of Achaia's warfaring,
Was smitten in the bath and died.
And Third, this Saviour or this last
   Doom from the deep. What end shall fall,
   Or peace, or death outsweeping all,
When night comes and the Wrath is past?

                       [*Exeunt.*

AESCHYLUS
THE EUMENIDES

➤➤➤ ◀◀◀

TRANSLATED
by
GILBERT MURRAY

CHARACTERS IN THE PLAY

The PYTHIAN PROPHETESS.
ORESTES.
The God APOLLO.
The Goddess PALLAS ATHENA.
The Ghost of CLYTEMNESTRA.
CHORUS OF FURIES (*Eumenides*).
CHORUS OF ATHENIAN CITIZENS.

The play was first produced in 458 B.C. at the same time as the other two plays in the trilogy, Agamemnon *and* Choëphoroe.

ARGUMENT

At the end of the *Choëphoroe*, Orestes goes mad, overcome by the horror of the deed he has been obliged, by divine command, to commit. He is already haunted by the Furies, 'his mother's wrathful hounds,' who are destined to pursue him over the earth until the sin is expiated through suffering. When the play opens, Orestes has taken refuge at the temple of Apollo, where he seeks the protection of the god whose will he has performed.

THE EUMENIDES

---

*The scene represents the front of the Temple of Apollo at
Delphi; great doors at the back lead to the inner shrine and
the central Altar. The Pythian* PROPHETESS *is standing before the Doors.*

   Prophetess. First of all Gods I worship in this prayer
Earth, the primeval prophet; after her
Themis, the Wise, who on her mother's throne—
So runs the tale—sat second; by whose own
Accepted will, with never strife nor stress,
Third reigned another earth-born Titaness,
Phoebe; from whom (for that he bears her name)
To Phoebus as a birthtide gift it came.
   He left his isle, he left his Delian seas,
He passed Athena's wave-worn promontories,
In haste this great Parnassus to possess
And Delphi, thronèd in the wilderness.
And with him came, to escort him and revere,
A folk born of Hephaistos, pioneer
Of God's way, making sweet a bitter land.
And much this people and the King whose hand
Then steered them, Delphos, glorified his name,
Till Zeus into his heart put mystic flame
And prophet here enthroned him, fourth in use:
So Loxias' lips reveal the thought of Zeus.
   These gods be foremost in all prayers of mine,
Who have held the Throne. Next, She before the shrine,
Pallas, is praisèd, and the Nymphs who keep
Yon old Corycian bird-belovèd steep,
Deep-caverned, where things blessèd come and go.
And Bromios walks the mountain, well I know,
Since first he led his Maenad host on high

[127]

And doomed King Pentheus like a hare to die.
And Pleistos' fountains and Poseidon's power
I call, and Him who brings the Perfect Hour,
Zeus, the Most Highest. With which prayers I go
To seat me, priestess, on the Throne. And, oh,
May God send blessing on mine entrance, more
And deeper than He e'er hath sent of yore!
    If there be present men of Greece but not
Of Delphi, let them enter as the lot
Ordains; I speak but as God leadeth me.

> [*She enters the Inner Shrine, and the stage is for
> a moment empty. Then she returns, grasping
> at the wall for support.*

Ah! Horrors, horrors, dire to speak or see,
From Loxias' chamber drive me reeling back.
My knees are weak beneath me, and I lack
The strength to fly. . . . O hands, drag me from here,
If feet fail! . . . An old woman, and in fear,
A thing of naught, a babe in helplessness!
I made my way into the Holy Place,
And there, at the inmost Altar of the world,
A man abhorred of God, his body hurled
Earthward in desperate prayer; blood on his hand
Yet reeking, and a naked new-drawn brand
Wreathed in beseeching wool, a suppliant's weed
Of snow-white fleece . . . so much mine eyes could read.
But out in front of him a rout unknown
Of women sleepeth, flung from throne to throne.
Women? Nay, never women! Gorgons more:
And yet not like the Gorgon shapes of yore. . . .
I saw a picture once of woman things — *the harpies*
That ravished Phineus' banquet. But no wings
Have these; all shadows, black, abominable.
The voices of their slumber rise and swell,
Back-beating, and their eyes drop gouts of gore.
Their garb, it is no garb to show before
God's altar nor the hearths of human kind.
I cannot read what lineage lies behind
These shapes, nor what land, having born such breed,
Hath trembled not before and shall not bleed

Hereafter. Let Apollo great in power
Take to his care the peril of this hour:
Being Helper, Prophet, Seer of things unseen,
The stainèd hearth he knoweth to make clean.

[*The* PROPHETESS *departs. The doors open and
reveal the inner shrine,* ORESTES *at the Altar,
the* FURIES *asleep about him, and* APOLLO *standing over them.*

Apollo. I fail thee not. For ever more I stay,
Or watching at thy side or far away,
Thy guard, and iron against thine enemies.
Even now my snares have closèd upon these.
The ragers sleep: the Virgins without love,
So gray, so old, whom never god above
Hath kissed, nor man, nor from the wilderness
One wild beast. They were born for wickedness
And sorrow; for in evil night they dwell,
And feed on the great darkness that is Hell,
Most hated by the Gods and human thought.
But none the less, fly thou and falter not.
For these shall hunt thee, ever on through earth
Unwandered, through the vast lands of the North,
The sea-ways and the cities ringed with sea.
But faint not. Clasp thy travail unto thee;
On till thou come to Pallas' Rock, and fold
Thine arms in prayer about her image old.
In Athens there be hearts to judge, there be
Words that bring peace; and I shall set thee free
At last from all this woe.—If thou didst kill
Thy mother, was it not my word and will?

Orestes. Not to betray thou knowest. Oh, ponder yet
One other lesson, Lord—not to forget!
Thy strength in doing can be trusted well.

[ORESTES *departs.*

Apollo. Remember! Let no fear thy spirit quell!
Do thou, O Hermes, brother of my blood,
Watch over him. Thou guide of man, make good
The name thou bearest, shepherding again
My suppliant. Him who pitieth suffering men
Zeus pitieth, and his ways are sweet on earth.

[129]

[*Exit* APOLLO. *Presently enter the* GHOST *of* CLY-
TEMNESTRA. *She watches the sleeping* FURIES.

Ghost. Ye sleep, O God, and what are sleepers worth?
'Tis you, have left me among all the dead
Dishonored. Always, for that blood I shed,
Rebuke and hissing cease not, and I go
Wandering in shame. Oh, hear! . . . For that old blow
I struck still I am hated, but for his
Who smote me, being of my blood, there is
No wrath in all the darkness: there is none
Cares for a mother murdered by her son.
Open thine heart to see this gash!—
    (*She shows the wound in her throat.*) In sleep
The heart hath many eyes and can see deep:
'Tis daylight makes man's fate invisible.
Oft of my bounty ye have lapt your fill;
Oft the sad peace of wineless cups to earth
I have poured, and midmurk feastings on your hearth
Burned, when no other god draws near to eat.
And all these things ye have cast beneath your feet,
And he is fled, fled lightly like a fawn
Out of your nets! With mocking he is gone
And twisting of the lips. . . . I charge you, hark!
This is my life, my death. Oh, shake the dark
From off you, Children of the Deep. 'Tis I,
Your dream, I, Clytemnestra, stand and cry.
      [*Moaning among the* FURIES.
Moan on, but he is vanished and forgot.
So strong the prayers of them that love me not!
          [*Moaning.*
Too sound ye sleep.—And have ye for the dead
No pity? . . . And my son, my murderer, fled!
          [*Groaning.*
Ye groan; ye slumber. Wake! . . . What task have ye
To do on earth save to work misery?
          [*Groaning.*
Can sleep and weariness so well conspire
To drain the fell she-dragon of her fire?
   [*Sharp repeated muttering: then words 'At him!
At him! Catch, catch, catch! Ah, beware!'*

[130]

Ah, hunting in your dreams, and clamorous yet,
Tired bloodhounds that can sleep but not forget!
  How now? Awake! Be strong! And faithful keep
Thy lust of pain through all the drugs of sleep.
  Thou feelst my scorn? Aye, feel and agonize
Within; such words are scourges to the wise.
Thy blood-mist fold about him, like a doom.
Waste him with vapor from thy burning womb.
A second chase is death! . . . Pursue! Pursue!

> [*The* GHOST *vanishes as the* FURIES *gradually wake.*

Leader of the Furies. Awake! Quick, waken her as I wake
  you!
Thou sleepest? Rise; cast slumber from thy brain
And search. Is our first hunt so all in vain?

  Furies (*speaking severally*). O rage, rage and wrath!
    Friends, they have done me wrong!
      Many and many a wrong I have suffered,
        mockeries all!
  Evil and violent deeds, a shame that lingereth long
    And bitter, bitter as gall!
  The beast is out of the toils, out of the toils and away!
    I slept, and I lost my prey.

What art thou, O Child of Zeus? A thief and a cozener!
    Hast broken beneath thy wheels them that were holy
      and old?
A godless man and an evil son, he but kneels in prayer,
    And straight he is ta'en to thy fold.
Thou hast chosen the man who spilt his mother's blood!
    Are these things just, thou God:

As a raging charioteer mid-grippeth his goad to bite
    Beneath the belly, beneath the flank, where the smart
      is hot,
There riseth out of my dreams Derision with hands to smite;
As a wretch at the block is scourged when the scourger hateth
  aright,
    And the shuddering pain dies not.

[131]

These be the deeds ye do, ye Gods of the younger race:
  Ye break the Law at your will; your high throne
   drips with gore,
The foot is wet and the head. There is blood in the Holy
  Place!
The Heart of Earth uplifteth its foulness in all men's face,
  Clean nevermore, nevermore!

Blood, thou holy Seer, there is blood on thy burning hearth.
  Thine inmost place is defiled, and thine was the will
   and the word.
Thou hast broken the Law of Heaven, exalted the things of
  Earth;
  The hallowed Portions of old thine hand hath blurred.

Thou knowest to hurt my soul; yea, but shalt save not him.
  The earth may open and hide, but never shall he be
   freed.
Defiling all he goes, there where in exile dim
  Many defilers more wait and bleed.
          [Enter APOLLO.

Apollo. Avaunt, I charge you! Get ye from my door!
Darken this visionary dome no more!
Quick, lest ye meet that snake of bitter wing
That leaps a-sudden from my golden string,
And in your agony spue forth again
The black froth ye have sucked from tortured men!
 This floor shall be no harbor to your feet.
Are there not realms where Law upon her seat
Smites living head from trunk? Where prisoners bleed
From gougèd eyes? Children with manhood's seed
Blasted are there; maimed foot and severed hand,
And stoning, and a moan through all the land
Of men impaled to die. There is the board
Whereat ye feast, and, feasting, are abhorred
Of heaven.—But all the shapes of you declare
Your souls within. Some reeking lion's lair
Were your fit dwelling, not this cloistered Hall
Of Mercy, which your foulness chokes withal.

Out, ye wild goats unherded! Out, ye drove
Accursed, that god nor devil dares to love!

[*During this speech the* FURIES *fly confusedly
from the Temple down into the Orchestra. The*
LEADER *turns.*

Leader. Phoebus Apollo, in thy turn give heed!
I hold thee not a partner in this deed;
Thou hast wrought it all. The gilt is thine alone.
Apollo. What sayst thou there?—One word, and then begone.
Leader. Thou spakest and this man his mother slew.
Apollo. I spoke, and he avenged his father. True.
Leader. Thou stoodest by, to accept the new-shed gore.
Apollo. I bade him turn for cleansing to my door.
Leader. Ha! And revilest us who guide his feet?
Apollo. Ye be not clean to approach this Mercy Seat.
Leader. We be by Law eternal what we be.
Apollo. And what is that? Reveal thy dignity.
Leader. We hunt from home his mother's murderer.
Apollo. A husband-murdering woman, what of her?
Leader. 'Twas not one blood in slayer and in slain.
Apollo. How? Would ye count as a light thing and vain
The perfect bond of Hera and high Zeus?
Yea, and thy word dishonoreth too the use
Of Cypris, whence love groweth to his best.
The fate-ordainèd meeting, breast to breast,
Of man and woman is a tie more sure
Than oath or pact, if Justice guards it pure.
If them so joined ye heed not when they slay,
Nor rise in wrath, nor smite them on their way,
Unrighteous is thine hunting of this man,
Orestes. Why on him is all thy ban
Unloosed? The other never broke thy rest . . .
But Pallas, child of Zeus, shall judge this quest.
Leader. I cleave to him. I leave him never more.
Apollo. Oh, hunt thy fill! Make sorrow doubly sore.
Leader. Abridge not thou the Portions of my lot.
Apollo. Keep thou thy portions. I will touch them not.
Leader. Thou hast thy greatness by the throne of God;
I . . . But the scent draws of that mother's blood.
I come! I come! I hunt him to the grave. . . .

[133]

[*The* FURIES *go out on the track of* ORESTES.

Apollo. 'Tis mine then to bring succor, and to save
My suppliant. Earth and Heaven are both afraid
For God's wrath, if one helpless is betrayed.

[APOLLO *returns behind the shrine, and the doors
close. When they open again, they reveal, in
place of Apollo's Central Altar, the Statue of*
ATHENA PARTHENOS: *the scene now represents
the Temple of Athena in Athens. Enter* ORESTES,
worn with travel and suffering.

Orestes. Pallas Athena, from Apollo's wing
I come; receive in peace this hunted thing
My sin no more polluteth, nor with hand
Unpurified before thy throne I stand.
A blunted edge, grief-worn and sanctified
By pain, where'er men traffic or abide,
On, on, o'er land and sea I have made my way,
True-purposed Loxias' bidding to obey.
At last I have found thy House; thine image I
Clasp, and here wait thy judgment till I die.

[*He throws himself down at the feet of the Statue,
but no answer comes. Presently enter the* FURIES,
following him.

Leader. Ha! Here he has passed. Spot reeketh upon spot.
Blood is a spy that points and babbles not.
Like hounds that follow some sore-wounded fawn,
We smell the way that blood and tears are gone,
And follow.—Oh, my belly gaspeth sore
With toils man-wasting; I can chase no more.
Through all the ways of the world I have shepherded
My lost sheep, and above the salt sea sped,
Wingless pursuing, swift as any sail.
And now 'tis here, meseemeth, he doth quail
And cower.—Aye, surely it is here; the smell
Of man's blood laughs to meet me. All is well.

Furies (*searching*). Ha, search, search again!
    Seek for him far and wide.
    Shall this man fly or hide
    And the unatonèd stain
    Of his mother's blood be vain?

[134]

Haha! Lo where he lies!
And comfort is in his eyes!
He hath made his arms a wreath
    For the knees of the Deathless One,
And her judgment challengeth
    On the deed his hands have done.
In vain! All in vain!
    When blood on the earth is shed,
    Blood of a mother dead,
Ye shall gather it not again.
    'Tis wet, 'tis vanishèd,
Down in the dust like rain.
    Thyself shalt yield instead,
Living, from every vein,
    Thine own blood, rich and red,
For our parchèd mouths to drain,
    Till my righteous heart be fed
With thy blood and thy bitter pain;
    Till I waste thee like the dead,
And cast thee among the slain,
    Till her wrong be comforted
And her wound no longer stain.

The Law thou then shalt see;
    That whoso of men hath trod
In sin against these three,
    Parent or Guest or God,
That sin is unforgot,
And the payment faileth not.
There liveth, for every man,
    Below, in the realm of Night,
A judge who straighteneth
The crooked; his name is Death.
All life his eye doth scan
    And recordeth right.

Orestes. I have known much evil, and have learnt therein
What divers roads man goes to purge his sin,
And when to speak and when be dumb; and eke
In this thing a wise master bids me speak.
The blood upon this hand is fallen asleep

[135]

And fades. And though a sin be ne'er so deep
'Twill age with the aging years. When this of mine
Was fresh, on Phoebus' hearth with blood of swine
'Twas washed and blurred. 'Twere a long tale since then,
To tell how I have spoke with many men
In scatheless parle. And now, with lips of grace,
Once more I pray the Lady of this place,
Athena, to mine aid. Let her but come;
Myself, mine Argive people and my home
Shall without war be hers, hers true of heart
And changeless. Therefore, wheresoe'er thou art,
In some far wilderness of Libyan earth,
By those Tritonid waters of thy birth;
Upgirt for deeds or veilèd on thy throne;
Or is it Phlegra's field thou brood'st upon,
Guiding the storm, like some bold Lord of War,
Oh, hear! A goddess heareth though afar:
Bring me deliverance in this mine hour!

           [He waits expectant, but there is no answer.
   Leader. Not Lord Apollo's, not Athena's power
Shall reach thee any more. Forgot, forgot,
Thou reelest back to darkness, knowing not
Where in man's heart joy dwelleth; without blood,
A shadow, flung to devils for their food!

   Wilt answer not my word? Wilt spurn thereat,
Thou that art mine, born, doomed, and consecrate
My living feast, at no high altar slain?
Hark thou this song to bind thee like a chain!

   Furies (as they move into position for the Dance).
         Up, let us tread the dance, and wind—
            The hour is come!—our shuddering spell.
            Show how this Band apportions well
         Their fated burdens to mankind.

         Behold, we are righteous utterly.
            The man whose hand is clean, no wrath
            From us shall follow: down his path
         He goeth from all evil free.

But whoso slays and hides withal
  His red hand, swift before his eyes
  True witness for the dead we rise:
We are with him to the end of all.

[*Being now in position they begin the Binding
    Song.*

Some Furies. Mother, who didst bear a being
  Dread to the eyeless and the seeing,
      Night, my Mother!
  Leto's Child would wrong me, tear
  From my clutch this trembling hare,
  My doomèd prey: he bore to slay,
  And shall he not the cleansing bear,
      He, none other?

*"The Witches'
Dance"*

Chorus. But our sacrifice to bind,
  Lo, the music that we wind,
  How it dazeth and amazeth
    And the will it maketh blind,
  As it moves without a lyre
  To the throb of my desire;
  'Tis a chain about the brain,
    'Tis a wasting of mankind.

*Try to put spell
around Orestes.*

Other Furies. Thus hath Fate, through weal and woe,
  For our Portion as we go
    Spun the thread:
  Whenso mortal man in sin
  'Brueth hand against his kin,
  Mine till death He wandereth,
  And freedom never more shall win,
    Not when dead.

Chorus. But our sacrifice to bind,
  Lo, the music that we wind,
  How it dazeth and amazeth
    And the will it maketh blind,
  As it moves without a lyre
  To the throb of my desire;

'Tis a chain about the brain,
'Tis a wasting of mankind.

Some Furies. Since the hour we were begot
Of this rite am I the priest;
Other gods may share it not;
Nor is any man nor beast
That dare eat the food we eat
Nor among us take his seat;
For no part have I nor lot
In the white robe of the feast.

Chorus. For the tale I make mine own
Is of houses overthrown,
When the Foe within the Dwelling
Slays a brother and is flown:
Up and after him, Io!
While the blood is still a-flow,
Though his strength be full and swelling,
We shall waste him, flesh from bone!

Other Furies. Would they take thee from the care
We have guarded thee withal?
Would the Gods disown our prayer
Till no Law be left at all?
Yea, because of blood that drips
As aforetime from our lips,
And the world's hate that we bear,
God hath cast us from His hall!

Chorus. I am on them as they fly,
With a voice out of the sky,
And my armèd heel is o'er them
To fall crashing from on high.
There be fliers far and fast,
But I trip them at the last,
And my arms are there before them,
And shall crush them ere they die!

Divers Furies. The glories of Man that were proud where the sunlight came,

Below in the dark are wasted and cast to shame;
    For he trembles at the hearing
    Of the Black Garments nearing,
    And the beating of the feet, like flame
He falls and knows not; the blow hath made blind his eyes;
And above hangs Sin, as a darkening of the skies,
    And a great voice swelling
    Like a mist about his dwelling,
And sobbing in the mist and cries.

For so it abideth: subtle are we to plan,
    Sure to fulfil, and forget not any Sin;
    And Venerable they call us, but none can win
    Our pardon for child of man.
Unhonored and undesired though our kingdom be,
    Where the sun is dead and no god in all the skies,
Great crags and trackless, alike for them that see,
    And them of the wasted eyes;

What mortal man but quaketh before my power,
    And boweth in worship to hear my rule of doom,
    God-given of old, fate-woven on the ageless loom
    And ripe to the perfect hour?
To the end of all abideth mine ancient Right,
    Whose word shall be never broke nor its deed undone,
Though my seat is below the Grave, in the place where sight
    Fails and there is no Sun.

                       [*Enter* ATHENA.

   Athena. Far off I heard the calling of my name,
Beside Scamander, where I took in claim
The new land which the Achaean lords and kings,
In royal spoil for many warfarings,
Gave, root and fruit for ever, as mine own
Exempted prize, to Theseus' sons alone.
Thence came I speeding, while behind me rolled
My wingless aegis, floating fold on fold.
   But these strange visitants . . . I tremble not
Beholding, yet I marvel. Who and what
Are ye? I speak to all. And who is he
Who round mine image clings so desperately?

                         [139]

[handwritten marginal note: possibly by machine*]*

But ye are like no earth-seed ever sown,
No goddess-shape that Heaven hath looked upon,
Nor any semblance born of human kind . . .
   Howbeit, ye have not wronged me. I were blind
To right and custom did I speak you ill.
   Leader. Virgin of God most high, have all thy will.
Still-weeping Night knows us the brood she bears;
The wronged ones in the darkness call us Prayers.
   Athena. I know your lineage and the names ye hold.
   Leader. Our office and our lot can soon be told.
   Athena. Make clear thy word, that all be understood.
   Leader. We hunt from home the shedder of man's blood.
   Athena. What end appoint ye to that flight of his?
   Leader. A land where none remembereth what joy is.
   Athena. And such a chase on this man thou wilt cry?
   Leader. Who dared to be his mother's murderer, aye.
   Athena. What goaded him? Some fear, some unseen wrath?
   Leader. What goad could drive a man on such a path?
   Athena (*looking at Orestes*). Why speaketh one alone, when
      two are there?
   Leader. He will not swear, nor challenge me to swear.
   Athena. Which wouldst thou, to seem righteous, or to be?
   Leader. What meanst thou there? Speak out thy subtlety.
   Athena. Let no bare oath the deeper right subdue.
   Leader. Try thou the cause, then, and give judgment true.
   Athena. Ye trust me this whole issue to decide?
   Leader. Who would not trust thee? True thou art and tried.
   Athena (*turning to Orestes*). Strange man, and what in turn
      hast thou to advance?
Thy land and lineage, and thy long mischance
Show first, then make thine answer to their laws.
If truly in the justice of thy cause
Trusting, thou clingest here in need so dire
To mine own shape, hard by my deathless fire,
In fearful prayer, as lost Ixîon prayed,
Make to all these thine answer unafraid.
   Orestes. Most high Athena, let me from the last
Of these thy questionings one fear outcast.
Pollution is not in me, nor with hand
Blood-reeking cleave I to thine altar-strand;

In sign whereof, behold, I have cast away
That silence which the man of blood alway
Observeth, till some hand, that hath the power
To cleanse the sins of man, new blood shall shower
Of swine upon him, drowning the old stain.
I have been cleansed again and yet again
In others' dwellings, both by blood that fell
And running rivers that have washed me well.
Be that care then forgot. My name and birth
Are quickly told. I am sprung of Argive earth;
My father's name was known upon thy lips,
Agamemnon, marshal of a thousand ships,
With whom thou madest Troy, that city of pride,
No more a city. He returning died,
Not kingly. 'Twas my mother black of heart
Met him and murdered, snaring him with art
Of spangled webs. . . . Alas, that robe of wrath,
That cried to heaven the blood-stain of the bath!
Then came long exile; then, returning, I
Struck dead my mother. Nought will I deny;
So, for my sire belovèd, death met death.
     And Loxias in these doings meriteth
His portion, who foretold strange agonies
To spur me if I left unsmitten these
That slew him. . . . Take me thou, and judge if ill
I wrought or righteously. I will be still
And praise thy judgment, whatsoe'er betide.
     Athena. This is a mystery graver to decide
Than mortal dreameth. Nor for me 'twere good
To sift the passionate punishments of blood.
Since thou hast cast thee on my altar stair
Perfect by suffering, from thy stains that were
Made clean and harmless, suppliant at my knee,
I, in my City's name, must pity thee
And chide not. Yet these too, I may not slight;
They have their portion in the Orb of Right
Eternal. If they are baffled of their will,
The wrath of undone Justice shall distil
Through all the air a poison; yea, a pall
Intolerable about the land shall fall

[141]

And groaning sickness. Doubtful thus it lies:
To cast them out or keep them in mine eyes
Were equal peril, and I must ponder sore.
Yet, seeing fate lays this matter at my door,
Myself not judging, I will judges find
In mine own City, who will make no blind
Oath-challenge to pursuer and pursued,
But follow this new rule, by me indued
As law for ever. Proofs and witnesses
Call ye on either side, and set to these
Your oaths. Such oath helps Justice in her need.
    I will go choose the noblest of the breed
Of Athens, and here bring them to decide
This bloody judgment even as truth is tried,
And then, their oath accomplished, to depart,
Right done, and no transgression in their heart.

        [*Exit* ATHENA. *The Shrine is closed,* ORESTES *re-
        maining inside at the foot of the image.*
Furies. This day there is a new Order born.
        If this long coil of judging and of strife
        Shall uplift the mother-murderer to life,
    Shall the World not mark it, and in scorn
        Go forth to do evil with a smile?
        Yea, for parents hereafter there is guile
            That waiteth, and great anguish; by a knife
    In a child's hand their bosom shall be torn.

No wrath shall be stirred by any deed,
        No doom from the Dark Watchers any more.
        Lo, to all death I cast wide the door!
And men, while they whisper of the need
    Of their neighbor, shall pray tremblingly within
    For some rest and diminishing of sin.
        They will praise the old medicine that of yore
Brought comfort, and marvel as they bleed.

        Vainly will they make their moan?
        Vainly cry in sore despite,
        'Help, ye Watchers on your throne,
            Help, O Right!'

Many a father so shall cry,
  Many a mother, new in pain;
Their vain sobbing floateth by:
  'The great House is fallen again!
      Law shall die!'

Times there be when Fear is good,
  And the Watcher in the breast
Needs must reign in masterhood.
      Aye, tis best
Through much straitening to be wise.
  Who that hath no fear at all
In the sunlight of his eyes,
  Man or City, but shall fall
      From Right somewise?

The life that walketh without rule,
The life that is a tyrant's fool,
      Thou shalt not praise.
O'er all man's striving variously
God looketh, but, where'er it be,
Gives to the Mean his victory.
And therefore know I and confess,
The doomèd child of Godlessness
Is Pride of Man, and Pride's excess;
Only from health of heart shall spring
What men desire, what poets sing,
      Stormless days.

Whate'er befall, the Throne of Right
Fear thou, and let no lucre bright
      Seen suddenly,
To spurn that Altar make thee blind;
For chastisement is hid behind,
And the End waiteth, and shall bind.
Wherefore I charge thee, through all stress
Thy mother and thy father bless:
Herein, O Man, lies holiness.
And next, of all within thy fold,

The stranger and the friendless hold
  In sanctity.
He that is righteous uncompelled and free
  His life's way taketh
Not without happiness; and utterly
Cast to destruction shall he never be.
But he who laugheth and is bold in sin,
From every port great gain he gathers in,
Rejoicing; but methinks shall cast away
All, with much haste and trembling, on the day
  When sails are stript by the edge of wind and sea
  And yard-arm breaketh.

He yearns, he strives, amid the whirling sea,
  But none shall hear;
And loud his Daemon laughs, saying 'This is he
  Who vaunted him these things should never be!'
Who now is weeping, weak in the endless foam,
And sees the foreland where beyond is home,
But shall not pass it: on the rocks of Right
Wrecked is his life's long glory; and the night
  Falls, and there lives from all his agony
  No word nor tear.

The scene is now set with seats for the Council of the Areopagus. Enter ATHENA, *the* JUDGES, *a* HERALD, *a crowd of* CITIZENS, *the* FURIES, ORESTES.

Athena. Herald, thine office! See that yonder crowds
Hold back, and let this piercer of the clouds,
Filled with man's breath, the Tuscan trumpet, blow
His fiery summons to the host below.
Then all be silence, while the people fill
This Council Hall. Thus shall my sovran will
And ordinance to this people, great and small,
Be known for ever, and upheld by all
Within our gates; and thus my wardens do
Justice this day, discerning false from true.
           [*Enter* APOLLO.

Areopagus - jurisdiction over religion + certain cases
of murder. Bfore 355 BC: Had previously supervised law
courts, controlled education of the young, + censorship of
the young. - see milton

THE EUMENIDES

Leader. Apollo, thou! Go, reign where thou art king!
What portion hast thou in this doom-saying?

Apollo. I come to bear my witness. This is one
Who in great anguish came to me alone
For refuge, and knelt suppliant at my shrine.
Therefore the cleansing of his stain is mine.
Likewise I share his plea, and on me take
What guilt he bears for that dead mother's sake.

Ope thou the court, O Pallas, and, as well
Thou canst, establish justice durable.

Athena. Ho! Opened is the Court; and yours the speech.
     (*To the* FURIES)
He who pursueth, speaking first, can teach
Best his whole grief, and how the evil grew.

Leader. Many are we, yet shall our words be few.
Make answer thou, point against point. And say
First this one thing: thy mother didst thou slay?

Orestes. I slew her. . . . Aye. Denied it cannot be.

Leader. Aha! The first of the three bouts to me!

Orestes. Too soon ye vaunt. I am not yet outsped.

Leader. How didst thou slay? That also must be said.

Orestes (*with an effort*). I will say it. I drew sword and
     clave her throat.

Leader. Who and what tempted thee? Who laid the plot?

Orestes. He who is with me now, and witnesseth.

Leader. God's prophet bade thee plot thy mother's death?

Orestes. Yes: and hath never failed me to this day.

Leader. And when the vote is cast, what wilt thou say?

Orestes. I fear not. Helpers from my father's grave.

Leader. Go, mother-murderer! Call the dead to save!

Orestes. Two stains of death lay mingled on her hand.

Leader. How two? Let these who judge thee understand.

Orestes. A husband and a father, both, she slew.

Leader. And death hath purged her. Shalt not thou die too?

Orestes. Ye never hunted her, for all her stain.

Leader. 'Twas not one blood in slayer and in slain.

Orestes. And are my mother's blood and my blood one?

Leader. How did she feed thee else beneath her zone?
Caitiff! Thy mother's blood wilt thou deny?

[145]

Orestes (*overcome*). I can no more. . . . Give witness, and
    reply.
Lord Phoebus, in my stead, if righteously
I slew. . . . I slew: denied it cannot be:
But rightly, or most foully—as thine own
Heart speaks, give judgment, and let all be known.
   Apollo. Ye judges of Athena's Court most high,
I come to speak before you faithfully,
Being God's prophet: therefore truth is mine.
Nor ever spake I from my throne divine
Of man nor woman, land nor city wall,
Save by command of Him who ruleth all,
Zeus, the Olympian Father. Is there Right
Holier than this, I charge ye think, or Might
More mighty? Follow ye the All-Father's will:
If oaths be strong, is Zeus not stronger still?
   Leader. 'Twas Zeus, thou tellest, laid this duty large
Upon thy lips? 'Twas Zeus who bade thee charge
This man to avenge his father and cast down,
As nothing worth, his mother's sacred crown?
   Apollo. Are these the same? That a great man, raised high
By royal scepter, given of God, should die,
And die by a woman's hand—and not in war
By Amazonian arrow, sped from far, . . .
But—Hear my tale, O Pallas, and ye too
Who sit enthronèd to sift false from true;
He came from battle after sufferings sore
But greater glories, and she stood before
The gate to greet and praise him, strewed his **path**
With crimson robes and led him to his bath—
A marble bed!—and o'er the end thereof
Laid the great web and curtained it above,
To ensnare him as he rose; then, in the wide
Unending folds, she smote him and he died!
So died a man, ye hear it from my lips,
All-honored, War-Lord of a thousand ships;
And such a wife was she! Be stern, and smite
The guilty, ye who sit to establish right!
   Leader. Doth Zeus count fatherhood so high a thing?
Who cast in bonds his father and his king,

Old Cronos? Are these things not contrary?
I charge ye, judges, hearken his reply.
    Apollo. Ye worms of hate, O ye that Gods abhor,
Bonds can be loosened; there is cure therefor,
And many and many a plan in God's great mind
To free the prisoners whom he erst did bind.
But once the dust hath drunk the blood of men
Murdered, there is no gathering it again.
For that no magic doth my Father know,
Though all things else he changeth high and low
Or fixeth, and no toil is in his breath.
    Leader. Is that thy pleading against this man's death?
The kindred blood, his mother's blood, the well
Of his own life, he hath spilt. How shall he dwell
In Argos? In his home? What altar-stair,
When Argos worships, will receive his prayer?
What love-bowl of the brethren cleanse his hand?
    Apollo. That too I answer; mark and understand.
The mother to the child that men call hers
Is no true life-begetter, but a nurse
Of live seed. 'Tis the sower of the seed
Alone begetteth. Woman comes at need,
A stranger, to hold safe in trust and love
That bud of new life—save when God above
Wills that it die. And would ye proof of this,
There have been fathers where no mother is.
Whereof a perfect witness standeth nigh,
Athena Pallas, child of the Most High,
A thought-begotten unconceivèd bloom,
No nursling of the darkness of the womb,
But such a flower of life as goddess ne'er
Hath born in heaven nor ever more shall bear.
    Pallas, in all things it is mine to swell
In power thy people and thy citadel;
And therefore to thine Altar did I send
This suppliant, that hereafter to the end
Of mortal time he may be true to thee,
And plant his spear by thine unfalteringly,
And on through generations yet unborn
Argos observe the pact her King hath sworn.

[147]

Athena. Now shall I charge upon their faith these men
To cast true stones, or would ye speak again?
Leader. Shot is our every arrow: I but stay
To learn how ends the issue of the day.
Athena. How shall I cast a judgment in this cause
Unblamed of you, and of the eternal laws?
Apollo. Ye have heard what ye have heard. Strangers, revere
Your oaths, and cast your judgment without fear.
Athena. Hear now mine ordinance, ye who have striven
This day to give, what none before hath given,
True judgment o'er spilt blood. O Attic Folk,
Henceforth for ever, under Aegeus' yoke,
This Council and this Judgment Seat by me
Are stablisht. On this mountain shall it be,
Here in the Amazon's most virgin hold,
Who came in wrath for Theseus' wrongs of old
Embattled, and this fortress against ours,
Hill against hill, towers against soaring towers,
Built, and to Ares on the rock with flame
Gave sacrifice: whence comes its awful name,
The Rock, the Mount, of Ares. All things here
Being holy, Reverence and her sister, Fear,
In darkness as in daylight shall restrain
From all unrighteousness the sons of men,
While Athens' self corrupt not her own law.
With mire and evil influx ye can flaw
Fair water till no lips may drink thereof.
I charge you, citizens, enfold and love
That spirit that nor anarch is nor thrall;
And casting away Fear, yet cast not all;
For who that hath no fear is safe from sin?
That Fear which is both Ruth and Law within
Be yours, and round your city and your land
Shall be upraised a rampart, yea, a hand
Of strong deliverance, which no sons of men,
From the Isle of Pelops to the Scythian fen,
Possess nor know, this Council of the Right,
Untouched of lucre, terrible to smite,
And swift and merciful, a guard to keep
Vigil above my people while they sleep.

Which here I establish. Let these words advise
My city evermore.—I charge you, rise
And lift your stones of doom and judge, alway
Your oath remembering. I have said my say.

> [*The* JUDGES *rise and go one by one past the two
> urns, casting their stones as they pass.*

Leader. Behold, an awful presence moveth yet
Within your land, which mock not nor forget!

Apollo. The will of Zeus, by my lips ministered,
I charge you make not fruitless nor unfeared!

Leader. And what wouldst thou with blood, having therein
No place? Henceforth thine altars are unclean!

Apollo. Did Zeus, then, sin, who bowed his head to spare
Blood-red Ixîon for his burning prayer?

Leader. Thou speakest: but my Law, if it be broke,
Shall come again in wrath to haunt this folk.

Apollo. Thou hast no honor more 'mid things divine,
Or old or new: the victory shall be mine.

Leader. So in Admetus' House thou didst betray
The Fates, to make man deathless past his day.

Apollo. Shall not a god regard his worshipper
Then chiefliest, when in peril and in prayer?

Leader. The ancient boundaries thou didst desecrate,
Thou mad'st a drunkard of Eternal Fate!

Apollo. True Justice thou canst know not. Thou shalt spue
Thy venom forth, and none give heed thereto.

Leader. Women are we, and old; and thou dost ride
Above us, trampling, in thy youth and pride.
Howbeit, I wait to know the end, being still
In doubt to work this City good or ill.

Athena. One judgment still remains. I, at the last,
To set Orestes free this stone will cast:
For, lo, no mother bare me: I approve
In all—save only that I know not love—
The man's way. Flesh and spirit I am His
Who gave me life. And in this coil it is
No dire deed that a woman, who had slain
Her mate and house-lord, should be quelled again.
Wherefore I judge that here, if equal be
The votes ye cast, Orestes shall go free.

Ye judges, haste: on you this office turns:
And cast the gathered sea-stones from the urns.
    Orestes. Apollo, Lord, what shall the issue be?
    Leader. O Night, O dark-eyed Mother, dost thou see?
    Orestes. Is it the noose of death, or life and light?
    Leader. My law down-trodden or enthroned in right?
    Apollo. Divide the fallen sea-stones as is due,
Strangers, and in the count see all be true.
An absent voice hath made life ruinous,
And one cast pebble built a fallen house.
        [*The scrutineers bring their results to* ATHENA.
    Athena. This prisoner, since the stones for ill and good
Are equal, hath escaped the doom of blood.
    Orestes. O Pallas, O deliverer of my race,
Thou hast led back the wanderer to his place,
The homeless to his home; and men shall say
'Once more he is an Argive, and this day
Dwells in his father's riches, by the word
Of Pallas, Loxias, and Zeus the Third,
Who saveth all and all accomplisheth.'
'Twas He of old who saw my father's death,
And pitied; He who saw pursuing me
My mother's ministers, and set me free.
    Pallas, to this thy people and thy clime
Through all the long years of ensuing Time
I swear, ere I depart to mine own land,
This oath. No captain of an Argive band
Shall ever against Athens raise his spear.
Yea, and if any break this law, I swear
Myself out of the grave bewilderment
Shall set before their host, and discontent,
Disheartened roads and rivers evil-starred,
Till back they turn, bowed down by toils too hard
For bearing. But if still with vow unbroke,
Through storm or shine, for Pallas and her folk
Their lance is lifted, then to Argos too
My love shall be the greater, and hold true.
And fare thee well, O Pallas; fare you well,
All that within her ancient rampart dwell;

Iron may your grasp against all evil be,
And strong to save, and big with victory!

[*Exit* ORESTES.

    Furies. Woe on you, woe, ye younger gods!
      Ye have trampled the great Laws of old
Beneath your chariots! Ye have broke the rods
    Of justice, yea and torn them from my hold!
Mine office gone, unhappy and angered sore,
I rage alone. What have I any more
    To do? Or be? Shall not mine injury turn
      And crush this people? Shall not poison rain
      Upon them, even the poison of this pain
        Wherewith my heart doth burn?
  And up therefrom there shall a lichen creep,
      A leafless, childless, blight,
A stain in the earth man-slaying . . . O just Throne of Right!
      Have ye not suffered deep,
Deep, ye unhappy children of old Night,
      Born to be scorned and weep!
    Athena. I pray you, nay! Make not this bitter moan;
Ye are not conquered. Equal, stone for stone,
The judgment fell, in honesty of thought,
Not scorn of thee. From Zeus on high was brought
A shining witness; and the god, who gave
The word to slay, himself was here to save,
Lest this man for obedience to his will
Should perish. . . . And for this ye fain would spill
Your poison? Ah, take thought! Nor on our heads
Rain the strange dew a spirit's anger sheds,
Seed-ravening blight and mildews merciless,
Till all the land lie waste in fruitlessness.
Spare us, and, lo, I promise: here shall be
A home your own, a caverned mystery,
Where alway ye shall sit, enthroned in pride
And shining, by my people glorified.
    Furies. Woe on you, woe, ye younger gods!
      Ye have trampled the great Laws of old
Beneath your chariots! Ye have broke the rods
    Of justice, yea and torn them from my hold!
Mine office gone, unhappy and angered sore,

I rage alone. What have I any more
   To do? Or be? Shall not mine injury turn
      And crush this people? Shall not poison rain
      Upon them, even the poison of this pain
         Wherewith my heart doth burn?
And up therefrom there shall a lichen creep,
      A leafless, childless, blight,
A stain in the earth man-slaying . . . O just Throne of Right!
      Have ye not suffered deep,
Deep, ye unhappy children of old Night,
      Born to be scorned and weep!
   Athena. Ah, rage not. No dishonor comes you nigh;
Nor, being immortal, blast for these who die
Their little life and land. I, even as you,
Obey the supreme Father, yea, I too.
What boots it to say more? To me alone
The keys of that great treasure-house are known
Where sleep the lightnings.—But He needs them not!
Accept my word, and cast not here the hot
Fruits of a passion that turns all to ill:
Bid the dark tempest's bitter surge be still,
Thou great in glory, partner of my home!
From many miles of land to thee shall come
First-fruits for maidens wed, for children born;
Then shall ye bless this peace that we have sworn.
   Furies.   That this should fall on me,
         Me of the ancient way,
         The faithful of heart! To be
         Unclean, abominable,
         In the darkness where I dwell,
         And mine honor shorn away!
My breath is as a fire flung far and wide,
And a strange anguish stabbeth at my side.
Hear thou my wrath, O Mother, Night, mine own,
Hear what these young false-handed gods have wrought!
Mine immemorial honor is overthrown,
         And I am naught!
   Athena. Thine heaviness myself will help thee bear.
Older thou art than I, and surely ware
Of wisdom that I wot not: yet also

To me Zeus giveth both to think and know.
And if ye leave us for the stranger's shore,
This know I, that your heart shall still be sore
For Athens. Time's great river in its flow
From darkness shall but make her glory grow.
And here in honor at Erechtheus' side
Enthronèd, thou shalt garner gifts of pride
From men and women worshippers, in fair
Procession moving, richer and more rare
Than eye of man hath seen in other lands.
Such offering now awaits thee at my hands:
Blessing and blest, 'mid glories gladly given,
To share this land, the best beloved of Heaven.

> *Furies.*   That this should fall on me,
>   Me of the ancient way,
>   The faithful of heart! To be
>   Unclean, abominable,
>   In the darkness where I dwell,
>   And mine honor shorn away!
My breath is as a fire flung far and wide,
And a strange anguish stabbeth at my side.
Hear thou my wrath, O Mother, Night, mine own,
Hear what these young false-handed gods have wrought!
Mine immemorial honor is overthrown,
      And I am naught!

> *Athena.* I will not cease thine anger to assuage
With good words. None shall say that, in thine age
By younger gods and city-building men
Thou and thy law were mocked, cast out again
To walk the wilderness, exiles from hence.
If thou canst hold that spirit in reverence
Which hears Persuasion and which thinks again,
Whose understanding and whose peace doth reign
By God's appointment in my word and thought,
Here thou wilt stay. Or, if that please thee not,
Thou shalt not justly lay upon this land
Or wrath, or vengeance, or afflicting hand.
Stay, if ye will. Let this soil be your own
With Right made perfect and an ageless throne.

> *Leader.* Great Pallas, what abode shall be my lot?

[153]

Athena. A throne unwashed by tears; reject it not.
Leader. Say I consent; what shall mine office be?
Athena. No house shall prosper save by aid of thee.
Leader. Such greatness mine! Wilt thou thereof have care?
Athena. Yea; and through life uphold thy worshipper.
Leader. For dateless time thou giv'st me warranty?
Athena. How should I speak the thing that shall not be?
Leader. Thou wilt soften me. . . . Methinks mine anger
bends.
Athena. Stay, and that softened mood will find thee friends.
Leader. What spell upon the land wouldst have me lay?
Athena. All that brings Victory and not Dismay.
From earth and dewy sea—be this thy prayer—
From moving winds and the still dome of air
Let breaths of gladness and sweet sunlight come;
The fruit of flocks and fields round every home
Abundant flow and, year by year, be true.
The seeds of human life make fruitful, too,
Save in the ungodly: them thy Rule of Right
Shall uproot, as of old. For I delight,
Like one that tends his garden, to uprear
These plants of righteousness, untouched by fear
Of evil. Cast not on this soil of mine
Thy whet-stones of the blood, like poisonous wine
In young men's hearts, till rage and death be stirred.
Oh, take not from the fierce mate-murdering bird
The heart to give my people, the blind war
Within, that burneth most where brethren are.
War with the stranger, yes; no stint thereof;
Terror is there, and glory, and great love;
But not the mad bird-rage that slays at home.
Such let thine office be. And if there come
True-hearted war, I will not fail to uphold
This land victorious where great deeds are told.
            [*At a sign from the* LEADER, *the* FURIES *take for-
              mation for a Song of Blessing.*
Furies. A home with Pallas shall be mine.
    I will not give this City nay,
  The Fort of Heaven, which Zeus divine
    And faithful Ares hold in sway,

A shining loveliness to enfold
The altars of the gods of old.

For whom—so do I weave my prayer
And move with words of presage good—
All fortunes whereby life is fair,
, Like springing fountains, up shall flood,
From Earth's deep-bosomed caverns won
By wooing of the enthronèd Sun.

Athena. I love my City; and with plan
  Aforethought here have welcomed these,
  The Awarders great and hard to appease,
Whose realm is all the estate of man.

Justice is theirs: though many an one
  May meet their wrath in innocence,
  Not knowing why the wound nor whence,
That striketh. Some great evil done

Aforetime, with no payment just,
  Cast him to These. Strange wrath and hate
  Are round him, and he cries: but Fate,
Unanswering, grindeth him to dust.

Furies. No storm-wind—so I speak my prize—
  Shall breathe the blight that poisoneth trees;
No burning things that blind the eyes
  Of plants, shall pass her boundaries:
The groaning pest shall come not nigh,
Nor fruit upon the branches die.

The flocks shall browse in happy cheer,
  And Pan, the Shepherd, guard them true,
With twofold increase, as the year
  Repays her seeds in season due;
And deep-hid treasures of the ground
Shall be in God's due order found.

Athena. Ye Guardians, hear the word she hath said,
  And shall fulfil! Most potent hands

Hath great Erînys, in the lands
Where dwell the deathless and the dead.

And all this world of men declares
  Her visible act on right and wrong;
  How ône man's life she makes a song.
Another's a long mist of tears.

Furies. Let manhood's glory by no doom
    Of death untimely be defiled;
  Let life to maidens in their bloom
    Bring each a lover and a child.
  O whatsoever Gods have power,
  And Fates eternal, grant this dower!

  Ye Fates, our Mother's Sisterhood,
    Assigners true to all that be,
  To every house its ill and good,
    To every hour its potency.
  Righteous participants through all,
  Of Gods the most majestical.

Athena. With joy I hear their prescient song
    Touching my land; and much in pride
    I praise Persuasion gentle-eyed,
  Who guarded well my lips and tongue,

  When these were wrathful and denied;
    But Zeus, whose Word is in the Mart,
    Prevailed; and of our strife no part,
  Save strife in blessing, shall abide.

Furies. Let her who hungereth still for wrong,
    Faction, in Athens ne'er again
  Lift on the air her ravening song;
    Let not the dust of Pallas' Plain
  Drink the dark blood of any son
  By fury of revenge fordone.

  Rage not to smite the smiter, lest
    By rage the City's heart be torn:

Bless him that blesseth: in each breast
So shall a single love be born,
And 'gainst Her foes a single hate.
This also maketh firm a state.

Athena. Wise are they and have found the way
Of peace. And in each awful face
I see for you, my People, grace:
If ye are gentle, even as they,
And do them worship, this shall be
Your work: to guide through ill, through good,
Both land and town in that pure mood
Of truth that shuns iniquity.

[*The* JUDGES *and the concourse of* ATHENIANS
have now formed into procession, to escort the
FURIES *to their Cavern.*

Chorus of Athenians. Rejoice, rejoice! And as ye go your
ways
In rich apportionment of blissful days,
Farewell, farewell!

Furies. Ye folk within the wall, approved
To neighbor Jove's eternal eyes,
Ye lovers of the Well-beloved,
The Virgin Spirit, timely wise,
The wings of Pallas fold above you,
Therefore shall Zeus the Father love you.

Athena. Fare ye well also. I must go
Before you, guiding, to make bright
Your secret chambers with the light,
The holy light, they dared not know.

Come, and when deep beneath the veil
Of earth ye pass, 'mid offering high,
Hold down the evil that shall die,
Send up the good that shall prevail.

[157]

Ye sons of Cranaos, guide them, till
These Wanderers rest within your doors:
With them one City now is yours;
Be one in working and in will!

Chorus of Athenians. Rejoice, rejoice! I raise my voice
again,
To speak that bliss that overtowereth pain.
Farewell, farewell!

Furies. All things within the Wall that dwell,
All gods and men, that are or were;
All life from Pallas' citadel
Which draws its being, I am here:
These Dwellers in your gates adore,
And fear the tides of Life no more!

Athena. The prayers they have uttered o'er my land I praise;
And speed them on, 'mid many a torch's blaze,
To that most deep and subterranean end
Of wandering. Let these ministers, who tend
Mine image, follow; righteous warders they.
Let all the fullness of the land this day,
Children, and wives and women bent with years,
Come forth: do worship to these Wanderers
Accepted in their robes of crimson dye.
Let leap the flash of fire. This great Ally
Shall be revealed and proven in the fate
Of Athens, if her men be true and great.
Chorus of Athenians. Gather ye home; are ye great, do ye
crave adoration,
O childless Children of Night in the pride of your going?
(Give good words, O Folk of the Fold!)
Aeonian caverns of glory are yours, and oblation
Of worship, and sacrifice high, and praise overflowing.
(Give good words, O young men and old!)
Come with the Law that can pardon, the Judgment that know-
eth,
O Semnai, Semnai, watchers o'er people and land;

And joy be a-stream in your ways, as the fire that bloweth
    A-stream from beacon and brand.
                        [A cry of joy rises above the singing.
Outpour ye the Chalice of Peace where the torches are blend-
    ing:
  In Pallas the place it is found and the task it is done.
The Law that is Fate and the Father the All-Comprehending
    Are here met together as one.
        [Again a cry of joy as the Procession passes out of
        sight.

SOPHOCLES
OEDIPUS, KING OF THEBES

⇥⇥⇤⇤

TRANSLATED
by
GILBERT MURRAY

CHARACTERS IN THE PLAY

OEDIPUS, *supposed son of Polybus, King of Corinth; now elected King of Thebes.*

JOCASTA, *Queen of Thebes; widow of Laïus, the late King, and now wife to Oedipus.*

CREON, *a Prince of Thebes, brother to Jocasta.*

TIRESIAS, *an old blind seer.*

PRIEST OF ZEUS.

A STRANGER *from Corinth.*

A SHEPHERD *of King Laïus.*

A MESSENGER *from the Palace.*

CHORUS of the Elders of Thebes.

A Crowd of Suppliants, men, women, and children.

The date of the first production of the play is not known, but was probably about the year 429 B.C.

ARGUMENT

While Thebes was under the rule of Laïus and Jocasta there appeared a strange and monstrous creature, 'the riddling Sphinx,' 'the She-Wolf of the woven song,' who in some unexplained way sang riddles of death and slew the people of Thebes. Laïus went to ask aid of the oracle of Delphi, but was slain mysteriously on the road. Soon afterwards there came to Thebes a young Prince of Corinth, Oedipus, who had left his home and was wandering. He faced the Sphinx and read her riddle, whereupon she flung herself from her rock and died. The throne being vacant was offered to Oedipus, and with it the hand of the Queen Jocasta.

Some ten or twelve years afterwards a pestilence has fallen on Thebes. At this point the play begins.

OEDIPUS, KING OF THEBES

SCENE.—*Before the Palace of Oedipus at Thebes. A crowd of suppliants of all ages are waiting by the altar in front and on the steps of the Palace; among them the* PRIEST OF ZEUS. *As the Palace door opens and* OEDIPUS *comes out, all the suppliants with a cry move toward him in attitudes of prayer, holding out their olive branches, and then become still again as he speaks.*

Oedipus. My children, fruit of Cadmus' ancient tree
New springing, wherefore thus with bended knee
Press ye upon us, laden all with wreaths
And suppliant branches? And the city breathes
Heavy with incense, heavy with dim prayer
And shrieks to affright the Slayer.—Children, care
For this so moves me, I have scorned withal
Message or writing: seeing 'tis I ye call,
'Tis I am come, world-honored Oedipus.
　　Old Man, do thou declare—the rest have thus
Their champion—in what mood stand ye so still,
In dread or sure hope? Know ye not, my will
Is yours for aid 'gainst all? Stern were indeed
The heart that felt not for so dire a need.
　　Priest. O Oedipus, who holdest in thy hand
My city, thou canst see what ages stand
At these thine altars; some whose little wing
Scarce flieth yet, and some with long living
O'erburdened; priests, as I of Zeus am priest,
And chosen youths: and wailing hath not ceased
Of thousands in the market-place, and by
Athena's twofold temples and the dry
Ash of Ismênus' portent-breathing shore.
　　For all our ship, thou see'st, is weak and sore

[163]

Shaken with storms, and no more lighteneth
Her head above the waves whose trough is death.
She wasteth in the fruitless buds of earth,
In parchèd herds and travail without birth
Of dying women: yea, and midst of it
A burning and a loathly god hath lit
Sudden, and sweeps our land, this Plague of power;
Till Cadmus' house grows empty, hour by hour,
And Hell's house rich with steam of tears and blood.
    O King, not God indeed nor peer to God
We deem thee, that we kneel before thine hearth,
Children and old men, praying; but of earth
A thing consummate by thy star confessed
Thou walkest and by converse with the blest;
Who came to Thebes so swift, and swept away
The Sphinx's song, the tribute of dismay,
That all were bowed beneath, and made us free.
A stranger, thou, naught knowing more than we,
Nor taught of any man, but by God's breath
Filled, thou didst raise our life. So the world saith;
So we say.
          Therefore now, O Lord and Chief,
We come to thee again; we lay our grief
On thy head, if thou find us not some aid.
Perchance thou hast heard Gods talking in the shade
Of night, or eke some man: to him that knows,
Men say, each chance that falls, each wind that blows
Hath life, when he seeks counsel. Up, O chief
Of men, and lift thy city from its grief;
Face thine own peril! All our land doth hold
Thee still our saviour, for that help of old:
Shall they that tell of thee hereafter tell
'By him was Thebes raised up, and after fell!'
Nay, lift us till we slip no more. Oh, let
That bird of old that made us fortunate
Wing back; be thou our Oedipus again.
And let thy kingdom be a land of men,
Not emptiness. Walls, towers, and ships, they all
Are nothing with no men to keep the wall.
    Oedipus. My poor, poor children! Surely long ago

I have read your trouble. Stricken, well I know,
Ye all are, stricken sore: yet verily
Not one so stricken to the heart as I.
Your grief, it cometh to each man apart
For his own loss, none other's; but this heart
For thee and me and all of us doth weep.
Wherefore it is not to one sunk in sleep
Ye come with waking. Many tears these days
For your sake I have wept, and many ways
Have wandered on the beating wings of thought.
And, finding but one hope, that I have sought
And followed. I have sent Menoikeus' son,
Creon, my own wife's brother, forth alone
To Apollo's House in Delphi, there to ask
What word, what deed of mine, what bitter task,
May save my city.
                    And the lapse of days
Reckoned, I can but but marvel what delays
His journey. 'Tis beyond all thought that thus
He comes not, beyond need. But when he does,
Then call me false and traitor, if I flee
Back from whatever task God sheweth me.
    Priest. At point of time thou speakest. Mark the cheer
Yonder. Is that not Creon drawing near?
        [*They all crowd to gaze where* CREON *is approach-
        ing in the distance.*
    Oedipus. O Lord Apollo, help! And be the star
That guides him joyous as his seemings are!
    Priest. Oh! surely joyous! How else should he bear
That fruited laurel wreathed about his hair?
    Oedipus. We soon shall know.—'Tis not too far for one
Clear-voiced.
    (*Shouting*) Ho, brother! Prince! Menoikeus' son,
What message from the God?
    Creon (*from a distance*). Message of joy!
                                [*Enter* CREON.
I tell thee, what is now our worst annoy,
If the right deed be done, shall turn to good.
        [*The crowd, which has been full of excited hope,
        falls to doubt and disappointment.*
                    [165]

Oedipus. Nay, but what is the message? For my blood
Runs neither hot nor cold for words like those.

Creon. Shall I speak now, with all these pressing close,
Or pass within?—To me both ways are fair.

Oedipus. Speak forth to all! The grief that these men bear
Is more than any fear for mine own death.

Creon. I speak then what I heard from God.—Thus saith
Phoebus, our Lord and Seer, in clear command.
An unclean thing there is, hid in our land,
Eating the soil thereof: this ye shall cast
Out, and not foster till all help be past.

Oedipus. How cast it out? What was the evil deed?

Creon. Hunt the men out from Thebes, or make them bleed
Who slew. For blood it is that stirs to-day.

Oedipus. Who was the man they killed? Doth Phoebus say?

Creon. O King, there was of old King Laïus
In Thebes, ere thou didst come to pilot us.

Oedipus. I know: not that I ever saw his face.

Creon. 'Twas he. And Loxias now bids us trace
And smite the unknown workers of his fall.

Oedipus. Where in God's earth are they? Or how withal
Find the blurred trail of such an ancient stain?

Creon. In Thebes, he said.—That which men seek amain
They find. 'Tis things forgotten that go by.

Oedipus. And where did Laïus meet them? Did he die
In Thebes, or in the hills, or some far land?

Creon. To ask God's will in Delphi he had planned
His journey. Started and returned no more.

Oedipus. And came there nothing back? No message, nor
None of his company, that ye might hear?

Creon. They all were slain, save one man; blind with fear
He came, remembering naught—or almost naught.

Oedipus. And what was that? One thing has often brought
Others, could we but catch one little clue.

Creon. 'Twas not one man, 'twas robbers—that he knew—
Who barred the road and slew him: a great band.

Oedipus. Robbers? What robber, save the work was planned
By treason here, would dare a risk so plain?

Creon. So some men thought. But Laïus lay slain,
And none to avenge him in his evil day.

Oedipus. And what strange mischief, when your master lay
Thus fallen, held you back from search and deed?
    Creon. The dark-songed Sphinx was here. We had no heed
Of distant sorrows, having death so near.
    Oedipus. It falls on me then. I will search and clear
This darkness.—Well hath Phoebus done, and thou
Too, to recall that dead king, even now,
And with you for the right I also stand,
To obey the God and succor this dear land.
Nor is it as for one that touches me
Far off; 'tis for mine own sake I must see
This sin cast out. Whoe'er it was that slew
Laïus, the same wild hand may seek me too:
And caring thus for Laïus, is but care
For mine own blood.—Up! Leave this altar-stair,
Children. Take from it every suppliant bough.
Then call the folk of Thebes. Say, 'tis my vow
To uphold them to the end. So God shall crown
Our greatness, or for ever cast us down.

                          [He goes into the Palace.
    Priest. My children, rise.—The King most lovingly.
Hath promised all we came for. And may He
Who sent this answer, Phoebus, come confessed
Helper to Thebes, and strong to stay the pest.
        *[The suppliants gather up their boughs and stand
           at the side. The* CHORUS *of Theban elders enter.*

                Chorus.
    *(They speak of the Oracle which they have not yet
      heard, and cry to* APOLLO *by his special cry 'I-ê.')*
   A Voice, a Voice, that is borne on the Holy Way!
What art thou, O Heavenly One, O Word of the Houses of
    Gold?
Thebes is bright with thee, and my heart it leapeth;
    yet is it cold,
              And my spirit faints as I pray.
              I-ê! I-ê!
What task, O Affrighter of Evil, what task shall thy people
    essay?

One new as our new-come affliction,
    Or an old toil returned with the years?
Unveil thee, thou dread benediction,
    Hope's daughter and Fear's.

(*They pray to Athena, Artemis, and Apollo.*)
Zeus-Child that knowest not death, to thee I pray,
O Pallas; next to thy Sister, who calleth Thebes her own,
Artemis, named of Fair Voices, who sitteth her orbèd throne
    In the throng of the market way:
            And I-ê! I-ê!
Apollo, the Pure, the Far-smiter; O Three that keep evil away,
    If of old for our city's desire,
        When the death-cloud hung close to her brow,
    Ye have banished the wound and the fire,
        Oh! come to us now!

(*They tell of the Pestilence.*)
Wounds beyond telling; my people sick unto death;
    And where is the counselor, where is the sword of thought?
And Holy Earth in her increase perisheth:
    The child dies and the mother awaketh not.
            I-ê! I-ê!
We have seen them, one on another, gone as a bird is gone,
    Souls that are flame; yea, higher,
    Swifter they pass than fire,
        To the rocks of the dying Sun.

(*They end by a prayer to Athena.*)
Their city wasteth unnumbered; their children lie
    Where death hath cast them, unpitied, unwept upon.
The altars stand, as in seas of storm a high
    Rock standeth, and wives and mothers gray thereon
            Weep, weep and pray.
Lo, joy-cries to fright the Destroyer; a flash in the dark they
        rise,
    Then die by the sobs overladen.
    Send help, O heaven-born Maiden,
        Let us look on the light of her eyes!

(*To Zeus, that he drive out the Slayer.*)
And Ares, the abhorred
  Slayer, who bears no sword,
But shrieking, wrapped in fire, stands over me,
  Make that he turn, yea, fly
  Broken, wind-wasted, high
Down the vexed hollow of the Vaster Sea;
  Or back to his own Thrace,
  To harbor shelterless.
Where Night hath spared, he bringeth end by day.
  Him, Him, O thou whose hand
  Beareth the lightning brand,
O Father Zeus, now with thy thunder, slay and slay!

(*To Apollo, Artemis, and Dionysus.*)
Where is thy gold-strung bow,
  O Wolf-god, where the flow
Of living shafts unconquered, from all ills
  Our helpers? Where the white
  Spears of thy Sister's light,
Far-flashing as she walks the wolf-wild hills?
  And thou, O Golden-crown,
  Theban and named our own,
O Wine-gleam, Voice of Joy, for ever more
  Ringed with thy Maenads white,
  Bacchus, draw near and smite,
Smite with thy glad-eyed flame the God whom Gods abhor.

[*During the last lines* OEDIPUS *has come out from
    the Palace.*

Oedipus. Thou prayest: but my words if thou wilt hear
And bow thee to their judgment, strength is near
For help, and a great lightening of ill.
Thereof I come to speak, a stranger still
To all this tale, a stranger to the deed:
(Else, save that I were clueless, little need
Had I to cast my net so wide and far:)
Howbeit, I, being now as all ye are,
A Theban, to all Thebans high and low
Do make proclaim: if any here doth know

[169]

By what man's hand died Laïus, your King,
Labdacus' son, I charge him that he bring
To me his knowledge. Let him feel no fear
If on a townsman's body he must clear
Our guilt: the man shall suffer no great ill,
But pass from Thebes, and live where else he will.

[*No answer.*

Is it some alien from an alien shore
Ye know to have done the deed, screen him no more!
Good guerdon waits you now and a King's love
Hereafter.   Ha! If still ye will not move
But, fearing for yourselves or some near friend,
Reject my charge, then hearken to what end
Ye drive me.—If in this place men there be
Who know and speak not, lo, I make decree
That, while in Thebes I bear the diadem,
No man shall greet, no man shall shelter them,
Nor give them water in their thirst, nor share
In sacrifice nor shrift nor dying prayer,
But thrust them from our doors, the thing they hide
Being this land's curse. Thus hath the God replied
This day to me from Delphi, and my sword
I draw thus for the dead and for God's word.

    And lastly for the murderer, be it one
Hiding alone or more in unison,
I speak on him this curse: even as his soul
Is foul within him let his days be foul,
And life unfriended grind him till he die.
More: if he ever tread my hearth and I
Know it, be every curse upon my head
That I have spoke this day.
                    All I have said
I charge ye strictly to fulfil and make
Perfect, for my sake, for Apollo's sake,
And this land's sake, deserted of her fruit
And cast out from her gods. Nay, were all mute
At Delphi, still 'twere strange to leave the thing
Unfollowed, when a true man and a King
Lay murdered. All should search. But I, as now

Our fortunes fall—his crown is on my brow,
His wife lies in my arms, and common fate,
Had but his issue been more fortunate,
Might well have joined our children—since this red
Chance hath so stamped its heel on Laïus head,
I am his champion left, and, as I would
For mine own father, choose for ill or good
This quest, to find the man who slew of yore
Labdacus' son, the son of Polydore,
Son of great Cadmus whom Agenor old
Begat, of Thebes first master. And, behold,
For them that aid me not, I pray no root
Nor seed in earth may bear them corn nor fruit,
No wife bear children, but this present curse
Cleave to them close and other woes yet worse.
    Enough: ye other people of the land,
Whose will is one with mine, may Justice stand
Your helper, and all gods for evermore.
                       [The crowd disperses.
    Leader. O King, even while thy curse yet hovers o'er
My head, I answer thee. I slew him not,
Nor can I shew the slayer. But, Got wot,
If Phoebus sends this charge, let Phoebus read
Its meaning and reveal who did the deed.
    Oedipus. Aye, that were just, if of his grace he would
Reveal it. How shall man compel his God?
    Leader. Second to that, methinks, 'twould help us most. . . .
    Oedipus. Though it be third, speak! Nothing should be lost.
    Leader. To our High Seer on earth vision is given
Most like to that High Phoebus hath in heaven.
Ask of Tiresias: he could tell thee true.
    Oedipus. That also have I thought for. Aye, and two
Heralds have sent ere now. 'Twas Creon set
Me on.—I marvel that he comes not yet.
    Leader. Our other clues are weak, old signs and far.
    Oedipus. What signs? I needs must question all that are.
    Leader. Some travelers slew him, the tale used to be.
    Oedipus. The tale, yes: but the witness, where is he?
    Leader. The man hath heard thy curses. If he knows
The taste of fear, he will not long stay close.

Oedipus. He fear my words, who never feared the deed?
Leader. Well, there is one shall find him.—See, they lead
Hither our Lord Tiresias, in whose mind
All truth is born, alone of human kind.

> [*Enter* TIRESIAS *led by a young disciple. He is an
>   old blind man in a prophet's robe, dark, un-
>   kempt and sinister in appearance.*

Oedipus. Tiresias, thou whose mind divineth well
All Truth, the spoken and the unspeakable,
The things of heaven and them that walk the earth;
Our city . . . thou canst see, for all thy dearth
Of outward eyes, what clouds are over her.
In which, O gracious Lord, no minister
Of help, no champion, can we find at all
Save thee. For Phoebus—thou hast heard withal
His message—to our envoy hath decreed
One only way of help in this great need:
To find and smite with death or banishing,
Him who smote Laïus, our ancient King.
Oh, grudge us nothing! Question every cry
Of birds, and all roads else of prophecy
Thou knowest. Save our city: save thine own
Greatness: save me; save all that yet doth groan
Under the dead man's wrong! Lo, in thy hand
We lay us. And methinks, no work so grand
Hath man yet compassed, as, with all he can
Of chance or power, to help his fellow man.
Tiresias (*to himself*). Ah, me!
A fearful thing is knowledge, when to know
Helpeth no end. I knew this long ago,
But crushed it dead. Else had I never come.
Oedipus. What means this? Comest thou so deep in gloom?
Tiresias. Let me go back! Thy work shall weigh on thee
The less, if thou consent, and minè on me.
Oedipus. Prophet, this is not lawful; nay, nor kind
To Thebes, who feeds thee, thus to veil thy mind.
Tiresias. 'Tis that I like not thy mind, nor the way
It goeth. Therefore, lest I also stray . . .

> [*He moves to go off.* OEDIPUS *bars his road.*
Oedipus. Thou shalt not, knowing, turn and leave us! See,

We all implore thee, all, on bended knee.

Tiresias. Ye have no knowledge. What is mine I hold
For ever dumb, lest what is thine be told.

Oedipus. What wilt thou? Know and speak not? In my need
Be false to me, and let thy city bleed?

Tiresias. I will not wound myself nor thee. Why seek
To trap and question me? I will not speak.

Oedipus. Thou devil! ——

> [*Movement of* LEADER *to check him.*]
> Nay; the wrath of any stone

Would rise at him. It lies with thee to have done
And speak. Is there no melting in thine eyes!

Tiresias. Naught lies with me! With thee, with thee there lies,
I warrant, what thou ne'er hast seen nor guessed.

Oedipus (*to* LEADER, *who tries to calm him*). How can I hear
    such talk?—he maketh jest
Of the land's woe—and keep mine anger dumb?

Tiresias. Howe'er I hold it back, 'twill come, 'twill come.

Oedipus. The more shouldst thou declare it to thy King.

Tiresias. I speak no more. For thee, if passioning
Doth comfort thee, on, passion to thy fill!

> [*He moves to go.*]

Oedipus. 'Fore God, I am in wrath; and speak I will,
Nor stint what I see clear. 'Twas thou, 'twas thou,
Didst plan this murder; aye, and, save the blow,
Wrought it.—I know thou art blind; else I could swear
Thou, and thou only, art the murderer.

Tiresias (*returning*). So?—I command thee by thine own
    word's power,
To stand accurst, and never from this hour
Speak word to me, nor yet to these who ring
Thy throne. Thou art thyself the unclean thing.

Oedipus. Thou front of brass, to fling out injury
So wild! Dost think to bate me and go free?

Tiresias. I am free. The strong truth is in this heart.

Oedipus. What prompted thee? I swear 'twas not thine art.

Tiresias. 'Twas thou. I spoke not, save for thy command.

Oedipus. Spoke what? What was it? Let me understand.

Tiresias. Dost tempt me? Were my words before not plain!

Oedipus. Scarce thy full meaning. Speak the words again.

*Oed. thinks
it is counter-
charge.*

Tiresias. <u>Thou seek'st this man of blood: Thyself art he.</u>
Oedipus. 'Twill cost thee dear, twice to have stabbed at me!
Tiresias. Shall I say more, to see thee rage again?
Oedipus. Oh, take thy fill of speech: 'twill all be vain.
Tiresias. Thou livest with those near to thee in shame
Most deadly, seeing not thyself nor them.
    Oedipus. Thou think'st 'twill help thee, thus to speak and
      speak?
Tiresias. Surely, until the strength of Truth be weak.
    Oedipus. 'Tis weak to none save thee. Thou hast no part
In truth, thou blind man, blind eyes, ears and heart.
    Tiresias. More blind, more sad thy words of scorn, which
      none
Who hears but shall cast back on thee: soon, soon.
    Oedipus. Thou spawn of Night, not I nor any free
And seeing man would hurt a thing like thee.
    Tiresias. God is enough.—'Tis not my doom to fall
By thee. He knows and shall accomplish all.
    Oedipus (with a flash of discovery). Ha! Creon!—Is it his
      or thine, this plot?
    Tiresias. 'Tis thyself hates thee. Creon hates thee not.
    Oedipus. O wealth and majesty, O skill all strife
Surpassing on the fevered roads of life,
What is your heart but bitterness, if now
For this poor crown Thebes bound upon my brow,
A gift, a thing I sought not—for this crown
Creon the stern and true, Creon mine own
Comrade, comes creeping in the dark to ban
And slay me; sending first this magic-man
And schemer, this false beggar-priest, whose eye
Is bright for gold and blind for prophecy.
Speak, thou. When hast thou ever shown thee strong
For aid? The She-Wolf of the woven song
Came, and thy art could find no word, no breath,
To save thy people from her riddling death.
'Twas scarce a secret, that, for common men
To unravel. There was need of Seer-craft then.
And thou hadst none to show. No fowl, no flame,
No God revealed it thee. <u>'Twas I that came,
Rude Oedipus, unlearned in wizard's lore,</u>

self-satisfied

tendency to pride

And read her secret, and she spoke no more.
Whom now thou thinkest to hunt out, and stand
Foremost in honour at King Creon's hand.
I think ye will be sorry, thou and he
That shares thy sin-hunt. Thou dost look to me
An old man; else, I swear this day should bring
On thee the death thou plottest for thy King.

   Leader. Lord Oedipus, these be but words of wrath,
All thou hast spoke and all the Prophet hath.
Which skills not. We must join, for ill or well,
In search how best to obey God's oracle.

   Tiresias. King though thou art, thou needs must bear the
     right
Of equal answer. Even in me is might
For thus much, seeing I live no thrall of thine,
But Lord Apollo's; neither do I sign
Where Creon bids me.

              I am blind, and thou
Hast mocked my blindness. Yea, I will speak now.
Eyes hast thou, but thy deeds thou canst not see
Nor where thou art, nor what things dwell with thee.
Whence art thou born? Thou know'st not; and unknown,
On quick and dead, on all that were thine own,
Thou hast wrought hate. For that across thy path
Rising, a mother's and a father's wrath,
Two-handed, shod with fire, from the haunts of men
Shall scourge thee, in thine eyes now light, but then
Darkness. Aye, shriek! What harbor of the sea,
What wild Kithairon shall not cry to thee
In answer, when thou hear'st what bridal song,
What wind among the torches, bore thy strong
Sail to its haven, not of peace but blood.
Yea, ill things multitude on multitude
Thou seest not, which so soon shall lay thee low,
Low as thyself, low as thy children.—Go,
Heap scorn on Creon and my lips withal:
For this I tell thee, never was there fall
Of pride, nor shall be, like to thine this day.

   Oedipus. To brook such words from this thing? Out, I say!

Out to perdition! Aye, and quick, before . . .

[*The* LEADER *restrains him.*

Enough then!—Turn and get thee from my door.

Tiresias. I had not come hadst thou not called me here.

Oedipus. I knew thee not so dark a fool. I swear
'Twere long before I called thee, had I known.

Tiresias. Fool, say'st thou? Am I truly such an one?
The two who gave thee birth, they held me wise.

Oedipus. Birth? . . . Stop! Who were they? Speak thy
prophecies.

Tiresias. This day shall give thee birth and blot thee out.

Oedipus. Oh, riddles everywhere and words of doubt!

Tiresias. Aye. Thou wast their best reader long ago.

Oedipus. Laugh on. I swear thou still shalt find me so.

Tiresias. That makes thy pride and thy calamity.

Oedipus. I have saved this land, and care not if I die.

Tiresias. Then I will go.—Give me thine arm, my child.

Oedipus. Aye, help him quick.—To see him there makes
wild
My heart. Once gone, he will not vex me more.

Tiresias (turning again as he goes). I fear thee not; nor
will I go before
That word be spoken which I came to speak.
How canst thou ever touch me?—Thou dost seek
With threats and loud proclaim the man whose hand
Slew Laïus. Lo, I tell thee, he doth stand
Here. He is called a stranger, but these days
Shall prove him Theban true, nor shall he praise
His birthright. Blind, who once had seeing eyes,
Beggared, who once had riches, in strange guise,
His staff groping before him, he shall crawl
O'er unknown earth, and voices round him call:
'Behold the brother-father of his own
Children, the seed, the sower and the sown,
Shame to his mother's blood, and to his sire
Son, murderer, incest-worker.'
                              Cool thine ire
With thought of these, and if thou find that aught
Faileth, then hold my craft a thing of naught.

[*He goes out.* OEDIPUS *returns to the Palace.*

Chorus.

(They sing of the unknown murderer.)

What man, what man is he whom the voice of Delphi's cell
Hath named of the bloody hand, of the deed no tongue may
    tell?
        Let him fly, fly, for his need
        Hath found him; oh, where is the speed
That flew with the winds of old, the team of North-Wind's spell?
    For feet there be that follow. Yea, thunder-shod
    And girt with fire he cometh, the Child of God;
And with him are they that fail not, the Sin-Hounds risen
    from Hell.
For the mountain hath spoken, a voice hath flashed from amid
    the snows,
That the wrath of the world go seek for the man whom no man
    knows.
        Is he fled to the wild forest,
        To caves where the eagles nest?
O angry bull of the rocks, cast out from thy herd-fellows!
    Rage in his heart, and rage across his way,
    He toileth ever to beat from his ears away
The word that floateth about him, living, where'er he goes.

(And of the Prophet's strange accusation.)

Yet strange, passing strange, the wise augur and his lore;
    And my heart it cannot speak; I deny not nor assent,
But float, float in wonder at things after and before;
    Did there lie between their houses some old wrath unspent,
That Corinth against Cadmus should do murder by the way?
    No tale thereof they tell, nor no sign thereof they show;
Who dares to rise for vengeance and cast Oedipus away
        For a dark, dark death long ago!
Ah, Zeus knows, and Apollo, what is dark to mortal eyes;
    They are Gods. But a prophet, hath he vision more than
        mine?
Who hath seen? Who can answer? There be wise men and
    unwise.
    I will wait, I will wait, for the proving of the sign.
But I list not nor hearken when they speak Oedipus ill.
    We saw his face of yore, when the riddling singer passed;

And we knew him that he loved us, and we saw him great in
   skill.
      Oh, my heart shall uphold him to the last!

                                   [*Enter* CREON.

   Creon. Good brother citizens, a frantic word
I hear is spoken by our chosen Lord
Oedipus against me, and here am come
Indignant. If he dreams, 'mid all this doom
That weighs upon us, he hath had from me
Or deed or lightest thought of injury, . . .
'Fore God, I have no care to see the sun
Longer with such a groaning name. Not one
Wound is it, but a multitude, if now
All Thebes must hold me guilty,—aye, and thou
And all who loved me—of a deed so foul.
   Leader. If words were spoken, it was scarce the soul
That spoke them: 'twas some sudden burst of wrath.
   Creon. The charge was made, then, that Tiresias hath
Made answer false, and that I bribed him, I?
   Leader. It was—perchance for jest. I know not why.
   Creon. His heart beat true, his eyes looked steadily
And fell not, laying such a charge on me?
   Leader. I know not. I have no eyes for the thing
My masters do.—But see, here comes the King.

                      [*Enter* OEDIPUS *from the Palace.*

   Oedipus. How now, assassin? Walking at my gate
With eye undimmed, thou plotter demonstrate
Against this life, and robber of my crown?
God help thee! Me! What was it set me down
Thy butt? So dull a brain hast found in me
Aforetime, such a faint heart, not to see
Thy work betimes, or seeing not to smite?
Art thou not rash, this once! It needeth might
Of friends, it needeth gold, to make a throne
Thy quarry; and I fear me thou hast none.
   Creon. One thing alone I ask thee. Let me speak
As thou hast spoken; then, with knowledge, wreak
Thy judgment. I accept it without fear.
   Oedipus. More skill hast thou to speak than I to hear
Thee. There is peril found in thee and hate.

Creon. That one thing let me answer ere too late.

Oedipus. One thing be sure of, that thy plots are known.

Creon. The man who thinks that bitter pride alone
Can guide him, without thought—his mind is sick.

Oedipus. Who thinks to slay his brother with a trick
And suffer not himself, his eyes are blind.

Creon. Thy words are more than just. But say what kind
Of wrong thou fanciest I have done thee. Speak.

Oedipus. Didst urge me, or didst urge me not, to seek
A counsel from that man of prophecies?

Creon. So judged I then, nor now judge otherwise.

Oedipus. (*Suddenly seeing a mode of attack.*)
How many years have passed since Laïus . . .

　　　　　　　[*The words seem to choke him.*

Creon. Speak on. I cannot understand thee thus.

Oedipus. (*With an effort.*) Passed in that bloody tempest
　　from men's sight?

Creon. Long years and old. I scarce can tell them right.

Oedipus. At that time was this seer in Thebes, or how?

Creon. He was; most wise and honored, even as now.

Oedipus. At that time did he ever speak my name?

Creon. No. To mine ear at least it never came.

Oedipus. Held you no search for those who slew your King?

Creon. For sure we did, but found not anything.

Oedipus. How came the all-knowing seer to leave it so?

Creon. Ask him! I speak not where I cannot know.

Oedipus. One thing thou canst, with knowledge full, I wot.

Creon. Speak it. If true, I will conceal it not.

Oedipus. This: that until he talked with thee, the seer
Ne'er spoke of me as Laïus' murderer.

Creon. I know not if he hath so spoken now.
I heard him not.—But let me ask and thou
Answer me true, as I have answered thee.

Oedipus. Ask, ask! Thou shalt no murder find in me.

Creon. My sister is thy wife this many a day?

Oedipus. That charge it is not in me to gainsay.

Creon. Thou reignest, giving equal reign to her?

Oedipus. Always to her desire I minister.

Creon. Were we not all as one, she, thou and I?

Oedipus. Yes, thou false friend! There lies thy treachery.

Creon. Not so! Nay, do but follow me and scan
Thine own charge close. Think'st thou that any man
Would rather rule and be afraid than rule
And sleep untroubled? Nay, where lives the fool—
I know them not nor am I one of them—
Who careth more to bear a monarch's name
Than do a monarch's deeds? As now I stand
All my desire I compass at thy hand.
Were I the King, full half my deeds were done
To obey the will of others, not mine own.
Were that as sweet, when all the tale were told,
As this calm griefless princedom that I hold
And silent power? Am I so blind of brain
That ease with glory tires me, and I fain
Must change them? All men now give me God-speed,
All smile to greet me. If a man hath need
Of thee, 'tis me he calleth to the gate,
As knowing that on my word hangs the fate
Of half he craves. Is life like mine a thing
To cast aside and plot to be a King?
Doth a sane man turn villain in an hour?

For me, I never lusted thus for power
Nor bore with any man who turned such lust
To doing.—But enough. I claim but just
Question. Go first to Pytho; find if well
And true I did report God's oracle.
Next, seek in Thebes for any plots entwined
Between this seer and me; which if ye find,
Then seize and strike me dead. Myself that day
Will sit with thee as judge and bid thee Slay!
But damn me not on one man's guess.—'Tis all
Unjust: to call a traitor true, to call
A true man traitor with no cause nor end!
And this I tell thee. He who plucks a friend
Out from his heart hath lost a treasured thing
Dear as his own dear life.

> But Time shall bring
Truth back. 'Tis Time alone can make men know
What hearts are true; the false one day can show.
Leader. To one that fears to fall his words are wise,

O King; in thought the swift win not the prize.
Oedipus. When he is swift who steals against my reign
With plots, then swift am I to plot again.
Wait patient, and his work shall have prevailed
Before I move, and mine for ever failed.
Creon. How then? To banish me is thy intent?
Oedipus. Death is the doom I choose, not banishment.
Creon. Wilt never soften, never trust thy friend?
Oedipus. First I would see how traitors meet their end.
Creon. I see thou wilt not think.
Oedipus. I think to save
My life.
Creon. Think, too, of mine.
Oedipus. Thine, thou born knave!
Creon. Yes. . . . What, if thou art blind in everything?
Oedipus. The King must be obeyed.
Creon. Not if the King
Does evil.
Oedipus. To your King! Ho, Thebes, mine own!
Creon. Thebes is my country, not the King's alone.

> [OEDIPUS *has drawn his sword; the* CHORUS *show
> signs of breaking into two parties to fight for
> Oedipus or for Creon, when the door opens
> and* JOCASTA *appears on the steps.*

Leader. Stay, Princes, stay! See, on the Castle stair
The Queen Jocasta standeth. Show to her
Your strife. She will assuage it as is well.
Jocasta. Vain men, what would ye with this angry swell
Of words heart-blinded? Is there in your eyes
No pity, thus, when all our city lies
Bleeding, to ply your privy hates? . . . Alack,
My lord, come in!—Thou, Creon, get thee back
To thine own house. And stir not to such stress
Of peril griefs that are but nothingness.
Creon. Sister, it is the pleasure of thy lord,
Our King, to do me deadly wrong. His word
Is passed on me: 'tis banishment or death.
Oedipus. I found him . . . I deny not what he saith,
My Queen . . . with craft and malice practising
Against my life.

Creon.   Ye Gods, if such a thing
Hath once been in my thoughts, may I no more
See any health on earth, but, festered o'er
With curses, die!—Have done. There is mine oath.
    Jocasta. In God's name, Oedipus, believe him, both
For my sake, and for these whose hearts are all
Thine own, and for my brother's oath withal.

                                              [Strophe.

    Leader. Yield; consent; think! My Lord, I conjure thee!
    Oedipus. What would ye have me do?
    Leader. Reject not one who never failed his troth
Of old and now is strong in his great oath.
    Oedipus. Dost know what this prayer means?
    Leader.   Yea, verily!
    Oedipus.   Say then the meaning true.
    Leader. I would not have thee cast to infamy
               Of guilt, where none is proved,
One who hath sworn and whom thou once hast loved.
    Oedipus. 'Tis that ye seek? For me, then . . . understand
Well . . . ye seek death or exile from the land.
    Leader. No, by the God of Gods, the all-seeing Sun!
May he desert me here, and every friend
With him, to death and utterest malison,
    If e'er my heart could dream of such an end!
           But it bleedeth, it bleedeth sore,
              In a land half slain,
         If we join to the griefs of yore
             Griefs of you twain.
    Oedipus. Oh, let him go, though it be utterly
My death, or flight from Thebes in beggary.
'Tis thy sad lips, not his, that make me know
Pity. Him I shall hate, where'er he go.
    Creon. I see thy mercy moving full of hate
And slow; thy wrath came swift and desperate.
Methinks, of all the pain that such a heart
Spreadeth, itself doth bear the bitterest part.
    Oedipus. Oh, leave me and begone!
    Creon.   I go, wronged sore
By thee. These friends will trust me as before.

[CREON *goes.* OEDIPUS *stands apart lost in trouble of mind.*

[*Antistrophe.*

Leader. Queen, wilt thou lead him to his house again?

Jocasta. I will, when I have heard.

Leader. There fell some word, some blind imagining
Between them. Things known foolish yet can sting.

Jocasta. From both the twain it rose?

Leader.   From both the twain.

Jocasta.   Aye, and what was the word?

Leader. Surely there is enough of evil stirred,
          And Thebes heaves on the swell
     Of storm.—Oh, leave this lying where it fell.

Oedipus. So be it, thou wise counselor! Make slight
My wrong, and blunt my purpose ere it smite.

Leader. O King, not once I have answered. Visibly
          Mad were I, lost to all wise usages,
     To seek to cast thee from us. 'Twas from thee
          We saw of old blue sky and summer seas,
          When Thebes in the storm and rain
               Reeled, like to die.
          Oh, if thou canst, again
               Blue sky, blue sky . . . !

Jocasta. Husband, in God's name, say what hath ensued
Of ill, that thou shouldst seek so dire a feud.

Oedipus. I will, wife. I have more regard for thee
Than these.—Thy brother plots to murder me.

Jocasta. Speak on. Make all thy charge. Only be clear.

Oedipus. He says that I am Laïus' murderer.

Jocasta. Says it himself? Says he hath witnesses?

Oedipus. Nay, of himself he ventures nothing. 'Tis
This priest, this hellish seer, makes all the tale.

Jocasta. The seer?—Then tear thy terrors like a veil
And take free breath. A seer? No human thing
Born on the earth hath power for conjuring
Truth from the dark of God.

                    Come, I will tell
An old tale. There came once an oracle
To Laïus: I say not from the God
Himself, but from the priests and seers who trod

[183]

His sanctuary: if ever son were bred
From him and me, by that son's hand, it said,
Laïus must die. And he, the tale yet stays
Among us, at the crossing of three ways
Was slain by robbers, strangers. And my son—
God's mercy!—scarcely the third day was gone
When Laïus took, and by another's hand
Out on the desert mountain, where the land
Is rock, cast him to die. Through both his feet
A blade of iron they drove. Thus did we cheat
Apollo of his will. My child could slay
No father, and the King could cast away
The fear that dogged him, by his child to die
Murdered.—Behold the fruits of prophecy!
Which heed not thou! God needs not that a seer
Help him, when he would make his dark things clear.

    Oedipus. Woman, what turmoil hath thy story wrought
Within me! What up-stirring of old thought!

    Jocasta. What thought? It turns thee like a frightened thing.

    Oedipus. 'Twas at the crossing of three ways this King
Was murdered? So I heard or so I thought.

    Jocasta. That was the tale. It is not yet forgot.

    Oedipus. The crossing of three ways! And in what land?

    Jocasta. Phokis 'tis called. A road on either hand
From Delphi comes and Daulia, in a glen.

    Oedipus. How many years and months have passed since
       then?

    Jocasta. 'Twas but a little time before proclaim
Was made of thee for king, the tidings came.

    Oedipus. My God, what hast thou willed to do with me?

    Jocasta. Oedipus, speak! What is it troubles thee?

    Oedipus. Ask me not yet. But say, what build, what height
Had Laïus? Rode he full of youth and might?

    Jocasta. Tall, with the white new gleaming on his brow
He walked. In shape just such a man as thou.

    Oedipus. God help me! I much fear that I have wrought
A curse on mine own head, and knew it not.

    Jocasta. How sayst thou? O my King, I look on thee
And tremble.

    Oedipus (*to himself*). Horror, if the blind can see!

Answer but one thing and 'twill all be clear.

Jocasta. Speak. I will answer though I shake with fear.

Oedipus. Went he with scant array, or a great band
Of armèd followers, like a lord of land?

Jocasta. Four men were with him, one a herald; one
Chariot there was, where Laïus rode alone.

Oedipus. Aye me! 'Tis clear now.

                      Woman, who could bring
To Thebes the story of that manslaying?

Jocasta. A house-thrall, the one man they failed to slay.

Oedipus. The one man . . . ? Is he in the house to-day?

Jocasta. Indeed no. When he came that day, and found
Thee on the throne where once sat Laïus crowned,
He took my hand and prayed me earnestly
To send him to the mountain heights, to be
A herdsman, far from any sight or call
Of Thebes. And there I sent him. 'Twas a thrall
Good-hearted, worthy a far greater boon.

Oedipus. Canst find him? I would see this herd, and soon.

Jocasta. 'Tis easy. But what wouldst thou with the herd?

Oedipus. I fear mine own voice, lest it spoke a word
Too much; whereof this man must tell me true.

Jocasta. The man shall come.—My lord, methinks I too
Should know what fear doth work thee this despite.

Oedipus. Thou shalt. When I am tossed to such an height
Of dark foreboding, woman, when my mind
Faceth such straits as these, where should I find
A mightier love than thine?

                   My father—thus
I tell thee the whole tale—was Polybus,
In Corinth King; my mother Meropê
Of Dorian line. And I was held to be
The proudest in Corinthia, till one day
A thing befell: strange was it, but no way
Meet for such wonder and such rage as mine.
A feast it was, and some one flushed with wine
Cried out at me that I was no true son
Of Polybus. Oh, I was wroth! That one
Day I kept silence, but the morrow morn
I sought my parents, told that tale of scorn

And claimed the truth; and they rose in their pride
And smote the mocker. . . . Aye, they satisfied
All my desire; yet still the cavil gnawed
My heart, and still the story crept abroad.

  At last I rose—my father knew not, nor
My mother—and went forth to Pytho's floor
To ask. And God in that for which I came
Rejected me, but round me, like a flame,
His voice flashed other answers, things of woe,
Terror, and desolation. I must know
My mother's body and beget thereon
A race no mortal eye durst look upon,
And spill in murder mine own father's blood.

  I heard, and, hearing, straight from where I stood,
No landmark but the stars to light my way,
Fled, fled from the dark south where Corinth lay,
To lands far off, where never I might see
My doom of scorn fulfilled. On bitterly
I strode, and reached the region where, so saith
Thy tale, that King of Thebes was struck to death. . . .
Wife, I will tell thee true. As one in daze
I walked, till, at the crossing of three ways,
A herald, like thy tale, and o'er his head
A man behind strong horses charioted
Met me. And both would turn me from the path,
He and a thrall in front. And I in wrath
Smote him that pushed me—'twas a groom who led
The horses. Not a word the master said,
But watched, and as I passed him on the road
Down on my head his iron-branchèd goad
Stabbed. But, by heaven, he rued it! In a flash
I swung my staff and saw the old man crash
Back from his car in blood. . . . Then all of them
I slew.

       Oh, if that man's unspoken name
Had aught of Laïus in him, in God's eye
What man doth move more miserable than I,
More dogged by the hate of heaven! No man, kin
Nor stranger, any more may take me in;

No man may greet me with a word, but all
Cast me from out their houses. And withal
'Twas mine own self that laid upon my life
These curses.—And I hold the dead man's wife
In these polluting arms that spilt his soul. . . .
Am I a thing born evil? Am I foul
In every vein? Thebes now doth banish me,
And never in this exile must I see
Mine ancient folk of Corinth, never tread
The land that bore me; else my mother's bed
Shall be defiled, and Polybus, my good
Father, who loved me well, be rolled in blood.
If one should dream that such a world began
In some slow devil's heart, that hated man,
Who should deny him?—God, as thou art clean,
Suffer not this, oh, suffer not this sin
To be, that e'er I look on such a day!
Out of all vision of mankind away
To darkness let me fall ere such a fate
Touch me, so unclean and so desolate!

    Leader. I tremble too, O King; but till thou hear
From him who saw, oh, let hope conquer fear.

    Oedipus. One shred of hope I still have, and therefore
Will wait the herdsman's coming. 'Tis no more.

    Jocasta. He shall come. But what further dost thou seek?

    Oedipus. This. If we mark him close and find him speak
As thou hast, then I am lifted from my dread.

    Jocasta. What mean'st thou? Was there something that I
        said . . . ?

    Oedipus. Thou said'st he spoke of robbers, a great band,
That slaughtered Laïus' men. If still he stand
To the same tale, the guilt comes not my way.
One cannot be a band. But if he say
One lonely loin-girt man, then visibly
This is God's finger pointing toward me.

    Jocasta. Be sure of this. He told the story so
When first he came. All they that heard him know,
Not only I. He cannot change again
Now. And if change he should, O Lord of men,
No change of his can make the prophecy

Of Laïus' death fall true. He was to die
Slain by my son. So Loxias spake. . . . My son!
He slew no man, that poor deserted one
That died. . . . And I will no more turn mine eyes
This way nor that for all their prophecies.

Oedipus. Woman, thou counselest well. Yet let it not
Escape thee. Send and have the herdsman brought.

Jocasta. That will I.—Come. Thou knowest I ne'er would do
Nor think of aught, save thou wouldst have it so.

[JOCASTA *and* OEDIPUS *go together into the Palace.*

Chorus.
(*They pray to be free from such great sins as they
have just heard spoken of.*)

[*Strophe.*

Toward God's great mysteries, oh, let me move
   Unstainèd till I die
In speech or doing; for the Laws thereof
Are holy, walkers upon ways above,
   Born in the far blue sky;
Their father is Olympus uncreate;
   No man hath made nor told
Their being; neither shall Oblivion set
Sleep on their eyes, for in them lives a great
   Spirit and grows not old.

(*They wonder if these sins be all due to pride and if
Creon has guilty ambitions*) ;

[*Antistrophe.*

'Tis Pride that breeds the tyrant; drunken deep
   With perilous things is she,
Which bring not peace: up, reeling, steep on steep
She climbs, till lo, the rock-edge, and the leap
   To that which needs must be,

The land where the strong foot is no more strong!
   Yet is there surely Pride
That saves a city; God preserve it long!
I judge not. Only through all maze of wrong
   Be God, not man, my guide.

[188]

*(Or if Tiresias can really be a lying prophet with no
fear of God; they feel that all faith in oracles and
the things of God is shaken.)*

[*Strophe.*

Is there a priest who moves amid the altars
    Ruthless in deed and word,
Fears not the presence of his god, nor falters
    Lest Right at last be heard?
If such there be, oh, let some doom be given
    Meet for his ill-starred pride,

Who will not gain his gain where Justice is,
Who will not hold his lips from blasphemies,
Who hurls rash hands amid the things of heaven
    From man's touch sanctified.

    In a world where such things be,
        What spirit hath shield or lance
    To ward him secretly
        From the arrow that slays askance?
    If honor to such things be,
        Why should I dance my dance?

[*Antistrophe.*

I go no more with prayers and adorations
    To Earth's deep Heart of Stone,
Nor yet the Abantes' floor, nor where the nations
    Kneel at Olympia's throne,
Till all this dark be lightened, for the finger
    Of man to touch and know.
O Thou that rulest—if men rightly call
Thy name on earth—O Zeus, thou Lord of all
And Strength undying, let not these things linger
    Unknown, tossed to and fro.

    For faint is the oracle,
        And they thrust it aside, away;
    And no more visible
        Apollo to save or slay;
    And the things of God, they fail
        As mist on the wind away.

[189]

[JOCASTA *comes out from the Palace followed by
handmaids bearing incense and flowers.*

Jocasta. Lords of the land, the ways my thought hath trod
Lead me in worship to these shrines of God
With flowers and incense flame. So dire a storm
Doth shake the King, sin, dread and every form
Of grief the world knows. 'Tis the wise man's way
To judge the morrow by the yester day;
Which he doth never, but gives eye and ear
To all who speak, will they but speak of fear.

And seeing no word of mine hath power to **heal**
His torment, therefore forth to thee I steal,
O Slayer of the Wolf, O Lord of Light,
Apollo: thou art near us, and of right
Dost hold us thine: to thee in prayer I fall.

[*She kneels at the altar of Apollo Lukeios.*

Oh, show us still some path that is not all
Unclean; for now our captain's eyes are dim
With dread, and the whole ship must follow him.

No preparation for
his coming ——[*While she prays a* STRANGER *has entered and
begins to accost the Chorus.*

Stranger. Good masters, is there one of you could bring
My steps to the house of Oedipus, your King?
Or, better, to himself if that may be?

Leader. This is the house and he within; and she
Thou seest, the mother of his royal seed.

[JOCASTA *rises, anxious, from her prayer.*

Stranger. Being wife to such a man, happy indeed
And ringed with happy faces may she live!

Jocasta. To one so fair of speech may the Gods give
Like blessing, courteous stranger; 'tis thy due.
But say what leads thee hither. Can we do
Thy wish in aught, or hast thou news to bring?

Stranger. Good news, O Queen, for thee and for the King.

Jocasta. What is it? And from what prince comest thou?

Stranger. I come from Corinth.—And my tale, I trow,
Will give thee joy, yet haply also pain.

Jocasta. What news can have that twofold power? Be plain.

Stranger. 'Tis spoke in Corinth that the gathering
Of folk will make thy lord our chosen King.

[190]

Jocasta. How? Is old Polybus in power no more?

Stranger. Death has a greater power. His reign is o'er.

Jocasta. What say'st thou? Dead? . . . Oedipus' father dead?

Stranger. If I speak false, let me die in his stead.

Jocasta. Ho, maiden! To our master! Hie thee fast
And tell this tale.

> [*The maiden goes.*

Where stand ye at the last
Ye oracles of God? For many a year
Oedipus fled before that man, in fear
To slay him. And behold we find him thus
Slain by a chance death, not by Oedipus.

> [OEDIPUS *comes out from the Palace.*

Oedipus. Jocasta, thou I love to look upon,
Why call'st thou me from where I sat alone?

Jocasta. Give ear, and ponder from what this man tells
How end these proud priests and their oracles.

Oedipus. Whence comes he? And what word hath he for us?

Jocasta. From Corinth; bearing news that Polybus
Thy father is no more. He has found his death.

Oedipus. How?—Stranger, speak thyself. This that she
saith. . . .

Stranger. Is sure. If that is the first news ye crave,
I tell thee, Polybus lieth in his grave.

Oedipus. Not murdered? . . . How? Some passing of disease?

Stranger. A slight thing turns an old life to its peace.

Oedipus. Poor father! . . . 'tis by sickness he is dead?

Stranger. The growing years lay heavy on his head.

Oedipus. O wife, why then should man fear any more
The voice of Pytho's dome, or cower before
These birds that shriek above us? They foretold
Me for my father's murderer; and behold,
He lies in Corinth dead, and here am I
And never touched the sword. . . . Or did he die,
In grief for me who left him? In that way
I may have wrought his death. . . . But come what may,
He sleepeth in his grave and with him all
This deadly seercraft, of no worth at all.

Jocasta. Dear Lord, long since did I not show thee
    clear . . . ?
Oedipus. Indeed, yes. I was warped by mine own fear.
Jocasta. Now thou wilt cast it from thee, and forget.
Oedipus. Forget my mother? . . . It is not over yet.
Jocasta. What should man do with fear, who hath but Chance
Above him, and no sight nor governance
Of things to be? To live as life may run,
No fear, no fret, were wisest 'neath the sun.
And thou, fear not thy mother. Prophets deem
A deed wrought that is wrought but in a dream.
And he to whom these things are nothing, best
Will bear his burden.
    Oedipus.   All thou counselest
Were good, save that my mother liveth still.
And, though thy words be wise, for good or ill
Her I still fear.
    Jocasta.   Think of thy father's tomb!
Like light across our darkness it hath come.
    Oedipus. Great light; but while she lives I fly from her.
    Stranger. What woman, Prince, doth fill thee so with fear?
    Oedipus. Meropê, friend, who dwelt with Polybus.
    Stranger. What in Queen Meropê should fright thee thus?
    Oedipus. A voice of God, stranger, of dire import.
    Stranger. Meet for mine ears? Or of some secret sort?
    Oedipus. Nay, thou must hear, and Corinth. Long ago
Apollo spake a doom, that I should know
My mother's flesh, and with mine own hand spill
My father's blood.—'Tis that, and not my will,
Hath kept me always far from Corinth. So;
Life hath dealt kindly with me, yet men know
On earth no comfort like a mother's face.
    Stranger. 'Tis that, hath kept thee exiled in this place?
    Oedipus. That, and the fear too of my father's blood.
    Stranger. Then, surely, Lord . . . I came but for thy
    good . . .
'Twere well if from that fear I set thee free.
    Oedipus. Ah, couldst thou! There were rich reward for thee.
    Stranger. To say truth, I had hoped to lead thee home
Now, and myself to get some good therefrom.

Oedipus. Nay; where my parents are I will not go.
Stranger. My son, 'tis clear enough thou dost not know
Thine own road.
Oedipus.   How? Old man, in God's name, say.
Stranger. If this it is, keeps thee so long away
From Corinth.
Oedipus.   'Tis the fear lest that word break
One day upon me true.
Stranger.   - Fear lest thou take
Defilement from the two that gave thee birth?
Oedipus. 'Tis that, old man, 'tis that doth fill the earth
With terror.
Stranger.   Then thy terror all hath been
For nothing.
Oedipus.   How? Were not your King and Queen
My parents?
Stranger.   Polybus was naught to thee
In blood.
Oedipus.   How? He, my father!
Stranger.   That was he
As much as I, but no more.
Oedipus.   Thou art naught;
'Twas he begot me.
Stranger.   'Twas not I begot
Oedipus, neither was it he.
Oedipus.   What wild
Fancy, then, made him name me for his child?
Stranger. Thou wast his child—by gift. Long years ago
Mine own hand brought thee to him.
Oedipus.   Coming so,
From a strange hand, he gave me that great love?
Stranger. He had no child, and the desire thereof
Held him.
Oedipus.   And thou didst find somewhere—or buy—
A child for him?
Stranger.   I found it in a high
Glen of Kithairon.

[*Movement of* JOCASTA, *who stands riveted with
dread, unnoticed by the others.*

[193]

Oedipus.   Yonder? To what end
Wast traveling in these parts?
    Stranger.   I came to tend
The flocks here on the mountain.
    Oedipus.   Thou wast one
That wandered, tending sheep for hire?
    Stranger.   My son,
That day I was the saviour of a King.
    Oedipus. How saviour? Was I in some suffering
Or peril?
    Stranger.   Thine own feet a tale could speak.
    Oedipus. Ah me! What ancient pain stirs half awake
Within me!
    Stranger.   'Twas a spike through both thy feet.
I set thee free.
    Oedipus.   A strange scorn that, to greet
A babe new on the earth!
    Stranger.   From that they fain
Must call thee Oedipus, '*Who-walks-in-pain.*'
    Oedipus. Who called me so—father or mother? Oh,
In God's name, speak!
    Stranger.   I know not. He should know
Who brought thee.
    Oedipus.   So: I was not found by thee.
Thou hadst me from another?
    Stranger.   Aye; to me
One of the shepherds gave the babe, to bear
Far off.
    Oedipus.   What shepherd? Know'st thou not? Declare
All that thou knowest.
    Stranger.   By my memory, then,
I think they called him one of Laïus' men.
    Oedipus. That Laïus who was king in Thebes of old?
    Stranger. The same. My man did herding in his fold.
    Oedipus. Is he yet living? Can I see his face?
    Stranger.   [*Turning to the Chorus.*
Ye will know that, being natives to the place.
    Oedipus. How?—Is there one of you within my pale
Standing, that knows the shepherd of his tale?

Ye have seen him on the hills? Or in this town?
Speak! For the hour is come that all be known.

    Leader. I think 'twill be the Peasant Man, the same,
Thou hast sought long time to see.—His place and name
Our mistress, if she will, can tell most clear.

               [JOCASTA *remains as if she heard nothing.*

    Oedipus. Thou hear'st him, wife. The herd whose presence here
We craved for, is it he this man would say?

    Jocasta. He saith . . . What of it? Ask not; only pray
Not to remember. . . . Tales are vainly told.

    Oedipus. 'Tis mine own birth. How can I, when I hold
Such clues as these, refrain from knowing all?

    Jocasta. For God's love, no! Not if thou care'st at all
For thine own life. . . . My anguish is enough.

    Oedipus (*bitterly*). Fear not! . . . Though I be thrice of
    slavish stuff
From my third grand-dam down, it shames not thee.

    Jocasta. Ask no more. I beseech thee . . . Promise me!

    Oedipus. To leave the Truth half-found? 'Tis not my mood.

    Jocasta. I understand; and tell thee what is good.

    Oedipus. Thy good doth weary me.

    Jocasta.   O child of woe,
I pray God, I pray God, thou never know!

    Oedipus (*turning from her*). Go, fetch the herdsman
    straight!—This Queen of mine
May walk alone to boast her royal line.

    Jocasta.   [*She twice draws in her breath through her
            teeth, as if in some sharp pain.*
Unhappy one, goodbye! Goodbye before
I go: this once, and never never more!

        [*She comes towards him, then turns and goes into
        the palace.*

    Leader. King, what was that? She passed like one who flies
In very anguish. Dread is o'er mine eyes
Lest from this silence break some storm of wrong.

    Oedipus. Break what break will! My mind abideth strong
To know the roots, how low soe'er they be,
Which grew to Oedipus. This woman, she

[195]

prison on brink of discovery

Is proud, methinks, and fears my birth and name
Will mar her nobleness. But I, no shame
Can ever touch me. I am Fortune's child,
Not man's; her mother face hath ever smiled
Above me, and my brethren of the sky,
The changing Moons, have changed me low and high.
There is my lineage true, which none shall wrest
From me; who then am I to fear this quest?

Chorus.

(*They sing of Oedipus as the foundling of their own
Theban mountain, Kithairon, and doubtless of divine
birth.*)

[*Strophe.*

If I, O Kithairon, some vision can borrow
From seercraft, if still there is wit in the old,
Long, long, through the deep-orbèd Moon of the morrow—
So hear me, Olympus!—thy tale shall be told.
O mountain of Thebes, a new Theban shall praise thee,
One born of thy bosom, one nursed at thy springs;
And the old men shall dance to thy glory, and raise thee
To worship, O bearer of joy to my kings.
joyous
And thou, we pray,
contrast to later catastrophe Look down in peace, O Apollo; I-ê, I-ê!

[*Antistrophe.*

What Oread mother, unaging, unweeping,
Did bear thee, O Babe, to the Crag-walker Pan;
Or perchance to Apollo? He loveth the leaping
Of herds on the rock-ways unhaunted of man.
Or was it the lord of Cyllênê, who found thee,
Or glad Dionysus, whose home is the height,
Who knew thee his own on the mountain, as round thee
The White Brides of Helicon laughed for delight?
'Tis there, 'tis there,
The joy most liveth of all his dance and prayer.
Oedipus. If I may judge, ye Elders, who have ne'er
Seen him, methinks I see the shepherd there
Whom we have sought so long. His weight of years
Fits well with our Corinthian messenger's;

[196]

And, more, I know the men who guide his way,
Bondsmen of mine own house.

      Thou, friend, wilt say
Most surely, who hast known the man of old.
Leader. I know him well. A shepherd of the fold
Of Laïus, one he trusted more than all.

   [*The* SHEPHERD *comes in, led by two thralls. He
    is an old man and seems terrified.*

Oedipus. Thou first, our guest from Corinth: say withal
Is this the man?
Stranger.   This is the man, O King.
Oedipus.   [*Addressing the* SHEPHERD.
Old man! Look up, and answer everything
I ask thee.—Thou wast Laïus' man of old?
Shepherd. Born in his house I was, not bought with gold.
Oedipus. What kind of work, what way of life, was thine?
Shepherd. Most of my days I tended sheep or kine.
Oedipus. What was thy camping ground at midsummer?
Shepherd. Sometimes Kithairon, sometimes mountains near.
Oedipus. Saw'st ever there this man thou seëst now?
Shepherd. There, Lord? What doing?—What man meanest
  thou?
Oedipus.   [*Pointing to the* STRANGER.
Look! Hath he ever crossed thy path before?
Shepherd. I call him not to mind, I must think more.
Stranger. Small wonder that, O King! But I will throw
Light on his memories.—Right well I know
He knows the time when, all Kithairon through,
I with one wandering herd and he with two,
Three times we neighbored one another, clear
From spring to autumn stars, a good half-year.
At winter's fall we parted; he drove down
To his master's fold, and I back to mine own. . . .
Dost call it back, friend? Was it as I say?
Shepherd. It was. It was. . . . 'Tis all so far away.
Stranger. Say then: thou gavest me once, there in the wild,
A babe to rear far off as mine own child?
Shepherd.   [*His terror returning.*
What does this mean? To what end askest thou?

[197]

SOPHOCLES

Stranger.   [*Pointing to* OEDIPUS.

That babe has grown, friend. 'Tis our master now.

    Shepherd.   [*He slowly understands, then stands for a moment horror-struck.*

No, in the name of death! . . . Fool, hold thy peace.

                [*He lifts his staff at the* STRANGER.

    Oedipus. Ha, graybeard! Wouldst thou strike him?—'Tis not his

Offences, 'tis thine own we need to mend.

    Shepherd. Most gentle master, how do I offend?

    Oedipus. Whence came that babe whereof he questioneth?

    Shepherd. He doth not know . . . 'tis folly . . . what he saith.

    Oedipus. Thou wilt not speak for love; but pain maybe . . .

    Shepherd. I am very old. Ye would not torture me.

    Oedipus. Back with his arms, ye bondmen! Hold him so.

        [*The thralls drag back the Shepherd's arms, ready for torture.*

    Shepherd. Woe's me! What have I done? . . . What wouldst thou know?

    Oedipus. Didst give this man the child, as he doth say?

    Shepherd. I did. . . . Would God that I had died this day!

    Oedipus. 'Fore heaven, thou shalt yet, if thou speak not true.

    Shepherd. 'Tis more than death and darker, if I do.

    Oedipus. This dog, it seems, will keep us waiting.

    Shepherd.   Nay,

I said at first I gave it.

    Oedipus.   In what way

Came it to thee? Was it thine own child, or Another's?

    Shepherd.   Nay, it never crossed my door:

Another's.

    Oedipus.   Whose? What man, what house, of these

About thee?

    Shepherd.   In the name of God who sees,

Ask me no more!

    Oedipus.   If once I ask again,

Thou diest.

    Shepherd.   From the folk of Laïus, then,

It came.

Oedipus. A slave, or born of Laïus' blood?

Shepherd. There comes the word I dread to speak, O God!

Oedipus. And I to hear: yet heard it needs must be. *ment have*

Shepherd. Know then, they said 'twas Laïus' child. But she *truth at all costs*
Within, thy wife, best knows its fathering.

Oedipus. 'Twas she that gave it?

Shepherd. It was she, O King.

Oedipus. And bade you . . . what?

Shepherd. Destroy it.

Oedipus. Her own child? . . .
Cruel!

Shepherd. Dark words of God had made her wild.

Oedipus. What words?

Shepherd. The babe must slay his father; so
'Twas written.

Oedipus. Why didst thou, then, let him go
With this old man?

Shepherd. O King, my heart did bleed.
I thought the man would save him, past all need
Of fear, to his own distant home. . . . And he
Did save him, to great evil. Verily
If thou art he whom this man telleth of,
Know, to affliction thou art born.

Oedipus. Enough!
All will come true. . . . Thou Light, never again
May I behold thee, I in the eyes of men
Made naked, how from sin my being grew,
In sin I wedded and in sin I slew!

[*He rushes into the Palace. The* SHEPHERD *is led
away by the thralls.*

[*Strophe.*

Chorus. Nothingness, nothingness,
Ye Children of Man, and less
I count you, waking or dreaming!
And none among mortals, none,
Seeking to live, hath won
More than to seem, and to cease
Again from his seeming.
While ever before mine eyes

[199]

One fate, one ensample, lies—
Thine, thine, O Oedipus, sore
    Of God oppressèd—
What thing that is human more
Dare I call blessèd?

                                    [*Antistrophe.*

*uncertainty
of human destiny*

Straight his archery flew
To the heart of living; he knew
    Joy and the fullness of power,
O Zeus, when the riddling breath
Was stayed and the Maid of Death
Slain, and we saw him through
    The death-cloud, a tower!

For that he was called my king;
Yea, every precious thing
Wherewith men are honored, down
    We cast before him,
And great Thebes brought her crown
    And kneeled to adore him.

                                    [*Strophe.*

But now, what man's story is such bitterness to speak?
    What life hath Delusion so visited, and Pain,
            And swiftness of Disaster?
            O great King, our master,
How oped the one haven to the slayer and the slain?
And the furrows of thy father, did they turn not nor shriek,
    Did they bear so long silent thy casting of the grain?

                                    [*Antistrophe.*

'Tis Time, Time, desireless, hath shown thee what thou art;
    The long monstrous mating, it is judged and all its race.
            O child of him that sleepeth,
            Thy land weepeth, weepeth,
    Unfathered. . . . Would God, I had never seen thy face!
From thee in great peril fell peace upon my heart,
    In thee mine eye clouded and the dark is come apace.

                [*A* MESSENGER *rushes out from the Palace.*
    Messenger. O ye above this land in honor old
Exalted, what a tale shall ye be told,

What sights shall see, and tears of horror shed,
If still your hearts be true to them that led
Your sires! There runs no river, well I ween,
Not Phasis nor great Ister, shall wash clean
This house of all within that hideth—nay,
Nor all that creepeth forth to front the day,
Of purposed horror. And in misery
That woundeth most which men have willed to be.

 Leader. No lack there was in what we knew before
Of food for heaviness. What bring'st thou more?

 Messenger. One thing I bring thee first. . . . 'Tis quickly
  said.
Jocasta, our anointed queen, is dead.

 Leader. Unhappy woman! How came death to her?

 Messenger. By her own hand. . . . Oh, of what passed in
  there
Ye have been spared the worst. Ye cannot see.
Howbeit, with that which still is left in me
Of mind and memory, ye shall hear her fate.

 Like one entranced with passion, through the gate
She passed, the white hands flashing o'er her head,
Like blades that tear, and fled, unswerving fled,
Toward her old bridal room, and disappeared
And the doors crashed behind her. But we heard
Her voice within, crying to him of old,
Her Laïus, long dead; and things untold
Of the old kiss unforgotten, that should bring
The lover's death and leave the loved a thing
Of horror, yea, a field beneath the plough
For sire and son: then wailing bitter-low
Across that bed of births unreconciled,
Husband from husband born and child from child.
And, after that, I know not how her death
Found her. For sudden, with a roar of wrath,
Burst Oedipus upon us. Then, I ween,
We marked no more what passion held the Queen,
But him, as in the fury of his stride,
'A sword! A sword! And show me here,' he cried,
'That wife, no wife, that field of bloodstained earth
Where husband, father, sin on sin, had birth,

Polluted generations!' While he thus
Raged on, some god—for sure 'twas none of us—
Showed where she was; and with a shout away,
As though some hand had pointed to the prey,
He dashed him on the chamber door. The straight
Door-bar of oak, it bent beneath his weight,
Shook from its sockets free, and in he burst
To the dark chamber.
               There we saw her first
Hanged, swinging from a noose, like a dead bird.
He fell back when he saw her. Then we heard
A miserable groan, and straight he found
And loosed the strangling knot, and on the ground
Laid her.—Ah, then the sight of horror came!
The pin of gold, broad-beaten like a flame,
He tore from off her breast, and, left and right,
Down on the shuddering orbits of his sight
Dashed it: 'Out! Out! Ye never more shall see
Me nor the anguish nor the sins of me.
Ye looked on lives whose like earth never bore,
Ye knew not those my spirit thirsted for:
Therefore be dark for ever!'
                  Like a song
His voice rose, and again, again, the strong
And stabbing hand fell, and the massacred
And bleeding eyeballs streamed upon his beard,
Wild rain, and gouts of hail amid the rain.
    Behold affliction, yea, afflictions twain
From man and woman broken, now made one
In downfall. All the riches yester sun
Saw in this house were rich in verity.
What call ye now our riches? Agony,
Delusion, Death, Shame, all that eye or ear
Hath ever dreamed of misery, is here.
    Leader. And now how fares he? Doth the storm abate?
    Messenger. He shouts for one to open wide the gate
And lead him forth, and to all Thebes display
His father's murderer, his mother's. . . . Nay,
Such words I will not speak. And his intent
Is set, to cast himself in banishment

Out to the wild, not walk 'mid human breed
Bearing the curse he bears. Yet sore his need
Of strength and of some guiding hand. For sure
He hath more burden now than man may endure.
    But see, the gates fall back, and that appears
Which he who loathes shall pity—yea, with tears.

> [OEDIPUS *is led in, blinded and bleeding. The Old
> Men bow down and hide their faces; some of
> them weep.*

Chorus. Oh, terrible! Oh, sight of all
    This life hath crossed, most terrible!
      Thou man more wronged than tongue can tell,
  What madness took thee? Do there crawl
      Live Things of Evil from the deep
      To leap on man? Oh, what a leap
  Was His that flung thee to thy fall!
Leader. O fallen, fallen in ghastly case,
      I dare not raise mine eyes to thee;
      Fain would I look and ask and see,
    But shudder sickened from thy face.
Oedipus. Oh, pain; pain and woe!
      Whither? Whither?
   They lead me and I go;
    And my voice drifts on the air
      Far away.
    Where, Thing of Evil, where
      Endeth thy leaping hither?
Leader. In fearful ends, which none may hear nor say.

Oedipus. Cloud of the dark mine own   [*Strophe.*
      For ever, horrible,
        Stealing, stealing, silent, unconquerable,
        Cloud that no wind, no summer can dispel!
    Again, again I groan,
  As through my heart together crawl the strong
   Stabs of this pain and memories of old wrong.
Leader. Yea, twofold hosts of torment hast thou there,
    The stain to think on and the pain to bear.

Oedipus. O Friend, thou mine own   [*Antistrophe.*
    Still faithful, minister
    Steadfast abiding alone of them that were,
    Dost bear with me and give the blind man care?
  Ah me! Not all unknown
  Nor hid thou art. Deep in this dark a call
  Comes and I know thy voice in spite of all.
Leader. O fearful sufferer, and could'st thou kill
  Thy living orbs? What God made blind thy will?

Oedipus. 'Tis Apollo; all is Apollo,   [*Strophe.*
  O ye that love me, 'tis he long time hath planned
    These things upon me evilly, evilly,
    Dark things and full of blood.
  I knew not; I did but follow
  His way; but mine the hand
    And mine the anguish. What were mine eyes to me
    When naught to be seen was good?
Leader. 'Tis even so; and Truth doth speak in thee.
Oedipus. To see, to endure, to hear words kindly spoken,
    Should I have joy in such?
    Out, if ye love your breath,
  Cast me swift unto solitude, unbroken
    By word or touch.
    Am I not charged with death,
      Most charged and filled to the brim
    With curses? And what man saith
    God hath so hated him?
Leader. Thy bitter will, thy hard calamity,
  Would I had never known nor looked on thee!
               [*Antistrophe.*
Oedipus. My curse, my curse upon him,
    That man whom pity held in the wilderness,
    Who saved the feet alive from the blood-fetter
    And loosed the barb thereof!
  That babe—what grace was done him,
    Had he died shelterless,
    He had not laid on himself this grief to bear,
    And all who gave him love.
Leader. I, too, O Friend, I had been happier.

Oedipus. Found not the way to his father's blood, nor shaken
  The world's scorn on his mother,
    The child and the groom withal;
But now, of murderers born, of God forsaken,
  Mine own son's brother;
   All this, and if aught can fall
    Upon man more perilous
  And elder in sin, lo, all
    Is the portion of Oedipus.
 Leader. How shall I hold this counsel or thy mind
True? Thou wert better dead than living blind.
 Oedipus. That this deed is not well and wisely wrought
Thou shalt not show me; therefore school me not.
Think, with what eyes hereafter in the place
Of shadows could I see my father's face,
Or my poor mother's? Both of whom this hand
Hath wronged too deep for man to understand.
Or children—born as mine were born, to see
Their shapes should bring me joy? Great God! To me
There is no joy in city nor in tower
Nor temple, from all whom, in this mine hour,
I that was chief in Thebes alone, and ate
The King's bread, I have made me separate
For ever. Mine own lips have bid the land
Cast from it one so evil, one whose hand
To sin was dedicate, whom God hath shown
Birth-branded . . . and my blood the dead King's own!
All this myself have proved. And can I then
Look with straight eyes into the eyes of men?
I trow not. Nay, if any stop there were
To dam this fount that welleth in mine ear
For hearing, I had never blenched nor stayed
Till this vile shell were all one dungeon made,
Dark, without sound. 'Tis thus the mind would fain
Find peace, self-prisoned from a world of pain.
 O wild Kithairon, why was it thy will
To save me? Why not take me quick and kill,
Kill, before ever I could make men know
The thing I am, the thing from which I grow?
Thou dead King, Polybus, thou city wall

Of Corinth, thou old castle I did call
My father's, what a life did ye begin,
What splendor rotted by the worm within,
When ye bred me! O Crossing of the Roads,
O secret glen and dusk of crowding woods,
O narrow footpath creeping to the brink
Where meet the Three! I gave you blood to drink.
Do you remember? 'Twas my life-blood, hot
From my own father's heart. Have ye forgot
What deed I did among you, and what new
And direr deed I fled from you to do?
O flesh, horror of flesh! . . .
                      But what is shame
To do should not be spoken. In God's name,
Take me somewhere far off and cover me
From sight, or slay, or cast me to the sea
Where never eye may see me any more.
   What? Do ye fear to touch a man so sore
Stricken? Nay, tremble not. My misery
Is mine, and shall be borne by none but me.
   Leader. Lo, yonder comes for answer to thy prayer
Creon, to do and to decree. The care
Of all our land is his, now thou art weak.
   Oedipus. Alas, what word to Creon can I speak,
How make him trust me more? He hath seen of late
So vile a heart in me, so full of hate.
                           [*Enter* CREON.

   Creon. Not to make laughter, Oedipus, nor cast
Against thee any evil of the past
I seek thee, but. . . Ah God! ye ministers,
Have ye no hearts? Or if for man there stirs
No pity in you, fear at least to call
Stain on our Lord the Sun, who feedeth all;
Nor show in nakedness a horror such
As this, which never mother Earth may touch,
Nor God's clean rain nor sunlight. Quick within!
Guide him.—The ills that in a house have been
They of the house alone should know or hear.
   Oedipus. In God's name, since thou hast undone the fear
Within me, coming thus, all nobleness,

[206]

To one so vile, grant me one only grace.
For thy sake more I crave it than mine own.
   Creon. Let me first hear what grace thou wouldst be shown.
   Oedipus. Cast me from Thebes . . . now, quick . . . where
    none may see
My visage more, nor mingle words with me.
   Creon. That had I done, for sure, save that I still
Tremble, and fain would ask Apollo's will.
   Oedipus. His will was clear enough, to stamp the unclean
Thing out, the bloody hand, the heart of sin.
   Creon. 'Twas thus he seemed to speak; but in this sore
Strait we must needs learn surer than before.
   Oedipus. Thou needs must trouble God for one so low?
   Creon. Surely; thyself will trust his answer now.
   Oedipus. I charge thee more . . . and, if thou fail, my sin
Shall cleave to thee. . . . For her who lies within,
Make as thou wilt her burial. 'Tis thy task
To tend thine own. But me: let no man ask
This ancient city of my sires to give
Harbor in life to me. Set me to live.
On the wild hills and leave my name to those
Deeps of Kithairon which my father chose,
And mother, for my vast and living tomb.
As they, my murderers, willed it, let my doom
Find me. For this my very heart doth know,
No sickness now, nor any mortal blow,
Shall slay this body. Never had my breath
Been thus kept burning in the midst of death,
Save for some frightful end. So, let my way
Go where it listeth.
                   But my children—Nay,
Creon, my sons will ask thee for no care.
Men are they, and can find them everywhere
What life needs. But my two poor desolate
Maidens. . . . There was no table ever set
Apart for them, but whatso royal fare
I tasted, they were with me and had share
In all. . . . Creon, I pray, forget them not.
And if it may be, go, bid them be brought,

> [CREON *goes and presently returns with the two*
> *princesses.* OEDIPUS *thinks he is there all the*
> *time.*

That I may touch their faces, and so weep. . . .
Go, Prince. Go, noble heart! . . .
If I might touch them, I should seem to keep
And not to have lost them, now mine eyes are gone. . . .
What say I?
In God's name, can it be I hear mine own
Beloved ones sobbing? Creon of his grace
Hath brought my two, my dearest, to this place.
Is it true?

    Creon. 'Tis true. I brought them, for in them I know
Thy joy is, the same now as long ago.

    Oedipus. God bless thee, and in this hard journey give
Some better guide than mine to help thee live.

Children! Where are ye? Hither; come to these
Arms of your . . . brother, whose wild offices
Have brought much darkness on the once bright eyes
Of him who grew your garden; who, nowise
Seeing nor understanding, digged a ground
The world shall shudder at. Children, my wound
Is yours too, and I cannot meet your gaze
Now, as I think me what remaining days
Of bitter living the world hath for you.
What dance of damsels shall ye gather to,
What feast of Thebes, but quick ye shall turn home,
All tears, or ere the feast or dancers come?
And, children, when ye reach the years of love,
Who shall dare wed you, whose heart rise above
The peril, to take on him all the shame
That cleaves to my name and my children's name?
God knows, it is enough! . . .
My flowers, ye needs must die, waste things, bereft
And fruitless.

             Creon, thou alone art left
Their father now, since both of us are gone
Who cared for them. Oh, leave them not alone
To wander masterless, these thine own kin,

And beggared. Neither think of them such sin
As ye all know in me, but let their fate
Touch thee. So young they are, so desolate—
Of all save thee. True man, give me thine hand,
And promise.

[OEDIPUS *and* CREON *clasp hands.*

If your age could understand,
Children, full many counsels I could give.
But now I leave this one word: Pray to live
As life may suffer you, and find a road
To travel easier than your father trod.

Creon. Enough thy heart hath poured its tears; now back
into thine house repair.

Oedipus. I dread the house, yet go I must.

Creon. Fair season maketh all things fair.

Oedipus. One oath then give me, and I go.

Creon. Name it, and I will answer thee.

Oedipus. To cast me from this land.

Creon. A gift not mine but God's thou askest me.

Oedipus. I am a thing of God abhorred.

Creon. The more, then, will he grant thy prayer.

Oedipus. Thou givest thine oath?

Creon. I see no light; and, seeing not, I may not swear.

Oedipus. Then take me hence. I care not.

Creon. Go in peace, and give these children o'er.

Oedipus. Ah no! Take not away my daughters!

[*They are taken from him.*

Creon. Seek not to be master more.
Did not thy masteries of old forsake thee when the end was
near?

Chorus. Ye citizens of Thebes, behold; 'tis Oedipus that
passeth here,
Who read the riddle-word of Death, and mightiest stood of
mortal men,
And Fortune loved him, and the folk that saw him turned and
looked again.
Lo, he is fallen, and around great storms and the outreaching
sea!

Therefore, O Man, beware, and look toward the end of things
    that be,
The last of sights, the last of days; and no man's life account
    as gain
Ere the full tale be finished and the darkness find him without
    pain.

          [OEDIPUS *is led into the house and the doors close*
            on him.

SOPHOCLES
ANTIGONE

≫≫⋘

TRANSLATED
by
ROBERT WHITELAW

CHARACTERS IN THE PLAY

ANTIGONE }
ISMENE   } *daughters of Oedipus.*

CREON, *King of Thebes.*

A SENTINEL.

HAEMON, *Son of Creon.*

TIRESIAS, *the blind prophet.*

A MESSENGER.

EURYDICE, *the wife of Creon.*

SECOND MESSENGER.

CHORUS OF THEBAN ELDERS

ARGUMENT

Oedipus, blind and degraded, has been exiled from Thebes. He leaves behind him a curse upon his two sons, Polynices and Eteocles, for not having resisted those who expelled him. Creon, brother of Jocasta, governs Thebes as regent, and is persuaded by Eteocles to banish Polynices, the elder brother. The latter takes refuge at Argos, where he marries the daughter of king Adrastus and persuades him to join in invading Thebes. Before the conflict, Polynices goes to Oedipus, now at Colonos, to secure his forgiveness and blessing. The old king only reiterates his curse, and prophesies that victory shall be with neither, but that both shall fall, slain by each other's hands. Antigone implores Polynices to abandon his enterprise but honor forbids. He goes, with a parting prayer that his sisters will see that in death he is not dishonored, but receives duly his funeral rites. The prophecy is fulfilled and the brothers are transfixed by each other's spears. Since Eteocles had died defending his native city, he was entitled to his funeral rites. But as Polynices had died while invading his native state at the head of an alien army, and was thus guilty of the greatest crime a citizen could commit, it is decreed that his body shall be left a prey to birds and dogs on the spot where he fell—a fate regarded with peculiar horror by the Greeks, since the funeral rites were believed to determine the welfare of the departed in the next world. It is at this point the play opens.

ANTIGONE

SCENE.—*An open space before the royal palace at* THEBES.
Enter ANTIGONE *and* ISMENE.

Antigone. Ismene, sister mine, one life with me,
Knowest thou of the burden of our race
Aught that from us yet living Zeus holds back?
Nay, for nought grievous and nought ruinous,
No shame and no dishonor, have I not seen
Poured on our hapless heads, both thine and mine.
And even now what edict hath the prince
Uttered, men say, to all this Theban folk?
Thou knowest it and hast heard? or 'scapes thy sense,
Aimed at thy friends, the mischief of thy foes?
   Ismene. To me of friends, Antigone, no word
Hath come, or sweet or bitter, since that we
Two sisters of two brothers were bereaved,
Both on a day slain by a twofold blow:
And, now that vanished is the Argive host
Ev'n with the night fled hence, I know no more,
If that I fare the better or the worse.
   Antigone. I knew full well, and therefore from the gates
O' the court I led thee hither, alone to hear.
   Ismene. There's trouble in thy looks: thy tidings tell.
   Antigone. Yea, hath not Creon, of our two brothers slain,
Honored with burial one, disdained the other?
For Eteocles, they say, he in the earth
With all fair rites and ceremony hath laid,
Nor lacks he honor in the world below;
But the poor dust of Polynices dead
Through Thebes, 'tis said, the edict has gone forth
That none may bury, none make moan for him,
But leave unwept, untombed, a dainty prize

[213]

For ravening birds that gloat upon their prey.
So hath our good lord Creon to thee and me
Published, men say, his pleasure—ay, to *me*—
And hither comes, to all who know it not
Its purport to make plain, nor deems the thing
Of slight account, but, whoso does this deed,
A public death by stoning is his doom.
Thou hast it now; and quickly shall be proved
If thou art noble, or base from noble strain.

    Ismene. O rash of heart, if this indeed be so,
What help in me, to loosen or to bind?

       Antigone. Consider, toil and pain if thou wilt share.

       Ismene. On what adventure bound? What wouldst thou do?

       Antigone. To lift his body, wilt thou join with me?

       Ismene. Wouldst thou indeed rebel, and bury him?

       Antigone. My brother I will bury, and thine no less,
Whether thou wilt or no: no traitress I.

       Ismene. O all too bold—when Creon hath forbid?

       Antigone. My rights to hinder is no right of his.

       Ismene. Ah, sister, yet think how our father died,
Wrapt in what cloud of hate and ignominy
By his own sins, self-proved, and both his eyes
With suicidal hand himself he stabbed:
Then too his mother-wife, two names in one,
Fordid with twisted noose her woeful life;
Last, our two brothers in one fatal day
Drew sword, O miserable, and each to each
Dealt mutual slaughter with unnatural hands:
And now shall we twain, who alone are left,
Fall like the rest, and worse—in spite of law,
And scorning kings, their edicts and their power?
Oh rather let us think, 'tis not for us,
Who are but women, to contend with men:
And the king's word is mighty, and to this,
And harsher words than this, we needs must bow.
Therefore will I, imploring of the dead
Forgiveness, that I yield but as I must,
Obey the king's commandment: for with things
Beyond our reach 'twere foolishness to meddle.

Antigone. I'll neither urge thee, nor, if now thou'dst help
My doing, should I thank thee for thine aid.
Do thou after thy kind: thy choice is made:
I'll bury him; doing this, so let me die.
So with my loved one loved shall I abide,
My crime a deed most holy: for the dead
Longer have I to please than these on earth.
There I shall dwell for ever: be it thine
To have scorned what gods have hallowed, if thou wilt.

Ismene. Nay, nothing do I scorn: but, how to break
My country's law—I am witless of the way.

Antigone. For thee such plea may serve: I go to heap
The earth upon my brother, whom I love.

Ismene. Alas, unhappy, how I fear for thee!

Antigone. Fear not for me: guide thine own fate aright.

Ismene. Yet breathe this purpose to no ear but mine:
Keep thou thy counsel well—and so will I.

Antigone. Oh speak: for much more hatred thou wilt get,
Concealing, than proclaiming it to all.

Ismene. This fever at thy heart by frost is fed.

Antigone. But, whom I most should please, they most are
    pleased.

Ismene. So wouldst thou: but thou canst not as thou wouldst.

Antigone. Why, then, when strength shall fail me, I will
    cease.

Ismene. Not to attempt the impossible is best.

Antigone. Hated by me, and hated by the dead—
To him a hateful presence evermore—
Thou shouldst be, and thou shalt be, speaking thus.
But leave me, and the folly that is mine,
This worst to suffer—not the worst—since still
A worse remains, no noble death to die.

Ismene. Go if thou wilt: but going know thyself
Senseless, yet to thy friends a friend indeed.

            [*Exeunt.*
            [*Strophe.*

Chorus. Lo, the sun upspringing!
Fairest light we hail thee
Of all dawns that on Thebes the seven-gated
Ever broke! Eye of golden day!

Over Dirce's fount appearing,
Hence the Argive host white-shielded,
That in complete arms came hither,
Headlong homeward thou didst urge
Faster still with shaken rein.
At call of Polynices, stirred
By bitter heat of wrangling claims,
Against our land they gathered, and they swooped
Down on us—like an eagle, screaming hoarse,
White-clad, with wings of snow—
With shields a many and with waving crests.

[*Antistrophe.*

- But above our dwellings,
With his spears that thirsted
For our blood, at each gate's mouth of the seven
Gaping round, paused the foe—and went,
Ere his jaws with blood were sated,
Or our circling towers the torch-flame
Caught and kindled: so behind him
Raged intense the battle-din—
While for life the Serpent fought.
For Zeus the tongue of vaunting pride
Hates with exceeding hate; he marked
That torrent army's onward flood, superb
With clank of gold, and with his brandished fire
Smote down who foremost climbed
To shout his triumph on our ramparts' heights.

[*Strophe.*

Hurled from that height with swift reverse,
The unpitying earth received him as he fell,
And quenched the brand he fain had flung,
And quelled the mad endeavor,
The frantic storm-gusts of his windy hate.
So fared it then with him;
Nor less elsewhere great Ares dealt
Against the foemen thunderous blows—
Our trace-horse on the right.
For seven chieftains at our seven gates
Met each his equal foe: and Zeus,
Who foiled their onset, claims from all his due,

The brazen arms, which on the field they left:
Save that infuriate pair,
Who, from one father and one mother sprung.
Against each other laid in rest
Their spears, victorious both,
And each by other share one equal death.

[*Antistrophe.*

But now of Victory be glad:
She meets our gladness with an answering smile,
And Thebes, the many-charioted,
Hears far resound her praises:
Now then with war have done, and strife forget!
All temples of the gods
Fill we with song and night-long dance;
And, Theban Bacchus, this our mirth
Lead thou, and shake the earth!
But lo the ruler of this Theban land,
Son of Menoeceus, Creon comes,
Crowned by these new and strange events, he comes—
By will of heav'n our new-created king,
What counsel pondering?
Who by his sovereign will hath now convoked,
In solemn conference to meet,
The elders of the state;
Obedient to whose summons, we are here.

[*Enter* CREON.

Creon. Sirs, it hath pleased the gods to right again
Our Theban fortunes, by sore tempest tossed:
And by my messenger I summoned hither
You out of all the state; first, as I knew you
To the might o' the throne of Laïus loyal ever:
Also, when Oedipus upheld the state,
And when he perished, to their children still
Ye with a constant mind were faithful found:
Now they are gone: both on one fatal field
An equal guilt atoned with equal doom,
Slayers of each other, by each other slain:
And I am left, the nearest to their blood,
To wield alone the scepter and the realm.
There is no way to know of any man

The spirit and the wisdom and the will,
Till he stands proved, ruler and lawgiver.
For who, with a whole city to direct,
Yet cleaves not to those counsels that are best,
But locks his lips in silence, being afraid,
I held and hold him ever of men most base:
And whoso greater than his country's cause
Esteems a friend, I count him nothing worth.
For, Zeus who seeth all be witness now,
Nor for the safety's sake would I keep silence,
And see the ruin on my country fall,
Nor would I deem an enemy to the state
Friend to myself; remembering still that she,
She only brings us safe: on board of her
Our friends we make—no friends, if she be lost.
So for the good of Thebes her laws I frame:
And such the proclamation I set forth,
Touching the sons of Oedipus, ev'n now—
Eteocles, who fighting for this land
In battle has fall'n, more valiant none than he,
To bury, and no funeral rite omit
To brave men paid—their solace in the grave:
Not so his brother, Polynices: he,
From exile back returning, utterly
With fire his country and his fathers' gods
Would fain have burnt, fain would with kinsmen's blood
Have slaked his thirst, or dragged us captive hence:
Therefore to all this city it is proclaimed
That none may bury, none make moan for him,
But leave him lying all ghastly where he fell,
Till fowls o' the air and dogs have picked his bones.
So am I purposed: not at least by me
Shall traitors be preferred to honest men:
But, whoso loves this city, him indeed
I shall not cease to honor, alive or dead.
   Chorus. Creon, son of Menoeceus, 'tis thy pleasure
The friend and foe of Thebes so to requite:
And, whatso pleases thee, that same is law,
Both for our Theban dead and us who live.
   Creon. Look to it, then, my bidding is performed.

[218]

Chorus. Upon some younger man impose this burden.
Creon. To watch the body, sentinels are set.
Chorus. What service more then wouldst thou lay on us?
Creon. That ye resist whoever disobeys.
Chorus. Who is so senseless that desires to die?
Creon. The penalty is death: yet hopes deceive,
And men wax foolish oft through greed of gain.

[*Enter* SENTINEL.

    Sentinel. That I come hither, king, nimble of foot,
And breathless with my haste, I'll not profess:
For many a doubtful halt upon the way,
And many a wheel to the right-about, I had,
Oft as my prating heart gave counsel, 'Fool,
What ails thee going into the lion's mouth?'
Then, 'Blockhead, wilt thou tarry? if Creon learns
This from another man, shalt thou not smart?'
So doubtfully I fared, reluctant-slow,
And, if the way was short, 'twas long to me.
But to come hither to thee prevailed at last,
And, though the speech be nought, yet I will speak.
For I have come fast clutching at the hope
That nought's to suffer but what fate decrees.
    Creon. What is it that hath troubled thus thy mind?
    Sentinel. First for myself this let me say: the deed
I neither did, nor saw who was the doer,
And 'twere not just that I should suffer harm.
    Creon. Wisely, thyself in covert, at the mark
Thou aimest: some shrewd news, methinks, thou'lt tell.
    Sentinel. Danger to face, well may a man be cautious.
    Creon. Speak then, and go thy way, and make an end.
    Sentinel. Now I will speak. Some one ev'n now hath buried
The body and is gone; with thirsty dust
Sprinkling it o'er, and paying observance due.
    Creon. How? By what man was dared a deed so rash?
    Sentinel. I cannot tell. No mattock's stroke indeed,
Nor spade's upcast was there: hard was the ground,
Baked dry, unbroken: track of chariot-wheels
Was none, nor any sign who did this thing.
But he who kept the watch at earliest dawn
Showed to us all—a mystery, hard to clear.

[219]

Not buried was the dead man, but concealed,
With dust besprinkled, as for fear of sin:
And neither of dog, nor any beast of prey,
That came, that tore the body, found we trace.
Then bitter words we bandied to and fro,
Denouncing each the other; and soon to blows
Our strife had grown—was none would keep the peace—
For every one was guilty of the deed,
And none confessed, but all denied they knew.
And we were fain to handle red-hot iron,
Or walk through fire barefoot, or swear by heaven,
That neither had we done it, nor had shared
His secret with who planned it or who wrought.
So all in vain we questioned: and at last
One spake, and all who heard him, bowed by fear,
Bent to the earth their faces, knowing not
How to gainsay, nor doing what he said
How we might 'scape mischance. This deed to thee
He urged that we should show, and hide it not.
And his advice prevailed; and by the lot
To luckless me this privilege befell.
Unwilling and unwelcome is my errand,
A bearer of ill news, whom no man loves.
    Chorus. O king, my thought hath counseled me long since,
Haply this deed is ordered by the gods.
    Creon. Cease, ere my wrath is kindled at thy speech,
Lest thou be found an old man and a fool.
Intolerably thou pratest of the gods,
That they to yonder dead man have respect.
Yea, for what service with exceeding honor
Sought they his burial, who came here to burn
Their pillared shrines and temple-offerings,
And of their land and of their laws make havoc?
Or seest thou that the gods allow the wicked?
Not so: but some impatient of my will
Among my people made a murmuring,
Shaking their heads in secret, to the yoke
With stubborn necks unbent, and hearts disloyal.
Full certainly I know that they with bribes
Have on these men prevailed to do this deed.

Of all the evils current in this world
Most mischievous is gold. This hath laid waste
Fair cities, and unpeopled homes of men:
Many an honest heart hath the false lure
Of gold seduced to walk in ways of shame;
And hence mankind are versed in villanies,
And of all godless acts have learnt the lore.
But, who took hire to execute this work,
Wrought to their own undoing at the last.
Since, if the dread of Zeus I still revere,
Be well assured—and what I speak I swear—
Unless the author of this burial
Ye find, and in my sight produce him here,
For you mere death shall not suffice, until
Gibbeted alive this outrage ye disclose,
That ye may know what gains are worth the winning,
And henceforth clutch the wiselier, having learnt
That to seek gain in all things is not well.
For from ill-gotten pelf the lives of men
Ruined than saved more often shall ye see.

   Sentinel. May I speak a word, or thus am I dismissed?
   Creon. Know'st thou not that ev'n now thy voice offends?
   Sentinel. Do I afflict thy hearing or thy heart?
   Creon. Where I am pained, it skills not to define.
   Sentinel. The doer grieves thy mind, but I thine ears.
   Creon. That thou wast born to chatter, 'tis too plain.
   Sentinel. And therefore not the doer of this deed.
   Creon. At thy life's cost thou didst it, bought with gold.
   Sentinel. Alas!
'Tis pity, men should judge, yet judge amiss.
   Creon. Talk you of 'judging' glibly as you may—
Who did this deed, I'll know, or ye shall own
That all your wondrous winnings end in loss.
   Sentinel. With all my heart I wish he may be found:
But found or no—for that's as fortune will—
I shall not show my face to you again.
Great cause I have to thank the gracious gods,
Saved past all hope and reckoning even now.
               [*Exeunt* CREON *and* SENTINEL.

Chorus. Many are the wonders of the world,　　　[*Strophe.*
And none so wonderful as Man.
Over the waters wan
His storm-vext bark he steers,
While the fierce billows break
Round his path, and o'er his head:
And the Earth-mother, first of gods,
The ageless, the indomitable,
With his ploughing to and fro
He wearieth, year by year:
In the deep furrow toil the patient mules.

　　　　　　　　　　　　　　　　　　　[*Antistrophe.*

The birds o' the air he snares and takes
All the light-hearted fluttering race:
And tribes of savage beasts,
And creatures of the deep,
Meshed in his woven toils,
Own the master-mind of man.
Free lives of upland and of wild
By human arts are curbed and tamed:
See the horse's shaggy neck
Submissive to the yoke—
And strength untired of mountain-roaming bulls.

　　　　　　　　　　　　　　　　　　　[*Strophe.*

Language withal he learnt,
And Thought that as the wind is free,
And aptitudes of civic life:
Ill-lodged no more he lies,
His roof the sky, the earth his bed,
Screened now from piercing frost and pelting rain;
All-fertile in resource, resourceless never
Meets he the morrow; only death
He wants the skill to shun:
But many a fell disease the healer's art hath foiled.

　　　　　　　　　　　　　　　　　　　[*Antistrophe.*

So soaring far past hope,
The wise inventiveness of man
Finds diverse issues, good and ill:
If from their course he wrests
The firm foundations of the state,

[222]

Laws, and the justice he is sworn to keep—
High in the city, cityless I deem him,
Dealing with baseness: overbold,
May he my hearth avoid,
Nor let my thoughts with his, who does such deeds, agree!

                 [*Re-enter* SENTINEL, *bringing in* ANTIGONE.

What strange portentous sight is this,
I doubt my eyes, beholding? This—
How shall I gainsay what I know?—
This maiden *is*—Antigone!
Daughter of Oedipus,
Hapless child of a hapless sire,
What hast thou done? It cannot be
That thou hast transgressed the king's command—
That, taken in folly, *thee* they bring!

   Sentinel. This same is she that did the burial:
We caught her in the act. But where's the king?

   Chorus. Back from the palace in good time he comes.

                     [*Re-enter* CREON.

   Creon. What chance is this, to which my steps are timed?

   Sentinel. Nothing, sir king, should men swear not to do;
For second thoughts to first thoughts give the lie.
Hither, I made full sure, I scarce should come
Back, by your threats beruffled as I was.
Yet here, surprised by most unlooked-for joy,
That trifles all delights that e'er I knew,
I bring you—though my coming breaks my oath—
This maiden, whom, busied about the corpse,
We captured. This time were no lots to throw:
My own good fortune this, and none but mine.
Now therefore, king, take her yourself and try her,
And question as you will: but I have earned
Full clearance and acquittal of this coil.

   Creon. Where, on what manner, was your captive taken?

   Sentinel. Burying the man, we took her: all is told.

   Creon. Art thou advised of this? Is it the truth?

   Sentinel. I say I saw her burying the body,
That you forbade. Is that distinct and clear?

   Creon. How! Was she seen, and taken in the act?

   Sentinel. So it fell out. When I had gone from hence

With thy loud threats yet sounding in my ears,
We swept off all the dust that hid the limbs,
And to the light stripped bare the clammy corpse,
And on the hill's brow sat, and faced the wind,
Choosing a spot clear of the body's stench.
Roundly we chid each other to the work;
'No sleeping at your post there' was our word.
So did we keep the watch, till in mid-heaven
The sun's bright burning orb above us hung,
With fierce noon-heat: and now a sudden blast
Swept, and a storm of dust, that vexed the sky
And choked the plain, and all the leaves o' the trees
O' the plain were marred, and the wide heaven it filled:
We with shut eyes the heaven-sent plague endured.
And, when after long time its force was spent,
We saw this maiden, and a bitter cry
She poured, as of a wailing bird that sees
Her empty nest dismantled of its brood:
So she, when she espied the body bare,
Cried out and wept, and many a grievous curse
Upon their heads invoked by whom 'twas done.
And thirsty dust she sprinkled with her hands,
And lifted up an urn, fair-wrought of brass,
And with thrice-poured libations crowned the dead.
We saw it and we hasted, and at once,
All undismayed, our captive, hemmed her round,
And with the two offences charged her there,
Both first and last. Nothing did she deny,
But made me glad and sorry, owning all.
For to have slipped one's own neck from the noose
Is sweet, yet no one likes to get his friends
In trouble: but my nature is to make
All else of small account, so I am safe.

   Creon. Speak thou, who bendest on the earth thy gaze,
Are these things, which are witnessed, true or false?

   Antigone. I say I did it; I deny it not.

   Creon. So, sirrah, thou art free; go where thou wilt,
Loosed from the burden of this heavy charge.
But tell me thou—and let thy speech be brief—
The edict hadst thou heard, which this forbade?

Antigone. I could not choose but hear what all men heard.
Creon. And didst thou dare to disobey the law?
  Antigone. Nowise from Zeus, me thought, this edict came,
Nor Justice, that abides among the gods
In Hades, who ordained these laws for men.
Nor did I deem *thine* edicts of such force
That they, a mortal's bidding, should o'erride
Unwritten laws, eternal in the heavens.
Not of to-day or yesterday are these,
But live from everlasting, and from whence
They sprang, none knoweth. I would not, for the breach
Of these, through fear of any human pride,
To heaven atone. I knew that I must die:
How else? Without thine edict, that were so.
And if before my time, why, this were gain.
Compassed about with ills, who lives, as I,
Death, to such life as his, must needs be gain.
So is it to me to undergo this doom
No grief at all: but had I left my brother,
My mother's child, unburied where he lay,
Then I had grieved; but now this grieves me not.
Senseless I seem to thee, so doing? Belike
A senseless judgment finds me void of sense.
  Chorus. How in the child the sternness of the sire
Shows stern, before the storm untaught to bend!   *Unsympathetic*
  Creon. Yet know full well that such o'er-stubborn wills
Are broken most of all, as sturdiest steel,
Of an untempered hardness, fresh from forge,
Most surely snapped and shivered should ye see.
Lo how a little curb has strength enough
To tame the restive horse: for to a slave
His masters give no license to be proud.
Insult on insult heaped! Was't not enough
My promulgated laws to have transgressed,
But, having done it, face to face with me
She boasts of this and glories in the deed?
I surely am the woman, she the man,
If she defies my power, and I submit.
Be she my sister's child, or sprung from one
More near of blood than all my house to me,

Not so shall they escape my direst doom—
She and her sister: for I count her too
Guilty no less of having planned this work.
Go, call her hither: in the house I saw her
Raving ev'n now, nor mistress of her thoughts.
So oft the mind, revolving secret crime,
Makes premature disclosure of its guilt.
But this is hateful, when the guilty one,
Detected, thinks to glorify his fault.

   Antigone. To kill me—wouldst thou more with me than
     this?

   Creon. This is enough: I do desire no more.

   Antigone. Why dost thou then delay? I have no pleasure
To hear thee speak—have not and would not have:
Nor less distasteful is my speech to thee.
Yet how could I have won myself a praise
More honorable than this, of burying
My brother? This from every voice should win
Approval, might but fear men's lips unseal.
But kings are fortunate—not least in this,
That they may do and speak what things they will.

   Creon. All Thebes sees this with other eyes than thine.

   Antigone. They see as I, but bate their breath to thee.

   Creon. And art thou not ashamed, from them to differ?

   Antigone. To reverence a brother is not shameful.

   Creon. And was not he who died for Thebes thy brother?

   Antigone. One mother bore us, and one sire begat.

   Creon. Yet, honoring both, thou dost dishonor him.

   Antigone. He in the grave will not subscribe to this.

   Creon. How, if no less thou dost revere the guilty?

   Antigone. 'Twas not his slave that perished, but his brother.

   Creon. The enemy of this land: its champion he.

   Antigone. Yet Death of due observance must not fail.

   Creon. Just and unjust urge not an equal claim.

   Antigone. Perchance in Hades 'tis a holy deed.

   Creon. Hatred, not ev'n in death, converts to love.

   Antigone. Not in your hates, but in your loves, I'd share.

   Creon. Go to the shades, and, if thou'lt love, love there:
No woman, while I live, shall master me.

                             [*Enter* ISMENE.

Chorus. See, from the palace comes Ismene—
Sisterly drops from her eyes down-shedding:
Clouded her brows droop, heavy with sorrow;
And the blood-red tinge of a burning blush
Covers her beautiful downcast face.
Creon. Thou, who hast crept, a serpent in my home,
Draining my blood, unseen; and I knew not
Rearing two pests, to overset my throne;
Speak—wilt thou too confess that in this work
Thou hadst a hand, or swear thou didst not know?
Ismene. I'll say the deed was mine, if she consents:
My share of the blame I bear, and do not shrink.
Antigone. Justice forbids thy claim: neither didst thou
Agree, nor I admit thee to my counsels.
Ismene. I am not ashamed, in thine extremity,
To make myself companion of thy fate.
Antigone. Whose was the deed, know Hades and the dead:
I love not friends, who talk of friendliness.
Ismene. Sister, disdain me not, but let me pour
My blood with thine, an offering to the dead.
Antigone. Leave me to die alone, nor claim the work
Thou wouldst not help. My death will be enough.
Ismene. What joy have I to live, when thou art gone?
Antigone. Ask Creon that: thou art of kin to him.
Ismene. Why wilt thou grieve me with thy needless taunts?
Antigone. If I mock thee, 'tis with a heavy heart.
Ismene. What may I do to serve thee even now?
Antigone. Look to thyself: I grudge thee not thy safety.
Ismene. And may I not, unhappy, share thy death?
Antigone. Thou didst make choice to live, but I to die.
Ismene. Might I unsay my words, this were not so.
Antigone. Wise seemed we—thou to these, and I to those.
Ismene. But now our fault is equal, thine and mine.
Antigone. Take heart to live: for so thou dost: but I—
Dead is my life long since—to help the dead.
Creon. One of these two, methinks, proves foolish now;
The other's folly with her life began.
Ismene. Nay, for, O king, misfortunes of the wise
To madness turn the wisdom that they have.
Creon. 'Tis so with thee, choosing to share her guilt.

Ismene. How should I live alone, without my sister?
Creon. Call her not thine: thou hast no sister now.
Ismene. But wilt thou tear her from thy son's embrace?
Creon. Are there no women in the world but she?
Ismene. Not as their faith was plighted, each to each.
Creon. An evil wife I like not for my son.
Antigone. Haemon! beloved! hear not thy father's scorn.
Creon. Thou and thy love to me are wearisome.
Chorus. Wilt thou indeed snatch from thy son his bride?
Creon. 'Tis death that will unloose their marriage-bond.
Chorus. It seems thou art resolved that she must die?
Creon. Of that we are agreed. Delay no more:
Ye, servants, lead them in. For from this time
Women they needs must be, and range no more:
Since ev'n the bold may play the runaway,
When death he sees close-creeping on his life.

[ANTIGONE *and* ISMENE *are led into the palace.*
Chorus.   [*Strophe.*
Happy indeed is the life of the man who tastes not of trouble!
For when from the gods a house is shaken,
Fails nevermore the curse,
On most and on least of the race descending:
Like to a rolling wave,
By furious blasts from the Thraceward driven—
Out of the nethermost deeps, out of the fathomless gloom,
Casting up mire and blackness and storm-vext wrack of the
    sea—
And back, with a moan like thunder, from the cliffs the surf
    is hurled.

[*Antistrophe.*
So from of old to the Labdacid race comes sorrow on sorrow:
And, ev'n as the dead, so fare the living:
Respite from ills is none,
Nor one generation redeems another—
All will some god bring low.
Now o'er the last root of the house, fate-stricken,
Woe for the light that had shined, woe for the lingering hope!
Smooth over all is lying the blood-stained dust they have
    spread—

Rash speech, and a frantic purpose, and the gods who reign
below.

[*Strophe.*

What human trespass, Zeus,
May circumscribe thy power,
Which neither sleep o'ercomes,
That saps the strength of all things else,
Nor months that run their tireless course,
But thou for ever with an ageless sway
The dazzling splendor dost possess
Of thine Olympian home?
'Tis now as it hath ever been,
And still in years to come
The old order will not change:
Never from human life departs
The universal scourge of man,
His own presumptuous pride.

[*Antistrophe.*

Hope wings her daring flight,
By strong winds borne afar—
And some are blessed; and some
Are cheated of their vain desires,
That learn their folly all too late,
When in the fire they tread with scorchèd feet.
'Twas said of old—and time approves
The wisdom of the saw—
That, when in foolish ways, that end
In ruin, gods would lead
A mortal's mind astray,
Evil that man miscalls his good:
A brief while then he holds his course
By fatuous pride unscathed.
See, thy son Haemon comes hither, of all
Thy children the last? Comes he lamenting
The doom of the maiden, his bride Antigone—
And the frustrated hope of his marriage?

[*Enter* HAEMON.

Creon. Soon we shall know, better than seers could say.
My son, in anger art thou come to me,
Hearing the sentence, not to be reversed,

Which on thy destined bride I have pronounced?
Or am I still thy friend, do what I may?
   Haemon. Father, I am in thy hand: with thy wise counsels
Thou dost direct me; these I shall obey.
Not rightly should I deem of more account
The winning of a wife than thy good guidance.
   Creon. Be this thy dearest wish and next thy heart,
In all things to uphold thy father's will.
For to this end men crave to see grow up
Obedient children round them in their homes,
Both to requite their enemies with hate,
And render equal honor to their friends.
Whoso begets unprofitable children,
What shall be said of him, but that he gets
Grief for himself, loud laughter for his foes?
Never, my son, let for a woman's sake
Reason give way to sense, but know full well
Cold is the pleasure that he clasps, who woos
An evil woman to his board and bed.
What wounds so deeply as an evil friend?
Count then this maiden as thine enemy,
Loathe her, and give her leave, in that dark world
To which she goes, to marry with another.
For out of all the city since I found
Her only, and her openly, rebellious,
I shall not to the city break my word,
But she shall die. Let her appeal to Zeus,
And sing the sanctity of kindred blood—
What then? If in my own house I shall nurse
Rebellion, how shall strangers not rebel?
He who to his own kith and kin does right,
Will in the state deal righteously with all.
Of such a man I shall not fear to boast,
Well he can rule, and well he would obey,
And in the storm of battle at his post
Firm he would stand, a comrade staunch and true.
But praise from me that man shall never have,
Who either boldly thrusts aside the law
Or takes upon him to instruct his rulers,
Whom, by the state empowered, he should obey,

In little and in much, in right and wrong.
The worst of evils is to disobey.
Cities by this are ruined, homes of men
Made desolate by this; this in the battle
Breaks into headlong rout the wavering line;
The steadfast ranks, the many lives unhurt,
Are to obedience due. We must defend
The government and order of the state,
And not be governed by a wilful girl.
We'll yield our place up, if we must, to men;
To women that we stooped, shall not be said.
    Chorus. Unless an old man's judgment is at fault,
These words of thine, we deem, are words of wisdom.
    Haemon. Reason, my father, in the mind of man,
Noblest of all their gifts, the gods implant,
And how to find thy reasoning at fault,
I know not, and to learn I should be loth;
Yet for another it might not be amiss.
But I for thee am vigilant to mark
All that men say, or do, or find to blame.
Thy presence awes the simple citizen
From speaking words that shall not please thine ear,
But I hear what they whisper in the dark,
And how the city for this maid laments,
That of all women she the least deserving
Dies for most glorious deeds a death most cruel,
Who her own brother, fall'n among the slain,
Left not unburied there, to be devoured
By ravening dogs or any bird o' the air:—
'Should not her deed be blazoned all in gold?'
Upon the darkness still such whisper grows.
But I of all possessions that I have
Prize most, my father, thy prosperity.
Welldoing and fair fame of sire to son,
Of son to sire, is noblest ornament.
Cleave not, I pray thee, to this constant mind,
That what thou sayest, and nought beside, is truth.
For men who think that only they are wise,
None eloquent, right-minded none, but they,
Often, when searched, prove empty. 'Tis no shame,

Ev'n if a man be wise, that he should yet
Learn many things, and not hold out too stiffly.
Beside the torrent's course, of trees that bend
Each bough, thou seest, and every twig is safe;
Those that resist are by the roots uptorn.
And ships, that brace with stubborn hardihood
Their mainsheet to the gale, pursue their voyage
Keel-uppermost, their sailors' thwarts reversed.
Cease from thy wrath; be not inexorable:
For if despite my youth I too may think
My thought, I'll say that best it is by far
That men should be all-knowing if they may,
But if—as oft the scale inclines not so—
Why then, by good advice 'tis good to learn.

    Chorus. What in thy son's speech, king, is seasonable
'Tis fit thou shouldst receive: and thou in his:
For there is reason in the words of both.

    Creon. Shall I, grown gray with age, be taught indeed—
And by this boy—to think what he thinks right?

    Haemon. Nothing that is not right: though I am young,
Consider not my years, but how I act.

    Creon. Is this thine act—to honor the unruly?

    Haemon. Wrongdoers, dishonor—outrage, if thou wilt!

    Creon. Hath not this maiden caught this malady?

    Haemon. The general voice of Thebes says no to that.

    Creon. Shall Thebes prescribe to me how I must govern?

    Haemon. How all too young art thou in speaking thus!

    Creon. Whose business is't but mine how Thebes is
      governed?

    Haemon. A city is none, that to one man belongs.

    Creon. Is it not held, the city is the king's?

    Haemon. Finely thou'dst rule, alone, a land dispeopled!

    Creon. It seems this boy will plead the woman's cause.

    Haemon. Woman art thou? my care is all for thee.

    Creon. Shameless—is't right to wrangle with thy father?

    Haemon. I see that wrong for right thou dost mistake.

    Creon. Do I mistake, to reverence my office?

    Haemon. What reverence, heaven's honors to contemn?

    Creon. O hateful spirit, ruled by a woman's will!

    Haemon. To no base service shalt thou prove me bound.

[232]

Creon. Art thou not pleading all the time for her?
Haemon. For thee and me, and for the gods below.
Creon. Thou shalt not marry her, this side the grave.
Haemon. If she must die, she shall: but not alone.
Creon. Art grown so bold, thou dost fly out in threats?
Haemon. What threats, to argue with a foolish purpose?
Creon. Thou'lt rue—unwise—thy wisdom spent on me.
Haemon. Thou art my father; or wise I scarce had called
  thee.
Creon. Slave—to thy mistress babble, not to me.
Haemon. Wouldst thou have all the talking for thine own?
Creon. Is't come to this? But, by Olympus yonder,
Know well, thou shalt be sorry for these taunts,
Wherewith thou dost upbraid me. Slaves, what ho!
Bring that abhorrence hither, that she may die,
Now, in her bridegroom's sight, whilst here he stands.
Haemon. Neither in my sight—imagine no such thing—
Shall she be slain; nor shalt thou from this hour
Look with thine eyes upon my face again:
To friends who love thy madness I commit thee.

                        [Exit HAEMON.
  Chorus. Suddenly, sire, in anger he is gone:
Young minds grow desperate, by grief distemper'd.
  Creon. More than a man let him conceive and do;
He shall not save these maidens from their doom.
  Chorus. Both sisters art thou purposed to destroy?
  Creon. Not her whose hands sinned not; thou askest well.
  Chorus. What of the other? how shall she be slain?
  Creon. By paths untrodden of men I will conduct her,
And shut her, living, in a vault, rock-hewn,
And there, with food, no more than shall suffice
To avert the guilt of murder from the city,
To Hades, the one god whom she reveres,
She, praying not to die, either shall have
Her asking, or shall learn, albeit too late,
That to revere the dead is fruitless toil.

                        [Exit CREON.
                        [Strophe.
  Chorus. O Love, our conqueror, matchless in might,
Thou prevailest, O Love, thou dividest the prey;

In damask cheeks of a maiden
Thy watch through the night is set.
Thou roamest over the sea;
On the hills, in the shepherd's huts, thou art;
Nor of deathless gods, nor of short-lived men,
From thy madness any escapeth.

[*Antistrophe.*

Unjust, through thee, are the thoughts of the just,
Thou dost bend them, O Love, to thy will, to thy spite.
Unkindly strife thou hast kindled,
This wrangling of son with sire.
For great laws, throned in the heart,
To the sway of a rival power give place,
To the love-light flashed from a fair bride's eyes:
In her triumph laughs Aphrodite.
Me, even now, me also,
Seeing these things, a sudden pity
Beyond all governance transports:
The fountains of my tears
I can refrain no more,
Seeing Antigone here to the bridal chamber
Come, to the all-receiving chamber of Death.

[*Enter* ANTIGONE *surrounded by guards.*

  Antigone. Friends and my countrymen, ye see me
Upon the last of all my ways
Set forth, the Sun-god's latest light
Beholding, now and never more:
But Death, who giveth sleep to all,
Yet living leads me hence
To the Acherontian shore,
Of marriage rites amerced,
And me no bridal song hath ever sung,
But Acheron will make of me his bride.
  Chorus. Therefore renowned, with praise of men,
To yonder vault o' the dead thou goest,
By no slow-wasting sickness stricken,
Nor doomed to fall with those who win
The wages of the swords they drew,
But mistress of thyself, alive,
Alone of mortals the dark road

[234]

To deathward thou shalt tread.

Antigone. I heard of one, most piteous in her ending,
That stranger, child of Phrygian Tantalus,
On heights of Sipylus enclasped,
And ivy-like enchained,
By clinging tendrils of the branching rock,
Who day and night unceasingly
'Mid drizzle of rain and drift of snow
Slow-wasting in her place
Stands, as the tale is told,
Her lids surcharged with weeping, and her neck
And bosom drenched with falling of her tears:—
A fate most like to hers
Seals up with sleep these eyes of mine.

Chorus. She was a goddess, sprung from gods:
Mortals, of mortal birth, are we.
But for one dead to win with those
Who rank no lower than the gods—
Living and, after, when she died—
An equal lot, were much to hear.

Antigone. Ah, I am mocked! Nay, by our fathers' gods,
Withhold thy taunts till I am gone—
Gone and evanished from thy sight.
O Thebes, my city!
O wealthy men of Thebes!
But *ye* will witness—yes, to you I turn—
O fount Dircaean, and this sacred grove
Of Thebè the fair-charioted,
By what stern law, and how of friends unwept,
To that strange grave I go,
The massy dungeon for my burial heaped.
O luckless wight,
Exiled from earth nor housed below,
Both by the living and the dead disowned!

Chorus. To furthest brink of boldness thou didst stray,
And stumbling there, at foot of Justice' throne,
Full heavily, my daughter, hast thou fallen:
Yet of thy father's fault belike
This suffering pays the price.

Antigone. Thou hast touched, ev'n there, my bitterest pang
    of all,
A thrice-told tale, my father's grief—
And all our grievous doom that clung
About the famed Labdacidae.
O that incestuous bed
Of horror, and my father's sin—
The hapless mother who bore him to the light,
By him enclasped—wherefrom I luckless sprang:
With whom, accurst, unwedded,
I must go hence to dwell.
O brother, a bride ill-starred
Who to thy couch didst win,
How, being dead, me living thou hast slain!
    Chorus. Religion prompts the reverent deed:
But power, to whomso power belongs,
Must nowise be transgressed; and thee
A self-willed temper hath o'erthrown.
    Antigone. Unwept and unfriended,
Cheered by no song Hymenaeal—
Lo, I am led, heavy-hearted,
This road that awaits me.
The sacred light-giving eye in heaven
Now no more must I see, unhappy:
But for my fate not a tear falls,
Not a friend makes moan.

                                [*Re-enter* CREON.
    Creon. Know ye not, songs and weepings before death
That none would pretermit, were he allowed?
Hence with her, hence, and tarry not, but deep
In her tomb-prison, even as I have said,
Leave her alone, forsaken: to die, or else
Live, in that vault entombed, if so she will:
Since of this maiden's blood our hands are clean,
Only we ban her sojourn in the light.
    Antigone. O tomb! O nuptial chamber! O house deep-
    delved
In earth, safe-guarded ever! To thee I come,
And to my kin in thee, who many an one
Are with Persephone, dead among the dead:

And last of all, most miserably by far,
I thither am going, ere my life's term be done.
But a good hope I cherish, that, come there,
My father's love will greet me, yea and thine,
My mother—and thy welcome, brother dear:
Since, when ye died, I with mine own hands laved
And dressed your limbs, and poured upon your graves
Libations; and like service done to thee
Hath brought me, Polynices, now to this.
Yet well I honored thee, the wise will say:
Since not for children's sake would I, their mother,
Nor for my husband, slain, and moldering there,
Have travailed thus, doing despite to Thebes.
According to what law, do I speak this?
One husband slain, another might have been,
And children from another, losing this;
But, father and mother buried out of sight,
There can be born no brother any more.
Such was the law whereby I held thee first
In honor; but to Creon all mistaken,
O dear my brother, I seemed, and overbold—
And now, made captive thus, he leads me hence
No wife, no bride for ever—of marriage-joy
And nursery of children quite bereft:
So by my friends forsaken I depart,
Living, unhappy, to dim vaults of death.
Yet I transgressed—what ordinance of heaven?
Why to the gods, ill-fated, any more
Should I look up—whom call to succor—since
Impiety my piety is named?
But, if these things are pleasing to the gods,
I'll freely own I suffered for my fault;
If theirs the fault, who doomed me, may to them
No worse befall than they unjustly do!
    Chorus. Stormily still o'er the soul of the maiden
The selfsame gusts of passion sweep.
    Creon. Therefore, I warn them, ruth for their lingering,
To those who lead her, this shall cause.
    Antigone. Short shrift, swift death—ah! woe is me—
This speech portends.

Creon. Lay to thy soul no flattering hope,
That unfulfilled this doom may be.
    Antigone. O country of Thebes and my father's city,
And gods my progenitors,
Lo, how they lead me—now, and delay not.
O all ye princes of Thebes, behold me—
Of the race of your kings, me, sole surviving—
What things at the hands of what men I suffer,
For the fear of the gods I feared.

                                          [Exit ANTIGONE.
                                                 [Strophe.

    Chorus. Out of the sunlight so,
In brass-bound prison-courts,
Were pent the limbs of Danaë,
And in a living tomb sealed up from sight;
Albeit, O daughter, she as thou
Came of a noble line,
And that life-quickening treasure of his golden rain
She had in charge from Zeus to keep.
O dread mysterious power of fate,
That neither wealth nor war can quell,
Nor walls shut out, nor ships escape,
Dark-fleeing o'er the foam!

                                                 [Antistrophe.

And that Edonian king
Was bound, the choleric son
Of Dryas, splenetive and hot,
Fast in the rock by Dionysus chained.
Such fierce and fevered issue streams
From madness at the height.
With splenetive rash speech what madness had assailed
The vengeful god, too late he learned.
To women-worshippers inspired
Their torchlit revels he forbade,
And flutings that the Muses loved
Had silenced with his scorn.

                                                 [Strophe.

From the dark rock-portals of the divided sea
Here go the cliffs of Bosporus, and there
The savage Thracian coast

Of Salmydessus, where the neighbor-worshipped God
Of Battle saw the blinding blow accurst,
Dealt by that fierce stepdame,
Darkling descend on both the sons
Of Phineus—on their sightless orbs
That plead for vengeance, stricken through and stabbed
By the sharp shuttle in her murderous hands.

[*Antistrophe.*

Wasted with their sorrow, their mother's hapless fate
They hapless wept, and in their mother's shame
Had part, as those base-born:
Yet she from the old Erechtheid blood her birth derived,
And in deep caverns of the hills was nursed,
Amid her father's storms,
Child of the North-wind—up the steep
Hillsides no bounding foal so fleet,
A daughter of the gods: but her, O child,
Fate's everlasting hands availed to reach.

[*Enter* TIRESIAS, *a boy leading him.*

Tiresias. Princes of Thebes, we come—one sight for both
Our common road descrying, as behoves
Blind men to find their way by help of others.
Creon. What tidings, old Tiresias, dost thou bring?
Tiresias. Hear then the prophet, and attend his speech.
Creon. Have I aforetime from thy wisdom swerved?
Tiresias. So, clear of shoals, thou pilotest the state.
Creon. The service thou hast rendered I attest.
Tiresias. Once more on razor's edge thy fortunes stand.
Creon. Hearing thy speech, I shudder: tell me more.
Tiresias. My art's prognostications hear and judge.
For in my ancient sea, to watch the birds
In that their general gathering-place, I sat,
And heard an unintelligible noise,
A cry and clangor of birds, confused with rage;
And what fierce fray they waged with murderous claws,
I guessed too surely by the whirr of wings.
Scared by that sound, burnt-offerings I then
Essayed on blazing altars; but no flame
Leapt from the sacrifice; a clammy ooze
Reeked from the thighs, and 'mid the ashes dripped,

[239]

Smoking and sputtering; the gall disparted,
And on the air was spent; and the thighbones
Of the enfolding fat fell stripped and bare.
This from this boy I heard, whose eyes beheld
The failing signs of sacrifice obscure:
Others by me are guided, I by him.
And by thy will we are afflicted thus.
For now our hearths and altars every one
Have ravening dogs and birds fouled with the flesh
Of this poor fallen son of Oedipus;
And so no flame of victims burnt may move
Gods any more to hearken to our prayers,
And birds obscene flap thence their bodeful cries,
With fat of human carrion newly gorged.
Slight not, my son, such warning. For all men,
Both great and small, are liable to err:
But he who errs no more unfortunate
Or all unwise shall be, if having tripped
He rights the wrong nor stubbornly persists.
He who persists in folly is the fool.
Give death his due: stab not the fallen foe:
What valor is in this, to slay the slain?
Wisely I speak and well; and sweet it is
To hear good counsel, when it counsels gain.
    Creon. Old man, ye all, as bowmen at a mark,
Shoot at this man, and now with soothsaying
Ye practice on me—ye by whose sort long since
Mere merchandise and salework I am made.
Go to, get gain, and barter, if ye will,
Amber ye buy from Sardis, and fine gold
Of Ind: but him, I say, ye shall not bury:
No, not if eagles, ministers of Zeus
Should bear him piecemeal to their Master's throne,
Will I, for fear of such pollution, grant
Leave for his burial; knowing well that men
Soil not the stainless majesty of heaven.
But, aged seer, the wisest of mankind
Dishonorably may fall, who fairly speak
Dishonorable words, and all for gain.
    Tiresias. Alas!

Who knows, or who considers, in this world—
   Creon. What wilt thou say? What commonplace is this?
   Tiresias. How prudence is the best of all our wealth?
   Creon. As folly, I suppose, our deadliest hurt.
   Tiresias. Yet with this malady art thou possest.
   Creon. Reproaches I'll not bandy with the prophet.
   Tiresias. Saying that I falsely prophesy, thou dost.
   Creon. So are all prophets; 'tis a covetous race.
   Tiresias. Greed of base gain marks still the tyrant-sort.
   Creon. Knowest thou that of thy rulers this is said?
   Tiresias. I know; for thou through me didst save the state.
   Creon. Wise in thy craft art thou, but false at heart.
   Tiresias. Secrets, fast-locked, thou'lt move me to disclose.
   Creon. Unlock them, only speaking not for gain.
   Tiresias. So, for thy part indeed, methinks I shall.
   Creon. Think not that in my purpose thou shalt trade.
   Tiresias. But surely know that thou not many more
Revolving courses of the sun shalt pass,
Ere of thine own blood one, to make amends,
Dead for the dead, thou shalt have rendered up,
For that a living soul thou hast sent below,
And with dishonor in the grave hast lodged,
And that one dead thou holdest here cut off
From presence of the gods who reign below,
All rites of death, all obsequies denied—
With whom thou shouldst not meddle, nor the gods
In heaven, but of their due thou robb'st the dead.
Therefore of Hades and the gods for thee
The Avengers wait, with ruin slow yet sure,
To take thee in the pit which thou hast dug.
Do I speak this for gold? Thyself shalt judge:
For, yet a little while, and wailings loud
Of men and women in thy house shall show.
Think, of each city too what gathering rage,
That sees its mangled dead entombed in maws
Of dogs and all fierce beasts, or borne by kites
With stench unhallowed to its hearth-crowned heights.
So like a bowman have I launched at thee
In wrath, for thou provok'st me, shafts indeed
To pierce thy heart, and fail not, from whose smart

Thou'lt not escape. But now, boy, lead me home,
That he may vent his spleen on younger men,
And learn to keep a tongue more temperate,
And in his breast a better mind than now.

[*Exit* TIRESIAS.

Chorus. The man has prophesied dread things, O king,
And gone: and never have I known—not since
These temples changed their raven locks to snow—
That aught of false this city heard from him.

Creon. Yea, this I know, and much am I perplexed:
For hard it is to yield, but standing firm
I fear to pluck swift ruin on my pride.

Chorus. Son of Menoeceus, be advised in time.

Creon. Say then, what must I do? and I'll obey.

Chorus. Go, from her prison in the rock release
The maiden, and the unburied corpse inter.

Creon. Dost thou think this, and wouldst thou have me
yield?

Chorus. Yea, king, and quickly; for the gods cut short
With sudden scathe the foolishness of men.

Creon. Hardly indeed, but yet with forced consent
I'll do it, stooping to necessity.

Chorus. Do it, and go; leave not this task to others.

Creon. Even as I am, I'll go; and, servants, haste,
That hear and hear me not: axes in hand,
All to yon spot, far-seen, make good your speed.
But I, since this way now my mind is bent
Whom I myself have bound, myself will loose.
For now my heart misgives me, he lives best,
Whose feet depart not from the ancient ways.

[*Exit.*
[*Strophe.*

Chorus. Worshipped by many names—
Glory of Theban Semele,
Child of loud-thundering Zeus—
Haunting the famed Italian fields,
Whom as a prince the hospitable vale
Of the Eleusinian Dame reveres—
Bacchus, that hast thy home
In Thebes, the home of Bacchanals,

[242]

Beside Ismenus' fertile stream,
Where the fell dragon's teeth of old were sown:

[*Antistrophe.*

O'er the two-crested peak,
With nymphs Corycian in thy train,
By springs of Castaly,
The streaming levin lights thy path:
And from steep Nysa's hills, with ivy clad,
And that green slope, with clustering grapes
Empurpled to the sea,
When thou wouldst visit Theban streets,
A jocund company divine
With acclamation loud conducts thee forth,

[*Strophe.*

Thebes of all cities most thou honorest,
Thou with thy mother, whom the lightning slew:
And now, when Thebes is sick,
And all her people the sore plague hath stricken,
Hear us and come with healing feet
O'er the Parnassian hill,
Or the resounding strait:

[*Antistrophe.*

Come, whom fire-breathing stars in dance obey,
The master of the voices of the night,
Of Zeus the puissant son—
Come at our call, girt with thy Thyiad troop,
That follow, with thy frenzy filled,
Dancing the livelong night,
Iacchus, thee their lord.

[*Enter* MESSENGER.

Messenger. Neighbors of Cadmus, and the royal house
Of old Amphion, no man's life would I,
How high or low soever, praise or blame,
Since, who to-day has fortune, good or ill,
To-morrow's fortune lifts or lays him low;
No seer a constant lot foresees for men.
For Creon before was happy, as I deemed,
Who saved this land of Cadmus from its foes,
And the sole sovereignty of Thebes receiving
Prospered therein, with noble children blest.

[243]

Now all is lost. For, when the joys of life
Men have relinquished, no more life indeed
I count their living, but a living death.
For in thy house heap riches, if thou wilt;
Keep kingly state; yet, if no joy withal
Thou hast, for all things else, compared with pleasure,
I would not change the shadow of a smoke.
    Chorus. Of what grief now of princes wilt thou tell?
    Messenger. That one lies dead, whom those who live have
    slain.
    Chorus. Say, who is slain? And what man is the slayer?
    Messenger. Haemon is dead: his death no stranger's act.
    Chorus. Slain by himself, or by his father's hand?
    Messenger. Wroth with his pitiless sire, he slew himself.
    Chorus. O prophet, how thy prophecy comes true!
    Messenger. These things being so, consider of the rest.
    Chorus. Lo, hard at hand the miserable queen,
Eurydice: who from the house comes forth
Either by chance, or hearing of her son.

                                [*Enter* EURYDICE.

    Eurydice. Good townsmen all, your conference I heard,
As to the doors I came, intending now
Of Pallas to entreat her heavenly aid.
Even as I loosed the fastenings of the gate,
That opened wide, there smote my ears a word
Of sorrow all my own: backward I swooned,
Surprised by terror, in my maidens' arms:
But tell me now your tidings once again—
For not unlearned in sorrow, I shall hear.
    Messenger. Dear mistress, I will tell thee what I saw,
And not leave out one word of all the truth.
Why should I flatter thee with glozing words,
Too soon found false? Plain truth is ever best.
Thy husband hence I followed at the heels
To that high plain, where torn by dogs the body
Of Polynices lay, unpitied still.
A prayer we said to Hecate in the way
And Pluto, their displeasure to refrain,
Then, sprinkling with pure water, in new-stript boughs
Wrapped round and burned the fragments that remained.

A lofty funeral-mound of native earth
We heaped for him; then sought the maiden's bed,
Her bridal bed with Hades in the rock,
And from afar a voice of shrill lament
About the unhallowed chamber some one heard,
And came to Creon, and told it to his lord,
And in his ears, approaching, the wild cry
Rang doubtfully, till now there brake from him
A word of sharp despair, 'O wretched man,
What fear is at my heart? and am I going
The woefullest road that ever I have gone?
It is my son's voice greets me. Good servants, go,
Go nearer quickly; and standing by the tomb,
Even to the throat of the vault peer through and look,
Where the wrenched stone-work gapes, if Haemon's voice
I recognize indeed, or by the gods
Am cheated!' Crazed with his fear, he spake; and we
Looked, as he bade; and in the last of the tomb
We saw the maiden—hanged: about her neck
Some shred of linen had served her for a noose
And fallen upon her, clasping her, he lay,
Wailing his wasted passion in the grave,
His fatal father, and his luckless bride.
His father saw, and crying a bitter cry
Went in, and with a lamentable voice
Called him, 'O rash, what is it that thou hast done?
What wouldst thou? On what madness hast thou rushed?
My son, come forth: I pray thee—I implore.'
But with fierce eyes the boy glared at his sire
And looks of loathing, and for answer plucked
Forth a two-hilted sword, and would have struck,
But missed him, as he fled: and in that minute,
Wroth with himself, in his own side amain
Thrust deep the steel, unhappy; and conscious still
Folded the maiden in his fainting arms;
Then, gasping out his life in one sharp breath,
Pelted her pale cheek with the crimson shower.
Dead with the dead he lies, such nuptial rites
In halls of Hades, luckless, having won;
Teaching the world, that of all human ills

With human folly is none that may compare. *~~effective~~ → ~~the~~ ~~says nothing~~* [*Exit* EURYDICE.

Chorus. How should one deem of this? The queen, without
A word, of good or evil, has gone hence.

Messenger. Indeed, 'tis strange; but yet I feed on hope
That to lament in public for her son
She will not deign; but, as for private sorrow,
Will charge her women in the house to weep.
She is well tried in prudence, not to fail.

Chorus. I know not; but to me the too-much silence,
No less than clamorous grief, seems perilous.

Messenger. I will go hence to the house, and know, if aught
Of secret purpose in her raging heart
She hath kept locked from us. Thou sayest well:
The too-much silence may bode mischief too.

[*Exit* MESSENGER.

Chorus. Lo, the king comes hither himself, in his hands
The record, not doubtful its purport, bearing;
No grief (I dare to say) wrought by another,
But the weight of his own misdoing.

[*Enter* CREON *with the body of Haemon.*
[*Strophe.*

Creon. Alas my purblind wisdom's fatal fault,
Stubborn, and fraught with death!
Ye see us, sire and son,
The slayer and the slain.
O counsels all unblest!
Alas for thee, my son,
So young a life and so untimely quenched—
Gone from me, past recall—
Not by thy folly, but my own!

Chorus. Ah, how too late thou dost discern the truth!

Creon. Yea, to my cost I know: but then, methinks,
Oh then, some god with crushing weight
Leapt on me, drave me into frantic ways,
Trampling, alas for me,
In the base dust my ruined joy.
O toil and trouble of mortals—trouble and toil!

[*Enter* SECOND MESSENGER.

Second Messenger. Trouble, O king, thine own and none but
 thine,
Thou comest, methinks, part bearing in thy hands;
Part—in the house thou hast, and soon shalt see.
  Creon. What more, what worse than evil, yet remains?
  Second Messenger. Thy wife is dead, with desperate hand
    ev'n now
Self-slain, for this dead son for whom she lived.

                                              [*Antistrophe.*
  Creon. O harbor of Hades, never to be appeased,
Why art thou merciless?
What heavy news is this?
Harsh news to me of grief,
That slays me, slain before!
Ah me, the woeful news!
What sayest thou, what latest word is this?
Slaughter on slaughter heaped—
Slain both together, son and wife!
  Chorus. Behold and see: for now the doors stand wide.
  Creon. This second grief, ah me, my eyes behold.
What fate, ah what, remains behind?
My son I hold already in my arms:
And now, ah woe is me,
This other in my sight lies dead:
Mother and child—most piteous both to see!
  Second Messenger. Heartstricken at the altar as she fell,
She veiled her swooning eyelids, wailing loud
For Megareus, her son, who nobly died
Before, and for this other, and with her last
Breath cursed, the slayer of her children, thee.
  Creon. Ah me, will no one aim
Against my heart, made wild with fear,
With two-edged sword a deadly thrust?
O wretched that I am,
Fulfilled with sorrow, and made one with grief!
  Second Messenger. She did reproach thee, truly, ere she
    died,
And laid on thee the blame of both their deaths.
  Creon. What was the manner of her violent end?

Second Messenger. Pierced to the heart, by her own hand, she died,
Hearing her son's most lamentable fate.
    Creon. All, all on me this guilt must ever rest,
And on no head but mine.
O my poor son, I slew thee, even I:
Let no one doubt but that the deed was mine.
O servants, lead me quickly, lead me hence;
And let me be as one who is no more.
    Chorus. 'Tis counseled well, if well with ill can be:
For bad is best, when soonest out of sight.
    Creon. I care not, let it come:
Let come the best of all my fate,
The best, the last, that ends my days:
What care I? come what will—
That I no more may see another day.
    Chorus. Let be the future: mind the present need,
And leave the rest to whom the rest concerns.
    Creon. No other wish have I; that prayer is all.
    Chorus. Pray not at all: all is as fate appoints:
'Tis not in mortals to avert their doom.
    Creon. Oh lead me hence, unprofitable; who thee
Unwittingly have slain,
Child, and my wife, unhappy; and know not now
Which way to look to either: for all things
Are crooked that I handle, and a fate
Intolerable upon my life hath leapt.

                      [CREON *is led away.*

    Chorus. First of all happiness far is wisdom,
And to the gods that one fail not of piety.
But great words of the overweening
Lay great stripes to the backs of the boasters:
Taught by adversity,
Old age learns, too late, to be wise.

                           [*Exeunt.*

SOPHOCLES
OEDIPUS AT COLONOS

⇥⇤

TRANSLATED
by
LEWIS CAMPBELL

CHARACTERS IN THE PLAY

OEDIPUS, *old and blind.*

ANTIGONE ⎱ *his young daughters.*
ISMENE ⎰

AN ATHENIAN.

THESEUS, *King of Athens.*

CREON, *envoy from Thebes.*

POLYNICES, *the elder son of Oedipus.*

A MESSENGER.

CHORUS *of Village Guardians.*

The scene is laid at Colonos.

ARGUMENT

Oedipus had remained at Thebes for some time after his fall. But he was afterwards banished by the command of Creon, with the consent of his own sons. Their intention at first was to lay no claim to the throne. But by-and-by ambition prevailed with Eteocles, the younger-born, and he persuaded Creon and the citizens to banish his elder brother. Polynices took refuge at Argos, where he married the daughter of Adrastus and levied an army of auxiliaries to support his pretensions to the throne of Thebes. Before going into exile Oedipus had cursed his sons.

Antigone after a while fled forth to join her father and support him in his wanderings. Ismene also once brought him secret intelligence.

Years have now elapsed, and the Delphian oracle proclaims that if Oedipus dies in a foreign land the enemies of Thebes shall overcome her.

In ignorance of this fact, Oedipus, now aged as well as blind, and led by his daughter Antigone, appears before the grove of the Eumenides, at Colonos, in the neighborhood of Athens. He has felt an inward intimation, which is strengthened by some words of the oracle received by him long since at Delphi, that his involuntary crimes have been atoned for, and that the Avenging Deities will now receive him kindly and make his cause their own.

After some natural hesitation on the part of the village-councilors of Colonos, Oedipus is received with princely magnanimity by Theseus, who takes him under the protection of Athens, and defends him against the machinations of Creon.

Thus the blessing of the Gods, which Oedipus carried with him, is secured to Athens, and denied to Thebes. The craft of Creon and the prayers of Polynices alike prove unavailing. Then the man of many sorrows, whose essential nobleness has survived them all, passes away mysteriously from the sight of men.

OEDIPUS AT COLONOS

Oedipus. Antigone, child of the old blind sire,
What land is here, what people? Who to-day
Shall dole to Oedipus, the wandering exile,
Their meager gifts? Little I ask, and less
Receive with full contentment; for my woes,
And the long years ripening the noble mind,
Have schooled me to endure.—But, O my child,
If thou espiest where we may sit, though near
Some holy precinct, stay me and set me there,
Till we may learn where we are come. 'Tis ours
To hear the will of strangers and to obey.
    Antigone. Woe-wearied father, yonder city's wall
That shields her, looks far distant; but this ground
Is surely sacred, thickly planted over
With olive, bay and vine, within whose bowers
Thick-fluttering song-birds make sweet melody.
Here then repose thee on this unhewn stone.
Thou hast traveled far to-day for one so old.
    Oedipus. Seat me, my child, and be the blind man's guard.
    Antigone. Long time hath well instructed me in that.
    Oedipus. Now, canst thou tell me where we have set our
      feet?
    Antigone. Athens I know, but not the nearer ground.
    Oedipus. Ay, every man that met us in the way
Named Athens.
    Antigone.   Shall I go, then, and find out
The name of the spot?
    Oedipus.   Yes, if 'tis habitable.
    Antigone. It is inhabited. Yet I need not go.
I see a man even now approaching here.
    Oedipus. How? Makes he towards us? Is he drawing nigh?

Antigone. He is close beside us. Whatsoe'er thou findest
Good to be spoken, say it. The man is here.

[*Enter an* ATHENIAN.

Oedipus. O stranger, learning from this maid, who sees
Both for herself and me, that thou art come
With timely light to clear our troubled thought—

Athenian. Ere thou ask more, come forth from where thou
sittest!
Ye trench on soil forbidden human tread.

Oedipus. What soil? And to what Power thus consecrate?

Athenian. None may go near, nor dwell there. 'Tis possessed
By the dread sisters, children of Earth and Night.

Oedipus. What holy name will please them, if I pray?

Athenian. 'All-seeing Gentle Powers' the dwellers here
Would call them. But each land hath its own rule.

Oedipus. And gently may they look on him who now
Implores them, and will never leave this grove!

Athenian. What saying is this?

Oedipus.   The watchword of my doom.

Athenian. Yet dare I not remove thee, till the town
Have heard my purpose and confirm the deed.

Oedipus. By Heaven, I pray thee, stranger, scorn me not,
Poor wanderer that I am, but answer me.

Athenian. Make clear thy drift. Thou'lt get no scorn from
me.

Oedipus. Then, pray thee, tell me how ye name the place
Where now I sit.

Athenian.   The region all around
Is sacred. For 'tis guarded and possessed
By dread Poseidon, and the Titan mind
That brought us fire—Prometheus. But that floor
Whereon thy feet are resting, hath been called
The brazen threshold of our land, the stay
Of glorious Athens, and the neighboring fields
Are fain to honor for their patron-god
Thee, O Colonos, first of Knights, whose name

[*Pointing to a statue*

They bear in brotherhood and own for theirs.
Such, friend, believe me, is this place, not praised
In story, but of many a heart beloved.

Oedipus. Then is the land inhabited of men?
Athenian. By men, who name them from Colonos there.
Oedipus. Have they a lord, or sways the people's voice?
Athenian. Lord Theseus, child of Aegeus, our late king.
Oedipus. Will some one of your people bring him hither?
Athenian. Wherefore? What urgent cause requires his presence?
Oedipus. He shall gain mightily by granting little.
Athenian. Who can gain profit from the blind?
Oedipus.   The words
These lips shall utter, shall be full of sight.
   Athenian. Well, thou look'st nobly, but for thy hard fate.
This course is safe. Thus do. Stay where I found thee,
Till I go tell the neighbor townsmen here
Not of the city, but Colonos. They
Shall judge for thee to abide or to depart.

                                   [*Exit.*

   Oedipus. Tell me, my daughter, is the man away?
   Antigone. He is gone, father. I alone am near.
Speak what thou wilt in peace and quietness.
   Oedipus. Dread Forms of holy Fear, since in this land
Your sanctuary first gave my limbs repose,
Be not obdurate to my prayer, nor spurn
The voice of Phoebus, who that fateful day,
When he proclaimed my host of ills to come,
Told me of rest after a weary time,
Where else but here? 'When I should reach my bourne,
And find repose and refuge with the Powers
Of reverend name, my troubled life should end
With blessing to the men who sheltered me,
And curses on their race who banished me
And sent me wandering forth.' Whereof he vouched me
Sure token, or by earthquake, or by fire
From heaven, or thundrous voices. And I know
Some aëry message from your shrine hath drawn me
With wingèd whisper to·this grove. Not else
Had ye first met me coming, nor had I
Sate on your dread unchiselled seat of stone,
With dry cold lips greeting your sober shrine.
Then give Apollo's word due course, and give

[253]

Completion to my life, if in your sight
These toils and sorrows past the human bound
Seem not too little. Kindly, gentle powers,
Offspring of primal darkness, hear my prayer!
Hear it, Athenai, of all cities queen,
Great Pallas' foster-city! Look with ruth
On this poor shadow of great Oedipus,
This fading semblance of his kingly form.

    Antigone. Be silent now. There comes an aged band
With jealous looks to know thine errand here.

    Oedipus. I will be silent, and thine arm shall guide
My footstep under covert of the grove
Out of the path, till I make sure what words
These men will utter. Warily to observe
Is the prime secret of the prudent mind.

                                [Exeunt.

    Chorus (entering). Keep watch! Who is it? Look!
Where is he? Vanished! Gone! Oh where?
    Most uncontrolled of men!
    Look well, inquire him out,
    Search keenly in every nook!
    —Some wanderer is the aged wight,
    A wanderer surely, not a native here.
    Else never had he gone within
    The untrodden grove
Of these—unmarried, unapproachable in might,
    —Whose name we dare not breathe,
    But pass their shrine
    Without a look, without a word,
Uttering the unheard voice of reverential thought.
    But now, one comes, they tell, devoid of awe,
    Whom, peering all around this grove
    I find not, where he abideth.

    Oedipus (behind). Behold me! For I 'see by sound,'
As mortals say.

    Chorus. Oh, Oh!
With horror I see him, with horror hear him speak.

    Oedipus. Pray you, regard me not as a transgressor!

    Chorus. Defend us, Zeus! Who is that aged wight?

    Oedipus. Not one of happiest fate,

Or enviable, O guardians of this land!
'Tis manifest; else had I not come hither
Led by another's eyes, not moored my bark
On such a slender stay.

    Chorus. Alas! And are thine eyes
Sightless? O full of misery,
      As thou look'st full of years!
      But not, if I prevail,
      Shalt thou bring down this curse.
      Thou art trespassing. Yet keep thy foot
      From stumbling in that verdant, voiceless dell,
      Where running water as it fills
      The hallowed bowl,
Mingles with draughts of honey. Stranger, hapless one!
      Avoid that with all care.
      Away! Remove!
      Distance impedes the sound. Dost hear,
Woe-burdened wanderer? If aught thou carest to bring
      Before our council, leave forbidden ground,
      And there, where all have liberty,
      Speak,—but till then, avaunt thee!
    Oedipus. Daughter, what must I think, or do?
    Antigone.   My sire!
We must conform us to the people's will,
Yielding ere they compel.
    Oedipus.   Give me thy hand.
    Antigone. Thou hast it.
    Oedipus.   —Strangers, let me not
Be wronged, when I have trusted you
And come from where I stood!
    Chorus. Assure thee, from this seat
No man shall drag thee off against thy will.
    Oedipus. Farther?
    Chorus.   Advance thy foot.
    Oedipus.   Yet more?
    Chorus.   Assist him onward,
Maiden, thou hast thy sight.
    Antigone. Come, follow, this way follow with thy darkened
    steps,

Father, the way I am leading thee.
Chorus. Content thee, sojourning in a strange land,
O man of woe!
To eschew whate'er the city holds in hate,
And honor what she loves!
Oedipus. Then do thou lead me, child,
Where with our feet secure from sin
We may be suffered both to speak and hear.
Let us not war against necessity.
Chorus. There! From that bench of rock
Go not again astray.
Oedipus. Even here?
Chorus. Enough, I tell thee.
Oedipus. May I sit?
Chorus. Ay, crouch thee low adown.
Crooking thy limbs, upon the stone.
Antigone. Father, this task is mine.—
Sink gently down into thy resting-place,
Oedipus. Woe is me!
Antigone. Supporting on this loving hand
Thy reverend aged form.
Oedipus. Woe, for my cruel fate!

[OEDIPUS *is seated.*

Chorus. Now thou unbendest from thy stubborn ways,
O man of woe!
Declare, what mortal wight thou art,
That, marked by troublous fortune, here art led.
What native country, shall we learn, is thine?
Oedipus. O strangers, I have none!
But do not—
Chorus. What dost thou forbid, old sir?
Oedipus. Do not, oh, do not ask me who I am,
Nor probe me with more question.
Chorus. What dost thou mean?
Oedipus. My birth is dreadful.
Chorus. Tell it forth.
Oedipus. What should I utter, O my child? Woe is me!
Chorus. Thy seed, thy father's name, stranger, pronounce!
Oedipus. Alas! What must I do? My child!
Antigone. Since no resource avails thee, speak!

Oedipus. I will. I cannot hide it further.

Chorus. Ye are long about it. Haste thee!

Oedipus.   Know ye of one
Begotten of Laïus?

Chorus.   Horror! Horror! Oh!

Oedipus. Derived from Labdacus?

Chorus.   O Heaven!

Oedipus. Fate-wearied Oedipus?

Chorus.   Art thou he?

Oedipus. Fear not my words.

Chorus.   Oh! Oh!

Oedipus. Unhappy me!

Chorus.   Oh!

Oedipus.   Daughter, what is coming?

Chorus. Away! Go forth. Leave ye the land. Begone!

Oedipus. And where, then, is the promise thou hast given?

Chorus. No doom retributive attends the deed
That wreaks prevenient wrong.
Deceit, matched with deceit, makes recompense
Of evil, not of kindness. Get thee forth!
Desert that seat again, and from this land
Unmooring speed thee away, lest on our state
Thou bring some further bale!

                                        [*Monody.*

Antigone. O strangers, full of reverent care!
Since ye cannot endure my father here,
Aged and blind,
Because ye have heard a rumor of the deeds
He did unknowingly,—yet, we entreat you,
Strangers, have pity on me, the hapless girl,
Who pray for mine own sire and for none else,
—Pray, looking in your eyes with eyes not blind,
As if a daughter had appeared to you.
Pleading for mercy to the unfortunate.
We are in your hands as in the hand of God,
Helpless. O then accord the unhoped-for boon!
By what is dear to thee, thy veriest own,
I pray thee,—chattel or child, or holier name!
Search through the world, thou wilt not find the man
Who could resist the leading of a God.

[257]

Chorus. Daughter of Oedipus, be well assured
We view with pity both thy case and his,
But fear of Heavenly wrath confines our speech
To that we have already said to you.
Oedipus. What profit lives in fame and fair renown
By unsubstantial rumor idly spread?
When Athens is extolled with peerless praise
For reverence, and for mercy!—She alone
The sufferer's shield, the exile's comforter!
What have I reaped hereof? Ye have raised me up
From yonder seat, and now would drive me forth
Fearing a name! For there is nought in me
Or deeds of mine to make you fear. My life
Hath more of wrong endured than of wrong done,
Were it but lawful to disclose to you
Wherefore ye dread me,—not my sin but theirs,
My mother's and my sire's. I know your thought.
Yet never can ye fasten guilt on me,
Who, though I had acted with the clear'st intent,
Were guiltless, for my deed requited wrong.
But as it was, all blindly I went forth
On that dire road, while they who planned my death
Planned it with perfect knowledge. Therefore, sirs,
By Heaven I pray you, as ye have bid me rise,
Protect your suppliant without fail; and do not
In jealous reverence for the blessed Gods
Rob them of truest reverence, but know this:—
God looks upon the righteousness of men
And their unrighteousness, nor ever yet
Hath one escaped who wrought iniquity.
Take part, then, with the Gods, nor overcloud
The golden fame of Athens with dark deeds;
But as ye have pledged your faith to shelter me,
Defend me and rescue, not rejecting me
Through mere abhorrence of my ruined face.
For on a holy mission am I come,
Sent with rich blessings for your neighbors here.
And when the head and sovereign of your folk
Is present, ye shall learn the truth at full.
Till then, be gracious to me, and not perverse.

Chorus. Thy meaning needs must strike our hearts with awe,
Old wanderer! so weighty are the words
That body it forth. Therefore we are content
The Lord of Athens shall decide this case.
    Oedipus. And where is he who rules this country, sirs?
    Chorus. He keeps his father's citadel. But one
Is gone to fetch him, he who brought us hither.
    Oedipus. Think you he will consider the blind man,
And come in person here to visit him?
    Chorus. Be sure he will,—when he hath heard thy name.
    Oedipus. And who will carry that?
    Chorus.   'Tis a long road;
But rumor from the lips of wayfarers
Flies far and wide, so that he needs must hear;
And hearing, never doubt but he will come.
So noised in every land hath been thy name,
Old sovereign,—were he sunk in drowsiness,
That sound would bring him swiftly to thy side.
    Oedipus. Well, may he come to bless his city and me!
When hath not goodness blessed the giver of good?

    Antigone. O Heavens! What shall I say, what think, my
      father?
    Oedipus. Daughter Antigone, what is it?
    Antigone.   I see
A woman coming toward us, mounted well
On a fair Sicilian palfrey, and her face
With brow-defending hood of Thessaly
Is shadowed from the sun. What must I think?
Is it she or no? Can the eye so far deceive?
It is. 'Tis not. Unhappy that I am,
I know not.—Yes, 'tis she. For drawing near
She greets me with bright glances, and declares
Beyond a doubt, Ismene's self is here.
    Oedipus. What say'st thou, daughter?
    Antigone.   That I see thy child,
My sister. Soon her voice will make thee sure.
                                [*Enter* ISMENE.
    Ismene. Father and sister!—names for ever dear!
Hard hath it been to find you, yea, and hard

I feel it now to look on you for grief.

Oedipus. Child, art thou here?

Ismene.   Father! O sight of pain!

Oedipus. Offspring and sister!

Ismene.   Woe for thy dark fate!

Oedipus. Hast thou come, daughter?

Ismene.   On a troublous way.

Oedipus. Touch me, my child!

Ismene.   I give a hand to both.

Oedipus. To her and me?

Ismene.   Three linked in one sad knot.

Oedipus. Child, wherefore art thou come?

Ismene.   In care for thee.

Oedipus. Because you missed me?

Ismene.   Ay, and to bring thee tidings,
With the only slave whom I could trust.

Oedipus.   And they,
Thy brethren, what of them? Were they not there
To take this journey for their father's good?

Ismene. Ask not of them. Dire deeds are theirs to-day.

Oedipus. How in all points their life obeys the law
Of Egypt, where the men keep house and weave
Sitting within-doors, while the wives abroad
Provide with ceaseless toil the means of life.
So in your case, my daughters, they who should
Have ta'en this burden on them, bide at home
Like maidens, while ye take their place, and lighten
My miseries by your toil. Antigone,
E'er since her childhood ended, and her frame
Was firmly knit, with ceaseless ministry
Still tends upon the old man's wandering,
Oft in the forest ranging up and down
Fasting and barefoot through the burning heat
Or pelting rain, nor thinks, unhappy maid,
Of home or comfort, so her father's need
Be satisfied. And thou, that camest before,
Eluding the Cadmeans, and didst tell me
What words Apollo had pronounced on me,
And when they banished me, stood'st firm to shield me.
What news, Ismene, bring'st thou to thy sire

To-day? What mission sped thee forth? I know
Thou com'st not idly, but with fears for me.
    Ismene. Father, I will not say what I endured
In searching out the place that sheltered thee.
To tell it o'er would but renew the pain.
But of the danger now encompassing
Thine ill-starred sons,—of that I came to speak.
At first they strove with Creon and declared
The throne should be left vacant and the town
Freed from pollution,—paying deep regard
In their debate to the dark heritage
Of ruin that o'ershadowed all thy race.
Far different is the strife which holds them now,
Since some great Power, joined to their sinful mind,
Incites them both to seize on sovereign sway.
Eteocles, in pride of younger years,
Robbed elder Polynices of his right,
Dethroned and banished him. To Argos then
Goes exiled Polynices, and obtains
Through intermarriage a strong favoring league,
Whose word is, 'Either Argos vanquishes
The seed of Cadmus or exalts their fame.'
This, father, is no tissue of empty talk,
But dreadful truth, nor can I tell where Heaven
Is to reveal his mercy to thy woe.
    Oedipus. And hadst thou ever hoped the Gods would care
For mine affliction, and restore my life?
    Ismene. I hope it now since this last oracle.
    Oedipus. What oracle hath been declared, my child?
    Ismene. That they shall seek thee forth, alive or dead,
To bring salvation to the Theban race.
    Oedipus. Who can win safety through such help as mine?
    Ismene. 'Tis said their victory depends on thee.
    Oedipus. When shrunk to nothing, am I indeed a man?
    Ismene. Yea, for the Gods uphold thee, who then destroyed.
    Oedipus. Poor work, to uphold in age who falls when young!
    Ismene. Know howsoe'er that Creon will be here
For this same end, ere many an hour be spent.
    Oedipus. For what end, daughter? Tell me in plain speech.
    Ismene. To set thee near their land, that thou may'st be

Beyond their borders, but within their power.

Oedipus. What good am I, thus lying at their gate?

Ismene. Thine inauspicious burial brings them woe.

Oedipus. There needs no oracle to tell one that.

Ismene. And therefore they would place thee near their land,
Where thou may'st have no power upon thyself.

Oedipus. Say then, shall Theban dust o'ershadow me?

Ismene. The blood of kindred cleaving to thy hand,
Father, forbids thee.

Oedipus.   Never, then, henceforth,
Shall they lay hold on me!

Ismene.   If that be true,
The brood of Cadmus shall have bale.

Oedipus.   What cause
Having appeared, will bring this doom to pass?

Ismene. Thy wrath, when they are marshaled at thy tomb.

Oedipus. From whom hast thou heard this?

Ismene.   Sworn messengers
Brought such report from Delphi's holy shrine.

Oedipus. Hath Phoebus so pronounced my destiny?

Ismene. So they declare who brought the answer back.

Oedipus. Did my sons hear?

Ismene.   They know it, both of them.

Oedipus. Villains, who, being informed of such a word,
Turned not their thoughts toward me, but rather chose
Ambition and a throne!

Ismene.   It wounds mine ear
To hear it spoken, but the news I bring
Is to that stern effect.

Oedipus.   Then I pray Heaven
The fury of their fate-appointed strife
May ne'er be quenched, but that the end may come
According to my wish upon them twain
To this contention and arbitrament
Of battle which they now assay and lift
The threatening spear! So neither he who wields
The sceptred power should keep possession still,
Nor should his brother out of banishment
Ever return:—who, when their sire—when I
Was shamefully thrust from my native land,

Checked not my fall nor saved me, but, for them,
I was driven homeless and proclaimed an exile.
Ye will tell me 'twas in reason that the State
Granted this boon to my express desire.
Nay; for in those first hours of agony,
When my heart raged, and it seemed sweetest to me
To die the death, and to be stoned with stones,
No help appeared to yield me that relief.
But after lapse of days, when all my pain
Was softened, and I felt that my hot spirit
Had run to fierce excess of bitterness
In wreaking mine offence—then, then the State
Drove me for ever from the land, and they,
Their father's sons, who might have saved their father,
Cared not to help him, but betrayed by them,
For lack of one light word, I wandered forth
To homeless banishment and beggary.
But these weak maidens to their nature's power
Have striven to furnish me with means to live
And dwell securely, girded round with love.
My sons have chosen before their father's life
A lordly throne and sceptred sovereignty.
But never shall they win me to their aid,
Nor shall the Theban throne for which they strive
Bring them desired content. That well I know,
Comparing with my daughter's prophecies
Those ancient oracles which Phoebus once
Spake in mine ear. Then let them send to seek me
Creon, or who is strongest in their State.
For if ye, strangers, will but add your might
To the protection of these awful Powers,
The guardians of your soil, to shelter me,
Ye shall acquire for this your State a saviour
Mighty to save, and ye shall vex my foes.
   Chorus. Thou art worthy of all compassion, Oedipus,
Thyself and these thy daughters. Now, moreover,
Since thou proclaim'st thyself our country s saviour
I would advise thee for the best.
   Oedipus.   Kind sir,
Be my good guide. I will do all thou biddest.

Chorus. Propitiate then these holy powers, whose grove
Received thee when first treading this their ground.

Oedipus. What are the appointed forms? Advise me, sirs.

Chorus. First see to it that from some perennial fount
Clean hands provide a pure drink-offering.

Oedipus. And when I have gotten this unpolluted draught?

Chorus. You will find bowls, formed by a skilful hand,
Whose brims and handles you must duly wreathe.

Oedipus. With leaves or flocks of wool, or in what way?

Chorus. With tender wool ta'en from a young ewe-lamb.

Oedipus. Well, and what follows to complete the rite?

Chorus. Next, make libation toward the earliest dawn.

Oedipus. Mean'st thou from those same urns whereof thou
speakest?

Chorus. From those three vessels pour three several streams,
Filling the last to the brim.

Oedipus.   With what contents
Must this be filled? Instruct me.

Chorus.   Not with wine,
But water and the treasure of the bee.

Oedipus. And when leaf-shadowed Earth has drunk of this,
What follows?

Chorus.   Thou shalt lay upon her then
From both thy hands a row of olive-twigs—
Counting thrice nine in all—and add this prayer—

Oedipus. That is the chief thing,—that I long to hear.

Chorus. As we have named them Gentle, so may they
From gentle hearts accord their suppliant aid;—
Be this thy prayer, or whoso prays for thee,
Spoken not aloud, but so that none may hear;
And in departing, turn not. This being done,
I can stand by thee without dread. But else,
I needs must fear concerning thee.

Oedipus.   My daughters,
Have ye both heard our friends who inhabit here?

Antigone. Yea, father; and we wait for thy command.

Oedipus. I cannot go. Two losses hinder me,
Two evils, want of strength and want of sight.
Let one of you go and perform this service.
One soul, methinks, in paying such a debt

May quit a million, if the heart be pure.
Haste, then, to do it. Only leave me not
Untended. For I cannot move alone
Nor without some one to support me and guide.
    Ismene. I will be ministrant. But let me know
Where I must find the place of offering.
    Chorus. Beyond this grove. And, stranger maid, if aught
Seem wanting, there is one at hand to show it.
    Ismene. Then to my task. Meantime, Antigone,
Watch by our sire. We must not make account
Of labor that supplies a parent's need.

                              [Exit.

    Chorus. Thy long since slumbering woe I would not wake
      again,
But yet I long to learn.
    Oedipus.   What hidden lore?
    Chorus.   The pain
That sprang against thy life with spirit-mastering force.
    Oedipus. Ah, sirs, as ye are kind, re-open not that source
Of unavoided shame.
    Chorus.   Friend, we would hear the tale
Told truly, whose wide voice doth hourly more prevail.
    Oedipus. Misery!
    Chorus.   Be not loth!
    Oedipus.   O bitterness!
    Chorus.   Consent.
For all thou didst require we gave to thy content.
    Oedipus. Oh, strangers, I have borne an all-too-willing
      brand,
Yet not of mine own choice.
    Chorus.   Whence? We would understand.
    Oedipus. Nought knowing of the curse she fastened on my
      head
Thebè in evil bands bound me.
    Chorus.   Thy mother's bed,
Say, didst thou fill? mine ear still echoes to the noise.
    Oedipus. 'Tis death to me to hear, but, these, mine only joys,
Friends, are my curse.
    Chorus.   O Heaven!

Oedipus.   The travail of one womb
Hath gendered all you see, one mother, one dark doom.
    Chorus. How? Are they both thy race, and—
    Oedipus.   Sister branches too,
Nursed at the self-same place with him from whom they grew.
    Chorus. O horror!
    Oedipus. Ay, not one, ten thousand charged me then!
    Chorus. O sorrow!
    Oedipus.   Never done, an ever-sounding strain.
    Chorus. O crime!
    Oedipus.   By me ne'er wrought.
    Chorus.   . But how?
    Oedipus.   The guerdon fell.
Would I had earned it not from those I served too well.
    Chorus. But, hapless, didst thou slay—
    Oedipus.   What seek ye more to know?
    Chorus. Thy father?
    Oedipus. O dismay! Ye wound me, blow on blow.
    Chorus. Thy hand destroyed him.
    Oedipus.   Yes. Yet lacks there not herein
A plea for my redress.
    Chorus.   How canst thou clear that sin?
    Oedipus. I'll tell thee. For the deed, 'twas proved mine,—
        Oh 'tis true!
Yet by Heaven's law I am freed:—I wist not whom I slew.

    Chorus. Enough. For lo! where Aegeus' princely son,
Theseus, comes hither, summoned at thy word.
                                    [*Enter* THESEUS.
    Theseus. From many voices in the former time
Telling thy cruel tale of sight destroyed
I have known thee, son of Laïus, and to-day
I know thee anew, in learning thou art here.
Thy raiment, and the sad change in thy face,
Proclaim thee who thou art, and pitying thee,
Dark-fated Oedipus, I fain would hear
What prayer or supplication thou preferrest
To me and to my city, thou and this
Poor maid who moves beside thee. Full of dread
Must be that fortune thou canst name, which I

Would shrink from, since I know of mine own youth,
How in strange lands a stranger as thou art
I bore the brunt of perilous circumstance
Beyond all others; nor shall any man,
Like thee an alien from his native home,
Find me to turn my face from succoring him.
I am a man and know it. To-morrow's good
Is no more mine than thine or any man's.

   Oedipus. Thy noble spirit, Theseus, in few words
Hath made my task of utterance brief indeed.
Thou hast told aright my name and parentage
And native city. Nought remains for me
But to make known mine errand, and our talk
Is ended.

   Theseus.   Tell me plainly thy desire.

   Oedipus. I come to offer thee this woe-worn frame,
As a free boon,—not goodly in outward view.
A better gift than beauty is that I bring.

   Theseus. What boon dost thou profess to have brought with
      thee?

   Oedipus. Thou shalt know by and by,—not yet awhile.

   Theseus. When comes the revelation of thine aid?

   Oedipus. When I am dead, and thou hast buried me.

   Theseus. Thou cravest the last kindness. What's between
Thou dost forget or else neglect.

   Oedipus.   Herein
One word conveys the assurance of the whole.

   Theseus. You sum up your petition in brief form.

   Oedipus. Look to it. Great issues hang upon this hour.

   Theseus. Mean'st thou in this the fortune of thy sons
Or mine?

   Oedipus.   I mean the force of their behest
Compelling my removal hence to Thebes.

   Theseus. So thy consent were sought, 'twere fair to yield.

   Oedipus. Once I was ready enough. They would not then.

   Theseus. Wrath is not wisdom in misfortune, man!

   Oedipus. Nay, chide not till thou knowest.

   Theseus.   Inform me, then!
I must not speak without just grounds.

Oedipus.   O Theseus,
I am cruelly harassed with wrong heaped on wrong.
   Theseus. Mean'st thou that prime misfortune of thy birth?
   Oedipus. No. That hath long been rumored through the
    world.
   Theseus. What, then, can be thy grief? If more than that,
'Tis more than human.
   Oedipus.   Here is my distress:—
I am made an outcast from my native land
By mine own offspring. And return is barred
For ever to the man who slew his sire.
   Theseus. How then should they require thee to go near,
And yet dwell separate?
   Oedipus.   The voice of Heaven
Will drive them to it.
   Theseus.   As fearing what reverse
Prophetically told?
   Oedipus.   Destined defeat
By Athens in the Athenian land.
   Theseus.   What source
Of bitterness 'twixt us and Thebes can rise?
   Oedipus. Dear son of Aegeus, to the Gods alone
Comes never Age nor Death. All else i' the world
Time, the all-subduer, merges in oblivion.
Earth and men's bodies weaken, fail, and perish:
Faith withers, breach of faith springs up and grows,
And neither men nor cities that are friends
Breathe the same spirit with continuing breath.
Love shall be turned to hate, and hate to love
With many hereafter, as with some to-day.
And though, this hour, between great Thebes and thee
No cloud be in the heaven, yet moving Time
Enfolds a countless brood of days to come,
Wherein for a light cause they shall destroy
Your now harmonious league with severing war,
Even where my slumbering form, buried in death,
Coldly shall drink the life-blood of my foes,
If Zeus be Zeus, and his son Phoebus true.
I would not speak aloud of mysteries.
Then let me leave where I began. Preserve

Thine own good faith, and thou shalt never say,
Unless Heaven's promise fail me, that for nought
Athens took Oedipus to dwell with her.
    Chorus. My lord, long since the stranger hath professed
Like augury of blessings to our land.
    Theseus. And who would dare reject his proffered good?
Whose bond with us of warrior amity
Hath ne'er been sundered,—and to-day he comes
A God-sent suppliant, whose sacred hand
Is rich with gifts for Athens and for me.
In reverent heed whereof I ne'er will scorn
The boon he brings, but plant him in our land.
And if it please our friend to linger here,
Ye shall protect him:—if to go with me
Best likes thee, Oedipus,—ponder, and use
Thy preference. For my course shall join with thine.
    Oedipus. Ye Heavens, reward such excellence!
    Theseus.   How, then?
Is it thy choice now to go home with me?
    Oedipus. Yea, were it lawful. But in this same spot—
    Theseus. What wouldst thou do? I'll not withstand thy will.
    Oedipus. I must have victory o'er my banishers.
    Theseus. Thy dwelling with us, then, is our great gain?
    Oedipus. Yes, if thou fail me not, but keep thy word.
    Theseus. Nay, fear not me! I will aye be true to thee.
    Oedipus. I will not bind thee, like a knave, with oaths.
    Theseus. Oaths were no stronger than my simple word.
    Oedipus. What will ye do, then?
    Theseus.   What is that thou fearest?
    Oedipus. They will come hither.
    Theseus.   Thy guards will see to that.
    Oedipus. Beware, lest, if you leave me—
    Theseus.   Tell not me,
I know my part.
    Oedipus.   Terror will have me speak.
    Theseus. Terror and I are strangers.
    Oedipus.   But their threats!
Thou canst not know—
    Theseus.   I know that none shall force
Thee from this ground against thy will. Full oft

Have threatening words in wrath been voluble,
Yet, when the mind regained her place again,
The threatened evil vanished. So to-day
Bold words of boastful meaning have proclaimed
Thy forcible adbuction by thy kin.
Yet shall they find (I know it) the voyage from Thebes,
On such a quest, long and scarce navigable.
Whate'er my thought, if Phoebus sent thee forth,
I would bid thee have no fear. And howsoe'er,
My name will shield thee from all injury.

    Chorus. Friend! in our land of conquering steeds thou art
      come
To this Heaven-fostered haunt, Earth's fairest home,
Gleaming Colonos, where the nightingale
In cool green covert warbleth ever clear,
True to the clustering ivy and the dear
      Divine, impenetrable shade,
From wildered boughs and myriad fruitage made,
Sunless at noon, stormless in every gale.
Wood-roving Bacchus there, with mazy round,
And his nymph nurses range the unoffended ground.

And nourished day by day with heavenly dew
Bright flowers their never-failing bloom renew,
From eldest time Dêo and Cora's crown
Full-flowered narcissus, and the golden beam
Of crocus, while Cephisus' gentle stream
      In runnels fed by sleepless springs
Over the land's broad bosom daily brings
His pregnant waters, never dwindling down.
The quiring Muses love to seek the spot
And Aphroditè's golden car forsakes it not.

Here too a plant, nobler than e'er was known
On Asian soil, grander than yet hath grown
In Pelops' mighty Dorian isle, unsown,
    Free, self-create, the conquering foeman's fear.
The kind oil-olive, silvery-green,
Chief nourisher of childish life, is seen

To burgeon best in this our mother-land.
No warrior, young, nor aged in command,
Shall ravage this, or scathe it with the spear;
For guardian Zeus' unslumbering eye
Beholds it everlastingly,
And Athens' gray-eyed Queen, dwelling for ever near.
Yet one more praise mightier than all I tell
O'er this my home, that Ocean loves her well,
And coursers love her, children of the wave.
To grace these roadways Prince Poseidon first
Framed for the horse, that else had burst
From man's control, the spirit-taming bit.
And the trim bark, rowed by strong arms, doth flit
O'er briny seas with glancing motion brave.
Lord of the deep! by that thy glorious gift
Thou hast established our fair town
For ever in supreme renown—
The Sea-nymphs' plashing throng glide not more smoothly
swift.

Antigone. O land exalted thus in blessing and praise,
Now is thy time to prove these brave words true.
Oedipus. What hath befallen, my daughter?
Antigone.   Here at hand,
Not unaccompanied, is Creon, father.
Oedipus. Dear aged friends, be it yours now to provide
My safety and the goal of my desire!
Chorus. It shall be so. Fear nought. I am old and weak,
But Athens in her might is ever young.

                              [*Enter* CREON.

Creon. Noble inhabiters of Attic ground,
I see as 'twere conceived within your eyes
At mine approach some new-engendered fear.
Nay, shrink not, nor let fall one fretful word.
I bring no menace with me, for mine age
Is feeble, and the state whereto I come
Is mighty,—none in Hellas mightier,—
That know I well. But I am sent to bring
By fair persuasion to our Theban plain
The reverend form of him now present here.

Nor came this mission from one single will,
But the commands of all my citizens
Are on me, seeing that it becomes my birth
To mourn his sorrows most of all the state.
Thou, then, poor sufferer, lend thine ear to me
And come. All Cadmus' people rightfully
Invite thee with one voice unto thy home,
I before all,—since I were worst of men,
Were I not pained at thy misfortunes, sir,
—To see thee wandering in the stranger's land
Aged and miserable, unhoused, unfed,
Singly attended by this girl, whose fall
To such a depth of undeservèd woe
I could not have imagined! Hapless maid!
Evermore caring for thy poor blind head,
Roving in beggary, so young, with no man
To marry her,—a mark for all mischance.
O misery, what deep reproach I have laid
On thee and me and our whole ill-starred race!
But who can hide evil that courts the day?
Thou, therefore, Oedipus, without constraint,
(By all the Gods of Cadmus' race I pray thee)
Remove this horror from the sight of men
By coming to the ancestral city and home
Of thy great sires,—bidding a kind farewell
To worthiest Athens, as is meet. But Thebes,
Thy native land, yet more deserves thy love.

    Oedipus. Thou unabashed in knavery, who canst frame
For every cause the semblance of a plea
Pranked up with righteous seeming, why again
Would'st thou contrive my ruin, and attempt
To catch me where I most were grieved being caught?
Beforetime, when my self-procurèd woes
Were plaguing me, and I would fain have rushed
To instant banishment, thou wouldst not then
Grant this indulgence to my keen desire.
But when I had fed my passion to the full,
And all my pleasure was to live at home,
Then 'twas thy cue to expel and banish me,
Nor was this name of kindred then so dear.

Now once again, when thou behold'st this city
And people joined in friendly bands with me,
Thou wouldst drag me from my promised resting-place,
Hiding hard policy with courtly show.
Strange kindness, to love men against their will!
Suppose, when thou wert eager in some suit,
No grace were granted thee, but all denied,
And when thy soul was sated, then the boon
Were offered, when such grace were graceless now;
—Poor satisfaction then were thine, I ween!
Even such a gift thou profferest me to-day,
Kind in pretense, but really full of evil.
These men shall hear me tell thy wickedness.
Thou comest to take me, not unto my home,
But to dwell outlawed at your gate, that so
Your Thebè may come off untouched of harm
From her encounter with Athenian men.
Ye shall not have me thus. But you shall have
My vengeful spirit ever in your land
Abiding for destruction,—and my sons
Shall have this portion in their father's ground,
To die thereon. Know I not things in Thebes
Better than thou? Yea, for 'tis mine to hear
Safer intelligencers,—Zeus himself,
And Phoebus, high interpreter of Heaven.
Thou bring'st a tongue suborned with false pretense,
Sharpened with insolence;—but in shrewd speech
Thou shalt find less of profit than of bane.
This thou wilt ne'er believe. Therefore begone!
Let me live here. For even such life as mine
Were not amiss, might I but have my will.

   Creon. Which of us twain, believ'st thou, in this talk
Hath more profoundly sinned against thy peace?

   Oedipus. If thou prevail'st with these men present here
Even as with me, I shall be well content.

   Creon. Unhappy man, will not even Time bring forth
One spark of wisdom to redeem thine age?

   Oedipus. Thou art a clever talker. But I know
No just man who in every cause abounds
With eloquent speech.

Creon.   'Tis not to abound in speech,
When one speaks fitting words in season.

Oedipus.   Oh!
As if thy words were few and seasonable!

Creon. Not in the dotard's judgment.

Oedipus.   Get thee gone!
I speak their mind as well—and dog not me
Beleaguering mine appointed dwelling-place!

Creon. These men shall witness—for thy word is naught;
And for thy spiteful answer to thy friends,
If once I seize thee—

Oedipus.   Who shall seize on me
Without the will of my protectors here?

Creon. Well, short of that, thou shalt have pain, I trow.

Oedipus. What hast thou done, that thou canst threaten
     thus?

Creon. One of thy daughters I have sent in charge.
This other, I myself will quickly take.

Oedipus. Oh, cruel!

Creon.   Soon thou'lt have more cause to cry.

Oedipus. Hast thou my child?

Creon.   I will have both ere long.

Oedipus. Dear friends, what will ye do? Will ye forsake
     me?
Will you not drive the offender from your land?

Chorus. Stranger, depart at once! Thou hast done wrong,
And wrong art doing.

Creon (*to attendants*). Now then, lead her away
By force, if she refuse to go with you.

Antigone. Ah me! unhappy! Whither shall I flee?
What aid of God or mortal can I find?

Chorus. What dost thou, stranger?

Creon.   I will lay no hand
On him, but on my kinswoman.

Oedipus.   Alas!
Lords of Colonos, will ye suffer it?

Chorus. Thou art transgressing, stranger.

Creon.   Nay, I stand
Within my right.

Chorus.   How so?

[274]

Creon. I take mine own.

Oedipus. Athens to aid!

Chorus. Stranger, forbear! What dost thou?
Let go, or thou shalt try thy strength with us.

Creon. Unhand me!

Chorus. Not while this intent is thine.

Creon. If you harm me, you will have war with Thebes.

Oedipus. Did I not tell you this would come?

Chorus. Release
The maid with speed.

Creon. Command where you have power.

Chorus. Leave hold, I say!

Creon. Away with her, say I!

Chorus. Come hither, neighbors, come!
My city suffers violence. Wrongful men
Are hurting her with force. Come hither to me!

Antigone. Unhappy, I am dragged away,—O strangers!

Oedipus. Where art thou, O my child?

Antigone. I go away
Against my will.

Oedipus. Reach forth thy hands, my daughter!

Antigone. I cannot.

Creon. Off with her!

Oedipus. Alas, undone!

[*Exit* ANTIGONE, *guarded.*

Creon. Thou shalt not have these staves henceforth to prop
Thy roaming to and fro. Take thine own way!
Since thou hast chosen to thwart thy nearest kin,—
Beneath whose orders, though a royal man,
I act herein,—and thine own native land.
The time will surely come when thou shalt find
That in this deed and all that thou hast done
In opposition to their friendly will,
Thou hast counseled foolishly against thy peace,
Yielding to anger, thy perpetual bane.

[*Going.*

Chorus. Stranger, stand where thou art!

Creon. Hands off, I say!

Chorus. Thou shalt not go, till thou restore the maids.

Creon. Soon, then, my city shall retain from you

A weightier cause of war. I will lay hands
Not on the maidens only.
    Chorus.   What wilt thou do?
    Creon. Oedipus I will seize and bear away.
    Chorus. Great Heaven forfend!
    Creon.   It shall be done forthwith,
Unless the ruler of this land prevent me.
    Oedipus. O shameless utterance! Wilt thou lay thy hold
On me?
    Creon.   Be silent! Speak no more!
    Oedipus.   No more?
May these dread Goddesses not close my lips
To this one prayer of evil against thee,
Thou villain, who, when I have lost mine eyes,
Bereavest me of all that I had left
To make my darkness light! Therefore I pray,
For this thy wrongful act, may He in heaven
Whose eye sees all things, Helios, give to thee
Slowly to wither in an age like mine!
    Creon. Men of this land, bear witness to his rage!
    Oedipus. They see us both, and are aware that I
Repay thee but with words for deeds of wrong.
    Creon. No longer will I curb my wrath. Though lonely
And cumbered by mine age, I will bear off
This man!
    Oedipus.   Me miserable!
    Chorus.   How bold thou art,
If standing here thou think'st to do this thing!
    Creon. I do.
    Chorus.   Then Athens is to me no city.
    Creon. Slight men prevail o'er strength in a just cause.
    Oedipus. Hear ye his words?
    Chorus.   He shall not make them good.
Be witness, Zeus!
    Creon.   Zeus knows more things than thou.
    Oedipus. Is not this violence?
    Creon.   Violence you must bear.
    Chorus. Come, chieftain of our land!
Come hither with all speed. They pass the bound.
                                  [*Enter* THESEUS.

Theseus. Wherefore that shouting? Daunted by what fear
Stayed ye me sacrificing to the God
Who guards this deme Colonos? Let me know
What cause so hastened my reluctant foot.
    Oedipus. Dear friend (I know thy voice addressing us),
One here hath lately done me cruel wrong.
    Theseus. Who is the wrong-doer, say, and what the deed?
    Oedipus. This Creon, whom thou seest, hath torn away
Two children that were all in all to me.
    Theseus. Can this be possible?
    Oedipus.   Thou hear'st the truth.
    Theseus. Then one of you run to the altar-foot
Hard by, and haste the people from the rite,
Horsemen and footmen at the height of speed
To race unto the parting of the roads
Where travelers from both gorges wont to meet.
Lest there the maidens pass beyond our reach
And I be worsted by this stranger's might
And let him laugh at me. Be swift! Away!
—For him, were I as wroth as he deserves,
He should not go unpunished from my hand.
But now he shall be ruled by the same law
He thought to enforce. Thou goest not from this ground
Till thou hast set these maids in presence here;
Since by thine act thou hast disgraced both me
And thine own lineage and thy native land,
Who with unlicensed inroad hast assailed
An ancient city, that hath still observed
Justice and equity, and apart from law
Ratifies nothing; and, being here, hast cast
Authority to the winds, and made thine own
Whate'er thou wouldst, bearing it off perforce,—
Deeming of me forsooth as nothing worth,
And of my city as one enslaved to foes
Or void of manhood. Not of Thebè's will
Come such wild courses. It is not her way
To foster men in sin, nor would she praise
Thy doing, if she knew that thou hast robbed
Me and the gods, dragging poor suppliant wights
From their last refuge at thy will.—I would not,

Had I perchance set foot within thy land,
Even were my cause most righteous, have presumed,
Without consent of him who bore chief sway,
To seize on any man, but would have known
How men should act who tread on foreign soil.
Thou bring'st disgrace on thine own mother-state
All undeservedly, and the lapse of years
Hath left thee agèd, but not wise.—Again
I bid those maids now to be brought with speed,
Unless thou would'st be made a sojourner
In Athens by compulsion. This I speak
Not with my lips alone, but from my will.

    Chorus. Stranger, dost thou perceive? Thy parentage
Is owned as noble, but thine evil deeds
Are blazoned visibly.

    Creon.   Great Aegeus' son!
Not as misprising this thy city's strength
In arms, or wisdom in debate, I dared
This capture, but in simple confidence
Thy citizens would not so envy me
My blood-relations, as to harbor them
Against my will,—nor welcome to their hearths
A man incestuous and a parricide,
The proved defiler of his mother's bed.
Such was the mount of Ares that I knew,
Seat of high wisdom, planted in their soil,
That suffers no such lawless runaways
To haunt within the borders of your realm.
Relying on that I laid my hands upon
This quarry; nor had done so, were it not
That bitterly he cursed myself and mine.
That moved me to requital, since even Age
Still bears resentment, till the power of death
Frees men from anger, as from all annoy.
Being sovereign here thou wilt do thy pleasure. I,
Though I have justice on my side, am weak
Through being alone. Yet if you meddle with me,
Old as I am, you'll find me dangerous.

    Oedipus. O boldness void of shame! Whom dost thou think
Thy obloquy most harms, this agèd head

Or thine, who hast thus let pass thy lips the crimes
I have borne unwittingly? So Heaven was pleased
To wreak some old offense upon our race.
Since in myself you will find no stain of sin
For which such ruinous error 'gainst myself
And mine own house might be the recompense.
Tell me, I pray thee, if a word from Heaven
Came to my father through the oracle
That he should die by his son's hand,—what right
Hast thou to fasten that reproach on me,
The child not yet begotten of my sire,
An unborn nothing, unconceived? Or if,
Born as I was to misery, I encountered
. And killed my father in an angry fray,
Nought knowing of what I did or whom I slew,
What reason is't to blame the unwitting deed?
And, oh, thou wretch! art not ashamed to force me
To speak that of my mother, thine own sister,
Which I will speak, for I will not keep silence,
Since thou hast been thus impious with thy tongue.
She was my mother, oh, the bitter word!
Though neither knew it, and having borne me, she
Became the mother of children to her son,
An infamous birth! Yet this I know, thy crime
Of speech against us both is voluntary.
But all involuntary was my deed
In marriage and is this mine utterance now.
No,—that shall not be called a bosom-sin,
Nor shall my name be sullied with the deed,
Thy tongue would brand on me, against my sire.
For answer me one question. If to-day,
Here, now, one struck at thee a murderous stroke,—
At thee, the righteous person,—wouldst thou ask
If such assailant were thy sire, or strike
Forthwith? Methinks, as one who cares to live,
You would strike before you questioned of the right,
Or reasoned of his kindred whom you slew.
Such was the net that snared me: such the woes
Heaven drew me to fulfil. My father's spirit,
Came he to life, would not gainsay my word.

But thou, to whom, beneath the garb of right,
No matter is too dreadful or too deep
For words, so rail'st on me, in such a presence.
Well thou dost flatter the great name of Theseus,
And Athens in her glory stablished here,
But midst thy fulsome praises thou forgettest
How of all lands that yield the immortal Gods
Just homage of true piety, this land
Is foremost. Yet from hence thou would'st beguile
Me, the aged suppliant. Nay, from hence thou would'st drag
Myself with violence, and hast reft away
My children. Wherefore I conjúre these powers,
With solemn invocation and appeal,
To come and take my part, that thou may'st know
What men they are who guard this hallowed realm.
    Chorus. My lord, the stranger deserves well. His fate
Is grievous, but the more demands our aid.
    Theseus. Enough of words. The captors and their prey
Are hasting;—we, they have wronged, are standing still.
    Creon. I am powerless here. What dost thou bid me do?
    Theseus. Lead us the way they are gone. I too must be
Thine escort, that if hereabout thou hast
Our maidens, thou mayest show them to my sight.
But if men flee and bear them, we may spare
Superfluous labor. Others hotly urge
That business, whom those robbers shall not boast
Before their Gods to have 'scaped out of this land.
Come, be our guide! Thou hast and hast not. Fortune
Hath seized thee seizing on thy prey. So quickly
Passes the gain that's got by wrongful guile.
Nay, thou shalt have no helper. Well I wot
Thou flew'st not to this pitch of truculent pride
Alone, or unsupported by intrigue;
But thy bold act hath some confederate here.
This I must look into, nor let great Athens
Prove herself weaker than one single man.
Hast caught my drift? Or is my voice as vain
Now, as you thought it when you planned this thing?
    Creon. I will gainsay nought of what thou utterest here.
But once in Thebes, I too shall know my course.

Theseus. Threaten, but go! Thou, Oedipus, remain
In quietness and perfect trust that I,
If death do not prevent me, will not rest
Till I restore thy children to thy hand.

Chorus. Soon shall the wheeling foes
    Clash with the din of brazen-throated War.
      Would I were there to see them close,
    Be the onset near or far!
    Whether at Daphnè's gorge to Phoebus dear,
      Or by the torch-lit shore
    Where kind maternal powers for evermore
    Guard golden mysteries of holy fear
      To nourish mortal souls
    Whose voice the seal of silent awe controls
    Imprinted by the Eumolpid minister.
      There, on that sacred way,
      Shall the divinest head
    Of royal Theseus, rouser of the fray,
    And those free maids, in their two squadrons led,
      Meet in the valorous fight
      That conquers for the right.

      Else, by the snow-capped rock,
    Passing to westward, they are drawing nigh
    The tract beyond the pasture high
      Where Oea feeds her flock.
    The riders ride, the rattling chariots flee
      At racing speed.—'Tis done!
    He shall be vanquished. Our land's chivalry
      Are valiant, valiant every warrior son
      Of Theseus.—On they run?
    Frontlet and bridle glancing to the light,
    Forward each steed is straining to the fight,
      Forward each eye and hand
      Of all that mounted band,
    Athena's knighthood, champions of her name
    And his who doth the mighty waters tame,
      Rhea's son that from of old
      Doth the Earth with seas enfold.

[281]

Strive they? Or is the battle still to be?
  An eager thought in me
Is pleading, 'Soon must they restore
The enduring maid, whose kinsmen vex her sore!'
To-day shall Zeus perform his will.
The noble cause wins my prophetic skill.
Oh! had I wings, and like a storm-swift dove
Poised on some aëry cloud might there descry
  The conflict from above,
Scouring the region with mine eye!

Sovran of Heaven, all-seeing Zeus, afford
  Unto this nation's lord
Puissance to crown the fair emprise,
Thou, and all-knowing Pallas, thy dread child!
Apollo, huntsman of the wild,
—Thou and thy sister, who doth still pursue
Swift many-spotted stags,—arise, arise,
With love we pray you, be our champions true!
  Yea, both together come
To aid our people and our home!
  Leader of Chorus. Ah, wanderer friend, thou wilt not have
    to accuse
Thy seer of falsehood. I behold the maids
This way once more in safe protection brought.
  Oedipus. Where? Is it true? How say you?
  Antigone.   Father, father!
Oh that some God would give thee once to see
The man whose royal virtue brings us hither!
  Oedipus. My daughters, are ye there?
  Antigone.   Saved by the arm
Of Theseus and his most dear ministers.
  Oedipus. Come near me, child, and let your father feel
The treasure he had feared for ever gone.
  Antigone. Not hard the boon which the heart longs to give.
  Oedipus. Where are ye, where?
  Antigone.   Together we draw near.
  Oedipus. Loved saplings of a solitary tree!
  Antigone. A father's heart hides all.
  Oedipus.   Staves of mine age!

Antigone. Forlorn supporters of an ill-starred life!

Oedipus. I have all I love; nor would the stroke of death
Be wholly bitter, with you standing by.
Press close to either side of me, my children;
Grow to your sire, and ye shall give me rest
From mine else lonely, hapless, wandering life.
And tell your tale as briefly as ye may,
Since at your age short speaking is enough.

Antigone. Here is our saviour. He shall tell thee all,
And shorten labor both for us and thee.

Oedipus. Think it not strange, dear friend, that I prolong
The unhoped-for greeting with my children here.
Full well I know, the joy I find in them
Springs from thee only, and from none beside.
Thou, thou alone hast saved them. May the Gods
Fulfil my prayer for thee and for thy land!
Since only in Athens, only here i' the world,
Have I found pious thought and righteous care,
And truth in word and deed. From a full heart
And thankful mind I thus requite thy love,
Knowing all I have is due to none but thee.
Extend to me, I pray thee, thy right hand,
O King, that I may feel thee, and may kiss,
If that be lawful, thy dear head! And yet
What am I asking? How can one like me
Desire of thee to touch an outlawed man,
On whose dark life all stains of sin and woe
Are fixed indelibly? I will not dare—
No, nor allow thee!—None but only they
Who have experience of such woes as mine
May share their wretchedness. Thou, where thou art
Receive my salutation, and henceforth
Continue in thy promised care of me
As true as to this moment thou hast proved.

Theseus. I marvel not at all if mere delight
In these thy daughters lengthened thy discourse,
Or led thee to address them before me.
That gives me not the shadow of annoy.
Nor am I careful to adorn my life
With words of praise, but with the light of deeds.

And thou hast proof of this. For I have failed
In nought of all I promised, agèd King!
Here stand I with thy children in full life
Unharmed in aught the foe had threatened them.
And now why vaunt the deeds that won the day,
When these dear maids will tell them in thine ear?
But let me crave thy counsel on a thing
That crossed me as I came. Small though it seem
When told, 'tis worthy of some wonder, too.
Be it small or great, men should not let things pass.

   Oedipus. What is it, O son of Aegeus? Let me hear,
I am wholly ignorant herein.

   Theseus.   We are told
One, not thy townsman, but of kin to thee,
Hath come in unawares, and now is found
Kneeling at great Poseidon's altar, where
I sacrificed, what time ye called me hither.

   Oedipus. What countryman, and wherefore suppliant there?

   Theseus. One thing alone I know. He craves of thee
Some speech, they say, that will not hold thee long.

   Oedipus. His kneeling there imports no trivial suit.

   Theseus. All he desires, they tell me, is to come,
Have speech with thee, and go unharmed away.

   Oedipus. Who can he be that kneels for such a boon?

   Theseus. Think, if at Argos thou a kinsman hast
Who might desire to obtain so much of thee.

   Oedipus. Dear friend! Hold there! No more!

   Theseus.   What troubles thee?

   Oedipus. Ask it not of me!

   Theseus.   What? Speak plainly forth.

   Oedipus. Thy words have shown me who the stranger is.

   Theseus. And who is he that I should say him nay?

   Oedipus. My son, O King,—hateful to me, whose tongue
Least of the world I could endure to hear.

   Theseus. What pain is there in hearing? Canst thou not
Hear, and refuse to do what thou mislikest?

   Oedipus. My Lord, I have come to loathe his very voice.
I pray thee, urge me not to yield in this.

   Theseus. Think that the God must be considered too;
The right of suppliants may compel thy care.

Antigone. Father, give ear, though I be young that speak.
Yield to the scruple of the King, who claims
This reverence for his people's God; and yield
To us who beg our brother may come near.
Take heart! He will not force thee from thy will.
What harm can come of hearkening? Wisdom's ways
Reveal themselves through words. He is thy son:
Whence, were his heartless conduct against thee
Beyond redemption impious, O my sire,
Thy vengeance still would be unnatural.
Oh let him!—Others have had evil sons
And passionate anger, but the warning voice
Of friends hath charmed their mood. Then do not thou
Look narrowly upon thy present griefs,
But on those ancient wrongs thou didst endure
From father and from mother. Thence thou wilt learn
That evil passion ever ends in woe.
Thy sightless eyes are no light argument
To warn thee through the feeling of thy loss.
Relent and hear us! 'Tis a mere disgrace
To beg so long for a just boon. The King
Is kind to thee. Be generous in return.
    Oedipus. Child, your dear pleading to your hard request
Hath won me. Let this be as ye desire.
Only, my lord, if he is to come near,
Let no man's power molest my liberty.
    Theseus. I need no repetition, aged friend,
Of that request. Vaunt will I not; but thou
Be sure, if Heaven protect me, thou art free.

    Chorus. Who, loving life, hath sought
        To outlive the appointed span,
      Shall be arraigned before my thought
        For an infatuate man.
      Since the added years entail
        Much that is bitter;—joy
      Flies out of ken, desire doth fail,
        The longed-for moments cloy.
      But when the troublous life,
        Be it less or more, is past,

With power to end the strife
　　Comes rescuing Death at last.
Lo! the dark bridegroom waits! No festal choir
Shall grace his destined hour, no dance, no lyre!
　　Far best were ne'er to be;
　　　But, having seen the day,
　　Next best by far for each to flee
　　　As swiftly as each may,
　　Yonder from whence he came:
　　　For once let Youth be there ·
　　With her light fooleries, who shall name
　　　The unnumbered brood of Care?
　　No trial spared, no fall!
　　　Feuds, battles, murders, rage,
　　Envy, and last of all,
　　　Despised, dim, friendless age!
Ay, there all evils, crowded in one room,
Each at his worst of ill, augment the gloom.

Such lot is mine, and round this man of woe,
　—As some gray headland of a northward shore
Bears buffets of all wintry winds that blow,—
　New storms of Fate are bursting evermore
　　In thundrous billows, borne
　　Some from the waning light,
Some through mid-noon, some from the rising
　　　morn,
　　Some from the realm of Night.

Antigone. Ah! **Who** comes here? Sure 'tis the Argive man
Approaching hitherward, weeping amain.
And, father, it is he!
　Oedipus.　　　　　Whom dost thou mean?
　Antigone. The same our thoughts have dwelt on all this
　　while,
Polynices. He is here.
　Polynices.　　　　What shall I do?
I stand in doubt which first I should lament,
My own misfortune or my father's woe,
Whom here I find an outcast in his age

[286]

With you, my sisters, in the stranger land,
Clothed in such raiment, whose inveterate filth
Horridly clings, wasting his reverend form,
While the gray locks over the eye-reft brow
Wave all unkempt upon the ruffling breeze.
And likewise miserable appears the store
He bears to nourish that time-wasted frame.
Wretch that I am! Too late I learn the truth,
And here give witness to mine own disgrace,
Which is as deep as thy distress. Myself
Declare it. Ask not others of my guilt.
But seeing that Zeus on his almighty throne
Keeps Mercy in all he doth to counsel him,
Thou, too, my father, let her plead with thee!
The evil that is done may yet be healed;
It cannot be augmented. Art thou silent?
O turn not from me, father! Speak but once!
Wilt thou not answer, but with shame dismiss me
Voiceless, nor make known wherefore thou art wroth?
O ye his daughters, one with me in blood,
Say, will not ye endeavor to unlock
The stern lips of our unrelenting sire?
Let him not thus reject in silent scorn
Without response the suppliant of Heaven!
   Antigone. Thyself, unhappy one, say why thou camest.
Speech ofttimes, as it flows, touching some root
Of pity or joy, or even of hate, hath stirred
The dumb to utterance.
   Polynices.   I will tell my need:—
First claiming for protector the dread God
From whose high altar he who rules this land
Hath brought me under safe-guard of his power,
Scatheless to speak and hear and go my way.
His word, I am well assured, will be made good,
Strangers, by you, and by my sisters twain,
And by our sire.—Now let me name mine errand.
I am banished, father, from our native land,
Because, being elder-born, I claimed to sit
Upon thy sovereign throne. For this offense
Eteocles, thy younger son, exiled me,

[287]

Not having won the advantage in debate
Or trial of manhood, but through guileful art
Gaining the people's will. Whereof I deem
Thy Fury the chief author; and thereto
Prophetic voices also testify.
For when I had come to Dorian Argolis,
I raised, through marriage with Adrastus' child,
An army bound in friendly league with me,
Led by the men who in the Apian land
Hold first pre-eminence and honor in war,
With whose aid levying all that mighty host
Of seven battalions, I have deeply sworn
Either to die, or drive from Theban ground
Those who such wrongs have wrought. So far, so well.
But why come hither? Father, to crave thine aid
With earnest supplication for myself
And for my firm allies, who at this hour,
Seven leaders of seven bands embattled there,
Encompass Thebè's plain. Amphiaráus,
Foremost in augury, foremost in war,
First wields his warlike spear. Next, Oeneus' son,
Aetolian Tydeus; then Etéoclus
Of Argive lineage; fourth, Hippomedon,
Sent by his father Tálaüs, and the fifth
Is Capaneus, who brags he will destroy
Thebè with desolating fire. The sixth,
Parthenopaeus, from the Arcadian glen
Comes bravely down, swift Atalanta's child,
Named from his mother's lingering maidenhood
Ere she conceived him. And the seventh am I,
Thy son, or if not thine, but the dire birth
Of evil Destiny, yet named thy son,
Who lead this dauntless host from Argolis
Against the Theban land. Now one and all
We pray thee on our knees, conjúring thee
As thou dost love these maids and thine own life,
My father, to forgive me, ere I go
To be revenged upon my brother there
Who drave me forth and robbed me of my throne.
If aught in prophecy deserves belief,

'Tis certain, whom thou favorest, those shall win.
Now by the wells whereof our fathers drank
And by the Gods they worshipped, hear our prayer,
Grant this petition: since alike in woe,
Alike in poverty and banishment,
Partakers of one destiny, thou and I
Cringe to the stranger for a dwelling-place.
Whilst he at home, the tyrant, woe is me,
Laughs at us both in soft luxurious pride.
Whose might, so thou wilt favor my design,
I will lightly scatter in one little hour;
And plant thee in thy Theban palace-home
Near to myself, hurling the usurper forth.
All this with thy consent I shall achieve,
But without thee, I forfeit life and all.

   Chorus. For his sake who hath brought him, Oedipus,
Say what is meet, and let him go in peace.

   Oedipus. Ay, were it not the lord of all this land
Theseus, that brought him to me and desired
He might hear words from me,—never again
Had these tones fallen upon his ear. But now
That boon is granted him: he shall obtain,
Ere he depart, such utterance of my tongue,
As ne'er shall give him joy;—ne'er comfort thee,
Villain, who when possessed of the chief power
Which now thy brother holds o'er Theban land,
Didst banish me, thy father, who stand here,
To live in exile, clothed with such attire,
That moves thy tears now that thine own estate
Is fallen into like depth of struggling woe.
But tears are bootless. Howsoe'er I live,
I must endure, and hold thee still my murderer.
'Tis thou hast girt me round with misery,
'Tis thou didst drive me forth, and driven by thee
I beg my bread, a wandering sojourner.
Yea, had these daughters not been born to me
To tend me, I were dead, for all thou hast done.
They have rescued, they have nursed me. They are men,
Not women, in the strength of ministry.
Ye are another's, not my sons.—For this

The eye of Destiny pursues thee still
Eager to light on thee with instant doom
If once that army move toward the town
Of ancient Thebes,—the *town;* no dearer name,
'City' or 'Country' shall beseem thy lip
Till ye both fall, stained with fraternal gore.
Long since I launched that curse against you twain
Which here again I summon to mine aid,
That ye may learn what duty children owe
To a parent, nor account it a light thing
That ye were cruel sons to your blind sire.
These maidens did not so. Wherefore my curse
Prevails against thy prayer for Thebè's throne,
If ancient Zeus, the eternal lawgiver,
Have primal Justice for his counselor.
Begone, renounced and fatherless for me,
And take with thee, vilest of villanous men,
This imprecation:—Vain be thine attempt
In levying war against thy father's race,
Frustrate be thy return to Argos' vale:
Die foully by a fratricidal hand,
And foully slay him who hath banished thee!
Further, I bid the horror-breathing gloom
Tartárean, of the vault that holds my sire,
To banish thee from that last home: I invoke
The Spirits who haunt this ground, and the fierce God
Who hath filled you both with this unnatural hate.—
Go now with all this in thine ears, and tell
The people of Cadmus and thy firm allies
In whom thou trustest, what inheritance
Oedipus hath divided to his sons.
    Chorus. 'Tis pity for thee, prince, to have come at all:
And now we bid thee go the way thou camest.
    Polynices. Alas! Vain enterprise, and hope undone!
Oh, my poor comrades! To what fatal end
I led you forth from Argos, woe is me!
I may not tell it you,—no, nor return.
In silence I must go to meet my doom.
Daughters of this inexorable sire,
Since now ye have heard his cruel curse on me,

Ah! in Heaven's name, my sisters, do not you
Treat me despitefully, but if, one day,
Our father's execration is fulfilled
And ye shall be restored to Theban ground,
Grace me with funeral honors and a tomb!
So shall this ample praise which ye receive
For filial ministration, in that day
Be more than doubled through your care for me.

    Antigone. Brother, I beg thee, listen to my prayer!
    Polynices. Dearest Antigone, speak what thou wilt.
    Antigone. Turn back thy host to Argos with all speed,
And ruin not thyself and Thebè too.
    Polynices. Impossible. If once I shrink for fear,
No longer may I lead them to the war.
    Antigone. But why renew thy rage? What benefit
Comes to thee from o'erturning thine own land?
    Polynices. 'Tis shameful to remain in banishment,
And let my brother mock my right of birth.
    Antigone. Then seest thou not how true unto their aim
Our father's prophecies of mutual death
Against you both are sped?
    Polynices.   He speaks his wish.
'Tis not for me to yield.
    Antigone.   O me, unhappy!
But who that hears the deep oracular sound
Of his dark words, will dare to follow thee?
    Polynices. They will not hear of danger from my mouth.
Wise generals tell of vantage, not of bale.
    Antigone. Art thou then so resolved, O brother mine?
    Polynices. I am. Retard me not! I must attend
To my dark enterprise, blasted and foiled
Beforehand by my father's angry curse.
But as for you, Heaven prosper all your way,
If ye will show this kindness in my death,
For nevermore in life shall ye befriend me!
Nay, cling to me no longer. Fare ye well.
Ye will behold my living form no more.
    Antigone. O misery!
    Polynices.   Bewail me not.
    Antigone.   And who

That saw thee hurrying forth to certain death
Would not bewail thee, brother?
   Polynices.   If fate wills,
Why, I must die.   *Antigone.*   Nay, but be ruled by me.
   Polynices. Give me not craven counsel.
   Antigone.   Woe is me,
To lose thee!
   Polynices.   Heaven hath power to guide the event
Or thus or otherwise. Howe'er it prove,
I pray that ye may ne'er encounter ill.
All men may know, ye merit nought but good.
        [*Exit. The sky is overcast—a storm is threatened.*

   Chorus. New trouble, strange trouble, deep-laden with doom,
From the sight-bereft stranger seems dimly to loom!
      Or peers Fate through the gloom?
She will move toward her mark or through shining or shade;
Since no purpose of Gods ever idly was made.
Time sees the fulfilment, who lifteth to-day
What was lowly, and trampleth the lofty to clay.
      Thunder! Heavens! what a sound!
   Oedipus. My children! Would but some one in the place
Haste hither Theseus, noblest among men!
   Antigone. Wherefore, my father? What is thy desire?
   Oedipus. These winged thunders of the Highest will soon
Bear me away to the Unseen. Send quickly!

   Chorus. Again, yonder crash through the fire-startled air
Wing'd from Zeus, rushes down, till my thin locks of hair,
      Stiff with fear, upward stare.
My soul shrinks and cowers, for yon gleam from on high
Darts again! Ne'er in vain hath it leapt from the sky,
But flies forth amain to what task Zeus hath given.
I fear the unknown fatal edict of Heaven!
      Lightning glares all around!

   Oedipus. My daughters, the divinely promised end
Here unavoidably descends on me.

Antigone. How dost thou know it? By what certain sign?
Oedipus. I know it perfectly. Let some one go
With speed to bring the lord of Athens hither.

Chorus. Great Heaven, how above me, beside me, around,
    Peals redoubled the soul-thrilling sound!
O our God, to this land, to our mother, if aught
Thou wouldst send with some darkness of destiny fraught,
Smile gently once more! With the good let me bear
    What of fortune soe'er,—
Taste no cup, touch no food, the doomed sinner may share.
    Zeus, to thee, Lord, I cry!

Oedipus. Is the King coming? Will he find me alive,
My daughters, and with reason undisturbed?
Antigone. Say wherefore dost thou crave with such desire
The clearness of an undistracted mind?
Oedipus. I would fully render from a grateful soul
The boon I promised, when I gained my suit.

Chorus (looking towards Athens). Come, my chief! come
    with speed! Or, if haply at hand,
    On the height where the curved altars stand,
Thou art hallowing with oxen in sacrifice slain
Yonder shrine of Poseidon, dread lord of the main,
Hie thee hither! Be swift! The blind stranger intends
    To thee, to thy friends,
To thy city, for burdens imposed, just amends.
    Haste thee, King! Hear our cry!
                      [*Enter* THESEUS.
Theseus. Why sounds again from hence your joint appeal,
Wherein the stranger's voice is loudly heard?
Is it some lightning-bolt new-fallen from Zeus,
Or cloud-born hail that is come rattling down?
From Heavens so black with storm nought can surprise.
Oedipus. Prince, thou art come to my desire. Some God
Hath happily directed this thy way.
Theseus. What is befallen? Son of Laïus, tell!
Oedipus. My path slopes downward, and before my death
I would confirm to Athens and to thee
My promised boon.

[293]

Theseus.   What sign dost thou perceive
That proves thine end so near?
     Oedipus.   The Gods themselves
With herald voices are proclaiming it,
Nought failing of the fore-appointed signs.
     Theseus. What are these tokens, aged monarch, say?
     Oedipus. The loud continual thunder, and the darts
That flash in volleys from the unconquered hand.
     Theseus. I may not doubt thee; for thy speech, I feel,
Hath ample witness of prophetic power.
What must I do?
     Oedipus.   I will instruct thee now,
Aegeus' great son! in rites that shall remain
An ageless treasure to thy countrymen.
I will presently, with no man guiding me,
Conduct thee to the spot, where I must die.
This is thy secret, not to be revealed
To any one of men, or where 'tis hid
Or whereabout it lies. So through all time
This neighboring mound shall yield thee mightier aid
Than many a shield and help of alien spears.
More shalt thou learn, too sacred to divulge,
When yonder thou art come thyself alone.
Since to none other of these citizens
Nor even unto the children of my love
May I disclose it. 'Tis for thee to keep
Inviolate while thou livest, and when thy days
Have ending, breathe it to the foremost man
Alone, and he in turn unto the next
Successively. So shalt thou ever hold
Athens unravaged by the dragon brood.
Cities are numberless, and any one
May lightly insult even those who dwell secure.
For the eye of Heaven though late yet surely sees
When, casting off respect, men turn to crime.
Erechtheus' heir! let that be far from thee!
A warning needless to a man so wise!
Now go we—for this leading of the God
Is urgent—to the place, nor loiter more.
This way, my children! follow me! For I

Am now your guide, as ye were mine. Come on!
Nay, touch me not, but leave me of myself
To find the holy sepulchre, wherein
This form must rest beneath Athenian soil.
Come this way! Come! This way are leading me
Guide Hermes and the Queen of realms below.
O Light, all dark to me! In former time
Bright seemed thy shining! Now thy latest ray
Sheds vital influence o'er this frame. I go
To hide the close of my disastrous life
With Hades. Kind Athenian friend, farewell!
May'st thou, thy followers, and this glorious land
Be happy, and in your endless happiness
Remember him who blessed you in his death.

                                  [Exeunt.

  Chorus. Prince of the Powers Unseen,
   Durst we with prayers adore
Thee and thy viewless Queen.
  Your aid, Aïdôneus, would our lips implore!
By no harsh-sounding doom
   Let him we love descend,
    With calm and cloudless end,
  In deep Plutonian dwelling evermore
To abide among the people of the tomb!
Long worn with many an undeservèd woe,
Just Gods will give thee glory there below.

Dread Forms, who haunt this floor,
  And thou, the Unconquered Beast,
  That hugely liest at rest
By the dim-shining adamantine door,
—Still from thy cavernous lair
  Gnarling, so legends tell,
  A tameless guard of Hell,—
Mayest thou this once thy vigilance forbear,
And leave large room for him now entering there.
Hear us, great Son of Darkness and the Deep;
On thee we call, God of the dreamless sleep!

                            [Enter MESSENGER.

Messenger. Athenian citizens, my briefest tale
Were to say singly, Oedipus is gone;
But to describe the scene enacted yonder
Craves no brief speech, nor was the action brief.
  Chorus. Then he is gone! Poor man!
  Messenger.   Know it once for all,
He hath left eternally the light of day.
  Chorus. Poor soul! What? Ended he with peace divine?
  Messenger. Ay, there is the main marvel. How he moved
From hence, thou knowest, for thou too wert here,
And saw'st that of his friends none guided him,
But he they loved was leader to them all.
Now, when he came to the steep pavement, rooted
With adamant foundation deep in Earth,
On one of many paths he took his stand
Near the stone basin, where Peirithoüs
And Theseus graved their everlasting league.
There, opposite the mass of Laurian ore,
Turned from the hollow pear-tree and the tomb
Of marble, he sate down, and straight undid
His travel-soiled attire, then called aloud
On both his children, and bade some one fetch
Pure water from a running stream. And they,
Hasting together to the neighboring hill
Of green Demeter, goddess of the Spring,
Brought back their sire's commission speedily,
And bathed, and clothed him with the sacred robe.
When he was satisfied, and nothing now
Remained undone of all he bade them do,
The God of darkness thundered, and the maids
Stood horror-stricken on hearing; then together
Fell at their father's knees and wept and wailed
Loudly and long with beating of the breast.
He, when that sound of sorrow pierced his ear,
Caressed them in his arms and said:—'My daughters,
From this day forth you have no more a father.
All that was mine is ended, and no longer
Shall ye continue your hard ministry
Of labor for my life.—And yet, though hard,
Not unendurable, since all the toil

Was rendered light through love, which ye can never
Receive on earth so richly, as from him
Bereaved of whom ye now shall live forlorn.'
Such was the talk, mingled with sobs and crying,
As each clung fast to each. But when they came
To an end of weeping and those sounds were stilled,
First all was silent; then a sudden voice
Hurried him onward, making each man's hair
Bristle on end with force of instant fear.
Now here, now there, not once but oftentimes,
A God called loudly, 'Oedipus, Oedipus!
Why thus delay our going? This long while
We are stayed for and thou tarriest. Come away!'
He, when he knew the summons of the God,
Gave word for royal Theseus to go near;
And when he came, said: 'Friend for ever kind,
Reach thy right hand, I pray thee (that first pledge)
To these my children:—daughters, yours to him!—
And give thy sacred word that thou wilt never
Betray these willingly: but still perform
All that thou mayest with true thought for their good.'
He, with grand calmness like his noble self,
Promised on oath to keep this friendly bond.
And when he had done so, Oedipus forthwith
Stroking his children with his helpless hands
Spake thus:—'My daughters, you must steel your hearts
To noble firmness, and depart from hence,
Nor ask to see or hear forbidden things.
Go, go at once! Theseus alone must stay
Sole rightful witness of these mysteries.'
Those accents were the last we all might hear.
Then, following the two maids, with checkless tears
And groans we took our way. But by and by,
At distance looking round, we saw,—not him,
Who was not there,—but Theseus all alone
Holding his hand before his eyes, as if
Some apparition unendurable
Had dazed his vision. In a little while,
We marked him making reverence in one prayer
To the Earth, and to the home of Gods on high.

But by what fate He perished, mortal man,
Save Theseus, none can say. No lightning-flash
From heaven, no tempest rising from the deep,
Caused his departure in that hour, but either
Some messenger from heaven, or, from beneath,
The lower part of Earth, where comes no pain,
Opening kindly to receive him in.
Not to be mourned, nor with a tearful end
Of sickness was he taken from the Earth,
But wondrously, beyond recorded fate.
If any deem my words unwise, I care not
In that man's judgment to be counted wise.

   Chorus. Where are those maidens and their escort? Say.
   Messenger. They are not far off, but here. The voice of
      weeping
Betokens all too plainly their approach.

   Antigone. Alas!
How manifold the inheritance of woe
Drawn from the troubled fountain of our birth!
Indelible, ineradicable grief!
For him erewhile
We had labor infinite and unrelieved,
And now in his last hour we have to tell
Of sights and sorrows beyond thought.
   Chorus.   How then?
   Antigone. Friends, ye might understand.
   Chorus.   Speak. Is he gone?
   Antigone. Gone! Even as heart could wish, had wishes
      power.
How else, when neither war, nor the wide sea
Encountered him, but viewless realms enwrapt him,
Wafted away to some mysterious doom?
Whence on our hearts a horror of night is fallen.
Woe's me! For whither wandering shall we find
Hard livelihood, by land or over sea?
   Ismene. I know not. Let dark Hades take me off
To lie in death with mine age-honored sire!
Death were far better than my life to be.
   Chorus. Noblest of maidens, ye must learn to bear

Meekly the sending of the Gods. Be not
On fire with grief. Your state is well assured.
   Antigone. If to be thus is well, then may one long
For evil to return. Things nowise dear
Were dear to me, whiles I had him to embrace.
O father! loved one! that art wearing now
The eternal robe of darkness underground,
Old as thou wert, think not this maid and I
Will cease from loving thee!
   Chorus.   He met his doom.
   Antigone. He met the doom he longed for.
   Chorus.   How was that?
   Antigone. In the strange land where he desired to die
He died. He rests in shadow undisturbed;
Nor hath he left a tearless funeral.
For these mine eyes, father, unceasingly
Mourn thee with weeping, nor can I subdue
This ever-mounting sorrow for thy loss.
Ah me! Would thou hadst not desired to die
Here among strangers, but alone with thee
There, in the desert, I had seen thee die!
   Ismene. Unhappy me! What destiny, dear girl,
Awaits us both, bereaved and fatherless?
   Chorus. His end was fortunate. He rests in peace.
Dear maidens, then desist from your complaint.
Sorrow is swift to overtake us all.

   Antigone. Thither again, dear girl, let us go speedily!
   Ismene. Say, for what end?
   Antigone.   Desire possesses me—
   Ismene. Whereof?
   Antigone. To see the darksome dwelling-place—
   Ismene. Of whom?
   Antigone.   Woe is me! Of him, our sire!
   Ismene.   But how
Can this be lawful? Seest thou not?
   Antigone.   How say'st thou?
Why this remonstrance?
   Ismene.   Seest thou not, again,
He hath no grave and no man buried him.

Antigone. Take me but where he lies. Then slay me there.

Ismene. Ah! woe is me, doubly unfortunate,
Forlorn and destitute, whither henceforth
For wretched comfort must we go?

Chorus.   Fear nought,
Dear maidens!

Ismene.   Where shall we find refuge?

Chorus.   Here,
Long since, your refuge is secure.

Antigone.   How so?

Chorus. No harm shall touch you.

Antigone.   I know that.

Chorus.   What then
Further engrosseth thee?

Antigone.   How to get home
I know not.

Chorus.   Seek not for it.

Antigone.   Weariness
O'erweighs me.

Chorus.   Hath it not before oppressed thee?

Antigone. Before, it vexed me; now it overwhelms.

Chorus. A mighty sea of misery is your lot.

Antigone. Woe is me! O Zeus! And whither must we go?
Unto what doom doth my Fate drive me now?

Chorus. Children, lament no longer. 'Tis not well
To mourn 'mongst those with whom the honored dead
Hath left the heirloom of his benison.

                                        [*Enter* THESEUS.

Antigone. Theseus, behold us falling at thy feet.

Theseus. What boon, my children, are ye bent to obtain?

Antigone. Our eyes would see our father's burial-place.

Theseus. 'Tis not permitted to go near that spot.

Antigone. O Athens' sovereign lord, what hast thou said?

Theseus. Dear children, 'twas your father's spoken will
That no man should approach his resting-place,
Nor human voice should ever violate
The mystery of the tomb wherein he lies.
He promised, if I truly kept this word,
My land would evermore be free from harm.
The power which no man may transgress and live,

The oath of Zeus, bore witness to our troth.
    Antigone. His wishes are enough. Then, pray thee, send
An escort to convey us to our home,
Primeval Thebes, if so we may prevent
The death that menaces our brethren there.
    Theseus. That will I; and in all that I may do
To prosper you and solace him beneath,—
Who even now passes to eternity,—
I must not falter. Come, lament no more.
His destiny hath found a perfect end.

SOPHOCLES
ELECTRA

→→》《←←

TRANSLATED
by
LEWIS CAMPBELL

CHARACTERS IN THE PLAY

AN OLD MAN, *formerly one of the retainers of Agamemnon.*
ORESTES, *son of Agamemnon and Clytemnestra.*
ELECTRA, *sister of Orestes.*
CHRYSOTHEMIS, *sister of Orestes and Electra.*
CLYTEMNESTRA, *Queen of Argos and Mycenae.*
AEGISTHUS, *usurping King of Argos and Mycenae, now husband of Clytemnestra.*
CHORUS *of Argive Women.*
PYLADES *appears with Orestes, but does not speak.*

The scene is laid in Mycenae, before the palace of the Pelopidae.

ARGUMENT

Agamemnon, on his return from Troy, had been murdered by his wife Clytemnestra and her paramour Aegisthus, who had usurped the Mycenean throne. Orestes, then a child, had been rescued by his sister Electra, and sent into Phocis with the one servant who remained faithful to his old master. The son of Agamemnon now returns, being of a full age, accompanied by this same attendant and his friend Pylades, with whom he has already concerted a plan for taking vengeance on his father's murderers, in obedience to the command of Apollo.

Orestes had been received in Phocis by Strophius, his father's friend. Another Phocian prince, named Phanoteus, was a friend of Aegisthus.

ELECTRA

Old Man. Son of the king who led the Achaean host
Erewhile beleaguering Troy, 'tis thine to-day
To see around thee what through many a year
Thy forward spirit hath sighed for. Argolis
Lies here before us, hallowed as the scene
Of Io's wildering pain: yonder, the mart
Named from the wolf-slaying God, and there, to our left,
Hera's famed temple. For we reach the bourn
Of far-renowned Mycenae, rich in gold.
And Pelops' fatal roofs before us rise,
Haunted with many horrors, whence my hand,
Thy murdered sire then lying in his gore,
Received thee from thy sister, and removed
Where I have kept thee safe and nourished thee
To this bright manhood thou dost bear, to be
The avenger of thy father's bloody death.
Wherefore, Orestes, and thou, Pylades,
Dearest of friends, though from a foreign soil,
Prepare your enterprise with speed. Dark night
Is vanished with her stars, and day's bright orb
Hath waked the birds of morn into full song.
Now, then, ere foot of man go forth, ye two
Knit counsels. 'Tis no time for shy delay:
The very moment for your act is come.
  Orestes. Kind faithful friend, how well thou mak'st appear
Thy constancy in service to our house!
As some good steed, aged, but nobly bred,
Slacks not his spirit in the day of war,
But points his ears to the fray, even so dost thou
Press on and urge thy master in the van.
Hear, then, our purpose, and if aught thy mind,
Keenly attent, discerns of weak or crude

In this I now set forth, admonish me.
    I, when I visited the Pythian shrine *Apollo's at Delphi*
Oracular, that I might learn whereby
To punish home the murderers of my sire,
Had word from Phoebus which you straight shall hear:
'No shielded host, but thine own craft, O King!
The righteous death-blow to thine arm shall bring.'
Then, since the will of Heaven is so revealed,
Go thou within, when Opportunity
Shall marshal thee the way, and gathering all
Their business, bring us certain cognizance.
Age and long absence are a safe disguise; *strained (credulity)*
They never will suspect thee who thou art.
And let thy tale be that another land,
Phocis, hath sent thee forth, and Phanoteus,
Than whom they have no mightier help in war.
Then, prefaced with an oath, declare thy news,
Orestes' death by dire mischance, down-rolled
From wheel-borne chariot in the Pythian course.
So let the fable be devised; while we,
As Phoebus ordered, with luxuriant locks
Shorn from our brows, and fair libations, crown
My father's sepulchre, and thence return
Bearing aloft the shapely vase of bronze
That's hidden hard by in brushwood, as thou knowest,
And bring them welcome tidings, that my form
Is fallen ere now to ashes in the fire.
How should this pain me, in pretense being dead,
Really to save myself and win renown?
No saying bodes men ill, that brings them gain.
Oft have I known the wise, dying in word,
Return with glorious salutation home.
So lightened by this rumor shall mine eye
Blaze yet like bale-star on mine enemies.
O native earth! and Gods that hold the land,
Accept me here, and prosper this my way!
Thou, too, paternal hearth! To thee I come, *he is confident*
Justly to cleanse thee by behest from heaven. *that he is doing right*
Send me not bootless, Gods, but let me found
A wealthy line of fair posterity!

[306]

I have spoken. To thy charge! and with good heed
Perform it. We go forth. The Occasion calls,
Great taskmaster of enterprise to men.

    Electra (within). Woe for my hapless lot!

    Old Man. Hark! from the doors, my son, methought there
      came
A moaning cry, as of some maid within.

    Orestes. Can it be poor Electra? Shall we stay,
And list again the lamentable sound?

    Old Man. Not so. Before all else begin the attempt
To execute Apollo's sovereign will,
Pouring libation to thy sire: this makes
Victory ours, and our success assured.

                    [Exeunt. Enter ELECTRA.
                            [Monody.

    Electra. O purest light!
And air by earth alone
Measured and limitable, how oft have ye
Heard many a piercing moan,
Many a blow full on my bleeding breast,
When gloomy night
Hath slackened pace and yielded to the day!
And through the hours of rest,
Ah! well 'tis known
To my sad pillow in yon house of woe,
What vigil of scant joyance keeping,
Whiles all within are sleeping,
For my dear father without stint I groan,
Whom not in bloody fray
The War-god in the stranger-land
Received with hospitable hand,
But she that is my mother, and her groom,
As woodmen fell the oak,
Cleft through the skull with murdering stroke.
And o'er this gloom
No ray of pity, save from only me,
Goes forth on thee,
My father, who didst die
A cruel death of piteous agony.
But ne'er will I

Cease from my crying and sad mourning lay,
While I behold the sky,
Glancing with myriad fires, or this fair day.
But, like some brood-bereavèd nightingale,
With far-heard wail,
Here at my father's door my voice shall sound.
O home beneath the ground!
Hades unseen, and dread Persephonè,
And darkling Hermes, and the Curse revered,
And ye, Erinyës, of mortals feared,
Daughters of Heaven, that ever see
Who die unjustly, who are wronged i' the bed
Of those they wed,
Avenge our father's murder on his foe!
Aid us, and send my brother to my side;
Alone I cannot longer bide
The oppressive strain of strength-o'ermastering woe.

    Chorus (*entering*). O sad Electra, child
Of a lost mother, why still flow
Unceasingly with lamentation wild
For him who through her treachery beguiled,
Inveigled by a wife's deceit,
Fallen at the foul adulterer's feet,
Most impiously was quelled long years ago?
Perish the cause! if I may lawfully pray so.

    Electra. O daughters of a noble line,
Ye come to soothe me from my troublous woe.
        I see, I know:
Your love is not unrecognized of mine.
But yet I will not seem as I forgot,
Or cease to mourn my hapless father's lot.
        Oh, of all love
That ever may you move,
This only boon I crave—
Leave me to rave!

    Chorus. Lament, nor praying breath
Will raise thy sire, our honored chief,
From that dim multitudinous gulf of death.
Beyond the mark, due grief that measureth,

Still pining with excess of pain
Thou urgest lamentation vain,
That from thy woes can bring thee no relief.
Why hast thou set thy heart on unavailing grief?
   Electra. Senseless were he who lost from thought
A noble father, lamentably slain!
       I love thy strain,
Bewildered mourner, bird divinely taught,
For 'Itys,' 'Itys,' ever heard to pine.
O Niobè, I hold thee all divine,
       Of sorrows queen,
Who with all tearful mien
Insepulchred in stone
Aye makest moan.
   Chorus. Not unto thee alone hath sorrow come,
Daughter, that thou shouldst carry grief so far
Beyond those dwellers in the palace-home
       Who of thy kindred are
And own one source with thee.
       What life hath she,
Chrysothemis, and Iphianassa bright,
       And he whose light
Is hidden afar from taste of horrid doom,
Youthful Orestes, who shall come
To fair Mycenae's glorious town,
Welcomed as worthy of his sire's renown,
Sped by great Zeus with kindly thought,
And to this land with happiest omen brought?
   Electra. Awaiting him I endlessly endure;
Unwed and childless still I go,
       With tears in constant flow,
Girt round with misery that finds no cure.
But he forgets his wrong and all my teaching.
What message have I sent beseeching,
But baffled flies back idly home?
Ever he longs, he saith, but, longing, will not come.
   Chorus. Take heart, dear child! still mighty in the sky
Is Zeus who ruleth all things and surveys.
Commit to him thy grief that surgeth high,
       And walk in safer ways,

Let not hate vex thee sore,
          Nor yet ignore
The cause of hate and sorrow in thy breast.
          Time bringeth rest:
All is made easy through his power divine.
The heir of Agamemnon's line
Who dwells by Crisa's pastoral strand
Shall yet return unto his native land;
And he shall yet regard his own
Who reigns beneath upon his Stygian throne.

Electra. Meanwhile my life falls from me in despair.
Years pass and patience nought avails:
          My heart within me fails:
Orphaned I pine without protecting care;
And like a sojourner all unregarded
At slave-like labor unrewarded
I toil within my father's hall
Thus meanly attired, and starved, a table-serving thrall.

Clyt. has been mistress here.

Chorus. Sad was thy greeting when he reached the strand,
Piteous thy crying where thy father lay
          On that fell day
When the bronze edge with dire effect was driven.
          By craft 'twas planned,
By frenzied lust the blow was given:
Mother and father of a monstrous birth,
Whether a God there wrought or mortal of the Earth.

Electra. O day beyond all days that yet have rolled
Most hateful in thy course of light!
          O horror of that night!
O hideous feast, abhorr'd, not to be told!
How could I bear it, when my father's eye
Saw death advancing from the ruthless pair,
          Conjoint in cruel villany,
By whom my life was plunged in black despair?
Oh, to the workers of such deeds as these
          May great Olympus' Lord
Return of evil still afford,
Nor let them wear the gloss of sovran ease!

Chorus. Take thought to keep thy crying within bound.
Doth not thy sense enlighten thee to see

How recklessly
Even now thou winnest undeservèd woe?
          Still are thou found
To make thy misery overflow
Through self-bred gloomy strife. But not for long
Shall one alone prevail who strives against the strong.
          Electra. 'Twas dire oppression taught me my complaint
I know my rage a quenchless fire:
                    But nought, however dire,
Shall visit this my frenzy with restraint,
Or check my lamentation while I live.
Dear friends, kind women of true Argive breed,
Say, who can timely counsel give
Or word of comfort suited to my need?
Beyond all cure shall this my cause be known.
                    No counsels more! Ah leave,
Vain comforters, and let me grieve
With ceaseless pain, unmeasured in my moan.
          Chorus. With kind intent
Full tenderly my words are meant;
Like a true mother pressing heart to heart,
I pray thee, do not aggravate thy smart.
          Electra. But have my miseries a measure? Tell.
                    Can it be well
To pour forgetfulness upon the dead?
                    Hath mortal head
Conceived a wickedness so bold?
O never may such brightness shine for me,
                    Nor let me peaceful be
With aught of good my life may still enfold,
If from wide echoing of my father's name
The wings of keen lament I must withhold.
                    Sure holy shame
And pious care would vanish among men,
If he, mere earth and nothingness, must lie
In darkness, and his foes shall not again
Render him blood for blood in amplest penalty.
          Leader of Chorus. Less from our own desires, my child,
          we came,
Than for thy sake. But, if we speak amiss,

[311]

Take thine own course. We still will side with thee.
   Electra. Full well I feel that too impatiently
I seem to multiply the sounds of woe.
Yet suffer me, dear women! Mighty force
Compels me. Who that had a noble heart
And saw her father's cause, as I have done,
By day and night more outraged, could refrain?
Are my woes lessening? Are they not in bloom?—
My mother full of hate and hateful proved,
Whilst I in my own home must dwell with these,
My father's murderers, and by them be ruled,
Dependent on their bounty even for bread.
And then what days suppose you I must pass,
When I behold Aegisthus on the throne
That was my father's; when I see him wear
Such robes, and pour libations by the hearth
Where he destroyed him; lastly, when I see
Their crowning insolence,—our regicide
Laid in my father's chamber beside her,
My mother—if she still must bear the name
When resting in those arms? Her shame is dead.
She harbors with blood-guiltiness, and fears
No vengeance, but, as laughing at the wrong,
She watches for the hour wherein with guile
She killed our sire, and orders dance and mirth
That day o' the month, and joyful sacrifice
Of thanksgiving. But I within the house
Beholding, weep and pine, and mourn that feast
Of infamy, called by my father's name,
All to myself; for not even grief may flow
As largely as my spirit would desire.
That so-called princess of a noble race
O'ercrows my wailing with loud obloquy:
'Hilding! are you alone in grief? Are none
Mourning for loss of fathers but yourself?
'Fore the blest Gods! ill may you thrive, and ne'er
Find cure of sorrow from the powers below!'
So she insults: unless she hear one say
'Orestes will arrive': then standing close,
She shouts like one possessed into mine ear,

'These are your doings, this your work, I trow.
You stole Orestes from my gripe, and placed
His life with fosterers; but you shall pay
Full penalty.' So harsh is her exclaim.
And he at hand, the husband she extols,
Hounds on the cry, that prince of cowardice,
From head to foot one mass of pestilent harm,
Tongue-doughty champion of this women's-war.
I, for Orestes ever languishing
To end this, am undone. For evermore
Intending, still delaying, he wears out
All hope, both here and yonder. How, then, friends,
Can I be moderate, or feel the touch
Of holy resignation? Evil fruit
Cannot but follow on a life of ill.
   Chorus. Say, is Aegisthus near while thus you speak?
Or hath he left the palace? We would know.
   Electra. Most surely. Never think, if he were by,
I could stray out of door. He is abroad.
   Chorus. Then with less fear I may converse with thee.
   Electra. Ask what you will, for he is nowhere near.
   Chorus. First of thy brother I beseech thee tell,
How deem'st thou? Will he come, or still delay?
   Electra. His promise comes, but still performance sleeps.
   Chorus. Well may he pause who plans a dreadful deed.
   Electra. I paused not in his rescue from the sword.
   Chorus. Fear not. He will bestead you. He is true.
   Electra. But for that faith my life had soon gone by.
   Chorus. No more! I see approaching from the house
Thy sister by both parents of thy blood,
Chrysothemis; in her hand an offering,
Such as old custom yields to those below.
                 [*Enter* CHRYSOTHEMIS.
   Chrysothemis. What converse keeps thee now beyond the
     gates,
Dear sister? why this talk in the open day?
Wilt thou not learn after so long to cease
From vain indulgence of a bootless rage?
I know in my own breast that I am pained
By what thou griev'st at, and if I had power,

Chrys. brings out character of Electra — contrast method.

My censure of their deeds would soon be known.
But in misfortune I have chosen to sail
With lowered canvas, rather than provoke
With puny strokes invulnerable foes.
I would thou didst the like: though I must own
The right is on thy side, and not on mine.
But if I mean to dwell at liberty,
I must obey in all the stronger will.
 Electra. 'Tis strange and pitiful, thy father's child
Can leave him in oblivion and subserve
The mother. All thy schooling of me springs
From her suggestion, not of thine own wit.
Sure, either thou art senseless, or thy sense
Deserts thy friends. Treason or dullness then?
Choose!—You declared but now, if you had strength,
You would display your hatred of this pair.
Yet, when I plan full vengeance for my sire,
You aid me not, but turn me from the attempt.
What's this but adding cowardice to evil?
For tell me, or be patient till I show,
What should I gain by ceasing this my moan?
I live to vex them:—though my life be poor,
Yet that suffices, for I honor him,
My father,—if affection touch the dead.
You say you hate them, but belie your word,
Consorting with our father's murderers.
I then, were all the gifts in which you glory
Laid at my feet, will never more obey
This tyrant power. I leave you your rich board
And life of luxury. Ne'er be it mine to feed
On dainties that would poison my heart's peace!
I care not for such honor as thou hast.
Nor wouldst thou care if thou wert wise. But now,
Having the noblest of all men for sire,
Be called thy mother's offspring; so shall most
Discern thine infamy and traitorous mind
To thy dead father and thy dearest kin.
 Chorus. No anger, we entreat. Both have said well,
If each would learn of other, and so do.

usual character always trying to calm conflicted character.

Chrysothemis. For my part, women, use hath seasoned me
To her discourse. Nor had I spoken of this,
Had I not heard a horror coming on
That will restrain her from her endless moan.

Electra. Come speak it forth, this terror! I will yield,
If thou canst tell me worse than I endure.

Chrysothemis. I'll tell thee all I know. If thou persist
In these thy wailings, they will send thee far
From thine own land, and close thee from the day,
Where in a rock-hewn chamber thou may'st chant
Thine evil orisons in darkness drear.
Think of it, while there's leisure to reflect;
Or if thou suffer, henceforth blame me not.

Electra. And have they so determined on my life?

Chrysothemis. 'Tis certain; when Aegisthus comes again.

Electra. If that be all, let him return with speed!

Chrysothemis. Unhappy! why this curse upon thyself?

Electra. If this be their intent, why, let him come!

Chrysothemis. To work such harm on thee! What thought is this?

Electra. Far from mine eye to banish all your brood.

Chrysothemis. Art not more tender of the life thou hast?

Electra. Fair, to a marvel, is my life, I trow!

Chrysothemis. It would be, couldst thou be advised for good.

Electra. Never advise me to forsake my kin.

Chrysothemis. I do not: only to give place to power.

Electra. Thine be such flattery. 'Tis not my way.

Chrysothemis. Sure, to be wrecked by rashness is not well.

Electra. Let me be wrecked in 'venging my own sire.

Chrysothemis. I trust his pardon for my helplessness.

Electra. Such talk hath commendation from the vile.

Chrysothemis. Wilt thou not listen? Wilt thou ne'er be ruled?

Electra. No; not by thee! Let me not sink so low.

Chrysothemis. Then I will hie me on mine errand straight.

Electra. Stay; whither art bound? For whom to spend those gifts?

Chrysothemis. Sent by my mother to my father's tomb
To pour libations to him.

Electra.   How? To him?

Most hostile to her of all souls that are?

    Chrysothemis. Who perished by her hand—so thou wouldst
    say.

    Electra. What friend hath moved her? Who hath cared for
    this?

    Chrysothemis. Methinks 'twas some dread vision, seen by
    night.

    Electra. Gods of my father, O be with me now!

    Chrysothemis. What? are thou hopeful from the fear I spake
    of?

    Electra. Tell me the dream, and I will answer thee.

    Chrysothemis. I know but little of it.

    Electra.   Speak but that.
A little word hath ofttimes been the cause
Of ruin or salvation unto men.

    Chrysothemis. 'Tis said she saw our father's spirit come
Once more to visit the abodes of light;
Then take and firmly plant upon the hearth
The scepter which he bore of old, and now
Aegisthus bears: and out of this upsprang
A burgeoned shoot, that shadowed all the ground
Of loved Mycenae. So I heard the tale
Told by a maid who listened when the Queen
Made known her vision to the God of Day.
But more than this I know not, save that I
Am sent by her through terror of the dream.
And I beseech thee by the Gods we serve
To take my counsel and not rashly fall.
If thou repel me now, the time may come
When suffering shall have brought thee to my side.

    Electra. Now, dear Chrysothemis, of what thou bearest
Let nothing touch his tomb. 'Tis impious
And criminal to offer to thy sire
Rites and libations from a hateful wife.
Then cast them to the winds, or deep in dust
Conceal them, where no particle may reach
His resting-place: but lie in store for her
When she goes underground. Sure, were she not
Most hardened of all women that have been,
She ne'er had sent those loveless offerings

.To grace the sepulcher of him she slew.
For think how likely is the buried king
To take such present kindly from her hand,
Who slew him like an alien enemy,
Dishonored even in death, and mangled him,
And wiped the death-stain with his flowing locks—
Sinful purgation! Think you that you bear
In those cold gifts atonement for her guilt?
It is not possible. Wherefore let be.
But take a ringlet from thy comely head,
And this from mine, that lingers on my brow
Longing to shade his tomb. Ah, give it to him,
All I can give, and this my maiden-zone,
Not daintily adorned, as once erewhile.
Then, humbly kneeling, pray that from the ground
He would arise to help us 'gainst his foes,
And grant his son Orestes with high hand
Strongly to trample on his enemies;
That in our time to come from ampler stores
We may endow him, than are ours to-day.
I cannot but imagine that his will
Hath part in visiting her sleep with fears.
But howsoe'er, I pray thee, sister mine,
Do me this service, and thyself, and him,
Dearest of all the world to me and thee,
The father of us both, who rests below.
   Chorus. She counsels piously; and thou, dear maid,
If thou art wise, wilt do her bidding here. *out of character(?)*
   Chrysothemis. Yea, when a thing is right, it is not well
Idly to wrangle, but to act with speed.
Only, dear friends, in this mine enterprise,
Let me have silence from your lips, I pray;
For should my mother know of it, sharp pain
Will follow yet my bold adventurous feat.
                                 [*Exit* CHRYSOTHEMIS.

1st stasimon

  Chorus. An erring seer am I,
     Of sense and wisdom lorn,
     If this prophetic Power of right,
     O'ertaking the offender, come not nigh
       Ere many an hour be born.

[317]

Yon vision of the night,
That lately breathed into my listening ear,
Hath freed me, O my daughter, from all fear.
Sweet was that bodement. He doth not forget,
The Achaean lord that gave thee being, nor yet
The bronzen-griding axe, edged like a spear,
Hungry and keen, though dark with stains of time,
That in the hour of hideous crime
Quelled him with cruel butchery:
That, too, remembers, and shall testify.

From ambush deep and dread
With power of many a hand
And many hastening feet shall spring
The Fury of the adamantine tread,
    Visiting Argive land
    Swift recompense to bring
For eager dalliance of a blood-stained pair
Unhallowed, foul, forbidden. No omen fair,—
Their impious course hath fixed this in my soul,—
Nought but black portents full of blame shall roll
Before their eyes that wrought or aided there.
Small force of divination would there seem
In prophecy or solemn dream,
Should not this vision of the night
Reach harbor in reality aright.

O chariot-course of Pelops, full of toil!
    How wearisome and sore
Hath been thine issue to our native soil!—
Since, from the golden car
Hurled to the deep afar,
    Myrtilus sank and slept,
Cruelly plucked from that fell chariot-floor,
This house unceasingly hath kept
Crime and misfortune mounting evermore.
                              [*Enter* CLYTEMNESTRA.

Clytemnestra. Again you are let loose and range at will.
Ay, for Aegisthus is not here, who barred
Your rashness from defaming your own kin

[318]

Beyond the gates. But now he's gone from home,
You heed not me: though you have noised abroad
That I am bold in crime, and domineer
Outrageously, oppressing thee and thine.
I am no oppressor, but I speak thee ill,
For thou art ever speaking ill of me—
Still holding forth thy father's death, that I
Have done it. So I did: I know it well:
That I deny not; for not I alone
But Justice slew him; and if you had sense,
To side with Justice ought to be your part.
For who but he of all the Greeks, your sire,
For whom you whine and cry, who else but he
Took heart to sacrifice unto the Gods
Thy sister?—having less of pain, I trow,
In getting her, than I, that bore her, knew!
Come, let me question thee! On whose behalf
Slew he my child? Was't for the Argive host?
What right had they to traffic in my flesh?—
Menelaüs was his brother. Wilt thou say
He slew my daughter for his brother's sake?
How then should he escape me? Had not he,
Menelaüs, children twain, begotten of her
Whom to reclaim that army sailed to Troy?
Was Death then so enamored of my seed,
That he must feast thereon and let theirs live?
Or was the God-abandoned father's heart
Tender toward them and cruel to my child?
Doth this not argue an insensate sire?
I think so, though your wisdom may demur.
And could my lost one speak, she would confirm it.
For my part, I can dwell on what I have done
Without regret. You, if you think me wrong,
Bring reasons forth and blame me to my face!

Electra. Thou canst not say this time that I began
And brought this on me by some taunting word.
But, so you'd suffer me, I would declare
The right both for my sister and my sire.

Clytemnestra. Thou hast my sufferance. Nor would hearing
vex,

[319]

If ever thus you tuned your speech to me.
    Electra. Then I will speak. You say you slew him. Where
Could there be found confession more depraved,
Even though the cause were righteous? But I'll prove
No rightful vengeance drew thee to the deed,
But the vile bands of him you dwell with now.
Or ask the huntress Artemis, what sin
She punished, when she tied up all the winds
Round Aulis.—I will tell thee, for her voice
Thou ne'er may'st hear! 'Tis rumored that my sire,
Sporting within the goddess' holy ground,
His foot disturbed a dappled hart, whose death
Drew from his lips some rash and boastful word.
Wherefore Latona's daughter in fell wrath
Stayed the army, that in quittance for the deer
My sire should slay at the altar his own child.
So came her sacrifice. The Achaean fleet
Had else no hope of being launched to Troy
Nor to their homes. Wherefore, with much constraint
And painful urging of his backward will,
Hardly he yielded;—not for his brother's sake.
But grant thy speech were sooth, and all were done
In aid of Menelaüs; for this cause
Hadst thou the right to slay him? What high law
Ordaining? Look to it, in establishing
Such precedent thou dost not lay in store
Repentance for thyself. For if by right
One die for one, thou first wilt be destroyed
If Justice find thee.—But again observe
The hollowness of thy pretended plea.
Tell me, I pray, what cause thou dost uphold
In doing now the basest deed of all,
Chambered with the blood-guilty, with whose aid
Thou slewest our father in that day. For him
You now bear children—ousting from their right
The stainless offspring of a holy sire. — *he is perfect in his ways*
How should this plead for pardon? Wilt thou say
Thus thou dost 'venge thy daughter's injury?
O shameful plea? Where is the thought of honor,
If foes are married for a daughter's sake?—

Enough. No words can move thee. Thy rash tongue
With checkless clamor cries that we revile
Our mother. Nay, no mother, but the chief
Of tyrants to us! For my life is full
Of weariness and misery from thee
And from thy paramour. While he abroad,
Orestes, our one brother, who escaped
Hardly from thy attempt, unhappy boy!
Wears out his life, victim of cross mischance.
Oft hast thou taunted me with fostering him
To be thy punisher. And this, be sure,
Had I but strength, I had done. Now for this word,
Proclaim me what thou wilt,—evil in soul,
Or loud in cursing, or devoid of shame:
For if I am infected with such guilt,
Methinks my nature is not fallen from thine.
    Chorus (*looking at* CLYTEMNESTRA). I see her fuming with
      fresh wrath: the thought
Of justice enters not her bosom now.
    Clytemnestra. What thought of justice should be mine for
      her,
Who at her age can so insult a mother?
Will shame withhold her from the wildest deed?
    Electra. Not unashamed, assure thee, I stand here,
Little as thou mayest deem it. Well I feel
My acts untimely and my words unmeet.
But your hostility and treatment force me
Against my disposition to this course.
Harsh ways are taught by harshness.
    Clytemnestra.   Brazen thing!
Too true it is that words and deeds of mine
Are evermore informing thy harsh tongue.
    Electra. The shame is yours, because the deeds are yours.
My words are but their issue and effect.
    Clytemnestra. By sovereign Artemis, whom still I serve,
You'll rue this boldness when Aegisthus comes.
    Electra. See now, your anger bears you off, and ne'er
Will let you listen, though you gave me leave.
    Clytemnestra. Must I not even sacrifice in peace
From your harsh clamor, when you've had your say?

Electra. I have done. I check thee not. Go, sacrifice!
Accuse not me of hindering piety.

    Clytemnestra (to an attendant). Then lift for me those fruit-
        ful offerings,
While to Apollo, before whom we stand,
I raise my supplication for release
From doubts and fears that shake my bosom now.
And, O defender of our house! attend
My secret utterance. No friendly ear
Is that which hearkens for my voice. My thought
Must not be blazoned with her standing by,
Lest through her envious and wide-babbling tongue
She fill the city full of wild surmise.
List, then, as I shall speak: and grant the dreams
Whose twofold apparition I to-night
Have seen, if good their bodement, be fulfilled:
If hostile, turn their influence on my foes.
And yield not them their wish that would by guile
Thrust me from this high fortune, but vouchsafe
That ever thus exempt from harms I rule
The Atridae's home and kingdom, in full life,
Partaking with the friends I live with now
All fair prosperity, and with my children,
Save those who hate and vex me bitterly.
Lykeian Phoebus, favorably hear   .
My prayer, and grant to all of us our need!
More is there, which, though I be silent here,
A God should understand. No secret thing
Is hidden from the all-seeing sons of Heaven.

                          [Enter the OLD MAN.

    Old Man. Kind dames and damsels, may I clearly know
If these be King Aegisthus' palace-halls?

    Chorus. They are, sir; you yourself have guessed aright.

    Old Man. May I guess further that in yonder dame
I see his queen? She looks right royally.

    Chorus. 'Tis she,—no other,—whom your eyes behold.

    Old Man. Princess, all hail! To thee and to thy spouse
I come with words of gladness from a friend.

    Clytemnestra. That auspice I accept. But I would first
Learn from thee who of men hath sent thee forth?

                          [322]

Old Man. Phanoteus the Phocian, with a charge of weight.
Clytemnestra. Declare it, stranger. Coming from a friend,
Thou bring'st us friendly tidings, I feel sure.
Old Man. Orestes' death. Ye have the sum in brief.
Electra. Ah me! undone! This day hath ruined me.
Clytemnestra. What? Let me hear again. Regard her not.
Old Man. Again I say it, Orestes is no more.
Electra. Undone! undone! Farewell to life and hope!
Clytemnestra (*to* ELECTRA). See thou to thine own case!
  (*To* OLD MAN). Now, stranger, tell me
In true discourse the manner of his death.
Old Man. For that I am here, and I will tell the whole.
He, entering on the great arena famed
As Hellas' pride, to win a Delphian prize,
On hearing the loud summons of the man
Calling the foot-race, which hath trial first,
Came forward, a bright form, admired by all.
And when his prowess in the course fulfilled
The promise of his form, he issued forth
Dowered with the splendid meed of victory.—
To tell a few out of the many feats
Of such a hero were beyond my power.
Know then, in brief, that of the prizes set
For every customary course proclaimed
By order of the judges, the whole sum
Victoriously he gathered, happy deemed
By all; declared an Argive, and his name
Orestes, son of him who levied once
The mighty armament of Greeks for Troy.
So fared he then: but when a God inclines
To hinder happiness, not even the strong
Are scatheless. So, another day, when came
At sunrise the swift race of charioteers,
He entered there with many a rival car:—
One from Achaia, one from Sparta, two
Libyan commanders of the chariot-yoke;
And he among them fifth, with steeds of price
From Thessaly;—the sixth Aetolia sent
With chestnut mares; the seventh a Magnete man;
The eighth with milk-white colts from Oeta's vale;

[323]

The ninth from god-built Athens; and the tenth
Boeotia gave to make the number full.
Then stood they where the judges of the course
Had posted them by lot, each with his team;
And sprang forth at the brazen trumpet's blare.
Shouting together to their steeds, they shook
The reins, and all the course was filled with noise
Of rattling chariots, and the dust arose
To heaven. Now all in a confusèd throng
Spared not the goad, each eager to outgo
The crowded axles and the snorting steeds;
For close about his nimbly circling wheels
And stooping sides fell flakes of panted foam.
Orestes, ever nearest at the turn,
With whirling axle seemed to graze the stone,
And loosing with free rein the right-hand steed
That pulled the side-rope, held the near one in.
　　So for a time all chariots upright moved,
But soon the Oetaean's hard-mouthed horses broke
From all control, and wheeling as they passed
From the sixth circuit to begin the seventh,
Smote front to front against the Barcan car.
And when that one disaster had befallen,
Each dashed against his neighbor and was thrown,
Till the whole plain was strewn with chariot-wreck.
Then the Athenian, skilled to ply the rein,
Drew on one side, and heaving to, let pass
The rider-crested surge that rolled i' the midst.
Meanwhile Orestes, trusting to the end,
Was driving hindmost with tight rein; but now,
Seeing him left the sole competitor,
Hurling fierce clamor through his steeds, pursued:
So drave they yoke by yoke—now this, now that
Pulling ahead with car and team. Orestes,
Ill-fated one, each previous course had driven
Safely without a check, but after this,
In letting loose again the left-hand rein,
He struck the edge of the stone before he knew,
Shattering the axle's end, and tumbled prone,
Caught in the reins, that dragged him with sharp thongs.

Then as he fell to the earth the horses swerved,
And roamed the field. The people when they saw
Him fallen from out the car, lamented loud
For the fair youth, who had achieved before them
Such glorious feats, and now had found such woe,—
Dashed on the ground, then tossed with legs aloft
Against the sky,—until the charioteers,
Hardly restraining the impetuous team,
Released him, covered so with blood that none,—
No friend who saw—had known his hapless form.
Which then we duly burned upon the pyre.
And straightway men appointed to the task
From all the Phocians bear his mighty frame—
Poor ashes! narrowed in a brazen urn,—
That he may find in his own fatherland
His share of sepulture.—Such our report,
Painful to hear, but unto us, who saw,
The mightiest horror that e'er met mine eye.

    Chorus. Alas! the stock of our old masters, then,
Is utterly uprooted and destroyed.

    Clytemnestra. O heavens! what shall I say? That this is
      well?
Or terrible, but gainful? Hard my lot,
To save my life through my calamity!

    Old Man. Lady, why hath my speech disheartened thee?

    Clytemnestra. To be a mother hath a marvelous power:
No injury can make one hate one's child.

    Old Man. Then it should seem our coming was in vain.

    Clytemnestra. In vain? Nay, verily; thou, that hast brought
Clear evidences of his fate, who, sprung
From my life's essence, severed from my breast
And nurture, was estranged in banishment,
And never saw me from the day he went
Out from this land, but for his father's blood
Threatened me still with accusation dire;
That sleep nor soothed at night nor sweetly stole
My senses from the day, but, all my time,
Each instant led me on the way to death!—
But this day's chance hath freed me from all fear
Of him, and of this maid: who being at home

Troubled me more, and with unmeasured thirst
Kept draining my life-blood; but now her threats
Will leave us quiet days, methinks, and peace
Unbroken.—How then shouldst thou come in vain?
  Electra. O misery! 'Tis time to wail thy fate,
Orestes, when, in thy calamity,
Thy mother thus insults thee. Is it well?
  Clytemnestra. 'Tis well that he is gone, not that you live.
  Electra. Hear, 'venging spirits of the lately dead!
  Clytemnestra. The avenging spirits have heard and answered
    well.
  Electra. Insult us now, for thou art fortunate!
  Clytemnestra. You and Orestes are to quench my pride.
  Electra. Our pride is quenched. No hope of quenching thee!
  Clytemnestra. A world of good is in thy coming, stranger,
Since thou hast silenced this all-clamorous tongue.
  Old Man. Then I may go my way, seeing all is well.
  Clytemnestra. Nay, go not yet! That would disgrace alike
Me and the friend who sent you to our land.
But come thou in, and leave her out of door
To wail her own and loved ones' overthrow.
                    [*Exeunt* CLYTEMNESTRA *and* OLD MAN.
  Electra. Think you the wretch in heartfelt agony
Weeps inconsolably her perished son?
She left us with a laugh! O misery!
How thou hast ruined me, dear brother mine,
By dying! Thou hast torn from out my heart
The only hope I cherished yet, that thou
Living wouldst come hereafter to avenge
Thy father's woes and mine. Where must I go?
Since I am left of thee and of my sire
Bereaved and lonely, and once more must be
The drudge and menial of my bitterest foes,
My father's murderers. Say, is it well?
Nay, nevermore will I consort with these,
But sinking here before the palace gate,
Thus, friendless, I will wither out my life.
Hereat if any in the house be vexed,
Let them destroy me; for to take my life

Were kindness, and to live is only pain:
Life hath not kindled my desires with joy.

    Chorus 1. O ever-blazing sun!
O lightning of the eternal Sire!
Can ye behold this done
And tamely hide your all-avenging fire?
    Electra. Ah me!
    Chorus 2.   My daughter, why these tears?
    Electra. Woe!
    Chorus 3.   Weep not, calm thy fears.
    Electra. You kill me.
    Chorus 4.   How?
    Electra.   To breathe
A hope for one beneath
So clearly sunk in death,
'Tis to afflict me more
Already pining sore.
    Chorus 5. One in a woman's toils
Was tangled, buried by her glittering coils,
Who now beneath—
    Electra.   Ah woe!
    Chorus 6. Rules with a spirit unimpaired and strong.
    Electra. O dreadful!
    Chorus 7.   Dreadful was the wrong.
    Electra. But she was quelled.
    Chorus 8.   Ay.
    Electra.   True!
That faithful mourner knew
A brother's aid. But I
Have no man now. The one
I had, is gone, is gone.
Rapt into nothingness.
    Chorus 9. Thou are wrung with sore distress.
    Electra. I know it. Too well I know,
Taught by a life of woe,
Where horror dwells without relief.
    Chorus 10. Our eyes have seen thy grief.
    Electra. Then comfort not again—
    Chorus 11. Whither now turns thy strain?

Electra. One utterly bereft,
Seeing no hope is left,
Of help from hands owning the same great sire.
  Chorus 12. 'Tis nature's debt.
  Electra.   To expire
On sharp-cut dragging thongs,
'Midst wildly trampling throngs
Of swiftly racing hoofs, like him,
Poor hapless one?
  Chorus 13.   Vast, dim,
And boundless was the harm.
  Electra. Yea, severed from mine arm,
By strangers kept—
  Chorus 14.   O pain!
  Electra. Hidden he must remain,
Of me unsepulchered, unmourned, unwept.
                              [*Enter* CHRYSOTHEMIS.
  Chrysothemis. Driven by delight, dear sister, I am come,
Reckless of dignity, with headlong speed.
For news I bear of joy and sweet relief
From ills that drew from thee thy ceaseless moan.
  Electra. Whence couldst thou hear of succor for my woes,
That close in darkness without hope of dawn?
  Chrysothemis. Here is Orestes, learn it from my mouth,
As certainly as you now look on me.
  Electra. What? Art thou mad, unhappy one, to laugh
Over thine own calamity and mine?
  Chrysothemis. No, by our father's hearth, I say not this
In mockery. I tell you he is come.
  Electra. Me miserable! Who hath given thine ear
The word that so hath wrought on thy belief?
  Chrysothemis. Myself am the eyewitness; no one else
Gained my belief, but proofs I clearly saw.
  Electra. What sign hath so engrossed thine eye, poor girl?
What sight hath fired thee with this quenchless glow?
  Chrysothemis. But list to me, I pray thee, that henceforth
Thou mayest account me clear-eyed, or a fool!
  Electra. By all means, if it pleasure thee, say on.
  Chrysothemis. Well, I will tell thee all I saw:—I came
Unto the ancient tomb that holds our sire;

[328]

And from the topmost mound I marked a stream
Of milk fresh-flowing, and his resting-place
Ringed round with garlands of all flowers that blow.
I marveled at the sight, and peered about,
Lest some one might be nearer than we knew.
But finding all was quiet in the spot,
I ventured closer to the tomb, and there,
Hard by the limit, I beheld a curl
Of hair new-shorn, with all the gloss of youth.
And straight it struck my heart, as with a sense
Of something seen, ah me! long, long ago,
And told me that my sight encountered here
The token of Orestes, dearest soul.
Then, clasping it, I did not cry aloud,
But straight mine eyes were filled with tears of joy;
And now as much as then I feel assured
He and none else bestowed this ornament.
To whom beyond thyself and me belongs
Such consecration? And I know this well,
I did it not,—nor thou. Impossible!
Thou canst not worship even the blessèd Gods
Forth of this roof, unpunished. And, most sure,
Our mother is not minded so to act,
Nor, had she done it, could we fail to know.
This offering comes then of Orestes' hand.
Take courage, dear one. Not one fate pursues
One house perpetually, but changeth still.
Ours was a sullen Genius, but perchance
This day begins the assurance of much good.
    Electra. Oh how I pity thine infatuate mind!
    Chrysothemis. Why? Dost thou find no comfort in my
      news?
    Electra. You know not where you roam. Far wide! far wide!
    Chrysothemis. Not know? when I have seen it with mine
      eyes?
    Electra. Dear, he is dead. Look not to him, poor girl!
Salvation comes to thee no more from him.
    Chrysothemis. Oh me, unfortunate! Who told thee this?
    Electra. He who stood by and saw his life destroyed.
    Chrysothemis. Amazement seizes me. Where is that man?

Electra. Right welcome to the mother there within.

Chrysothemis. Me miserable! Who then can have decked
With all those ceremonies our father's tomb?

Electra. I cannot but suppose some hand hath brought
These gifts in memory of Orestes dead.

Chrysothemis. O cruel fate! While I in ecstasy
Sped with such news, all ignorant, it seems,
Of our dire fortune; and, arriving, find
Fresh sorrows added to the former woe.

Electra. It is so, sister; yet if thou wilt list
To me, thou mayest disperse this heaviness.

Chrysothemis. What? Shall I raise the dead again to life?

Electra. I did not mean so. I am not so fond.

Chrysothemis. What bid you then that I have power to do?

Electra. To endure courageously what I enjoin.

Chrysothemis. So it make profit, I will not refuse.

Electra. Remember, without toil no plan may thrive!

Chrysothemis. I know it, and will aid thee to my power.

Electra. Then hearken my resolve. Thou seëst now,
We have no friendly succor in the world;
But death has taken all, and we are left
Two only. I, so long as I could hear
My brother lived and flourished, still had hope
He would arise to wreak his father's blood.
But now that he is gone, to thee I turn,
To help thy sister boldly to destroy
The guilty author of our father's death,
Aegisthus.—Wherefore hide it from thee now?
—Yea, sister! Till what term wilt thou remain
Inactive? To what end? What hope is yet
Left standing? Surely thou hast cause to grieve,
Robbed of thy father's opulent heritage,
And feeling bitterly the creeping years
That find thee still a virgin and unwed.
Nay, nor imagine thou shalt ever know
That blessing. Not so careless of his life
Is King Aegisthus, as to risk the birth
Of sons from us, to his most certain fall.
But if thou wilt but follow my resolve,
First thou shalt win renown of piety

From our dead father, and our brother too,
Who rest beneath the ground, and shalt be free
For evermore in station as in birth,
And nobly matched in marriage, for the good
Draw gazers to them still. Then seest thou not
What meed of honor, if thou dost my will,
Thou shalt apportion to thyself and me?
For who, beholding us, what citizen,
What foreigner, will not extend the hand
Of admiration, and exclaim, 'See, friends,
These scions of one stock, these noble twain,
These that have saved their father's house from woe,
Who once when foes were mighty, set their life
Upon a cast, and stood forth to avenge
The stain of blood! Who will not love the pair
And do them reverence? Who will not give
Honor at festivals, and in the throng
Of popular resort, to these in chief,
For their high courage and their bold emprise?'
Such fame will follow us in all the world,
Living or dying, still to be renowned.
Ah, then, comply, dear sister; give thy sire
This toil—this labor to thy brother give;
End these my sufferings, end thine own regret:
The well-born cannot bear to live in shame.
    Chorus. In such affairs, for those who speak and hear
Wise thoughtfulness is still the best ally.
    Chrysothemis. True, noble women, and before she spake
Sound thought should have prevented the rash talk
That now hath proved her reckless. What wild aim
Beckons thee forth in arming this design
Whereto thou wouldst demand my ministry?
Dost not perceive, thou art not man but woman,
Of strength inferior to thine enemies,—
Their Genius daily prospering more and more,
Whilst ours is dwindling into nothingness?
Who then that plots against a life so strong
Shall quit him of the danger without harm?
Take heed we do not add to our distress
Should some one hear of this our colloquy.

Small help and poor advantage 'twere for us
To win brief praise and then inglorious die.
Nay, death is not so hateful as when one
Desiring death is balked of that desire.
And I beseech thee, ere in utter ruin
We perish and make desolate our race,
Refrain thy rage. And I will guard for thee
In silence these thy words unrealized;
If thou wilt learn this wisdom from long time,
Having no strength, to bend before the strong.
    Chorus. Comply. Than prudence and a heedful mind,
No fairer treasure can be found for men.
    Electra. Thy words have not surprised me. Well I knew
The good I offered would come back with scorn.
I, all alone and with a single hand,
Must do this. For it shall not rest undone.
    Chrysothemis. Would thou hadst been thus minded when our sire
Lay dying! In one act thou hadst compassed all.
    Electra. My spirit was the same: my mind was less.
    Chrysothemis. Be such the life-long temper of thy mind!
    Electra. Thine admonition augurs little aid.
    Chrysothemis. Yea. For the attempt would bring me certain bane.
    Electra. I envy thee thy prudence, hate thy fear.
    Chrysothemis. Even when thou speak'st me fair, I will endure it.
    Electra. Take heart. That never will be thine from me.
    Chrysothemis. Long time remains to settle that account.
    Electra. I find no profit in thee. Go thy way.
    Chrysothemis. Profit there is, hadst thou a mind to learn.
    Electra. Go to thy mother and declare all this!
    Chrysothemis. I am not so in hatred of thy life.
    Electra. Yet know the shame thou wouldst prepare for me.
    Chrysothemis. No, no! Not shame, but care for thine estate.
    Electra. Must I still follow as thou thinkest good?
    Chrysothemis. When thou hast wisdom, thou shalt be the guide.
    Electra. 'Tis hard when error wears the garb of sense.
    Chrysothemis. Right. That is the misfortune of your case.

Electra. Why? Feel you not the justice of my speech?
Chrysothemis. Justice may chance to bring me injury.
Electra. I care not, I, to live by such a rule.
Chrysothemis. Well, if you do it, you will find me wise.
Electra. Well, I will do it, nought dismayed by thee.
Chrysothemis. Speak you plain sooth? and will you not be
    counseled?
Electra. No, for bad counsel is of all most hateful.
Chrysothemis. You take the sense of nothing that I say.
Electra. Long since, not newly, my resolve is firm.
Chrysothemis. Then I will go. Thy heart will ne'er be
    brought
To praise my words, nor I thine action here.
Electra. Then go within! I will not follow thee,
Though thou desire it vehemently. None
Would be so fond to hunt on a cold trail.
Chrysothemis. If this seem wisdom to thee, then be wise
Thy way: but in the hour of misery,
When it hath caught thee, thou wilt praise my words.

                                   [*Exit* CHRYSOTHEMIS.

Chorus. Wise are the birds of air
      That with true filial care
For those provide convenient food
Who gave them birth, who wrought their good.
Why will not men the like perfection prove?
      Else, by the fires above,
      And heavenly Rectitude,
Fierce recompense they shall not long elude.
O darkling rumor, world-o'er-wandering voice
That piercest to the shades beneath the ground,
To dead Atrides waft a sound
Of sad reproach, not bidding him rejoice.
      Stained is the ancestral hall,
      Broken the battle-call,
That heretofore his children twain
In loving concord did sustain.
Alone, deserted, vexed, Electra sails,
      Storm-tossed with rugged gales,
      Lamenting evermore
Like piteous Philomel, and pining sore

For her lost father;—might she but bring down
That twofold Fury, caring not for death,
But ready to resign her breath.
What maid so worthy of a sire's renown?
None who inherit from a noble race,
    Complying with things base
Will let their ancient glory be defiled.
    So 'twas thy choice, dear child,
Through homeless misery to win a twofold prize,
    Purging the sin and shame
    That cloud the Argive name,
So to be called most noble and most wise.
May'st thou surpass thy foes in wealth and power
    As o'er thee now they tower!
Since I have found thee, not in bright estate,
    Nor blessed by wayward fate,
But through thy loyalty to Heaven's eternal cause
    Wearing the stainless crown
    Of perfectest renown,
And richly dowered by the mightiest laws.

[*Enter* ORESTES *and* PYLADES, *with the urn.*

Orestes. Say, dames and damsels, have we heard aright,
And speed we to the goal of our desire?
    Chorus. And what desire or quest hath brought thee hither?
    Orestes. I seek Aegisthus' dwelling all this while.
    Chorus. Welcome. The tongue that told thee hath no blame.
    Orestes. Which of you all will signify within
Our joint arrival,—not unwelcome here.
    Chorus. This maiden, if the nearest should report.
    Orestes. Mistress, wilt thou go yonder and make known,
That certain Phocians on Aegisthus wait?
    Electra. Oh! can it be that you are come to bring
Clear proofs of the sad rumor we have heard?
    Orestes. I know not what ye have heard. Old Strophius
Charged me with tidings of Orestes' fate.
    Electra. What, stranger? How this terror steals on me!
    Orestes. Bearing scant remnants of his body dead
In this small vase thou seest, we bring them home.
    Electra. O sorrow! thou art here: I see full well

[334]

That burden of my heart in present view.

    Orestes. If thou hast tears for aught Orestes suffered,
Know that he lies within this vessel's room.

    Electra. Ah, sir! by all in Heaven, if yonder urn
Hide him, ah! give it once into my hand,
That o'er that dust I may lament and mourn
Myself and mine own house and all our woe!

    Orestes. Bring it and give her, whosoe'er she be.
For not an enemy—this petition shows it—
But of his friends or kindred, is this maid.

                      [The urn is given into ELECTRA'S *hands.*

    Electra. O monument of him whom o'er all else
I loved! sole relic of Orestes' life,
How cold in this thy welcome is the hope
Wherein I decked thee as I sent thee forth!
Then bright was thy departure, whom I now
Bear lightly, a mere nothing, in my hands.
Would I had gone from life, ere I dispatched
Thee from my arms that saved thee to a land
Of strangers, stealing thee from death! For then
Thou hadst been quiet on that far-off day,
And had thy portion in our father's tomb.
Now thou hast perished in the stranger land
Far from thy sister, lorn and comfortless.
And I, O wretchedness! neither have bathed
And laid thee forth, nor from the blazing fire
Collected the sad burden, as was meet:
But thou, when foreign hands have tended thee,
Com'st a small handful in a narrow shell.
Woe for the constant care I spent on thee
Of old all vainly, with sweet toil! For never
Wast thou thy mother's darling, nay, but mine,
And I of all the household most thy nurse,
While 'sister, sister,' was thy voice to me.
But now all this is vanished in one day,
Dying in thy death. Thou hast carried all away
As with a whirlwind, and art gone. No more
My father lives: thyself art lost in death:
I am dead, who lived in thee. Our enemies
Laugh loudly, and she maddens in her joy,

Our mother most unmotherly, of whom
Thy secret missives ofttimes told me, thou
Wouldst be the punisher. But that fair hope
The hapless Genius of thy lot and mine
Hath reft away, and gives thee thus to me,—
For thy loved form thy dust and fruitless shade
O bitterness! O piteous sight! Woe! woe!
Oh! sent on thy dire journey, dearest one,
How thou hast ruined me! Thou hast indeed,
Dear brother! Then receive me to thyself,
Hide me in this thy covering, there to dwell,
Me who am nothing, with thy nothingness,
For ever! Yea, when thou wert here above,
I ever shared with thee in all, and now
I would not have thee shut me from thy tomb.
Oh! let me die and follow thee! the dead,
My mind assures me now, have no more pain.
    Chorus. Electra, think! Thou hadst a mortal sire,
And mortal was thy brother. Grieve not far.
    Orestes. O me! What shall I speak, or which way turn
The desperate word? I cannot hold my tongue.
    Electra. What pain o'ercomes thee? Wherefore speak'st thou
      so?
    Orestes. Can this be famed Electra I behold?
    Electra. No other. In sad case, as you may see.
    Orestes. Ah! deep indeed was this calamity!
    Electra. Is't possible that thou shouldst grieve for me?
    Orestes. O ruined form! abandoned to disgrace!
    Electra. 'Tis me you mean, stranger, I feel it now.
    Orestes. Woe's me! Untrimmed for bridal, hapless maid!
    Electra. Why this fixed gaze, O stranger! that deep groan?
    Orestes. How all unknowing was I of mine ill!
    Electra. What thing hath passed to make it known to thee?
    Orestes. The sight of thee attired with boundless woe.
    Electra. And yet thine eye sees little of my pain.
    Orestes. Can aught be still more hateful to be seen?
    Electra. I have my dwelling with the murderers—
    Orestes. Of whom? What evil would thy words disclose?
    Electra. Of him who gave me birth. I am their slave.
    Orestes. Whose power compels thee to this sufferance?

Recognition scene

Electra. One called my mother, most unmotherly.
Orestes. How? by main force, or by degrading shames?
Electra. By force and shames, and every kind of evil.
Orestes. And is there none to succor or prevent?
Electra. None. Him I had, you give me here in dust.
Orestes. How mine eye pities thee this while, poor maid!
Electra. Know now, none ever pitied me but you.
Orestes. None ever came whose heart like sorrow wrung.
Electra. Is't possible we have some kinsman here?
Orestes. I will tell it, if these women here be friendly.
Electra. They are. They may be trusted. Only speak.
Orestes. Let go yon vase, that thou may'st learn the whole.
Electra. Nay, by the Gods! be not so cruel, sir!
Orestes. Obey me and thou shalt not come to harm.
Electra. Ah, never rob me of what most I love!
Orestes. You must not hold it.
Electra.   O me miserable
For thee, Orestes, if I lose thy tomb!
Orestes. Speak no rash word. Thou hast no right to mourn.
Electra. No right to mourn my brother who is gone?
Orestes. Such utterance belongs not to thy tongue.
Electra. Oh, am I thus dishonored of the dead?
Orestes. Far from dishonor. But this ne'er was thine.
Electra. Is't not Orestes' body that I bear?
Orestes. Nay, but the idle dressing of a tale.
Electra. And where is his poor body's resting-place?
Orestes. Nowhere. Seek not the living with the dead.
Electra. My son, what saidst thou?
Orestes.   Nought but what is true.
Electra. Doth he yet live?
Orestes.   If I have life in me.
Electra. Art thou Orestes?
Orestes.   Let my signet here, — *the token*
That was our father's, tell thine eyes, I am.
Electra. O day of days!
Orestes.   Time hath no happier hour.
Electra. Is it thy voice?
Orestes.   Hearken not otherwhere.
Electra. Have my arms caught thee?
Orestes.   Hold me so for aye!

Electra. O dearest women, Argives of my home!
Ye see Orestes, dead in craft, but now
By that same craft delivered and preserved.
    Chorus. We see, dear daughter, and the gladsome tear
Steals from our eye to greet the bright event.
    Electra. Offspring of him I loved beyond all telling!
Ah! thou art come,—hast found me, eye to eye
Behold'st the face thou didst desire to see.
    Orestes. True, I am here; but bide in silence still.
    Electra. Wherefore?
    Orestes. Hush! speak not loud, lest one within should
      hearken.
    Electra. By ever-virgin Artemis, ne'er will I
Think worthy of my fear
This useless mass of woman-cowardice
Burdening the house within,
Not peering out of door.
    Orestes. Yet know that women too have might in war.
Of that methinks thou hast feeling evidence.
    Electra. Ah me! thou hast unveiled
And thrust before my gaze
That burning load of my distress
No time will soothe, no remedy will heal.
    Orestes. I know that too. But when we are face to face
With the evildoers,—then let remembrance work.
    Electra. All times alike are fit with instant pain
Justly to mind me of that dreadful day;
Even now but hardly hath my tongue been free.
    Orestes. Yes, that is it. Therefore preserve this boon.
    Electra. Whereby?
    Orestes. Put limits to unseasonable talk.
    Electra. Ah! brother, who, when thou art come,
Could find it meet to exchange
Language for silence, as thou bidst me do?
Since beyond hope or thought
Was this thy sight to me.
    Orestes. God gave me to your sight when so he willed.
    Electra. O heaven of grace beyond
The joy I knew but now!
If God hath brought thee to our roof,

A miracle of bounty then is here.
   Orestes. I hate to curb the gladness of thy spirit,
But yet I fear this ecstasy of joy.
   Electra. Oh! after all these years,
Now thou at length hast sped
Thy dearest advent on the wished-for way,
Do not, in all this woe
Thou seest surrounding me—
   Orestes. What means this prayer?
   Electra.   Forbid me not my joy,
Nor make me lose the brightness of thy face!
   Orestes. Deep were my wrath at him who should attempt it.
   Electra. Is my prayer heard?
   Orestes.   Why doubt it?
   Electra.   Friends, I learned
A tale beyond my thought; and hearing I restrained
My passion, voiceless in my misery,
Uttering no cry. But now
I have thee safe; now, dearest, thou art come,
With thy blest countenance, which I
Can ne'er forget, even at the worst of woe.
   Orestes. A truce now to unnecessary words. *iambic trimeter again*
My mother's vileness and Aegisthus' waste,
Draining and squandering with spendthrift hand
Our patrimony, tell me not anew.
Such talk might stifle opportunity.
But teach me, as befits the present need,
What place may serve by lurking vigilance
Or sudden apparition to o'erwhelm
Our foes in the adventure of to-day.
And, when we pass within, take heedful care
Bright looks betray thee not unto our mother.
But groan as for the dire calamity
Vainly reported:—Let's achieve success,
Then with free hearts we may rejoice and laugh.
   Electra. Dear brother, wheresoe'er thy pleasure leads,
My will shall follow, since the joys I know,
Not from myself I took them, but from thee.
And ne'er would I consent thy slightest grief
Should win for me great gain. Ill should I then

Serve the divinity of this high hour!
Thou knowest how matters in the palace stand.
Thou hast surely heard, Aegisthus is from home,
And she, our mother, is within. Nor fear
She should behold me with a smiling face.
Mine ancient hate of her hath sunk too deep.
And from the time I saw thee, tears of joy
Will cease not. Wherefore should I stint their flow?
I, who in this thy coming have beheld
Thee dead and living? Strangely hast thou wrought
On me;—that should my father come alive,
I would not think the sight were miracle,
But sober truth. Since such thy presence, then,
Lead as thy spirit prompts. For I alone
Of two things surely had achievèd one,
Noble deliverance or a noble death.
 Orestes. Be silent; for I hear within the house
A footstep coming forth.
 Electra (loudly). Strangers, go in!
For none within the palace will reject
Your burden, nor be gladdened by the event.
          [Enter the OLD MAN.
 Old Man. O lost in folly and bereft of soul!
Is't that your care for life hath ebbed away,
Or were you born without intelligence,
When fallen, not near, but in the midst of ill,
And that the greatest, ye perceive it not?
Had I not watched the doors this while, your deeds
Had gone within the palace ere yourselves.
But, as things are, my care hath fenced you round.
Now, then, have done with long-protracted talk,
And this insatiable outburst of joy,
And enter, for in such attempts as these
Delay is harmful: and 'tis more than time.
 Orestes. But how shall I find matters there within?
 Old Man. Well. You are shielded by their ignorance.
 Orestes. That means you have delivered me as dead.
 Old Man. Alone of dead men thou art here above.
 Orestes. Doth this delight them, or how went the talk?
 Old Man. I will report, when all is done. Meanwhile,

[340]

Know, all is well with them, even what is evil.

Electra. Who is this, brother? I beseech thee, tell.

Orestes. Dost not perceive?

Electra.   I cannot even imagine.

Orestes. Know'st not into whose hands thou gav'st me once?

Electra. Whose hands? How say you?

Orestes.   His, who through thy care
Conveyed me secretly to Phocis' plain.

Electra. What! is this he, whom I, of all the band,
Found singly faithful in our father's death?

Orestes. He is that man. No more!

Electra.   O gladsome day!
Dear only savior of our father's house,
How camest thou hither? Art thou he indeed,
That didst preserve Orestes and myself
From many sorrows? O dear hands, kind feet,
Swift in our service,—how couldst thou so long
Be near, nor show one gleam, but didst destroy
My heart with words, hiding the loveliest deeds?
Father!—in thee methinks I see my father.
O welcome! thou of all the world to me
Most hated and most loved in one short hour.

Old Man. Enough, dear maiden! Many nights and days
Are circling hitherward, that shall reveal
In clear recountment all that came between.

But to you two that stand beside I tell,
Now is your moment, with the Queen alone,
And none of men within; but if you pause,
Know that with others of profounder skill
You'll have to strive, more than your present foes.

Orestes. Then, Pylades, we need no more to dwell
On words, but enter on this act with speed,
First worshipping the holy shrines o' the Gods
That were my father's, harbored at the gate.

[*They pass within.* ELECTRA *remains in an atti-
tude of prayer.*

Electra. O King Apollo! hear them graciously,
And hear me too, that with incessant hand
Honored thee richly from my former store!
And now, fierce slayer, I importune thee,

[341]

And woo thee with such gifts as I can give,
Be kindly aidant to this enterprise,
And make the world take note, what meed of bane
Heaven still bestows on man's iniquity.

[ELECTRA *goes within.*

Chorus. Lo, where the War-god moves
  With soft, sure footstep, on to his design,
  Breathing hot slaughter of an evil feud!
  Even now the inevitable hounds that track
  Dark deeds of hideous crime
  Are gone beneath the covert of the domes.
  Not long in wavering suspense shall hang
  The dreaming presage of my wistful soul.

  For lo! within is led
  With crafty tread the avenger of the shades,
  Even to his father's throne of ancient power,
  And in his hand the bright new-sharpened death!
  And Hermes, Maia's son,
  Is leading him, and hath concealed the guile
  Even to the fatal end in clouds of night.
  His time of weary waiting all is o'er.

[*Re-enter* ELECTRA.

Electra. O dearest women! they are even now
About it. Only bide in silence still.
  Chorus. What is the present scene?
  Electra.   She decks the vase
For burial, and they both are standing by.
  Chorus. And wherefore hast thou darted forth?
  Electra.   To watch
Aegisthus' coming, that he enter not
At unawares.
  Clytemnestra (*within*). Ah! ah! Woe for the house,
Desert of friends, and filled with hands of death!
  Electra. A cry within! Did ye not hear it, friends?
  Chorus. Would I had not! I heard, and shivered through.
  Clytemnestra (*within*). Oh me! Alas, Aegisthus! where art
    thou?
  Electra. Hark! yet again that sound!

[342]

[handwritten marginalia:] Her emotions registered while murder is going on.

Clytemnestra (*within*).　　　　　O son, have pity!
Pity the womb that bare thee.
　　Electra.　　　　　　　Thou hadst none
For him, nor for his father, in that day.
　　Half-Chorus. Poor city! hapless race!
Thy destiny to-day
Wears thee away, away.
What morn shall see thy face?
　　Clytemnestra (*within*). **Oh, I am** smitten!
　　Electra.　　　　　　Give a second stroke,
If thou hast power.
　　Clytemnestra (*within*).　　　Oh me! again, again!
　　Electra. Would thou wert shrieking for Aegisthus too!
　　Chorus. The curse hath found, and they in earth who lie
Are living powers to-day.
Long dead, they drain away
The streaming blood of those who made them die.
　　　　　　　　　　[*Enter* ORESTES *and* PYLADES.
Behold, they come, they come!
His red hand dripping as he moves
With drops of sacrifice the War-god loves.
My 'wildered heart is dumb.
　　Electra. How is it with you, brother?
　　Orestes.　　　　　　　If Apollo
Spake rightfully, the state within is well.
　　Electra. Wretched one, is she dead?
　　Orestes.　　　　　　No more have fear
Thou shalt be slighted by thy mother's will.
　　Chorus. Cease, for I see Aegisthus near in view.
　　Electra. In, in again, boys!
　　Orestes.　　　　　　Where do ye behold
The tyrant?
　　Electra.　　To our hand from yonder gate
He comes with beaming look.
　　Half-Chorus. Haste, with what speed ye may,
Stand on the doorway stone,
That, having thus much done,
Ye may do all to-day.
　　Orestes. Fear not: we will perform it.

Electra.   Speed ye now:
Follow your thought.
    Orestes.   We are already there.
    Electra. Leave matters here to me. All shall go well.
                       [*Exit* ORESTES *with* PYLADES.
    Chorus. Few words, as if in gentleness, 'twere good
To utter in his ear,
That, eager and unware,
One step may launch him on the field of blood.
                       [*Enter* AEGISTHUS.
    Aegisthus. Which of you know where are the Phocian men
Who brought the news I hear, Orestes' life
Hath suffered shipwreck in a chariot-race?
You, you I question, you in former time
So fearless! You methinks most feelingly
Can tell us, for it touches you most near.
    Electra. I know: assure thee. Else had I not heard
The dearest of all fortunes to my heart.
    Aegisthus. Where are the strangers then? Enlighten me.
    Electra. Yonder. Their hostess entertained them well.
    Aegisthus. And did they certainly report him dead?
    Electra. Not only so. They showed him to our sight.
    Aegisthus. May this clear evidence be mine to see?
    Electra. I envy not the sight that waits you there.
    Aegisthus. Against their wont thy words have given me joy.
    Electra. Much joy be thine, if this be joy to thee!
    Aegisthus. Silence, I say! Wide let the gates be flung!
For all the Myceneans to behold
And all in Argolis, that if but one
Hath heretofore been buoyed on empty hopes
Fixed in Orestes, seeing him now dead,
He may accept my manage, and not wait
For our stern chastisement to teach him sense.
    Electra. My lesson is already learnt: at length
I am schooled to labor with the stronger will.
          [*The body of* CLYTEMNESTRA *is disclosed under a
                veil:* ORESTES *standing by.*
    Aegisthus. Zeus! Divine envy surely hath laid low
The form I here behold. But if the truth
Provoke Heaven's wrath, be it unexpressed.—Unveil!

Off with all hindrance, that mine eye may see,
And I may mourn my kinsman as I should.
 Orestes. Thyself put forth thy hand. Not mine but thine
To look and speak with kindness to this corse.
 Aegisthus. I will, for thou advisest well; but thou,
Call Clytemnestra, if she be within.

          [AEGISTHUS *lifts the shroud.*
 Orestes. She is beside thee, gaze not otherwhere.
 Aegisthus. What do I see! oh!
 Orestes.   Why so strange? Whom fear you?
 Aegisthus. Who are the men into whose midmost toils
All hapless I am fallen?
 Orestes.   Ha! knowest thou not
Thou hast been taking living men for dead?
 Aegisthus. I understand that saying. Woe is me!
I know, Orestes' voice addresseth me.
 Orestes. A prophet! How wert thou so long deceived?
 Aegisthus. Undone, undone! Yet let me speak one word.
 Electra. Brother, by Heaven, no more! Let him not speak.
When death is certain, what do men in woe
Gain from a little time? Kill him at once!
And, killed, expose him to such burial
From dogs and vultures, as beseemeth such,
Far from our view. Nought less will solace me
For the remembrance of a life of pain.
 Orestes. Go in and tarry not. No contest this
Of verbal question, but of life or death.
 Aegisthus. Why drive you me within? If this you do
Be noble, why must darkness hide the deed?
Why not destroy me out of hand?
 Orestes.   Command not!
Enter, and in the place where ye cut down
My father, thou shalt yield thy life to me.
 Aegisthus. Is there no help but this abode must see
The past and future ills of Pelops' race?
 Orestes. Thine anyhow. That I can prophesy
With perfect inspiration to thine ear.
 Aegisthus. The skill you boast belonged not to your sire.
 Orestes. You question and delay. Go in!
 Aegisthus.   Lead on.

Orestes. Nay, go thou first.
Aegisthus.   That I may not escape thee?
Orestes. No, that thou may'st not have thy wish in death.
I may not stint one drop of bitterness.
And would this doom were given without reprieve,
If any try to act beyond the law,
To kill them. Then the wicked would be few.

   Leader of Chorus. O seed of Atreus! how triumphantly
Through grief and hardness thou hast freedom found,
With full achievement in this onset crowned!

EURIPIDES
ELECTRA

➤➤ ⬅⬅

TRANSLATED
by
GILBERT MURRAY

CHARACTERS IN THE PLAY

CLYTEMNESTRA, *Queen of Argos and Mycenae; widow of Agamemnon.*
ELECTRA, *daughter of Agamemnon and Clytemnestra.*
ORESTES, *son of Agamemnon and Clytemnestra, now in banishment.*
A PEASANT, *husband of Electra.*
AN OLD MAN, *formerly servant to Agamemnon.*
PYLADES, *son of Strophios, King of Phocis; friend to Orestes.*
AEGISTHUS, *usurping King of Argos and Mycenae, now husband of
    Clytemnestra.*
The Heroes CASTOR *and* POLYDEUCES.
CHORUS *of Argive Women, with their Leader.*
FOLLOWERS *of Orestes;* HANDMAIDS *of Clytemnestra.*

*The scene is laid in the mountains of Argos. The play was first produced
    between the years 414 and 412 B.C.*

ARGUMENT

The vengeance of Orestes has been treated by each of the three tragedians: by Sophocles in his *Electra*, by Aeschylus in the *Choëphoroe*, and
by Euripides in the present play. In Aeschylus' play it is the dead king,
Agamemnon, who dominates the action, called forth from his sleep by
the chants of the Libation-Bearers and the prayers of his children. But
to Euripides, as to Sophocles, Electra is the central figure, 'a woman
shattered in childhood by the shock of an experience too terrible for a
girl to bear; a poisoned and a haunted woman, eating her heart in
ceaseless broodings of hate and love, alike unsatisfied'—*A-lektra*, 'the
Unmated.'

ELECTRA

The scene represents a hut on a desolate mountain side; the river Inachus is visible in the distance. The time is the dusk of early dawn, before sunrise. The PEASANT *is discovered in front of the hut.*

Peasant. Old gleam on the face of the world, I give thee
    hail,
River of Argos land, where sail on sail
The long ships met, a thousand, near and far.
When Agamemnon walked the seas in war;
Who smote King Priam in the dust, and burned
The storied streets of Ilion, and returned
Above all conquerors, heaping tower and fane
Of Argos high with spoils of Eastern slain.

  So in far lands he prospered; and at home
His own wife trapped and slew him. 'Twas the doom
Aegisthus wrought, son of his father's foe.

  Gone is that King, and the old spear laid low
That Tantalus wielded when the world was young.
Aegisthus hath his queen, and reigns among
His people. And the children here alone,
Orestes and Electra, buds unblown
Of man and womanhood, when forth to Troy
He shook his sail and left them—lo, the boy
Orestes, ere Aegisthus' hand could fall,
Was stolen from Argos—borne by one old thrall,
Who served his father's boyhood, over seas
Far off, and laid upon King Strophios' knees
In Phocis, for the old king's sake. But here
The maid Electra waited, year by year,
Alone, till the warm days of womanhood
Drew nigh and suitors came of gentle blood

[349]

In Hellas. Then Aegisthus was in fear
Lest she be wed in some great house, and bear
A son to avenge her father. Close he wrought
Her prison in his house, and gave her not
To any wooer. Then, since even this
Was full of peril, and the secret kiss
Of some bold prince might find her yet, and rend
Her prison walls, Aegisthus at the end
Would slay her. Then her mother, she so wild
Aforetime, pled with him and saved her child.
Her heart had still an answer for her lord
Murdered, but if the child's blood spoke, what word
Could meet the hate thereof? After that day
Aegisthus thus decreed: whoso should slay
The old king's wandering son, should win rich meed
Of gold; and for Electra, she must wed
With me, not base of blood—in that I stand
True Mycenaean—but in gold and land
Most poor, which maketh highest birth as naught.
So from a powerless husband shall be wrought
A powerless peril. Had some man of might
Possessed her, he had called perchance to light
Her father's blood, and unknown vengeances
Risen on Aegisthus yet.
                        Aye, mine she is:
But never yet these arms—the Cyprian knows
My truth!—have clasped her body, and she goes
A virgin still. Myself would hold it shame
To abase this daughter of a royal name.
I am too lowly to love violence. Yea,
Orestes too doth move me, far away,
Mine unknown brother! Will he ever now
Come back and see his sister bowed so low?
    Doth any deem me fool, to hold a fair
Maid in my room and seek no joy, but spare
Her maidenhood? If any such there be,
Let him but look within. The fool is he
In gentle things, weighing the more and less
Of love by his own heart's untenderness.

[As he ceases ELECTRA *comes out of the hut. She is in mourning garb, and carries a large pitcher on her head. She speaks without observing the* PEASANT'S *presence.*

Electra. Dark shepherdess of many a golden star,
Dost see me, Mother Night? And how this jar
Hath worn my earth-bowed head, as forth and fro
For water to the hillward springs I go?
Not for mere stress of need, but purpose set,
That never day nor night God may forget
Aegisthus' sin: aye, and perchance a cry
Cast forth to the waste shining of the sky
May find my father's ear. . . . The woman bred
Of Tyndareus, my mother—on her head
Be curses!—from my house hath outcast me;
She hath borne children to our enemy;
She hath made me naught, she hath made Orestes naught. . . .

[As the bitterness of her tone increases, the PEAS-
ANT *comes forward.*

Peasant. What wouldst thou now, my sad one, ever fraught
With toil to lighten my toil? And so soft
Thy nurture was! Have I not chid thee oft,
And thou wilt cease not, serving without end?

Electra (turning to him with impulsive affection).
O friend, my friend, as God might be my friend,
Thou only hast not trampled on my tears.
Life scarce can be so hard, 'mid many fears
And many shames, when mortal heart can find
Somewhere one healing touch, as my sick mind
Finds thee. . . . And should I wait thy word, to endure
A little for thine easing, yea, or pour
My strength out in thy toiling fellowship?
Thou hast enough with fields and kine to keep;
'Tis mine to make all bright within the door.
'Tis joy to him that toils, when toil is o'er,
To find home waiting, full of happy things.

Peasant. If so it please thee, go thy way. The springs
Are not far off. And I before the morn
Must drive my team afield, and sow the corn

[351]

In the hollows.—Not a thousand prayers can gain
A man's bare bread, save an he work amain.

> [ELECTRA *and the* PEASANT *depart on their several*
> *ways. After a few moments there enter stealthily*
> *two armed men,* ORESTES *and* PYLADES.

Orestes. Thou art the first that I have known in deed
True and my friend, and shelterer of my need.
Thou only, Pylades, of all that knew,
Hast held Orestes of some worth, all through
These years of helplessness, wherein I lie
Downtrodden by the murderer—yea, and by
The murderess, my mother! . . . I am come,
Fresh from the cleansing of Apollo, home
To Argos—and my coming no man yet
Knoweth—to pay the bloody twain their debt
Of blood. This very night I crept alone
To my dead father's grave, and poured thereon
My heart's first tears and tresses of my head
New-shorn, and o'er the barrow of the dead
Slew a black lamb, unknown of them that reign
In this unhappy land. . . . I am not fain
To pass the city gates, but hold me here
Hard on the borders. So my road is clear
To fly if men look close and watch my way;
If not, to seek my sister. For men say
She dwelleth in these hills, no more a maid
But wedded. I must find her house, for aid
To guide our work, and learn what hath betid
Of late in Argos.—Ha, the radiant lid
Of Dawn's eye lifteth! Come, friend; leave we now
This trodden path. Some worker of the plough,
Or serving damsel at her early task
Will presently come by, whom we may ask
If here my sister dwells. But soft! Even now
I see some bondmaid there, her death-shorn brow
Bending beneath its freight of well-water.
Lie close until she pass; then question her.
A slave might help us well, or speak some sign
Of import to this work of mine and thine.

[The two men retire into ambush. ELECTRA *enters,
returning from the well.*

Electra.   Onward, O laboring tread,
             As on move the years;
           Onward amid thy tears,
             O happier dead!

[Strophe.

Let me remember. I am she,
Agamemnon's child, and the mother of me
Clytemnestra, the evil Queen,
Helen's sister. And folk, I ween,
That pass in the streets call yet my name
Electra. . . . God protect my shame!
    For toil, toil is a weary thing,
      And life is heavy about my head;
  And thou far off, O Father and King,
      In the lost lands of the dead.
A bloody twain made these things be;
One was thy bitterest enemy,
And one the wife that lay by thee.

[Antistrophe.

Brother, brother, on some far shore
Hast thou a city, is there a door
That knows thy footfall, Wandering One?
Who left me, left me, when all our pain
Was bitter about us, a father slain,
And a girl that wept in her room alone.
    Thou couldst break me this bondage sore,
      Only thou, who art far away,
  Loose our father, and wake once more. . . .
      Zeus, Zeus, dost hear me pray? . . .
The sleeping blood and the shame and the doom!
O feet that rest not, over the foam
Of distant seas, come home, come home!

[Strophe.

  What boots this cruse that I carry?
    O, set free my brow!
  For the gathered tears that tarry

Through the day and the dark till now,
Now in the dawn are free,
    Father, and flow beneath
The floor of the world, to be
    As a song in the house of Death:
From the rising up of the day
They guide my heart alway,
The silent tears unshed,
And my body mourns for the dead;
My cheeks bleed silently,
    And these bruisèd temples keep
Their pain, remembering thee
    And thy bloody sleep.

Be rent, O hair of mine head!

As a swan crying alone
    Where the river windeth cold.
For a loved, for a silent one,
    Whom the toils of the fowler hold,
I cry, Father, to thee,
O slain in misery!

                        [*Antistrophe.*

The water, the wan water,
    Lapped him, and his head
Drooped in the bed of slaughter
    Low, as one wearièd;
Woe for the edgèd axe,
    And woe for the heart of hate,
Houndlike about thy tracks,
    O conqueror desolate,
From Troy over land and sea,
Till a wife stood waiting thee;
Not with crowns did she stand,
Nor flowers of peace in her hand;
With Aegisthus' dagger drawn
    For her hire she strove,
Through shame and through blood alone;
    And won her a traitor's love.

[*As she ceases there enter from right and left the*
CHORUS, *consisting of women of Argos, young
and old, in festal dress.*

[*Strophe.*

Chorus. (*Some Women.*)
    Child of the mighty dead,
      Electra, lo, my way
  To thee in the dawn hath sped,
    And the cot on the mountain gray,
      For the Watcher hath cried this day:
  He of the ancient folk,
    The walker of waste and hill,
  Who drinketh the milk of the flock;
    And he told of Hera's will;
  For the morrow's morrow now
    They cry her festival,
  And before her throne shall bow
      Our damsels all.
Electra. Not unto joy, nor sweet
    Music, nor shining of gold,
  The wings of my spirit beat.
    Let the brides of Argos hold
      Their dance in the night, as of old;
  I lead no dance; I mark
    No beat as the dancers sway;
  With tears I dwell in the dark,
    And my thought is of tears alway,
    To the going down of the day.
  Look on my wasted hair
  And raiment. . . . This that I bear,
  Is it meet for the King my sire,
    And her whom the King begot?
  For Troy, that was burned with fire
    And forgetteth not?

[*Antistrophe.*

Chorus. (*Other Women.*)
    Hera is great!—Ah, come,
      Be kind; and my hand shall bring
  Fair raiment, work of the loom,
    And many a golden thing,

For joyous robe-wearing.
Deemest thou this thy woe
　　Shall rise unto God as prayer,
Or bend thine haters low?
　　Doth God for thy pain have care?
Not tears for the dead nor sighs,
　　But worship and joy divine
Shall win thee peace in thy skies,
　　　O daughter mine!

Electra. No care cometh to God
　　For the voice of the helpless; none
For the crying of ancient blood.
　　Alas for him that is gone,
　　And for thee, O wandering one:
That now, methinks, in a land
　　Of the stranger must toil for hire,
And stand where the poor men stand,
　　A-cold by another's fire,
　　O son of the mighty sire:
While I in a beggar's cot
On the wrecked hills, changing not,
　　Starve in my soul for food;
　　But our mother lieth wed
In another's arms, and blood
　　　Is about her bed.

Leader. On all of Greece she wrought great jeopardy,
Thy mother's sister, Helen,—and on thee.

　　　　[ORESTES *and* PYLADES *move out from their con-
　　　　cealment;* ORESTES *comes forward:* PYLADES
　　　　beckons to two ARMED SERVANTS *and stays
　　　　with them in the background.*

Electra. Woe's me! No more of wailing! Women, flee!
Strange armèd men beside the dwelling there
Lie ambushed! They are rising from their lair.
Back by the road, all you. I will essay
The house; and may our good feet save us!

　　Orestes (between ELECTRA *and the hut).* Stay,
Unhappy woman! Never fear my steel.

　　Electra (in utter panic). O bright Apollo! Mercy! See, I
　　kneel;

Slay me not.

Orestes.　　　Others I have yet to slay
Less dear than thou.

Electra.　　　　Go from me! Wouldst thou lay
Hand on a body that is not for thee?

Orestes. None is there I would touch more righteously.

Electra. Why lurk'st thou by my house? And why a sword?

Orestes. Stay. Listen! Thou wilt not gainsay my word.

Electra. There—I am still. Do what thou wilt with me.
Thou art too strong.

Orestes.　　　A word I bear to thee . . .
Word of thy brother.

Electra.　　　　Oh, friend! More than friend!
Living or dead?

Orestes.　　　He lives; so let me send
My comfort foremost, ere the rest be heard.

Electra. God love thee for the sweetness of thy word!

Orestes. God love the twain of us, both thee and me.

Electra. He lives! Poor brother! In what land weareth he
His exile?

Orestes.　　　Not one region nor one lot
His wasted life hath trod.

Electra.　　　　He lacketh not
For bread?

Orestes.　　　Bread hath he; but a man is weak
In exile.

Electra. What charge laid he on thee? Speak.

Orestes. To learn if thou still live, and how the storm,
Living, hath struck thee.

Electra.　　　That thou seest; this form
Wasted . . .

Orestes.　　　Yea, riven with the fire of woe.
I sigh to look on thee.

Electra.　　　My face; and, lo,
My temples of their ancient glory shorn.

Orestes. Methinks thy brother haunts thee, being forlorn;
Aye, and perchance thy father, whom they slew. . . .

Electra. What should be nearer to me than those two?

Orestes. And what to him, thy brother, half so dear
As thou?

[357]

EURIPIDES

Electra. His is a distant love, not near
At need.
Orestes. But why this dwelling place, this life
Of loneliness?
Electra (with sudden bitterness). Stranger, I am a wife. . . .
O better dead!
Orestes. That seals thy brother's doom!
What Prince of Argos . . . ?
Electra. Not the man to whom
My father thought to give me.
Orestes. Speak; that I
May tell thy brother all.
Electra. 'Tis there, hard by,
His dwelling, where I live, far from men's eyes.
Orestes. Some ditcher's cot, or cowherd's, by its guise!
Electra (struck with shame for her ingratitude).
A poor man; but true-hearted and to me
God-fearing.
Orestes. How? What fear of God hath he?
Electra. He hath never held my body to his own.
Orestes. Hath he some vow to keep? Or is it done
To scorn thee?
Electra. Nay; he only scorns to sin
Against my father's greatness.
Orestes. But to win
A princess! Doth his heart not leap for pride?
Electra. He honoreth not the hand that gave the bride.
Orestes. I see. He trembles for Orestes' wrath?
Electra. Aye, that would move him. But beside, he hath
A gentle heart.
Orestes. Strange! A good man. . . . I swear
He well shall be requited.
Electra. Whensoe'er
Our wanderer comes again!
Orestes. Thy mother stays
Unmoved 'mid all thy wrong?
Electra. A lover weighs
More than a child in any woman's heart.
Orestes. But what end seeks Aegisthus, by such art
Of shame?

[358]

Electra. <u>To make mine unborn children low</u>
<u>And weak, even as my husband.</u>
 Orestes.   Lest there grow
From thee the avenger?
 Electra.   Such his purpose is:
For which may I requite him!
 Orestes.   And of this
Thy virgin life—Aegisthus knows it?
 Electra.   Nay,
We speak it not. It cometh not his way.
 Orestes. These <u>women hear us. Are they friends to thee?</u>
 Electra. Aye, friends and true. They will keep faithfully
All words of mine and thine.
 Orestes (*trying her*).   Thou art well stayed
With friends. And could Orestes give thee aid
In aught, if e'er . . .
 Electra.   Shame on thee! Seest thou not?
Is it not time?
 Orestes (*catching her excitement*).   How time? And if
   he sought
To slay, how should he come at his desire?
 Electra. By daring, as they dared who slew his sire!
 Orestes. Wouldst thou dare with him, if he came, thou too,
To slay her? ·
 Electra.   Yes; with the same axe that slew
My father!
 Orestes.   'Tis thy message? And thy mood
Unchanging?
 Electra.   <u>Let me shed my mother's blood,</u>
<u>And I die happy.</u>
 Orestes.   God! . . . I would that now
Orestes heard thee here.
 Electra.   Yet, wottest thou,
Though here I saw him, I should know him not.
 Orestes. Surely. Ye both were children, when they wrought
Your parting.
 Electra.   One alone in all this land
Would know his face.
 Orestes.   The thrall, methinks, whose hand
Stole him from death—or so the story ran?

Electra. He taught my father, too, an old old man
Of other days than these.
    Orestes.   Thy father's grave . . .
He had due rites and tendance?
    Electra.   What chance gave,
My father had, cast out to rot in the sun.
    Orestes. God, 'tis too much! . . . To hear of such things
      done
Even to a stranger, stings a man. . . . But speak,
Tell of thy life, that I may know, and seek
Thy brother with a tale that must be heard
Howe'er it sicken. If mine eyes be blurred,
Remember, 'tis the fool that feels not. Aye,
Wisdom is full of pity; and thereby
Men pay for too much wisdom with much pain.
    Leader. My heart is moved as this man's. I would fain
Learn all thy tale. Here dwelling on the hills
Little I know of Argos and its ills.
    Electra. If I must speak—and at love's call, God knows,
I fear not—I will tell thee all; my woes,
My father's woes, and—O, since thou hast stirred
This storm of speech, thou bear him this my word—
His woes and shame! Tell of this narrow cloak
In the wind; this grime and reek of toil, that choke
My breathing; this low roof that bows my head
After a king's. This raiment . . . thread by thread,
'Tis I must weave it, or go bare—must bring,
Myself, each jar of water from the spring.
No holy day for me, no festival,
No dance upon the green! From all, from all
I am cut off. No portion hath my life
Mid wives of Argos, being no true wife.
No portion where the maidens throng to praise
Castor—my Castor, whom in ancient days,
Ere he passed from us and men worshipped him,
They named my bridegroom!—
                       And she, she! . . . The grim
Troy spoils gleam round her throne, and by each hand
Queens of the East, my father's prisoners, stand,
A cloud of Orient webs and tangling gold.

And there upon the floor, the blood, the old
Black blood, yet crawls and cankers, like a rot
In the stone! And on our father's chariot
The murderer's foot stands glorying, and the red
False hand uplifts that ancient staff, that led
The armies of the world! . . . Aye, tell him how
The grave of Agamemnon, even now,
Lacketh the common honor of the dead; *melodramatic*
A desert barrow, where no tears are shed,
No tresses hung, no gift, no myrtle spray.
And when the wine is in him, so men say,
Our mother's mighty master leaps thereon,
Spurning the slab, or pelteth stone on stone,
Flouting the lone dead and the twain that live:
'Where is thy son Orestes? Doth he give
Thy tomb good tendance? Or is all forgot?'
So is he scorned because he cometh not. . . .
    O stranger, on my knees, I charge thee, tell
This tale, not mine, but of dumb wrongs that swell
Crowding—and I the trumpet of their pain,
This tongue, these arms, this bitter burning brain;
These dead shorn locks, and he for whom they died!
His father slew Troy's thousands in their pride:
He hath but one to kill. . . . O God, but one!
Is he a man, and Agamemnon's son?
    Leader. But hold: is this thy husband from the plain, *short day!*
His labor ended, hasting home again?

                                    [*Enter the* PEASANT.
    Peasant. Ha, who be these? Strange men in arms before
My house! What would they at this lonely door?
Seek they for me?—Strange gallants should not stay
A woman's going.
    Electra.   Friend and helper!—Nay,
Think not of any evil. These men be
Friends of Orestes, charged with words for me! . . .
Strangers, forgive his speech.
    Peasant.   What word have they
Of him? At least he lives and sees the day?
    Electra. So fares their tale—and sure I doubt it not!
    Peasant. And ye two still are living in his thought,

Thou and his father?
  Electra.   In his dreams we live.
An exile hath small power.
  Peasant.   And did he give
Some privy message?
  Electra.   None: they come as spies
For news of me.
  Peasant.   Thine outward news their eyes
Can see; the rest, methinks, thyself will tell.
  Electra. They have seen all, heard all. I trust them well.
  Peasant. Why were our doors not open long ago?
Be welcome, strangers both, and pass below
My lintel. In return for your glad words
Be sure all greeting that mine house affords
Is yours.—Ye followers, bear in their gear!·
Gainsay me not; for his sake are ye dear
That sent you to our house; and though my part
In life be low, I am no churl at heart.

> [*The* PEASANT *goes to the* ARMED SERVANTS *at the
> back, to help them with the baggage.*

  Orestes (aside to Electra). Is this the man that shields thy
    maidenhood
Unknown, and will not wrong thy father's blood?
  Electra. He is called my husband. 'Tis for him I toil.
  Orestes. How dark lies honor hid! And what turmoil
In all things human: sons of mighty men
Fallen to naught, and from ill seed again
Good fruit: yea, famine in the rich man's scroll
Writ deep, and in poor flesh a lordly soul.
As, lo, this man, not great in Argos, not
With pride of house uplifted, in a lot
Of unmarked life hath shown a prince's grace.

> [*To the* PEASANT, *who has returned.*

All that is here of Agamemnon's race,
And all that lacketh yet, for whom we come,
Do thank thee, and the welcome of thy home
Accept with gladness.—Ho, men; hasten ye
Within!—This open-hearted poverty
Is blither to my sense than feasts of gold.
  Lady, thine husband's welcome makes me bold;

Yet would thou hadst thy brother, before all
Confessed, to greet us in a prince's hall!
Which may be, even yet. Apollo spake
The word; and surely, though small store I make
Of man's divining, God will fail us not.

       [ORESTES *and* PYLADES *go in, following the*
         SERVANTS.

Leader. O never was the heart of hope so hot
Within me. How? So moveless in time past,
Hath Fortune girded up her loins at last?

  Electra. Now know'st thou not thine own ill furniture,
To bid these strangers in, to whom for sure
Our best were hardship, men of gentle breed?

  Peasant. Nay, if the men be gentle, as indeed
I deem them, they will take good cheer or ill
With even kindness.

  Electra.   'Twas ill done; but still—
Go, since so poor thou art, to that old friend
Who reared my father. At the realm's last end
He dwells, where Tanaos river foams between
Argos and Sparta. Long time hath he been
An exile 'mid his flocks. Tell him what thing
Hath chanced on me, and bid him haste and bring
Meat for the strangers' tending.—Glad, I trow,
That old man's heart will be, and many a vow
Will lift to God, to learn the child he stole
From death, yet breathes.—I will not ask a dole
From home; how should my mother help me? Nay,
I pity him that seeks that door, to say
Orestes liveth!

  Peasant.   Wilt thou have it so?
I will take word to the old man. But go
Quickly within, and whatso there thou find
Set out for them. A woman, if her mind
So turn, can light on many a pleasant thing
To fill her board. And surely plenishing
We have for this one day.—'Tis in such shifts
As these, I care for riches, to make gifts
To friends, or lead a sick man back to health
With ease and plenty. Else small aid is wealth

For daily gladness; once a man be done
With hunger, rich and poor are all as one.

*last appearance
in the play*   [*The* PEASANT *goes off to the left;* ELECTRA *goes
into the house.*

[*Strophe.*

Chorus.   O for the ships of Troy, the beat
     Of oars that shimmered
Innumerable, and dancing feet
     Of Nereids glimmered;
And dolphins, drunken with the lyre,
Across the dark blue prows, like fire,
     Did bound and quiver,
To cleave the way for Thetis' son,
Fleet-in-the-wind Achilles, on
To war, to war, till Troy be won
     Beside the reedy river.

[*Antistrophe.*

Up from Euboea's caverns came
     The Nereids, bearing
Gold armor from the Lords of Flame,
     Wrought for his wearing:
Long sought those daughters of the deep,
Up Pelion's glen, up Ossa's steep
     Forest enchanted,
Where Peleus reared alone, afar,
His lost sea-maiden's child, the star
Of Hellas, and swift help of war
     When weary armies panted.

[*Strophe.*

There came a man from Troy, and told
     Here in the haven,
How, orb on orb, to strike with cold
The Trojan, o'er that targe of gold,
     Dread shapes were graven.
All round the level rim thereof
Perseus, on wingèd feet, above
     The long seas hied him;
The Gorgon's wild and bleeding hair
He lifted; and a herald fair,

[364]

He of the wilds, whom Maia bare,
  God's Hermes, flew beside him.

                              [*Antistrophe.*

But midmost, where the boss rose higher,
    A sun stood blazing,
And wingèd steeds, and stars in choir,
Hyad and Pleiad, fire on fire,
    For Hector's dazing:
Across the golden helm, each way,
Two taloned Sphinxes held their prey,
    Song-drawn to slaughter:
And round the breastplate ramping came
A mingled breed of lion and flame,
Hot-eyed to tear that steed of fame
    That found Pirene's water.

                              [*Epode.*

The red red sword with steeds four-yoked
    Black-maned, was graven,
That labored, and the hot dust smoked
    Cloudwise to heaven.
Thou Tyndarid woman! Fair and tall
Those warriors were, and o'er them all
    One king great-hearted,
Whom thou and thy false love did slay:
Therefore the tribes of Heaven one day
For these thy dead shall send on thee
An iron death: yea, men shall see
The white throat drawn, and blood's red spray,
    And lips in terror parted.

[*As they cease, there enters from the left a very
    OLD MAN, bearing a lamb, a wineskin, and a
    wallet.*

Old Man. Where is my little Princess? Ah, not now;
But still my queen, who tended long ago
The lad that was her father. . . . How steep-set
These last steps to her porch! But faint not yet:
Onward, ye failing knees and back with pain
Bowed, till we look on that dear face again.
                              [*Enter* ELECTRA.

Ah, daughter, is it thou?—Lo, here I am,
With gifts from all my store; this suckling lamb
Fresh from the ewe, green crowns for joyfulness,
And creamy things new-curdled from the press.
And this long-storèd juice of vintages
Forgotten, cased in fragrance: scant it is,
But passing sweet to mingle nectar-wise
With feebler wine.—Go, bear them in; mine eyes . . .
Where is my cloak?—They are all blurred with tears.

    Electra. What ails thine eyes, old friend? After these years
Doth my low plight still stir thy memories?
Or think'st thou of Orestes, where he lies
In exile, and my father? Aye, long love
Thou gavest him, and seest the fruit thereof
Wasted, for thee and all who love thee!

    Old Man.   **All**
Wasted! And yet 'tis that lost hope withal
I cannot brook. But now I turned aside
To see my master's grave. All, far and wide,
Was silence; so I bent these knees of mine
And wept and poured drink-offerings from the wine
I bear the strangers, and about the stone
Laid myrtle sprays. And, child, I saw thereon
Just at the censer slain, a fleecèd ewe,
Deep black, in sacrifice: the blood was new
About it: and a tress of bright brown hair
Shorn as in mourning, close. Long stood I there
And wondered, of all men what man had gone
In mourning to that grave.—My child, 'tis none
In Argos. Did there come . . . Nay, mark me now . . .
Thy brother in the dark, last night, to bow
His head before that unadorèd tomb?

    O come, and mark the color of it. Come
And lay thine own hair by that mourner's tress!
A hundred little things make likenesses
In brethren born, and show the father's blood.

    Electra (trying to mask her excitement and resist the contagion of his). Old heart, old heart, is this a wise man's
        mood? . . .
O, not in darkness, not in fear of men,

Shall Argos find him, when he comes again,
Mine own undaunted . . . Nay, and if it were,
What likeness could there be? My brother's hair
Is as a prince's and a rover's, strong
With sunlight and with strife: not like the long
Locks that a woman combs. . . . And many a head
Hath this same semblance, wing for wing, tho' bred
Of blood not ours. . . . 'Tis hopeless. Peace, old man.

Old Man. The footprints! Set thy foot by his, and scan
The track of frame and muscles, how they fit!

Electra. That ground will take no footprint! All of it
Is bitter stone. . . . It hath? . . . And who hath said
There should be likeness in a brother's tread *criticism of Aesch.?*
And sister's? His is stronger every way. *failure to show Electra's*

Old Man. But hast thou nothing . . . ? If he came this day *pessimism*
And sought to show thee, is there no one sign *also it has*
Whereby to know him? . . . Stay; the robe was thine, *made old*
Work of thy loom, wherein I wrapt him o'er *man alert to*
That night, and stole him through the murderers' door. *possibility of Orestes being near.*

Electra. Thou knowest, when Orestes was cast out
I was a child. . . . If I did weave some clout
Of raiment, would he keep the vesture now
He wore in childhood? Should my weaving grow
As his limbs grew? . . . 'Tis lost long since. No more!
O, either 'twas some stranger passed, and shore
His locks for very ruth before that tomb:
Or, if he found perchance, to seek his home,
Some spy . . .

Old Man. The strangers! Where are they? I fain
Would see them, aye, and bid them answer plain . . . *dramatic convenience*

Electra. Here at the door! How swift upon the thought!

[*Enter* ORESTES *and* PYLADES.

Old Man. High-born: albeit for that I trust them not.
The highest oft are false. . . . Howe'er it be,

[*Approaching them.*

I bid the strangers hail!

Orestes. All hail to thee,
Graybeard!—Prithee, what man of all the King
Trusted of old, is now this broken thing?

Electra. 'Tis he that trained my father's boyhood.

[367]

Orestes.   How?
And stole from death thy brother? Sayest thou?
   Electra. This man was his deliverer, if it be
Deliverance.
   Orestes.   How his old eye pierceth me,
As one that testeth silver and alloy!
Sees he some likeness here?
   Electra.   Perchance 'tis joy,
To see Orestes' comrade, that he feels.
   Orestes. None dearer.—But what ails the man? He reels
Dizzily back.
   Electra.   I marvel. I can say
No more.
   Old Man (in a broken voice). Electra, mistress, daughter,
     pray!
Pray unto God!
   Electra.   Of all the things I crave,
The thousand things, or all that others have,
What should I pray for?
   Old Man.   Pray thine arms may hold
At last this treasure-dream of more than gold
God shows us!
   Electra. God, I pray thee! . . . Wouldst thou more?
   Old Man. Gaze now upon this man, and bow before
Thy dearest upon earth!
   Electra.   I gaze on thee!
O, hath time made thee mad?
   Old Man.   Mad, that I see
Thy brother?
   Electra.   My . . . I know not what thou say'st:
I looked not for it . . .
   Old Man.   I tell thee, here confessed
Standeth Orestes, Agamemnon's son!
   Electra. A sign before I trust thee! O, but one!
How dost thou know . . . ?
   Old Man.   There, by his brow, I see
The scar he made, that day he ran with thee
Chasing thy fawn, and fell.
   Electra (in a dull voice).   A scar? 'Tis so.
I see a scar.

Old Man.   And fearest still to throw
Thine arms round him thou lovest?
    Electra.   O, no more!
Thy sign hath conquered me. . . . (*throwing herself into*
    ORESTES' *arms*).   At last, at last!
Thy face like light! And do I hold thee fast,
Unhoped for?
    Orestes.   Yea, at last! And I hold thee.
    Electra. I never knew . . .
    Orestes.   I dreamed not.
    Electra.   Is it he,
Orestes?
    Orestes.   Thy defender, yea, alone
To fight the world! Lo, this day have I thrown
A net, which once unbroken from the sea
Drawn home, shall . . . O, and it must surely be!
Else men shall know there is no God, no light
In Heaven, if wrong to the end shall conquer right.
    Chorus. Comest thou, comest thou now,
        Chained by the years and slow,
          O Day long sought?
        A light on the mountains cold
        Is lit, yea, a fire burneth.
        'Tis the light of one that turneth
        From roamings manifold,
        Back out of exile old
          To the house that knew him not.

        Some spirit hath turned our way,
          Victory visible,
        Walking at thy right hand,
        Belovèd; O lift this day
        Thine arms, thy voice, as a spell;
        And pray for thy brother, pray,
        Treading the perilous land,
          That all be well!
    Orestes. Enough; this dear delight is mine at last
Of thine embracing; and the hour comes fast
When we shall stand again as now we stand,
And stint not.—Stay, Old Man: thou, being at hand

At the edge of time, advise me, by what way
Best to requite my father's murderers. Say,
Have I in Argos any still to trust;
Or is the love, once borne me, trod in dust,
Even as my fortunes are? Whom shall I seek?
By day or night? And whither turn, to wreak
My will on them that hate us? Say.

    Old Man.   My son.
In thine adversity, there is not one
Will call thee friend. Nay, that were treasure-trove,
A friend to share, not faltering from love,
Fair days and foul the same. Thy name is gone
Forth to all Argos, as a thing o'erthrown
And dead. Thou hast not left one spark to glow
With hope in one friend's heart! Hear all, and know:
Thou hast God's fortune and thine own right hand,
Naught else, to conquer back thy fatherland.

    Orestes. The deed, the deed! What must we do?

    Old Man.   Strike down
Aegisthus . . . and thy mother.

    Orestes.   'Tis the crown
My race is run for. But how find him?

    Old Man.   Not
Within the city walls, however hot
Thy spirit.

    Orestes.   Ha! With watchers doth he go
Begirt, and mailèd pikemen?

    Old Man.   Even so:
He lives in fear of thee, and night nor day
Hath slumber.

    Orestes.   That way blocked!—'Tis thine to say
What next remains.

    Old Man.   I will; and thou give ear.
A thought has found me!

    Orestes.   All good thoughts be near,
For thee to speak and me to understand!

    Old Man. But now I saw Aegisthus, close at hand
As here I journeyed.

    Orestes.   That good word shall trace
My path for me! Thou saw'st him? In what place?

[370]

Old Man. Out on the pastures where his horses stray.
Orestes. What did he there so far?—A gleam of day
Crosseth our darkness.

Old Man.   'Twas a feast, methought,
Of worship to the wild-wood nymphs he wrought.

Orestes. The watchers of men's birth? Is there a son
New born to him, or doth he pray for one
That cometh?

[*Movement of* ELECTRA.

Old Man.   More I know not; he had there
A wreathèd ox, as for some weighty prayer.

Orestes. What force was with him? Not his serfs alone?

Old Man. No Argive lord was there; none but his own
Household.

Orestes.   Not any that might know my race,
Or guess?

Old Man.   Thralls, thralls; who ne'er have seen thy
          face.

Orestes. Once I prevail, the thralls will welcome me!

Old Man. The slaves' way, that; and no ill thing for thee!

Orestes. How can I once come near him?

Old Man.   Walk thy ways
Hard by, where he may see thee, ere he slays
His sacrifice.

Orestes.   How? Is the road so nigh?

Old Man. He cannot choose but see thee, passing by,
And bid thee stay to share the beast they kill.

Orestes. A bitter fellow-feaster, if God will!

Old Man. And then . . . then swift be heart and brain, to
          see
God's chances!

Orestes.   Aye. Well hast thou counseled me.
But . . . where is she?

Old Man.   In Argos now, I guess;
But goes to join her husband, ere the press
Of the feast.

Orestes.   Why goeth not my mother straight
Forth at her husband's side?

Old Man.   She fain will wait
Until the gathered country-folk be gone.

[371]

Orestes. Enough! She knows what eyes are turned upon
Her passings in the land!
   Old Man.   Aye, all men hate
The unholy woman.
   Orestes.   How then can I set
My snare for wife and husband in one breath?
   Electra (*coming forward*). Hold! It is I must work our
     mother's death.
   Orestes. If that be done, I think the other deed
Fortune will guide.
   Electra.   This man must help our need,
One friend alone for both.
   Old Man. He will, he will!
Speak on. What cunning hast thou found to fill
Thy purpose?
   Electra.   Get thee forth, Old Man, and quick
Tell Clytemnestra . . . tell her I lie sick,
New-mothered of a man-child.
   Old Man.   Thou hast borne
A son! But when?
   Electra. Let this be the tenth morn.
Till then a mother stays in sanctity,
Unseen.
   Old Man.   And if I tell her, where shall be
The death in this?
   Electra.   That word let her but hear,
Straight she will seek me out!
   Old Man.   The queen! What care
Hath she for thee, or pain of thine?
   Electra.   She will;
And weep my babe's low station!
   Old Man.   Thou hast skill
To know her, child; say on.
   Electra.   But bring her here,
Here to my hand; the rest will come.
   Old Man.   I swear,
Here at the gate she shall stand palpable!
   Electra. The gate: the gate that leads to me and Hell.
   Old Man. Let me but see it, and I die content.
   Electra. First, then, my brother: see his steps be bent

Old Man. Straight yonder where Aegisthus makes his
prayer!

Electra. Then seek my mother's presence, and declare
My news.

Old Man. Thy very words, child, as tho' spoke
From thine own lips!

Electra.   Brother, thine hour is struck.
Thou standest in the van of war this day.

Orestes (rousing himself). Aye, I am ready. . . . I will go
my way,
If but some man will guide me.

Old Man.   Here am I,
To speed thee to the end, right thankfully.

Orestes (turning as he goes and raising his hands to heaven).
Zeus of my sires, Zeus of the lost battle,

Electra. Have pity; have pity; we have earned it well!

Old Man. Pity these twain, of thine own body sprung!

Electra. O Queen o'er Argive altars, Hera high,

Orestes. Grant us thy strength, if for the right we cry.

Old Man. Strength to these twain, to right their father's
wrong!

Electra. O Earth, deep Earth, to whom I yearn in vain,

Orestes. And deeper thou, O father darkly slain,

Old Man. Thy children call, who love thee: hearken thou!

Orestes. Girt with thine own dead armies, wake, O wake!

Electra. With all that died at Ilion for thy sake . . .

Old Man. And hate earth's dark defilers; help us now!

Electra. Dost hear us yet, O thou in deadly wrong,
Wronged by my mother?

Old Man.   Child, we stay too long.
He hears; be sure he hears!

Electra.   And while he hears,
I speak this word for omen in his ears:
'Aegisthus dies, Aegisthus dies.' . . . Ah me,
My brother, should it strike not him, but thee,
This wrestling with dark death, behold, I too
Am dead that hour. Think of me as one true,
Not one that lives. I have a sword made keen
For this, and shall strike deep.

                    I will go in

And make all ready. If there come from thee
Good tidings, all my house for ecstasy
Shall cry; and if we hear that thou art dead,
Then comes the other end!—Lo, I have said.
   Orestes. I know all, all.
   Electra.   Then be a man to-day!

               [ORESTES *and the* OLD MAN *depart.*

O Women, let your voices from this fray
Flash me a fiery signal, where I sit,
The sword across my knees, expecting it.
For never, though they kill me, shall they touch
My living limbs!—I know my way thus much.

               [*She goes into the house.*
               [*Strophe.*

Chorus.
      When white-haired folk are met
        In Argos about the fold,
      A story lingereth yet,
      A voice of the mountains old,
        That tells of the Lamb of Gold:
      A lamb from a mother mild,
        But the gold of it curled and beat;
      And Pan, who holdeth the keys of the wild,
        Bore it to Atreus' feet:
      His wild reed pipes he blew,
        And the reeds were filled with peace,
      And a joy of singing before him flew,
        Over the fiery fleece:
      And up on the basèd rock,
        As a herald cries, cried he:
      'Gather ye, gather, O Argive folk,
        The King's Sign to see,
      The sign of the blest of God,
        For he that hath this, hath all!'
      Therefore the dance of praise they trod
        In the Atreïd brethren's hall.

               [*Antistrophe.*

      They opened before men's eyes
        That which was hid before,
      The chambers of sacrifice,

The dark of the golden door,
  And fires on the altar floor.
And bright was every street,
  And the voice of the Muses' tree,
The carven lotus, was lifted sweet;
  When afar and suddenly,
Strange songs, and a voice that grew:
  'Come to your king, ye folk!
Mine, mine, is the Golden Ewe!'
  'Twas dark Thyestes spoke.
For, lo, when the world was still,
  With his brother's bride he lay,
And won her to work his will,
  And they stole the Lamb away!
Then forth to the folk strode he,
  And called them about his fold,
And showed that Sign of the King to be,
  The fleece and the horns of gold.

Then, then, the world was changed;
  And the Father, where they ranged,
Shook the golden stars and glowing,
  And the great Sun stood deranged
In the glory of his going.

Lo, from that day forth, the East
Bears the sunrise on his breast,
And the flaming Day in heaven
  Down the dim ways of the West
Driveth, to be lost at even.

The wet clouds to Northward beat;
  And Lord Ammon's desert seat
Crieth from the South, unslaken,
  For the dews that once were sweet,
For the rain that God hath taken.

[Antistrophe.

'Tis a children's tale, that old
  Shepherds on far hills have told;
And we reck not of their telling,

*his
scepticism*

Deem not that the Sun of gold
Ever turned his fiery dwelling,

Or beat backward in the sky,
For the wrongs of man, the cry
Of his ailing tribes assembled,
To do justly, ere they die!
Once, men told the tale, and trembled;

Fearing God, O Queen: whom thou
Hast forgotten, till thy brow
With old blood is dark and daunted.
And thy brethren, even now,
Walk among the stars, enchanted.

Leader. Ha, friends, was that a voice? Or some dream sound
Of voices shaketh me, as underground
God's thunder shuddering? Hark, again, and clear!
It swells upon the wind.—Come forth and hear!
Mistress, Electra!

[ELECTRA, *a bare sword in her hand, comes
from the house.*

Electra. Friends! Some news is brought?
How hath the battle ended?
Leader. I know naught.
There seemed a cry as of men massacred!
Electra. I heard it too. Far off, but still I heard.
Leader. A distant floating voice . . . Ah, plainer now!
Electra. Of Argive anguish!—Brother, is it thou?
Leader. I know not. Many confused voices cry . . .
expects the worst *Electra.* Death, then for me! That answer bids me die.
Leader. Nay, wait! We know not yet thy fortune. Wait!
Electra. No messenger from him!—Too late, too late!
Leader. The message yet will come. 'Tis not a thing
So light of compass, to strike down a king.

[*Enter a* MESSENGER, *running.*

Messenger. Victory, Maids of Argos, Victory!
Orestes . . . all that love him, list to me! . . .
Hath conquered! Agamemnon's murderer lies
Dead! O give thanks to God with happy cries!

Electra. Who art thou? I mistrust thee. . . . 'Tis a plot!
Messenger. Thy brother's man. Look well. Dost know me
    not?
    Electra. Friend, friend; my terror made me not to see
Thy visage. Now I know and welcome thee.
How sayst thou? He is dead, verily dead,
My father's murderer . . . ?
    Messenger.   Shall it be said
Once more? I know again and yet again
Thy heart would hear. Aegisthus lieth slain!
    Electra. Ye Gods! And thou, O Right, that seest all,
Art come at last? . . . But speak; how did he fall?
How swooped the wing of death? . . . I crave to hear.
    Messenger. Forth of this hut we set our faces clear
To the world, and struck the open chariot road;
Then on toward the pasture lands, where stood
The great Lord of Mycenae. In a set
Garden beside a channeled rivulet,
Culling a myrtle garland for his brow,
He walked: but hailed us as we passed: 'How now,
Strangers! Who are ye? Of what city sprung,
And whither bound?' 'Thessalians,' answered young
Orestes: 'to Alpheüs journeying,
With gifts to Olympian Zeus.' Whereat the King:
'This while, beseech you, tarry, and make full
The feast upon my hearth. We slay a bull
Here to the Nymphs. Set forth at break of day
To-morrow, and 'twill cost you no delay.
But come'—and so he gave his hand, and led
The two men in—'I must not be gainsaid;
Come to the house. Ho, there; set close at hand
Vats of pure water, that the guests may stand
At the altar's verge, where falls the holy spray.'
Then quickly spake Orestes: 'By the way
We cleansed us in a torrent stream. We need
No purifying here. But if indeed
Strangers may share thy worship, here are we
Ready, O King, and swift to follow thee.'
    So spoke they in the midst. And every thrall
Laid down the spears they served the King withal,

[handwritten marginalia: the familiar mess's speech]

And hied him to the work. Some bore amain
The death-vat, some the corbs of hallowed grain;
Or kindled fire, and round the fire and in
Set cauldrons foaming; and a festal din
Filled all the place. Then took thy mother's lord
The ritual grains, and o'er the altar poured
Its due, and prayed: 'O Nymphs of Rock and Mere,
With many a sacrifice for many a year,
May I and she who waits at home for me,
My Tyndarid Queen, adore you. May it be
Peace with us always, even as now; and all
Ill to mine enemies'—meaning withal
Thee and Orestes. Then my master prayed
Against that prayer, but silently, and said
No word, to win once more his fatherland.
Then in the corb Aegisthus set his hand,
Took the straight blade, cut from the proud bull's head
A lock, and laid it where the fire was red;
Then, while the young men held the bull on high,
Slew it with one clean gash; and suddenly
Turned on thy brother: 'Stranger, every true
Thessalian, so the story goes, can hew
A bull's limbs clean, and tame a mountain steed.
Take up the steel, and show us if indeed
Rumor speak true.' Right swift Orestes took
The Dorian blade, back from his shoulders shook
His brochèd mantle, called on Pylades
To aid him, and waved back the thralls. With ease
Heelwise he held the bull, and with one glide
Bared the white limb; then stripped the mighty hide
From off him, swifter than a runner runs
His furlongs, and laid clean the flank. At once
Aegisthus stooped, and lifted up with care
The ominous parts, and gazed. No lobe was there;
But lo, strange caves of gall, and, darkly raised,
The portal vein boded to him that gazed
Fell visitations. Dark as night his brow
Clouded. Then spake Orestes: 'Why art thou
Cast down so sudden?' 'Guest,' he cried, 'there be
Treasons from whence I know not, seeking me.

Of all my foes, 'tis Agamemnon's son;
His hate is on my house, like war.' 'Have done!'
Orestes cried: 'thou fear'st an exile's plot,
Lord of a city? Make thy cold heart hot
With meat.—Ho, fling me a Thessalian steel!
This Dorian is too light. I will unseal
The breast of him.' He took the heavier blade,
And clave the bone. And there Aegisthus stayed,
The omens in his hand, dividing slow
This sign from that; till, while his head bent low,
Up with a leap thy brother flashed the sword,
Then down upon his neck, and cleft the cord
Of brain and spine. Shuddering the body stood
One instant in an agony of blood,
And gasped and fell. The henchmen saw, and straight
Flew to their spears, a host of them to set
Against those twain. But there the twain did stand
Unfaltering, each his iron in his hand,
Edge fronting edge. Till 'Hold,' Orestes calls: *Cowardly way*
'I come not as in wrath against these walls   *of killing Aeg.*
And mine own people. One man righteously
I have slain, who slew my father. It is I,
The wronged Orestes! Hold, and smite me not,
Old housefolk of my father!' When they caught
That name, their lances fell. And one old man,
An ancient in the house, drew nigh to scan
His face, and knew him. Then with one accord
They crowned thy brother's temples, and outpoured
Joy and loud songs. And hither now he fares
To show the head, no Gorgon, that he bears,
But that Aegisthus whom thou hatest! Yea,
Blood against blood, his debt is paid this day.

> [*He goes off to meet the others*—ELECTRA *stands
> as though stupefied.*

Chorus. Now, now thou shalt dance in our dances,
   Beloved, as a fawn in the night!
The wind is astir for the glances
   Of thy feet; thou art robed with delight.
He hath conquered, he cometh to free us
   With garlands new-won,

More high than the crowns of Alpheüs,
    Thine own father's son:
    Cry, cry, for the day that is won!

Electra. O Light of the Sun, O chariot wheels of flame,
O Earth and Night, dead Night without a name
That held me! Now mine eyes are raised to see,
And all the doorways of my soul flung free.
Aegisthus dead! My father's murderer dead!
  What have I still of wreathing for the head
Stored in my chambers? Let it come forth now
To bind my brother's and my conqueror's brow.

       [*Some garlands are brought out from the house to*
        ELECTRA.

Chorus. Go, gather thy garlands, and lay them
    As a crown on his brow, many-tressed,
    But our feet shall refrain not nor stay them:
    'Tis the joy that the Muses have blest.
For our king is returned as from prison,
    The old king, to be master again,
Our belovèd in justice re-risen:
    With guile he hath slain . . .
    But cry, cry in joyance again!

       [*There enter from the left* ORESTES *and* PYLADES,
        followed by some thralls.

Electra. O conqueror, come! The king that trampled Troy
Knoweth his son Orestes. Come in joy,
Brother, and take to bind thy rippling hair
My crowns! . . . O what are crowns, that runners wear
For some vain race? But thou in battle true
Hast felled our foe Aegisthus, him that slew
By craft thy sire and mine.

                    [*She crowns* ORESTES.
            And thou no less,
O friend at need, O reared in righteousness,
Take, Pylades, this chaplet from my hand.
'Twas half thy battle. And may ye two stand
Thus alway, victory-crowned, before my face!

                    [*She crowns* PYLADES.

  Orestes. Electra, first as workers of this grace
Praise thou the Gods, and after, if thou will,

Praise also me, as chosen to fulfil
God's work and Fate's.—Aye, 'tis no more a dream;
In very deed I come from slaying him.
Thou hast the knowledge clear, but lo, I bring
More also. See himself, dead!

> [*Attendants bring in the body of* AEGISTHUS *on a bier.*

                 Wouldst thou fling
This lord on the rotting earth for beasts to tear?
Or up, where all the vultures of the air
May glut them, pierce and nail him for a sign
Far off? Work all thy will. Now he is thine.

   Electra. It shames me; yet, God knows, I hunger sore—
   Orestes. What wouldst thou? Speak; the old fear nevermore
Need touch thee.
   Electra.   To let loose upon the dead
My hate! Perchance to rouse on mine own head
The sleeping hate of the world?— *and yet she is afraid*
   Orestes.   No man that lives
Shall scathe thee by one word.
   Electra.   Our city gives
Quick blame; and little love have men for me.
   Orestes. If aught thou hast unsaid, sister, be free
And speak. Between this man and us no bar
Cometh nor stint, but the utter rage of war.

> [*She goes and stands over the body. A moment's silence.*

   Electra. Ah me, what have I? What first flood of hate
To loose upon thee? What last curse to sate
My pain, or river of wild words to flow *Rather scummy*
Bank-high between? . . . Nothing? . . . And yet I know *of her to float in this fashion*
There hath not passed one sun, but through the long
Cold dawns, over and over, like a song,
I have said them—words held back, O, some day yet
To flash into thy face, would but the fret
Of ancient fear fall loose and let me free.
And free I am, now; and can pay to thee
At last the weary debt.
             Oh, thou didst kill
My soul within. Who wrought thee any ill,

That thou shouldst make me fatherless? Aye, me
And this my brother, loveless, solitary?
'Twas thou, didst bend my mother to her shame:
Thy weak hand murdered him who led to fame
The hosts of Hellas—thou, that never crossed
O'erseas to Troy! . . . God help thee, wast thou lost
In blindness, long ago, dreaming, some-wise,
She would be true with thee, whose sin and lies
Thyself had tasted in my father's place?
And then, that thou wert happy, when thy days
Were all one pain? Thou knewest ceaselessly
Her kiss a thing unclean, and she knew thee
A lord so little true, so dearly won!
So lost ye both, being in falseness one,
What fortune else had granted; she thy curse,
Who marred thee as she loved thee, and thou hers . . .
And on thy ways thou heardst men whispering,
'Lo, the Queen's husband yonder'—not 'the King.'
  And then the lie of lies that dimmed thy brow,
Vaunting that by thy gold, thy chattels, Thou
Wert Something; which themselves are nothingness,
Shadows, to clasp a moment ere they cease.
The thing thou art, and not the things thou hast,
Abideth, yea, and bindeth to the last
Thy burden on thee: while all else, ill-won
And sin-companioned, like a flower o'erblown,
Flies on the wind away.
                          Or didst thou find
In women . . . Women? . . . Nay, peace, peace! The blind
Could read thee. Cruel wast thou in thine hour,
Lord of a great king's house, and like a tower
Firm in thy beauty.
                    [*Starting back with a look of loathing.*
                    Ah, that girl-like face!
God grant, not that, not that, but some plain grace
Of manhood to the man who brings me love:
A father of straight children, that shall move
Swift on the wings of War.
                          So, get thee gone!
Naught knowing how the great years, rolling on,

Have laid thee bare, and thy long debt full paid.
O vaunt not, if one step be proudly made
In evil, that all Justice is o'ercast:
Vaunt not, ye men of sin, ere at the last
The thin-drawn marge before you glimmereth
Close, and the goal that wheels 'twixt life and death.

Leader. Justice is mighty. Passing dark hath been
His sin: and dark the payment of his sin.

Electra (*with a weary sigh, turning from the body*). Ah me!
Go some of you, bear him from sight,
That when my mother come, her eyes may light
On nothing, nothing, till she know the sword . . .

[*The body is borne into the hut.* PYLADES *goes
with it.*

Orestes (*looking along the road*). Stay, 'tis a new thing!
We have still a word
To speak . . .

Electra. What? Not a rescue from the town
Thou seëst?

Orestes. 'Tis my mother comes: my own
Mother, that bare me.

[*He takes off his crown.*

Electra (*springing, as it were, to life again, and moving
where she can see the road*). Straight into the snare!
Aye, there she cometh.—Welcome in thy rare
Chariot! All welcome in thy brave array!

Orestes. What would we with our mother? Didst thou say
Kill her?

Electra (*turning on him*). What? Is it pity? Dost thou fear
To see thy mother's shape?

Orestes. 'Twas she that bare
My body into life. She gave me suck.
How can I strike her?

Electra. Strike her as she struck
Our father!

Orestes (*to himself, brooding*). Phoebus, God, was all thy
mind
Turned unto darkness?

Electra. If thy God be blind,
Shalt thou have light?

Orestes (*as before*). Thou, thou, didst bid me kill
My mother: which is sin.
    Electra.   How brings it ill
To thee, to raise our father from the dust?
    Orestes. I was a clean man once. Shall I be thrust
From men's sight, blotted with her blood?
    Electra.   Thy blot
Is black as death if him thou succor not!
    Orestes. Who shall do judgment on me, when she dies?
    Electra. Who shall do judgment, if thy father lies
Forgotten?
    Orestes (*turning suddenly to* ELECTRA). Stay! How if some
      fiend of Hell,
Hid in God's likeness, spake that oracle?
    Electra. In God's own house? I trow not.
    Orestes.   And I trow
It was an evil charge!
                     [*He moves away from her.*
    Electra (*almost despairing*). To fail me now!
To fail me now! A coward!—O brother, no!
    Orestes. What shall it be, then? The same stealthy blow . . .
    Electra. That slew our father! Courage! thou hast slain
Aegisthus.
    Orestes.   Aye. So be it.—I have ta'en
A path of many terrors: and shall do
Deeds horrible. 'Tis God will have it so. . . .
Is this the joy of battle, or wild woe?
                   [*He goes into the House.*
    Leader. O Queen o'er Argos thronèd high,
        O Woman, sister of the twain,
        God's Horsemen, stars without a stain,
    Whose home is in the deathless sky,
        Whose glory in the sea's wild pain,
    Toiling to succor men that die:
    Long years above us hast thou been,
        God-like for gold and marveled power:
        Ah, well may mortal eyes this hour
    Observe thy state: All hail, O Queen!
        [*Enter from the right* CLYTEMNESTRA *on a chariot,
        accompanied by richly dressed Handmaidens.*

Clytemnestra. Down from the wain, ye dames of Troy, and
   hold
Mine arm as I dismount. . . . *pride?*

               [*Answering* ELECTRA's *thought.*
             The spoils and gold.
Of Ilion I have sent out of my hall
To many shrines. These bondwomen are all   *conscience*
I keep in mine own house . . . Deemst thou the cost
Too rich to pay me for the child I lost—
Fair though they be?
   Electra.   Nay, Mother, here am I
Bond likewise, yea, and homeless, to hold high
Thy royal arm!
   Clytemnestra. Child, the war-slaves are here;
Thou needst not toil.
   Electra.   What was it but the spear
Of war, drove me forth too? Mine enemies
Have sacked my father's house, and, even as these,
Captives and fatherless, made me their prey.
   Clytemnestra. It was thy father cast his child away,   *Debate*
A child he might have loved! . . . Shall I speak out?
(*Controlling herself*) Nay; when a woman once is caught about *scenes*
With evil fame, there riseth in her tongue
A bitter spirit—wrong, I know! Yet, wrong
Or right, I charge ye look on the deeds done;
And if ye needs must hate, when all is known,
Hate on! What profits loathing ere ye know?
   My father gave me to be his. 'Tis so.
But was it his to kill me, or to kill
The babes I bore? Yet, lo, he tricked my will
With fables of Achilles' love: he bore   *More info on the*
To Aulis and the dark ship-clutching shore, *trick on Iphigenia*
He held above the altar-flame, and smote,
Cool as one reaping, through the strainèd throat,
My white Iphigenia. . . . Had it been
To save some falling city, leaguered in
With foemen; to prop up our castle towers,
And rescue other children that were ours,
Giving one life for many, by God's laws
I had forgiven all! Not so. Because

Helen was wanton, and her master knew
No curb for her: for that, for that, he slew
My daughter!—Even then, with all my wrong,
No wild beast yet was in me. Nay, for long,
I never would have killed him. But he came,
At last, bringing that damsel, with the flame
Of God about her, mad and knowing all:
And set her in my room; and in one wall
Would hold two queens!—O wild are woman's eyes
And hot her heart. I say not otherwise.
But, being thus wild, if then her master stray
To love far off, and cast his own away,
Shall not her will break prison too, and wend
Somewhere to win some other for a friend?
And then on us the world's curse waxes strong
In righteousness! The lords of all the wrong
Must hear no curse!—I slew him. I trod then
The only road: which led me to the men
He hated. Of the friends of Argos whom
Durst I have sought, to aid me to the doom
I craved?—Speak if thou wouldst, and fear not me,
If yet thou deemst him slain unrighteously.

    Leader. Thy words be just, yet shame their justice brings;
A woman true of heart should bear all things
From him she loves. And she who feels it not,
I cannot reason of her, nor speak aught.

    Electra. Remember, Mother, thy last word of grace,
Bidding me speak, and fear not, to thy face.

    Clytemnestra. So said I truly, child, and so say still.

    Electra. Wilt softly hear, and after work me ill?

    Clytemnestra. Not so, not so. I will but pleasure thee.

    Electra. I answer then. And, Mother, this shall be
My prayer of opening, where hangs the whole:
Would God that He had made thee clean of soul!
Helen and thou—O, face and form were fair,
Meet for men's praise; but sisters twain ye were,
Both things of naught, a stain on Castor's star.
And Helen slew her honor, borne afar
In wilful ravishment: but thou didst slay
The highest man of the world. And now wilt say

'Twas wrought in justice for thy child laid low
At Aulis? . . . Ah, who knows thee as I know?
Thou, thou, who long ere aught of ill was done
Thy child, when Agamemnon scarce was gone,
Sate at the looking-glass, and tress by tress
Didst comb the twinèd gold in loneliness.
When any wife, her lord being far away,
Toils to be fair, O blot her out that day
As false within! What would she with a cheek
So bright in strange men's eyes, unless she seek
Some treason? None but I, thy child, could so
Watch thee in Hellas: none but I could know
Thy face of gladness when our enemies
Were strong, and the swift cloud upon thine eyes
If Troy seemed falling, all thy soul keen-set
Praying that he might come no more! . . . And yet
It was so easy to be true. A king
Was thine, not feebler, not in anything
Below Aegisthus; one whom Hellas chose
For chief beyond all kings. Aye, and God knows,
How sweet a name in Greece, after the sin
Thy sister wrought, lay in thy ways to win.
Ill deeds make fair ones shine, and turn thereto
Men's eyes.—Enough: but say he wronged thee; slew
By craft thy child:—what wrong had I done, what
The babe Orestes? Why didst render not
Back unto us, the children of the dead,
Our father's portion? Must thou heap thy bed
With gold of murdered men, to buy to thee
Thy strange man's arms? Justice! Why is not he
Who cast Orestes out, cast out again?
Not slain for me whom doubly he hath slain,
In living death, more bitter than of old
My sister's? Nay, when all the tale is told
Of blood for blood, what murder shall we make,
I and Orestes, for our father's sake?

    Clytemnestra. Aye, child; I know thy heart, from long ago.
Thou hast alway loved him best. 'Tis oft-time so:
One is her father's daughter, and one hot
To bear her mother's part. I blame thee not . . .

Yet think not I am happy, child; nor flown
With pride now, in the deeds my hand hath done . . .
  [*Seeing* ELECTRA *unsympathetic, she checks her-*
      self.
  But thou art all untended, comfortless
Of body and wild of raiment; and thy stress
Of travail scarce yet ended! . . . Woe is me!
'Tis all as I have willed it. Bitterly
I wrought against him, to the last blind deep
Of bitterness. . . . Woe's me!
    Electra.   Fair days to weep,
When help is not! Or stay: though he lie cold
Long since, there lives another of thy fold
Far off; there might be pity for thy son?
    Clytemnestra. I dare not! . . . Yes, I fear him. 'Tis mine
      own
Life, and not his, comes first. And rumor saith
His heart yet burneth for his father's death.
    Electra. Why dost thou keep thine husband ever hot
Against me?
    Clytemnestra. 'Tis his mood. And thou art not
So gentle, child!
    Electra.   My spirit is too sore!
Howbeit, from this day I will no more
Hate him.
    Clytemnestra (with a flash of hope). O daughter!—Then,
      indeed, shall he,
I promise, never more be harsh to thee!
    Electra. He lieth in my house, as 'twere his own.
'Tis that hath made him proud.
    Clytemnestra.   Nay, art thou flown
To strife again so quick, child?
    Electra.   Well; I say
No more; long have I feared him, and alway
Shall fear him, even as now!
    Clytemnestra.   Nay, daughter, peace!
It bringeth little profit, speech like this . . .
Why didst thou call me hither?
    Electra.   It reached thee,
My word that a man-child is born to me?

[388]

Do thou make offerings for me—for the rite
I know not—as is meet on the tenth night.
I cannot; I have borne no child till now.

Clytemnestra. Who tended thee? 'Tis she should make the
vow.

Electra. None tended me. Alone I bare my child.

Clytemnestra. What, is thy cot so friendless? And this wild
So far from aid?

Electra. Who seeks for friendship sake
A beggar's house?

Clytemnestra. I will go in, and make
Due worship for thy child, the Peace-bringer.
To all thy need I would be minister.
Then to my lord, where by the meadow side
He prays the woodland nymphs.

Ye handmaids, guide
My chariot to the stall, and when ye guess
The rite draws near its end, in readiness
Be here again. Then to my lord! . . . I owe
My lord this gladness, too.

[*The Attendants depart;* CLYTEMNESTRA, *left alone,
proceeds to enter the house.*

Electra. Welcome below
My narrow roof! But have a care withal,
A grime of smoke lies deep upon the wall.
Soil not thy robe! . . .

Not far now shall it be,
The sacrifice God asks of me and thee.
The bread of Death is broken, and the knife
Lifted again that drank the Wild Bull's life:
And on his breast . . . Ha, Mother, hast slept well
Aforetime? Thou shalt lie with him in Hell.
That grace I give to cheer thee on thy road;
Give thou to me—peace from my father's blood!

[*She follows her mother into the house.*

Chorus. Lo, the returns of wrong.
The wind as a changèd thing
Whispereth overhead
Of one that of old lay dead

In the water lapping long:
　　My King, O my King!

A cry in the rafters then
　　Rang, and the marble dome:
'Mercy of God, not thou,
'Woman! To slay me now,
'After the harvests ten
　　'Now, at the last, come home!'

O fate shall turn as the tide,
　　Turn, with a doom of tears
For the flying heart too fond;
A doom for the broken bond.
She hailed him there in his pride,
　　Home from the perilous years,

In the heart of his wallèd lands,
　　In the Giants' cloud-capt ring;
Herself, none other, laid
The hone to the axe's blade;
She lifted it in her hands,
　　The woman, and slew her king.

Woe upon spouse and spouse,
　　Whatso of evil sway
Held her in that distress!
Even as a lioness
Breaketh the woodland boughs
　　Starving, she wrought her way.

Voice of Clytemnestra. O Children, Children; in the name
　　of God,
Slay not your mother!
　　A Woman.　　　　　Did ye hear a cry
Under the rafters?
　　Another.　　　　I weep too, yea, I;
Down on the mother's heart the child hath trod!
　　　　　　　　　　　　[*A death-cry from within.*
　　Another. God bringeth Justice in his own slow tide.
　　　　Aye, cruel is thy doom; but thy deeds done

Evil, thou piteous woman, and on one
   Whose sleep was by thy side!
     [*The doors burst open, and* ORESTES *and* ELECTRA
       come forth in disorder. Attendants bring out
       the bodies of CLYTEMNESTRA *and* AEGISTHUS.

Leader. Lo, yonder, in their mother's new-spilt gore
   Red-garmented and ghastly, from the door
   They reel. . . . O horrible! Was it agony
   Like this, she boded in her last wild cry?
   There lives no seed of man calamitous,
   Nor hath lived, like this seed of Tantalus.

Orestes. O Dark of the Earth, O God,
     Thou to whom all is plain;
   Look on my sin, my blood,
     This horror of dead things twain:
   Gathered as one they lie
   Slain; and the slayer was I,
     I, to pay for my pain!

Electra. Let tear rain upon tear,
     Brother: but mine is the blame.
   A fire stood over her,
     And out of the fire I came,
   I, in my misery. . . .
   And I was the child at her knee.
     'Mother' I named her name.

Chorus. Alas for Fate, for the Fate of thee,
   O Mother, Mother of Misery:
   And Misery, lo, hath turned again,
   To slay thee, Misery and more,
   Even in the fruit thy body bore.
   Yet hast thou Justice, Justice plain,
     For a sire's blood spilt of yore!

Orestes. Apollo, alas for the hymn
     Thou sangest, as hope in mine ear!
   The Song was of Justice dim,
     But the Deed is anguish clear;
   And the Gift, long nights of fear,
     Of blood and of wandering,
     Where cometh no Greek thing,
   Nor sight, nor sound on the air.

Yea, and beyond, beyond,
   Roaming—what rest is there?
Who shall break bread with me?
Who, that is clean, shall see
And hate not the blood-red hand,
   His mother's murderer?

Electra. And I? What clime shall hold
   My evil, or roof it above?
I cried for dancing of old,
   I cried in my heart for love:
What dancing waiteth me now?
What love that shall kiss my brow
   Nor blench at the brand thereof?

Chorus. Back, back, in the wind and rain
   Thy driven spirit wheeleth again.
Now is thine heart made clean within
That was dark of old and murder-fraught.
But, lo, thy brother; what hast thou wrought . . .
Yea, though I love thee . . . what woe, what sin,
   On him, who willed it not!

Orestes. Saw'st thou her raiment there,
   Sister, there in the blood?
   She drew it back as she stood,
She opened her bosom bare,
   She bent her knees to the earth,
   The knees that bent in my birth . . .
And I . . . Oh, her hair, her hair . . .
      [He breaks into inarticulate weeping.

Chorus. Oh, thou didst walk in agony,
   Hearing thy mother's cry, the cry
   Of wordless wailing, well know I.

Electra. She stretched her hand to my cheek,
   And there brake from her lips a moan;
   'Mercy, my child, my own!'
Her hand clung to my cheek;
   Clung, and my arm was weak;
   And the sword fell and was gone.

Chorus. Unhappy woman, could thine eye
   Look on the blood, and see her lie,
   Thy mother, where she turned to die?

Orestes. I lifted over mine eyes
    My mantle: blinded I smote,
  As one smiteth a sacrifice;
    And the sword found her throat.
Electra. I gave thee the sign and the word;
    I touched with mine hand thy sword.
Leader. Dire is the grief ye have wrought.
Orestes. Sister, touch her again:
    Oh, veil the body of her;
    Shed on her raiment fair,
  And close that death-red stain.
    Mother! And didst thou bear,
  Bear in thy bitter pain,
    To life, thy murderer?
  [*The two kneel over the body of* CLYTEMNESTRA,
    and cover her with raiment.
Electra. On her that I loved of yore,
    Robe upon robe I cast:
  On her that I hated sore.
Chorus. O House that hath hated sore,
    Behold thy peace at the last!
Leader. Ha, see: above the roof-tree high
    There shineth . . . Is some spirit there
    Of earth or heaven? That thin air
  Was never trod by things that die!
    What bodes it now that forth they fare,
  To men revealèd visibly?
  [*There appears in the air a vision of* CASTOR *and*
    POLYDEUCES. *The mortals kneel or veil their*
    faces.
  Castor. Thou Agamemnon's Son, give ear! 'Tis we,
Castor and Polydeuces, call to thee,
God's Horsemen and thy mother's brethren twain.
An Argive ship, spent with the toiling main,
We bore but now to peace, and, here withal
Being come, have seen thy mother's bloody fall,
Our sister's. Righteous is her doom this day,
But not thy deed. And Phoebus, Phoebus . . . Nay;
He is my lord; therefore I hold my peace.
Yet though in light he dwell, no light was this

He showed to thee, but darkness! Which do thou
Endure, as man must, chafing not. And now
Fare forth where Zeus and Fate have laid thy life.
   The maid Electra thou shalt give for wife
To Pylades; then turn thy head and flee
From Argos' land. 'Tis never more for thee
To tread this earth where thy dead mother lies.
And, lo, in the air her Spirits, bloodhound eyes,
Most horrible yet Godlike, hard at heel
Following shall scourge thee as a burning wheel,
Speed-maddened. Seek thou straight Athena's land,
And round her awful image clasp thine hand,
Praying: and she will fence them back, though hot
With flickering serpents, that they touch thee not,
Holding above thy brow her gorgon shield.
   There is a hill in Athens, Ares' field,
Where first for that first death by Ares done
On Halirrhothius, Poseidon's son,
Who wronged his daughter, the great Gods of yore
Held judgment: and true judgments evermore
Flow from that Hill, trusted of man and God.
There shalt thou stand arraignèd of this blood;
And of those judges half shall lay on thee
Death, and half pardon; so shalt thou go free.
For Phoebus in that hour, who bade thee shed
Thy mother's blood, shall take on his own head
The stain thereof. And ever from that strife
The law shall hold, that when, for death or life
Of one pursued, men's voices equal stand,
Then Mercy conquereth.—But for thee, the band
Of Spirits dread, down, down, in very wrath,
Shall sink beside that Hill, making their path
Through a dim chasm, the which shall aye be trod
By reverent feet, where men may speak with God.
But thou forgotten and far off shalt dwell,
By great Alpheüs waters, in a dell
Of Arcady, where that gray Wolf-God's wall
Stands holy. And thy dwelling men shall call
Orestes' Town. So much to thee be spoke.
But this dead man, Aegisthus, all the folk

Shall bear to burial in a high green grave
Of Argos. For thy mother, she shall have
Her tomb from Menelaus, who hath come
This day, at last, to Argos, bearing home
Helen. From Egypt comes she, and the hall
Of Proteus, and in Troy hath ne'er at all
Set foot. 'Twas but a wraith of Helen, sent
By Zeus, to make much wrath and ravishment.

So forth for home, bearing the virgin bride,
Let Pylades make speed, and lead beside
Thy once-named brother, and with golden store
Stablish his house far off on Phocis' shore.

Up, gird thee now to the steep Isthmian way,
Seeking Athena's blessèd rock; one day,
Thy doom of blood fulfilled and this long stress
Of penance past, thou shalt have happiness.

Leader (*looking up*). Is it for us, O Seed of Zeus,
            To speak and hear your words again?
Castor.   Speak: of this blood ye bear no stain.
Electra. I also, sons of Tyndareus,
            My kinsmen; may my word be said?
Castor.   Speak: on Apollo's head we lay
            The bloody doings of this day.
Leader.   Ye Gods, ye brethren of the dead,
            Why held ye not the deathly herd
            Of Kêres back from off this home?
Castor.   There came but that which needs must come
            By ancient Fate and that dark word
            That rang from Phoebus in his mood.
Electra. And what should Phoebus seek with me,
            Or all God's oracles that be,
            That I must bear my mother's blood?
Castor.   Thy hand was as thy brother's hand,
            Thy doom shall be as his. One stain,
            From dim forefathers on the twain
            Lighting, hath sapped your hearts as sand.
Orestes (*who has never raised his head, nor spoken to the*
   Gods). After so long, sister, to see
            And hold thee, and then part, then part,

By all that chained thee to my heart
Forsaken, and forsaking thee!

Castor. Husband and house are hers. She bears
No bitter judgment, save to go
Exiled from Argos.

Electra. And what woe,
What tears are like an exile's tears?

Orestes. Exiled and more am I; impure,
A murderer in a stranger's hand!

Castor. Fear not. There dwells in Pallas' land
All holiness. Till then endure!

[ORESTES *and* ELECTRA *embrace.*

Orestes. Aye, closer; clasp my body well,
And let thy sorrow loose, and shed,
As o'er the grave of one new dead,
Dead evermore, thy last farewell!

[*A sound of weeping.*

Castor. Alas, what would ye? For that cry
Ourselves and all the sons of heaven
Have pity. Yea, our peace is riven
By the strange pain of these that die.

Orestes. No more to see thee! *Electra.* Nor thy breath
Be near my face! *Orestes.* Ah, so it ends.

Electra. Farewell, dear Argos. All ye friends,
Farewell! *Orestes.* O faithful unto death,
Thou goest? *Electra.* Aye, I pass from you,
Soft-eyed at last. *Orestes.* Go, Pylades,
And God go with you! Wed in peace
My tall Electra, and be true.

[ELECTRA *and* PYLADES *depart to the left.*

Castor. Their troth shall fill their hearts.—But on:
Dread feet are near thee, hounds of prey,
Snake-handed, midnight-visaged, yea,
And bitter pains their fruit! Begone!

[ORESTES *departs to the right.*

But hark, the far Sicilian sea
Calls, and a noise of men and ships
That labor sunken to the lips
In bitter billows; forth go we,

Through the long leagues of fiery blue,
  With saving; not to souls unshriven;
  But whoso in his life hath striven
To love things holy and be true,

Through toil and storm we guard him; we
  Save, and he shall not die!—Therefore,
  O praise the lying man no more,
Nor with oath-breakers sail the sea:
  Farewell, ye walkers on the shore
Of death! A God hath counseled ye.
                [CASTOR *and* POLYDEUCES *disappear.*
Chorus. Farewell, Farewell!—But he who can so fare,
  And stumbleth not on mischief anywhere,
        Blessèd on earth is he!

EURIPIDES
IPHIGENIA IN TAURIS

➤➤ ⫷⫷

TRANSLATED
by
GILBERT MURRAY

CHARACTERS IN THE PLAY

IPHIGENIA, *eldest daughter of Agamemnon, King of Argos; supposed to have been sacrificed by him to Artemis at Aulis.*

ORESTES, *her brother; pursued by Furies for killing his mother, Clytemnestra, who had murdered Agamemnon.*

PYLADES, *Prince of Phokis, friend to Orestes.*

THOAS, *King of Tauris, a savage country beyond the Symplêgades.*

A HERDSMAN.

A MESSENGER.

CHORUS of Captive Greek Women, handmaids to Iphigenia.

The Goddess PALLAS ATHENA.

The play was first performed between the years 414 and 412 B.C.

ARGUMENT

It will be remembered that Agamemnon, when ready to sail with all the powers of Greece against Troy, was bound by weather at Aulis. The medicine-man, Calchas, explained that Artemis demanded the sacrifice of his daughter, Iphigenia, who was then at home with her mother, Clytemnestra. Odysseus and Agamemnon sent for the maiden on the pretext that she was to be married to the famous young hero, Achilles; she was brought to Aulis and treacherously slaughtered—or, at least, so the people thought. In reality Artemis at the last moment saved Iphigenia, rapt her away from mortal eyes, and set her down in the land of the Tauri to be her priestess. These Tauri possessed an image of Artemis which had fallen from heaven, and kept up a savage rite of sacrificing to it all strangers who were cast on their shores. Iphigenia, obedient to her goddess, and held by 'the spell of the altar,' had to consecrate the victims as they went in to be slain. So far only barbarian strangers had come; she waited half in horror, half in a rage of revenge, for the day when she should have to sacrifice a Greek. The first Greek that came was her own brother, Orestes, who had been sent by Apollo to take the image of Artemis and bear it to Attica, where it should no more þe stained with human sacrifice.

IPHIGENIA IN TAURIS

*The Scene shows a great and barbaric Temple on a desolate
sea-coast. An altar is visible stained with blood. There are
spoils of slain men hanging from the roof.* IPHIGENIA, *in the
dress of a Priestess, comes out from the Temple.*

Iphigenia. Child of the man of torment and of pride
Tantalid Pelops bore a royal bride
On flying steeds from Pisa. Thence did spring
Atreus: from Atreus, linkèd king with king,
Menelaus, Agamemnon. His am I
And Clytemnestra's child: whom cruelly
At Aulis, where the strait of shifting blue
Frets with quick winds, for Helen's sake he slew,
Or thinks to have slain; such sacrifice he swore
To Artemis on that deep-bosomed shore.
 For there Lord Agamemnon, hot with joy
To win for Greece the crown of conquered Troy,
For Menelaus' sake through all distress
Pursuing Helen's vanished loveliness,
Gathered his thousand ships from every coast
Of Hellas: when there fell on that great host
Storms and despair of sailing. Then the King
Sought signs of fire, and Calchas answering
Spake thus: 'O Lord of Hellas, from this shore
No ship of thine may move for evermore,
Till Artemis receive in gift of blood
Thy child, Iphigenia. Long hath stood
Thy vow, to pay to Her that bringeth light
Whatever birth most fair by day or night
The year should bring. That year thy queen did bear
A child—whom here I name of all most fair.
See that she die.'

So from my mother's side
By lies Odysseus won me, to be bride
In Aulis to Achilles. When I came,
They took me and above the altar flame
Held, and the sword was swinging to the gash,
When, lo, out of their vision in a flash
Artemis rapt me, leaving in my place
A deer to bleed; and on through a great space
Of shining sky upbore and in this town
Of Tauris the Unfriended set me down;
Where o'er a savage people savagely
King Thoas rules. This is her sanctuary
And I her priestess. Therefore, by the rite
Of worship here, wherein she hath delight—
Though fair in naught but name. . . . But Artemis
Is near; I speak no further. Mine it is
To consecrate and touch the victim's hair;
Doings of blood unspoken are the care
Of others, where her inmost chambers lie.
Ah me!
But what dark dreams, thou clear and morning sky,
I have to tell thee, could that bring them ease!
Meseemed in sleep, far over distant seas,
I lay in Argos, and about me slept
My maids: and, lo, the level earth was swept
With quaking like the sea. Out, out I fled,
And, turning, saw the cornice overhead
Reel, and the beams and mighty door-trees down
In blocks of ruin round me overthrown.
One single oaken pillar, so I dreamed,
Stood of my father's house; and hair, meseemed,
Waved from its head all brown: and suddenly
A human voice it had, and spoke. And I,
Fulfilling this mine office, built on blood
Of unknown men, before that pillar stood,
And washed him clean for death, mine eyes astream
With weeping.
                    And this way I read my dream.
Orestes is no more: on him did fall
My cleansing drops.—The pillar of the hall

Must be the man first-born; and they on whom
My cleansing falls, their way is to the tomb.
    Therefore to my dead brother will I pour
Such sacrifice, I on this bitter shore
And he beyond great seas, as still I may,
With all those maids whom Thoas bore away
In war from Greece and gave me for mine own.
But wherefore come they not? I must be gone
And wait them in the temple, where I dwell.

                                        [*She goes into the Temple.*
Voice. Did some one cross the pathway? Guard thee well.
Another Voice. I am watching. Every side I turn mine eye.

                        [*Enter* ORESTES *and* PYLADES. *Their dress shows
                        they are travelers:* ORESTES *is shaken and dis-
                        traught.*

Orestes. How, brother? And is this the sanctuary
At last, for which we sailed from Argolis?
Pylades. For sure, Orestes. Seest thou not it is?
Orestes. The altar, too, where Hellene blood is shed.
Pylades. How like long hair those blood-stains, tawny red!
Orestes. And spoils of slaughtered men—there by the thatch.
Pylades. Aye, first-fruits of the harvest, when they catch
Their strangers!—'Tis a place to search with care.

                        [*He searches, while* ORESTES *sits.*
Orestes. O God, where hast thou brought me? What new
    snare
Is this?—I slew my mother; I avenged
My father at thy bidding; I have ranged
A homeless world, hunted by shapes of pain,
And circling trod in mine own steps again.
At last I stood once more before thy throne
And cried thee question, what thing should be done
To end these miseries, wherein I reel
Through Hellas, mad, lashed like a burning wheel;
And thou didst bid me seek . . . what land but this
Of Tauri, where thy sister Artemis
Her altar hath, and seize on that divine
Image which fell, men say, into this shrine
From heaven. This I must seize by chance or plot
Or peril—clearer word was uttered not—

And bear to Attic earth. If this be done,
I should have peace from all my malison.
    Lo, I have done thy will. I have pierced the seas
Where no Greek man may live.—Ho, Pylades,
Sole sharer of my quest: hast seen it all?
What can we next? Thou seest this circuit wall
Enormous? Must we climb the public stair,
With all men watching? Shall we seek somewhere
Some lock to pick, some secret bolt or bar—
Of all which we know nothing? Where we are,
If one man mark us, if they see us prize
The gate, or think of entrance anywise,
'Tis death.—We still have time to fly for home:
Back to the galley quick, ere worse things come!
    Pylades. To fly we dare not, brother. 'Twere a thing
Not of our custom; and ill work, to bring
God's word to such reviling.—Let us leave
The temple now, and gather in some cave
Where glooms the cool sea ripple. But not where
The ship lies; men might chance to see her there
And tell some chief; then certain were our doom.
But when the fringèd eye of Night be come
Then we must dare, by all ways foul or fine,
To thieve that wondrous Image from its shrine.
Ah, see; far up, between each pair of beams
A hollow one might creep through! Danger gleams
Like sunshine to a brave man's eyes, and fear
Of what may be is no help anywhere.
    Orestes. Aye; we have never braved these leagues of way
To falter at the end. See, I obey
Thy words. They are ever wise. Let us go mark
Some cavern, to lie hid till fall of dark.
God will not suffer that bad things be stirred
To mar us now, and bring to naught the word
Himself hath spoke. Aye, and no peril brings
Pardon for turning back to sons of kings.

> [*They go out towards the shore. After they are
> gone, enter gradually the* WOMEN OF THE
> CHORUS.

Chorus. Peace! Peace upon all who dwell
  By the Sister Rocks that clash in the swell
   Of the Friendless Seas.
  O Child of Leto, thou,
  Dictynna mountain-born,
  To the cornice gold-inlaid,
  To the pillared sanctities,
  We come in the cold of morn,
  We come with virgin brow,
  Pure as our oath was sworn,
  Handmaids of thine handmaid
  Who holdeth the stainless keys.

  From Hellas, that once was ours,
  We come before thy gate,
  From the land of the western seas,
  The horses and the towers,
  The wells and the garden trees,
  And the seats where our fathers sate.
Leader. What tidings, ho? With what intent
  Hast called me to thy shrine and thee,
  O child of him who crossed the sea
  To Troy with that great armament,
  The thousand prows, the myriad swords?
  I come, O child of Atreid Lords.
   [IPHIGENIA, *followed by* ATTENDANTS, *comes from*
    the Temple.
Iphigenia. Alas, O maidens mine,
  I am filled full of tears:
  My heart filled with the beat
  Of tears, as of dancing feet,
  A lyreless joyless line,
  And music meet for the dead.

  For a whisper is in mine ears,
  By visions borne on the breath
  Of the Night that now is fled,
  Of a brother gone to death.
  Oh sorrow and weeping sore,
  For the house that no more is,

For the dead that were kings of yore
   And the labor of Argolis!
                    [*She begins the Funeral Rite.*
O Spirit, thou unknown,
Who bearest on dark wings
My brother, my one, mine own,
   I bear drink-offerings,
And the cup that bringeth ease
   Flowing through Earth's deep breast;
Milk of the mountain kine,
The hallowed gleam of wine,
The toil of murmuring bees:
   By these shall the dead have rest.
                    [*To an* ATTENDANT.
The golden goblet let me pour,
And that which Hades thirsteth for.

O branch of Agamemnon's tree
   Beneath the earth, as to one dead,
This cup of love I pour to thee.
   Oh, pardon, that I may not shed
One lock of hair to wreathe thy tomb,
   One tear; so far, so far am I
From what to me and thee was home,
   And where in all men's fantasy,
   Butchered, O God! I also lie.
Chorus. Woe; woe: I too with refluent melody,
   An echo wild of the dirges of the Asian,
I, thy bond maiden, cry to answer thee:
   The music that lieth hid in lamentation,
The song that is heard in the deep hearts of the dead,
   That the Lord of dead men 'mid his dancing singeth,
   And never joy-cry, never joy it bringeth;
   Woe for the house of Kings in desolation,
Woe for the light of the sceptre vanishèd.

From kings in Argos of old, from joyous kings,
      The beginning came:
Then peril swift upon peril, flame cn flame:
The dark and wheeling coursers, as wild with wings,

The cry of one betrayed on a drowning shore,
The sun that blanched in heaven, the world that changed—
Evil on evil and none alone!—deranged
By the Golden Lamb and the wrong grown ever more;
Blood following blood, sorrow on sorrow sore!
So come the dead of old, the dead in wrath,
Back on the seed of the high Tantalidae;
Surely the Spirit of Life an evil path
      Hath hewed for thee.
   Iphigenia. From the beginning the Spirit of my life
Was an evil spirit. Alas for my mother's zone,
And the night that bare me! From the beginning Strife,
As a book to read, Fate gave me for mine own.
They wooed a bride for the strikers down of Troy—
Thy first-born, Mother: was it for this, thy prayer?—
A hind of slaughter to die in a father's snare,
Gift of a sacrifice where none hath joy.

      They set me on a royal wain;
        Down the long sand they led me on,
      A bride new-decked, a bride of bane,
        In Aulis to the Nereid's son.
      And now estranged for evermore
        Beyond the far estranging foam
      I watch a flat and herbless shore,
        Unloved, unchilded, without home
      Or city: never more to meet
        For Hera's dance with Argive maids,
      Nor round the loom 'mid singing sweet
        Make broideries and storied braids,
      Of writhing giants overthrown
      And clear-eyed Pallas. . . . All is gone!
      Red hands and ever-ringing ears:
      The blood of men that friendless die,
      The horror of the strangers' cry
      Unheard, the horror of their tears.

      But now, let even that have rest:
      I weep for him in Argos slain,
      The brother whom I knew, Ah me,

A babe, a flower; and yet to be—
There on his mother's arms and breast—
The crowned Orestes, lord of men!

Leader of the Chorus. Stay, yonder from some headland of
   the sea
There comes—methinks a herdsman, seeking thee.

   [*Enter a* HERDSMAN. IPHIGENIA *is still on her knees.*

Herdsman. Daughter of Clytemnestra and her king,
Give ear! I bear news of a wondrous thing.

Iphigenia. What news, that should so mar my obsequies?

Herdsman. A ship hath passed the blue Symplêgades,
And here upon our coast two men are thrown,
Young, bold, good slaughter for the altar-stone
Of Artemis!

                              [*She rises.*
                  Make all the speed ye may;
'Tis not too much. The blood-bowl and the spray!

Iphigenia. Men of what nation? Doth their habit show?

Herdsman. Hellenes for sure, but that is all we know.

Iphigenia. No name? No other clue thine ear could seize?

Herdsman. We heard one call his comrade 'Pylades.'

Iphigenia. Yes. And the man who spoke—his name was
   what?

Herdsman. None of us heard. I think they spoke it not.

Iphigenia. How did ye see them first, how make them fast?

Herdsman. Down by the sea, just where the surge is
   cast. . . .

Iphigenia. The sea? What is the sea to thee and thine?

Herdsman. We came to wash our cattle in the brine.

Iphigenia. Go back, and tell how they were taken; show
The fashion of it, for I fain would know
All.—'Tis so long a time, and never yet,
Never, hath Greek blood made this altar wet.

Herdsman. We had brought our forest cattle where the seas
Break in long tides from the Symplêgades.
A bay is there, deep eaten by the surge
And hollowed clear, with cover near the verge
Where purple-fishers camp. These twain were there
When one of mine own men, a forager,

Spied them, and tiptoed whispering back: 'God save
Us now! Two things unearthly by the wave
Sitting!' We looked, and one of pious mood
Raised up his hands to heaven and praying stood:
'Son of the white Sea Spirit, high in rule,
Storm-lord Palaemon, Oh, be merciful:
Or sit ye there the warrior twins of Zeus,
Or something loved of Him, from whose great thews
Was born the Nereids' fifty-fluted choir.'
  Another, flushed with folly and the fire
Of lawless daring, laughed aloud and swore
'Twas shipwrecked sailors skulking on the shore,
Our rule and custom here being known, to slay
All strangers. And most thought this was the way
To follow, and seek out for Artemis
The blood-gift of our people.
                              Just at this
One of the strangers started from his seat,
And stood, and upward, downward, with a beat
His head went, and he groaned, and all his arm
Trembled. Then, as a hunter gives alarm,
He shrieked, stark mad and raving: 'Pylades,
Dost see her there?—And there—Oh, no one sees!—
A she-dragon of Hell, and all her head
Agape with fangèd asps, to bite me dead.
She hath no face, but somewhere from her cloak
Bloweth a wind of fire and bloody smoke:
The wings' beat fans it: in her arms, Ah see!
My mother, dead gray stone, to cast on me
And crush. . . . Help, help! The crowd on me behind. . . .'
  No shapes at all were there. 'Twas his sick mind
Which turned the herds that lowed and barking hounds
That followed, to some visionary sounds
Of Furies. For ourselves, we did but sit
And watch in silence, wondering if the fit
Would leave him dead. When suddenly out shone
His sword, and like a lion he leaped upon
Our herds, to fight his Furies! Flank and side
He stabbed and smote them, till the foam was dyed
Red at the waves' edge. Marry, when we saw

The cattle hurt and falling, no more law
We gave, but sprang to arms and blew the horn
For help—so strong they looked and nobly born
For thralls like us to meet, that pair unknown.

Well, a throng gathered ere much time was gone;
When suddenly the whirl of madness slips
From off him and he falls, quite weak, his lips
Dropping with foam. When once we saw him fall
So timely, we were at him one and all
To pelt and smite. The other watched us come,
But knelt and wiped those lips all dank with foam
And tended the sick body, while he held
His cloak's good web above him for a shield;
So cool he was to ward off every stone
And all the while care for that stricken one.

Then rose the fallen man, calm now and grave,
Looked, and saw battle bursting like a wave
That bursts, and knew that peril close at hand
Which now is come, and groaned. On every hand
We stood, and stoned and stoned, and ceased not. Aye,
'Twas then we heard that fearful battle-cry:
'Ho, Pylades, 'tis death! But let it be
A gallant death! Draw sword and follow me.'

When those two swords came flashing, up the glen
Through the loose rocks we scattered back; but when
One band was flying, down by rocks and trees
Came others pelting: did they turn on these,
Back stole the first upon them, stone on stone.
'Twas past belief: of all those shots not one
Struck home. The goddess kept her fated prey
Perfect. Howbeit, at last we made our way
Right, left and round behind them on the sands,
And rushed, and beat the swords out of their hands,
So tired they scarce could stand. Then to the king
We bore them both, and he, not tarrying,
Sends them to thee, to touch with holy spray—
And then the blood-bowl!

                I have heard thee pray,
Priestess, ere now for such a draft as this.
Aye, slay but these two chiefs to Artemis

And Hellas shall have paid thy debt, and know
What blood was spilt in Aulis long ago.
    Leader. I marvel that one mad, whoe'er he be,
Should sail from Hellas to the Friendless Sea.
    Iphigenia. 'Tis well. Let thy hand bring them, and mine own
Shall falter not till here God's will be done.

                           [*Exit* HERDSMAN.

O suffering heart, not fierce thou wast of old
To shipwrecked men. Nay, pities manifold
Held thee in fancy homeward, lest thy hand
At last should fall on one of thine own land.
But now, for visions that have turned to stone
My heart, to know Orestes sees the sun
No more, a cruel woman waits you here,
Whoe'er ye be, and one without a tear.
    'Tis true: I know by mine own evil will:
One long in pain, if things more suffering still
Fall to his hand, will hate them for his own
Torment. . . . And no great wind hath ever blown,
No ship from God hath passed the Clashing Gate,
To bring me Helen, who hath earned my hate,
And Menelaus, till I mocked their prayers
In this new Aulis, that is mine, not theirs:
Where Greek hands held me lifted, like a beast
For slaughter, and my throat bled. And the priest
My father! . . . Not one pang have I forgot.
    Ah me, the blind half-prisoned arms I shot
This way and that, to find his beard, his knees,
Groping and wondering: 'Father, what are these
For bridal rites? My mother even now
Mid Argive women sings for me, whom thou . . .
What dost thou? She sings happy songs, and all
Is dance and sound of piping in the hall;
And here. . . . Is he a vampire, is he one
That fattens on the dead, thy Peleus' son—
Whose passion shaken like a torch before
My leaping chariot, lured me to this shore
To wed—'
           Ah me! And I had hid my face,
Burning, behind my veil. I would not press

Orestes to my arms . . . who now is slain! . . .
I would not kiss my sister's lips again,
For shame and fullness of the heart to meet
My bridegroom. All my kisses, all my sweet
Words were stored up and hid: I should come back
So soon to Argos!
        And thou, too: alack,
Brother, if dead thou art, from what high things
Thy youth is outcast, and the pride of kings
Fallen!
      And this the goddess deemeth good!
If ever mortal hand be dark with blood;
Nay, touch a new-made mother or one slain
In war, her ban is on him. 'Tis a stain
She driveth from her outer walls; and then
Herself doth drink this blood of slaughtered men?
Could ever Leto, she of the great King
Beloved, be mother to so gross a thing?
These tales be lies, false as those feastings wild
Of Tantalus and Gods that tore a child.
This land of murderers to its god hath given
Its own lust; evil dwelleth not in heaven.

                           [She goes into the Temple.

                               [Strophe.

Chorus. Dark of the sea, dark of the sea,
   Gates of the warring water,
One, in the old time, conquered you,
A wingèd passion that burst the blue,
When the West was shut and the Dawn lay free
   To the pain of Inachus' daughter.

But who be these, from where the rushes blow
On pale Eurôtas, from pure Dirce's flow,
   That turn not neither falter,
Seeking Her land, where no man breaketh bread
Her without pity, round whose virgin head
Blood on the pillars rusts from long ago,
   Blood on the ancient altar.

[Antistrophe.

A flash of the foam, a flash of the foam,
  A wave on the oarblade welling,
And out they passed to the heart of the blue:
A chariot shell that the wild winds drew.
Is it for passion of gold they come,
  Or pride to make great their dwelling?

For sweet is Hope, yea, to much mortal woe
So sweet that none may turn from it nor go,
  Whom once the far voice calleth,
To wander through fierce peoples and the gleam
Of desolate seas, in every heart a dream:
And these she maketh empty die, and lo,
  To that man's hand she falleth.

[Strophe.

Through the Clashing Rocks they burst:
  They passed by the Cape unsleeping
Of Phineus' sons accurst:
They ran by the star-lit bay
  Upon magic surges sweeping,
Where folk on the waves astray
Have seen, through the gleaming gray,
Ring behind ring, men say,
  The dance of the old Sea's daughters.

The guiding oar abaft
  It rippled and it dinned,
And now the west wind laughed
  And now the south-west wind;
And the sail was full in flight,
And they passed by the Island White:

Birds, birds, everywhere,
  White as the foam, light as the air;
And ghostly Achilles raceth there,
  Far in the Friendless Waters.

[Antistrophe.

'Ah, would that Leda's child . . .
  (So prayeth the priestess maiden)
From Troy, that she beguiled,

Hither were borne, to know
    What sin on her soul is laden!
Hair twisted, throat held low,
Head back for the blood to flow,
To die by the sword.' . . . Ah no!
    One hope my soul yet hideth.

A sail, a sail from Greece,
    Fearless to cross the sea,
With ransom and with peace
    To my sick captivity.
O home, to see thee still,
And the old walls on the hill!
Dreams, dreams, gather to me!
Bear me on wings over the sea;
O joy of the night, to slave and free,
    One good thing that abideth!   .

Leader. But lo, the twain whom Thoas sends,
    Their arms in bondage graspèd sore;
    Strange offering this, to lay before
The Goddess! Hold your peace, O friends.

Onward, still onward, to this shrine
    They lead the first-fruits of the Greek.
    'Twas true, the tale he came to speak,
That watcher of the mountain kine.

O holy one, if it afford
    Thee joy, what these men bring to thee,
    Take thou their sacrifice, which we,
By law of Hellas, hold abhorred.
        [*Enter* ORESTES *and* PYLADES, *bound, and guarded*
            by TAURIANS. *Re-enter* IPHIGENIA.
Iphigenia. So be it.
My foremost care must be that nothing harms
The temple's holy rule.—Untie their arms.
That which is hallowed may no more be bound.
You, to the shrine within! Let all be found
As the law bids, and as we need this day.

[ORESTES *and* PYLADES *are set free; some* AT-
TENDANTS *go into the Temple.*

Ah me!
What mother then was yours, O strangers, say,
And father? And your sister, if you have
A sister: both at once, so young and brave
To leave her brotherless! Who knows when heaven
May send that fortune? For to none is given
To know the coming nor the end of woe;
So dark is God, and to great darkness go
His paths, by blind chance mazèd from our ken.
    Whence are ye come, O most unhappy men?
From some far home, methinks, ye have found this shore
And far shall stay from home for evermore.
    Orestes. Why weepest thou, woman, to make worse the smart
Of that which needs must be, whoe'er thou art?
I count it not for gentleness, when one
Who means to slay, seeks first to make undone
By pity that sharp dread. Nor praise I him,
With hope long dead, who sheddeth tears to dim
The pain that grips him close. The evil so
Is doubled into twain. He doth but show
His feeble heart, and, as he must have died,
Dies.—Let ill fortune float upon her tide
And weep no more for us. What way this land
Worships its god we know and understand.
    Iphigenia. Say first . . . which is it men call Pylades?
    Orestes. 'Tis this man's name, if that will give thee ease.
    Iphigenia. From what walled town of Hellas cometh he?
    Orestes. Enough!—How would the knowledge profit thee?
    Iphigenia. Are ye two brethren of one mother born?
    Orestes. No, not in blood. In love we are brothers sworn.
    Iphigenia. Thou also hast a name: tell me thereof.
    Orestes. Call me Unfortunate. 'Tis name enough.
    Iphigenia. I asked not that. Let that with Fortune lie.
    Orestes. Fools cannot laugh at them that nameless die.
    Iphigenia. Why grudge me this? Hast thou such mighty
        fame?
    Orestes. My body, if thou wilt, but not my name.
    Iphigenia. Nor yet the land of Greece where thou wast bred?

[415]

Orestes. What gain to have told it thee, when I am dead?
Iphigenia. Nay: why shouldst thou deny so small a grace?
Orestes. Know then, great Argos was my native place.
Iphigenia. Stranger! The truth! . . . From Argos art thou come?
Orestes. Mycenae, once a rich land, was my home.
Iphigenia. 'Tis banishment that brings thee here—or what?
Orestes. A kind of banishment, half forced, half sought.
Iphigenia. Wouldst thou but tell me all I need of thee!
Orestes. 'Twere not much added to my misery.
Iphigenia. From Argos! . . . Oh, how sweet to see thee here!
Orestes. Enjoy it, then. To me 'tis sorry cheer.
Iphigenia. Thou knowest the name of Troy? Far doth it flit.
Orestes. Would God I had not; nay, nor dreamed of it.
Iphigenia. Men fable it is fallen beneath the sword?
Orestes. Fallen it is. Thou hast heard no idle word.
Iphigenia. Fallen! At last!—And Helen taken too?
Orestes. Aye; on an evil day for one I knew.
Iphigenia. Where is she? I too have some anger stored. . . .
Orestes. In Sparta! Once more happy with her lord!
Iphigenia. Oh, hated of all Greece, not only me!
Orestes. I too have tasted of her wizardry.
Iphigenia. And came the armies home, as the tales run?
Orestes. To answer that were many tales in one.
Iphigenia. Oh, give me this hour full! Thou wilt soon die.
Orestes. Ask, if such longing holds thee. I will try.
Iphigenia. A seer called Calchas! Did he ever come . . . ?
Orestes. Calchas is dead, as the news went at home.
Iphigenia. Good news, ye gods!—Odysseus, what of him?
Orestes. Not home yet, but still living, as men deem.
Iphigenia. Curse him! And may he see his home no more.
Orestes. Why curse him? All his house is stricken sore.
Iphigenia. How hath the Nereid's son, Achillès, sped?
Orestes. Small help his bridal brought him! He is dead.
Iphigenia. A false fierce bridal, so the sufferers tell!
Orestes. Who art thou, questioning of Greece so well?
Iphigenia. I was Greek. Evil caught me long ago.
Orestes. Small wonder, then, thou hast such wish to know.
Iphigenia. That war-lord, whom they call so high in bliss.

Orestes. None such is known to me. What name was his?
Iphigenia. They called him Agamemnon, Atreus' son.
Orestes. I know not. Cease.—My questioning is done.
Iphigenia. 'Twill be such joy to me! How fares he? Tell!
Orestes. Dead. And hath wrecked another's life as well.
Iphigenia. Dead? By what dreadful fortune? Woe is me!
Orestes. Why sighst thou? Had he any link with thee?
Iphigenia. I did but think of his old joy and pride.
Orestes. His own wife foully stabbed him, and he died.
Iphigenia. O God!
I pity her that slew . . . and him that slew.
Orestes. Now cease thy questions. Add no word thereto.
Iphigenia. But one word. Lives she still, that hapless wife?
Orestes. No. Her own son, her first-born, took her life.
Iphigenia. O shipwrecked house! What thought was in his
brain?
Orestes. Justice on her, to avenge his father slain.
Iphigenia. Alas!
A bad false duty bravely hath he wrought.
Orestes. Yet God, for all his duty, helps him not.
Iphigenia. And not one branch of Atreus' tree lives on?
Orestes. Electra lives, unmated and alone.
Iphigenia. The child they slaughtered . . . is there word of
her?
Orestes. Why, no, save that she died in Aulis there.
Iphigenia. Poor child! Poor father, too, who killed and
lied!
Orestes. For a bad woman's worthless sake she died.
Iphigenia. The dead king's son, lives he in Argos still?
Orestes. He lives, now here, now nowhere, bent with ill.
Iphigenia. O dreams, light dreams, farewell! Ye too were
lies.
Orestes. Aye; the gods too, whom mortals deem so wise,
Are nothing clearer than some wingèd dream;
And all their ways, like man's ways, but a stream
Of turmoil. He who cares to suffer least,
Not blind, as fools are blinded, by a priest,
Goes straight . . . to what death, those who know him know.
Leader. We too have kinsmen dear, but, being low,
None heedeth, live they still or live they not.

Iphigenia (*with sudden impulse*). Listen! For I am fallen
    upon a thought,
Strangers, of some good use to you and me,
Both. And 'tis thus most good things come to be,
When different eyes hold the same way for fair.
    Stranger, if I can save thee, wilt thou bear
To Argos and the friends who loved my youth
Some word? There is a tablet which, in ruth
For me and mine ill works, a prisoner wrote,
Ta'en by the king in war. He knew 'twas not
My will that craved for blood, but One on high
Who holds it righteous her due prey shall die.
And since that day no Greek hath ever come
Whom I could save and send to Argos home
With prayer for help to any friend: but thou,
I think, dost loathe me not; and thou dost know
Mycenae and the names that fill my heart.
Help me! Be saved! Thou also hast thy part,
Thy life for one light letter. . . . (ORESTES *looks at* PYLADES.)
                            For thy friend,
The law compelleth. He must bear the end
By Artemis ordained, apart from thee.
    Orestes. Strange woman, as thou biddest let it be,
Save one thing. 'Twere for me a heavy weight
Should this man die. 'Tis I and mine own fate
That steer our goings. He but sails with me
Because I suffer much. It must not be
That by his ruin I should 'scape mine own,
And win thy grace withal. 'Tis simply done.
Give him the tablet. He with faithful will
Shall all thy hest in Argolis fulfil.
And I . . . who cares may kill me. Vile is he
Who leaves a friend in peril and goes free
Himself. And, as it chances, this is one
Right dear to me; his life is as my own.
    Iphigenia. O royal heart! Surely from some great seed
This branch is born, that can so love indeed.
God grant the one yet living of my race
Be such as thou! For not quite brotherless
Am even I, save that I see him not,

Strangers. . . . Howbeit, thy pleasure shall be wrought.
This man shall bear the message, and thou go
To death. So greatly thou wilt have it so!

Orestes. Where is the priest who does this cruelty?

Iphigenia. 'Tis I. This altar's spell is over me.

Orestes. A grievous office and unblest, O maid.

Iphigenia. What dare I do? The law must be obeyed.

Orestes. A girl to hold a sword and stab men dead!

Iphigenia. I shall but sign the water on thy head.

Orestes. And who shall strike me, if I needs must ask?

Iphigenia. There be within these vaults who know their task.

Orestes. My grave, when they have finished their desire?

Iphigenia. A great gulf of the rock, and holy fire.

Orestes. Woe's me!
Would that my sister's hand could close mine eyes!

Iphigenia. Alas, she dwelleth under distant skies,
Unhappy one, and vain is all thy prayer.
Yet, Oh, thou art from Argos: all of care
That can be, I will give and fail thee not.
Rich raiment to thy burial shall be brought,
And oil to cool thy pyre in golden floods,
And sweet that from a thousand mountain buds
The murmuring bee hath garnered, I will throw
To die with thee in fragrance. . . .

                                    I must go
And seek the tablet from the Goddess' room
Within.—Oh, do not hate me for my doom!

Watch them, ye servitors, but leave them free.

It may be, past all hoping, it may be,
My word shall sail to Argos, to his hand
Whom most I love. How joyous will he stand
To know, past hope, that here on the world's rim
His dead are living, and cry out for him!

                              [She goes into the Temple.

                                        [Strophe.

Chorus. Alas, we pity thee; surely we pity thee:
Who are given over to the holy water,

The drops that fall deadly as drops of blood.

Orestes. I weep not, ye Greek maidens: but farewell.

[*Antistrophe.*

Chorus. Aye, and rejoice with thee; surely rejoice with thee,
Thou happy rover from the place of slaughter;
   Thy foot shall stand again where thy father's stood.

Pylades. While he I love must die? 'Tis miserable.

Divers Women of the Chorus.

   A. Alas, the deathward faring of the lost!
   B. Woe, woe; thou too shalt move to misery.
   C. Which one shall suffer most?
   D. My heart is torn by two words evenly,
      For thee should I most sorrow, or for thee?

Orestes. By heaven, is thy thought, Pylades, like mine?

Pylades. O friend, I cannot speak.—But what is thine?

Orestes. Who can the damsel be? How Greek her tone
Of question, all of Ilion overthrown,
And how the kings came back, the wizard flame
Of Calchas, and Achilles' mighty name,
And ill-starred Agamemnon. With a keen
Pity she spoke, and asked me of his queen
And children. . . . The strange woman comes from there
By race, an Argive maid.—What aileth her
With tablets, else, and questionings as though
Her own heart beat with Argos' joy or woe?

Pylades. Thy speech is quicker, friend, else I had said
The same; though surely all men visited
By ships have heard the fall of the great kings.
But let that be: I think of other things. . . .

   Orestes. What? If thou hast need of me, let it be said.

   Pylades. I cannot live for shame if thou art dead.
I sailed together with thee; let us die
Together. What a coward slave were I,
Creeping through Argos and from glen to glen
Of wind-torn Phocian hills! And most of men—
For most are bad—will whisper how one day
I left my friend to die and made my way
Home. They will say I watched the sinking breath
Of thy great house and plotted for thy death
To wed thy sister, climb into thy throne. . . .

I dread, I loathe it.—Nay, all ways but one
Are shut. My last breath shall go forth with thine,
Thy bloody sword, thy gulf of fire be mine
Also. I love thee and I dread men's scorn.

 Orestes. Peace from such thoughts! My burden can be
  borne;
But where one pain sufficeth, double pain
I will not bear. Nay, all that scorn and stain
That fright thee, on mine own head worse would be
If I brought death on him who toiled for me.
It is no bitter thing for such an one
As God will have me be, at last to have done
With living. Thou art happy; thy house lies
At peace with God, unstainèd in men's eyes;
Mine is all evil fate and evil life. . . .
Nay, thou once safe, my sister for thy wife—
So we agreed—in sons of hers and thine
My name will live, nor Agamemnon's line
Be blurred for ever like an evil scroll.
Back! Rule thy land! Let life be in thy soul!
And when thou art come to Hellas, and the plain
Of Argos where the horsemen ride, again—
Give me thy hand!—I charge thee, let there be
Some death-mound and a graven stone for me.
My sister will go weep thereat, and shear
A tress or two. Say how I ended here,
Slain by a maid of Argolis, beside
God's altar, in mine own blood purified.

 And fare thee well. I have no friend like thee
For truth and love, O boy that played with me,
And hunted on Greek hills, O thou on whom
Hath lain the hardest burden of my doom!
Farewell. The Prophet and the Lord of Lies
Hath done his worst. Far out from Grecian skies
With craft forethought he driveth me, to die
Where none may mark how ends his prophecy!
I trusted in his word. I gave him all
My heart. I slew my mother at his call;
For which things now he casts me here to die.

 Pylades. Thy tomb shall fail thee not. Thy sister I

Will guard for ever. I, O stricken sore,
Who loved thee living and shall love thee more
Dead. But for all thou standest on the brink,
God's promise hath not yet destroyed thee. Think!
How oft, how oft the darkest hour of ill
Breaks brightest into dawn, if Fate but will!

Orestes. Enough. Nor god nor man can any more
Aid me. The woman standeth at the door.

[*Enter* IPHIGENIA *from the Temple.*

Iphigenia. Go ye within; and have all things of need
In order set for them that do the deed.
There wait my word.

[ATTENDANTS *go in.*

Ye strangers, here I hold
The many-lettered tablet, fold on fold.
Yet . . . one thing still. No man, once unafraid
And safe, remembereth all the vows he made
In fear of death. My heart misgiveth me,
Lest he who bears my tablet, once gone free,
Forget me here and set my charge at naught.

Orestes. What wouldst thou, then? Thou hast some troubling
thought.

Iphigenia. His sworn oath let him give, to bear this same
Tablet to Argos, to the friend I name.

Orestes. And if he give this oath, wilt thou swear too?

Iphigenia. What should I swear to do or not to do?

Orestes. Send him from Tauris safe and free from ill.

Iphigenia. I promise. How else could he do my will?

Orestes. The King will suffer this?

Iphigenia. Yes: I can bend
The King, and set upon his ship thy friend.

Orestes. Choose then what oath is best, and he will swear.

Iphigenia (*to* PYLADES, *who has come up to her*). Say: 'To
thy friend this tablet I will bear.'

Pylades (*taking the tablet*). Good. I will bear this tablet
to thy friend.

Iphigenia. And I save thee beyond this kingdom's end.

Pylades. What god dost thou invoke to witness this?

Iphigenia. Her in whose house I labor, Artemis.

Pylades. And I the Lord of Heaven, eternal Zeus.

Iphigenia. And if thou fail me, or thine oath abuse . . . ?
Pylades. May I see home no more. And thou, what then?
Iphigenia. May this foot never tread Greek earth again.
Pylades. But stay: there is one chance we have forgot.
Iphigenia. A new oath can be sworn, if this serve not.
Pylades. In one case set me free. Say I be crossed
With shipwreck, and, with ship and tablet lost
And all I bear, my life be saved alone:
Let not this oath be held a thing undone,
To curse me.
    Iphigenia. Nay, then, many ways are best
To many ends. The words thou carriest
Enrolled and hid beneath that tablet's rim,
I will repeat to thee, and thou to him
I look for. Safer so. If the scrip sail
Unhurt to Greece, itself will tell my tale
Unaided: if it drown in some wide sea,
Save but thyself, my words are saved with thee.
    Pylades. For thy sake and for mine 'tis fairer so.
Now let me hear his name to whom I go
In Argolis, and how my words should run.
    Iphigenia (*repeating the words by heart*). Say: 'To Orestes,
      Agamemnon's son,
She that was slain in Aulis, dead to Greece
Yet quick, Iphigenia sendeth peace':
    Orestes. Iphigenia! Where? Back from the dead?
    Iphigenia. 'Tis I. But speak not, lest thou break my thread.—
'Take me to Argos, brother, ere I die,
Back from the Friendless Peoples and the high
Altar of Her whose bloody rites I wreak.'
    Orestes (*aside*). Where am I, Pylades? How shall I speak?
    Iphigenia. 'Else one in grief forsaken shall, like shame,
Haunt thee.'
    Pylades (*aside*). Orestes!
    Iphigenia (*overhearing him*). Yes: that is the name.
    Pylades. Ye Gods above!
    Iphigenia.   Why callest thou on God
For words of mine?
    Pylades.   'Tis nothing. 'Twas a road
My thoughts had turned. Speak on.—No need for us

To question; we shall hear things marvelous.

Iphigenia. Tell him that Artemis my soul did save,
I wot not how, and to the altar gave
A fawn instead; the which my father slew,
Not seeing, deeming that the sword he drew
Struck me. But she had borne me far away
And left me in this land.—I charge thee, say
So much. It all is written on the scroll.

Pylades. An easy charge thou layest on my soul,
A glad oath on thine own. I wait no more,
But here fulfil the service that I swore.
Orestes, take this tablet which I bear
To thine own hand, thy sister's messenger.

Orestes. I take it, but I reck not of its scrip
Nor message. Too much joy is at my lip.
Sister! Belovèd! Wildered though I be,
My arms believe not, yet they crave for thee.
Now, filled with wonder, give me my delight!

[*He goes to embrace her. She stands speechless.*

Leader. Stranger, forbear! No living man hath right
To touch that robe. The Goddess were defiled!

Orestes. O Sister mine, O my dead father's child,
Agamemnon's child; take me and have no fear,
Beyond all dreams 'tis I thy brother here.

Iphigenia. My brother? Thou? . . . Peace! Mock at me
no more.
Argos is bright with him and Nauplia's shore.

Orestes. Unhappy one! Thou hast no brother there.

Iphigenia. Orestes . . . thou? Whom Clytemnestra bare?

Orestes. To Atreus' firstborn son, thy sire and mine.

Iphigenia. Thou sayst it: Oh, give me some proof, some
sign!

Orestes. What sign thou wilt. Ask anything from home.

Iphigenia. Nay, thou speak: 'tis from thee the sign should
come.

Orestes. That will I.—First, old tales Electra told.
Thou knowest how Pelops' princes warred of old?

Iphigenia. I know: the Golden lamb that wrought their
doom.

Orestes. Thine own hand wove that story on the loom. . . .

Iphigenia. How sweet! Thou movest near old memories.
Orestes. With a great Sun back beaten in the skies.
Iphigenia. Fine linen threads I used. The memories come.
Orestes. And mother gave thee shrift-water from home
For Aulis. . . .
Iphigenia.   I remember. Not so fair
A day did drink that water!
Orestes.   And thine hair
They brought us for thy dying gift, and gave
To mother.
Iphigenia. Yes: for record on the grave
I sent it, where this head should never lie.
Orestes. Another token, seen of mine own eye.
The ancient lance that leapt in Pelops' hand,
To win his bride, the virgin of the land,
And smite Oenomaus, in thy chamber hid. . . .
Iphigenia (*falling into his arms*). Belovèd! Oh, no other,
    for indeed
                Belovèd art thou! In mine arms at last,
                    Orestes far away.
Orestes. And thou in mine, the evil dreaming past,
                Back from the dead this day!
    Yet through the joy tears, tears and sorrow loud
    Are o'er mine eyes and thine eyes, like a cloud.
Iphigenia. Is this the babe I knew,
                The little babe, light lifted like a bird?
        O heart of mine, too blest for any word,
                What shall I say or do?
        Beyond all wonders, beyond stories heard,
                This joy is here and true.
Orestes. Could we but stay thus joined for evermore!
Iphigenia. A joy is mine I may not understand,
        Friends, and a fear, lest sudden from my hand
                This dream will melt and soar
        Up to the fiery skies from whence it came.
        O Argos land, O hearth and holy flame
                That old Cyclôpes lit,
            I bless ye that he lives, that he is grown,
        A light and strength, my brother and mine own;
                I bless your name for it.

Orestes. One blood we are; so much is well. But Fate,
Sister, hath not yet made us fortunate.
    Iphigenia. O most unfortunate! Did I not feel,
        Whose father, misery-hearted, at my bare
            Throat held the steel?
    Orestes. Woe's me! Methinks even now I see thee there.
    Iphigenia. No love-song of Achilles! Crafty arms
        Drew me to that cold sleep,
    And tears, blind tears amid the altar psalms
        And noise of them that weep—
    That was my cleansing!
    Orestes.   My heart too doth bleed,
To think our father wrought so dire a deed.
    Iphigenia. My life hath known no father. Any road
        To any end may run,
As god's will drives; else . . .
    Orestes.   Else, unhappy one,
Thyself had spilt this day thy brother's blood!
    Iphigenia. Ah God, my cruel deed! . . . 'Twas horrible.
'Twas horrible. . . . O brother! Did my heart
        Endure it? . . . And things fell
Right by so frail a chance; and here thou art.
        Bloody my hand had been,
        My heart heavy with sin.
        And now, what end cometh?
    Shall Chance yet comfort me,
    Finding a way for thee
    Back from the Friendless Strand,
      Back from the place of death—
    Ere yet the slayers come
    And thy blood sink in the sand—
    Home unto Argos, home? . . .
    Hard heart, so swift to slay,
    Is there to life no way? . . .
    No ship! . . . And how by land? . ₒ ₒ
        A rush of feet
    Out to the waste alone.
        Nay: 'twere to meet
    Death, amid tribes unknown
    And trackless ways of the waste. . ₒ ₒ

Surely the sea were best.
Back by the narrow bar
   To the Dark Blue Gate! . . .
  Ah God, too far, too far! . . .
    Desolate! Desolate!
What god or man, what unimagined flame,
  Can cleave this road where no road is, and bring
To us last wrecks of Agamemnon's name,
    Peace from long suffering?

Leader. Lo, deeds of wonder and beyond surmise,
Not as tales told, but seen of mine own eyes.

Pylades. Men that have found the arms of those they love
Would fain long linger in the joy thereof.
But we, Orestes, have no respite yet
For tears or tenderness. Let us forget
All but the one word Freedom, calling us
To live, not die by altars barbarous.
Think not of joy in this great hour, nor lose
Fortune's first hold. Not thus do wise men use.

Orestes. I think that Fortune watcheth o'er our lives,
Surer than we. But well said: he who strives
Will find his gods strive for him equally.

Iphigenia. He shall not check us so, nor baffle me
Of this one word. How doth Electra move
Through life? Ye twain are all I have to love.

Orestes. A wife and happy: this man hath her hand.

Iphigenia. And what man's son is he, and of what land?

Orestes. Son of King Strophios he is called of men.

Iphigenia. Whom Atreus' daughter wed?—My kinsman then.

Orestes. Our cousin, and my true and only friend.

Iphigenia. He was not born, when I went to mine end.

Orestes. No, Strophios had no child for many a year.

Iphigenia. I give thee hail, husband of one so dear.

Orestes. My more than kinsman, saviour in my need!

Iphigenia. But mother. . . . Speak: how did ye dare that
    deed?

Orestes. Our father's wrongs. . . . But let that story be.

Iphigenia. And she to slay her king! What cause had she?

Orestes. Forget her! . . . And no tale for thee it is.

Iphigenia. So be it.—And thou art Lord of Argolis?

Orestes. Our uncle rules. I walk an exile's ways.
Iphigenia. Doth he so trample on our fallen days?
Orestes. Nay: there be those that drive me, Shapes of Dread.
Iphigenia. Ah!
That frenzy on the shore! 'Tis as they said. . . .
Orestes. They saw me in mine hour. It needs must be.
Iphigenia. 'Twas our dead mother's Furies hounding thee!
Orestes. My mouth is bloody with the curb they ride.
Iphigenia. What brought thee here beyond the Friendless
Tide?
Orestes. What leads me everywhere—Apollo's word.
Iphigenia. Seeking what end?—Or may the tale be heard?
Orestes. Nay, I can tell thee all. It needs must be
The whole tale of my days of misery.
When this sore evil that we speak not of
Lit on my hand, this way and that they drove
My body, till the God by diverse paths
Led me to Athens, that the nameless Wraths
Might bring me before judgment. For that land
A pure tribunal hath, where Ares' hand,
Red from an ancient stain, by Zeus was sent
For justice. Thither came I; and there went
God's hate before me, that at first no man
Would give me shelter. Then some few began
To pity, and set out for me aloof
One table. There I sate within their roof,
But without word they signed to me, as one
Apart, unspoken to, unlooked upon,
Lest touch of me should stain their meat and sup.
And every man in measure filled his cup
And gave me mine, and took their joy apart,
While I sat silent; for I had no heart
To upbraid the hosts that fed me. On I wrought
In my deep pain, feigning to mark them not.
And now, men say, mine evil days are made
A rite among them and the cups are laid
Apart for each. The rule abideth still.
Howbeit, when I was come to Ares' Hill
They gave me judgment. On one stone I stood,
On one she that was eldest of the brood

That hunted me so long. And many a word
Touching my mother's death was spoke and heard,
Till Phoebus rose to save me. Even lay
The votes of Death and Life; when, lo, a sway
Of Pallas' arm, and free at last I stood
From that death grapple. But the Shapes of Blood—
Some did accept the judgment, and of grace
Consent to make their house beneath that place
In darkness. Others still consented not,
But clove to me the more, like bloodhounds hot
On the dying; till to Phoebus' house once more
I crept, and cast me starving on the floor
Facing the Holy Place, and made my cry:
'Lord Phoebus, here I am come, and here will die,
Unless thou save me, as thou hast betrayed.'
And, lo, from out that dark and golden shade
A voice: 'Go, seek the Taurian citadel:
Seize there the carven Artemis that fell
From heaven, and stablish it on Attic soil.
So comes thy freedom.'

                               [IPHIGENIA *shrinks.*

                  Sister, in this toil
Help us!—If once that image I may win
That day shall end my madness and my sin:
And thou, to Argos o'er the sundering foam
My many-oarèd barque shall bear thee home.
    O sister loved and lost, O pitying face,
Help my great peril; help our father's race.
For lost am I and perished all the powers
Of Pelops, save that heavenly thing be ours!
    Leader. Strange wrath of God hath fallen, like hot rain,
On Tantalus' house: he leadeth them through pain.
    Iphigenia. Long ere you came my heart hath yearned to be
In Argos, brother, and so near to thee:
But now—thy will is mine. To ease thy pain,
To lift our father's house to peace again,
And hate no more my murderers—aye, 'tis good.
Perchance to clean this hand that sought thy blood,
And save my people . . .
                  But the goddess' eyes,

How dream we to deceive them? Or what wise
Escape the King, when on his sight shall fall
The blank stone of the empty pedestal? . . .
I needs must die. . . . What better can I do?

And yet, one chance there is: could I but go
Together with the image: couldst thou bear
Both on the leaping seas! The risk were fair.
But how?
        Nay, I must wait then and be slain:
Thou shalt walk free in Argolis again,
And all life smile on thee. . . . Dearest, we need
Not shrink from that. I shall by mine own deed
Have saved thee. And a man gone from the earth
Is wept for. Women are but little worth.

    Orestes. My mother, and then thou? It may not be.
This hand hath blood enough. I stand with thee
One-hearted here, be it for life or death,
And either bear thee, if God favoreth,
With me to Greece and home, or else lie here
Dead at thy side.—But mark me: if thou fear
Lest Artemis be wroth, how can that be?
Hath not her brother's self commanded me
To bear to Greece her image?—Oh, he knew
Her will! He knew that in this land we two
Must meet once more. All that so far hath past
Doth show his work. He will not at the last
Fail. We shall yet see Argos, thou and I.

    Iphigenia. To steal for thee the image, yet not die
Myself! 'Tis that we need. 'Tis that doth kill
My hope. Else. . . . Oh, God knows I have the will!

    Orestes. How if we slew your savage king?

    Iphigenia.   Ah, no:
He sheltered me, a stranger.

    Orestes.   Even so,
If it bring life for me and thee, the deed
May well be dared.

    Iphigenia.   I could not. . . . Nay; indeed
I thank thee for thy daring.

    Orestes.   Canst thou hide
My body in the shrine?

Iphigenia.   There to abide
Till nightfall, and escape?
Orestes.   Even so; the night
Is the safe time for robbers, as the light
For just men.
Iphigenia.   There be sacred watchers there
Who needs must see us.
Orestes.   Gods above! What prayer
Can help us then?
Iphigenia.   I think I dimly see
One chance.
Orestes.   What chance? Speak out thy fantasy.
Iphigenia. On thine affliction I would build my way.
Orestes. Women have strange devices.
Iphigenia.   I would say
Thou com'st from Hellas with thy mother's blood
Upon thee.
Orestes.   Use my shame, if any good
Will follow.
Iphigenia.   Therefore, an offense most high
It were to slay thee to the goddess!
Orestes.   Why?
Though I half guess.
Iphigenia.   Thy body is unclean.—
Oh, I will fill them with the fear of sin!
Orestes. What help is that for the Image?
Iphigenia.   I will crave
To cleanse thee in the breaking of the wave.
Orestes. That leaves the goddess still inside her shrine,
And 'tis for her we sailed.
Iphigenia.   A touch of thine
Defiled her. She too must be purified.
Orestes. Where shall it be? Thou knowest where the tide
Sweeps up in a long channel?
Iphigenia.   Yes! And where
Your ship, I guess, lies moored.
Orestes.   Whose hand will bear—
Should it be thine?—the Image from her throne?
Iphigenia. No hand of man may touch it save mine own.
Orestes. And Pylades—what part hath he herein?

Iphigenia. The same as thine. He bears the self-same sin.

Orestes. How wilt thou work the plan—hid from the king,
Or known?

Iphigenia.   To hide it were a hopeless thing. . . .
Oh, I will face him, make him yield to me.

Orestes. Well, fifty oars lie waiting on the sea.

Iphigenia. Aye, there comes thy work, till an end be made.

Orestes. Good. It needs only that these women aid
Our secret. Do thou speak with them, and find
Words of persuasion. Power is in the mind
Of woman to wake pity.—For the rest,
God knoweth: may it all end for the best!

Iphigenia. O women, you my comrades, in your eyes
I look to read my fate. In you it lies,
That either I find peace, or be cast down
To nothing, robbed forever of mine own—
Brother, and home, and sister pricelessly
Beloved.—Are we not women, you and I,
A broken race, to one another true,
And strong in our shared secrets? Help me through
This strait; keep hid the secret of our flight,
And share our peril! Honor shineth bright
On her whose lips are steadfast. . . . Heaven above!
Three souls, but one in fortune, one in love,
Thou seest us go—is it to death or home?
If home, then surely, surely, there shall come
Part of our joy to thee. I swear, I swear
To aid thee also home. . . .

> [*She goes to one after another, and presently
> kneels embracing the knees of the* LEADER.

                    I make my prayer
By that right hand; to thee, too, by that dear
Cheek; by thy knees; by all that is not here
Of things beloved, by mother, father, child—
Thou hadst a child!—How say ye? Have ye smiled
Or turned from me? For if ye turn away,
I and my brother are lost things this day.

Leader. Be of good heart, sweet mistress. Only go
To happiness. No child of man shall know
From us thy secret. Hear me, Zeus on high!

Iphigenia (*rising*). God bless you for that word, and fill
    your eye
With light!—

[*Turning to* ORESTES *and* PYLADES.
But now, to work! Go thou, and thou,
In to the deeper shrine. King Thoas now
Should soon be here to question if the price
Be yet paid of the strangers' sacrifice.

[ORESTES *and* PYLADES *go in.*
Thou Holy One, that on the shrouded sand
Of Aulis saved me from a father's hand
Blood-maddened, save me now, and save these twain.
Else shall Apollo's lips, through thy disdain,
Be no more true nor trusted in men's eyes.
Come from the friendless shore, the cruel skies,
Come back: what mak'st thou here, when o'er the sea
A clean and joyous land doth call for thee?

[*She follows the men into the Temple.*

[*Strophe.*
Chorus. Bird of the sea rocks, of the bursting spray,
    O halcyon bird,
That wheelest crying, crying, on thy way;
Who knoweth grief can read the tale of thee:
One love long lost, one song for ever heard
    And wings that sweep the sea.

Sister, I too beside the sea complain,
    A bird that hath no wing.
Oh, for a kind Greek market-place again,
For Artemis that healeth woman's pain;
    Here I stand hungering.
Give me the little hill above the sea,
The palm of Delos fringèd delicately,
The young sweet laurel and the olive-tree
    Gray-leaved and glimmering;
O Isle of Leto, Isle of pain and love;
The Orbèd Water and the spell thereof;
Where still the Swan, minstrel of things to be,
    Doth serve the Muse and sing!

[433]

[Antistrophe.

Ah, the old tears, the old and blinding tears
    I gave God then,
When my town fell, and noise was in mine ears
Of crashing towers, and forth they guided me
Through spears and lifted oars and angry men
    Out to an unknown sea.
They bought my flesh with gold, and sore afraid
    I came to this dark East
To serve, in thrall to Agamemnon's maid,
This Huntress Artemis, to whom is paid
    The blood of no slain beast;
Yet all is bloody where I dwell, Ah me!
Envying, envying that misery
That through all life hath endured changelessly.
    For hard things borne from birth
Make iron of man's heart, and hurt the less.
'Tis change that paineth; and the bitterness
Of life's decay when joy hath ceased to be
    That makes dark all the earth.

[Strophe.

    Behold,
    Two score and ten there be
    Rowers that row for thee,
And a wild hill air, as if Pan were there,
    Shall sound on the Argive sea,
    Piping to set thee free.

    Or is it the stricken string
    Of Apollo's lyre doth sing
Joyously, as he guideth thee
    To Athens, the land of spring;
    While I wait wearying?

    Oh, the wind and the oar,
    When the great sail swells before,
With sheets astrain, like a horse on the rein;
    And on, through the race and roar,
    She feels for the farther shore.

[434]

    Ah me,   [*Antistrophe.*
  To rise upon wings and hold
  Straight on up the steeps of gold
Where the joyous Sun in fire doth run,
  Till the wings should faint and fold
  O'er the house that was mine of old:

  Or watch where the glade below
  With a marriage dance doth glow,
And a child will glide from her mother's side
  Out, out, where the dancers flow:
  As I did, long ago.
  Oh, battles of gold and rare
  Raiment and starrèd hair,
And bright veils crossed amid tresses tossed
  In a dusk of dancing air!
  O Youth and the days that were!

      [*Enter* KING THOAS, *with Soldiers.*
 Thoas. Where is the warden of this sacred gate,
The Greek woman? Is her work ended yet
With those two strangers? Do their bodies lie
Aflame now in the rock-cleft sanctuary?
 Leader. Here is herself, O King, to give thee word.
    [*Enter, from the Temple,* IPHIGENIA, *carrying the
     Image on high.*
 Thoas. How, child of Agamemnon! Hast thou stirred
From her eternal base, and to the sun
Bearest in thine own arms, the Holy One?
 Iphigenia. Back Lord! No step beyond the pillared way.
 Thoas. But how? Some rule is broken?
 Iphigenia.   I unsay
That word. Be all unspoken and unwrought!
 Thoas. What means this greeting strange? Disclose thy
  thought.
 Iphigenia. Unclean the prey was that ye caught, O King.
 Thoas. Who showed thee so? Thine own imagining?
 Iphigenia. The Image stirred and shuddered from its seat.
 Thoas. Itself? . . . Some shock of earthquake loosened it.
 Iphigenia. Itself. And the eyes closed one breathing space.
 Thoas. But why? For those two men's bloodguiltiness?

Iphigenia. That, nothing else. For, Oh, their guilt is sore.
Thoas. They killed some of my herdsmen on the shore?
Iphigenia. Their sin was brought from home, not gathered here.
Thoas. What? I must know this.—Make thy story clear.
Iphigenia (she puts the Image down and moves nearer to Thoas). The men have slain their mother?
Thoas. God! And these Be Greeks!
Iphigenia. They both are hunted out of Greece.
Thoas. For this thou has brought the Image to the sun?
Iphigenia. The fire of heaven can cleanse all malison.
Thoas. How didst thou first hear of their deed of shame?
Iphigenia. When the Image hid its eyes, I questioned them.
Thoas. Good. Greece hath taught thee many a subtle art.
Iphigenia. Ah, they too had sweet words to move my heart.
Thoas. Sweet words? How, did they bring some news of Greece?
Iphigenia. Orestes, my one brother, lives in peace.
Thoas. Surely! Good news to make thee spare their lives. . . .
Iphigenia. My father too in Argos lives and thrives.
Thoas. While thou didst think but of the goddess' laws!
Iphigenia. Do I not hate all Greeks? Have I not cause?
Thoas. Good cause. But now. . . . What service should be paid?
Iphigenia. The Law of long years needs must be obeyed.
Thoas. To work then, with thy sword and handwashing!
Iphigenia. First I must shrive them with some cleansing thing.
Thoas. What? Running water, or the sea's salt spray?
Iphigenia. The sea doth wash all the world's ills away.
Thoas. For sure. 'Twill make them cleaner for the knife.
Iphigenia. And my hand, too, cleaner for all my life.
Thoas. Well, the waves lap close by the temple floor.
Iphigenia. We need a secret place. I must do more.
Thoas. Some rite unseen? 'Tis well. Go where thou wilt.
Iphigenia. The Image likewise must be purged of guilt.
Thoas. The stain hath touched it of that mother's blood?
Iphigenia. I durst not move it else, from where it stood.

Thoas. How good thy godliness and forethought! Aye,
Small wonder all our people hold thee high.

Iphigenia. Dost know then what I fain would have?

Thoas.   'Tis thine to speak and it shall be.

Iphigenia. Put bondage on the strangers both. . . .

Thoas.   Why bondage? Whither can they flee?

Iphigenia. Put not thy faith in any Greek.

Thoas (to Attendants).   Ho, men! some thongs and
     fetters, go!

Iphigenia. Stay; let them lead the strangers here, outside
     the shrine. . . .

Thoas.   It shall be so.

Iphigenia. And lay dark raiment on their heads. . . .

Thoas.   To veil them, lest the Sun should see.

Iphigenia. And lend me some of thine own spears.

Thoas.   This company shall go with thee.

Iphigenia. Next, send through all the city streets a herald.

Thoas.   Aye; and what to say?

Iphigenia. That no man living stir abroad.

Thoas.   The stain of blood might cross their way.

Iphigenia. Aye, sin like theirs doth spread contagion.

Thoas (to an Attendant).   Forth, and publish my
     command. . . .

Iphigenia. That none stir forth—nor look. . . .

Thoas.   Nor look.—How well thou carest for the land!

Iphigenia. For one whom I am bound to love.

Thoas.   Indeed, I think thou hat'st me not.

Iphigenia. And thou meanwhile, here at the temple, wait, O
     King, and. . . .

Thoas.   Wait for what?

Iphigenia. Purge all the shrine with fire.

Thoas.   'Twill all be clean before you come again.

Iphigenia. And while the strangers pass thee close, seeking
     the sea. . . .

Thoas.   What wouldst thou then?

Iphigenia. Put darkness on thine eyes.

Thoas.   Mine eyes might drink the evil of their crime?

Iphigenia. And, should I seem to stay too long. . . .

Thoas.   Too long? How shall I judge the time?

Iphigenia. Be not dismayed.

Thoas.   Perform thy rite all duly. We have time to spare.
Iphigenia. And God but grant this cleansing end as I desire!
Thoas.   I join thy prayer.
Iphigenia. The door doth open! See, they lead the strangers
   from the cell within,
And raiment holy and young lambs, whose blood shall shrive
   the blood of Sin.
And, lo, the light of sacred fires, and things of secret power,
   arrayed
By mine own hand to cleanse aright the strangers, to cleanse
   Leto's Maid.
                      [She takes up the Image again.
There passeth here a holy thing: begone, I charge ye, from the
   road,
O whoso by these sacred gates may dwell, hand-consecrate to
   God,
What man hath marriage in his heart, what woman goeth great
   with child,
Begone and tremble from this road: fly swiftly, lest ye be
   defiled.—
O Queen and Virgin, Leto-born, have pity! Let me cleanse this
   stain,
And pray to thee where pray I would: a clean house shall be
   thine again,
And we at last win happiness.—Behold, I speak but as I dare;
The rest . . . Oh, God is wise, and thou, my Mistress, thou
   canst read my prayer.
        [The procession passes out, THOAS *and the by-*
           standers veiled; Attendants in front, then
           IPHIGENIA *with the Image, then veiled Sol-*
           diers, then ORESTES *and* PYLADES *bound, the*
           bonds held by other veiled Soldiers following
           them. THOAS *goes into the Temple.*
                                [Strophe.

Chorus. Oh, fair the fruits of Leto blow:
    A Virgin, one, with joyous bow,
    And one a Lord of flashing locks,
     Wise in the harp, Apollo:
    She bore them amid Delian rocks,
     Hid in a fruited hollow.

But forth she fared from that low reef,
Sea-cradle of her joy and grief.
A crag she knew more near the skies
   And lit with wilder water,
That leaps with joy of Dionyse:
   There brought she son and daughter.
And there, behold, an ancient Snake,
Wine-eyed, bronze-gleaming in the brake
Of deep-leaved laurel, ruled the dell
   Sent by old Earth from under
Strange caves to guard her oracle—
   A thing of fear and wonder.

Thou, Phoebus, still a new-born thing,
   Meet in thy mother's arms to lie,
Didst kill the Snake and crown thee king,
   In Pytho's land of prophecy:
Thine was the tripod and the chair
Of golden truth; and thronèd there,
Hard by the streams of Castaly,
   Beneath the untrodden portal
Of Earth's mid stone there flows from thee
   Wisdom for all things mortal.

                   [*Antistrophe.*

He slew the Snake; he cast, men say,
Themis, the child of Earth, away
From Pytho and her hallowed stream;
   Then Earth, in dark derision,
Brought forth the Peoples of the Dream
   And all the tribes of Vision.

And men besought them; and from deep
Confusèd underworlds of sleep
They showed blind things that erst had been
And are and yet shall follow,
So did avenge that old Earth Queen
   Her child's wrong on Apollo.
Then swiftly flew that conquering one
To Zeus on high, and round the throne
Twining a small indignant hand,

Prayed him to send redeeming
To Pytho from that troublous band
   Sprung from the darks of dreaming.

Zeus laughed to see the babe, I trow,
So swift to claim his golden rite;
He laughed and bowed his head, in vow
To still those voices of the night.
And so from out the eyes of men
That dark dream-truth was lost again;
And Phoebus, thronèd where the throng
   Prays at the golden portal,
Again doth shed in sunlit song
   Hope unto all things mortal.
               [*Enter a* MESSENGER, *running.*

Messenger. Ho, watchers of the fane! Ho, altar-guard,
Where is King Thoas gone? Undo the barred
Portals, and call the King! The King I seek.

Leader. What tidings—if unbidden I may speak?

Messenger. The strangers both are gone, and we beguiled,
By some dark plot of Agamemnon's child:
Fled from the land! And on a barque of Greece
They bear the heaven-sent shape of Artemis.

Leader. Thy tale is past belief.—Go, swiftly on,
And find the King. He is but newly gone.

Messenger. Where went he? He must know of what has
    passed!

Leader. I know not where he went. But follow fast
And seek him. Thou wilt light on him ere long.

Messenger. See there! The treason of a woman's tongue!
Ye all are in the plot, I warrant ye!

Leader. Thy words are mad! What are the men to me? . . .
Go to the palace, go!

Messenger (*seeing the great knocker on the Temple door*).
             I will not stir
Till word be come by this good messenger
If Thoas be within these gates or no.—
               [*Thundering at the door.*
Ho, loose the portals! Ye within! What ho!
Open, and tell our master one doth stand

Without here, with strange evil in his hand.

[Enter THOAS *from the Temple.*

Thoas. Who dares before this portal consecrate
Make uproar and lewd battering of the gate?
Thy noise hath broke the Altar's ancient peace.

Messenger. Ye Gods! They swore to me—and bade me cease
My search—the King was gone. And all the while . . . !

Thoas. These women? How? What sought they by such
     guile?

Messenger. Of them hereafter!—Give me first thine ear
For greater things. The virgin minister
That served our altar, she hath fled from this
And stolen the dread Shape of Artemis,
With those two Greeks. The cleansing was a lie.

Thoas. She fled?—What wild hope whispered her to fly?

Messenger. The hope to save Orestes. Wonder on!

Thoas. Orestes—how? Not Clytemnestra's son?

Messenger. And our pledged altar-offering. 'Tis the same.

Thoas. O marvel beyond marvel! By what name
More rich in wonder can I name thee right?

Messenger. Give not thy mind to that. Let ear and sight
Be mine awhile; and when thou hast heard the whole
Devise how to best trap them ere the goal.

Thoas. Aye, tell thy tale. Our Tauric seas stretch far,
Where no man may escape my wand of war.

Messenger. Soon as we reached that headland of the sea,
Whereby Orestes' barque lay secretly,
We soldiers holding, by thine own commands,
The chain that bound the strangers, in our hands,
There Agamemnon's daughter made a sign,
Bidding us wait far off, for some divine
And secret fire of cleansing she must make.
We could but do her will. We saw her take
The chain in her own hands and walk behind.
Indeed thy servants bore a troubled mind,
O King, but how do else? So time went by.
Meanwhile to make it seem she wrought some high
Magic, she cried aloud: then came the long
Drone of some strange and necromantic song,
As though she toiled to cleanse that blood; and there

Sat we, that long time, waiting. Till a fear
O'ertook us, that the men might slip their chain
And strike the priestess down and plunge amain
For safety: yet the dread our eyes to fill
With sights unbidden held us, and we still
Sat silent. But at last all spoke as one,
Forbid or not forbid, to hasten on
And find them. On we went, and suddenly,
With oarage poised, like wings upon the sea,
An Argive ship we saw, her fifty men
All benched, and on the shore, with every chain
Cast off, our strangers, standing by the stern!
The prow was held by stay-poles: turn by turn
The anchor-cable rose; some men had strung
Long ropes into a ladder, which they swung
Over the side for those two Greeks to climb.
    The plot was open, and we lost no time
But flew to seize the cables and the maid,
And through the stern dragged out the steering-blade,
To spoil her course, and shouted: 'Ho, what way
Is this, to sail the seas and steal away
An holy image and its minister?
What man art thou, and what man's son, to bear
Our priestess from the land?' And clear thereon
He spoke: 'Orestes, Agamemnon's son,
And brother to this maid, whom here in peace
I bear, my long lost sister, back to Greece.'
    We none the less clung fast to her, and strove
To drag her to thy judgment-seat. Thereof
Came trouble and bruised jaws. For neither they
Nor we had weapons with us. But the way
Hard-beaten fist and heel from those two men
Rained upon ribs and flank—again, again . . .
To touch was to fall gasping! Aye, they laid
Their mark on all of us, till back we fled
With bleeding crowns, and some with blinded eyes,
Up a rough bank of rock. There on the rise
We found good stones and stood, and fought again.
    But archers then came out, and sent a rain
Of arrows from the poop, and drove us back.

And just then—for a wave came, long and black,
And swept them shoreward—lest the priestess' gown
Should feel the sea, Orestes stooping down
Caught her on his left shoulder: then one stride
Out through the sea, the ladder at the side
Was caught, and there amid the benches stood
The maid of Argos and the carven wood
Of heaven, the Image of God's daughter high.

   And up from the mid galley rose a cry:
'For Greece! For Greece, O children of the shores
Of storm! Give way, and let her feel your oars;
Churn the long waves to foam. The prize is won,
The prize we followed, on and ever on,
Friendless beyond the blue Symplêgades.'

   A roar of glad throats echoed down the breeze
And fifty oars struck, and away she flew.
And while the shelter lasted, she ran true
Full for the harbor-mouth; but ere she well
Reached it, the weather caught her, and the swell
Was strong. Then sudden in her teeth a squall
Drove the sail bellying back. The men withal
Worked with set teeth, kicking against the stream.
But back, still back, striving as in a dream,
She drifted. Then the damsel rose and prayed:
'O Child of Leto, save thy chosen maid
From this dark land to Hellas, and forgive
My theft this day, and let these brave men live.
Dost thou not love thy brother, Holy One?
What marvel if I also love mine own?'

   The sailors cried a paean to her prayers,
And set those brown and naked arms of theirs,
Half-mad with strain, quick swinging chime on chime
To the helmsman's shout. But vainly; all the time
Nearer and nearer rockward they were pressed.
One of our men was wading to his breast,
Some others roping a great grappling-hook,
While I sped hot-foot to the town, to look
For thee, my Prince, and tell thee what doth pass.

   Come with me, Lord. Bring manacles of brass
And bitter bonds. For now, unless the wave

Fall sudden calm, no mortal power can save
Orestes. There is One that rules the sea
Who grieved for Troy and hates her enemy:
Poseidon's self will give into thine hand
And ours this dog, this troubler of the land—
The priestess, too, who, recking not what blood
Ran red in Aulis, hath betrayed her god!

Leader. Woe, woe! To fall in these men's hands again,
Mistress, and die, and see thy brother slain!

Thoas. Ho, all ye dwellers of my savage town
Set saddle on your steeds, and gallop down
To watch the heads, and gather what is cast
Alive from this Greek wreck. We shall make fast,
By God's help, the blasphemers.—Send a corps
Out in good boats a furlong from the shore;
So we shall either snare them on the seas
Or ride them down by land, and at our ease
Fling them down gulfs of rock, or pale them high
On stakes in the sun, to feed our birds and die.

Women: you knew this plot. Each one of you
Shall know, before the work I have to do
Is done, what torment is.—Enough. A clear
Task is afoot. I must not linger here.

[*While* THOAS *is moving off, his men shouting and
running before and behind him, there comes a
sudden blasting light and thunder-roll, and*
ATHENA *is seen in the air confronting them.*

Athena. Ho, whither now, so hot upon the prey,
King Thoas? It is I that bid thee stay,
Athena, child of Zeus. Turn back this flood
Of wrathful men, and get thee temperate blood.

Apollo's word and Fate's ordainèd path
Have led Orestes here, to escape the wrath
Of Them that Hate. To Argos he must bring
His sister's life, and guide that Holy Thing
Which fell from heaven, in mine own land to dwell.
So shall his pain have rest, and all be well.
Thou hast heard my speech, O King. No death from thee
May snare Orestes between rocks and sea:

Poseidon for my love doth make the sore
Waves gentle, and set free his laboring oar.

And thou, O far away—for, far or near
A goddess speaketh and thy heart must hear—
Go on thy ways, Orestes, bearing home
The Image and thy sister. When ye come
To god-built Athens, lo, a land there is
Half hid on Attica's last boundaries,
A little land, hard by Karystus' Rock,
But sacred. It is called by Attic folk
Halae. Build there a temple, and bestow
Therein thine Image, that the world may know
The tale of Tauris and of thee, cast out
From pole to pole of Greece, a blood-hound rout
Of ill thoughts driving thee. So through the whole
Of time to Artemis the Tauropole
Shall men make hymns at Halae. And withal
Give them this law. At each high festival,
A sword, in record of thy death undone,
Shall touch a man's throat, and the red blood run—
One drop, for old religion's sake. In this
Shall live that old red rite of Artemis.

And thou, Iphigenia, by the stair
Of Brauron in the rocks, the Key shalt bear
Of Artemis. There shalt thou live and die,
And there have burial. And a gift shall lie
Above thy shrine, fair raiment undefiled
Left upon earth by mothers dead with child.

Ye last, O exiled women, true of heart
And faithful found, ye shall in peace depart,
Each to her home: behold Athena's will.

Orestes, long ago on Ares' Hill
I saved thee, when the votes of Death and Life
Lay equal: and henceforth, when men at strife
So stand, mid equal votes of Life and Death,
My law shall hold that Mercy conquereth.

Begone. Lead forth thy sister from this shore
In peace; and thou, Thoas, be wroth no more.
    Thoas. Most high Athena, he who bows not low
His head to God's word spoken, I scarce know
How such an one doth live. Orestes hath
Fled with mine Image hence. . . . I bear no wrath.
Nor yet against his sister. There is naught,
Methinks, of honor in a battle fought
'Gainst gods. The strength is theirs. Let those two fare
Forth to thy land and plant mine Image there.
I wish them well.
                These bondwomen no less
I will send free to Greece and happiness,
And stay my galleys' oars, and bid this brand
Be sheathed again, Goddess, at thy command.
    Athena. 'Tis well, O King. For that which needs must be
Holdeth the high gods as it holdeth thee.

Winds of the north, O winds that laugh and run,
Bear now to Athens Agamemnon's son:
Myself am with you, o'er long leagues of foam
Guiding my sister's hallowed Image home.
                        [She floats away.

    Chorus (Some Women).
           Go forth in bliss, O ye whose lot
           God shieldeth, that ye perish not!
    Others. O great in our dull world of clay,
           And great in heaven's undying gleam,
    Pallas, thy bidding we obey:
    And bless thee, for mine ears have heard
    The joy and wonder of a word
           Beyond my dream, beyond my dream.

EURIPIDES
MEDEA

➤➤➤◄◄◄

TRANSLATED
by
GILBERT MURRAY

CHARACTERS IN THE PLAY

MEDEA, *daughter of Aiêtês, King of Colchis.*

JASON, *chief of the Argonauts; nephew of Pelias, King of Iôlcos in Thessaly.*

CREON, *ruler of Corinth.*

AEGEUS, *King of Athens.*

NURSE *of Medea.*

TWO CHILDREN *of Jason and Medea.*

ATTENDANT *on the children.*

A MESSENGER.

CHORUS *of Corinthian Women, with their* LEADER.

SOLDIERS *and* ATTENDANTS.

The scene is laid in Corinth. The play was first acted when Pythodôrus was Archon, Olympiad 87, year 1 (B.C. 431). Euphorion was first, Sophocles second, Euripides third, with Medea, Philoctetes, Dictys, *and the* Harvesters, *a Satyr-play.*

ARGUMENT

Jason, son of Aeson, King of Iôlcos, in Thessaly, began his life in exile. His uncle Pelias had seized the kingdom, and Jason was borne away to the mountains by night and given to Chiron, the Centaur. When he reached manhood, he came down to Iôlcos to demand his throne. Pelias, cowed but loath to yield, promised to give up the kingdom if Jason would make his way to the unknown land of Colchis to secure the soul of his kinsman Phrixus and the Golden Fleece. Jason gathered the most daring heroes of all Hellas, built the first ship, Argo, and set to sea. When he reached the land of Aiêtês, king of the Colchians, all means failed. The Argonauts were surrounded and destruction seemed sure, when suddenly, unasked, Aiêtês' daughter Medea, an enchantress, fell in love with Jason. She slew for him her own sleepless serpent, who guarded the fleece, deceived her father; and secured both the fleece and the soul of Phrixus. Finally, when her brother, Absyrtus, plotted to kill Jason, she stabbed him dead and fled with Jason over the seas. Jason could not avoid taking Medea with him though of course, in fifth-century Athens, no legal marriage was possible between a Greek and a barbarian from Colchis. Upon their return to Iôlcos, Pelias was still determined to keep the kingdom. Medea, resolved to do her lover another act of service, persuaded Pelias that he could renew his youth, and in the process he died in agony. Medea and Jason had to fly for their lives, and directed their flight to Corinth where the ruler, now growing old, had an only daughter. Jason doubtless felt it necessary to free himself somehow from this wild beast of a woman who was ruining his life. He accepted the hand of the princess, and when Medea became violent, did not intervene to save her from exile.

MEDEA

---

*The Scene represents the front of Medea's House in Corinth.
A road to the right leads towards the royal castle, one on the
left to the harbor. The* Nurse *is discovered alone.*

Nurse. Would God no Argo e'er had winged the seas
To Colchis through the blue Symplêgades:
No shaft of riven pine in Pêlion's glen
Shaped that first oar-blade in the hands of men
Valiant, who won, to save King Pelias' vow,
The fleece All-golden! Never then, I trow,
Mine own princess, her spirit wounded sore
With love of Jason, to the encastled shore
Had sailed of old Iôlcos: never wrought
The daughters of King Pelias, knowing not,
To spill their father's life: nor fled in fear,
Hunted for that fierce sin, to Corinth here
With Jason and her babes. This folk at need
Stood friend to her, and she in word and deed
Served alway Jason. Surely this doth bind,
Through all ill days, the hurts of humankind,
When man and woman in one music move.
   But now, the world is angry, and true love
Sick as with poison. Jason doth forsake
My mistress and his own two sons, to make
His couch in a king's chamber. He must wed:
Wed with this Creon's child, who now is head
And chief of Corinth. Wherefore sore betrayed
Medea calleth up the oath they made,
They two, and wakes the claspèd hands again
The troth surpassing speech, and cries amain
On God in heaven to mark the end, and how
Jason hath paid his debt.

All fasting now
And cold, her body yielded up to pain,
Her days a waste of weeping, she hath lain,
Since first she knew that he was false. Her eyes
Are lifted not; and all her visage lies
In the dust. If friends will speak, she hears no more
Than some dead rock or wave that beats the shore:
Only the white throat in a sudden shame
May writhe, and all alone she moans the name
Of father, and land, and home, forsook that day
For this man's sake, who casteth her away.
Not to be quite shut out from home . . . alas,
She knoweth now how rare a thing that was!
Methinks she hath a dread, not joy, to see
Her children near. 'Tis this that maketh me
Most tremble, lest she do I know not what.
Her heart is no light thing, and useth not
To brook much wrong. I know that woman, aye,
And dread her! Will she creep alone to die
Bleeding in that old room, where still is laid
Lord Jason's bed? She hath for that a blade
Made keen. Or slay the bridegroom and the king,
And win herself God knows what direr thing?
'Tis a fell spirit. Few, I ween, shall stir
Her hate unscathed, or lightly humble her.

Ha! 'Tis the children from their games again,
Rested and gay; and all their mother's pain
Forgotten! Young lives ever turn from gloom!

[*The* CHILDREN *and their* ATTENDANT *come in.*

Attendant. Thou ancient treasure of my lady's room,
What mak'st thou here before the gates alone,
And alway turning on thy lips some moan
Of old mischances? Will our mistress be
Content, this long time to be left by thee?

Nurse. Gray guard of Jason's children, a good thrall
Hath his own grief, if any hurt befall
His master's. Aye, it holds one's heart! . . . Meseems
I have strayed out so deep in evil dreams,
I longed to rest me here alone, and cry
Medea's wrongs to this still Earth and Sky.

Attendant. How? Are the tears yet running in her eyes?

Nurse. 'Twere good to be like thee! . . . Her sorrow lies
Scarce wakened yet, not half its perils wrought.

Attendant. Mad spirit! . . . if a man may speak his thought
Of masters mad.—And nothing in her ears
Hath sounded yet of her last cause for tears!

> [*He moves towards the house, but the* NURSE
> *checks him.*

Nurse. What cause, old man? . . . Nay, grudge me not one
    word.

Attendant. 'Tis nothing. Best forget what thou hast heard.

Nurse. Nay, housemate, by thy beard! Hold it not hid
From me. . . . I will keep silence if thou bid.

Attendant. I heard an old man talking, where he sate
At draughts in the sun, beside the fountain gate,
And never thought of me, there standing still
Beside him. And he said 'twas Creon's will,
Being lord of all this land, that she be sent, *[to be banished]*
And with her her two sons, to banishment.
Maybe 'tis all false. For myself, I know
No further, and I would it were not so.

Nurse. Jason will never bear it—his own sons
Banished,—however hot his anger runs
Against their mother!

Attendant.   Old love burneth low
When new love wakes, men say. He is not now
Husband nor father here, nor any kin.

Nurse. But this is ruin! New waves breaking in
To wreck us, ere we are righted from the old!

Attendant. Well, hold thy peace. Our mistress will be told
All in good time. Speak thou no word hereof.

Nurse. My babes! What think ye of your father's love?
God curse him not, he is my master still:
But, oh, to them that loved him, 'tis an ill
Friend. . . .

Attendant. And what man on earth is different? How?
Hast thou lived all these years, and learned but now
That every man more loveth his own head
Than other men's? He dreameth of the bed *[his estimate of Jason]*
Of this new bride, and thinks not of his sons.

[451]

Nurse. Go: run into the house, my little ones:
All will end happily! . . . Keep them apart:
Let not their mother meet them while her heart
Is darkened. Yester night I saw a flame
Stand in her eye, as though she hated them,
And would I know not what. For sure her wrath
Will never turn nor slumber, till she hath . . .
Go: and if some must suffer, may it be
Not we who love her, but some enemy!
    Voice (*within*). Oh shame and pain: O woe is me!
    Would I could die in my misery!
                [*The* CHILDREN *and the* ATTENDANT *go in.*
Nurse. Ah, children, hark! She moves again
    Her frozen heart, her sleeping wrath.
    In, quick! And never cross her path,
    Nor rouse that dark eye in its pain;

    That fell sea-spirit, and the dire
        Spring of a will untaught, unbowed.
        Quick, now!—Methinks this weeping cloud
    Hath in its heart some thunder-fire,

    Slow gathering, that must flash ere long.
        I know not how, for ill or well,
        It turns, this uncontrollable
    Tempestuous spirit, blind with wrong.

Voice (*within*). Have I not suffered? Doth it call
    No tears? . . . Ha, ye beside the wall
    Unfathered children, God hate you
    As I am hated, and him, too,
        That gat you, and this house and all!

Nurse. For pity! What have they to do,
        Babes, with their father's sin? Why call
        Thy curse on these? . . . Ah, children, all
    These days my bosom bleeds for you.

    Rude are the wills of princes: yea,
        Prevailing alway, seldom crossed,

On fitful winds their moods are tossed:
'Tis best men tread the equal way.

Aye, not with glory but with peace
   May the long summers find me crowned:
   For gentleness—her very sound
Is magic, and her usages
All wholesome: but the fiercely great
   Hath little music on his road,
   And falleth, when the hand of God
Shall move, most deep and desolate.
       [*During the last words the* LEADER *of the Chorus*
        has entered. Other women follow her.

Leader. I heard a voice and a moan,
   A voice of the eastern seas:
   Hath she found not yet her ease?
      Speak, O agèd one.
   For I stood afar at the gate,
   And there came from within a cry,
   And wailing desolate.
    Ah, no more joy have I,
   For the griefs this house doth see,
   And the love it hath wrought in me.

Nurse. There is no house! 'Tis gone. The lord
   Seeketh a prouder bed: and she
   Wastes in her chamber, nor one word
    Will hear of care or charity.

Voice (*within*). O Zeus, O Earth, O Light,
   Will the fire not stab my brain?
   What profiteth living? Oh,
   Shall I not lift the slow
   Yoke, and let Life go,
  As a beast out in the night,
   To lie, and be rid of pain?

Chorus (*Some Women*). A. 'O Zeus, O Earth, O Light':
   The cry of a bride forlorn

Heard ye, and wailing born
Of lost delight?

B. Why weariest thou this day,
    Wild heart, for the bed abhorrèd,
The cold bed in the clay?
Death cometh though no man pray,
    Ungarlanded, unadorèd.
        Call him not thou.

C. If another's arms be now
        Where thine have been,
        On his head be the sin:
Rend not thy brow!

D. All that thou sufferest,
        God seeth: Oh, not so sore
Waste nor weep for the breast
    That was thine of yore.

Voice (within). Virgin of Righteousness,
    Virgin of hallowed Troth,
    Ye marked me when with an oath
    I bound him; mark no less
    That oath's end. Give me to see
    Him and his bride, who sought
    My grief when I wronged her not,
    Broken in misery,
    And all her house. . . . O God,
    My mother's home, and the dim
    Shore that I left for him,
    And the voice of my brother's blood. . . .

Nurse. Oh, wild words! Did ye hear her cry
        To them that guard man's faith forsworn,
        Themis and Zeus? . . . This wrath new-born
    Shall make mad workings ere it die.

Chorus (Other Women). A. Would she but come to seek
    Our faces, that love her well,

[454]

And take to her heart the spell
    Of words that speak?

B. Alas for the heavy hate
    And anger that burneth ever!
Would it but now abate,
Ah God, I love her yet.
    And surely my love's endeavor
      Shall fail not here.

C. Go: from that chamber drear
      Forth to the day
Lead her, and say, Oh, say
    That we love her dear.

D. Go, lest her hand be hard
    On the innocent: Ah, let be!
For her grief moves hitherward,
    Like an angry sea.
Nurse. That will I: though what words of mine
Or love shall move her? Let them lie
With the old lost labors! . . . Yet her eye—
Know ye the eyes of the wild kine,

The lion flash that guards their brood?
  So looks she now if any thrall
  Speak comfort, or draw near at all
My mistress in her evil mood.

              [*The* NURSE *goes into the house.*
Chorus (A Woman). Alas, the bold blithe bards of old
    That all for joy their music made,
For feasts and dancing manifold,
    That Life might listen and be glad.

But all the darkness and the wrong,
    Quick deaths and dim heart-aching things,
Would no man ease them with a song
    Or music of a thousand strings?

Then song had served us in our need.
    What profit, o'er the banquet's swell

That lingering cry that none may heed?
The feast hath filled them: all is well!

Others. I heard a song, but it comes no more.
Where the tears ran over:
A keen cry but tired, tired:
A woman's cry for her heart's desired,
For a traitor's kiss and a lost lover.
But a prayer, methinks, yet riseth sore
To God, to Faith, God's ancient daughter—
The Faith that over sundering seas
Drew her to Hellas, and the breeze
Of midnight shivered, and the door
Closed of the salt unsounded water.

[*During the last words* MEDEA *has come out from
the house.*

Medea. Women of Corinth, I am come to show
My face, lest ye despise me. For I know
Some heads stand high and fail not, even at night
Alone—far less like this, in all men's sight:
And we, who study not our wayfarings
But feel and cry—Oh we are drifting things,
And evil! For what truth is in men's eyes,
Which search no heart, but in a flash despise
A strange face, shuddering back from one that ne'er
Hath wronged them? . . . Sure, far-comers anywhere,
I know, must bow them and be gentle. Nay,
A Greek himself men praise not, who alway
Should seek his own will recking not. . . . But I—
This thing undreamed of, sudden from on high,
Hath sapped my soul: I dazzle where I stand,
The cup of all life shattered in my hand,
Longing to die—O friends! He, even he,
Whom to know well was all the world to me,
The man I loved, hath proved most evil.—Oh,
Of all things upon earth that bleed and grow,
A herb most bruised is woman. We must pay
Our store of gold, hoarded for that one day,
To buy us some man's love; and lo, they bring
A master of our flesh! There comes the sting

[456]

Of the whole shame. And then the jeopardy,
For good or ill, what shall that master be;
Reject she cannot: and if he but stays
His suit, 'tis shame on all that woman's days.
So thrown amid new laws, new places, why,
'Tis magic she must have, or prophecy—
Home never taught her that—how best to guide
Toward peace this thing that sleepeth at her side.
And she who, laboring long, shall find some way
Whereby her lord may bear with her, nor fray
His yoke too fiercely, blessed is the breath
That woman draws! Else, let her pray for death.
Her lord, if he be wearied of the face
Withindoors, gets him forth; some merrier place
Will ease his heart: but she waits on, her whole
Vision enchainèd on a single soul.
And then, forsooth, 'tis they that face the call
Of war, while we sit sheltered, hid from all
Peril!—False mocking! Sooner would I stand
Three times to face their battles, shield in hand,
Than bear one child.

                But peace! There cannot be
Ever the same tale told of thee and me.
Thou hast this city, and thy father's home,
And joy of friends, and hope in days to come:
But I, being cityless, am cast aside
By him that wedded me, a savage bride
Won in far seas and left—no mother near,
No brother, not one kinsman anywhere
For harbor in this storm. Therefore of thee
I ask one thing. If chance yet ope to me
Some path, if even now my hand can win
Strength to requite this Jason for his sin,
Betray me not! Oh, in all things but this,
I know how full of fears a woman is,
And faint at need, and shrinking from the light
Of battle: but once spoil her of her right
In man's love, and there moves, I warn thee well,
No bloodier spirit between heaven and hell.

    Leader. I will betray thee not. It is but just,

Thou smite him.—And that weeping in the dust
And stormy tears, how should I blame them? . . . Stay:
'Tis Creon, lord of Corinth, makes his way
Hither, and bears, methinks, some word of weight.

[*Enter from the right* CREON, *the King, with armed
Attendants.*

Creon. Thou woman sullen-eyed and hot with hate
Against thy lord, Medea, I here command
That thou and thy two children from this land
Go forth to banishment. Make no delay:
Seeing ourselves, the King, are come this day
To see our charge fulfilled; nor shall again
Look homeward ere we have led thy children twain
And thee beyond our realm's last boundary.

Medea. Lost! Lost!
Mine haters at the helm with sail flung free
Pursuing; and for us no beach nor shore
In the endless waters! . . . Yet, though stricken sore,
I still will ask thee, for what crime, what thing
Unlawful, wilt thou cast me out, O King?

Creon. What crime? I fear thee, woman—little need
To cloak my reasons—lest thou work some deed
Of darkness on my child. And in that fear
Reasons enough have part. Thou comest here
A wise-woman confessed, and full of lore
In unknown ways of evil. Thou art sore
In heart, being parted from thy lover's arms.
And more, thou hast made menace . . . so the alarms
But now have reached mine ear . . . on bride and groom,
And him who gave the bride, to work thy doom
Of vengeance. Which, ere yet it be too late,
I sweep aside. I choose to earn thine hate
Of set will now, not palter with the mood
Of mercy, and hereafter weep in blood.

Medea. 'Tis not the first nor second time, O King,
That fame hath hurt me, and come nigh to bring
My ruin. . . . How can any man, whose eyes
Are wholesome, seek to rear his children wise
Beyond men's wont? Much helplessness in arts
Of common life, and in their townsmen's hearts

[458]

Envy deep-set . . . so much their learning brings!
Come unto fools with knowledge of new things,
They deem it vanity, not knowledge. Aye,
And men that erst for wisdom were held high,
Feel thee a thorn to fret them, privily
Held higher than they. So hath it been with me.
A wise-woman I am; and for that sin
To divers ill names men would pen me in;
A seed of strife; an eastern dreamer; one
Of brand not theirs; one hard to play upon . . .
Ah, I am not so wondrous wise!—And now,
To thee, I am terrible! What fearest thou?
What dire deed? Do I tread so proud a path—
Fear me not thou!—that I should brave the wrath
Of princes? Thou: what hast thou ever done
To wrong me? Granted thine own child to one
Whom thy soul chose.—Ah, *him* out of my heart
I hate; but thou, meseems, hast done thy part
Not ill. And for thine houses' happiness
I hold no grudge. Go: marry, and God bless
Your issues. Only suffer me to rest
Somewhere within this land. Though sore oppressed,
I will be still, knowing mine own defeat.

    Creon. Thy words be gentle: but I fear me yet
Lest even now there creep some wickedness
Deep hid within thee. And for that the less
I trust thee now than ere these words began.
A woman quick of wrath, aye, or a man,
Is easier watching than the cold and still.

    Up, straight, and find thy road! Mock not my will
With words. This doom is passed beyond recall;
Nor all thy crafts shall help thee, being withal
My manifest foe, to linger at my side.

    Medea (*suddenly throwing herself down and clinging to
      Creon*). Oh, by thy knees! By that new-wedded bride . . .

    Creon. 'Tis waste of words. Thou shalt not weaken me.

    Medea. Wilt hunt me? Spurn me when I kneel to thee?

    Creon. 'Tis mine own house that kneels to me, not thou.

    Medea. Home, my lost home, how I desire thee now!

Creon. And I mine, and my child, beyond all things.
Medea. O Loves of man, what curse is on your wings!
Creon. Blessing or curse, 'tis as their chances flow.
Medea. Remember, Zeus, the cause of all this woe!
Creon. Oh, rid me of my pains! Up, get thee gone!
Medea. What would I with thy pains? I have mine own.
Creon. Up: or, 'fore God, my soldiers here shall fling . . .
Medea. Not that! Not that! . . . I do but pray, O
    King . . .
Creon. Thou wilt not? I must face the harsher task?
Medea. I accept mine exile. 'Tis not that I ask.
Creon. Why then so wild? Why clinging to mine hand?
Medea (rising). For one day only leave me in thy land
At peace, to find some counsel, ere the strain
Of exile fall, some comfort for these twain,
Mine innocents; since others take no thought,
It seems, to save the babes that they begot.
    Ah! Thou wilt pity them! Thou also art
A father: thou hast somewhere still a heart
That feels. . . . I reck not of myself: 'tis they
That break me, fallen upon so dire a day.
    Creon. Mine is no tyrant's mood. Aye, many a time
Ere this my tenderness hath marred the chime
Of wisest counsels. And I know that now
I do mere folly. But so be it! Thou
Shalt have this grace . . . But this I warn thee clear,
If once the morrow's sunlight find thee here
Within my borders, thee or child of thine,
Thou diest! . . . Of this judgment not a line
Shall waver nor abate. So linger on,
If thou needs must, till the next risen sun;
No further. . . . In one day there scarce can be
Those perils wrought whose dread yet haunteth me.
                     [*Exit* CREON *with his suite.*

Chorus. O woman, woman of sorrow,
    Where wilt thou turn and flee?
What town shall be thine to-morrow,
    What land of all lands that be,
What door of a strange man's home?
    Yea, God hath hunted thee,

Medea, forth to the foam
Of a trackless sea.
Medea. Defeat on every side; what else?—But Oh,
Not here the end is: think it not! I know
For bride and groom one battle yet untried,
And goodly pains for him that gave the bride.

Dost dream I would have groveled to this man,
Save that I won mine end, and shaped my plan
For merry deeds? My lips had never deigned
Speak word with him: my flesh been never stained
With touching. . . . Fool, Oh, triple fool! It lay
So plain for him to kill my whole essay
By exile swift: and, lo, he sets me free
This one long day: wherein mine haters three
Shall lie here dead, the father and the bride
And husband—mine, not hers! Oh, I have tried
So many thoughts of murder to my turn,
I know not which best likes me. Shall I burn
Their house with fire? Or stealing past unseen
To Jason's bed—I have a blade made keen
For that—stab, breast to breast, that wedded pair?
Good, but for one thing. When I am taken there,
And killed, they will laugh loud who hate me. . . .
Nay,
I love the old way best, the simple way
Of poison, where we too are strong as men.
Ah me!
And they being dead—what place shall hold me then?
What friend shall rise, with land inviolate
And trusty doors, to shelter from their hate
This flesh? . . . None anywhere! . . . A little more
I needs must wait: and, if there ope some door
Of refuge, some strong tower to shield me, good:
In craft and darkness I will hunt this blood.
Else, if mine hour be come and no hope nigh,
Then sword in hand, full-willed and sure to die,
I yet will live to slay them. I will wend
Man-like, their road of daring to the end.
So help me She who of all Gods hath been

The best to me, of all my chosen queen
And helpmate, Hecatê, who dwells apart,
The flame of flame, in my fire's inmost heart:
For all their strength, they shall not stab my soul
And laugh thereafter! Dark and full of dole
Their bridal feast shall be, most dark the day
They joined their hands, and hunted me away.

    Awake thee now, Medea! Whatso plot
Thou hast, or cunning, strive and falter not.
On to the peril-point! Now comes the strain
Of daring. Shall they trample thee again?
How? And with Hellas laughing o'er thy fall
While this thief's daughter weds, and weds withal
Jason? . . . A true king was thy father, yea,
And born of the ancient Sun! . . . Thou know'st the way;
And God hath made thee woman, things most vain
For help, but wondrous in the paths of pain.

                          [MEDEA *goes into the House.*
    Chorus. Back streams the wave on the ever-running river:
    Life, life is changed and the laws of it o'ertrod.
Man shall be the slave, the affrighted, the low-liver!
               Man hath forgotten God.
And woman, yea, woman, shall be terrible in story:
    The tales too, meseemeth, shall be other than of yore.
For a fear there is that cometh out of Woman, and a glory,
    And the hard hating voices shall encompass her no more!

The old bards shall cease, and their memory that lingers
    Of frail brides and faithless, shall be shriveled as with fire.
For they loved us not, nor knew us: and our lips were dumb, our fingers
               Could wake not the secret of the lyre.

Else, else, O God the Singer, I had sung amid their rages
    A long tale of Man and his deeds for good and ill.
But the old World knoweth—'tis the speech of all his ages—
    Man's wrong and ours: he knoweth and is still.

    Some Women. Forth from thy father's home
        Thou camest, O heart of fire,

To the Dark Blue Rocks, to the clashing foam,
　　To the seas of thy desire:

Till the Dark Blue Bar was crossed;
　　And, lo, by an alien river,
Standing, thy lover lost,
　　Void-armed for ever,

Forth yet again, O lowest
　　Of landless women, a ranger
Of desolate ways, thou goest,
　　From the walls of the stranger.

Others. And the great Oath waxeth weak;
　　And Ruth, as a thing outstriven,
Is fled, fled, from the shores of the Greek,
Away on the winds of heaven.

Dark is the house afar,
　　Where an old king called thee daughter;
All that was once thy star
　　In stormy water,

Dark: and, lo, in the nearer
　　House that was sworn to love thee,
Another, queenlier, dearer,
　　Is thronèd above thee.

　　　　　　　　　　[*Enter from the right* JASON.

Jason. Oft have I seen, in other days than these,
How a dark temper maketh maladies
No friend can heal. 'Twas easy to have kept
Both land and home. It needed but to accept
Unstrivingly the pleasure of our lords.
But thou, for mere delight in stormy words,
Wilt lose all! . . . Now thy speech provokes not me.
Rail on. Of all mankind let Jason be
Most evil; none shall check thee. But for these
Dark threats cast out against the majesties
Of Corinth, count as veriest gain thy path
Of exile. I myself, when princely wrath

Was hot against thee, strove with all good will
To appease the wrath, and wished to keep thee still
Beside me. But thy mouth would never stay
From vanity, blaspheming night and day
Our masters. Therefore thou shalt fly the land.

    Yet, even so, I will not hold my hand
From succoring mine own people. Here am I
To help thee, woman, pondering heedfully
Thy new state. For I would not have thee flung
Provisionless away—aye, and the young
Children as well; nor lacking aught that will
Of mine can bring thee. Many a lesser ill
Hangs on the heels of exile. . . . Aye, and though
Thou hate me, dream not that my heart can know
Or fashion aught of angry will to thee.

    Medea. Evil, most evil! . . . since thou grantest me
That comfort, the worst weapon left me now
To smite a coward. . . . Thou comest to me, thou,
Mine enemy! (*Turning to the* CHORUS) Oh, say, how call ye
    this,
To face, and smile, the comrade whom his kiss
Betrayed? Scorn? Insult? Courage? None of these:
'Tis but of all man's inward sicknesses
The vilest, that he knoweth not of shame
Nor pity! Yet I praise him that he came . . .
To me it shall bring comfort, once to clear
My heart on thee, and thou shalt wince to hear.

    I will begin with that, 'twixt me and thee,
That first befell. I saved thee. I saved thee—
Let thine own Greeks be witness, every one
That sailed on Argo—saved thee, sent alone
To yoke with yokes the bulls of fiery breath,
And sow that Acre of the Lords of Death;
And mine own ancient Serpent, who did keep
The Golden Fleece, the eyes that knew not sleep,
And shining coils, him also did I smite
Dead for thy sake, and lifted up the light
That bade thee live. Myself, uncounselèd,
Stole forth from father and from home, and fled
Where dark Iôlcos under Pelion lies,

[464]

With thee—Oh, single-hearted more than wise!
I murdered Pelias, yea, in agony,
By his own daughters' hands, for sake of thee;
I swept their house like War.—And hast thou then
Accepted all—O evil yet again!—
And cast me off and taken thee for bride
Another? And with children at thy side!
One could forgive a childless man. But no: *Euripidean*
I have borne thee children . . . *rhetoric*
                              Is sworn faith so low
And weak a thing? I understand it not.
Are the old gods dead? Are the old laws forgot,
And new laws made? Since not my passioning,
But thine own heart, doth cry thee for a thing
Forsworn.

      [*She catches sight of her own hand which she has
        thrown out to denounce him.*

          Poor, poor right hand of mine, whom he *apostrophe*
Did cling to, and these knees, so cravingly,
We are unclean, thou and I; we have caught the stain
Of bad men's flesh . . . and dreamed our dreams in vain.
  Thou comest to befriend me? Give me, then,
Thy counsel. 'Tis not that I dream again
For good from thee: but, questioned, thou wilt show
The viler. Say: now whither shall I go?
Back to my father? Him I did betray,
And all his land, when we two fled away.
To those poor Peliad maids? For them 'twere good
To take me in, who spilled their father's blood. . . .
Aye, so my whole life stands! There were at home
Who loved me well: to them I am become
A curse. And the first friends who sheltered me,
Whom most I should have spared, to pleasure thee
I have turned to foes. Oh, therefore hast thou laid
My crown upon me, blest of many a maid
In Hellas, now I have won what all did crave,
Thee, the world-wondered lover and the brave;
Who this day looks and sees me banished, thrown
Away with these two babes, all, all, alone . . .
Oh, merry mocking when the lamps are red:

'Where go the bridegroom's babes to beg their bread
In exile, and the woman who gave all
To save him?'
          O great God, shall gold withal
Bear thy clear mark, to sift the base and fine,
And o'er man's living visage runs no sign
To show the lie within, ere all too late?

    Leader. Dire and beyond all healing is the hate
When hearts that loved are turned to enmity.

    Jason. In speech at least, meseemeth, I must be
Not evil; but, as some old pilot goes
Furled to his sail's last edge, when danger blows
Too fiery, run before the wind and swell,
Woman, of thy loud storms.—And thus I tell
My tale. Since thou wilt build so wondrous high
Thy deeds of service in my jeopardy,
To all my crew and quest I know but one
Saviour, of Gods or mortals one alone,
The Cyprian. Oh, thou hast both brain and wit,
Yet underneath . . . nay, all the tale of it
Were graceless telling; how sheer love, a fire
Of poison-shafts, compelled thee with desire
To save me. But enough. I will not score
That count too close. 'Twas good help: and therefor
I give thee thanks, howe'er the help was wrought.
Howbeit, in my deliverance, thou hast got
Far more than given. A good Greek land hath been
Thy lasting home, not barbary. Thou hast seen
Our ordered life, and justice, and the long
Still grasp of law not changing with the strong
Man's pleasure. Then, all Hellas far and near
Hath learned thy wisdom, and in every ear
Thy fame is. Had thy days run by unseen
On that last edge of the world, where then had been
The story of great Medea? Thou and I . . .
What worth to us were treasures heapèd high
In rich kings' rooms; what worth a voice of gold
More sweet than ever rang from Orpheus old,
Unless our deeds have glory?
                    Speak I so,

[466]

Touching the Quest I wrought, thyself did throw
The challenge down. Next for thy cavilling
Of wrath at mine alliance with a king,
Here thou shalt see I both was wise, and free
From touch of passion, and a friend to thee
Most potent, and my children . . . Nay, be still!
    When first I stood in Corinth, clogged with ill
From many a desperate mischance, what bliss
Could I that day have dreamed of, like to this,
To wed with a king's daughter, I exiled
And beggared? Not—what makes thy passion wild—
From loathing of thy bed; not over-fraught
With love for this new bride; not that I sought
To upbuild mine house with offspring: 'tis enough,
What thou hast borne: I make no word thereof:
But, first and greatest, that we all might dwell
In a fair house and want not, knowing well
That poor men have no friends, but far and near
Shunning and silence. Next, I sought to rear
Our sons in nurture worthy of my race,
And, raising brethren to them, in one place
Join both my houses, and be all from now
Prince-like and happy. What more need hast thou
Of children? And for me, it serves my star
To link in strength the children that now are
With those that shall be.
                                      Have I counseled ill?
Not thine own self would say it, couldst thou still
One hour thy jealous flesh.—'Tis ever so!
Who looks for more in women? When the flow
Of love runs plain, why, all the world is fair:
But, once there fall some ill chance anywhere
To baulk that thirst, down in swift hate are trod
Men's dearest aims and noblest. Would to God
We mortals by some other seed could raise
Our fruits, and no blind women block our ways!
Then had there been no curse to wreck mankind.
    Leader. Lord Jason, very subtly hast thou twined
Thy speech: but yet, though all athwart thy will
I speak, this is not well thou dost, but ill,

[467]

Betraying her who loved thee and was true.

    Medea. Surely I have my thoughts, and not a few
Have held me strange. To me it seemeth, when
A crafty tongue is given to evil men
'Tis like to wreck, not help them. Their own brain
Tempts them with lies to dare and dare again,
Till . . . no man hath enough of subtlety.
As thou—be not so seeming-fair to me
Nor deft of speech. One word will make thee fall.
Wert thou not false, 'twas thine to tell me all,
And charge me help thy marriage path, as I
Did love thee; not befool me with a lie.

*then why
didn't you
tell me.*

    Jason. An easy task had that been! Aye, and thou
A loving aid, who canst not, even now,
Still that loud heart that surges like the tide!

    Medea. That moved thee not. Thine old barbarian bride,
The queen out of the east who loved thee sore,
She grew gray-haired, she served thy pride no more.

    Jason. Now understand for once! The girl to me
Is nothing, in this web of sovranty
I hold. I do but seek to save, even yet,
Thee: and for brethren to our sons beget
Young kings, to prosper all our lives again.

    Medea. God shelter me from prosperous days of pain,
And wealth that maketh wounds about my heart.

    Jason. Wilt change that prayer, and choose a wiser part?
Pray not to hold true sense for pain, nor rate
Thyself unhappy, being too fortunate.

    Medea. Aye, mock me; thou hast where to lay thine head,
But I go naked to mine exile.

    Jason.   Tread
Thine own path! Thou hast made it all to be.

    Medea. How? By seducing and forsaking thee?

    Jason. By those vile curses on the royal halls
Let loose. . . .

    Medea.   On thy house also, as chance falls,
I am a living curse.

    Jason.   Oh, peace! Enough
Of these vain wars! I will no more thereof.
If thou wilt take from all that I possess

Aid for these babes and thine own helplessness
Of exile, speak thy bidding. Here I stand
Full-willed to succor thee with stintless hand,
And send my signet to old friends that dwell
On foreign shores, who will entreat thee well.
Refuse, and thou shalt do a deed most vain.
But cast thy rage away, and thou shalt gain
Much, and lose little for thine anger's sake.

Medea. I will not seek thy friends. I will not take
Thy givings. Give them not. Fruits of a stem
Unholy bring no blessing after them.

Jason. Now God in heaven be witness, all my heart
Is willing, in all ways, to do its part
For thee and for thy babes. But nothing good
Can please thee. In sheer savageness of mood
Thou drivest from thee every friend. Wherefore
I warrant thee, thy pains shall be the more.

        [He goes slowly away.

Medea. Go: thou art weary for the new delight
Thou wooest, so long tarrying out of sight
Of her sweet chamber. Go, fulfil thy pride,
O bridegroom! For it may be, such a bride
Shall wait thee,—yea, God heareth me in this—
As thine own heart shall sicken ere it kiss.

Chorus. Alas, the Love that falleth like a flood,
  Strong-winged and transitory:
Why praise ye him? What beareth he of good
  To man, or glory?
Yet Love there is that moves in gentleness,
Heart-filling, sweetest of all powers that bless.
Loose not on me, O Holder of man's heart,
  Thy golden quiver,
Nor steep in poison of desire the dart
  That heals not ever.

The pent hate of the word that cavileth,
  The strife that hath no fill,
Where once was fondness; and the mad heart's breath
  For strange love panting still:
O Cyprian, cast me not on these; but sift,

Keen-eyed, of love the good and evil gift.
Make Innocence my friend, God's fairest star,
 Yea, and abate not
The rare sweet beat of bosoms without war,
 That love, and hate not.

Others. Home of my heart, land of my own,
 Cast me not, nay, for pity,
Out on my ways, helpless, alone,
Where the feet fail in the mire and stone,
 A woman without a city.
Ah, not that! Better the end:
 The green grave cover me rather,
If a break must come in the days I know,
And the skies be changed and the earth below;
For the weariest road that man may wend
 Is forth from the home of his father.

Lo, we have seen: 'tis not a song
 Sung, nor learned of another.
For whom hast thou in thy direst wrong
For comfort? Never a city strong
 To hide thee, never a brother.
Ah, but the man—cursed be he,
 Cursèd beyond recover,
Who openeth, shattering, seal by seal,
A friend's clean heart, then turns his heel,
Deaf unto love: never in me
 Friend shall he know nor lover.

> [*While* MEDEA *is waiting downcast, seated upon
> her door-step, there passes from the left a
> traveler with followers. As he catches sight of*
> MEDEA *he stops.*

Aegeus. Have joy, Medea! 'Tis the homeliest
Word that old friends can greet with, and the best.
 Medea (looking up, surprised). Oh, joy on thee, too,
 Aegeus, gentle king
Of Athens!—But whence com'st thou journeying?
 Aegeus. From Delphi now and the old encaverned stair. . . .

Medea. Where Earth's heart speaks in song? What mad'st
thou there?

Aegeus. Prayed heaven for children—the same search alway.

Medea. Children? Ah God! Art childless to this day?

Aegeus. So God hath willed. Childless and desolate.

Medea. What word did Phoebus speak, to change thy fate?

Aegeus. Riddles, too hard for mortal man to read.

Medea. Which I may hear?

Aegeus.   Assuredly: they need
A rarer wit.

Medea.   How said he?

Aegeus.   Not to spill
Life's wine, nor seek for more. . . .

Medea.   Until?

Aegeus.   Until
I tread the hearth-stone of my sires of yore.

Medea. And what should bring thee here, by Creon's shore?

Aegeus. One Pittheus know'st thou, high lord of Trozên?

Medea. Aye, Pelops' son, a man most pure of sin.

Aegeus. Him I would ask, touching Apollo's will.

Medea. Much use in God's ways hath he, and much skill.

Aegeus. And, long years back he was my battle-friend,
The truest e'er man had.

Medea.   Well, may God send
Good hap to thee, and grant all thy desire.

Aegeus. But thou . . . ? Thy frame is wasted, and the fire
Dead in thine eyes.

Medea.   Aegeus, my husband is
The falsest man in the world.

Aegeus.   What word is this?
Say clearly what thus makes thy visage dim?

Medea. He is false to me, who never injured him.

Aegeus. What hath he done? Show all, that I may see.

Medea. Ta'en him a wife; a wife, set over me
To rule his house.

Aegeus.   He hath not dared to do,
Jason, a thing so shameful?

Medea.   Aye, 'tis true:
And those he loved of yore have no place now.

Aegeus. Some passion sweepeth him? Or is it thou
He turns from?
Medea.   Passion, passion to betray
His dearest!
Aegeus.   Shame be his, so fallen away
From honor!
Medea.   Passion to be near a throne,
A king's heir!
Aegeus.   How, who gives the bride? Say on.
Medea. Creon, who o'er all Corinth standeth chief.
Aegeus. Woman, thou hast indeed much cause for grief.
Medea. 'Tis ruin.—And they have cast me out as well.
Aegeus. Who? 'Tis a new wrong this, and terrible.
Medea. Creon the king, from every land and shore. . . .
Aegeus. And Jason suffers him? Oh, 'tis too sore!
Medea. He loveth to bear bravely ills like these!
But, Aegeus, by thy beard, oh, by thy knees,
I pray thee, and I give me for thine own,
Thy suppliant, pity me! Oh, pity one
So miserable. Thou never wilt stand there
And see me cast out friendless to despair.
Give me a home in Athens . . . by the fire
Of thine own hearth! Oh, so may thy desire
Of children be fulfilled of God, and thou
Die happy! . . . Thou canst know not; even now
Thy prize is won! I, I will make of thee
A childless man no more. The seed shall be,
I swear it, sown. Such magic herbs I know.
Aegeus. Woman, indeed my heart goes forth to show
This help to thee, first for religion's sake,
Then for thy promised hope, to heal my ache
Of childlessness. 'Tis this hath made mine whole
Life as a shadow, and starved out my soul.
But thus it stands with me. Once make thy way
To Attic earth, I, as in law I may,
Will keep thee and befriend. But in this land,
Where Creon rules, I may not raise my hand
To shelter thee. Move of thine own essay
To seek my house, there thou shalt alway stay,
Inviolate, never to be seized again.

[472]

But come thyself from Corinth. I would fain
Even in foreign eyes be alway just.

Medea. 'Tis well. Give me an oath wherein to trust
And all that man could ask thou hast granted me.

Aegeus. Dost trust me not? Or what thing troubleth thee?

Medea. I trust thee. But so many, far and near,
Do hate me—all King Pelias' house, and here
Creon. Once bound by oaths and sanctities
Thou canst not yield me up for such as these
To drag from Athens. But a spoken word,
No more, to bind thee, which no God hath heard . . .
The embassies, methinks, would come and go:
They all are friends to thee. . . . Ah me, I know
Thou wilt not list to me! So weak am I,
And they full-filled with gold and majesty.

Aegeus. Methinks 'tis a far foresight, this thine oath.
Still, if thou so wilt have it, nothing loath
Am I to serve thee. Mine own hand is so
The stronger, if I have this plea to show
Thy persecutors: and for thee withal
The bond more sure.—On what God shall I call?

Medea. Swear by the Earth thou treadest, by the Sun,
Sire of my sires, and all the gods as one. . . .

Aegeus. To do what thing or not do? Make all plain.

Medea. Never thyself to cast me out again.
Nor let another, whatsoe'er his plea,
Take me, while thou yet livest and art free.

Aegeus. Never: so hear me, Earth, and the great star
Of daylight, and all other gods that are!

Medea. 'Tis well: and if thou falter from thy vow . . . ?

Aegeus. God's judgment on the godless break my brow!

Medea. Go! Go thy ways rejoicing.—All is bright
And clear before me. Go: and ere the night
Myself will follow, when the deed is done
I purpose, and the end I thirst for won.

[AEGEUS *and his train depart.*

Chorus. Farewell: and Maia's guiding Son
        Back lead thee to thy hearth and fire,
        Aegeus; and all the long desire
    That wasteth thee, at last be won:

Our eyes have seen thee as thou art,
A gentle and a righteous heart.
   Medea. God, and God's Justice, and ye blinding Skies!
At last the victory dawneth! Yea, mine eyes
See, and my foot is on the mountain's brow.
Mine enemies! Mine enemies, oh, now
Atonement cometh! Here at my worst hour
A friend is found, a very port of power
To save my shipwreck. Here will I make fast
Mine anchor, and escape them at the last
In Athens' wallèd hill.—But ere the end
'Tis meet I show thee all my counsel, friend:
Take it, no tale to make men laugh withal!
   Straightway to Jason I will send some thrall
To entreat him to my presence. Comes he here,
Then with soft reasons will I feed his ear,
How his will now is my will, how all things
Are well, touching this marriage-bed of kings
For which I am betrayed—all wise and rare
And profitable! Yet will I make one prayer,
That my two children be no more exiled
But stay. . . . Oh, not that I would leave a child
Here upon angry shores till those have laughed
Who hate me: 'tis that I will slay by craft
The king's daughter. With gifts they shall be sent,
Gifts to the bride to spare their banishment,
Fine robings and a carcanet of gold.
Which raiment let her once but take, and fold
About her, a foul death that girl shall die
And all who touch her in her agony.
Such poison shall they drink, my robe and wreath!
   Howbeit, of that no more. I gnash my teeth
Thinking on what a path my feet must tread
Thereafter. I shall lay those children dead—
Mine, whom no hand shall steal from me away!
Then, leaving Jason childless, and the day
As night above him, I will go my road
To exile, flying, flying from the blood
Of these my best-beloved, and having wrought
All horror, so but one thing reach me not,

The laugh of them that hate us.
                              Let it come!
What profits life to me? I have no home,
No country now, nor shield from any wrong.
That was my evil hour, when down the long
Halls of my father out I stole, my will
Chained by a Greek man's voice, who still, oh, still,
If God yet live, shall all requited be.
For never child of mine shall Jason see
Hereafter living, never child beget
From his new bride, who this day, desolate
Even as she made me desolate, shall die
Shrieking amid my poisons. . . . Names have I
Among your folk? One light? One weak of hand?
An eastern dreamer?—Nay, but with the brand
Of strange suns burnt, my hate, by God above,
A perilous thing, and passing sweet my love!
For these it is that make life glorious.

   Leader. Since thou hast bared thy fell intent to us
I, loving thee, and helping in their need
Man's laws, adjure thee, dream not of this deed!

   Medea. There is no other way.—I pardon thee
Thy littleness, who art not wronged like me.

   Leader. Thou canst not kill the fruit thy body bore!
   Medea. Yes: if the man I hate be pained the more.
   Leader. And thou made miserable, most miserable?
   Medea. Oh, let it come! All words of good or ill
Are wasted now.

        [*She claps her hands: the* NURSE *comes out from
        the house.*

        Ho, woman; get thee gone
And lead lord Jason hither. . . . There is none
Like thee, to work me these high services.
But speak no word of what my purpose is,
As thou art faithful, thou, and bold to try
All succors, and a woman even as I!

           [*The* NURSE *departs.*

   Chorus. The sons of Erechtheus, the olden,
     Whom high gods planted of yore
     In an old land of heaven upholden,

A proud land untrodden of war:
They are hungered, and, lo, their desire
    With wisdom is fed as with meat:
In their skies is a shining of fire,
    A joy in the fall of their feet:
And thither, with manifold dowers,
    From the North, from the hills, from the morn,
The Muses did gather their powers,
    That a child of the Nine should be born;
And Harmony, sown as the flowers,
    Grew gold in the acres of corn.

And Cephîsus, the fair-flowing river—
    The Cyprian dipping her hand
Hath drawn of his dew, and the shiver
    Of her touch is as joy in the land.
For her breathing in fragrance is written,
    And in music her path as she goes,
And the cloud of her hair, it is litten
    With stars of the wind-woven rose.
So fareth she ever and ever,
    And forth of her bosom is blown,
As dews on the winds of the river,
    An hunger of passions unknown,
Strong Loves of all godlike endeavor,
    Whom Wisdom shall throne on her throne.

Some Women. But Cephîsus the fair-flowing,
    Will he bear thee on his shore?
        Shall the land that succors all, succor thee,
    Who art foul among thy kind,
    With the tears of children blind?
Dost thou see the red gash growing,
        Thine own burden dost thou see?
            Every side, Every way,
    Lo, we kneel to thee and pray:
        By thy knees, by thy soul, O woman wild!
One at least thou canst not slay,
                Not thy child!

[476]

Others. Hast thou ice that thou shalt bind it
　　To thy breast, and make thee dead
　　　To thy children, to thine own spirit's pain?
　When the hand knows what it dares,
　When thine eyes look into theirs,
　Shalt thou keep by tears unblinded
　　Thy dividing of the slain?
　　　These be deeds not for thee:
　These be things that cannot be!
　　　Thy babes—though thine hardihood be fell,
　When they cling about thy knee,
　　　'Twill be well!

　　　　　　　　　　　　　　[Enter JASON.

　Jason. I answer to thy call. Though full of hate
Thou be, I yet will not so far abate
My kindness for thee, nor refuse mine ear.
Say in what new desire thou hast called me here.
　Medea. Jason, I pray thee, for my words but now
Spoken, forgive me. My bad moods. . . . Oh, thou
At least wilt strive to bear with them! There be
Many old deeds of love 'twixt me and thee.
Lo, I have reasoned with myself apart
And chidden: 'Why must I be mad, O heart
Of mine: and raging against one whose word
Is wisdom: making me a thing abhorred
To them that rule the land, and to mine own
Husband, who doth but that which, being done,
Will help us all—to wed a queen, and get
Young kings for brethren to my sons? And yet
I rage alone, and cannot quit my rage—
What aileth me?—when God sends harborage
So simple? Have I not my children? Know
I not we are but exiles, and must go
Beggared and friendless else?' Thought upon thought
So pressed me, till I knew myself full-fraught
With bitterness of heart and blinded eyes.
So now—I give thee thanks: and hold thee wise
To have caught this anchor for our aid. The fool
Was I; who should have been thy friend, thy tool;
Gone wooing with thee, stood at thy bed-side

Serving, and welcomed duteously thy bride.
But, as we are, we are—I will not say
Mere evil—women! Why must thou to-day
Turn strange, and make thee like some evil thing,
Childish, to meet my childish passioning?
See, I surrender: and confess that then
I had bad thoughts, but now have turned again
And found my wiser mind.

> [*She claps her hands.*

                    Ho, children! Run
Quickly! Come hither, out into the sun,

> [*The* CHILDREN *come from the house, followed by
> their* ATTENDANT.

And greet your father. Welcome him with us,
And throw quite, quite away, as mother does,
Your anger against one so dear. Our peace
Is made, and all the old bad war shall cease
For ever.—Go, and take his hand. . . .

> [*As the* CHILDREN *go to* JASON, *she suddenly bursts
> into tears. The* CHILDREN *quickly return to her:
> she recovers herself, smiling amid her tears.*

                              Ah me,
I am full of hidden horrors! . . . Shall it be
A long time more, my children, that ye live
To reach to me those dear, dear arms? . . . Forgive!
I am so ready with my tears to-day,
And full of dread. . . . I sought to smooth away
The long strife with your father, and, lo, now
I have all drowned with tears this little brow!

> [*She wipes the child's face.*

  Leader. O'er mine eyes too there stealeth a pale tear:
Let the evil rest, O God, let it rest here!
  Jason. Woman, indeed I praise thee now, nor say
Ill of thine other hour. 'Tis nature's way,
A woman needs must stir herself to wrath,
When work of marriage by so strange a path
Crosseth her lord. But thou, thine heart doth wend
The happier road. Thou hast seen, ere quite the end,
What choice must needs be stronger: which to do
Shows a wise-minded woman. . . . And for you,

[478]

Children, your father never has forgot
Your needs. If God but help him, he hath wrought
A strong deliverance for your weakness. Yea,
I think you, with your brethren, yet one day
Shall be the mightiest voices in this land.
Do you grow tall and strong. Your father's hand
Guideth all else, and whatso power divine
Hath alway helped him. . . . Ah, may it be mine
To see you yet in manhood, stern of brow,
Strong-armed, set high o'er those that hate me. . . .

            How?

Woman, thy face is turned. Thy cheek is swept
With pallor of strange tears. Dost not accept
Gladly and of good will my benisons?
 Medea. 'Tis nothing. Thinking of these little ones. . . .
 Jason. Take heart, then. I will guard them from all ill.
 Medea. I do take heart. Thy word I never will
Mistrust. Alas, a woman's bosom bears
But woman's courage, a thing born for tears.
 Jason. What ails thee?—All too sore thou weepest there.
 Medea. I was their mother! When I heard thy prayer
Of long life for them, there swept over me
A horror, wondering how these things shall be.
 But for the matter of my need that thou
Should speak with me, part I have said, and now
Will finish.—Seeing it is the king's behest
To cast me out from Corinth . . . aye, and best,
Far best, for me—I know it—not to stay
Longer to trouble thee and those who sway
The realm, being held to all their house a foe. . . .
Behold, I spread my sails, and meekly go
To exile. But our children. . . . Could this land
Be still their home awhile: could thine own hand
But guide their boyhood. . . . Seek the king, and pray
His pity, that he bid thy children stay!
 Jason. He is hard to move. Yet surely 'twere well done.
 Medea. Bid her—for thy sake, for a daughter's boon. . . .
 Jason. Well thought! Her I can fashion to my mind.
 Medea. Surely. She is a woman like her kind. . . .
Yet I will aid thee in thy labor; I

Will send her gifts, the fairest gifts that lie
In the hands of men, things of the days of old,
Fine robings and a carcanet of gold,
By the boys' hands.—Go, quick, some handmaiden,
And fetch the raiment.

> [*A handmaid goes into the house.*

Ah, her cup shall then
Be filled indeed! What more should woman crave,
Being wed with thee, the bravest of the brave,
And girt with raiment which of old the sire
Of all my house, the Sun, gave, steeped in fire,
To his own fiery race?

> [*The handmaid has returned bearing the Gifts.*

Come, children, lift
With heed these caskets. Bear them as your gift
To her, being bride and princess and of right
Blessed!—I think she will not hold them light.

Jason. Fond woman, why wilt empty thus thine hand
Of treasure? Doth King Creon's castle stand
In stint of raiment, or in stint of gold?
Keep these, and make no gift. For if she hold
Jason of any worth at all, I swear
Chattels like these will not weigh more with her.

Medea. Ah, chide me not! 'Tis written, gifts persuade
The gods in heaven; and gold is stronger made
Than words innumerable to bend men's ways.
Fortune is hers. God maketh great her days:
Young and a crownèd queen! And banishment
For those two babes. . . . I would not gold were spent,
But life's blood, ere that come.

My children, go
Forth into those rich halls, and, bowing low,
Beseech your father's bride, whom I obey,
Ye be not, of her mercy, cast away
Exiled: and give the caskets—above all
Mark this!—to none but her, to hold withal
And keep. . . . Go quick! And let your mother know
Soon the good tidings that she longs for. . . . Go!

> [*She goes quickly into the house.* JASON *and the*
> CHILDREN *with their* ATTENDANT *depart.*

[480]

Chorus. Now I have no hope more of the children's living;
  No hope more. They are gone forth unto death.
The bride, she taketh the poison of their giving:
  She taketh the bounden gold and openeth;
And the crown, the crown, she lifteth about her brow,
Where the light brown curls are clustering. No hope now!
O sweet and cloudy gleam of the garments golden!
  The robe, it hath clasped her breast and the crown her head.
Then, then, she decketh the bride, as a bride of olden
  Story, that goeth pale to the kiss of the dead.
For the ring hath closed, and the portion of death is there;
And she flieth not, but perisheth unaware.
  Some Women. O bridegroom, bridegroom of the kiss so cold,
Art thou wed with princes, art thou girt with gold,
      Who know'st not, suing
      For thy child's undoing,
  And, on her thou lovest, for a doom untold?
  How art thou fallen from thy place of old!
  Others. O Mother, Mother, what hast thou to reap,
When the harvest cometh, between wake and sleep?
      For a heart unslaken,
      For a troth forsaken,
Lo, babes that call thee from a bloody deep:
And thy love returns not. Get thee forth and weep!
          [*Enter the* ATTENDANT *with the two* CHILDREN:
            MEDEA *comes out from the house.*
  Attendant. Mistress, these children from their banishment
Are spared. The royal bride hath mildly bent
Her hand to accept thy gifts, and all is now
Peace for the children.—Ha, why standest thou
Confounded, when good fortune draweth near?
  Medea. Ah God!
  Attendant. This chimes not with the news I bear.
  Medea. O God, have mercy!
  Attendant. Is some word of wrath
Here hidden that I knew not of? And hath
My hope to give thee joy so cheated me?
  Medea. Thou givest what thou givest: I blame not thee.
  Attendant. Thy brows are all o'ercast: thine eyes are
      filled. . . .

Medea. For bitter need, Old Man! The gods have willed,
And my own evil mind, that this should come.
    Attendant. Take heart! Thy sons one day will bring thee
      home.
    Medea. Home? . . . I have others to send home. Woe's me!
    Attendant. Be patient. Many a mother before thee
Hath parted from her children. We poor things
Of men must needs endure what fortune brings.
    Medea. I will endure.—Go thou within, and lay
. All ready that my sons may need to-day.
                [*The* ATTENDANT *goes into the House.*
O children, children mine: and you have found
A land and home, where, leaving me discrowned
And desolate, forever you will stay,
Motherless children! And I go my way
To other lands, an exile, ere you bring
Your fruits home, ere I see you prospering
Or know your brides, or deck the bridal bed,
All flowers, and lift your torches overhead.

Oh, cursèd be mine own hard heart! 'Twas all
In vain, then, that I reared you up, so tall
And fair; in vain I bore you, and was torn
With those long pitiless pains, when you were born.
Ah, wondrous hopes my poor heart had in you,
How you would tend me in mine age, and do
The shroud about me with your own dear hands,
When I lay cold, blessèd in all the lands
That knew us. And that gentle thought is dead!
You go, and I live on, to eat the bread
Of long years, to myself most full of pain.
And never your dear eyes, never again,
Shall see your mother, far away being thrown
To other shapes of life. . . . My babes, my own,
Why gaze ye so?—What is it that ye see?—
And laugh with that last laughter? . . . Woe is me,
What shall I do?
               Women, my strength is gone,
Gone like a dream, since once I looked upon
Those shining faces. . . . I can do it not.
Good-bye to all the thoughts that burned so hot

Aforetime! I will take and hide them far,
Far, from men's eyes. Why should I seek a war
So blind: by these babes' wounds to sting again
Their father's heart, and win myself a pain
Twice deeper? Never, never! I forget
Henceforward all I labored for.

                          And yet,
What is it with me? Would I be a thing
Mocked at, and leave mine enemies to sting
Unsmitten? It must be. O coward heart,
Ever to harbor such soft words!—Depart
Out of my sight, ye twain.

                        [*The* CHILDREN *go in.*
                And they whose eyes
Shall hold it sin to share my sacrifice,
On their heads be it! My hand shall swerve not now.
   Ah, Ah, thou Wrath within me! Do not thou,
Do not. . . . Down, down, thou tortured thing, and spare
My children! They will dwell with us, aye, there
Far off, and give thee peace.

                 Too late, too late!
By all Hell's living agonies of hate,
They shall not take my little ones alive
To make their mock with! Howsoe'er I strive
The thing is doomed; it shall not escape now
From being. Aye, the crown is on the brow,
And the robe girt, and in the robe that high
Queen dying.

            I know all. Yet . . . seeing that I
Must go so long a journey, and these twain
A longer yet and darker, I would fain
Speak with them, ere I go.

           [*A handmaid brings the* CHILDREN *out again.*
               Come, children; stand
A little from me. There. Reach out your hand,
Your right hand—so—to mother: and good-bye!
          [*She kept them hitherto at arm's length: but at
            the touch of their hands, her resolution breaks
            down, and she gathers them passionately into
            her arms.*

Oh, darling hand! Oh, darling mouth, and eye,
And royal mien, and bright brave faces clear,
May you be blessèd, but not here! What here
Was yours, your father stole. . . . Ah God, the glow
Of cheek on cheek, the tender touch; and Oh,
Sweet scent of childhood. . . . Go! Go! . . . Am I blind? . . .
Mine eyes can see not, when I look to find
Their places. I am broken by the wings
Of evil. . . . Yea, I know to what bad things
I go, but louder than all thought doth cry
Anger, which maketh man's worst misery.

> [*She follows the* CHILDREN *into the house.*

Chorus. My thoughts have roamed a cloudy land,
    And heard a fierier music fall
    Than woman's heart should stir withal:
    And yet some Muse majestical,
    Unknown, hath hold of woman's hand
    Seeking for Wisdom—not in all:
    A feeble seed, a scattered band,
    Thou yet shalt find in lonely places,
    Not dead amongst us, nor our faces
    Turned away from the Muses' call.
And thus my thought would speak: that she
Who ne'er hath borne a child nor known
Is nearer to felicity:
Unlit she goeth and alone,
With little understanding what
A child's touch means of joy or woe,
And many toils she beareth not.
But they within whose garden fair
That gentle plant hath blown, they go
Deep-written all their days with care—
To rear the children, to make fast
Their hold, to win them wealth; and then
Much darkness, if the seed at last
Bear fruit in good or evil men!
And one thing at the end of all
Abideth, that which all men dread:
The wealth is won, the limbs are bred
To manhood, and the heart withal

Honest: and, lo, where Fortune smiled,
Some change, and what hath fallen? Hark!
'Tis death slow winging to the dark,
And in his arms what was thy child.
What therefore doth it bring of gain
To man, whose cup stood full before,
That God should send this one thing more
Of hunger and of dread, a door
Set wide to every wind of pain?

[MEDEA *comes out alone from the house.*

Medea. Friends, this long hour I wait on Fortune's eyes,
And strain my senses in a hot surmise
What passeth on that hill.—Ha! even now
There comes . . . 'tis one of Jason's men, I trow.
His wild-perturbèd breath doth warrant me
The tidings of some strange calamity.

[*Enter* MESSENGER.

Messenger. O dire and ghastly deed! Get thee away,
Medea! Fly! Nor let behind thee stay
One chariot's wing, one keel that sweeps the seas. . . .

Medea. And what hath chanced, to cause such flights as
  these?

Messenger. The maiden princess lieth—and her sire,
The king—both murdered by thy poison-fire.

Medea. Most happy tiding! Which thy name prefers
Henceforth among my friends and well-wishers.

Messenger. What say'st thou? Woman, is thy mind within
Clear, and not raving? Thou art found in sin
Most bloody wrought against the king's high head,
And laughest at the tale, and hast no dread?

Medea. I have words also that could answer well
Thy word. But take thine ease, good friend, and tell,
How died they? Hath it been a very foul
Death, prithee? That were comfort to my soul.

Messenger. When thy two children, hand in hand entwined,
Came with their father, and passed on to find
The new-made bridal rooms, Oh, we were glad,
We thralls, who ever loved thee well, and had
Grief in thy grief. And straight there passed a word
From ear to ear, that thou and thy false lord

Had poured peace offering upon wrath foregone.
A right glad welcome gave we them, and one
Kissed the small hand, and one the shining hair:
Myself, for very joy, I followed where
The women's rooms are. There our mistress . . . she
Whom now we name so . . . thinking not to see
Thy little pair, with glad and eager brow
Sate waiting Jason. Then she saw, and slow
Shrouded her eyes, and backward turned again,
Sick that thy children should come near her. Then
Thy husband quick went forward, to entreat
The young maid's fitful wrath. 'Thou wilt not meet
Love's coming with unkindness? Nay, refrain
Thy suddenness, and turn thy face again,
Holding as friends all that to me are dear,
Thine husband. And accept these robes they bear
As gifts: and beg thy father to unmake
His doom of exile on them—for my sake.'
When once she saw the raiment, she could still
Her joy no more, but gave him all his will.
And almost ere the father and the two
Children were gone from out the room, she drew
The flowerèd garments forth, and sate her down
To her arraying: bound the golden crown
Through her long curls, and in a mirror fair
Arranged their separate clusters, smiling there
At the dead self that faced her. Then aside
She pushed her seat, and paced those chambers wide
Alone, her white foot poising delicately—
So passing joyful in those gifts was she!—
And many a time would pause, straight-limbed, and wheel
Her head to watch the long fold to her heel
Sweeping. And then came something strange. Her cheek
Seemed pale, and back with crooked steps and weak
Groping of arms she walked, and scarcely found
Her old seat, that she fell not to the ground.
　　Among the handmaids was a woman old
And gray, who deemed, I think, that Pan had hold
Upon her, or some spirit, and raised a keen
Awakening shout; till through her lips was seen

A white foam crawling, and her eyeballs back
Twisted, and all her face dead pale for lack
Of life: and while that old dame called, the cry
Turned strangely to its opposite, to die
Sobbing. Oh, swiftly then one woman flew
To seek her father's rooms, one for the new
Bridegroom, to tell the tale. And all the place
Was loud with hurrying feet.

                            So long a space
As a swift walker on a measured way
Would pace a furlong's course in, there she lay
Speechless, with veilèd lids. Then wide her eyes
She oped, and wildly, as she strove to rise,
Shrieked: for two diverse waves upon her rolled
Of stabbing death. The carcanet of gold
That gripped her brow was molten in a dire
And wondrous river of devouring fire.
And those fine robes, the gift thy children gave—
God's mercy!—everywhere did lap and lave
The delicate flesh; till up she sprang, and fled,
A fiery pillar, shaking locks and head
This way and that, seeking to cast the crown
Somewhere away. But like a thing nailed down
The burning gold held fast the anadem,
And through her locks, the more she scattered them,
Came fire the fiercer, till to earth she fell
A thing—save to her sire—scarce nameable,
And strove no more. That cheek of royal mien,
Where was it—or the place where eyes had been?
Only from crown and temples came faint blood
Shot through with fire. The very flesh, it stood
Out from the bones, as from a wounded pine
The gum starts, where those gnawing poisons fine
Bit in the dark—a ghastly sight! And touch
The dead we durst not. We had seen too much.

  But that poor father, knowing not, had sped,
Swift to his daughter's room, and there the dead
Lay at his feet. He knelt, and groaning low,
Folded her in his arms, and kissed her: 'Oh,
Unhappy child, what thing unnatural hath

[487]

So hideously undone thee? Or what wrath
Of gods, to make this old gray sepulcher
Childless of thee? Would God but lay me there
To die with thee, my daughter!' So he cried.
But after, when he stayed from tears, and tried
To uplift his old bent frame, lo, in the folds
Of those fine robes it held, as ivy holds
Strangling among young laurel boughs. Oh, then
A ghastly struggle came! Again, again,
Up on his knee he writhed; but that dead breast
Clung still to his: till, wild, like one possessed,
He dragged himself half free; and, lo, the live
Flesh parted; and he laid him down to strive
No more with death, but perish; for the deep
Had risen above his soul. And there they sleep,
At last, the old proud father and the bride,
Even as his tears had craved it, side by side.

    For thee—Oh, no word more! Thyself will know
How best to baffle vengeance. . . . Long ago
I looked upon man's days, and found a gray
Shadow. And this thing more I surely say,
That those of all men who are counted wise,
Strong wits, devisers of great policies,
Do pay the bitterest toll. Since life began,
Hath there in God's eye stood one happy man?
Fair days roll on, and bear more gifts or less
Of fortune, but to no man happiness.

                    [*Exit* MESSENGER.

    Chorus (*Some Women*). Wrath upon wrath, meseems, this
        day shall fall
From God on Jason! He hath earned it all.
    Other Women. O miserable maiden, all my heart
Is torn for thee, so sudden to depart
From thy king's chambers and the light above
To darkness, all for sake of Jason's love!
    Medea. Women, my mind is clear. I go to slay
My children with all speed, and then, away
From hence; not wait yet longer till they stand
Beneath another and an angrier hand
To die. Yea, howsoe'er I shield them, die

They must. And, seeing that they must, 'tis I
Shall slay them, I their mother, touched of none
Beside. Oh, up and get thine armor on,
My heart! Why longer tarry we to win
Our crown of dire inevitable sin?
Take up thy sword, O poor right hand of mine,
Thy sword: then onward to the thin-drawn line
Where life turns agony. Let there be naught
Of softness now: and keep thee from that thought,
'Born of thy flesh,' 'thine own belovèd.' Now,
For one brief day, forget thy children: thou
Shalt weep hereafter. Though thou slay them, yet
Sweet were they. . . . I am sore unfortunate.

[She goes into the house.

Chorus (Some Women). O Earth, our mother; and thou
    All-seër, arrowy crown
     Of Sunlight, manward now
      Look down, Oh, look down!
Look upon one accurst,
    Ere yet in blood she twine
    Red hands—blood that is thine!
O Sun, save her first!
She is thy daughter still,
    Of thine own golden line;
   Save her! Or shall man spill
     The life divine?
Give peace, O Fire that diest not! Send thy spell
   To stay her yet, to lift her afar, afar—
  A torture-changèd spirit, a voice of Hell
    Wrought of old wrongs and war!
Others. Alas for the mother's pain
    Wasted! Alas the dear
  Life that was born in vain!
   Woman, what mak'st thou here,
  Thou from beyond the Gate
   Where dim Symplêgades
   Clash in the dark blue seas,
The shores where death doth wait?
Why hast thou taken on thee,
   To make us desolate,

This anger of misery
And guilt of hate?
For fierce are the smitings back of blood once shed
Where love hath been: God's wrath upon them that kill,
And an anguished earth, and the wonder of the dead
Haunting as music still. . . .

[A cry is heard within.

A Woman. Hark! Did ye hear? Heard ye the children's cry?
Another. O miserable woman! O abhorred!
A Child within. What shall I do? What is it? Keep me fast
From mother!
The Other Child. I know nothing. Brother! Oh,
I think she means to kill us.
A Woman. Let me go!
I will—Help! Help!—and save them at the last.
A Child. Yes, in God's name! Help quickly ere we die!
The Other Child. She has almost caught me now. She has a
sword.

*[Many of the Women are now beating at the barred
door to get in. Others are standing apart.*

Women at the door. Thou stone, thou thing of iron! Wilt
verily
Spill with thine hand that life, the vintage stored
Of thine own agony?
The Other Women. A Mother slew her babes in days of
yore,
One, only one, from dawn to eventide,
Ino, god-maddened, whom the Queen of Heaven
Set frenzied, flying to the dark: and she
Cast her for sorrow to the wide salt sea,
Forth from those rooms of murder unforgiven,
Wild-footed from a white crag of the shore,
And clasping still her children twain, she died.
O Love of Woman, charged with sorrow sore,
What hast thou wrought upon us? What beside
Resteth to tremble for?

[Enter hurriedly JASON *and* ATTENDANTS.

Jason. Ye women by this doorway clustering
Speak, is the doer of the ghastly thing
Yet here, or fled? What hopeth she of flight?

Shall the deep yawn to shield her? Shall the height
Send wings, and hide her in the vaulted sky
To work red murder on her lords, and fly
Unrecompensed? But let her go! My care
Is but to save my children, not for her.
Let them she wronged requite her as they may.
I care not. 'Tis my sons I must some way
Save, ere the kinsmen of the dead can win
From them the payment of their mother's sin.

   Leader. Unhappy man, indeed thou knowest not
What dark place thou art come to! Else, God wot,
Jason, no word like these could fall from thee.

   Jason. What is it?—Ha! The woman would kill me?

   Leader. Thy sons are dead, slain by their mother's hand.

   Jason. How? Not the children. . . . I scarce understand. . . .
O God, thou hast broken me!

   Leader.   Think of those twain
As things once fair, that ne'er shall bloom again.

   Jason. Where did she murder them? In that old room?

   Leader. Open, and thou shalt see thy children's doom.

   Jason. Ho, thralls! Unloose me yonder bars! Make more
Of speed! Wrench out the jointing of the door.
And show my two-edged curse, the children dead,
The woman. . . . Oh, this sword upon her head. . . .

           [*While the* ATTENDANTS *are still battering at the
           door* MEDEA *appears on the roof, standing on
           a chariot of winged Dragons, in which are the
           children's bodies.*

   Medea. What make ye at my gates? Why batter ye
With brazen bars, seeking the dead and me
Who slew them? Peace! . . . And thou, if aught of mine
Thou needest, speak, though never touch of thine
Shall scathe me more. Out of his firmament
My fathers' father, the high Sun, hath sent
This, that shall save me from mine enemies' rage.

   Jason. Thou living hate! Thou wife in every age
Abhorrèd, blood-red mother, who didst kill
My sons, and make me as the dead: and still
Canst take the sunshine to thine eyes, and smell
The green earth, reeking from thy deed of hell;

[491]

I curse thee! Now, Oh, now mine eyes can see,
That then were blinded, when from savagery
Of eastern chambers, from a cruel land,
To Greece and home I gathered in mine hand
Thee, thou incarnate curse: one that betrayed
Her home, her father, her . . . Oh, God hath laid
Thy sins on me!—I knew, I knew, there lay
A brother murdered on thy hearth that day
When thy first footstep fell on Argo's hull. . . .
Argo, my own, my swift and beautiful!
    That was her first beginning. Then a wife
I made her in my house. She bore to life
Children: and now for love, for chambering
And men's arms, she hath murdered them! A thing
Not one of all the maids of Greece, not one,
Had dreamed of; whom I spurned, and for mine own
Chose thee, a bride of hate to me and death,
Tigress, not woman, beast of wilder breath
Than Skylla shrieking o'er the Tuscan sea.
Enough! No scorn of mine can reach to thee,
Such iron is o'er thine eyes. Out from my road,
Thou crime-begetter, blind with children's blood!
And let me weep alone the bitter tide
That sweepeth Jason's days, no gentle bride
To speak with more, no child to look upon
Whom once I reared . . . all, all for ever gone!
    Medea. An easy answer had I to this swell
Of speech, but Zeus our father knoweth well,
All I for thee have wrought, and thou for me.
So let it rest. This thing was not to be,
That thou shouldst live a merry life, my bed
Forgotten and my heart uncomforted,
Thou nor thy princess: nor the king that planned
Thy marriage drive Medea from his land,
And suffer not. Call me what thing thou please,
Tigress or Skylla from the Tuscan seas:
My claws have gripped thine hearth, and all things shine.
    Jason. Thou too hast grief. Thy pain is fierce as mine.
    Medea. I love the pain, so thou shalt laugh no more.
    Jason. Oh, what a womb of sin my children bore!

MEDEA

Medea. Sons, did ye perish for your father's shame?
Jason. How? It was not my hand that murdered them.
Medea. 'Twas thy false wooings, 'twas thy trampling pride.
Jason. Thou hast said it! For thy lust of love they died.
Medea. And love to women a slight thing should be?
Jason. To women pure!—All thy vile life to thee!
Medea. Think of thy torment. They are dead, they are dead!
Jason. No: quick, great God; quick curses round thy head!
Medea. The Gods know who began this work of woe.
Jason. Thy heart and all its loathliness they know.
Medea. Loathe on. . . . But, Oh, thy voice. It hurts me sore.
Jason. Aye, and thine me. Wouldst hear me then no more?
Medea. How? Show me but the way. 'Tis this I crave.
Jason. Give me the dead to weep, and make their grave.
Medea. Never! Myself will lay them in a still
Green sepulcher, where Hera by the Hill
Hath precinct holy, that no angry men
May break their graves and cast them forth again
To evil. So I lay on all this shore
Of Corinth a high feast for evermore
And rite, to purge them yearly of the stain
Of this poor blood. And I, to Pallas' plain
I go, to dwell beside Pandion's son,
Aegeus.—For thee, behold, death draweth on,
Evil and lonely, like thine heart: the hands
Of thine old Argo, rotting where she stands,
Shall smite thine head in twain, and bitter be
To the last end thy memories of me.

   [*She rises on the chariot and is slowly borne away.*
Jason. May They that hear the weeping child
   Blast thee, and They that walk in blood!
Medea. Thy broken vows, thy friends beguiled
   Have shut for thee the ears of God.
Jason. Go, thou art wet with children's tears!
Medea. Go thou, and lay thy bride to sleep.
Jason. Childless, I go, to weep and weep.
Medea. Not yet! Age cometh and long years.
Jason. My sons, mine own!
Medea.   Not thine, but mine . . .
Jason. . . . Who slew them!

[493]

Medea.   Yes: to torture thee.

Jason. Once let me kiss their lips, once twine
     Mine arms and touch. . . . Ah, woe is me!

Medea. Wouldst love them and entreat? But now
     They were as nothing.

Jason.   At the last,
     O God, to touch that tender brow!

Medea. Thy words upon the wind are cast.

Jason. Thou, Zeus, wilt hear me. All is said
     For naught. I am but spurned away
   And trampled by this tigress, red
     With children's blood. Yet, come what may,
  So far as thou hast granted, yea,
     So far as yet my strength may stand,
  I weep upon these dead, and say
     Their last farewell, and raise my hand
  To all the daemons of the air
     In witness of these things; how she
     Who slew them, will not suffer me
  To gather up my babes, nor bear
  To earth their bodies; whom, O stone
  Of women, would I ne'er had known!
     Nor gotten, to be slain by thee!
                    [He casts himself upon the earth.

Chorus. Great treasure halls hath Zeus in heaven,
     From whence to man strange dooms be given,
          Past hope or fear.
  And the end men looked for cometh not,
  And a path is there where no man thought:
        So hath it fallen here.

EURIPIDES

HIPPOLYTUS

⇻⟫⟪⇺

TRANSLATED
by
GILBERT MURRAY

CHARACTERS IN THE PLAY

The Goddess APHRODITE.
HIPPOLYTUS, *son of Theseus and the Amazon Hippolyta.*
HUNTSMEN.
AN OLD HUNTSMAN.
THE NURSE *of Phaedra.*
PHAEDRA, *daughter of Minos, King of Crete, and wife of Theseus.*
THESEUS, *King of Athens and Trozên.*
A HENCHMAN *of Hippolytus.*
The Goddess ARTEMIS.
ATTENDANTS.
CHORUS of TROZENIAN WOMEN, *with their* LEADER.

The scene is laid in Trozên.

ARGUMENT

Hippolytus, the son of Theseus and the Amazon Hippolyta, has lived a chaste and virtuous life, devoted to the worship of Artemis. In his enjoyment of Artemis' favor, he scorns the Goddess of Love, and boasts that she can have no power over him. Aphrodite, resenting Hippolytus' disregard of her, announces her determination to avenge this neglect. She causes Phaedra, Theseus' second wife, to fall in love against her will with Hippolytus, and thus intends to bring about the young man's ruin. At this point the play opens.

HIPPOLYTUS

---

*The scene represents the front of the royal castle of Trozên,
the chief door being in the center, facing the audience. Two
statues are visible, that of* ARTEMIS *on the right, that of*
APHRODITE *or* CYPRIS *on the left. The goddess* APHRODITE
is discovered alone.

Aphrodite. Great among men, and not unnamed am I,
The Cyprian, in God's inmost halls on high.
And wheresoe'er from Pontus to the far
Red West men dwell, and see the glad Day-star,
And worship Me, the pious hearts I bless,
And wreck that life that lives in stubbornness.
For that there is, even in a great God's mind,
That hungereth for the praise of human kind.
  So runs my word; and soon the very deed
Shall follow. For this Prince of Theseus' seed,
Hippolytus, child of that dead Amazon,
And reared by saintly Pittheus in his own
Strait ways, hath dared, alone of all Trozên,
To hold me least of spirits and most mean,
And spurns my spell and seeks no woman's kiss.
But great Apollo's sister, Artemis,
He holds of all most high, gives love and praise,
And through the wild dark woods for ever strays,
He and the Maid together, with swift hounds
To slay all angry beasts from out these bounds,
To more than mortal friendship consecrate!
  I grudge it not. No grudge know I, nor hate;
Yet, seeing he hath offended, I this day
Shall smite Hippolytus. Long since my way
Was opened, nor needs now much labor more.
  For once from Pittheus' castle to the shore

Of Athens came Hippolytus over-seas
Seeking the vision of the Mysteries.
And Phaedra there, his father's Queen high-born,
Saw him, and, as she saw, her heart was torn
With great love, by the working of my will.
And for his sake, long since, on Pallas' hill,
Deep in the rock, that Love no more might roam,
She built a shrine, and named it *Love-at-home:*
And the rock held it, but its face alway
Seeks Trozên o'er the seas. Then came the day
When Theseus, for the blood of kinsmen shed,
Spake doom of exile on himself, and fled,
Phaedra beside him, even to this Trozên.
And here that grievous and amazèd Queen,
Wounded and wondering, with ne'er a word,
Wastes slowly; and her secret none hath heard
Nor dreamed.
         But never thus this love shall end!
To Theseus' ear some whisper will I send,
And all be bare! And that proud Prince, my foe,
His sire shall slay with curses. Even so
Endeth that boon the great Lord of the Main
To Theseus gave, the Three Prayers not in vain.
  And she, not in dishonor, yet shall die.
I would not rate this woman's pain so high
As not to pay mine haters in full fee
That vengeance that shall make all well with me.

  But soft, here comes he, striding from the chase,
Our Prince Hippolytus!—I will go my ways.—
And hunters at his heels: and a loud throng
Glorying Artemis with praise and song!
Little he knows that Hell's gates opened are,
And this his last look on the great Day-star!

      [APHRODITE *withdraws, unseen by* HIPPOLYTUS
       and a band of huntsmen, who enter from the
       left, singing. They pass the Statue of APHRO-
       DITE *without notice.*

Hippolytus. Follow, O follow me,
Singing on your ways

Her in whose hand are we,
Her whose own flock we be,
The Zeus-Child, the Heavenly;
    To Artemis be praise!
    Huntsmen. Hail to thee, Maiden blest,
Proudest and holiest:
God's Daughter, great in bliss,
Leto-born, Artemis!
Hail to thee, Maiden, far
Fairest of all that are,
    Yea, and most high thine home,
Child of the Father's hall;
Hear, O most virginal,
Hear, O most fair of all,
    In high God's golden dome.

[*The huntsmen have gathered about the altar of*
ARTEMIS. HIPPOLYTUS *now advances from them,*
and approaches the Statue with a wreath in his
hand.

Hippolytus. To thee this wreathèd garland, from a green
And virgin meadow bear I, O my Queen,
Where never shepherd leads his grazing ewes
Nor scythe has touched. Only the river dews
Gleam, and the spring bee sings, and in the glade
Hath Solitude her mystic garden made.
    No evil hand may cull it: only he
Whose heart hath known the heart of Purity,
Unlearned of man, and true whate'er befall.
Take therefore from pure hands this coronal,
O mistress loved, thy golden hair to twine.
For, sole of living men, this grace is mine,
To dwell with thee, and speak, and hear replies
Of voice divine, though none may see thine eyes.
    Oh, keep me to the end in this same road!

[*An* OLD HUNTSMAN, *who has stood apart from*
the rest, here comes up to HIPPOLYTUS.

Huntsman. My Prince—for 'Master' name I none but God—
Gave I good counsel, wouldst thou welcome it?
    Hippolytus. Right gladly, friend; else were I poor of wit.

Huntsman. Knowest thou one law, that through the world
has won?
Hippolytus. What wouldst thou? And how runs thy law?
Say on.
Huntsman. It hates that Pride that speaks not all men fair!
Hippolytus. And rightly. Pride breeds hatred everywhere.
Huntsman. And good words love, and grace in all men's
sight?
Hippolytus. Aye, and much gain withal, for trouble slight.
Huntsman. How deem'st thou of the Gods? Are they the
same?
Hippolytus. Surely: we are but fashioned on their frame.
Huntsman. Why then wilt thou be proud, and worship
not . . .
Hippolytus. Whom? If the name be speakable, speak out!
Huntsman. She stands here at thy gate: the Cyprian Queen!
Hippolytus. I greet her from afar: my life is clean.
Huntsman. Clean? Nay, proud, proud; a mark for all to
scan!
Hippolytus. Each mind hath its own bent, for God or man.
Huntsman. God grant thee happiness . . . and wiser thought!
Hippolytus. These Spirits that reign in darkness like me not.
Huntsman. What the Gods ask, O Son, that man must pay!
Hippolytus (*turning from him to the others*). On, hunts-
men, to the Castle! Make your way
Straight to the feast room; 'tis a merry thing
After the chase, a board of banqueting.
And see the steeds be groomed, and in array
The chariot dight. I drive them forth to-day.

> [*He pauses, and makes a slight gesture of reverence
> to the Statue on the left. Then to the* OLD
> HUNTSMAN.

That for thy Cyprian, friend, and nought beside!

> [HIPPOLYTUS *follows the huntsmen, who stream
> off by the central door into the Castle. The*
> OLD HUNTSMAN *remains.*

Huntsman (*approaching the Statue and kneeling*). O
Cyprian—for a young man in his pride
I will not follow!—here before thee, meek,
In that one language that a slave may speak,

I pray thee; Oh, if some wild heart in froth
O youth surges against thee, be not wroth
For ever! Nay, be far and hear not then:
Gods should be gentler and more wise than men!

[*He rises and follows the others into the Castle.
The·Orchestra is empty for a moment, then there enter
from right and. left several Trozenian women,
young and old. Their number eventually amounts
to fifteen.*]

Chorus. There riseth a rock-born river,
        Of Ocean's tribe, men say;
    The crags of it gleam and quiver,
        And pitchers dip in the spray:
A woman was there with raiment white
To bathe and spread in the warm sunlight,
    And she told a tale to me there by the river,
        The tale of the Queen and her evil day:

    How, ailing beyond allayment,
        Within she hath bowed her head,
    And with shadow of silken raiment
        The bright brown hair bespread.
For three long days she hath lain forlorn,
Her lips untainted of flesh or corn,
    For that secret sorrow beyond allayment
        That steers to the far sad shore of the dead.

Some Women. Is this some Spirit, O child of man?
Doth Hecat hold thee perchance, or Pan?
Doth She of the Mountains work her ban,
    Or the dread Corybantes bind thee?

Others. Nay, is it sin that upon thee lies,
Sin of forgotten sacrifice,
In thine own Dictynna's sea-wild eyes?
    Who in Limna here can find thee;
For the Deep's dry floor is her easy way,
And she moves in the salt wet whirl of the spray.

Other Women. Or doth the Lord of Erechtheus' race,
Thy Theseus, watch for a fairer face,
For secret arms in a silent place,
    Far from thy love or chiding?

[501]

Others. Or hath there landed, amid the loud
   Hum of Piraeus' sailor-crowd,
   Some Cretan venturer, weary-browed,
      Who bears to the Queen some tiding;
   Some far home-grief, that hath bowed her low,
   And chained her soul to a bed of woe?
An Older Woman. Nay—know ye not?—this burden hath
      alway lain
   On the devious being of woman; yea, burdens twain,
   The burden of Wild Will and the burden of Pain.
   Through my heart once that wind of terror sped;
      But I, in fear confessèd,
   Cried from the dark to Her in heavenly bliss,
   The Helper of Pain, the Bow-Maid Artemis:
   Whose feet I praise for ever, where they tread
      Far off among the blessèd!
The Leader. But see, the Queen's gray nurse at the door,
Sad-eyed and sterner, methinks, than of yore,
      With the Queen. Doth she lead her hither,
To the wind and sun?—Ah, fain would I know
What strange betiding hath blanched that brow,
      And made that young life wither.

               [*The* NURSE *comes out from the central door, fol-
               lowed by* PHAEDRA, *who is supported by two
               handmaids. They make ready a couch for*
               PHAEDRA *to lie upon.*

Nurse. O sick and sore are the days of men!
What wouldst thou? What shall I change again?
Here is the Sun for thee; here is the sky;
And thy weary pillows wind-swept lie,
      By the castle door.
But the cloud of thy brow is dark, I ween;
And soon thou wilt back to thy bower within:
So swift to change is the path of thy feet,
And near things hateful, and far things sweet;
      So was it before!

Oh, pain were better than tending pain!
For that were single, and this is twain,
With grief of heart and labor of limb.

Yet all man's life is but ailing and dim,
  And rest upon earth comes never.
But if any far-off state there be,
Dearer than life to mortality;
The hand of the Dark hath hold thereof,
And mist is under and mist above.
And so we are sick for life, and cling
On earth to this nameless and shining thing.
For other life is a fountain sealed,
And the deeps below us are unrevealed,
  And we drift on legends for ever!

[PHAEDRA *during this has been laid on her couch:
  she speaks to the handmaids.*

Phaedra. Yes; lift me: not my head so low.
  There, hold my arms.—Fair arms they seem!—
My poor limbs scarce obey me now!
Take off that hood that weighs my brow,
  And let my long hair stream.
Nurse. Nay, toss not, Child, so feveredly.
  The sickness best will win relief
By quiet rest and constancy.
  All men have grief.
Phaedra (not noticing her). Oh for a deep and dewy spring,
  With runlets cold to draw and drink!
And a great meadow blossoming,
Long-grassed, and poplars in a ring,
  To rest me by the brink!
Nurse. Nay, Child! Shall strangers hear this tone
  So wild, and thoughts so fever-flown?
Phaedra. Oh, take me to the Mountain! Oh,
  Past the great pines and through the wood,
Up where the lean hounds softly go,
  A-whine for wild things' blood,
And madly flies the dappled roe.
O God, to shout and speed them there,
An arrow by my chestnut hair
Drawn tight, and one keen glimmering spear—
  Ah! if I could!
Nurse. What wouldst thou with them—fancies all:—
  Thy hunting and thy fountain brink?

What wouldst thou? By the city wall
Canst hear our own brook plash and fall
    Downhill, if thou wouldst drink.
Phaedra. O Mistress of the Sea-lorn Mere
    Where horse-hoofs beat the sand and sing,
O Artemis, that I were there
'To tame Enetian steeds and steer
    Swift chariots in the ring!
Nurse. Nay, mountainward but now thy hands
    Yearned out, with craving for the chase;
And now toward the unseaswept sands
    Thou roamest, where the coursers pace!
    O wild young steed, what prophet knows
The power that holds thy curb, and throws
    Thy swift heart from its race?
        [*At these words* PHAEDRA *gradually recovers her-
        self and pays attention.*
Phaedra. What have I said? Woe's me! And where
    Gone straying from my wholesome mind?
What? Did I fall in some god's snare?
    —Nurse, veil my head again, and blind
    Mine eyes.—There is a tear behind
    That lash.—Oh, I am sick with shame!
        Aye, but it hath a sting,
    To come to reason; yet the name
        Of madness is an awful thing.—
    Could I but die in one swift flame
        Unthinking, unknowing!
Nurse. I veil thy face, Child.—Would that so
    Mine own were veiled for evermore,
    So sore I love thee! . . . Though the lore
Of long life mocks me, and I know
How love should be a lightsome thing
    Not rooted in the deep o' the heart;
    With gentle ties, to twine apart
If need so call, or closer cling.—
Why do I love thee so? O fool,
    O fool, the heart that bleeds for twain,
    And builds, men tell us, walls of pain,
To walk by love's unswerving rule,

The same for ever, stern and true!
　　For 'Thorough' is no word of peace:
　　'Tis 'Naught-too-much' makes trouble cease,
And many a wise man bows thereto.

> [*The* LEADER OF THE CHORUS *here approaches the*
> NURSE.

Leader. Nurse of our Queen, thou watcher old and true,
We see her great affliction, but no clue
Have we to learn the sickness. Wouldst thou tell
The name and sort thereof, 'twould like us well.

Nurse. Small leechcraft have I, and she tells no man.

Leader. Thou know'st no cause? Nor when the unrest
　　began?

Nurse. It all comes to the same. She will not speak.

Leader (*turning and looking at* PHAEDRA). How she is
　　changed and wasted! And how weak!

Nurse. 'Tis the third day she hath fasted utterly.

Leader. What, is she mad? Or doth she seek to die?

Nurse. I know not. But to death it sure must lead.

Leader. 'Tis strange that Theseus takes hereof no heed.

Nurse. She hides her wound, and vows it is not so.

Leader. Can he not look into her face and know?

Nurse. Nay, he is on a journey these last days.

Leader. Canst thou not force her, then? Or think of ways
To trap the secret of the sick heart's pain?

Nurse. Have I not tried all ways, and all in vain?
Yet will I cease not now, and thou shalt tell
If in her grief I serve my mistress well!

> [*She goes across to where* PHAEDRA *lies; and pres-*
> *ently, while speaking, kneels by her.*

Dear daughter mine, all that before was said
Let both of us forget; and thou instead
Be kindlier, and unlock that prisoned brow.
And I, who followed then the wrong road, now
Will leave it and be wiser. If thou fear
Some secret sickness, there be women here
To give thee comfort.

> [PHAEDRA *shakes her head.*

　　　　　　No; not secret? Then
Is it a sickness meet for aid of men?

EURIPIDES

Speak, that a leech may tend thee.
                                        Silent still?
Nay, Child, what profits silence? If 'tis ill
This that I counsel, make me see the wrong:
If well, then yield to me.
                            Nay, Child, I long
For one kind word, one look!
              [PHAEDRA *lies motionless. The* NURSE *rises.*
                                        Oh, woe is me!
Women, we labor here all fruitlessly,
All as far off as ever from her heart!
She ever scorned me, and now hears no part
Of all my prayers!
                        [*Turning to* PHAEDRA *again.*
                    Nay, hear thou shalt, and be,
If so thou will, more wild than the wild sea;
But know, thou art thy little ones' betrayer!
If thou die now, shall child of thine be heir
To Theseus' castle? Nay, not thine, I ween,
But hers! That barbèd Amazonian Queen
Hath left a child to bend thy children low,
A bastard royal-hearted—sayst not so?—
Hippolytus . . .
    Phaedra.   Ah!
          [*She starts up, sitting, and throws the veil off.*
    Nurse.   That stings thee?
    Phaedra.   Nurse, most sore
Thou hast hurt me! In God's name, speak that name no more.
    Nurse. Thou seest? Thy mind is clear; but with thy mind
Thou wilt not save thy children, nor be kind
To thine own life.
    Phaedra.   My children? Nay, most dear
I love them.—Far, far other grief is here.
    Nurse (after a pause, wondering). Thy hand is clean, O
        Child, from stain of blood?
    Phaedra. My hand is clean; but is my heart, O God?
    Nurse. Some enemy's spell hath made thy spirit dim?
    Phaedra. He hates me not that slays me, nor I him.
    Nurse. Theseus, the King, hath wronged thee in man's wise?
    Phaedra. Ah, could but I stand guiltless in his eyes!

Nurse. O speak! What is this death-fraught mystery?

Phaedra. Nay, leave me to my wrong. I wrong not thee.

Nurse (*suddenly throwing herself in supplication at* PHAEDRA'S *feet*). Not wrong me, whom thou wouldst all desolate leave!

Phaedra (*rising and trying to move away*). What wouldst thou? Force me? Clinging to my sleeve?

Nurse. Yea, to thy knees; and weep; and let not go!

Phaedra. Woe to thee, Woman, if thou learn it, woe!

Nurse. I know no bitterer woe than losing thee.

Phaedra. I am lost! Yet the deed shall honor me.

Nurse. Why hide what honors thee? 'Tis all I claim!

Phaedra. Why, so I build up honor out of shame!

Nurse. Then speak, and higher still thy fame shall stand.

Phaedra. Go, in God's name!—Nay, leave me; loose my hand!

Nurse. Never, until thou grant me what I pray.

Phaedra (*yielding, after a pause*). So be it. I dare not tear that hand away.

Nurse (*rising and releasing* PHAEDRA). Tell all thou wilt, Daughter. I speak no more.

Phaedra (*after a long pause*). Mother, poor Mother, that didst love so sore!

Nurse. What mean'st thou, Child? The Wild Bull of the Tide?

Phaedra. And thou, sad sister, Dionysus' bride!

Nurse. Child! wouldst thou shame the house where thou wast born?

Phaedra. And I the third, sinking most all-forlorn!

Nurse (*to herself*). I am all lost and feared. What will she say?

Phaedra. From there my grief comes, not from yesterday.

Nurse. I come no nearer to thy parable.

Phaedra. Oh, would that thou couldst tell what I must tell!

Nurse. I am no seer in things I wot not of.

Phaedra (*again hesitating*). What is it that they mean, who say men . . . love?

Nurse. A thing most sweet, my Child, yet dolorous.

Phaedra. Only the half, belike, hath fallen on us!

Nurse (*starting*). On thee? Love?—Oh, what sayst thou?
   What man's son?

Phaedra. What man's? There was a Queen, an Amazon . . .

Nurse. Hippolytus, sayst thou?

Phaedra (*again wrapping her face in the veil*).

                    Nay, 'twas thou, not I!

   [PHAEDRA *sinks back on the couch and covers her
      face again. The* NURSE *starts violently from her
      and walks up and down.*

Nurse. O God! what wilt thou say, Child? Wouldst thou try
To kill me?—Oh, 'tis more than I can bear;
Women, I will no more of it, this glare
Of hated day, this shining of the sky.
I will fling down my body, and let it lie
Till life be gone!

                Women, God rest with you,
My works are over! For the pure and true
Are forced to evil, against their own heart's vow,
And love it!

            [*She suddenly sees the Statue of Cypris, and stands
               with her eyes riveted upon it.*

            Ah, Cyprian! No god art thou,
But more than god, and greater, that hath thrust
Me and my queen and all our house to dust!

            [*She throws herself on the ground close to the
               statue.*

Chorus (*Some Women*). O Women, have ye heard? Nay,
   dare ye hear
   The desolate cry of the young Queen's misery?

A Woman. My Queen, I love thee dear,
   Yet liefer were I dead than framed like thee.

Others. Woe, woe to me for this thy bitter bane,
Surely the food man feeds upon is pain!

   Others. How wilt thou bear thee through this livelong day,
   Lost, and thine evil naked to the light?

Strange things are close upon us—who shall say
   How strange?—save one thing that is plain to sight,
The stroke of the Cyprian and the fall thereof
On thee, thou child of the Isle of fearful Love!

[PHAEDRA *during this has risen from the couch and comes forward collectedly. As she speaks the* NURSE *gradually rouses herself, and listens more calmly.*

Phaedra. O Women, dwellers in this portal-seat
Of Pelops' land, gazing toward my Crete,
How oft, in other days than these, have I
Through night's long hours thought of man's misery,
And how this life is wrecked! And, to mine eyes,
Not in man's knowledge, not in wisdom, lies
The lack that makes for sorrow. Nay, we scan
And know the right—for wit hath many a man—
But will not to the last end strive and serve.
For some grow too soon weary, and some swerve
To other paths, setting before the Right
The diverse far-off image of Delight;
And many are delights beneath the sun!
Long hours of converse; and to sit alone
Musing—a deadly happiness!—and Shame:
Though two things there be hidden in one name,
And Shame can be slow poison if it will!

   This is the truth I saw then, and see still;
Nor is there any magic that can stain
That white truth for me, or make me blind again.
Come, I will show thee how my spirit hath moved.
When the first stab came, and I knew I loved,
I cast about how best to face mine ill.
And the first thought that came, was to be still
And hide my sickness.—For no trust there is
In man's tongue, that so well admonishes
And counsels and betrays, and waxes fat
With griefs of its own gathering!—After that
I would my madness bravely bear, and try
To conquer by mine own heart's purity.

   My third mind, when these two availed me naught
To quell love, was to die—

                    [*Motion of protest among the Women.*
                         the best, best thought—
—Gainsay me not—of all that man can say!
I would not have mine honor hidden away;

Why should I have my shame before men's eyes
Kept living? And I knew, in deadly wise,
Shame was the deed and shame the suffering;
And I a woman, too, to face the thing,
Despised of all!
                          Oh, utterly accurst
Be she of women, whoso dared the first
To cast her honor out to a strange man!
'Twas in some great house, surely, that began
This plague upon us; then the baser kind,
When the good led toward evil, followed blind
And joyous! Cursed be they whose lips are clean
And wise and seemly, but their hearts within
Rank with bad daring! How can they, O Thou
That walkest on the waves, great Cyprian, how
Smile in their husbands' faces, and not fall,
Not cower before the Darkness that knows all,
Aye, dread the dead still chambers, lest one day
The stones find voice, and all be finished!
                                               Nay,
Friends, 'tis for this I die; lest I stand there
Having shamed my husband and the babes I bare.
In ancient Athens they shall some day dwell,
My babes, free men, free-spoken, honorable,
And when one asks their mother, proud of me!
For, oh, it cows a man, though bold he be,
To know a mother's or a father's sin.

'Tis written, one way is there, one, to win
This life's race, could man keep it from his birth,
A true clean spirit. And through all this earth
To every false man, that hour comes apace
When Time holds up a mirror to his face,
And girl-like, marveling, there he stares to see
How foul his heart! Be it not so with me!

    Leader of Chorus. Ah God, how sweet is virtue, and how
        wise,
And honor its due meed in all men's eyes!
    Nurse (who has now risen and recovered herself). Mistress,
        a sharp swift terror struck me low
A moment since, hearing of this thy woe.

But now—I was a coward! And men say
Our second thought the wiser is alway.
   This is no monstrous thing; no grief too dire
To meet with quiet thinking. In her ire
A most strong goddess hath swept down on thee.
Thou lovest. Is that so strange? Many there be
Beside thee! . . . And because thou lovest, wilt fall
And die! And must all lovers die, then? All
That are or shall be? A blithe law for them!
Nay, when in might she swoops, no strength can stem
Cypris; and if man yields him, she is sweet;
But is he proud and stubborn? From his feet
She lifts him, and—how think you?—flings to scorn!
   She ranges with the stars of eve and morn,
She wanders in the heaving of the sea,
And all life lives from her.—Aye, this is she
That sows Love's seed and brings Love's fruit to birth;
And great Love's brethren are all we on earth!
   Nay, they who con gray books of ancient days
Or dwell among the Muses, tell—and praise—
How Zeus himself once yearned for Semelê;
How maiden Eôs in her radiancy
Swept Kephalos to heaven away, away,
For sore love's sake. And there they dwell, men say,
And fear not, fret not; for a thing too stern
Hath met and crushed them!
                    And must thou, then, turn
And struggle? Sprang there from thy father's blood
Thy little soul all lonely? Or the god
That rules thee, is he other than our gods?
   Nay, yield thee to men's ways, and kiss their rods!
How many, deem'st thou, of men good and wise,
Know their own home's blot, and avert their eyes?
How many fathers, when a son has strayed
And toiled beneath the Cyprian, bring him aid,
Not chiding? And man's wisdom e'er hath been
To keep what is not good to see, unseen!
   A straight and perfect life is not for man;
Nay, in a shut house, let him, if he can,
'Mid sheltered rooms, make all lines true. But here,

Out in the wide sea fallen, and full of fear,
Hopest thou so easily to swim to land?
    Canst thou but set thine ill days on one hand
And more good days on the other, verily,
O child of woman, life is well with thee!
               [*She pauses, and then draws nearer to* PHAEDRA.
Nay, dear my daughter, cease thine evil mind,
Cease thy fierce pride! For pride it is, and blind,
To seek to outpass gods!—Love on and dare:
A god hath willed it! And, since pain is there,
Make the pain sleep! Songs are there to bring calm,
And magic words. And I shall find the balm,
Be sure, to heal thee. Else in sore dismay
Were men, could not we women find our way!

    Leader of the Chorus. Help is there, Queen, in all this
        woman says,
To ease thy suffering. But 'tis thee I praise;
Albeit that praise is harder to thine ear
Than all her chiding was, and bitterer!

    Phaedra. Oh, this it is hath flung to dogs and birds
Men's lives and homes and cities—fair false words!
Oh, why speak things to please our ears? We crave
Not that. 'Tis honor, honor, we must save!

    Nurse. Why prate so proud? 'Tis no words, brave nor base,
Thou cravest; 'tis a man's arms!
                [PHAEDRA *moves indignantly.*
                Up and face
The truth of what thou art, and name it straight!
Were not thy life thrown open here for Fate
To beat on; hadst thou been a woman pure
Or wise or strong; never had I for lure
Of joy nor heartache led thee on to this!
But when a whole life one great battle is,
To win or lose—no man can blame me then.

    Phaedra. Shame on thee! Lock those lips, and ne'er again
Let word nor thought so foul have harbor there!

    Nurse. Foul, if thou wilt: but better than the fair
For thee and me. And better, too, the deed
Behind them, if it save thee in thy need,
Than that word Honor thou wilt die to win!

Phaedra. Nay, in God's name,—such wisdom and such sin
Are all about thy lips!—urge me no more.
For all the soul within me is wrought o'er
By Love; and if thou speak and speak, I may
Be spent, and drift where now I shrink away.
  Nurse. Well, if thou wilt!—'Twere best never to err,
But, having erred, to take a counselor
Is second.—Mark me now. I have within
Love-philters, to make peace where storm hath been,
That, with no shame, no scathe of mind, shall save
Thy life from anguish; wilt but thou be brave!

                              [*To herself, reflecting.*
Ah, but from him, the well-beloved, some sign
We need, or word, or raiment's hem, to twine
Amid the charm, and one spell knit from twain.
  Phaedra. Is it a potion or a salve? Be plain.
  Nurse. Who knows? Seek to be helped, Child, not to know.
  Phaedra. Why art thou ever subtle? I dread thee, so.
  Nurse. Thou wouldst dread everything!—What dost thou
    dread?
  Phaedra. Lest to his ear some word be whisperèd.
  Nurse. Let be, Child! I will make all well with thee!
—Only do thou, O Cyprian of the Sea,
Be with me! And mine own heart, come what may,
Shall know what ear to seek, what word to say!

            [*The* NURSE, *having spoken these last words in
            prayer apart to the Statue of Cypris, turns back
            and goes into the house.* PHAEDRA *sits pensive
            again on her couch till toward the end of the
            following Song, when she rises and bends close
            to the door.*

  Chorus. Erôs, Erôs, who blindest, tear by tear,
    Men's eyes with hunger; thou swift Foe, that pliest
  Deep in our hearts joy like an edgèd spear;
  Come not to me with Evil haunting near,
  Wrath on the wind, nor jarring of the clear
    Wing's music as thou fliest!
  There is no shaft that burneth, not in fire,
  Not in wild stars, far off and flinging fear,
  As in thine hands the shaft of All Desire,

[513]

Erôs, Child of the Highest!
In vain, in vain, by old Alpheüs' shore
The blood of many bulls doth stain the river,
And all Greece bows on Phœbus' Pythian floor;
Yet bring we to the Master of Man no store,
The Keybearer, who standeth at the door
Close-barred, where hideth ever
The heart of the shrine. Yea, though he sack man's life
Like a sacked city, and moveth evermore
Girt with calamity and strange ways of strife,
Him have we worshiped never!

There roamed a Steed in Oechalia's wild,
A Maid without yoke, without Master,
And Love she knew not, that far King's child:
But he came, he came, with a song in the night,
With fire, with blood; and she strove in flight,
A Torrent Spirit, a Maenad white,
Faster and vainly faster,
Sealed unto Heracles by the Cyprian's Might.
Alas, thou Bride of Disaster!

O Mouth of Dirce, O god-built wall,
That Dirce's wells run under,
Ye know the Cyprian's fleet footfall!
Ye saw the heavens around her flare,
When she lulled to her sleep that Mother fair
Of Twy-born Bacchus, and decked her there
The Bride of the bladed Thunder.
For her breath is on all that hath life, and she floats in the
air,
Bee-like, death-like, a wonder.

[*During the last lines* PHAEDRA *has approached
the door and is listening.*

Phaedra. Silence, ye Women! Something is amiss.
Leader. How? In the house?—Phaedra, what fear is this?
Phaedra. Let me but listen! There are voices. Hark!
Leader. I hold my peace: yet is thy presage dark.
Phaedra. Oh, misery!

O God, that such a thing should fall on me!
   Leader. What sound, what word,
O Woman, Friend, makes that sharp terror start
Out at thy lips? What ominous cry half-heard
     Hath leapt upon thine heart?
   Phaedra. I am undone!—Bend to the door and hark,
Hark what a tone sounds there, and sinks away!
   Leader. Thou art beside the bars. 'Tis thine to mark
The castle's floating message. Say, Oh, say
     What thing hath come to thee?
   Phaedra (calmly). Why, what thing should it be?
The son of that proud Amazon speaks again
In bitter wrath: speaks to my handmaiden!
   Leader. I hear a noise of voices, nothing clear.
For thee the din hath words, as through barred locks
     Floating, at thy heart it knocks.
   Phaedra. 'Pander of Sin' it says.—Now canst thou hear?—
And there: 'Betrayer of a master's bed.'
   Leader. Ah me, betrayed! Betrayed!
Thy secret brought to light, and ruin near,
     By her thou heldest dear,
By her that should have loved thee and obeyed!
   Phaedra. Aye, I am slain. She thought to help my fall
With love instead of honor, and wrecked all.
   Leader. Where wilt thou turn thee, where?
And what help seek, O wounded to despair?
   Phaedra. I know not, save one thing, to die right soon.
For such as me God keeps no other boon.

                [*The door in the center bursts open, and* HIPPO-
            LYTUS *comes forth, closely followed by the*
            NURSE. PHAEDRA *cowers aside.*
   Hippolytus. O Mother Earth, O Sun that makest clean,
What poison have I heard, what speechless sin!
   Nurse. Hush, O my Prince, lest others mark, and guess . . .
   Hippolytus. I have heard horrors! Shall I hold my peace?
   Nurse. Yea, by this fair right arm, Son, by thy pledge . . .
   Hippolytus. Down with that hand! Touch not my garment's
     edge!
   Nurse. Oh, by thy knees, be silent or I die!

Hippolytus. Why, when thy speech was all so guiltless? Why?

Nurse. It is not meet, fair Son, for every ear!

Hippolytus. Good words can bravely forth, and have no fear.

Nurse. Thine oath, thine oath! I took thine oath before!

Hippolytus. 'Twas but my tongue, 'twas not my soul that swore.

Nurse. O Son, what wilt thou? Wilt thou slay thy kin?

Hippolytus. I own no kindred with the spawn of sin!

[*He flings her from him.*

Nurse. Nay, spare me! Man was born to err; oh, spare!

Hippolytus. O God, why hast Thou made this gleaming snare,
Woman, to dog us on the happy earth?
Was it Thy will to make Man, why his birth
Through Love and Woman? Could we not have rolled
Our store of prayer and offering, royal gold,
Silver and weight of bronze before Thy feet,
And bought of God new child-souls, as were meet
For each man's sacrifice, and dwelt in homes
Free, where nor Love nor Woman goes and comes?

How, is that daughter not a bane confessed,
Whom her own sire sends forth—(He knows her best!)—
And, will some man but take her, pays a dower!
And he, poor fool, takes home the poison-flower;
Laughs to hang jewels on the deadly thing
He joys in; labors for her robe-wearing,
Till wealth and peace are dead. He smarts the less
In whose high seat is set a Nothingness,
A woman naught availing. Worst of all
The wise deep-thoughted! Never in my hall
May she sit throned who thinks and waits and sighs!
For Cypris breeds most evil in the wise,
And least in her whose heart has naught within;
For puny wit can work but puny sin.

Why do we let their handmaids pass the gate?
Wild beasts were best, voiceless and fanged, to wait
About their rooms, that they might speak with none,
Nor ever hear one answering human tone!
But now dark women in still chambers lay

Plans that creep out into the light of day
On handmaids' lips—

[Turning to the NURSE.
As thine accursèd head
Braved the high honor of my Father's bed,
And came to traffic. . . . Our white torrent's spray
Shall drench mine ears to wash those words away!
And couldst thou dream that *I* . . . ? I feel impure
Still at the very hearing! Know for sure,
Woman, naught but mine honor saves ye both.
Hadst thou not trapped me with that guileful oath,
No power had held me secret till the King
Knew all! But now, while he is journeying,
I too will go my ways and make no sound.
And when he comes again, I shall be found
Beside him, silent, watching with what grace
Thou and thy mistress greet him face to face!
Then shall I have the taste of it, and know
What woman's guile is.—Woe upon you, woe!
How can I too much hate you, while the ill
Ye work upon the world grows deadlier still?
Too much? Make woman pure, and wild Love tame,
Or let me cry for ever on their shame!

[He goes off in fury to the left. PHAEDRA *still
cowering in her place begins to sob.*
Phaedra. Sad, sad and evil-starred
Is Woman's state.
What shelter now is left or guard?
What spell to loose the iron knot of fate?
And this thing, O my God,
O thou sweet Sunlight, is but my desert!
I cannot fly before the avenging rod
Falls, cannot hide my hurt.
What help, O ye who love me, can come near,
What god or man appear, .
To aid a thing so evil and so lost?
Lost, for this anguish presses, soon or late,
To that swift river that no life hath crossed.
No woman ever lived so desolate!

Leader of the Chorus. Ah me, the time for deeds is gone;
the boast
Proved vain that spake thine handmaid; and all lost!
   [*At these words* PHAEDRA *suddenly remembers the*
    NURSE, *who is cowering silently where* HIPPO-
    LYTUS *had thrown her from him. She turns*
    upon her.

Phaedra. O wicked, wicked, wicked! Murderess heart
To them that loved thee! Hast thou played thy part?
Am I enough trod down?
       May Zeus, my sire,
Blast and uproot thee! Stab thee dead with fire!
Said I not—Knew I not thine heart?—to name
To no one soul this that is now my shame?
And thou couldst not be silent! So no more
I die in honor. But enough; a store
Of new words must be spoke and new things thought.
This man's whole being to one blade is wrought
Of rage against me. Even now he speeds
To abase me to the King with thy misdeeds;
Tell Pittheus; fill the land with talk of sin!
  Cursèd be thou, and whoso else leaps in
To bring bad aid to friends that want it not.
   [*The* NURSE *has raised herself, and faces* PHAEDRA,
    downcast but calm.

Nurse. Mistress, thou blamest me; and all thy lot
So bitter sore is, and the sting so wild,
I bear with all. Yet, if I would, my Child,
I have mine answer, couldst thou hearken aught.
  I nursed thee, and I love thee; and I sought
Only some balm to heal thy deep despair,
And found—not what I sought for. Else I were
Wise, and thy friend, and good, had all sped right.
So fares it with us all in the world's sight.

Phaedra. First stab me to the heart, then humor me
With words! 'Tis fair; 'tis all as it should be!

Nurse. We talk too long, Child. I did ill; but, oh,
There is a way to save thee, even so!

Phaedra. A way? No more ways! One way hast thou trod
Already, foul and false and loathed of god!

Begone out of my sight; and ponder how
Thine own life stands! I need no helpers now.

> [*She turns from the* NURSE, *who creeps abashed
> away into the Castle.*

Only do ye, high Daughters of Trozên,
Let all ye hear be as it had not been;
Know naught, and speak of naught! 'Tis my last prayer.

Leader. By God's pure daughter, Artemis, I swear,
No word will I of these thy griefs reveal!

Phaedra. 'Tis well. But now, yea, even while I reel
And falter, one poor hope, as hope now is,
I clutch at in this coil of miseries;
To save some honor for my children's sake;
Yea, for myself some fragment, though things break
In ruin around me. Nay, I will not shame
The old proud Cretan castle whence I came,
I will not cower before King Theseus' eyes,
Abased, for want of one life's sacrifice!

Leader. What wilt thou? Some dire deed beyond recall?

Phaedra (musing). Die; but how die?

Leader.   Let not such wild words fall!

Phaedra (turning upon her). Give thou not such light
    counsel! Let me be
To sate the Cyprian that is murdering me!
To-day shall be her day; and, all strife past,
Her bitter Love shall quell me at the last.

Yet, dying, shall I die another's bane!
He shall not stand so proud where I have lain
Bent in the dust! Oh, he shall stoop to share
The life I live in, and learn mercy there!

> [*She goes off wildly into the Castle.*

Chorus. Could I take me to some cavern for mine hiding,
    In the hill-tops where the Sun scarce hath trod;
Or a cloud make the home of mine abiding,
    As a bird among the bird-droves of God!
      Could I wing me to my rest amid the roar
      Of the deep Adriatic on the shore,
Where the waters of Eridanus are clear,
    And Phaëthon's sad sisters by his grave

Weep into the river, and each tear
  Gleams, a drop of amber, in the wave.

To the strand of the Daughters of the Sunset,
  The Apple-tree, the singing and the gold;
Where the mariner must stay him from his onset,
  And the red wave is tranquil as of old;
    Yea, beyond that Pillar of the End
    That Atlas guardeth, would I wend;
Where a voice of living waters never ceaseth
  In God's quiet garden by the sea,
And Earth, the ancient life-giver, increaseth
  Joy among the meadows, like a tree.

O shallop of Crete, whose milk-white wing
Through the swell and the storm-beating,
  Bore us thy Prince's daughter,
Was it well she came from a joyous home
To a far King's bridal across the foam?
  What joy hath her bridal brought her?
Sure some spell upon either hand
Flew with thee from the Cretan strand,
Seeking Athena's tower divine;
And there, where Munychus fronts the brine,
Crept by the shore-flung cables' line,
  The curse from the Cretan water!

And, for that dark spell that about her clings,
Sick desires of forbidden things
  The soul of her rend and sever;
The bitter tide of calamity
Hath risen above her lips; and she,
  Where bends she her last endeavor?
She will hie her alone to her bridal room,
And a rope swing slow in the rafters' gloom;
And a fair white neck shall creep to the noose,
A-shudder with dread, yet firm to choose
The one strait way for fame, and lose
  The Love and the pain for ever.

[*The Voice of the* NURSE *is heard from within, cry-ing, at first inarticulately, then clearly.*

Voice. Help ho! The Queen! Help, whoso hearkeneth!
Help! Theseus' spouse caught in a noose of death!

A Woman. God, is it so soon finished? That bright head
Swinging beneath the rafters! Phaedra dead!

Voice. O haste! This knot about her throat is made
So fast! Will no one bring me a swift blade?

A Woman. Say, friends, what think ye? Should we haste within,
And from her own hand's knotting loose the Queen?

Another. Nay, are there not men there? 'Tis an ill road
In life, to finger an another's load.

Voice. Let it lie straight! Alas! the cold white thing
That guards his empty castle for the King!

A Woman. Ah! 'Let it lie straight!' Heard ye what she said?
No need for helpers now; the Queen is dead!

[*The Women, intent upon the voices from the Castle, have not noticed the approach of* THESEUS. *He enters from the left; his dress and the garland on his head show that he has returned from some oracle or special abode of a God. He stands for a moment perplexed.*

Theseus. Ho, Women, and what means this loud acclaim
Within the house? The vassals' outcry came
To smite mine ears far off. It were more meet
To fling out wide the Castle gates, and greet
With joy a herald from God's Presence!

[*The confusion and horror of the Women's faces gradually affects him. A dirge-cry comes from the Castle.*

How?
Not Pittheus? Hath Time struck that hoary brow?
Old is he, old, I know. But sore it were,
Returning thus, to find his empty chair!

[*The Women hesitate; then the* LEADER *comes forward.*

Leader. O Theseus, not on any old man's head
This stroke falls. Young and tender is the dead.

Theseus. Ye Gods! One of my children torn from me?

Leader. Thy motherless children live, most grievously.

Theseus. How sayst thou? What? My wife? . . .

                     Say how she died.

Leader. In a high death-knot that her own hands tied.

Theseus. A fit of the old cold anguish—Tell me all—
That held her? Or did some fresh thing befall?

Leader. We know no more. But now arrived we be,
Theseus, to mourn for thy calamity.

         [THESEUS *stays for a moment silent, and puts his
            hand to his brow. He notices the wreath.*

Theseus. What? And all garlanded I come to her
With flowers, most evil-starred God's-messenger!

Ho, varlets, loose the portal bars; undo
The bolts; and let me see the bitter view
Of her whose death hath brought me to mine own.

         [*The great central door of the Castle is thrown
            open wide, and the body of* PHAEDRA *is seen
            lying on a bier, surrounded by a group of
            Handmaids, wailing.*

The Handmaids. Ah me, what thou hast suffered and hast
    done:

A deed to wrap this roof in flame!
Why was thine hand so strong, thine heart so bold?
Wherefore, O dead in anger, dead in shame,
The long, long wrestling ere thy breath was cold?

        O ill-starred Wife,
What brought this blackness over all thy life?

        [*A throng of Men and Women has gradually
           collected.*

Theseus. Ah me, this is the last
—Hear, O my countrymen!—and bitterest
Of Theseus' labors! Fortune all unblest,
How hath thine heavy heel across me passed!
Is it the stain of sins done long ago,
        Some fell God still remembereth,
That must so dim and fret my life with death?
I cannot win to shore; and the waves flow
Above mine eyes, to be surmounted not.

        Ah wife, sweet wife, what name
        Can fit thine heavy lot?

Gone like a wild bird, like a blowing flame,
In one swift gust, where all things are forgot!
      Alas! this misery!
Sure 'tis some stroke of God's great anger rolled
      From age to age on me,
For some dire sin wrought by dim kings of old.
  Leader. Sire, this great grief hath come to many an one,
A true wife lost. Thou art not all alone.
  Theseus. Deep, deep beneath the Earth,
      Dark may my dwelling be,
And Night my heart's one comrade, in the dearth,
O Love, of thy most sweet society.
This is my death, O Phaedra, more than thine.
                [He turns suddenly on the ATTENDANTS.
Speak who speak can? What was it? What malign
Swift stroke, O heart discounseled, leapt on thee?
          [He bends over PHAEDRA; *then, as no one speaks,*
            looks fiercely up.
What, will ye speak? Or are they dumb as death,
This herd of thralls, my high house harboreth?
          [There is no answer. He bends again over
            PHAEDRA.
Ah me, why shouldst thou die?
A wide and royal grief I here behold,
Not to be borne in peace, not to be told.
      As a lost man am I,
My children motherless and my house undone,
      Since thou art vanished quite,
Purest of hearts that e'er the wandering Sun
Touched, or the star-eyed splendor of the Night.
                [He throws himself beside the body.
  Chorus. Unhappy one, O most unhappy one!
    With what strange evil is this Castle vexed!
Mine eyes are molten with the tears that run
    For thee and thine; but what thing follows next?
      I tremble when I think thereon!
      [They have noticed that there is a tablet with writ-
        ing fastened to the dead woman's wrist. THE-
        SEUS *also sees it.*
  Theseus. Ha, what is this that hangs from her dear hand?

A tablet! It would make me understand
Some dying wish, some charge about her bed
And children. 'Twas the last prayer, ere her head
Was bowed for ever.

> *[Taking the tablet.*

                   Fear not, my lost bride,
No woman born shall lie at Theseus' side,
Nor rule in Theseus' house!

                     A seal! Ah, see
How her gold signet here looks up at me,
Trustfully. Let me tear this thread away,
And read what tale the tablet seeks to say.

> *[He proceeds to undo and read the tablet. The*
> Chorus *breaks into horrified groups.*

Some Women. Woe, woe! God brings to birth
A new grief here, close on the other's tread!
        My life hath lost its worth.
May all go now with what is finishèd!
The castle of my King is overthrown,
A house no more, a house vanished and gone!
   Other Women. O God, if it may be in any way,
Let not this house be wrecked! Help us who pray!
I know not what is here: some unseen thing
That shows the Bird of Evil on the wing.

> *[*Theseus *has read the tablet and breaks out in*
> *uncontrollable emotion.*

   Theseus. Oh, horror piled on horror!—Here is writ . . .
Nay, who could bear it, who could speak of it?
   Leader. What, O my King? If I may hear it, speak!
   Theseus. Doth not the tablet cry aloud, yea, shriek,
Things not to be forgotten?—Oh, to fly
And hide mine head! No more a man am I.
Ah, God, what ghastly music echoes here!
   Leader. How wild thy voice! Some terrible thing is near.
   Theseus. No; my lips' gates will hold it back no more;
       This deadly word,
That struggles on the brink and will not o'er,
       Yet will not stay unheard.

> *[He raises his hand, to make proclamation to all*
> *present.*

Ho, hearken all this land!

> [*The people gather expectantly about him.*

Hippolytus by violence hath laid hand
On this my wife, forgetting God's great eye.

> [*Murmurs of amazement and horror;* THESEUS,
> *apparently calm, raises both arms to heaven.*

Therefore, O Thou my Father, hear my cry,
Poseidon! Thou didst grant me for mine own
Three prayers; for one of these, slay now my son,
Hippolytus; let him not outlive this day,
If true thy promise was! Lo, thus I pray.

Leader. Oh, call that wild prayer back! O King, take heed!
I know that thou wilt live to rue this deed.

Theseus. It may not be.—And more, I cast him out
From all my realms. He shall be held about
By two great dooms. Or by Poseidon's breath
He shall fall swiftly to the house of Death;
Or wandering, outcast, o'er strange land and sea
Shall live and drain the cup of misery.

Leader. Ah, see! here comes he at the point of need.
Shake off that evil mood, O King: have heed
For all thine house and folk.—Great Theseus, hear!

> [THESEUS *stands silent in fierce gloom.* HIPPO-
> LYTUS *comes in from the right.*

Hippolytus. Father, I heard thy cry, and sped in fear
To help thee.—But I see not yet the cause
That racked thee so.—Say, Father, what it was.

> [*The murmurs in the crowd, the silent gloom of
> his Father, and the horror of the Chorus-
> women gradually work on* HIPPOLYTUS *and
> bewilder him. He catches sight of the bier.*

Ah, what is that! Nay, Father, not the Queen
Dead! (*Murmurs in the crowd.*)
　　　　'Tis most strange. 'Tis passing strange, I ween.
'Twas here I left her. Scarce an hour hath run
Since here she stood and looked on this same sun.
What is it with her? Wherefore did she die?

> [THESEUS *remains silent. The murmurs increase.*

Father, to thee I speak. Oh, tell me, why,
Why art thou silent? What doth silence know

Of skill to stem the bitter flood of woe?
And human hearts in sorrow crave the more
For knowledge, though the knowledge grieve them sore.
It is not love, to veil thy sorrows in
From one most near to thee, and more than kin.

    Theseus (to himself). Fond race of men, so striving and so
      blind,
Ten thousand arts and wisdoms can ye find,
Desiring all and all imagining:
But ne'er have reached nor understood one thing,
To make a true heart there where no heart is!

    Hippolytus. That were indeed beyond man's mysteries,
To make a false heart true against his will.
But why this subtle talk? It likes me ill,
Father; thy speech runs wild beneath this blow.

    Theseus (as before). O would that God had given us here
      below
Some test of love, some sifting of the soul,
To tell the false and true! Or through the whole
Of men two voices ran, one true and right,
The other as chance willed it; that we might
Convict the liar by the true man's tone,
And not live duped forever, every one!

    Hippolytus (misunderstanding him; then guessing at some-
      thing of the truth). What? Hath some friend proved
      false?
          Or in thine ear
Whispered some slander? Stand I tainted here,
Though utterly innocent?
                    [Murmurs from the crowd.
              Yea, dazed am I;
'Tis thy words daze me, falling all awry,
Away from reason, by fell fancies vexed!

    Theseus. O heart of man, what height wilt venture next?
What end comes to thy daring and thy crime?
For if with each man's life 'twill higher climb,
And every age break out in blood and lies
Beyond its fathers, must not God devise
Some new world far from ours, to hold therein
Such brood of all unfaithfulness and sin?

Look, all, upon this man, my son, his life
Sprung forth from mine! He hath defiled my wife;
And standeth here convicted by the dead,
A most black villain!

[HIPPOLYTUS *falls back with a cry and covers his
face with his robe.*

Nay, hide not thine head!
Pollution, is it? Thee it will not stain.
Look up, and face thy Father's eyes again!
   Thou friend of Gods, of all mankind elect;
Thou the pure heart, by thoughts of ill unflecked!
I care not for thy boasts. I am not mad,
To deem that Gods love best the base and bad.
   Now is thy day! Now vaunt thee; thou so pure,
No flesh of life may pass thy lips! Now lure
Fools after thee; call Orpheus King and Lord;
Make ecstasies and wonders! Thumb thine hoard
Of ancient scrolls and ghostly mysteries—
Now thou art caught and known!

Shun men like these,
I charge ye all! With solemn words they chase
Their prey, and in their hearts plot foul disgrace.
   My wife is dead.—'Ha, so that saves thee now?'
That is what grips thee worst, thou caitiff, thou!
What oaths, what subtle words, shall stronger be
Than this dead hand, to clear the guilt from thee?
   'She hated thee,' thou sayest; 'the bastard born
Is ever sore and bitter as a thorn
To the true brood.'—A sorry bargainer
In the ills and goods of life thou makest her,
If all her best-beloved she cast away
To wreak blind hate on thee!—What, wilt thou say,
'Through every woman's nature one blind strand
Of passion winds, that men scarce understand?'—
Are we so different? Know I not the fire
And perilous flood of a young man's desire,
Desperate as any woman, and as blind,
When Cypris stings? Save that the man behind
Has all men's strength to aid him. Nay, 'twas thou . . .
   But what avail to wrangle with thee now,

When the dead speaks for all to understand,
A perfect witness!
                                Hie thee from this land
To exile with all speed. Come never more
To god-built Athens, not to the utmost shore
Of any realm where Theseus' arm is strong!
What? Shall I bow my head beneath this wrong,
And cower to thee? Not Isthmian Sinis so
Will bear men witness that I laid him low,
Nor Skiron's rocks, that share the salt sea's prey,
Grant that my hand hath weight vile things to slay!
    Leader. Alas! whom shall I call of mortal men
Happy? The highest are cast down again.
    Hippolytus. Father, the hot strained fury of thy heart
Is terrible. Yet, albeit so swift thou art
Of speech, if all this matter were laid bare,
Speech were not then so swift; nay, nor so fair . . .
                          [*Murmurs again in the crowd.*
I have no skill before a crowd to tell
My thoughts. 'Twere best with few, that know me well.—
Nay, that is natural; tongues that sound but rude
In wise men's ears, speak to the multitude
With music.
          None the less, since there is come
This stroke upon me, I must not be dumb,
But speak perforce. . . . And there will I begin
Where thou beganst, as though to strip my sin
Naked, and I not speak a word!
                   Dost see
This sunlight and this earth? I swear to thee
There dwelleth not in these one man—deny
All that thou wilt!—more pure of sin than I.
    Two things I know on earth: God's worship first;
Next to win friends about me, few, that thirst
To hold them clean of all unrighteousness.
Our rule doth curse the tempters, and no less
Who yieldeth to the tempters.—How, thou say'st,
'Dupes that I jest at?' Nay; I make a jest
Of no man. I am honest to the end,
Near or far off, with him I call my friend.

And most in that one thing, where now thy mesh
Would grip me, stainless quite! No woman's flesh
Hath e'er this body touched. Of all such deed
Naught wot I, save what things a man may read
In pictures or hear spoke; nor am I fain,
Being virgin-souled, to read or hear again.

   My life of innocence moves thee not; so be it.
Show then what hath seduced me; let me see it.
Was that poor flesh so passing fair, beyond
All women's loveliness?

                         Was I some fond
False plotter, that I schemed to win through her
Thy castle's heirdom? Fond indeed I were!
Nay, a stark madman! 'But a crown,' thou say'st,
'Usurped, is sweet.' Nay, rather most unblest
To all wise-hearted; sweet to fools and them
Whose eyes are blinded by the diadem.
In contests of all valor fain would I
Lead Hellas; but in rank and majesty
Not lead, but be at ease, with good men near
To love me, free to work and not to fear.
That brings more joy than any crown or throne.
        [*He sees from the demeanor of* THESEUS *and of
            the crowd that his words are not winning them,
            but rather making them bitterer than before.
            It comes to his lips to speak the whole truth.*
I have said my say; save one thing . . . one alone.

   O had I here some witness in my need,
As I was witness! Could she hear me plead,
Face me and face the sunlight; well I know,
Our deeds would search us out for thee, and show
Who 'lies!

            But now, I swear—so hear me both,
The Earth beneath and Zeus who Guards the Oath—
I never touched this woman that was thine!
No words could win me to it, nor incline
My heart to dream it. May God strike me down,
Nameless and fameless, without home or town,
An outcast and a wanderer of the world;
May my dead bones rest never, but be hurled

From sea to land, from land to angry sea,
If evil is my heart and false to thee!

> [*He waits a moment; but sees that his Father is
> unmoved. The truth again comes to his lips.*]

If 'twas some fear that made her cast away
Her life . . . I know not. More I must not say.
Right hath she done when in her was no right;
And Right I follow to mine own despite!

Leader. It is enough! God's name is witness large,
And thy great oath, to assoil thee of this charge.

Theseus. Is not the man a juggler and a mage,
Cool wits and one right oath—what more?—to assuage
Sin and the wrath of injured fatherhood!

Hippolytus. Am I so cool? Nay, Father, 'tis thy mood
That makes me marvel! By my faith, wert thou
The son, and I the sire; and deemed I now
In very truth thou hadst my wife assailed,
I had not exiled thee, nor stood and railed,
But lifted once mine arm, and struck thee dead!

Theseus. Thou gentle judge! Thou shalt not so be sped
To simple death, nor by thine own decree.
Swift death is bliss to men in misery.
Far off, friendless forever, thou shalt drain
Amid strange cities the last dregs of pain!

Hippolytus. Wilt verily cast me now beyond thy pale,
Not wait for Time, the lifter of the veil?

Theseus. Aye, if I could, past Pontus, and the red
Atlantic marge! So do I hate thine head.

Hippolytus. Wilt weigh nor oath nor faith nor prophet's
word
To prove me? Drive me from thy sight unheard?

Theseus. This tablet here, that needs no prophet's lot
To speak from, tells me all. I ponder not
Thy fowls that fly above us! Let them fly.

Hippolytus. O ye great Gods, wherefore unlock not I
My lips, ere yet ye have slain me utterly,
Ye whom I love most? No. It may not be!
The one heart that I need I ne'er should gain
To trust me. I should break mine oath in vain.

Theseus. Death! but he chokes me with his saintly tone!—

Up, get thee from this land! Begone! Begone!
 Hippolytus. Where shall I turn me? Think. To what friend's
  door
Betake me, banished on a charge so sore?
 Theseus. Whoso delights to welcome to his hall
Vile ravishers . . . to guard his hearth withal!
 Hippolytus. Thou seekst my heart, my tears? Aye, let it be
Thus! I am vile to all men, and to thee!
 Theseus. There was a time for tears and thought; the time
Ere thou didst up and gird thee to thy crime.
 Hippolytus. Ye stones, will ye not speak? Ye castle walls!
Bear witness if I be so vile, so false!
 Theseus. Aye, fly to voiceless witnesses! Yet here
A dumb deed speaks against thee, and speaks clear!
 Hippolytus. Alas!
Would I could stand and watch this thing, and see
My face, and weep for very pity of me!
 Theseus. Full of thyself, as ever. Not a thought
For them that gave thee birth; nay, they are naught!
 Hippolytus. O my wronged Mother! O my birth of shame!
May none I love e'er bear a bastard's name!
 Theseus (in a sudden blaze of rage). Up, thralls, and drag
  him from my presence! What?
'Tis but a foreign felon! Heard ye not?
      [*The thralls still hesitate in spite of his fury.*
 Hippolytus. They touch me at their peril! Thine own hand
Lift, if thou canst, to drive me from the land.
 Theseus. That will I straight, unless my will be done!
      [HIPPOLYTUS *comes close to him and kneels.*
Nay! Not for thee my pity! Get thee gone!
    [HIPPOLYTUS *rises, makes a sign of submission,*
     and slowly moves away. THESEUS, *as soon as*
     he sees him going, turns rapidly and enters the
     Castle. The door is closed again. HIPPOLYTUS
     has stopped for a moment before the Statue
     of ARTEMIS, *and, as* THESEUS *departs, breaks*
     out in prayer.
 Hippolytus. So; it is done! O dark and miserable!
I see it all, but see not how to tell
The tale.—O thou belovèd, Leto's Maid,

Chase-comrade, fellow-rester in the glade,
Lo, I am driven with a caitiff's brand
Forth from great Athens! Fare ye well, O land
And city of old Erechtheus! Thou, Trozên,
What riches of glad youth mine eyes have seen
In thy broad plain! Farewell! This is the end;
The last word, the last look!

       Come, every friend
And fellow of my youth that still may stay,
Give me god-speed and cheer me on my way.
Ne'er shall ye see a man more pure of spot
Than me, though mine own Father loves me not!

    [HIPPOLYTUS *goes away to the right, followed by*
      many Huntsmen and other young men. The rest
      of the crowd has by this time dispersed, except
      the Women of the Chorus and some Men of the
      Chorus of Huntsmen.

Chorus (*Men*). Surely the thought of the Gods hath balm
 in it alway, to win me
Far from my griefs; and a thought, deep in the dark of my
 mind,
Clings to a great Understanding. Yet all the spirit within me
 Faints, when I watch men's deeds matched with the guerdon
  they find.

    For Good comes in Evil's traces,
    And the Evil the Good replaces;
    And Life, 'mid the changing faces,
     Wandereth weak and blind.

Women. What wilt thou grant me, O God? Lo, this is the
  prayer of my travail—
Some well-being; and chance not very bitter thereby;
A Spirit uncrippled by pain; and a mind not deep to unravel
 Truth unseen, nor yet dark with the brand of a lie.

    With a veering mood to borrow
    Its light from every morrow,
    Fair friends and no deep sorrow,
     Well could man live and die!

Men. Yet my spirit is no more clean,
    And the weft of my hope is torn,
    For the deed of wrong that mine eyes have seen,

The lie and the rage and the scorn;
A Star among men, yea, a Star
    That in Hellas was bright,
By a Father's wrath driven far
    To the wilds and the night.
Oh, alas for the sands of the shore!
    Alas for the brakes of the hill,
Where the wolves shall fear thee no more,
    And thy cry to Dictynna is still!

Women. No more in the yoke of thy car
    Shall the colts of Enetia fleet;
Nor Limna's echoes quiver afar
    To the clatter of galloping feet.
The sleepless music of old,
    That leaped in the lyre,
Ceaseth now, and is cold,
    In the halls of thy sire.
The bowers are discrowned and unladen
    Where Artemis lay on the lea;
And the love-dream of many a maiden
    Lost, in the losing of thee.

A Maiden. And I, even I,
    For thy fall, O Friend,
        Amid tears and tears,
    Endure to the end
        Of the empty years,
Of a life run dry.
    In vain didst thou bear him,
        Thou Mother forlorn!
    Ye Gods that did snare him,
Lo, I cast in your faces
        My hate and my scorn!
Ye love-linkèd Graces,
    (Alas for the day!)
        Was he naught, then, to you,
    That ye cast him away,
        The stainless and true,
From the old happy places?

Leader. Look yonder! Surely from the Prince 'tis one
That cometh, full of haste and woe-begone.

[533]

[A Henchman *enters in haste.*

Henchman. Ye women, whither shall I go to seek
King Theseus? Is he in this dwelling? Speak!
    Leader. Lo, where he cometh through the Castle gate!

[Theseus *comes out from the Castle.*

    Henchman. O King, I bear thee tidings of dire weight
To thee, aye, and to every man, I ween,
From Athens to the marches of Trozên.
    Theseus. What? Some new stroke hath touched, unknown
        to me,
The sister cities of my sovranty?
    Henchman. Hippolytus is . . . Nay, not dead; but stark
Outstretched, a hairsbreadth this side of the dark.
    Theseus (*as though unmoved*). How slain? Was there some
        other man, whose wife
He had like mine defiled, that sought his life?
    Henchman. His own wild team destroyed him, and the dire
Curse of thy lips.
              The boon of thy great Sire
Is granted thee, O King, and thy son slain.
    Theseus. Ye Gods! And thou, Poseidon! Not in vain
I called thee Father; thou hast heard my prayer!
How did he die? Speak on. How closed the snare
Of Heaven to slay the shamer of my blood?
    Henchman. 'Twas by the bank of beating sea we stood,
We thralls, and decked the steeds, and combed each mane;
Weeping; for word had come that ne'er again
The foot of our Hippolytus should roam
This land, but waste in exile by thy doom.
    So stood we till he came, and in his tone
No music now save sorrow's, like our own,
And in his train a concourse without end
Of many a chase-fellow and many a friend.
At last he brushed his sobs away, and spake:
'Why this fond loitering? I would not break
My Father's law.—Ho, there! My coursers four
And chariot, quick! This land is mine no more.'
    Thereat, be sure, each man of us made speed.
Swifter than speech we brought them up, each steed
Well dight and shining, at our Prince's side.

He grasped the reins upon the rail: one stride
And there he stood, a perfect charioteer,
Each foot in its own station set. Then clear
His voice rose, and his arms to heaven were spread:
'O Zeus, if I be false, strike thou me dead!
But, dead or living, let my Father see
One day, how falsely he hath hated me!'
    Even as he spake, he lifted up the goad
And smote; and the steeds sprang. And down the road
We henchmen followed, hard beside the rein,
Each hand, to speed him, toward the Argive plain
And Epidaurus.
                So we made our way
Up toward the desert region, where the bay
Curls to a promontory near the verge
Of our Trozên, facing the southward surge
Of Saron's gulf. Just there an angry sound,
Slow-swelling, like God's thunder underground,
Broke on us, and we trembled. And the steeds
Pricked their ears skyward, and threw back their heads.
And wonder came on all men, and affright,
Whence rose that awful voice. And swift our sight
Turned seaward, down the salt and roaring sand.
    And there, above the horizon, seemed to stand
A wave unearthly, crested in the sky;
Till Skiron's Cape first vanished from mine eye,
Then sank the Isthmus hidden, then the rock
Of Epidaurus. Then it broke, one shock
And roar of gasping sea and spray flung far,
And shoreward swept, where stood the Prince's car.
    Three lines of wave together raced, and, full
In the white crest of them, a wild Sea-Bull
Flung to the shore, a fell and marvelous Thing.
The whole land held his voice, and answering
Roared in each echo. And all we, gazing there,
Gazed seeing not; 'twas more than eyes could bear.
    Then straight upon the team wild terror fell.
Howbeit, the Prince, cool-eyed and knowing well
Each changing mood a horse has, gripped the reins
Hard in both hands; then as an oarsman strains

Up from his bench, so strained he on the thong,
Back in the chariot swinging. But the young
Wild steeds bit hard the curb, and fled afar;
Nor rein nor guiding hand nor morticed car
Stayed them at all. For when he veered them round,
And aimed their flying feet to grassy ground,
In front uprose that Thing, and turned again
The four great coursers, terror-mad. But when
Their blind rage drove them toward the rocky places,
Silent, and ever nearer to the traces,
It followed, rockward, till one wheel-edge grazed.

  The chariot tript and flew, and all was mazed
In turmoil. Up went wheel-box with a din,
Where the rock jagged, and nave and axle-pin.
And there—the long reins round him—there was he
Dragging, entangled irretrievably.
A dear head battering at the chariot side,
Sharp rocks, and ripped flesh, and a voice that cried:
'Stay, stay, O ye who fattened at my stalls,
Dash me not into nothing!—O thou false
Curse of my Father!—Help! Help, whoso can,
An innocent, innocent and stainless man!'

  Many there were that labored then, I wot,
To bear him succor, but could reach him not,
Till—who knows how?—at last the tangled rein
Unclasped him, and he fell, some little vein
Of life still pulsing in him.

        All beside,
The steeds, the hornèd Horror of the Tide,
Had vanished—who knows where?—in that wild land.

  O King, I am a bondsman of thine hand;
Yet love nor fear nor duty me shall win
To say thine innocent son hath died in sin.
All women born may hang themselves, for me,
And swing their dying words from every tree
On Ida! For I know that he was true!

   Leader. O God, so cometh new disaster, new
Despair! And no escape from what must be!

   Theseus. Hate of the man thus stricken lifted me
At first to joy at hearing of thy tale:

But now, some shame before the Gods, some pale
Pity for mine own blood, hath o'er me come.
I laugh not, neither weep, at this fell doom.
  Henchman. How then? Behoves it bear him here, or how
Best do thy pleasure?—Speak, Lord. Yet if thou
Wilt mark at all my word, thou wilt not be
Fierce-hearted to thy child in misery.
  Theseus. Aye, bring him hither. Let me see the face
Of him who durst deny my deep disgrace
And his own sin; yea, speak with him, and prove
His clear guilt by God's judgments from above.

> [*The* HENCHMAN *departs to fetch* HIPPOLYTUS,
> THESEUS *sits waiting in stern gloom, while the*
> CHORUS *sing. At the close of their song a Divine*
> *Figure is seen approaching on a cloud in the*
> *air and the voice of* ARTEMIS *speaks.*

Chorus. Thou comest to bend the pride
    Of the hearts of God and man,
  Cypris; and by thy side,
    In earth-encircling span,
  He of the changing plumes,
  The Wing that the world illumes,
As over the leagues of land flies he,
Over the salt and sounding sea.

  For mad is the heart of Love,
    And gold the gleam of his wing;
  And all to the spell thereof
    Bend, when he makes his spring;
  All life that is wild and young
    In mountain and wave and stream,
  All that of earth is sprung,
    Or breathes in the red sunbeam;
Yea, and Mankind. O'er all a royal throne,
Cyprian, Cyprian, is thine alone!

A Voice from the Cloud. O thou that rulest in Aegeus' Hall,
    I charge thee, hearken!
                Yea, it is I,
  Artemis, Virgin of God most High.

Thou bitter King, art thou glad withal
    For thy murdered son?
For thine ear bent low to a lying Queer,
For thine heart so swift amid things unseen?
Lo, all may see what end thou hast won!
Go, sink thine head in the waste abyss;
Or aloft to another world than this,
    Birdwise with wings,
    Fly far to thine hiding,
Far over this blood that clots and clings;
For in righteous men and in holy things
    No rest is thine nor abiding!

        [*The cloud has become stationary in the air.*

Hear, Theseus, all the story of thy grief!
Verily, I bring but anguish, not relief;
Yet, 'twas for this I came, to show how high
And clean was thy son's heart, that he may die
Honored of men; aye, and to tell no less
The frenzy, or in some sort the nobleness,
Of thy dead wife. One Spirit there is, whom we
That know the joy of white virginity,
Most hate in heaven. She sent her fire to run
In Phaedra's veins, so that she loved thy son.
Yet strove she long with love, and in the stress
Fell not, till by her Nurse's craftiness
Betrayed, who stole, with oaths of secrecy,
To entreat thy son. And he, most righteously,
Nor did her will, nor, when thy railing scorn
Beat on him, broke the oath that he had sworn,
For God's sake. And thy Phaedra, panic-eyed,
Wrote a false writ, and slew thy son, and died,
Lying; but thou wast nimble to believe!

        [THESEUS, *at first bewildered, then dumbfounded,*
          now utters a deep groan.

It stings thee, Theseus?—Nay, hear on, and grieve
Yet sorer. Wottest thou three prayers were thine
Of sure fulfilment, from thy Sire divine?
Hast thou no foes about thee, then, that one—
Thou vile King!—must be turned against thy son?
The deed was thine. Thy Sea-born Sire but heard

The call of prayer, and bowed him to his word.
But thou in his eyes and in mine art found
Evil, who wouldst not think, nor probe, nor sound
The deeps of prophet's lore, nor day by day
Leave Time to search; but, swifter than man may,
Let loose the curse to slay thine innocent son!
   Theseus. O Goddess, let me die!
   Artemis. Nay; thou hast done
A heavy wrong; yet even beyond this ill
Abides for thee forgiveness. 'Twas the will
Of Cypris that these evil things should be,
Sating her wrath. And this immutably
Hath Zeus ordained in heaven: no God may thwart
A God's fixed will; we grieve but stand apart.
Else, but for fear of the Great Father's blame,
Never had I to such extreme of shame
Bowed me, be sure, as here to stand and see
Slain him I loved best of mortality!
   Thy fault, O King, its ignorance sunders wide
From very wickedness; and she who died
By death the more disarmed thee, making dumb
The voice of question. And the storm has come
Most bitterly of all on thee! Yet I
Have mine own sorrow, too. When good men die,
There is no joy in heaven, albeit our ire
On child and house of the evil falls like fire.

      [*A throng is seen approaching;* HIPPOLYTUS *enters,
        supported by his attendants.*

   Chorus. Lo, it is he! The bright young head
        Yet upright there!
   Ah, the torn flesh and the blood-stained hair;
        Alas for the kindred's trouble!
   It falls as fire from a God's hand sped,
        Two deaths, and mourning double.
   Hippolytus. Ah, pain, pain, pain!
O unrighteous curse! O unrighteous sire!
No hope.—My head is stabbed with fire,
And a leaping spasm about my brain.
   Stay, let me rest. I can no more.
O fell, fell steeds that my own hand fed,

Have ye maimed me and slain, that loved me of yore?
—Soft there, ye thralls! No trembling hands
As ye lift me, now!—Who is that that stands
At the right?—Now firm, and with measured tread,
Lift one accursèd and stricken sore
      By a father's sinning.

Thou, Zeus, dost see me? Yea, it is I;
The proud and pure, the server of God,
The white and shining in sanctity!
To a visible death, to an open sod,
      I walk my ways;
And all the labor of saintly days
      Lost, lost, without meaning!

      Ah God, it crawls
        This agony, over me!
      Let be, ye thralls!
        Come, Death, and cover me;
     Come, O thou Healer blest!

      But a little more,
        And my soul is clear,
      And the anguish o'er!
        Oh, a spear, a spear!
     To rend my soul to its rest!

Oh, strange, false Curse! Was there some blood-stained head,
Some father of my line, unpunishèd,
     Whose guilt lived in his kin,
And passed, and slept, till after this long day
It lights. . . . Oh, why on me? Me, far away
     And innocent of sin?

    O words that cannot save!
  When will this breathing end in that last deep
Pain that is painlessness? 'Tis sleep I crave.
  When wilt thou bring me sleep,
Thou dark and midnight magic of the grave!

Artemis. Sore-stricken man, bethink thee in this stress,
Thou dost but die for thine own nobleness.
  Hippolytus. Ah!
O breath of heavenly fragrance! Though my pain
Burns, I can feel thee and find rest again.
The Goddess Artemis is with me here.
  Artemis. With thee and loving thee, poor sufferer!
  Hippolytus. Dost see me, Mistress, nearing my last sleep?
  Artemis. Aye, and would weep for thee, if Gods could weep.
  Hippolytus. Who now shall hunt with thee or hold thy
    quiver?
  Artemis. He dies; but my love cleaves to him for ever.
  Hippolytus. Who guide thy chariot, keep thy shrine-flowers
    fresh?
  Artemis. The accursèd Cyprian caught him in her mesh!
  Hippolytus. The Cyprian? Now I see it!—Aye, 'twas she.
  Artemis. She missed her worship, loathed thy chastity!
  Hippolytus. Three lives by her one hand! 'Tis all clear now.
  Artemis. Yea, three; thy father and his Queen and thou.
  Hippolytus. My father; yea, he too is pitiable!
  Artemis. A plotting Goddess tripped him, and he fell.
  Hippolytus. Father, where art thou? . . . Oh, thou sufferest
    sore!
  Theseus. Even unto death, child. There is joy no more.
  Hippolytus. I pity thee in this coil; aye, more than me.
  Theseus. Would I could lie there dead instead of thee!
  Hippolytus. Oh, bitter bounty of Poseidon's love!
  Theseus. Would God my lips had never breathed thereof!
  Hippolytus (*gently*). Nay, thine own rage had slain me
    then, some wise!
  Theseus. A lying spirit had made blind mine eyes!
  Hippolytus. Ah me!
Would that a mortal's curse could reach to God!
  Artemis. Let be! For not, though deep beneath the sod
Thou liest, not unrequited nor unsung
Shall this fell stroke, from Cypris' rancor sprung,
Quell thee, mine own, the saintly and the true!
  My hand shall win its vengeance, through and through
Piercing with flawless shaft what heart soe'er
Of all men living is most dear to Her.

Yea, and to thee, for this sore travail's sake,
Honors most high in Trozên will I make;
For yokeless maids before their bridal night
Shall shear for thee their tresses; and a rite
Of honoring tears be thine in ceaseless store;
And virgins' thoughts in music evermore
Turn toward thee, and praise thee in the Song
Of Phaedra's far-famed love and thy great wrong.

O seed of ancient Aegeus, bend thee now
And clasp thy son. Aye, hold and fear not thou!
Not knowingly hast thou slain him; and man's way,
When Gods send error, needs must fall astray.

And thou, Hippolytus, shrink not from the King,
Thy father. Thou wast born to bear this thing.

Farewell! I may not watch man's fleeting breath,
Nor stain mine eyes with the effluence of death.
And sure that Terror now is very near.

[*The cloud slowly rises and floats away.*

Hippolytus. Farewell, farewell, most Blessèd! Lift thee clear
Of soiling men! Thou wilt not grieve in heaven
For my long love! . . . Father, thou art forgiven.
It was Her will. I am not wroth with thee. . . .
I have obeyed Her all my days! . . .

Ah me,
The dark is drawing down upon mine eyes;
It hath me! . . . Father! . . . Hold me! Help me rise!

Theseus (*supporting him in his arms*). Ah, woe How dost
thou torture me, my son!

Hippolytus. I see the Great Gates opening. I am gone.

Theseus. Gone? And my hand red-reeking from this thing!

Hippolytus. Nay, nay; thou art assoiled of manslaying.

Theseus. Thou leav'st me clear of murder? Sayst thou so?

Hippolytus. Yea, by the Virgin of the Stainless Bow!

Theseus. Dear Son! Ah, now I see thy nobleness!

Hippolytus. Pray that a true-born child may fill my place.

Theseus. Ah me, thy righteous and godfearing heart!

Hippolytus. Farewell;

A long farewell, dear Father, ere we part!

[THESEUS *bends down and embraces him passion-
ately.*

[542]

Theseus. Not yet!—O hope and bear while thou hast breath!
Hippolytus. Lo, I have borne my burden. This is death. . . .
Quick, Father; lay the mantle on my face.

      [THESEUS *covers his face with a mantle and rises.*
Theseus. Ye bounds of Pallas and of Pelops' race,
What greatness have ye lost!

                Woe, woe is me!
Thou Cyprian, long shall I remember thee!
    Chorus. On all this folk, both low and high,
      A grief hath fallen beyond men's fears.
    There cometh a throbbing of many tears,
      A sound as of waters falling.
      For when great men die,
    A mighty name and a bitter cry
      Rise up from a nation calling.

      [*They move into the Castle, carrying the body of*
      HIPPOLYTUS.

ARISTOPHANES
THE CLOUDS

✥

TRANSLATED
by
BENJAMIN BICKLEY ROGERS

CHARACTERS IN THE PLAY

STREPSIADES, *a countryman compelled by the War to live in Athens.*
PHEIDIPPIDES, *son of Strepsiades.*
SERVANT *of Strepsiades.*
STUDENTS *of Socrates.*
SOCRATES, *the philosopher.*
RIGHT LOGIC.
WRONG LOGIC.
PASIAS } *creditors of Strepsiades.*
AMYNIAS }
A WITNESS.
CHAEREPHON, *a disciple of Socrates.*
CHORUS *of Clouds.*

ARGUMENT

The comedy of the *Clouds* was aimed at the Sophistical system of education, that subtle and insidious disease which was sapping the very life of the old Athenian character, and which for a money payment taught men to argue not for Truth, but for Victory; to assail all traditional belief; and to pride themselves on their ability to take up a bad cause and make it triumph over the right.

No satirist ever had a nobler object, and probably no man ever lived who could have carried it out with more sustained wit and vigor than Aristophanes has done in the comedy before us. But in order to assail the system on the public stage, it was necessary for the poet to select some representative individual to personify the ideas he was seeking to ridicule. And in Socrates the poet found precisely the individual he required—a native Athenian universally known, whose demeanor and habits lent themselves readily to caricature, and who might reasonably be considered a Sophist. What matter if he did not in all respects conform to the type which Aristophanes was setting himself to combat; if he kept no school or Phrontisterium, took no money from his pupils, had not (like the Wrong Logic) risen from poverty to affluence, and so on? The suggestion (which every Athenian would know to be unfounded) that Socrates did these things was as purely farcical as the presentation of the philosopher himself suspended in a basket betwixt heaven and earth.

The play was produced at the Great Dionysia in the year 423 B.C., when it placed last. Some years afterwards Aristophanes revised the comedy, and it is this revised edition which has come down to us.

THE CLOUDS

Strepsiades.　　　O dear! O dear!
O Lord! O Zeus! these nights, how long they are.
Will they ne'er pass? will the day never come?
Surely I heard the cock crow, hours ago.
Yet still my servants snore. These are new customs.
O 'ware of war for many various reasons;
One fears in war even to flog one's servants.
And here's this hopeful son of mine wrapped up
Snoring and sweating under five thick blankets.
Come, we'll wrap up and snore in opposition.
　　　　　　　　　　　　　　　　[Tries to sleep.
But I can't sleep a wink, devoured and bitten
By ticks, and bugbears, duns, and race-horses,
All through this son of mine. *He* curls his hair,
And sports his thoroughbreds, and drives his tandem;
Even in dreams he rides: while I—I'm ruined,
Now that the Moon has reached her twentieths,
And paying-time comes on. Boy! light a lamp,
And fetch my ledger: now I'll reckon up
Who are my creditors, and what I owe them.
Come, let me see then. *Fifty pounds to Pasias!*
Why fifty pounds to Pasias? what were they for?
O, for the hack from Corinth. O dear! O dear!
I wish my eye had been hacked out before—
　　Pheidippides (in his sleep). You are cheating, Philon;
　　　keep to your own side.
　　Strepsiades. Ah! there it is! that's what has ruined me!
Even in his very sleep he thinks of horses.
　　Pheidippides (in his sleep). How many heats do the war-
　　　chariots run?
　　Strepsiades. A pretty many heats you have run your father.
Now then, what debt assails me after Pasias?

[547]

A curricle and wheels. Twelve pounds. Amynias.
 Pheidippides (in his sleep). Here, give the horse a roll, and
 take him home.
 Strepsiades. You have **rolled** me *out* of house and home,
 my boy,
Cast in some suits already, while some swear
They'll seize my goods for payment.
 Pheidippides.   Good, my father,
What makes you toss so restless all night long?
 Strepsiades. There's a bumbailiff from the mattress bites me.
 Pheidippides. Come now, I prithee, let me sleep in peace.
 Strepsiades. Well then, you sleep; only be sure of this,
These debts will fall on your own head at last.
Alas, alas!
For ever cursed be that same match-maker,
Who stirred me up to marry your poor mother.
Mine in the country was the pleasantest life,
Untidy, easy-going, unrestrained,
Brimming with olives, sheepfolds, honey-bees.
Ah! then I married—I a rustic—her
A fine town-lady, niece of Megacles.
A regular, proud, luxurious, Coesyra.
This wife I married, and we came together,
I rank with wine-lees, fig-boards, greasy woolpacks;
She all with scents, and saffron, and tongue-kissings,
Feasting, expense, and lordly modes of loving.
She was not idle though, she was too fast.
I used to tell her, holding out my cloak,
Threadbare and worn; *Wife, you're too fast by half.*
 Servant-Boy. Here's no more oil remaining in the lamp.
 Strepsiades. O me! what made you light the tippling lamp?
Come and be whipp'd.
 Servant.   Why, what would you whip me for?
 Strepsiades. Why did you put one of those thick wicks in?
Well, when at last to me and my good woman
This hopeful son was born, our son and heir,
Why then we took to wrangle on the name.
She was for giving him some knightly name,
'Callippides,' 'Xanthippus,' or 'Charippus':
I wished 'Pheidonides,' his grandsire's name.

Thus for some time we argued: till at last
We compromised it in Pheidippides.
This boy she took, and used to spoil him, saying,
Oh! when you are driving to the Acropolis, clad
Like Megacles, in your purple; whilst I said
Oh! when the goats you are driving from the fells,
Clad like your father, in your sheepskin coat.
Well, he cared nought for my advice, but soon
A galloping consumption caught my fortunes.
Now cogitating all night long, I've found
One way, one marvelous transcendent way,
Which if he'll follow, we may yet be saved.
So,—but, however, I must rouse him first;
But how to rouse him kindliest? that's the rub.
Pheidippides, my sweet one.

   Pheidippides.   Well, my father.
   Strepsiades. Shake hands, Pheidippides, shake hands and
     kiss me.
   Pheidippides. There; what's the matter?
   Strepsiades.   Dost thou love me, boy?
   Pheidippides. Ay! by Poseidon there, the God of horses.
   Strepsiades. No, no, not that: miss out the God of horses.
That God's the origin of all my evils.
But if you love me from your heart and soul,
My son, obey me.
   Pheidippides. .   Very well: what in?
   Strepsiades. Strip with all speed, strip off your present
     habits,
And go and learn what I'll advise you to.
   Pheidippides. Name your commands.
   Strepsiades.   Will you obey?
   Pheidippides.   I will,
By Dionysus!
   Strepsiades.   Well then, look this way.
See you that wicket and the lodge beyond?
   Pheidippides. I see: and prithee what is that, my father?
   Strepsiades. That is the thinking-house of sapient souls.
There dwell the men who teach—aye, who persuade us,
That Heaven is one vast fire-extinguisher
Placed round about us, and that we're the cinders.

Aye, and they'll teach (only they'll want some money),
How one may speak and conquer, right or wrong.
    Pheidippides. Come, tell their names.
    Strepsiades.   Well, I can't quite remember,
But they're deep thinkers, and true gentlemen.
    Pheidippides. Out on the rogues! I know them. Those rank
    pedants,
Those palefaced, barefoot vagabonds you mean:
That Socrates, poor wretch, and Chaerephon.
    Strepsiades. Oh! Oh! hush! hush! don't use those foolish
    words;
But if the sorrows of my barley touch you,
Enter their Schools and cut the Turf for ever.
    Pheidippides. I wouldn't go, so help me Dionysus,
For all Leogoras's breed of Phasians!
    Strepsiades. Go, I beseech you, dearest, dearest son,
Go and be taught.
    Pheidippides.   And what would you have me learn?
    Strepsiades. 'Tis known that in their Schools they keep two
    Logics,
The Worse, Zeus save the mark, the Worse and Better.
This Second Logic then, I mean the Worse one,
They teach to talk unjustly and—prevail.
Think then, you only learn that Unjust Logic,
And all the debts, which I have incurred through you,—
I'll never pay, no, not one farthing of them.
    Pheidippides. I will not go. How could I face the knights
With all my color worn and torn away!
    Strepsiades. O! then, by Earth, you have eat your last of
    mine,
You, and your coach-horse, and your sigma-brand:
Out with you! Go to the crows, for all I care.
    Pheidippides. But uncle Megacles won't leave me long
Without a horse: I'll go to him: good-bye.
    Strepsiades. I'm thrown, by Zeus, but I won't long lie
    prostrate.
I'll pray the Gods and send myself to school:
I'll go at once and try their thinking-house.
Stay: how can I, forgetful, slow, old fool,
Learn the nice hair-splittings of subtle Logic?

Well, go I must. 'Twont do to linger here.
Come on, I'll knock the door. Boy! Ho there, boy!

Student (*within*). O, hang it all! who's knocking at the door?

Strepsiades. Me! Pheidon's son: Strepsiades of Cicynna.

Student. Why, what a clown you are! to kick our door,
In such a thoughtless, inconsiderate way!
You've made my cogitation to miscarry.

Strepsiades. Forgive me: I'm an awkward country fool.
But tell me, what was that I made miscarry?

Student. 'Tis not allowed: Students alone may hear.

Strepsiades. O that's all right: you may tell *me:* I'm come
To be a student in your thinking-house.

Student. Come then. But they're high mysteries, remember.
'Twas Socrates was asking Chaerephon,
How many feet of its own a flea could jump.
For one first bit the brow of Chaerephon,
Then bounded off to Socrates's head.

Strepsiades. How did he measure this?

Student.   Most cleverly.
He warmed some wax, and then he caught the flea,
And dipped its feet into the wax he'd melted:
Then let it cool, and there were Persian slippers!
These he took off, and so he found the distance.

Strepsiades. O Zeus and king, what subtle intellects!

Student. What would you say then if you heard another,
Our Master's own?

Strepsiades.   O come, do tell me that.

Student. Why, Chaerephon was asking him in turn,
Which theory did he sanction; that the gnats
Hummed through their mouth, or backwards, through the tail?

Strepsiades. Aye, and what said your Master of the gnat?

Student. He answered thus: the entrail of the gnat
Is small: and through this narrow pipe the wind
Rushes with violence straight towards the tail;
There, close against the pipe, the hollow rump
Receives the wind, and whistles to the blast.

Strepsiades. So then the rump is trumpet to the gnats!
O happy, happy in your entrail-learning!
Full surely need he fear nor debts nor duns,

Who knows about the entrails of the gnats.

Student. And yet last night a mighty thought we lost
Through a green lizard.

Strepsiades. Tell me, how was that?

Student. Why, as Himself, with eyes and mouth wide open,
Mused on the moon, her paths and revolutions,
A lizard from the roof squirted full on him.

Strepsiades. He, he, he, he. I like the lizard's spattering
Socrates.

Student. Then yesterday, poor we, we'd got no dinner.

Strepsiades. Hah! what did he devise to do for barley?

Student. He sprinkled on the table—some fine ash—
He bent a spit—he grasped it compass-wise—
And—filched a mantle from the Wrestling School.

Strepsiades. Good heavens! Why Thales was a fool to this!
O open, open, wide the study door,
And show me, show me, show me Socrates.
I die to be a student. Open, open!
O Heracles, what kind of beasts are these!

Student. Why, what's the matter? what do you think they're
like?

Strepsiades. Like? why those Spartans whom we brought
from Pylus:
What makes them fix their eyes so on the ground?

Student. They seek things underground.

Strepsiades. O! to be sure,
Truffles! You there, don't trouble about that!
I'll tell you where the best and finest grow.
Look! why do these stoop down so very much?

Student. They're diving deep into the deepest secrets.

Strepsiades. Then why's their rump turned up towards the
sky?

Student. It's taking private lessons on the stars.

[*To the other Students.*
Come, come: get in: HE'll catch us presently.

Strepsiades. Not yet! not yet! just let them stop one moment,
While I impart a little matter to them.

Student. No, no: they must go in: 'twould never do
To expose themselves too long to the open air.

Strepsiades. O! by the Gods, now, what are these? do tell
me?

Student. This is Astronomy.

Strepsiades. And what is this?

Student. Geometry.

Strepsiades. Well, what's the use of that?

Student. To mete out lands.

Strepsiades. What, for allotment grounds?

Student. No, but all lands.

Strepsiades. A choice idea, truly.
Then every man may take his choice, you mean.

Student. Look; here's a chart of the whole world. Do you
see?
This city's Athens.

Strepsiades. Athens? I like that.
I see no dicasts sitting. That's not Athens.

Student. In very truth, this is the Attic ground.

Strepsiades. And where then are my townsmen of Cicynna?

Student. Why, thereabouts; and here, you see, Euboea:
Here, reaching out a long way by the shore.

Strepsiades. Yes, overreached by us and Pericles.
But now, where's Sparta?

Student. Let me see: O, here.

Strepsiades. Heavens! how near us. O do please manage this,
To shove her off from us, a long way further.

Student. We can't do that, by Zeus.

Strepsiades. The worse for you.
Hallo! who's that? that fellow in the basket?

Student. That's HE.

Strepsiades. Who's HE?

Student. Socrates.

Strepsiades. Socrates!
You sir, call out to him as loud as you can.

Student. Call him yourself: I have not leisure now.

Strepsiades. Socrates! Socrates!
Sweet Socrates!

Socrates. Mortal! why call'st thou me?

Strepsiades. O, first of all, please tell me what you are doing.

Socrates. I walk on air, and contem-plate the Sun.

Strepsiades. O then from a basket you contemn the Gods,

[553]

And not from the earth, at any rate?
   Socrates.   Most true.
I could not have searched out celestial matters
Without suspending judgment, and infusing
My subtle spirit with the kindred air.
If from the ground I were to seek these things,
I could not find: so surely doth the earth
Draw to herself the essence of our thought.
The same too is the case with water-cress.
   Strepsiades. Hillo! what's that?
Thought draws the essence into water-cress?
Come down, sweet Socrates, more near my level,
And teach the lessons which I come to learn.
   Socrates. And wherefore art thou come?
   Strepsiades.   To learn to speak.
For owing to my horrid debts and duns,
My goods are seized, I'm robbed, and mobbed, and plundered.
   Socrates. How did you get involved with your eyes open?
   Strepsiades. A galloping consumption seized my money.
Come now: do let me learn the unjust Logic
That can shirk debts: now do just let me learn it.
Name your own price, by all the Gods I'll pay it.
   Socrates. The Gods! why you must know the Gods with us
Don't pass for current coin.
   Strepsiades.   Eh? what do you use then?
Have you got iron, as the Byzantines have?
   Socrates. Come, would you like to learn celestial matters.
How their truth stands?
   Strepsiades.   Yes, if there's any truth.
   Socrates. And to hold intercourse with yon bright Clouds,
Our virgin Goddesses?
   Strepsiades.   Yes, that I should.
   Socrates. Then sit you down upon that sacred bed.
   Strepsiades. Well, I am sitting.
   Socrates.   Here then, take this chaplet.
   Strepsiades. Chaplet? why? why? now, never, Socrates:
Don't sacrifice poor me, like Athamas.
   Socrates. Fear not: our entrance-services require
All to do this.
   Strepsiades.   But what am I to gain?

Socrates. You'll be the flower of talkers, prattlers, gossips:
Only keep quiet.
Strepsiades.   Zeus! your words come true!
I shall be flour indeed with all this peppering.

Socrates. Old man sit you still, and attend to my will,
                              and hearken in peace to my prayer,
O Master and King, holding earth in your swing,
                              O measureless infinite Air;
And thou glowing Ether, and Clouds who enwreathe her
                    with thunder, and lightning, and storms,
Arise ye and shine, bright Ladies Divine,
                              to your student in bodily forms.
Strepsiades. No, but stay, no, but stay, just one moment I
          pray,
                    while my cloak round my temples I wrap.
To think that I've come, stupid fool, from my home,
                              with never a waterproof cap!
Socrates. Come forth, come forth, dread Clouds, and to earth
                              your glorious majesty show;
Whether lightly ye rest on the time-honored crest
                              of Olympus environed in snow,
Or tread the soft dance 'mid the stately expanse
                              of Ocean, the nymphs to beguile,
Or stoop to enfold with your pitchers of gold,
                              the mystical waves of the Nile,
Or around the white foam of Maeotis ye roam,
                              or Mimas all wintry and bare,
O hear while we pray, and turn not away
                    from the rites which your servants prepare.
Chorus.   Clouds of all hue,
     Rise we aloft with our garments of dew.
     Come from old Ocean's unchangeable bed,
     Come, till the mountain's green summits we tread,
     Come to the peaks with their landscapes untold,
     Gaze on the Earth with her harvests of gold,
     Gaze on the rivers in majesty streaming,
         Gaze on the lordly, invincible Sea,
     Come, for the Eye of the Ether is beaming,
         Come, for all Nature is flashing and free.

Let us shake off this close-clinging dew
From our members eternally new,
And sail upwards the wide world to view.
    Come away! Come away!
Socrates. O Goddesses mine, great Clouds and divine,
    ye have heeded and answered my prayer.
Heard ye their sound, and the thunder around,
    as it thrilled through the tremulous air?
Strepsiades. Yes, by Zeus, and I shake, and I'm all of a quake,
    and I fear I must sound a reply,
Their thunders have made my soul so afraid,
    and those terrible voices so nigh:
So if lawful or not, I must run to a pot,
    by Zeus, if I stop I shall die.
Socrates. Don't act in our schools like those Comedy-fools
    with their scurrilous scandalous ways.
Deep silence be thine: while this Cluster divine
    their soul-stirring melody raise.
Chorus.   Come then with me,
Daughters of Mist, to the land of the free.
Come to the people whom Pallas hath blest,
Come to the soil where the Mysteries rest;
Come, where the glorified Temple invites
The pure to partake of its mystical rites:
Holy the gifts that are brought to the Gods,
    Shrines with festoons and with garlands are crowned,
Pilgrims resort to the sacred abodes,
    Gorgeous the festivals all the year round.
And the Bromian rejoicings in Spring,
When the flutes with their deep music ring,
And the sweetly-toned Choruses sing
    Come away! Come away!
Strepsiades. O Socrates pray, by all the Gods, say,
    for I earnestly long to be told,
Who are these that recite with such grandeur and might?
    are they glorified mortals of old?
Socrates. No mortals are there, but Clouds of the air,
    great Gods who the indolent fill:

[556]

These grant us discourse, and logical force,
         and the art of persuasion instil,
And periphrasis strange, and a power to arrange,
         and a marvelous judgment and skill.

Strepsiades. So then when I heard their omnipotent word,
         my spirit felt all of a flutter,
And it yearns to begin subtle cobwebs to spin
         and about metaphysics to stutter,
And together to glue an idea or two,
         and battle away in replies:
So if it's not wrong, I earnestly long
         to behold them myself with my eyes.

Socrates. Look up in the air, towards Parnes out there,
         for I see they will pitch before long
These regions about.

Strepsiades.   Where? point me them out.

Socrates.   They are drifting, an infinite throng,
And their long shadows quake over valley and brake.

Strepsiades.   Why, whatever's the matter to-day?
I can't see, I declare.

Socrates.   By the Entrance; look there!

Strepsiades.   Ah, I just got a glimpse, by the way.

Socrates. There, now you must see how resplendent they be,
         or your eyes must be pumpkins, I vow.

Strepsiades. Ah! I see them proceed; I should think so
  indeed:
         great powers! they fill everything now.

Socrates. So then till this day that celestials were they,
         you never imagined or knew?

Strepsiades. Why, no, on my word, for I always had heard
         they were nothing but vapor and dew.

Socrates. O, then I declare, you can't be aware
         that 'tis these who the sophists protect,
Prophets sent beyond sea, quacks of every degree,
         fops signet-and-jewel-bedecked,
Astrological knaves, and fools who their staves
         of dithyrambs proudly rehearse—
'Tis the Clouds who all these support at their ease,
         because they exalt them in verse.

Strepsiades. 'Tis for this then they write of 'the on-rushin' might

      o' the light-stappin' rain-drappin' Cloud,'
And the 'thousand black curls whilk the Tempest-lord whirls,'
      and the 'thunder-blast stormy an' loud,'
And 'birds o' the sky floatin' upwards on high,'
      and 'air-water leddies' which 'droon
Wi' their saft falling dew the gran' Ether sae blue,'
      and then in return they gulp doon
Huge gobbets o' fishes an' bountifu' dishes
      o' mavises prime in their season.
Socrates. And is it not right such praise to requite?
Strepsiades.   Ah, but tell me then what is the reason
That if, as you say, they are Clouds, they to-day
      as women appear to our view?
For the ones in the air are not women, I swear.
Socrates.   Why, what do they seem then to you?
Strepsiades. I can't say very well, but they straggle and swell

      like fleeces spread out in the air;
Not like women they flit, no, by Zeus, not a bit,
      but these have got noses to wear.
Socrates. Well, now then, attend to this question, my friend.
Strepsiades.   Look sharp, and propound it to me.
Socrates. Didst thou never espy a Cloud in the sky,
      which a centaur or leopard might be,
Or a wolf, or a cow?
Strepsiades.   Very often, I vow:
      and show me the cause, I entreat.
Socrates. Why, I tell you that these become just what they please,

      and whenever they happen to meet
One shaggy and wild, like the tangle-haired child
      of old Xenophantes, their rule
Is at once to appear like Centaurs, to jeer
      the ridiculous look of the fool.
Strepsiades. What then do they do if Simon they view,
      that fraudulent harpy to shame?
Socrates. Why, his nature to show to us mortals below,
      a wolfish appearance they frame.

Strepsiades. O, they then I ween having yesterday seen
                 Cleonymus quaking with fear,
(Him who threw off his shield as he fled from the field),
               metamorphosed themselves into deer.
Socrates. Yes, and now they espy soft Cleisthenes nigh,
             and therefore as women appear.
Strepsiades. O then without fail, All hail! and All hail!
                my welcome receive; and reply
With your voices so fine, so grand and divine,
               majestical Queens of the Sky!
Chorus. Our welcome to thee, old man, who wouldst see
           the marvels that science can show:
And thou, the high-priest of this subtlety feast,
           say what would you have us bestow?
Since there is not a sage for whom we'd engage
           our wonders more freely to do,
Except, it may be, for Prodicus; he
         for his knowledge may claim them, but you,
For that sideways you throw your eyes as you go,
          and are all affectation and fuss;
No shoes will you wear, but assume the grand air
          on the strength of your dealings with us.
Strepsiades. O Earth! what a sound, how august and pro-
found!
          it fills me with wonder and awe.
Socrates. These, these then alone, for true Deities own,
          the rest are all Godships of straw.
Strepsiades. Let Zeus be left out: He's a God beyond doubt:
          come, that you can scarcely deny.
Socrates. Zeus, indeed! there's no Zeus: don't you be so
obtuse.
Strepsiades.   No Zeus up aloft in the sky!
Then, you first must explain, who it is sends the rain;
          or I really must think you are wrong.
Socrates. Well then, be it known, these send it alone:
          I can prove it by arguments strong.
Was there ever a shower seen to fall in an hour
          when the sky was all cloudless and blue?
Yet on a fine day, when the Clouds are away,
          he might send one, according to you.

Strepsiades. Well, it must be confessed, that chimes in with
the rest:

                     your words I am forced to believe.
Yet before, I had dreamed that the rain-water streamed

                  from Zeus and his chamber-pot sieve.
But whence then, my friend, does the thunder descend?

              that does make me quake with affright!
   Socrates. Why 'tis they, I declare, as they roll through the
air.
   Strepsiades.   What the Clouds? did I hear you aright?
   Socrates. Ay: for when to the brim filled with water they
swim,

                by Necessity carried along,
They are hung up on high in the vault of the sky,

             and so by Necessity strong
In the midst of their course, they clash with great force,

             and thunder away without end.
   Strepsiades. But is it not He who compels this to be?

            does not Zeus this Necessity send?
   Socrates. No Zeus have we there, but a Vortex of air.
   Strepsiades.   What! Vortex? that's something, I own.
I knew not before, that Zeus was no more,

           but Vortex was placed on his throne!
But I have not yet heard to what cause you referred

           the thunder's majestical roar.
   Socrates. Yes, 'tis they, when on high full of water they fly,

          and then, as I told you before,
By Compression impelled, as they clash, are compelled

          a terrible clatter to make.
   Strepsiades. Come, how can that be? I really don't see.
   Socrates.   Yourself as my proof I will take.
Have you never then eat the broth-puddings you get

          when the Panathenaea comes round,
And felt with what might your bowels all night

          in turbulent tumult resound?
   Strepsiades. By Apollo, 'tis true, there's a mighty to-do,

         and my belly keeps rumbling about;
And the puddings begin to clatter within

         and kick up a wonderful rout:

Quite gently at first, papapax, papapax,

> but soon pappapappax away,

Till at last, I'll be bound, I can thunder as loud,

> papapappappapappax, as They.

Socrates. Shalt thou then a sound so loud and profound

> from thy belly diminutive send,

And shall not the high and the infinite Sky

> go thundering on without end?

For both, you will find, on an impulse of wind

> and similar causes depend.

Strepsiades. Well, but tell me from Whom comes the bolt
through the gloom,

> with its awful and terrible flashes;

And wherever it turns, some it singes and burns,

> and some it reduces to ashes!

For this 'tis quite plain, let who will send the rain,

> that Zeus against perjurers dashes.

Socrates. And how, you old fool of a dark-ages school,

> and an antediluvian wit,

If the perjured they strike, and not all men alike,

> have they never Cleonymus hit?

Then of Simon again, and Theorus explain:

> known perjurers, yet they escape.

But he smites his own shrine with his arrows divine,

> and 'Sunium, Attica's cape,'

And the ancient gnarled oaks: now what prompted those
strokes?

> *They* never forswore I should say.

Strepsiades. Can't say that they do: your words appear true.

> Whence comes then the thunderbolt, pray?

Socrates. When a wind that is dry, being lifted on high,

> is suddenly pent into these,

It swells up their skin, like a bladder, within,

> by Necessity's changeless decrees:

Till, compressed very tight, it bursts them outright,

> and away with an impulse so strong,

That at last by the force and the swing of its course,

> it takes fire as it whizzes along.

Strepsiades. That's exactly the thing that I suffered one
Spring,

at the great feast of Zeus, I admit:
I'd a paunch in the pot, but I wholly forgot

about making the safety-valve slit.
So it spluttered and swelled, while the saucepan I held,

till at last with a vengeance it flew:
Took me quite by surprise, dung-bespattered my eyes,

and scalded my face black and blue!
Chorus. O thou who wouldst fain great wisdom attain,

and comest to us in thy need,
All Hellas around shall thy glory resound,

such a prosperous life thou shalt lead:
So thou art but endued with a memory good,

and accustomed profoundly to think,
And thy soul wilt inure all wants to endure,

and from no undertaking to shrink,
And art hardy and bold, to bear up against cold,

and with patience a supper thou losest:
Nor too much dost incline to gymnastics and wine,

but all lusts of the body refusest:
And esteemest it best, what is always the test

of a truly intelligent brain,
To prevail and succeed whensoever you plead,

and hosts of tongue-conquests to gain
Strepsiades. But as far as a sturdy soul is concerned

and a horrible restless care,
And a belly that pines and wears away

on the wretchedest, frugalest fare,
You may hammer and strike as long as you like;

I am quite invincible there.
Socrates. Now then you agree in rejecting with me

the Gods you believed in when young,
And *my* creed you'll embrace *'I believe in wide space,*

in the Clouds, in the eloquent Tongue.'
Strepsiades. If I happened to meet other Gods in the street,

I'd show the cold shoulder, I vow.
No libation I'll pour: not one victim more

on their altars I'll sacrifice now.

Chorus. Now be honest and true, and say what we shall do:
             since you never shall fail of our aid,
If you hold us most dear in devotion and fear,
             and will ply the philosopher's trade.
Strepsiades. O Ladies Divine, small ambition is mine:
             I only most modestly seek,
Out and out for the rest of my life to be best
             of the children of Hellas to speak.
Chorus. Say no more of your care, we have granted your
    prayer:
             and know from this moment, that none
More acts shall pass through in the People than you:
             such favor from us you have won.
Strepsiades. Not acts, if you please: I want nothing of these:
             this gift you may quickly withdraw;
But I wish to succeed, just enough for my need,
             and to slip through the clutches of law.
Chorus. This then you shall do, for your wishes are few:
             not many nor great your demands,
So away with all care from henceforth, and prepare
             to be placed in our votaries' hands.
Strepsiades. This then will I do, confiding in you,
             for Necessity presses me sore,
And so sad is my life, 'twixt my cobs and my wife,
             that I cannot put up with it more.
So now, at your word, I give and afford
My body to these, to treat as they please,
To have and to hold, in squalor, in cold,
In hunger and thirst, yea by Zeus, at the worst,
To be flayed out of shape from my heels to my nape
So along with my hide from my duns I escape,
And to men may appear without conscience or fear,
Bold, hasty, and wise, a concocter of lies,
A rattler to speak, a dodger, a sneak,
A regular claw of the tables of law,
A shuffler complete, well worn in deceit,
A supple, unprincipled, troublesome cheat;
A hang-dog accurst, a bore with the worst,
In the tricks of the jury-courts thoroughly versed.
If all that I meet this praise shall repeat,

Work away as you choose, I will nothing refuse,
Without any reserve, from my head to my shoes.
You shan't see me wince though my gutlets you mince,
And these entrails of mine for a sausage combine,
Served up for the gentlemen students to dine.

Chorus. Here's a spirit bold and high
Ready-armed for any strife.
(*To* STREPSIADES). If you learn what I can teach
                         Of the mysteries of speech,
Your glory soon shall reach
To the summit of the sky.

Strepsiades. And what am I to gain?
Chorus.   With the Clouds you will obtain
The most happy, the most enviable life.
Strepsiades. Is it possible for me Such felicity to see?
Chorus. Yes, and men shall come and wait
                         In their thousands at your gate,
     Desiring consultations and advice
On an action or a pleading
                         From the man of light and leading,
     And you'll pocket many talents in a trice.
(*To* SOCRATES). Here, take the old man, and do all that you
     can,
                    your new-fashioned thoughts to instill,
And stir up his mind with your notions refined,
                    and test him with judgment and skill.
Socrates. Come now, you tell me something of your habits:
For if I don't know them, I can't determine
What engines I must bring to bear upon you.
Strepsiades. Eh! what? Not going to storm me, by the Gods?
Socrates. No, no: I want to ask you a few questions.
First: is your memory good?
Strepsiades.   Two ways, by Zeus:
If I'm owed anything, I'm mindful, very:
But if I owe, (Oh, dear!) forgetful, very.
Socrates. Well then: have you the gift of speaking in you?
Strepsiades. The gift of speaking, no: of cheating, yes.
Socrates. No? how then can you learn?
Strepsiades.   Oh, well enough.
Socrates. Then when I throw you out some clever notion.

About the laws of nature, you must catch it.

    Strepsiades. What! must I snap up sapience, in dog-fashion?

    Socrates. Oh! why the man's an ignorant old savage:

I fear, my friend, that you'll require the whip.

Come, if one strikes you, what do you do?

    Strepsiades.   I'm struck:

Then in a little while I call my witness:

Then in another little while I summon him.

    Socrates. Put off your cloak.

    Strepsiades.   Why, what have I done wrong?

    Socrates. O, nothing, nothing: all go in here naked.

    Strepsiades. Well, but I have not come with a search-warrant.

    Socrates. Fool! throw it off.

    Strepsiades.   Well, tell me this one thing;

If I'm extremely careful and attentive,

Which of your students shall I most resemble?

    Socrates. Why, Chaerephon. You'll be his very image.

    Strepsiades. What! I shall be half-dead! O luckless me!

    Socrates. Don't chatter there, but come and follow me;

Make haste now, quicker, here.

    Strepsiades.   Oh, but do first

Give me a honied cake: Zeus! how I tremble,

To go down there, as if to see Trophonius.

    Socrates. Go on! why keep you pottering round the door?

    Chorus. Yes! go, and farewell; as your courage is great,

            So bright be your fate.

    May all good fortune his steps pursue,

      Who now, in his life's dim twilight haze,

    Is game such venturesome things to do,

    To steep his mind in discoveries new,

      To walk, a novice, in wisdom's ways.

O Spectators, I will utter

                 honest truths with accents free,

Yea! by mighty Dionysus,

               Him who bred and nurtured me.

So may I be deemed a poet,

               and this day obtain the prize,

As till that unhappy blunder

             I had always held you wise,

And of all my plays esteeming
> this the wisest and the best,

Served it up for your enjoyment,
> which had, more than all the rest,

Cost me thought, and time, and labor:
> then most scandalously treated,

I retired in mighty dudgeon,
> by unworthy foes defeated.

This is why I blame your critics,
> for whose sake I framed the play:

Yet the clever ones amongst you
> even now I won't betray.

No! for ever since from judges
> unto whom 'tis joy to speak,

Brothers Profligate and Modest
> gained the praise we fondly seek,

When, for I was yet a Virgin,
> and it was not right to bear,

I exposed it, and Another
> did the foundling nurse with care,

But 'twas ye who nobly nurtured,
> ye who brought it up with skill;—

From that hour I proudly cherish
> pledges of your sure good will.

Now then comes its sister hither,
> like Electra in the Play,

Comes in earnest expectation
> kindred minds to meet to-day;

She will recognize full surely,
> if she find, her brother's tress.

And observe how pure her morals:
> who, to notice her first dress,

Enters not with filthy symbols
> on her modest garments hung,

Jeering bald-heads, dancing ballets,
> for the laughter of the young.

In this play no wretched graybeard
> with a staff his fellow pokes,

So obscuring from the audience
> all the poorness of his jokes.

No one rushes in with torches,
                    no one groans, *'Oh, dear! Oh, dear!'*
Trusting in its genuine merits
                    comes this play before you here.
Yet, though such a hero-poet,
                    I, the bald-head, do not grow
Curling ringlets: neither do I
                    twice or thrice my pieces show.
Always fresh ideas sparkle,
                    always novel jests delight,
Nothing like each other, save that
                    all are most exceeding bright.
I am he who floored the giant,
                    Cleon, in his hour of pride,
Yet when down I scorned to strike him,
                    and I left him when he died!
But the others, when a handle
                    once Hyperbolus did lend,
Trample down the wretched caitiff,
                    and his mother, without end.
In his Maricas the Drunkard,
                    Eupolis the charge began,
Shamefully my 'Knights' distorting,
                    as he is a shameful man,
Tacking on the tipsy beldame,
                    just the ballet-dance to keep,
Phrynichus's prime invention,
                    eat by monsters of the deep.
Then Hermippus on the caitiff
                    opened all his little skill,
And the rest upon the caitiff
                    are their wit exhausting still;
And my simile to pilfer
                    'of the Eels' they all combine.
Whoso laughs at their productions,
                    let him not delight in mine.
But for you who praise my genius,
                    you who think my writings clever,
Ye shall gain a name for wisdom,
                    yea! for ever and for ever

O mighty God, O heavenly King,
First unto Thee my prayer I bring,
O come, Lord Zeus, to my choral song;—
And Thou, dread Power, whose resistless hand
Heaves up the sea and the trembling land,
Lord of the trident, stern and strong;—
And Thou who sustainest the life of us all
Come, Ether, our parent. O come to my call;—
And Thou who floodest the world with light,
Guiding thy steeds through the glittering sky,
To men below and to Gods on high
A Potentate heavenly-bright!

O most sapient wise spectators,
                    hither turn attention due,
We complain of sad ill-treatment,
                    we've a bone to pick with you:
We have ever helped your city,
                    helped with all our might and main;
Yet you pay us no devotion,
                    that is why we now complain.
We who always watch around you.
                    For if any project seems
Ill-concocted, then we thunder,
                    then the rain comes down in streams.
And, remember, very lately,
                    how we knit our brows together,
'Thunders crashing, lightnings flashing,'
                    never was such awful weather;
And the Moon in haste eclipsed her,
                    and the Sun in anger swore
He would curl his wick within him
                    and give light to you no more,
Should you choose that mischief-worker,
                    Cleon, whom the Gods abhor,
Tanner, Slave, and Paphlagonian,
                    to lead out your hosts to war.
Yet you chose him! yet you chose him!
                    For they say that Folly grows

Best and finest in this city,

               but the gracious Gods dispose
Always all things for the better,

               causing errors to succeed:
And how this sad job may profit,

               surely he who runs may read.
Let the Cormorant be convicted,

               in command, of bribes and theft,
Let us have him gagged and muzzled,

               in the pillory chained and left,
Then again, in ancient fashion,

               all that ye have erred of late,
Will turn out your own advantage,

               and a blessing to the State.

    'Phoebus, my king, come to me still.'
    Thou who holdest the Cynthian hill,
      The lofty peak of the Delian isle;—
    And Thou, his sister, to whom each day
    Lydian maidens devoutly pray
      In Thy stately gilded Ephesian pile;—
    And Athene, our Lady, the queen of us all,
    With the Aegis of God, O come to my call;—
    And Thou whose dancing torches of pine
    Flicker, Parnassian glades along,
    Dionysus, Star of Thy Maenad throng,
      Come, Reveller most divine!

We, when we had finished packing,

               and prepared our journey down,
Met the Lady Moon, who charged us

               with a message for your town.
First, All hail to noble Athens,

               and her faithful true Allies;
Then, she said, your shameful conduct

               made her angry passions rise,
Treating her so ill who always

               aids you, not in words, but clearly;
Saves you, first of all, in torchlight

               every month a drachma nearly,

So that each one says, if business
     calls him out from home by night,
'Buy no link, my boy, this evening,
     for the Moon will lend her light.'
Other blessings too she sends you,
     yet you will not mark your days
As she bids you, but confuse them,
     jumbling them all sorts of ways,
And, she says, the Gods in chorus
     shower reproaches on her head,
When in bitter disappointment
     they go supperless to bed,
Not obtaining festal banquets
     duly on the festal day;
Ye are badgering in the law-courts
     when ye should arise and slay!
And full oft when we celestials
     some strict fast are duly keeping,
For the fate of mighty Memnon,
     or divine Sarpedon weeping,
Then you feast and pour libations:
     and Hyperbolus of late
Lost the crown he wore so proudly
     as Recorder of the Gate,
Through the wrath of us immortals:
     so perchance he'll rather know
Always all his days in future
     by the Lady Moon to go.
 Socrates. Never by Chaos, Air, and Respiration,
Never, no never have I seen a clown
So helpless, and forgetful, and absurd!
Why if he learns a quirk or two he clean
Forgets them ere he has learnt them: all the same,
I'll call him out of doors here to the light.
Take up your bed, Strepsiades, and come!
 Strepsiades. By Zeus, I can't: the bugs make such resistance.
 Socrates. Make haste. There, throw it down, and listen.
 Strepsiades.   Well!
 Socrates. Attend to me: what shall I teach you first
That you've not learnt before? Which will you have,

Measures or rhythms or the right use of words?

Strepsiades. Oh! measures to be sure: for very lately
A grocer swindled me of full three pints.

Socrates. I don't mean that: but which do you like the best
Of all the measures; six feet, or eight feet?

Strepsiades. Well, I like nothing better than the yard.

, *Socrates.* Fool! don't talk nonsense.

Strepsiades. What will you bet me now
That two yards don't exactly make six feet?

Socrates. Consume you! what an ignorant clown you are!
Still, perhaps you can learn tunes more easily.

Strepsiades. But will tunes help me to repair my fortunes?

Socrates. They'll help you to behave in company:
If you can tell which kind of tune is best
For the sword-dance, and which for finger music.

Strepsiades. For fingers! aye, but I know that.

Socrates. Say on, then.

Strepsiades. What is it but this finger? though before,
Ere this was grown, I used to play with that.

Socrates. Insufferable dolt!

Strepsiades. Well but, you goose,
I don't want to learn this.

Socrates. What *do* you want then?

Strepsiades. Teach me the Logic! teach me the unjust Logic!

Socrates. But you must learn some other matters first:
As, what are males among the quadrupeds.

Strepsiades. I should be mad indeed not to know that.
The Ram, the Bull, the Goat, the Dog, the Fowl.

Socrates. Ah! there you are! there's a mistake at once!
You call the male and female fowl the same.

Strepsiades. How! tell me how.

Socrates. Why fowl and fowl of course.

Strepsiades. That's true though! what then shall I say in
future?

Socrates. Call one a fowless and the other a fowl.

Strepsiades. A fowless? Good! Bravo! Bravo! by Air.
Now for that one bright piece of information
I'll give you a barley bumper in your trough.

Socrates. Look there, a fresh mistake; you called it trough,
Masculine, when it's feminine.

[571]

Strepsiades.   How, pray?
How did I make it masculine?
    Socrates.   Why 'trough,'
Just like 'Cleonymus.'
    Strepsiades.   I don't quite catch it.
    Socrates. Why 'trough,' 'Cleonymus,' both masculine.
    Strepsiades. Ah, but Cleonymus has got no trough,
His bread is kneaded in a rounded mortar:
Still, what must I say in future?
    Socrates.   What! why call it
A 'troughess,' female, just as one says 'an actress.'
    Strepsiades. A 'troughess,' female?
    Socrates.   That's the way to call it.
    Strepsiades. O 'troughess' then and Miss Cleonymus.
    Socrates. Still you must learn some more about these names;
Which are the names of men and which of women.
    Strepsiades. Oh, I know which are women.
    Socrates.   Well, repeat some.
    Strepsiades. Demetria, Cleitagora, Philinna.
    Socrates. Now tell me some men's names.
    Strepsiades.   O yes, ten thousand.
Philon, Melesias, Amynias.
    Socrates. Hold! I said men's names: these are women's
    names.
    Strepsiades. No, no, they're men's.
    Socrates.   They are *not* men's, for how
Would you address Amynias if you met him?
    Strepsiades. How? somehow thus: 'Here, here, Amynia!'
    Socrates. Amynia! a woman's name, you see.
    Strepsiades. And rightly too; a sneak who shirks all service!
But all know this: let's pass to something else.
    Socrates. Well, then, you get into the bed.
    Strepsiades.   And then?
    Socrates. Excogitate about your own affairs.
    Strepsiades. Not there: I do beseech, not there: at least
Let me excogitate on the bare ground.
    Socrates. There is no way but this.
    Strepsiades.   O luckless me!
How I shall suffer from the bugs to-day.

Socrates. Now then survey in every way,
             with airy judgment sharp and quick:
Wrapping thoughts around you thick:
And if so be in one you stick,
Never stop to toil and bother,
  Lightly, lightly, lightly leap,
To another, to another;
   Far away be balmy sleep.
Strepsiades. Ugh! Ugh! Ugh! Ugh! Ugh!
Chorus. What's the matter? where's the pain?
Strepsiades. Friends! I'm dying. From the bed
  Out creep bugbears scantly fed.
  And my ribs they bite in twain,
  And my life-blood out they suck,
  And my manhood off they pluck,
  And my loins they dig and drain,
  And I'm dying, once again.
Chorus. O take not the smart so deeply to heart.
Strepsiades.   Why, what can I do?
  Vanished my skin so ruddy of hue,
  Vanished my life-blood, vanished my shoe,
  Vanished my purse, and what is still worse
  As I hummed an old tune till my watch should be past,
  I had very near vanished myself at the last.

Socrates. Hallo there, are you pondering?
Strepsiades.   Eh! what? I?
Yes to be sure.
Socrates.   And what have your ponderings come to?
Strepsiades. Whether these bugs will leave a bit of me.
Socrates. Consume you, wretch!
Strepsiades.   Faith, I'm consumed already.
Socrates. Come, come, don't flinch: pull up the clothes
  again:
Search out and catch some very subtle dodge
To fleece your creditors.
Strepsiades.   O me, how can I
Fleece any one with all these fleeces on me?
               [Puts his head under the clothes.
  Socrates. Come, let me peep a moment what he's doing.

[573]

Hey! he's asleep!

Strepsiades.   No, no! no fear of that!

Socrates. Caught anything?

Strepsiades.   No, nothing.

Socrates.   Surely, something.

Strepsiades. Well, I had something in my hand, I'll own.

Socrates. Pull up the clothes again, and go on pondering.

Strepsiades. On what? now do please tell me, Socrates.

Socrates. What is it that you want? first tell me that.

Strepsiades. You have heard a million times what 'tis I
    want:

My debts! my debts! I want to shirk my debts.

Socrates. Come, come, pull up the clothes: refine your
    thoughts

With subtle wit: look at the case on all sides:

Mind you divide correctly.

Strepsiades.   Ugh! O me.

Socrates. Hush: if you meet with any difficulty

Leave it a moment: then return again

To the same thought: then lift and weigh it well.

Strepsiades. Oh, here, dear Socrates!

Socrates.   Well, my old friend.

Strepsiades. I've found a notion how to shirk my debts.

Socrates. Well then, propound it.

Strepsiades.   What do you think of this?

Suppose I hire some grand Thessalian witch

To conjure down the Moon, and then I take it

And clap it into some round helmet-box,

And keep it fast there, like a looking-glass,—

Socrates. But what's the use of that?

Strepsiades.   The use, quotha:

Why if the Moon should never rise again,

I'd never pay one farthing.

Socrates.   No! why not?

Strepsiades. Why, don't we pay our interest by the month?

Socrates. Good! now I'll proffer you another problem.

Suppose an action: damages, five talents:

Now tell me how you can evade that same.

Strepsiades. How! how! can't say at all: but I'll go seek.

Socrates. Don't wrap your mind for ever round yourself,

But let your thoughts range freely through the air,
Like chafers with a thread about their feet.

Strepsiades. I've found a bright evasion of the action:
Confess yourself, 'tis glorious.

Socrates. But what is it?

Strepsiades. I say, haven't you seen in druggists' shops
That stone, that splendidly transparent stone,
By which they kindle fire?

Socrates. The burning-glass?

Strepsiades. That's it: well then, I'd get me one of these,
And as the clerk was entering down my case,
I'd stand, like this, some distance towards the sun,
And burn out every line.

Socrates. By the Three Graces,
A clever dodge!

Strepsiades. O me, how pleased I am
To have a debt like that clean blotted out.

Socrates. Come, then, make haste and snap up this.

Strepsiades. Well, what?

Socrates. How to prevent an adversary's suit
Supposing you were sure to lose it; tell me.

Strepsiades. O, nothing easier.

Socrates. How, pray?

Strepsiades. Why thus,
While there was yet one trial intervening,
Ere mine was cited, I'd go hang myself.

Socrates. Absurd!

Strepsiades. No, by the Gods, it isn't though:
They could not prosecute me were I dead.

Socrates. Nonsense! Be off: I'll try no more to teach you.

Strepsiades. Why not? do, please: now, please do, Socrates.

Socrates. Why you forget all that you learn, directly.
Come, say what you learnt first: there's a chance for you.

Strepsiades. Ah! what was first?—Dear me: whatever was
it?—
Whatever's that we knead the barley in?—
Bless us, what was it?

Socrates. Be off, and feed the crows,
You most forgetful, most absurd old dolt!

Strepsiades. O me! what will become of me, poor wretch!

[575]

I'm clean undone: I haven't learnt to speak.——
O gracious Clouds, now do advise me something.
 Chorus. Our counsel, ancient friend, is simply this,
To send your son, if you have one at home,
And let him learn this wisdom in your stead.
 Strepsiades. Yes! I've a son, quite a fine gentleman:
But he won't learn, so what am I to do?
 Chorus. What! is he master?
 Strepsiades.   Well: he's strong and vigorous,
And he's got some of the Coesyra blood within him:
Still I'll go for him, and if he won't come
By all the Gods I'll turn him out of doors.
Go in one moment, I'll be back directly.

 Chorus. Dost thou not see how bounteous we our favors free
     Will shower on you,
    Since whatsoe'er your will prepare
     This dupe will do.
But now that you have dazzled and
          elated so your man,
Make haste and seize whate'er you please
         as quickly as you can,
For cases such as these, my friend,
       are very prone to change and bend.

 Strepsiades. Get out! you shan't stop here: so help me
  Mist!
Be off, and eat up Megacles's columns.
 Pheidippides. How now, my father? what's i' the wind
  to-day?
You're wandering; by Olympian Zeus, you are.
 Strepsiades. Look there! Olympian Zeus! you blockhead
  you,
Come to *your* age, and yet believe in Zeus!
 Pheidippides. Why prithee, what's the joke?
 Strepsiades.   'Tis so preposterous
When babes like you hold antiquated notions.
But come and I'll impart a thing or two,
A wrinkle, making you a man indeed.
But, mind: don't whisper this to any one.

Pheidippides. Well, what's the matter?

Strepsiades.   Didn't you swear by Zeus?

Pheidippides. I did.

Strepsiades.   See now, how good a thing is learning.
There is no Zeus, Pheidippides.

Pheidippides.   Who then?

Strepsiades. Why Vortex reigns, and he has turned out Zeus.

Pheidippides. Oh me, what stuff.

Strepsiades.   Be sure that this is so.

Pheidippides. Who says so, pray?

Strepsiades.   The Melian—Socrates,
And Chaerephon, who knows about the flea-tracks.

Pheidippides. And are you come to such a pitch of madness
As to put faith in brain-struck men?

Strepsiades.   O hush!
And don't blaspheme such very dexterous men
And sapient too: men of such frugal habits
They never shave, nor use your precious ointment,
Nor go to baths to clean themselves: but you
Have taken *me* for a corpse and cleaned me out.
Come, come, make haste, do go and learn for me.

  Pheidippides. What can one learn from them that is worth
    knowing?

Strepsiades. Learn! why, whatever's clever in the world:
And you shall learn how gross and dense you are.
But stop one moment: I'll be back directly.

  Pheidippides. O me! what must I do with my mad father?
Shall I indict him for his lunacy,
Or tell the undertakers of his symptoms?

  Strepsiades. Now then! you see this, don't you? what do
    you call it?

Pheidippides. That? why a fowl.

Strepsiades.   Good! now then, what is this?

Pheidippides. That's a fowl too.

Strepsiades.   What both! Ridiculous!
Never say that again, but mind you always
Call this a fowless and the other a fowl.

  Pheidippides. A fowless! These then are the mighty secrets
You have picked up amongst those earth-born fellows.

Strepsiades. And lots besides: but everything I learn
I straight forget: I am so old and stupid.
    Pheidippides. And this is what you have lost your mantle
      for?
    Strepsiades. It's very absent sometimes: 'tisn't lost.
    Pheidippides. And what have you done with your shoes,
      you dotard you?
    Strepsiades. Like Pericles, all for the best, I've lost them.
Come, come; go with me: humor me in this,
And then do what you like. Ah! I remember
How I to humor you, a coaxing baby,
With the first obol which my judgeship fetched me
Bought you a go-cart at the great Diasia.
    Pheidippides. The time will come when you'll repent of this.
    Strepsiades. Good boy to obey me. Hallo! Socrates.
Come here; come here; I've brought this son of mine.
Trouble enough, I'll warrant you.
    Socrates.   Poor infant,
Not yet aware of my suspension-wonders.
    Pheidippides. You'd make a wondrous piece of ware, sus-
      pended.
    Strepsiades. Hey! Hang the lad! Do you abuse the Master?
    Socrates. And look, 'suthspended'! In what foolish fashion
He mouthed the word with pouting lips agape.
How can *he* learn evasion of a suit,
Timely citation, damaging replies?
Hyperbolus, though, learnt them for a talent.
    Strepsiades. O never fear! he's very sharp, by nature.
For when he was a little chap, *so* high,
He used to build small baby-houses, boats,
Go-carts of leather, darling little frogs
Carved from pomegranates, you can't think how nicely!
So now, I prithee, teach him both your Logics,
The Better, as you call it, and the Worse
Which with the worse cause can defeat the Better;
Or if not both, at all events the Worse.
    Socrates. Aye, with his own ears he shall hear them argue.
I shan't be there.
    Strepsiades.   But please remember this,
Give him the knack of reasoning down all Justice.

Right Logic. Come show yourself now
with your confident brow.
—To the stage, if you dare!

Wrong Logic. 'Lead on where you please':
I shall smash you with ease,
If an audience be there.

Right Logic. **You'll** smash me, you say! And who are *you,* pray?

Wrong Logic. A Logic, like you.

Right Logic. But the Worst of the two.

Wrong Logic. Yet you I can drub whom my Better they dub.

Right Logic. By what artifice taught?

Wrong Logic. By original thought.

Right Logic. Aye, truly your trade so successful is made.
By means of these noodles of ours, I'm afraid.

Wrong Logic. Not noodles, but wise.

Right Logic. I'll smash you and your lies!

Wrong Logic. By what method, forsooth?

Right Logic. By speaking the Truth.

Wrong Logic. Your words I will meet, and entirely defeat:
There never *was* Justice or Truth, I repeat.

Right Logic. No Justice! you say?

Wrong Logic. Well, where does it stay?

Right Logic. With the Gods in the air.

Wrong Logic. If Justice be there,
How comes it that Zeus could his father reduce,
Yet live with their Godships unpunished and loose?

Right Logic. Ugh! Ugh! These evils come thick,
I feel awfully sick,
A bason, quick, quick!

Wrong Logic. You're a useless old drone with one foot in the grave!

Right Logic. You're a shameless, unprincipled, dissolute knave!

Wrong Logic. Hey! a rosy festoon.

Right Logic. And a vulgar buffoon!

Wrong Logic. What? Lilies from *you?*

Right Logic. And a parricide too!

Wrong Logic. 'Tis with gold (you don't know it) you sprinkle my head.

[579]

Right Logic. O gold is it now? but it used to be lead!

Wrong Logic. But now it's a grace and a glory instead.

Right Logic. You're a little too bold.

Wrong Logic. You're a good deal too old.

Right Logic. 'Tis through you I well know not a stripling will go

To attend to the rules which are taught in the Schools;

But Athens one day shall be up to the fools.

Wrong Logic. How squalid your dress!

Right Logic. Yours is fine, I confess.

Yet of old, I declare, but a pauper you were;

And passed yourself off, our compassion to draw

As a Telephus, (Euripidéan)

Well pleased from a beggarly wallet to gnaw

At inanities Pandeletéan.

Wrong Logic. O me! for the wisdom you've mentioned in jest!

Right Logic. O me! for the folly of you, and the rest

Who you to destroy their children employ!

Wrong Logic. Him you never shall teach: you are quite out of date.

Right Logic. If not, he'll be lost, as he'll find to his cost:

Taught nothing by you but to chatter and prate.

Wrong·Logic. He raves, as you see: let him be, let him be.

Right Logic. Touch him if you dare! I bid you beware.

Chorus. Forbear, forbear to wrangle and scold!

Each of you show

You what you taught their fathers of old,

You let us know

Your system untried, that hearing each side

From the lips of the Rivals the youth may decide

To which of your schools he will go.

Right Logic. This then will I do.

Wrong Logic. And so will I too.

Chorus. And who will put in his claim to begin?

Wrong Logic. If *he* wishes, he may: I kindly give way:

And out of his argument quickly will I

Draw facts and devices to fledge the reply

Wherewith I will shoot him and smite and refute him.

And at last if a word from his mouth shall be heard

My sayings like fierce savage hornets shall pierce
  His forehead and eyes,
Till in fear and distraction he yields and he—dies!
    Chorus. With thoughts and words and maxims pondered well
      Now then in confidence let both begin:
    Try which his rival can in speech excel:
      Try which this perilous wordy war can win,
    Which all my votaries' hopes are fondly centered in.
O Thou who wert born our sires to adorn
                   with characters blameless and fair,
Say on what you please, say on and to these
                   your glorious Nature declare.
    Right Logic. To hear then prepare of the Discipline rare
              which flourished in Athens of yore
When Honor and Truth were in fashion with youth
            and Sobriety bloomed on our shore;
First of all the old rule was preserved in our school
         that 'boys should be seen and not heard':
And then to the home of the Harpist would come
            decorous in action and word
All the lads of one town, though the snow peppered down,
          in spite of all wind and all weather:
And they sang an old song as they paced it along,
        not shambling with thighs glued together:
'O the dread shout of War how it peals from afar,'
          or 'Pallas the Stormer adore,'
To some manly old air all simple and bare
          which their fathers had chanted before.
And should anyone dare the tune to impair
         and with intricate twistings to fill,
Such as Phrynis is fain, and his long-winded train,
        perversely to quaver and trill,
Many stripes would he feel in return for his zeal,
         as to genuine Music a foe.
And every one's thigh was forward and high
         as they sat to be drilled in a row,
So that nothing the while indecent or vile
        the eye of a stranger might meet;
And then with their hand they would smooth down the sand
       whenever they rose from their seat,

To leave not a trace of themselves in the place
>> for a vigilant lover to view.
They never would soil their persons with oil
>> but were inartificial and true.
Nor tempered their throat to a soft mincing note
>> and sighs to their lovers addressed:
Nor laid themselves out, as they strutted about,
>> to the wanton desires of the rest:
Nor would anyone dare such stimulant fare
>> as the head of the radish to wish:
Nor to make over bold with the food of the old,
>> the anise, and parsley, and fish:
Nor dainties to quaff, nor giggle and laugh,
>> nor foot within foot to enfold.

Wrong Logic. Faugh! this smells very strong of some musty old song,
>> and Chirrupers mounted in gold;
And Slaughter of beasts, and old-fashioned feasts.

Right Logic. Yet these are the precepts which taught
The heroes of old to be hardy and bold,
>> and the Men who at Marathon fought!
But now must the lad from his boyhood be clad
>> in a Man's all-enveloping cloak:
So that, oft as the Panathenaea returns,
>> I feel myself ready to choke
When the dancers go by with their shields to their thigh,
>> not caring for Pallas a jot.
You therefore, young man, choose me while you can;
>> cast in with my Method your lot;
And then you shall learn the forum to spurn,
>> and from dissolute baths to abstain,
And fashions impure and shameful abjure,
>> and scorners repel with disdain:
And rise from your chair if an elder be there,
>> and respectfully give him your place,
And with love and with fear your parents revere,
>> and shrink from the brand of Disgrace,
And deep in your breast be the Image impressed
>> of Modesty, simple and true,

Nor resort any more to a dancing-girl's door,

              nor glance at the harlotry crew,

Lest at length by the blow of the Apple they throw

           from the hopes of your Manhood you fall.

Nor dare to reply when your Father is nigh,

           nor 'musty old Japhet' to call

In your malice and rage that Sacred Old Age

          which lovingly cherished your youth.

    Wrong Logic. Yes, yes, my young friend, if to him you attend,

            by Bacchus I swear of a truth

You will scarce with the sty of Hippocrates vie,

          as a mammy-suck known even there!

    Right Logic. But then you'll excel in the games you love well,

          all blooming, athletic and fair:

Not learning to prate as your idlers debate

          with marvelous prickly dispute,

Nor dragged into Court day by day to make sport

          in some small disagreeable suit:

But you will below to the Academe go

          and under the olives contend

With your chaplet of reed, in a contest of speed

          with some excellent rival and friend:

All fragrant with woodbine and peaceful content,

          and the leaf which the lime blossoms fling,

When the plane whispers love to the elm in the grove

          in the beautiful season of Spring.

If then you'll obey and do what I say,

And follow with me the more excellent way,

Your chest shall be white, your skin shall be bright,

Your arms shall be tight, your tongue shall be slight,

And everything else shall be proper and right.

But if you pursue what men nowadays do,

You will have, to begin, a cold pallid skin,

Arms small and chest weak, tongue practised to speak,

Special laws very long, and the symptoms all strong

Which show that your life is licentious and wrong.

And your mind he'll prepare so that foul to be fair

And fair to be foul you shall always declare;

And you'll find yourself soon, if you listen to him,
With the filth of Antimachus filled to the brim!

Chorus. O glorious Sage! with loveliest Wisdom teeming!
Sweet on thy words does ancient Virtue rest!
Thrice happy they who watched thy Youth's bright beam-
ing!
Thou of the vaunted genius, do thy best;
This man has gained applause: His Wisdom stands con-
fessed.
And you with clever words and thoughts must needs your case
adorn
Else he will surely win the day, and you retreat with scorn.

Wrong Logic. Aye, say you so? why I have been
half-burst; I do so long
To overthrow his arguments
with arguments more strong.
I am the Lesser Logic? True:
these Schoolmen call me so,
Simply because I was the first
of all mankind to show
How old established rules and laws
might contradicted be:
And this, as you may guess, is worth
a thousand pounds to me,
To take the feebler cause, and yet
to win the disputation.
And mark me now, how I'll confute
his boasted Education!
You said that always from warm baths
the stripling must abstain:
Why must he? on what grounds do you
of these warm baths complain?
Right Logic. Why, it's the worst thing possible,
it quite unstrings a man.
Wrong Logic. Hold there: I've got you round the waist:
escape me if you can.
And first: of all the sons of Zeus
which think you was the best?

Which was the manliest? which endured
> more toils than all the rest?
Right Logic. Well, I suppose that Heracles
> was bravest and most bold.
Wrong Logic. And are the baths of Heracles
> so wonderfully cold?
Aha! you blame warm baths, I think.
Right Logic. This, this is what they say:
This is the stuff our precious youths
> are chattering all the day!
This is what makes them haunt the baths,
> and shun the manlier Games!
Wrong Logic. Well then, we'll take the Forum next:
> I praise it, and he blames.
But if it *was* so bad, do you think
> old Homer would have made
Nestor and all his worthies ply
> a real forensic trade?
Well: then he says a stripling's tongue
> should always idle be:
I say it should be used of course:
> so there we disagree.
And next he says you must be chaste.
> A most preposterous plan!
Come, tell me did you ever know
> one single blessed man
Gain the least good by chastity?
> come, prove I'm wrong: make haste.
Right Logic. Yes, many, many! Peleus gained
> a sword by being chaste.
Wrong Logic. A sword indeed! a wondrous meed
> the unlucky fool obtained.
Hyperbolus the Lamp-maker
> hath many a talent gained
By knavish tricks which I have taught:
> but not a sword, no, no!
Right Logic. Then Peleus did to his chaste life
> the bed of Thetis owe.
Wrong Logic. And then she cut and ran away!
> for nothing so engages

[585]

A woman's heart as forward warmth,
old shred of those dark Ages!
For take this chastity, young man:
sift it inside and out:
Count all the pleasures, all the joys,
it bids you live without:
No kind of dames, no kind of games,
no laughing, feasting, drinking,—
Why, life itself is little worth
without these joys, I'm thinking.
Well, I must notice now the wants
by Nature's self implanted;
You love, seduce, you can't help that,
you're caught, convicted. Granted.
You're done for; you can't say one word:
while if you follow me
Indulge your genius, laugh and quaff,
hold nothing base to be.
Why if you're in adultery caught,
your pleas will still be ample:
You've done no wrong, you'll say, and then
bring Zeus as your example.
He fell before the wondrous powers
by Love and Beauty wielded:
And how can you, the Mortal, stand,
where He, the Immortal, yielded?
Right Logic. Aye, but suppose in spite of all,
he must be wedged and sanded.
Won't he be probed, or else can you
prevent it? now be candid.
Wrong Logic. And what's the damage if it should be so?
Right Logic. What greater damage can the young man
know?
Wrong Logic. What will you do, if this dispute I win?
Right Logic. I'll be for ever silent.
Wrong Logic. Good, begin.
The Counselor: from whence comes he?
Right Logic. From probed adulterers.
Wrong Logic. I agree.
The Tragic Poets: whence are they?

Right Logic. From probed adulterers.
Wrong Logic.   So I say.
    The Orators: what class of men?
Right Logic. All probed adulterers.
Wrong Logic.   Right again.
    You feel your error, I'll engage,
    But look once more around the stage,
    Survey the audience, which they be,
    Probed or not Probed.
Right Logic.   I see, I see.
Wrong Logic. Well, give your verdict.
Right Logic.   It must go
    For probed adulterers: him I know,
    And him, and him: the Probed are most.
Wrong Logic. How stand we then?
Right Logic.   I own, I've lost.
    O Cinaeds, Cinaeds, take my robe!
    Your words have won, to you I run
    To live and die with glorious Probe!

Socrates. Well, what do you want? to take away your son
At once, or shall I teach him how to speak?
    Strepsiades. Teach him, and flog him, and be sure you well
Sharpen his mother wit, grind the one edge
Fit for my little law-suits, and the other,
Why, make that serve for more important matters.
    Socrates. Oh, never fear! He'll make a splendid sophist.
    Strepsiades. Well, well, I hope he'll be a poor pale rascal.

Chorus. Go: but in us the thought is strong,
                you will repent of this ere long.
Now we wish to tell the Judges
                all the blessings they shall gain
If, as Justice plainly warrants,
                we the worthy prize obtain.
First, whenever in the Season
                ye would fain your fields renew,
All the world shall wait expectant
                till we've poured our rain on you:

Then of all your crops and vineyards
        we will take the utmost care
So that neither drought oppress them,
        nor the heavy rain impair.
But if anyone amongst you
        dare to treat our claims with scorn,
Mortal he, the Clouds immortal,
        better had he ne'er been born!
He from his estates shall gather
        neither corn, nor oil, nor wine,
For whenever blossoms sparkle
        on the olive or the vine
They shall all at once be blighted:
        we will ply our slings so true.
And if ever we behold him
        building up his mansions new,
With our tight and nipping hailstones
        we will all his tiles destroy.
But if he, his friends or kinsfolk,
        would a marriage-feast enjoy,
All night long we'll pour in torrents:
        so perchance he'll rather pray
To endure the drought of Egypt,
        than decide amiss to-day!

Strepsiades. The fifth, the fourth, the third, and then the
  second,
And then that day which more than all the rest
I loathe and shrink from and abominate,
Then comes at once that hateful Old-and-New day.
And every single blessed dun has sworn
He'll stake his gage, and ruin and destroy me.
And when I make a modest small request,
'O my good friend, part don't exact at present,
And part defer, and part remit,' they swear
So they shall never touch it, and abuse me
As a rank swindler, threatening me with actions.
Now let them bring their actions! Who's afraid?
Not I: if these have taught my son to speak.
But here's the door: I'll knock and soon find out.

Boy! Ho there, boy!

Socrates.   I clasp Strepsiades.

Strepsiades. And I clasp you: but take this meal-bag first.
'Tis meet and right to glorify one's Tutors.
But tell me, tell me, has my son yet learnt
That Second Logic which he saw just now?

Socrates. He hath.

Strepsiades.   Hurrah! great Sovereign Knavery!

Socrates. You may escape whatever suit you please.

Strepsiades. What, if I borrowed before witnesses?

Socrates. Before a thousand, and the more the merrier.

Strepsiades. 'Then shall my song be loud and deep.'
Weep, obol-weighers, weep, weep, weep,
Ye, and your principals, and compound interests,
For ye shall never pester me again.
Such a son have I bred,
(He is within this door),
Born to inspire my foemen with dread,
Born his old father's house to restore:
Keen and polished of tongue is he,
He my Champion and Guard shall be,
He will set his old father free,
Run you, and call him forth to me.
'O my child! O my sweet! come out, I entreat;
'Tis the voice' of your sire.

Socrates. Here's the man you require.

Strepsiades. Joy, joy of my heart!

Socrates. Take your son and depart.

Strepsiades. O come, O come, my son, my son,
O dear! O dear!
O joy, to see your beautiful complexion!
Aye now you have an aspect Negative
And Disputative, and our native query
Shines forth there 'What d'ye say?' You've the true face
Which rogues put on, of injured innocence.
You have the regular Attic look about you.
So now, you save me, for 'twas you undid me.

Pheidippides. What is it ails you?

Strepsiades.   Why the Old-and-New day?

Pheidippides. And is there such a day as Old-and-New?

Strepsiades. Yes: that's the day they mean to stake their
gages.

Pheidippides. They'll lost them if they stake them. What! do
you think

That one day can be two days, both together?

Strepsiades. Why, can't it be so?

Pheidippides.   Surely not; or else

A woman might at once be old and young.

Strepsiades. Still, the law says so.

Pheidippides.   True: but I believe

They don't quite understand it.

Strepsiades.   You explain it.

Pheidippides. Old Solon had a democratic turn.

Strepsiades. Well, but that's nothing to the Old-and-New.

Pheidippides. Hence then he fixed that summonses be issued

For these two days, the old one and the new one,

So that the gage be staked on the New-month.

Strepsiades. What made him add 'the old' then?

Pheidippides.   I will tell you.

He wished the litigants to meet on *that* day

And compromise their quarrels: if they could not,

Then let them fight it out on the New-month.

Strepsiades. Why then do Magistrates receive the stakes

On the Old-and-New instead of the New-month?

Pheidippides. Well, I believe they act like the Foretasters.

They wish to bag the gage as soon as possible,

And thus they gain a whole day's foretaste of it.

Strepsiades. Aha! poor dupes, why sit ye mooning there,

Game for us Artful Dodgers, you dull stones,

You ciphers, lambkins, butts piled up together!

Oh! my success inspires me, and I'll sing

Glad eulogies on me and thee, my son.

> '*Man, most blessed, most divine,*
> *What a wondrous wit is thine,*
> *What a son to grace thy line,*'
> Friends and neighbors day by day
>   Thus will say,

When with envious eyes my suits they see you win:

But first I'll feast you, so come in, my son, come in.

Pasias. What! must a man lost his own property!

No: never, never. Better have refused
With a bold face, than be so plagued as this.
See! to get paid my own just debts, I'm forced
To drag you to bear witness, and what's worse
I needs must quarrel with my townsman here.
Well, I won't shame my country, while I live,
I'll go to law, I'll summon him.
  Strepsiades.   Hallo!
 Pasias. To the next Old-and-New.
 Strepsiades.   Bear witness, all!
He named two days. You'll summon me; what for?
 Pasias. The fifty pounds I lent you when you bought
That iron-gray.
 Strepsiades.   Just listen to the fellow!
The whole world knows that I detest all horses.
 Pasias. I swear you swore by all the Gods to pay me.
 Strepsiades. Well, now I swear I won't: Pheidippides
Has learnt since then the unanswerable Logic.
 Pasias. And will you therefore shirk my just demand?
 Strepsiades. Of course I will: else why should he have
  learnt it?
 Pasias. And will you dare forswear it by the Gods?
 Strepsiades. The Gods indeed! What Gods?
 Pasias. Poseidon, Hermes, Zeus.
 Strepsiades.   By Zeus I would,
Though I gave twopence halfpenny for the privilege.
 Pasias. O then confound you for a shameless rogue!
 Strepsiades. Hallo! this butt should be rubbed down with
  salt.
 Pasias. Zounds! you deride me!
 Strepsiades.   Why 'twill hold four gallons.
 Pasias. You 'scape me not, by Mighty Zeus, and all
The Gods!
 Strepsiades.   I wonderfully like the Gods;
An oath by Zeus is sport to knowing ones.
 Pasias. Sooner or later you'll repent of this.
Come do you mean to pay your debts or don't you?
Tell me, and I'll be off.
 Strepsiades.   Now do have patience;
I'll give you a clear answer in one moment.

Pasias. What do you think he'll do?

Witness. I think he'll pay you.

Strepsiades. Where is that horrid dun? O here: now tell me
What you call this.

Pasias. What I call that? a trough.

Strepsiades. Heavens! what a fool: and do *you* want your
    money?
I'd never pay one penny to a fellow
Who calls my troughess, trough. So there's your answer.

Pasias. Then you won't pay me?

Strepsiades. No, not if I know it.
Come put your best foot forward, and be off:
March off, I say, this instant!

Pasias. May I die
If I don't go at once and stake my gage!

Strepsiades. No don't: the fifty pounds are loss enough:
And really on my word I would not wish you
To lose this too just for one silly blunder.

Amynias. Ah me! Oh! Oh! Oh!

Strepsiades. Hallo! who's that making that horrible noise?
Not one of Carcinus's sniveling Gods?

Amynias. Who cares to know what I am? what imports it?
An ill-starred man.

Strepsiades. Then keep it to yourself.

Amynias. 'O heavy fate!' 'O Fortune, thou hast broken
My chariot wheels!' 'Thou hast undone me, Pallas!'

Strepsiades. How! has Tlepolemus been at you, man?

Amynias. Jeer me not, friend, but tell your worthy son
To pay me back the money which I lent him:
I'm in a bad way and the times are pressing.

Strepsiades. What money do you mean?

Amynias. Why what he borrowed.

Strepsiades. You *are* in a bad way, I really think.

Amynias. Driving my four-wheel out I fell, by Zeus.

Strepsiades. You rave as if you'd fall'n times out-of-mind.

Amynias. I rave? how so? I only claim my own.

Strepsiades. You can't be quite right, surely.

Amynias. Why, what mean you?

Strepsiades. I shrewdly guess your brain's received a shake.

Amynias. I shrewdly guess that you'll receive a summons
If you don't pay my money.
    Strepsiades.   Well then, tell me,
Which theory do you side with, that the rain
Falls fresh each time, or that the Sun draws back
The same old rain, and sends it down again?
    Amynias. I'm very sure I neither know nor care.
    Strepsiades. Not care! good heavens! And do *you* claim
        your money,
So unenlightened in the Laws of Nature?
    Amynias. If you're hard up then, pay me back the Interest
At least.
    Strepsiades.   Int-er-est? what kind of a beast is that?
    Amynias. What else than day by day and month by month
Larger and larger still the silver grows
As time sweeps by?
    Strepsiades.   Finely and nobly said.
What then! think you the Sea is larger now
Than 'twas last year?
    Amynias.   No surely, 'tis no larger:
It is not right it should be.
    Strepsiades.   And do you then,
Insatiable grasper! when the Sea,
Receiving all these Rivers, grows no larger,
Do you desire your silver to grow larger?
Come now, you prosecute your journey off!
Here, fetch the whip.
    Amynias.   Bear witness, I appeal.
    Strepsiades. Be off! what, won't you? Gee up, sigma-grand!
    Amynias. I say! a clear assault!
    Strepsiades.   You won't be off?
I'll stimulate you; Zeus! I'll goad your haunches.
Aha! you run: I thought I'd stir you up
You and your phaetons, and wheels, and all!

    Chorus. What a thing it is to long for matters which are
      wrong!
              For you see how this old man
              Is seeking, if he can
              His creditors trepan:

And I confidently say
That he will this very day
Such a blow
Amid his prosperous cheats receive,
that he will deeply deeply grieve.

For I think that he has won what he wanted for his son,
And the lad has learned the way
All justice to gainsay,
Be it what or where it may:
That he'll trump up any tale,
Right or wrong, and so prevail.
This I know.
Yea! and perchance the time will come
when he shall wish his son were dumb.

Strepsiades.   Oh! Oh!
Help! Murder! Help! O neighbors, kinsfolk, townsmen,
Help, one and all, against this base assault,
Ah! Ah! my cheek! my head! O luckless me!
Wretch! do you strike your father?
Pheidippides.   Yes, Papa.
Strepsiades. See! See! he owns he struck me.
Pheidippides.   To be sure.
Strepsiades. Scoundrel! and parricide! and house-breaker.
Pheidippides. Thank you: go on, go on: do please go on.
I am quite delighted to be called such names!
Strepsiades. O probed Adulterer.
Pheidippides.   Roses from your lips.
Strepsiades. Strike you your father?
Pheidippides.   O dear yes: what's more,
I'll prove I struck you justly.
Strepsiades.   Struck me justly!
Villain! how can you strike a father justly?
Pheidippides. Yes, and I'll demonstrate it, if you please.
Strepsiades. Demonstrate this?
Pheidippides.   O yes, quite easily.
Come, take your choice, which Logic do you choose?
Strepsiades. Which what?

Pheidippides.   Logic: the Better or the Worse?
Strepsiades. Ah, then, in very truth I've had you taught
To reason down all Justice, if you think
You can prove this, that it is just and right
That fathers should be beaten by their sons!
    Pheidippides. Well, well, I think I'll prove it, if you'll listen,
So that even you won't have one word to answer.
    Strepsiades. Come, I should like to hear what you've to say.

Chorus. 'Tis yours, old man, some method to contrive
            This fight to win:
    He would not without arms wherewith to strive
            So bold have been.
    He knows, be sure, whereon to trust.
    His eager bearing proves he must.

So come and tell us from what cause
                        this sad dispute began;
Come, tell us how it first arose:
                        do tell us if you can.
    Strepsiades. Well from the very first I will
                        the whole contention show:
'Twas when I went into the house
                        to feast him, as you know,
I bade him bring his lyre and sing,
                        the supper to adorn,
Some lay of old Simonides,
                        as, how the Ram was shorn:
But he replied, to sing at meals
                        was coarse and obsolete;
Like some old beldame humming airs
                        the while she grinds her wheat.
    Pheidippides. And should you not be thrashed who told
                        your son, from food abstaining
To SING! as though you were, forsooth
                        cicalas entertaining.
    Strepsiades. You hear him! so he said just now
                        or e'er high words began:
And next he called Simonides
                        a very sorry man.

And when I heard him, I could scarce
                            my rising wrath command;
Yet so I did, and him I bid
                            take myrtle in his hand
And chant some lines from Aeschylus,
                            but he replied with ire,
'Believe me, I'm not one of those
                            who Aeschylus admire,
That rough, unpolished, turgid bard,
                            that mouther of bombast!'
When he said this, my heart began
                            to heave extremely fast;
Yet still I kept my passion down,
                            and said, 'Then prithee you,
Sing one of those new-fangled songs
                            which modern striplings do.'
And he began the shameful tale
                            Euripides has told
How a brother and a sister lived
                            incestuous lives of old.
Then, then I could no more restrain,
                            but first I must confess
With strong abuse I loaded him,
                            and so, as you may guess,
We stormed and bandied threat for threat:
                            till out at last he flew,
And smashed and thrashed and thumped and bumped
                            and bruised me black and blue.
  Pheidippides. And rightly too, who coolly dared
                            Euripides to blame,
Most sapient bard.
    Strepsiades.   Most sapient bard!
                            you, what's your fitting name?
Ah! but he'll pummel me again.
    Pheidippides.   He will: and justly too.
    Strepsiades. What! justly, heartless villain! when
                            'twas I who nurtured you.
I knew your little lisping ways,
                            how soon, you'd hardly think,

If you cried 'bree!' I guessed your wants,
     and used to give you drink:
If you said 'mamm!' I fetched you bread
     with fond discernment true,
And you could hardly say 'Cacca!'
     when through the door I flew
And held you out a full arm's length
     your little needs to do:
   But now when I was crying
   That I with pain was dying,
   You brute! you would not tarry
   Me out of doors to carry,
   But choking with despair
   I've been and done it there.
Chorus. Sure all young hearts are palpitating now
   To hear him plead,
  Since if those lips with artful words avow
   The daring deed,
  And once a favoring verdict win,
  A fig for every old man's skin.
O thou! who rakest up new thoughts
     with daring hands profane.
Try all you can, ingenious man,
     that verdict to obtain.
 Pheidippides. How sweet it is these novel arts,
     these clever words to know,
And have the power established rules
     and laws to overthrow.
Why in old times when horses were
     my sole delight, 'twas wonder
If I could say a dozen words
     without some awful blunder!
But now that he has made me quit
     that reckless mode of living,
And I have been to subtle thoughts
     my whole attention giving,
I hope to prove by logic strict
     'tis right to beat my father.
 Strepsiades. O! buy your horses back, by Zeus,
     since I would ten times rather

Have to support a four-in-hand,

        so I be struck no more.

Pheidippides. Peace. I will now resume the thread

        where I broke off before.

And first I ask: when I was young,

        did you not strike me then?

Strepsiades. Yea: for I loved and cherished you.

   Pheidippides.   Well, solve me this again,

Is it not just that I your son

        should cherish you alike,

And strike you, since, as you observe,

        to cherish means to strike?

What! must my body needs be scourged

        and pounded black and blue

And yours be scathless? was not I

        as much freeborn as you?

'Children are whipped, and shall not sires be whipped?'

Perhaps you'll urge that children's minds

        alone are taught by blows:—

Well: Age is Second Childhood then:

        that everybody knows.

And as by old experience Age

        should guide its steps more clearly,

So when they err, they surely should

        be punished more severely.

   Strepsiades. But Law goes everywhere for me:

        deny it, if you can.

   Pheidippides. Well was not he who made the law,

        a man, a mortal man,

As you or I, who in old times

        talked over all the crowd?

And think you that to you or me

        the same is not allowed,

To change it, so that sons by blows

        should keep their fathers steady?

Still, we'll be liberal, and blows

        which we've received already

We will forget, we'll have no ex-

        post-facto legislation.

—Look at the game-cocks, look at all
                                                    the animal creation,
Do not *they* beat their parents? Aye:
                                        I say then, that in fact
They are as we, except that they
                                        no special laws enact.
    Strepsiades. Why don't you then, if always where
                                        the game-cock leads you follow,
Ascend your perch to roost at night,
                                        and dirt and ordure swallow?
    Pheidippides. The case is different there, old man,
                                        as Socrates would see.
    Strepsiades. Well then you'll blame yourself at last,
                                        if you keep striking me.
    Pheidippides. How so?
    Strepsiades.   Why, if it's right for me to punish you
my son,
You can, if you have got one, yours.
    Pheidippides. Aye, but suppose I've none.
Then having gulled me you will die,
                                        while I've been flogged in vain.
    Strepsiades. Good friends! I really think he has
                                        some reason to complain.
I must concede he has put the case
                                        in quite a novel light:
I really think we should be flogged
                                        unless we act aright!
  Pheidippides. Look to a fresh idea then.
    Strepsiades.   He'll be my death I vow.
    Pheidippides. Yet then perhaps you will not grudge
                                        ev'n what you suffer now.
    Strepsiades. How! will you make me like the blows
                                        which I've received to-day?
    Pheidippides. Yes, for I'll beat my mother too.
    Strepsiades.   What! What is that you say!
Why, this is worse than all.
    Pheidippides.   But what, if as I proved the other,
By the same Logic I can prove
                                        'tis right to beat my mother?
    Strepsiades. Aye! what indeed! if this you plead,

[599]

> If this you think to win,
> Why then, for all I care, you may
> To the Accursed Pit convey
> Yourself with all your learning new,
> Your master, and your Logic too,
> And tumble headlong in.

O Clouds! O Clouds! I owe all this to you!
Why did I let you manage my affairs!
 Chorus. Nay, nay, old man, you owe it to yourself.
Why didst thou turn to wicked practices?
 Strepsiades. Ah, but ye should have asked me that before,
And not have spurred a poor old fool to evil.
 Chorus. Such is our plan. We find a man
> On evil thoughts intent,
> Guide him along to shame and wrong,
> Then leave him to repent.

 Strepsiades. Hard words, alas! yet not more hard than just.
It was not right unfairly to keep back
The money that I borrowed. Come, my darling,
Come and destroy that filthy Chaerephon
And Socrates; for they've deceived us both!
 Pheidippides. No. I will lift no hand against my Tutors.
 Strepsiades. Yes do, come, reverence Paternal Zeus.
 Pheidippides. Look there! Paternal Zeus! what an old fool.
Is there a Zeus?
 Strepsiades.   There is.
 Pheidippides.   There is *no* Zeus.
Young Vortex reigns, and he has turned out Zeus.
 Strepsiades. No Vortex reigns: that was my foolish thought
All through this vortex here. Fool that I was,
To think a piece of earthenware a God.
 Pheidippides. Well, rave away, talk nonsense to yourself.
 Strepsiades. Oh! fool, fool, fool, how mad I must have been
To cast away the Gods, for Socrates.
Yet Hermes, gracious Hermes, be not angry
Nor crush me utterly, but look with mercy
On faults to which his idle talk hath led me.
And lend thy counsel; tell me, had I better
Plague them with lawsuits, or how else annoy them.
            [Affects to listen.

Good: your advice is good: I'll have no lawsuits,
I'll go at once and set their house on fire,
The prating rascals. Here, here, Xanthias,
Quick, quick here, bring your ladder and your pitchfork,
Climb to the roof of their vile thinking-house,
Dig at their tiles, dig stoutly, an' thou lovest me,
Tumble the very house about their ears.
And someone fetch me here a lighted torch,
And I'll soon see if, boasters as they are,
They won't repent of what they've done to me.
    Student 1. O dear! O dear!
    Strepsiades. Now, now, my torch, send out a lusty flame.
    Student 1. Man! what are you at there?
    Strepsiades.   What am I at? I'll tell you.
I'm splitting straws with your house-rafters here.
    Student 2. Oh me! who's been and set our house on fire?
    Strepsiades. Who was it, think you, that you stole the cloak
      from?
    Student 3. O Murder! Murder!
    Strepsiades.   That's the very thing,
Unless this pick prove traitor to my hopes,
Or I fall down, and break my blessed neck.
    Socrates. Hallo! what are you at, up on our roof?
    Strepsiades. I walk on air, and contemplate the Sun.
    Socrates. O! I shall suffocate. O dear! O dear!
    Chaerephon. And I, poor devil, shall be burnt to death.
    Strepsiades. For with what aim did ye insult the Gods,
And pry around the dwellings of the Moon?
Strike, smite them, spare them not, for many reasons,
BUT MOST BECAUSE THEY HAVE BLASPHEMED THE GODS!
    Chorus. Lead out of the way: for I think we may say
We have acted our part very fairly to-day.

ARISTOPHANES
THE BIRDS

⊰⊱

TRANSLATED
by
BENJAMIN BICKLEY ROGERS

CHARACTERS IN THE PLAY

EUELPIDES ⎱ *two old Athenians.*
PEISTHETAERUS ⎰

THE PLOVER-PAGE

THE HOOPOE.

A PRIEST.

A POET.

AN ORACLE-MONGER.

METON, *the astronomer.*

A COMMISSIONER.

A STATUTE-SELLER.

A MESSENGER.

A GUARD.

The Goddess IRIS.

A HERALD.

A SIRE-STRIKER.

CINESIAS, *a dithyrambic poet.*

A SYCOPHANT.

PROMETHEUS.

The God POSEIDON.

The God HERACLES.

A TRIBALLIAN.

A SERVANT.

CHORUS of BIRDS.

ARGUMENT

This play was produced at the time when the Sicilian expedition was in the full tide of success, and apparently was on the point of obtaining a triumphant issue. Athens was full of the wildest speculations and the most far-reaching ambitions. These feelings are mirrored in the present comedy. Two elderly Athenians leave the city and go to sojourn with the Birds, whom they persuade to claim the sovereignty of the world, and to build up an enormous wall in the Mid-air, so that no sacrifices offered by men can henceforth reach the sky; and the Gods are presently starved into submission.

Thus did Aristophanes caricature the high schemes and ambitions which were then in the air; not as *encouraging* them, for his caricature is fantastic and ludicrous in the extreme; yet not as *discouraging* them, since even his fantastic adventure is crowned with a brilliant success.

THE BIRDS

Euelpides. Straight on do you bid me go, where the tree
    stands?

Peisthetaerus. O hang it all! mine's croaking back again.

Euelpides. Why are we wandering up and down, you rogue?
This endless spin will make an end of *us*.

Peisthetaerus. To think that I, poor fool, at a crow's bidding,
Should trudge about, an hundred miles and more!

Euelpides. To think that I, poor wretch, at a daw's bidding,
Should wear the very nails from off my feet!

Peisthetaerus. Why, where we are, I've not the least idea.

Euelpides. Could you from hence find out your fatherland?

Peisthetaerus. No, that would pose even—Execestides!

Euelpides. O, here's a nuisance!

Peisthetaerus.   Go *you* there, then, friend.

Euelpides. I call Philocrates a regular cheat,
The fool that sells the bird-trays in the market.
He swore these two would lead us straight to Tereus,
The hoopoe, made a bird in that same market.
So then this daw, this son of Tharreleides,
We bought for an obol, and that crow for three.
But what knew they? Nothing, but how to—bite!
Where are you gaping now? Do you want to lead us
Against the rocks? There's no road here, I tell you.

Peisthetaerus. No, nor yet here; not even the tiniest path.

Euelpides. Well, but what says your crow about the road?

Peisthetaerus. By Zeus, she croaks quite differently now.

Euelpides (*shouting*). WHAT DOES SHE SAY ABOUT THE
    ROAD?

Peisthetaerus.   She says
She'll gnaw my fingers off: that's all she says.

Euelpides. Now isn't it a shame that when we are here
Ready and willing as two men can be

[605]

To go to the ravens, we can't find the way.
For we are sick, spectators, with a sickness
Just the reverse of that which Sacas has.
He, no true townsman, would perforce press in;
Whilst we, with rights of tribe and race unchallenged,
Townsmen mid townsmen, no man scaring us,
Spread both our—feet, and flew away from home.
Not that we hate our city, as not being
A prosperous mighty city, free for all
To spend their wealth in, paying fines and fees.
Aye, the cicalas chirp upon the boughs
One month, or two; but our Athenians chirp
Over their lawsuits all their whole life long.
That's why we are journeying on this journey now,
Trudging along with basket, pot, and myrtles,
To find some quiet easy-going spot,
Where we may settle down, and dwell in peace.
Tereus, the hoopoe, is our journey's aim,
To learn if he, in any place he has flown to,
Has seen the sort of city that we want.

Peisthetaerus. You there!

Euelpides.   What now?

Peisthetaerus.   My crow keeps croaking upwards
Ever so long.

Euelpides.   And here's my jackdaw gaping
Up in the air, as if to show me something.
There must be birds about, I am sure of that.
Let's make a noise and we shall soon find out.

Peisthetaerus. Then harkye; bang your leg against the rock.

Euelpides. And you, your head; and there'll be twice the
     noise.

Peisthetaerus. Well, take a stone and knock.

Euelpides.   Yes, I'll do that.
Boy! Boy!

Peisthetaerus.   Eh! What! do you call the hoopoe 'Boy'?
You should call 'Whoop-ho there,' not 'Boy' of course.

Euelpides. O, Whoop-ho there! What, must I knock again?
Whoop-ho!

Plover-Page. Whoever are these? Who calls my master?

Euelpides. Apollo shield us, what a terrible gape!

[606]

Plover-Page. These be two bird-catchers. O dear, O dear!
Euelpides (*aside*). As nasty-speaking, as unpleasant-looking!
Plover-Page. Ye shall both die!
Euelpides.   O, we're not men.
Plover-Page.   What then?
Euelpides. Well, I'm the Panic-struck, a Libyan bird.
Plover-Page. Nonsense!
Euelpides.   No nonsense: look for yourself and see.
Plover-Page. And he—what bird is he? come, won't you
    answer?
Peisthetaerus. I? I'm a pheasant, and a yellow-tailed one.
Euelpides. But O by all the Gods, whatever are you?
Plover-Page. A serving-bird.
Euelpides.   What, vanquished by some gamecock
In fight?
Plover-Page.   No, but my master, when he first
Became a hoopoe, prayed that I might turn
Into a bird, to be his servant still.
Euelpides. What, does a bird require a serving-bird?
Plover-Page. *He* does, as having been a man, I fancy.
So when he wants to taste Phaleric sardines,
I run for the sardines, catching up a dish.
Does he want soup? then where's the pot and ladle?
I run for the ladle.
Euelpides.   A regular running-page.
Now harkye, Plover-page, run in and call
Your master out.
Plover-Page.   Great Zeus! he has just been eating
Myrtles and midges, and is gone to roost.
Euelpides. But still, do wake him.
Plover-Page.   Well, I know he won't
Like to be waked, still for your sake I'll do it.
Peisthetaerus. Confound the bird! he frightened me to death.
Euelpides. O dear! O dear! my heart went pit-a-pat,
My daw's gone too.
Peisthetaerus (*severely*).   Gone! O you coward you,
You LET him go!
Euelpides.   Well, didn't you fall down,
And let your crow go?
Peisthetaerus.   No, I didn't. No!

Euelpides. Where is she then?
Peisthetaerus. She flew away herself.
Euelpides. You didn't let her go. You're a brave boy!
Hoopoe. Throw wide the wood, that I may issue forth!
Euelpides. O Heracles, why what in the world is this?
What feathering's here? What style of triple-cresting?
Hoopoe. Who be the folk that seek me?
Euelpides. The Twelve Gods
Would seem to have wrought your ruin.
Hoopoe. What, do you jeer me,
Seeing the way I'm feathered? Strangers, I
Was once a man.
Euelpides. It's not at you we're laughing.
Hoopoe. What is it then?
Euelpides. Your beak looks rather funny.
Hoopoe. This is the way that Sophocles disfigures
The manly form of Tereus in his Play.
Euelpides. What, are you Tereus? Are you bird or peacock?
Hoopoe. I am a bird.
Euelpides. Then, where are all your feathers?
Hoopoe. They've fallen off!
Euelpides. What! from disease, or why?
Hoopoe. No, but in winter-time all birds are wont
To moult their feathers, and then fresh ones grow.
But tell me what *ye* are.
Euelpides. We? mortal men.
Hoopoe. And of what race?
Euelpides. Whence the brave galleys come.
Hoopoe. Not dicasts, are ye?
Euelpides. No, the other sort.
We're anti-dicasts.
Hoopoe. Grows that seedling there?
Euelpides. Aye in the country you can find a few,
If you search closely.
Hoopoe. But what brings you hither?
Euelpides. To talk with you a little.
Hoopoe. What about?
Euelpides. You were a man at first, as we are now,
And had your creditors, as we have now,

And loved to shirk your debts, as we do now;
And then you changed your nature, and became
A bird, and flew round land and sea, and know
All that men feel, and all that birds feel too.
That's why we are come as suppliants here, to ask
If you can tell us of some city, soft
As a thick rug, to lay us down within.

    Hoopoe. Seek ye a mightier than the Cranaan town?
    Euelpides. A mightier, no; a more commodious, yes.
    Hoopoe. Aristocratic?
    Euelpides.   Anything but that!
I loathe the very name of Scellias' son.
    Hoopoe. What sort of city would ye like?
    Euelpides.   Why, one
Where my worst trouble would be such as this;
A friend at daybreak coming to my door
And calling out *O by Olympian Zeus,*
Take your bath early: then come round to me,
You and your children, to the wedding banquet
I'm going to give. Now pray don't disappoint me,
Else, keep your distance, when my money's—gone.
    Hoopoe. Upon my word, you are quite in love with troubles!
And *you?*
    Peisthetaerus.   I love the like.
    Hoopoe.   But tell me what.
    Peisthetaerus. To have the father of some handsome lad
Come up and chide me with complaints like these,
Fine things I hear of you, Stilbonides,
You met my son returning from the baths,
And never kissed, or hugged, or fondled him,
You, his paternal friend! You're a nice fellow.
    Hoopoe. Poor Poppet, you are in love with ills indeed.
Well, there's the sort of city that ye want
By the Red Sea.
    Euelpides.   Not by the sea! Not where
The Salaminian, with a process-server
On board, may heave in sight some early morn.
But can't you mention some Hellenic town?
    Hoopoe. Why don't ye go and settle down in Elis,
At Lepreus?

Euelpides.   Leprous! I was never there,
But for Melanthius' sake I loathe the name.
    Hoopoe. Well then, the Opuntians up in Locris, there's
The place to dwell in!
    Euelpides.   I become Opuntius!
No thank you, no, not for a talent of gold.
But this, this bird-life here, you know it well,
What is this like?
    Hoopoe.   A pleasant life enough.
Foremost and first you don't require a purse.
    Euelpides. There goes a grand corrupter of our life!
    Hoopoe. Then in the gardens we enjoy the myrtles,
The cress, the poppy, the white sesame.
    Euelpides. Why, then, ye live a bridegroom's jolly life.
    Peisthetaerus. Oh! Oh!
O the grand scheme I see in the birds' reach,
And power to grasp it, if ye'd trust to me!
    Hoopoe. Trust you in what?
    Peisthetaerus.   What? First don't fly about
In all directions, with your mouths wide open.
That makes you quite despised. With *us*, for instance,
If you should ask the flighty people there,
Who is that fellow? Teleas would reply,
The man's a bird, a flighty feckless bird,
Inconsequential, always on the move.
    Hoopoe. Well blamed, i'faith; but what we ought to do,
Tell us.
    Peisthetaerus.   Live all together: found one State.
    Hoopoe. What sort of State are birds to found, I wonder.
    Peisthetaerus. Aye, say you so? You who have made the most
Idiotic speech, **look down.**
    Hoopoe.   **I do.**
    Peisthetaerus.   Look up.
    Hoopoe. I do.
    Peisthetaerus.   **Twirl round** your head.
    Hoopoe.   Zeus! I shall be
A marvelous gainer, if I twist my neck!
    Peisthetaerus. What did you see?
    Hoopoe.   I saw the clouds and sky.

Peisthetaerus. And is not that the Station of the Birds?

Hoopoe. Station?

Peisthetaerus.   As one should say, their habitation.
Here while the heavens revolve, and yon great dome
Is moving round, ye keep your Station still.
Make this your city, fence it round with walls,
And from your Station is evolved your State.
So ye'll be lords of men, as now of locusts,
And Melian famine shall destroy the Gods.

Hoopoe. Eh! how?

Peisthetaerus.   The Air's betwixt the Earth and Sky.
And just as we, if we would go to Pytho,
Must crave a grant of passage from Boeotia,
Even so, when men slay victims to the Gods,
Unless the Gods pay tribute, ye in turn
Will grant no passage for the savory steam
To rise through Chaos, and a realm not theirs.

Hoopoe. Hurrah!
O Earth! ods traps, and nets, and gins, and snares,
This is the nattiest scheme that e'er I heard of!
So with your aid I'm quite resolved to found
The city, if the other birds concur.

Peisthetaerus. And who shall tell them of our plan?

Hoopoe.   Yourself.
O they're not mere barbarians, as they were
Before I came. I've taught them language now.

Peisthetaerus. But how to call them hither?

Hoopoe.   That's soon done.
I've but to step within the coppice here,
And wake my sleeping nightingale, and then
We'll call them, both together. Bless the birds,
When once they hear our voices, they'll come running.

Peisthetaerus. You darling bird, now don't delay one instant.
O I beseech you get at once within
Your little copse, and wake the nightingale!

                              [*The* HOOPOE's *Serenade.*

Hoopoe. Awake, my mate!
Shake off thy slumbers, and clear and strong
Let loose the floods of thy glorious song,
The sacred dirge of thy mouth divine

For sore-wept Itys, thy child and mine;
Thy tender trillings his name prolong
With the liquid note of thy tawny throat;
Through the leafy curls of the woodbine sweet
The pure sound mounts to the heavenly seat,
And Phoebus, lord of the golden hair,
As he lists to thy wild plaint echoing there,
Draws answering strains from his ivoried lyre,
Till he stirs the dance of the heavenly choir,
And calls from the blessed lips on high
Of immortal Gods, a divine reply
To the tones of thy witching melody.

> [*The sound of a flute is heard within, imitating the nightingale's song.*

Euelpides. O Zeus and King, the little birdie's voice!
O how its sweetness honied all the copse!
Peisthetaerus. Hi!
Euelpides.   Well?
Peisthetaerus.   Keep quiet.
Euelpides.   Why?
Peisthetaerus.   The Hoopoe here
Is going to favor us with another song.

> [*The Bird-call by the* HOOPOE *and Nightingale conjointly; the Nightingale's song being imitated, as before, by the flute.*

Hoopoe. Whoop-ho! Whoop-ho!
          Whoop-hoop-hoop-hoop-hoop-ho!
Hoi! Hoi! Hoi! Come, come, come, come, come!

> [*The land-birds.*

Come hither any bird with plumage like my own;
Come hither ye that batten on the acres newly sown,
     On the acres by the farmer neatly sown;
And the myriad tribes that feed on the barley and the seed,
The tribes that lightly fly, giving out a gentle cry;
And ye who round the clod, in the furrow-riven sod,
With voices sweet and low, twitter flitter to and fro,
     Singing *tío, tio, tío, tiotinx;*
And ye who in the gardens a pleasant harvest glean,
Lurking in the branches of the ivy ever green;
And ye who top the mountains with gay and airy flight;

And ye who in the olive and the arbutus delight;
Come hither one and all, come flying to our call,
   Triotó, triotó, totobrinx.

                              [The marsh-birds.

Ye that snap up the gnats, shrilly voiced,
   Mid the deep water-glens of the fens,
Or on Marathon's expanse haunt the lea, fair to see,
   Or career o'er the swamps, dewy-moist,
And the bird with the gay mottled plumes, come away,
   Francolín! Francolín! come away!

                                [The sea-birds.

Ye with the halcyons flitting delightedly
Over the surge of the infinite Sea,
Come to the great Revolution awaiting us,
Hither, come hither, come hither to me.
Hither, to listen to wonderful words,
Hither we summon the taper-necked birds.

For hither has come a shrewd old file,
Such a deep old file, such a sharp old file,
His thoughts are new, new deeds he'll do,
Come here, and confer with this shrewd old file.
Come hither! Come hither! Come hither!
Toro-toro-toro-torotinx!
Kikkabau, kikkabau!
Toro-toro-toro-toro-lililinx!

Peisthetaerus. See any bird?
  Euelpides.   By Apollo no, not I,
Though up I gaze with mouth and eyes wide open.
  Peisthetaerus. Methinks the Hoopoe played the lapwing's
    trick,
Went in the copse, and whooped, and whooped for nothing.
  Hoopoe. Torotinx! Torotinx.
  Peisthetaerus. Comrade, here's a bird approaching,
                     coming to receive our visit.
  Euelpides. Aye by Zeus, what bird do you call it?
                     Surely not a peacock, is it?
  Peisthetaerus. That the Hoopoe here will teach us.
                Prithee, friend, what bird is he?

Hoopoe. That is not a common object,
                            such as you can always see;
That's a marsh-bird.
    Euelpides. Lovely creature! nice and red like flaming flame.
    Hoopoe. So he should be, for Flamingo
                            is the lovely creature's name.

    Euelpides. Hi there!
    Peisthetaerus.   What? The row you're making!
    Euelpides.   Here's another, full in view.
    Peisthetaerus. Aye by Zeus, another truly,
                            with a foreign aspect too.
Who is he, the summit-ascending,
                    Muse-prophetical, wondrous bird?
    Hoopoe. He's a Median.
    Peisthetaerus.   He a Median! Heracles, the thing's absurd.
How on earth without a camel
                            could a Median hither fly?
    Euelpides. Here they're coming; here's another,
                            with his crest erected high.
    Peisthetaerus. Goodness gracious, that's a hoopoe;
                            yes, by Zeus, another one!
Are not *you* the only Hoopoe?
    Hoopoe.   I'm his grandsire; he's the son
Of the Philocléan hoopoe:
                            as with you a name will pass,
Callias siring Hipponicus, Hipponicus Callias.
    Peisthetaerus. O then that is Callias is it?
                            How his feathers moult away!
    Hoopoe. Aye, the simple generous creature,
                            he's to parasites a prey.
And the females flock around him,
                            plucking out his feathers too.
    Peisthetaerus. O Poseidon, here's another;
                            here's a bird of brilliant hue!
What's the name of this, I wonder.
    Hoopoe.   That's a Glutton styled by us.
    Peisthetaerus. Is there then another Glutton
                            than our own Cleonymus?
    Euelpides. Our Cleonymus, I fancy,
                            would have thrown his crest away.

Peisthetaerus. But what means the crest-equipment
                              of so many birds, I pray?
Are they going to race in armor?
   Hoopoe.   No, my worthy friend, they make
Each his dwelling, like the Carians,
                              on the crests for safety's sake.
Peisthetaerus. O Poseidon, what the mischief!
                              see the birds are everywhere
Fluttering onward.
   Euelpides. King Apollo, what a cloud! O! O! look there,
Now we cannot see the entrance
                              for the numbers crowding in.
Peisthetaerus. Here you see a partridge coming,
                              there by Zeus a francolin,
Here a widgeon onward hurries,
                              there's a halcyon, sure as fate.
Euelpides. Who's behind her?
Peisthetaerus. That's a clipper; he's the lady halcyon's mate.
Euelpides. Can a clipper be a bird then?
Peisthetaerus.   Sporgilus is surely so.
Here's an owl.
   Euelpides. And who to Athens brought an owl, I'd like to
      know.
Peisthetaerus. Jay and turtle, lark and sedgebird,
                              thyme-finch, ring-dove first, and then
Rock-dove, stock-dove, cuckoo, falcon,
                              fiery-crest, and willow wren,
Lammergeyer, porphyrion, kestrel,
                              waxwing, nuthatch, water-hen.
Euelpides (*singing*). Ohó for the birds, Ohó! Ohó!
                              Ohó for the blackbirds, ho!
How they twitter, how they go,
                              shrieking and screaming to and fro.
Goodness! are they going to charge us?
                              They are gazing here, and see
All their beaks they open widely.
   Peisthetaerus.   That is what occurs to me.
Chorus. Wh-wh-wh-wh-wh-wh-wh-wh-where may he be
      that was calling for me? In what locality pastureth he?

[615]

Hoopoe. I am ready, waiting here;

never from my friends I stir.

Chorus. Te-te-te-te-te-te-te-te-teach me, I pray, in an amicable
way,

what is the news you have gotten to say.

Hoopoe. News amazing! News auspicious!

News delightful, safe, and free!

Birds! Two men of sublest genius

hither have arrived to me.

Chorus.   Who! What! When! say that again.

Hoopoe. Here, I say, have come two elders,

traveling to the birds from man,

And the stem they are bringing with them

of a most stupendous plan.

Chorus. You who have made the greatest error

since my callow life began,

What do you say?

Hoopoe.   Now don't be nervous.

Chorus.   What is the thing you have done to me?

Hoopoe. I've received two men, enamored

of your sweet society.

Chorus. You have really dared to do it?

Hoopoe.   Gladly I the deed avow.

Chorus. And the pair are now amongst us?

Hoopoe.   Aye, if I'm amongst you now.

Chorus.   O! O! Out upon you!

We are cheated and betrayed,

we have suffered shame and wrong!

For our comrade and our friend

who has fed with us so long,

He has broken every oath, and his holy plighted troth,

And the old social customs of our clan.

He has led us unawares into wiles, and into snares,

He has given us a prey, all helpless and forlorn,

To those who were our foes

from the time that they were born,

To vile and abominable Man!

But for him, our bird-companion,

comes a reckoning by and by;

As for these two old deceivers,

       they shall suffer instantly,
Bit by bit we'll tear and rend them.
 Peisthetaerus.   Here's a very horrid mess.
 Euelpides. Wretched man, 'twas you that caused it,

       you and all your cleverness!
Why you brought me I can't see.
 Peisthetaerus.   Just that you might follow me.
 Euelpides. Just that I might die of weeping.
 Peisthetaerus.   What a foolish thing to say!
Weeping will be quite beyond you,

      when your eyes are pecked away.
 Chorus. On! On! In upon them!
Make a very bloody onset,

      spread your wings about your foes,
Assail them and attack them,

      and surround them and enclose.
Both, both of them shall die,

      and their bodies shall supply
 A rare dainty pasture for my beak.
For never shall be found any distant spot of ground,
Or shadowy mountain covert, or foamy Ocean wave,
Or cloud in Ether floating,

      which these reprobates shall save
 From the doom that upon them I will wreak.
On then, on, my flying squadrons,

      now's the time to tear and bite,
Tarry ye not an instant longer.

      Brigadier, advance our right.
 Euelpides. Here it comes! I'm off, confound them.
 Peisthetaerus.   Fool, why can't you remain with me?
 Euelpides. What! that these may tear and rend me?
 Peisthetaerus.   How can you hope from birds to flee?
 Euelpides. Truly, I haven't the least idea.
 Peisthetaerus.   Then it is I the affair must guide.
Seize we a pot and, the charge awaiting,

      here we will combat side by side.
 Euelpides. Pot! and how can a pot avail us?
 Peisthetaerus.   Never an owl will then come near.
 Euelpides. What of these birds of prey with talons?

Peisthetaerus.   Snatch up a spit, like a hoplite's spear,
Planting it firmly there before you.
Euelpides.   What shall I do about my eyes?
Peisthetaerus. Take a platter, or take a saucer,
                         holding it over them buckler-wise.
Euelpides. What a skilful neat contrivance!
                         O you clever fellow you,
In your military science Nicias you far outdo!
Chorus. Eleleleu! advance! no loitering;
                         level your beaks and charge away.
Shatter the pot at once to pieces;
                         worry, and scratch, and tear, and flay!
Hoopoe. O, whatever is your purpose? is your villainy so
     great,
You would slay two worthy persons,
                         kinsmen, clansmen, of my mate?
Men who never sought to harm you,
                         would you tear and lacerate?
Chorus. Why, I wonder, should we spare them,
                         more than ravening beasts of prey?
Shall we ever find, for vengeance,
                         enemies more rank than they?
Hoopoe. Enemies, I grant, by nature,
                         very friends in heart and will;
Here they come with kindly purpose,
                         useful lessons to instil.
Chorus. What, they come with words of friendship?
                         What, you really then suppose
They will teach us useful lessons,
                         they our fathers' fathers' foes?
Hoopoe. Yet to clever folk a foeman
                         very useful hints may show;
Thus, that foresight brings us safety,
                         from a friend we ne'er should know,
But the truth is forced upon us, very quickly, by a foe.
Hence it is that all the Cities,
                         taught by foe, and not by friend,
Learn to build them ships of battle,
                         and their lofty walls extend;

[618]

So by this, a foeman's, teaching
> children, home, and wealth defend.
Chorus. Well, I really think 'tis better
> that their errand we should know;
I admit that something useful
> may be taught us by a foe.
Peisthetaerus (*to* EUELPIDES). Now their anger grows more
slack;
> now we had better just draw back.
Hoopoe (*to* CHORUS). This is right and friendly conduct,
> such as I deserve from you.
Chorus. Well, I am sure that we have never
> gone against you hitherto.
Peisthetaerus. Now they are growing a deal more peaceful,
> now is the time the pot to ground,
Now we may lower the platters twain.
Nay, but the spit we had best retain,
Walking within the encampment's bound,
Letting our watchful glances skim
Over the edge of the pot's top rim;
Never a thought of flight must strike us.
Euelpides. Well, but tell me, suppose we die,
Where in the world will our bodies lie?
Peisthetaerus. They shall be buried in Cerameicus,
That will be done at the public cost,
For we will say that our lives we lost
Gallantly fighting the public foe,
(Yea, we will tell the commanders so,)
Gallantly fighting at Orneae.
Chorus. Fall back, fall back to your ranks once more,
And stand at ease as ye stood before,
And lay your wrath on the ground, in line
With your angry mood, as a warrior should;
We'll ask the while who the men may be,
And whence they come, and with what design.
Hey, Hoopoe, hey! to you I speak.
Hoopoe. What is it that to learn you seek?
Chorus. Whence are these visitors and who?
Hoopoe. From clever Hellas strangers two.

[619]

Chorus. What's their aim?　Canst thou tell
Why they came　Here to dwell?
Hoopoe. Love of you,　Love of your
Life and ways　Was the lure.
Here they fain　Would remain
Comrades true　　All their days.
Chorus. Hey, hey, what do you say?
What is the tale they tell?
Hoopoe.　　　　In brief,
'Tis something more than past belief.
Chorus. But wherefore is he come? What is it
He seeks to compass by his visit?
Think you he's got some cunning plan
Whereby, allied with us, he can
Assist a friend, or harm a foe?
What brings him here, I'd like to know.
Hoopoe. Too great, too great, for thought or words,
The bliss he promises the birds.
All things are yours, he says, whate'er
Exists in space, both here and there,
And to and fro, and everywhere.
Chorus. Mad a little, eh?
Hoopoe. More sane than words can say.
Chorus. Wide awake?
Hoopoe.　　　　Wide as day.
The subtlest cunningest fox,
All scheme, invention, craft; wit, wisdom, paradox.
Chorus. His speech, his speech, bid him begin it.
The things you show excite me so,
　I'm fit to fly this very minute.
Hoopoe. Now you and you, take back this panoply,
And hang it up, God bless it, out of sight
Within the kitchen there, beside the Jack.
But you (*to* PEISTHETAERUS) the things we summoned them
　to hear
Expound, declare.
　Peisthetaerus.　　By Apollo no, not I,
Unless they pledge me such a treaty-pledge
As that small jackanapes who makes the swords
Pledged with his wife, to wit that they'll not bite me

Nor pull me about, nor scratch my—
   Chorus.   Fie, for shame!
Not *this?* no, no!
   Peisthetaerus.   *My eyes,* I was going to say.
   Chorus. I pledge it.
   Peisthetaerus.   Swear!
   Chorus.   I swear on these conditions:
So may I win by every judge's vote,
And the whole Theater's.
   Peisthetaerus.   AND SO YOU SHALL.
   Chorus. But if I'm false, then by one vote alone.
   Hoopoe. O yes! O yes! Hoplites, take up your arms
And march back homewards; there await the orders
We're going to publish on the notice-boards.
   Chorus. Full of wiles, full of guiles, at all times, in all ways,
Are the children of Men; still we'll hear what he says.
         Thou hast haply detected
Something good for the Birds which we never suspected;
      Some power of achievement, too high
For my own shallow wit by itself to descry.
         But if aught you espy,
Tell it out; for whate'er of advantage shall fall
To ourselves by your aid, shall be common to all.
So expound us the plan you have brought us, my man,
           not doubting, it seems, of success.
And don't be afraid, for the treaty we made
           we won't be the first to transgress.
   Peisthetaerus. I am hot to begin, and my spirit within
           is fermenting the tale to declare.
And my dough I will knead, for there's nought to
           impede. Boy, bring me a wreath for my hair,
And a wash for my hands.
   Euelpides.   Why, what mean these commands?
           Is a dinner in near contemplation?
   Peisthetaerus. No dinner, I ween; 'tis a SPEECH that I mean,
           a stalwart and brawny oration,
Their spirit to batter, and shiver and shatter.
        (*To the Birds*) So sorely I grieve for your lot
Who once in the prime and beginning of time
        were Sovereigns—

Chorus.   We Sovereigns! of what?
Peisthetaerus. Of all that you see; of him and of me;
                              of Zeus up above on his throne;
A lineage older and nobler by far
                    than the Titans and Cronos ye own,
And than Earth.
Chorus. And than Earth!
Peisthetaerus.   By Apollo 'tis true.
Chorus.   And I never had heard it before!
Peisthetaerus. Because you've a blind uninquisitive mind,
                    unaccustomed on Aesop to pore.
The lark had her birth, so he says, before Earth;
                    then her father fell sick and he died.
She laid out his body with dutiful care,
                    but a grave she could nowhere provide;
For the Earth was not yet in existence; at last,
                    by urgent necessity led,
When the fifth day arrived, the poor creature contrived
                    to bury her sire in her head.
Euelpides. So the sire of the lark, give me leave to remark,
                    on the crest of a headland lies dead.
Peisthetaerus. If therefore, by birth, ye are older than Earth,
                    if before all the Gods ye existed,
By the right of the firstborn the scepter is yours;
                    your claim cannot well be resisted.
Euelpides. I advise you to nourish and strengthen your beak,
                    and to keep it in trim for a stroke.
Zeus won't in a hurry the scepter restore
                    to the woodpecker tapping the oak.
Peisthetaerus. In times prehistoric 'tis easily proved,
                    by evidence weighty and ample,
That Birds, and not Gods, were the Rulers of men,
                    and the Lords of the world; for example,
Time was that the Persians were ruled by the Cock,
                    a King autocratic, alone;
The scepter he wielded or ever the names
                    'Megabazus,' 'Darius' were known;
And the 'Persian' he still by the people is called
                    from the Empire that once was his own.

Euelpides. And thus, to this hour, the symbol of power
                  on his head you can always detect:
Like the Sovereign of Persia, alone of the Birds,
                      he stalks with tiara erect.
Peisthetaerus. So mighty and great was his former estate,
                so ample he waxed and so strong,
That still the tradition is potent, and still,
               when he sings in the morning his song,
At once from their sleep all mortals upleap,
             the cobblers, the tanners, the bakers,
The potters, the bathmen, the smiths, and the shield-
             and-the-musical-instrument-makers;
And some will at eve take their sandals and leave.
Euelpides. I can answer for that, to my cost.
'Twas all through his crowing at eve that my cloak,
             the softest of Phrygians, I lost.
I was asked to the Tenth-day feast of a child;
           and I drank ere the feast was begun;
Then I take my repose; and anon the cock crows;
           so thinking it daybreak I run
To return from the City to Halimus town;
           but scarce I emerge from the wall,
When I get such a whack with a stick on my back
           from a rascally thief, that I fall,
And he skims off my cloak from my shoulders or e'er
           for assistance I'm able to bawl.
Peisthetaerus. Then a Kite was the Sovereign of Hellas of
  old,
           and ruled with an absolute sway.
Chorus. The Sovereign of Hellas!
Peisthetaerus.   And, taught by his rule,
           we wallow on earth to this day
When a Kite we espy.
Euelpides.   By Bacchus, 'twas I
           saw a Kite in the air; so I wallow
Then raising my eyne from my posture supine,
           I give such a gulp that I swallow
O what but an obol I've got in my mouth,
           and am forced to return empty-handed.

[623]

Peisthetaerus. And the whole of Phoenice and Egypt was erst
          by a masterful Cuckoo commanded.
When his loud cuckoo-cry was resounding on high,
          at once the Phoenicians would leap
All hands to the plain, rich-waving with grain,
          their wheat and their barley to reap.
Euelpides. So that's why we cry to the circumcised *Hi!*
          Cuckoo! To the plain! Cuckoo!
Peisthetaerus. And whene'er in the cities of Hellas a chief
          to honor and dignity grew,
Menelaus or King Agamemnon perchance,
          your rule was so firm and decided
That a bird on his scepter would perch, to partake
          of the gifts for his Lordship provided.
Euelpides. Now of that I declare I was never aware;
          and I oft have been filled with amaze,
When Priam so noble and stately appeared,
          with a bird, in the Tragedy-plays.
But the bird was no doubt for the gifts looking out,
          to Lysicrates brought on the sly.
Peisthetaerus. But the strongest and clearest of proofs is
  that Zeus
          who at present is Lord of the sky
Stands wearing, as Royalty's emblem and badge,
          an Eagle erect on his head,
Our Lady an owl, and Apollo forsooth,
          as a lackey, a falcon instead.
Euelpides. By Demeter, 'tis true; that is just what they do;
          but tell me the reason, I pray.
Peisthetaerus. That the bird may be ready and able, whene'er
          the sacrificed inwards we lay,
As custom demands, in the deity's hands,
          to seize before Zeus on the fare.
And none by the Gods, but all by the Birds,
          were accustomed aforetime to swear:
And Lampon will vow by the Goose even now,
          whenever he's going to cheat you:
So holy and mighty they deemed you of old,
          with so deep a respect did they treat you!

Now they treat you as knaves,
                                    and as fools, and as slaves;
    Yea they pelt you as though ye were mad.
No safety for you can the Temples ensure,
For the bird-catcher sets his nooses and nets,
And his traps, and his toils, and his bait, and his lure,
And his lime-covered rods in the shrine of the Gods!
Then he takes you, and sets you for sale in the lump;
And the customers, buying, come poking and prying
        And twitching and trying,
To feel if your bodies are tender and plump.
And if they decide on your flesh to sup
They don't just roast you and serve you up,
But over your bodies, as prone ye lie,
They grate their cheese and their silphium too,
        And oil and vinegar add,
Then a gravy, luscious and rich, they brew,
And pour it in soft warm streams o'er you,
As though ye were carrion noisome and dry.
    Chorus. O man. 'tis indeed a most pitiful tale
Thou hast brought to our ears; and I can but bewail
        Our fathers' demerit,
Who born such an Empire as this to inherit
        Have lost it, have lost it, for me!
But now thou art come, by good Fortune's decree,
        Our Saviour to be,
And under thy charge, whatsoever befall,
I will place my own self, and my nestlings, and all.
Now therefore do you tell us what we must do;
                        since life is not worth our retaining,
Unless we be Lords of the world as before,
                        our ancient dominion regaining.
    Peisthetaerus. Then first I propose that the Air ye enclose,
                and the space 'twixt the Earth and the sky,
Encircling it all with a brick-builded wall,
                        like Babylon's, solid and high;
And there you must place the abode of your race,
                and make them one State, and one nation.
    Euelpides. O Porphyrion! O Cebriones!
                    how stupendous the fortification!

Peisthetaerus. When the wall is complete, send a messenger fleet,

                 the empire from Zeus to reclaim.

And if he deny, or be slow to comply,

              nor retreat in confusion and shame,

Proclaim ye against him a Holy War,

                and announce that no longer below,

On their lawless amours through these regions of yours,

                will the Gods be permitted to go.

No more through the air (to their Alopes fair,

              their Alcmenas, their Semeles wending)

May they post in hot love, as of old, from above,

              for if ever you catch them descending,

You will clap on their dissolute persons a seal,

                their evil designs to prevent!

And then let another ambassador-bird

              to men with this message be sent,

That the Birds being Sovereigns, to them must be paid

              all honor and worship divine,

And the Gods for the future to them be postponed.

              Now therefore assort and combine

Each God with a bird, whichever will best

              with his nature and attributes suit;

If to Queen Aphrodite a victim ye slay,

              first sacrifice grain to the coot;

If a sheep to Poseidon ye slay, to the duck

              let wheat as a victim be brought;

And a big honey-cake for the cormorant make,

              if ye offer to Heracles aught.

Bring a ram for King Zeus! But ye first must produce

              for our Kinglet, the gold-crested wren,

A masculine midge, full formed and entire,

              to be sacrificed duly by men.

Euelpides. I am tickled and pleased with the sacrificed midge.

              Now thunder away, great Zan!

Chorus. But men, will they take us for Gods, and not daws,—

              do ye really believe that they can—

If they see us on wings flying idly about?

Peisthetaerus.   Don't say such ridiculous things!
Why, Hermes, and lots of the deities too,
                              go flying about upon wings.
There is Victory, bold on her pinions of gold;
                    and then, by the Powers, there is Love;
And Iris, says Homer, shoots straight through the skies,
                              with the ease of a terrified dove.
Euelpides. And the thunderbolt flies upon wings, I surmise:
                    what if Zeus upon us let it fall?
Peisthetaerus. But suppose that mankind, being stupid and
    blind,
                              should account you as nothing at all,
And still in the Gods of Olympus believe—
                    why then, like a cloud, shall a swarm
Of sparrows and rooks settle down on their stooks,
                    and devour all the seed in the farm.
Demeter may fill them with grain, if she will,
                    when hungry and pinched they entreat her.
Euelpides. O no, for by Zeus, she will make some excuse;
                    that is always the way with Demeter.
Peisthetaerus. And truly the ravens shall pluck out the eyes
                    of the oxen that work in the plough,
Of the flocks and the herds, as a proof that the Birds
                    are the Masters and Potentates now.
Apollo the leech, if his aid they beseech,
                    may cure them; but then they must pay!
Euelpides. Nay but hold, nay but hold, nor begin till I've
    sold
                              my two little oxen I pray.
Peisthetaerus. But when once to esteem you as God, and as
    Life,
                    and as Cronos and Earth they've begun,
And as noble Poseidon, what joys shall be theirs!
Chorus.   Will you kindly inform me of one?
Peisthetaerus. The delicate tendrils and bloom of the vine
                    no more shall the locusts molest,
One gallant brigade of the kestrels and owls
                    shall rid them at once of the pest.
No more shall the mite and the gall-making blight
                    the fruit of the fig-tree devour;

Of thrushes one troop on their armies shall swoop,
>> and clear them all off in an hour.
Chorus. But how shall we furnish the people with wealth?
>> It is wealth that they mostly desire.
Peisthetaerus. Choice blessings and rare ye shall give them
whene'er
>> they come to your shrine to inquire.
To the seer ye shall tell when 'tis lucky and well
>> for a merchant to sail o'er the seas,
So that never a skipper again shall be lost.
Chorus. What, 'never'? Explain if you please.
Peisthetaerus. Are they seeking to know when a voyage
to go?
>> The Birds shall give answers to guide them.
Now stick to the land, there's a tempest at hand!
>> *Now sail!* and good luck shall betide them.
Euelpides. A galley for me; I am off to the sea!
>> No longer with you will I stay.
Peisthetaerus. The treasures of silver long since in the earth
>> by their forefathers hidden away
To men ye shall show, for the secret ye know.
>> How often a man will declare,
There is no one who knows where my treasures repose,
>> *if it be not a bird of the air.*
Euelpides. My galley may go; I will buy me a hoe,
>> and dig for the crock and the casket.
Chorus. But Health, I opine, is a blessing divine;
>> can we give it to men if they ask it?
Peisthetaerus. If they've plenty of wealth, they'll have plenty
of health;
>> ye may rest quite assured that they will.
Did you ever hear tell of a man that was well,
>> when faring remarkably ill?
Chorus. Long life 'tis Olympus alone can bestow;
>> so can men live as long as before?
Must they die in their youth?
Peisthetaerus. Die? No! why in truth
>> their lives by three hundred or more
New years ye will lengthen.
Chorus. Why, whence will they come?

Peisthetaerus. From your own inexhaustible store.
What! dost thou not know that the noisy-tongued crow
                lives five generations of men?
Euelpides. O fie! it is plain they are fitter to reign
                than the Gods; let us have them again.
Peisthetaerus. Ay fitter by far!
No need for their sakes to erect and adorn
Great temples of marble with portals of gold.
Enough for the birds on the brake and the thorn
And the evergreen oak their receptions to hold.
Or if any are noble, and courtly, and fine,
The tree of the olive will serve for their shrine.
No need, when a blessing we seek, to repair
To Delphi or Ammon, and sacrifice there;
We will under an olive or arbutus stand
     With a present of barley and wheat,
And piously lifting our heart and our hand
     The birds for a boon we'll entreat,
And the boon shall be ours, and our suit we shall gain
At the cost of a few little handfuls of grain.

Chorus. I thought thee at first of my foemen the worst;
            and lo, I have found thee the wisest
And best of my friends, and our nation intends
             to do whatsoe'er thou advisest.
     A spirit so lofty and rare
     Thy words have within me excited,
     That I lift up my soul, and I swear
     That if Thou wilt with Me be united
     In bonds that are holy and true
     And honest and just and sincere,
     If our hearts are attuned to one song,
     We will march on the Gods without fear;
     The scepter—MY scepter, MY due,—
     They shall not be handling it long!
So all that by muscle and strength can be done,
            we Birds will assuredly do;
But whatever by prudence and skill must be won,
           we leave altogether to you.

Hoopoe. Aye and, by Zeus, the time is over now
For drowsy nods and Nicias-hesitations.
We must be up and doing! And do you,
Or e'er we start, visit this nest of mine,
My bits of things, my little sticks and straws;
And tell me what your names are.
    Peisthetaerus.   That's soon done.
My name is Peisthetaerus.
    Hoopoe.   And your friend's?
    Peisthetaerus. Euelpides of Crio.
    Hoopoe.   Well, ye are both
Heartily welcome.
    Peisthetaerus.   Thank you.
    Hoopoe.   Come ye in.
    Peisthetaerus. Aye, come we in; you, please, precede us.
    Hoopoe.   Come.
    Peisthetaerus. But—dear! what was it? step you back a
    moment.
O yes,—but tell us, how can he and I
Consort with you, we wingless and you winged?
    Hoopoe. Why, very well.
    Peisthetaerus.   Nay, but in Aesop's fables
There's something, mind you, told about the fox
How ill it fared, consorting with an eagle.
    Hoopoe. O never fear; for there's a little root
Which when ye have eaten, ye will both be winged.
    Peisthetaerus. That being so, we'll enter. Xanthias there,
And Manodorus, bring along the traps.
    Chorus. O stay, and O stay!
    Hoopoe.   Why what ails you to-day?
    Chorus. Take the gentlemen in, and regale them, we say
But O for the nightingale peerless in song,
               who chants in the choir of the Muses her lay;
Our sweetest and best, fetch her out of the nest,
               and leave her awhile with the Chorus to play.
    Peisthetaerus. O do, by Zeus, grant them this one request;
Fetch out the little warbler from the reeds.
    Euelpides. Yes, fetch her out by all the Gods, that so
We too may gaze upon the nightingale.
    Hoopoe. Well, if you wish it, so we'll have it. Procne,

Come hither, dear, and let the strangers see you.

Peisthetaerus. Zeus, what a darling lovely little bird!
How fair, and tender!

Euelpides.   O the little love,
Wouldn't I like to be her mate this instant!

Peisthetaerus. And O the gold she is wearing, like a girl.

Euelpides. Upon my word, I've half a mind to kiss her!

Peisthetaerus. Kiss her, you fool! Her beak's a pair of spits.

Euelpides. But I would treat her like an egg, and strip
The egg-shell from her poll, and kiss her so.

Hoopoe. Come, go we in.

Peisthetaerus.   Lead on, and luck go with us.

Chorus. O darling! O tawny-throat!
          Love, whom I love the best,
          Dearer than all the rest,
          Playmate and partner in
               All my soft lays,
          Thou art come! Thou art come!
          Thou hast dawned on my gaze,
          I have heard thy sweet note,
          Nightingále! Nightingále!
Thou from thy flute   Softly-sounding canst bring
Music to suit   With our songs of the Spring:
          Begin then I pray
     Our own anapaestic address to essay.

Ye men who are dimly existing below,
               who perish and fade as the leaf,
Pale, woebegone, shadowlike, spiritless folk,
               life feeble and wingless and brief,
Frail castings in clay, who are gone in a day,
               like a dream full of sorrow and sighing,
Come listen with care to the Birds of the air,
               the ageless, the deathless, who flying
In the joy and the freshness of Ether, are wont
               to muse upon wisdom undying.
We will tell you of things transcendental; of Springs
               and of Rivers the mighty upheaval;

The nature of Birds; and the birth of the Gods:
        and of Chaos and Darkness primeval.
When this ye shall know, let old Prodicus go,
        and be hanged without hope of reprieval.
THERE WAS Chaos at first, and Darkness, and Night,
        and Tartarus vasty and dismal;
But the Earth was not there, nor the Sky, nor the Air,
        till at length in the bosom abysmal
Of Darkness an egg, from the whirlwind conceived,
        was laid by the sable-plumed Night.
And out of that egg, as the Seasons revolved,
        sprang Love, the entrancing, the bright,
Love brilliant and bold with his pinions of gold,
        like a whirlwind, refulgent and sparkling!
Love hatched us, commingling in Tartarus wide,
        with Chaos, the murky, the darkling,
And brought us above, as the firstlings of love,
        and first to the light we ascended.
There was never a race of Immortals at all
        till Love had the universe blended;
Then all things commingling together in love,
        there arose the fair Earth, and the Sky,
And the limitless Sea; and the race of the Gods,
        the Blessed, who never shall die.
So we than the Blessed are older by far;
        and abundance of proof is existing
That we are the children of Love, for we fly,
        unfortunate lovers assisting.
And many a man who has found, to his cost,
        that his powers of persuasion have failed,
And his loves have abjured him for ever, again
        by the power of the Birds has prevailed;
For the gift of a quail, or a Porphyry rail,
        or a Persian, or goose, will regain them.
And the chiefest of blessings ye mortals enjoy,
        by the help of the Birds ye obtain them.
'Tis from us that the signs of the Seasons in turn,
        Spring, Winter, and Autumn are known.
When to Libya the crane flies clanging again,
        it is time for the seed to be sown,

And the skipper may hang up his rudder awhile,
                    and sleep after all his exertions,
And Orestes may weave him a wrap to be warm
                    when he's out on his thievish excursions.
Then cometh the kite, with its hovering flight,
                    of the advent of Spring to tell,
And the Spring sheep-shearing begins; and next,
                    your woolen attire you sell,
And buy you a lighter and daintier garb,
                    when you note the return of the swallow.
Thus your Ammon, Dodona, and Delphi are we;
                    we are also your Phoebus Apollo.
For whatever you do, if a trade you pursue,
                    or goods in the market are buying,
Or the wedding attend of a neighbor and friend,
                    first you look to the Birds and their flying.
And whene'er you of omen or augury speak,
                    'tis a bird you are always repeating;
A Rumor's a bird, and a sneeze is a bird,
                    and so is a word or a meeting,
A servant's a bird, and an ass is a bird.
                    It must therefore assuredly follow
That the Birds are to you (I protest it is true)
                    your prophetic divining Apollo.

Then take us for Gods, as is proper and fit,
And Muses Prophetic ye'll have at your call
Spring, winter, and summer, and autumn and all.
And we won't run away from your worship, and sit
Up above in the clouds, very stately and grand,
Like Zeus in his tempers: but always at hand
Health and wealth we'll bestow, as the formula runs,
On yourselves, and your sons, and the sons of your
    sons;
And happiness, plenty, and peace shall belong
To you all; and the revel, the dance, and the song,
And laughter, and youth, and the milk of the birds
    We'll supply, and we'll never forsake you.
Ye'll be quite overburdened with pleasures and joys,
    So happy and blest we will make you.

·O woodland Muse,
   tío, tio, tío, tiotinx,
Of varied plume, with whose dear aid
On the mountain top, and the sylvan glade,
   tío, tio, tío, tiotinx,
I, sitting up aloft on a leafy ash, full oft,
   tío, tio, tío, tiotinx,
Pour forth a warbling note from my little tawny throat,
Pour festive choral dances to the mountain mother's praise,
And to Pan the holy music of his own immortal lays;
   totótotótotótotótotinx,
   Whence Phrynichus of old,
   Sipping the fruit of our ambrosial lay,
   Bore, like a bee, the honied store away,
   His own sweet songs to mould.
   tio, tío, tio, tío, tiotinx.

Is there anyone amongst you,
          O spectators, who would lead
With the birds a life of pleasure,
          let him come to us with speed.
All that here is reckoned shameful,
          all that here the laws condemn,
With the birds is right and proper,
          you may do it all with them.
Is it here by law forbidden
          for a son to beat his sire?
That a chick should strike his father,
          strutting up with youthful ire,
Crowing *Raise your spur and fight me,*
          that is what the birds admire.
Come you runaway deserter,
          spotted o'er with marks of shame,
Spotted Francolin we'll call you,
          that, with us, shall be your name.
You who style yourself a tribesman,
          Phrygian pure as Spintharus,
Come and be a Phrygian linnet,
          of Philemon's breed, with us.

Come along, you slave and Carian,

                             Execestides to wit,

Breed with us your Cuckoo-rearers,

                         they'll be guildsmen apt and fit.

Son of Peisias, who to outlaws

                           would the city gates betray,

Come to us, and be a partridge

                       (*cockerel like the cock,* they say),

We esteem it no dishonor

                       knavish partridge-tricks to play.

    Even thus the Swans,

      tío, tio, tío, tiotinx,

  Their clamorous cry were erst up-raising,

  With clatter of wings Apollo praising,

      tío, tio, tío, tiotinx,

As they sat in serried ranks on the river Hebrus' banks.

      tío, tio, tío, tiotinx,

Right upward went the cry

               through the cloud and through the sky.

Quailed the wild-beast in his covert,

                   and the bird within her nest,

And the still and windless Ether

                lulled the ocean-waves to rest.

   totótotótotótotótotinx,

    Loudly Olympus rang!

Amazement seized the kings; and every Grace

And every Muse within that heavenly place

    Took up the strain, and sang.

    tio, tío, tio, tío, tiotinx.

Truly to be clad in feather

                is the very best of things.

Only fancy, dear spectators,

                 had you each a brace of wings,

Never need you, tired and hungry,

                   at a Tragic Chorus stay,

You would lightly, when it bored you,

                 spread your wings and fly away,

Back returning, after luncheon,

                 to enjoy our Comic Play.

Never need a Patrocleides,
> sitting here, his garment stain;
When the dire occasion seized him,
> he would off with might and main
Flying home, then flying hither,
> lightened and relieved, again.
If a gallant should the husband
> on the Council-bench behold
Of a gay and charming lady,
> one whom he had loved of old,
Off at once he'd fly to greet her,
> have a little converse sweet,
Then be back, or e'er ye missed him,
> calm and smiling in his seat.
Is not then a suit of feathers
> quite the very best of things?
Why, Diitrephes was chosen,
> though he had but wicker wings,
First a Captain, then a Colonel,
> till from nothing he of late
Has become a tawny cock-horse,
> yea a pillar of the State!

Peisthetaerus. Well, here we are. By Zeus, I never saw
In all my life a sight more laughable.
Euelpides. What are you laughing at?
Peisthetaerus. At your flight-feathers.
I'll tell you what you're like, your wings and you,
Just like a gander, sketched by some cheap-Jack.
Euelpides. And you, a blackbird, with a bowl-cropped
noddle.
Peisthetaerus. These shafts of ridicule are winged by nought
But our own plumes, as Aeschylus would say.
Chorus. What's the next step?
Peisthetaerus. First we must give the city
Some grand big name: and then we'll sacrifice
To the high Gods.
Euelpides. That's my opinion also.
Chorus. Then let's consider what the name shall be.

Peisthetaerus. What think you of that grand Laconian name,
Sparta?
Euelpides.   What! Sparta for my city? No.
I wouldn't use esparto for my pallet,
Not if I'd cords; by Heracles, not I.
Peisthetaerus. How shall we name it then?
Chorus.   Invent some fine
Magniloquent name, drawn from these upper spaces
And clouds.
Peisthetaerus.   What think you of Cloudcuckoobury?
Chorus. Good! Good!
You have found a good big name, and no mistake.
Euelpides. Is this the great Cloudcuckoobury town
Where all the wealth of Aeschines lies hid,
And all Theagenes's?
Peisthetaerus.   Best of all,
This is the plain of Phlegra, where the Gods
Outshot the giants at the game of Brag.
Euelpides. A glistering sort of a city? Who shall be
Its guardian God? For whom shall we weave the Peplus?
Peisthetaerus. Why not retain Athene, City-keeper?
Euelpides. And how can that be a well-ordered State,
Where she, a woman born, a Goddess, stands
Full-armed, and Cleisthenes assumes a spindle?
Peisthetaerus. And who shall hold the citadel's Storkade?
Chorus. A bird of ours, one of the Persian breed,
Everywhere noted as the War-god's own
Armipotent cockerel.
Euelpides.   O, Prince Cockerel? Yes,
He's just the God to perch upon the rocks.
Peisthetaerus. Now, comrade, get you up into the air,
And lend a hand to those that build the wall.
Bring up the rubble; strip, and mix the mortar;
Run up the ladder with the hod; fall off;
Station the sentinels; conceal the fire;
Round with the alarum bell; go fast asleep;
And send two heralds, one to heaven above,
And one to earth below; and let them come
From thence, for me.
Euelpides.   And you, remaining here,

Be hanged—for me!

Peisthetaerus.　　　Go where I send you, comrade,
Without your help there, nothing will be done.
But I, to sacrifice to these new Gods,
Must call the priest to regulate the show.
Boy! Boy! take up the basket and the laver.

Chorus. I'M WITH you, you'll find me quite willing:
　　　I highly approve of your killing
　　　A lambkin, to win us the favor divine,
　　　Mid holy processionals, stately and fine.
　　　Up high, up high, let the Pythian cry,
　　　The Pythian cry to the God be sent;
　　　Let Chaeris play the accompaniment.

Peisthetaerus. O stop that puffing! Heracles, what's this?
Faith, I've seen many a sight, but never yet
A mouth-band-wearing raven! Now then, priest,
To the new Gods commence the sacrifice.
　　　Priest. I'll do your bidding. Where's the basket-bearer?
　　　　　　　Let us pray
To the Hestia-bird of the household shrine,
And the Kite that watches her feasts divine,
And to all the Olympian birds and birdesses,
　　　Peisthetaerus. O Sunium-hawking, King of the Sea—mew,
　　　　hail!
　　　Priest. And to the holy Swan, the Pythian and Delian one,
And to thee too, Quail-guide Leto,
And to Artemis the Thistle-finch,
　　　Peisthetaerus. Aye, Thistle-finch; no more Colaenis now!
　　　Priest. And to Sabazius the Phrygian linnet; and then
To Rhea the Great Mother of Gods and men;
　　　Peisthetaerus. Aye, Ostrich-queen, Cleocritus's Mother!
　　　Priest. That they may grant health and salvation
To the whole Cloudcuckooburian nation,
　　　For themselves and the Chians,
　　　Peisthetaerus. I like the Chians everywhere tacked on.
　　　Priest. And to the hero-birds and sons of heroes,
And to the Porphyrion rail;
And to the pelican white, and pelican gray;

And to the eagle, and to the capercaillie;
And to the peacock, and to the sedgewarbler;
And to the teal, and to the skua;
And to the heron, and to the gannet;
And to the blackcap, and to the titmouse;—
    Peisthetaerus. Stop, stop your calling, hang you. O, look
    here.
To what a victim, idiot, are you calling
Ospreys and vultures? Don't you see that one
One single kite could carry off the whole?
Get away hence, you and your garlands too!
Myself alone will sacrifice this victim.

    Chorus. ONCE MORE as the laver they're bringing,
        Once more I my hymns must be singing,
        Hymns holy and pious, the Gods to invite—
        One alone, only one,—to our festival rite.
        Your feast for two, I am sure won't do.
        For what you are going to offer there.
        Is nothing at all but horns and hair.

    Peisthetaerus. Let us pray,
Offering our victim to the feathery gods.

    Poet (*singing*). Cloudcuckoobury
              With praise and glory crown,
        Singing, O Muse,
              Of the new and happy town!
    Peisthetaerus. Whatever's this? Why, who in the world are
    you?
    Poet. O I'm a warbler, carolling sweet lays,
        An eager meager servant of the Muses,
          As Homer says.
    Peisthetaerus. What! you a slave and wear your hair so
    long?
    Poet. No, but all we who teach sweet choral lays
        Are eager meager servant of the Muses,
          As Homer says.
    Peisthetaerus. That's why your cloak so meager seems, no
    doubt.

But, poet, what ill wind has blown you hither?

Poet. Oh I've been making, making lovely songs,
Simonideans, virgin songs, and sweet
Dithyrambic songs, on your Cloudcuckooburies.

Peisthetaerus. When did you first begin these lovely songs?

Poet. Long, long ago, O yes! Long, long ago!

Peisthetaerus. Why, is not this the City's Tenth-day feast?
I've just this instant given the child its name.

Poet. But fleet, as the merry many-twinkling horses' feet,
The airy fairy Rumor of the Muses.
Aetna's Founder, father mine,
Whose name is the same as the holy altar flame,
Give to me what thy bounty chooses
To give me willingly of thine.

Peisthetaerus. He'll cause us trouble now, unless we give him
Something, and so get off. Hallo, you priest,
Why, you've a jerkin and a tunic too;
Strip, give the jerkin to this clever poet.
Take it; upon my word you *do* seem cold.

Poet. This little kindly gift the Muse
Accepts with willing condescension;
But let me to an apt remark
Of Pindar call my lord's attention.

Peisthetaerus. The fellow does not seem inclined to leave us.

Poet. Out among the Scythians yonder
See poor Straton wander, wander,
Poor poor Straton, not possessed
of a whirly-woven vest.
All inglorious comes, I trow, leather jerkin, if below
No soft tunic it can show.
Conceive my drift, I pray.

Peisthetaerus. Aye, I conceive you want the tunic too.
Off with it, you. Needs must assist a Poet.
There, take it, and depart.

Poet.   Yes, I'll depart,
And make to the city pretty songs like this;
O Thou of the golden throne,
Sing Her, the quivering, shivering;
I came to the plains many-sown,

I came to the snowy, the blowy.
      Alalae!
Peisthetaerus. Well, well, but now you surely have escaped
From all those shiverings, with that nice warm vest.
This is, by Zeus, a plague I never dreamed of
That he should find our city out so soon.
Boy, take the laver and walk round once more.
Now hush!
    Oracle-Monger. Forbear! touch not the goat awhile.
    Peisthetaerus. Eh? Who are you?
    Oracle-Monger.   A soothsayer.
    Peisthetaerus.   You be hanged!
    Oracle-Monger. O think not lightly, friend, of things divine;
Know I've an oracle of Bakis, bearing
On your Cloudcuckooburies.
    Peisthetaerus.   Eh? then why
Did you not soothsay that before I founded
My city here?
    Oracle-Monger.   The Power within forbade me.
    Peisthetaerus. Well, well, there's nought like hearing what
      it says.
    Oracle-Monger. 𝕹𝖆𝖞 𝖇𝖚𝖙 𝖎𝖋 𝖔𝖓𝖈𝖊 𝖌𝖗𝖆𝖞 𝖈𝖗𝖔𝖜𝖘
                      𝖆𝖓𝖉 𝖜𝖔𝖑𝖇𝖊𝖘 𝖘𝖍𝖆𝖑𝖑 𝖇𝖊 𝖇𝖆𝖓𝖉𝖎𝖓𝖌 𝖙𝖔𝖌𝖊𝖙𝖍𝖊𝖗,
𝕺𝖚𝖙 𝖎𝖓 𝖙𝖍𝖊 𝖒𝖎𝖉𝖜𝖆𝖞 𝖘𝖕𝖆𝖈𝖊,
                      𝖙𝖜𝖎𝖝𝖙 𝕮𝖔𝖗𝖎𝖓𝖙𝖍 𝖆𝖓𝖉 𝕾𝖎𝖈𝖞𝖔𝖓, 𝖉𝖜𝖊𝖑𝖑𝖎𝖓𝖌,
    Peisthetaerus. But what in the world have I to do with
      Corinth?
    Oracle-Monger. Bakis is riddling: Bakis means the Air.
𝕱𝖎𝖗𝖘𝖙 𝖙𝖔 𝕻𝖆𝖓𝖉𝖔𝖗𝖆 𝖔𝖋𝖋𝖊𝖗
                      𝖆 𝖜𝖍𝖎𝖙𝖊-𝖋𝖑𝖊𝖊𝖈𝖊𝖉 𝖗𝖆𝖒 𝖋𝖔𝖗 𝖆 𝖛𝖎𝖈𝖙𝖎𝖒.
𝕹𝖊𝖝𝖙, 𝖜𝖍𝖔 𝖋𝖎𝖗𝖘𝖙 𝖘𝖍𝖆𝖑𝖑 𝖆𝖗𝖗𝖎𝖛𝖊
                      𝖒𝖞 𝖛𝖊𝖗𝖘𝖊𝖘 𝖕𝖗𝖔𝖕𝖍𝖊𝖙𝖎𝖈 𝖊𝖝𝖕𝖔𝖚𝖓𝖉𝖎𝖓𝖌,
𝕲𝖎𝖛𝖊 𝖍𝖎𝖒 𝖆 𝖇𝖗𝖆𝖓𝖉=𝖓𝖊𝖜 𝖈𝖑𝖔𝖆𝖐
                      𝖆𝖓𝖉 𝖆 𝖕𝖆𝖎𝖗 𝖔𝖋 𝖊𝖝𝖈𝖊𝖑𝖑𝖊𝖓𝖙 𝖘𝖆𝖓𝖉𝖆𝖑𝖘.
    Peisthetaerus. Are sandals in it?
    Oracle-Monger.   Take the book and see.
𝕲𝖎𝖛𝖊 𝖍𝖎𝖒 𝖒𝖔𝖗𝖊𝖔𝖛𝖊𝖗 𝖆 𝖈𝖚𝖕,
                      𝖆𝖓𝖉 𝖋𝖎𝖑𝖑 𝖍𝖎𝖘 𝖍𝖆𝖓𝖉𝖘 𝖜𝖎𝖙𝖍 𝖙𝖍𝖊 𝖎𝖓𝖜𝖆𝖗𝖉𝖘.
    Peisthetaerus. Are inwards in it?
    Oracle-Monger.   Take the book and see.
𝕻𝖔𝖚𝖙𝖍, 𝖉𝖎𝖛𝖎𝖓𝖊𝖑𝖞 𝖎𝖓𝖘𝖕𝖎𝖗𝖊𝖉,
                      𝖎𝖋 𝖙𝖍𝖔𝖚 𝖉𝖔𝖘𝖙 𝖆𝖘 𝕴 𝖇𝖎𝖉, 𝖙𝖍𝖔𝖚 𝖘𝖍𝖆𝖑𝖙 𝖘𝖚𝖗𝖊𝖑𝖞
𝕾𝖔𝖆𝖗 𝖎𝖓 𝖙𝖍𝖊 𝖈𝖑𝖔𝖚𝖉𝖘 𝖆𝖘 𝖆𝖓 𝕰𝖆𝖌𝖑𝖊;
                      𝖗𝖊𝖋𝖚𝖘𝖊, 𝖆𝖓𝖉 𝖙𝖍𝖔𝖚 𝖓𝖊'𝖊𝖗 𝖘𝖍𝖆𝖑𝖙 𝖇𝖊𝖈𝖔𝖒𝖊 𝖆𝖓

𝔈agle, or even a dove,

> or a woodpecker tapping the oak-tree.

Peisthetaerus. Is all that in it?

Oracle-Monger. Take the book and see.

Peisthetaerus. O how unlike your oracle to mine,
Which from Apollo's words I copied out;
But if a cheat, an impostor,

> presume to appear uninvited,

𝔗roubling the sacred rites,

> and lusting to taste of the inwards,

ℌit him betwixt the ribs

> with all your force and your fury.

Oracle-Monger. You're jesting surely.

Peisthetaerus. Take the book and see.

𝔖ee that ye spare not the rogue,

> though he soar in the clouds as an 𝔈agle,

𝔜ea, be he 𝔏ampon himself

> or even the great 𝔇iopeithes.

Oracle-Monger. Is all that in it?

Peisthetaerus. Take the book and see.
Get out! be off, confound you!

> [*Striking him.*

Oracle-Monger. O! O! O!

Peisthetaerus. There, run away and soothsay somewhere else.

Meton. I come amongst you—

Peisthetaerus. Some new misery this!
Come to do what? What's your scheme's form and outline?
What's your design? What buskin's on your foot?

Meton. I come to land-survey this Air of yours,
And mete it out by acres.

Peisthetaerus. Heaven and Earth!
Whoever are you?

Meton (scandalized). Whoever am I! I'm METON,
Known throughout Hellas and Colonus.

Peisthetaerus. Aye,
And what are *these?*

Meton. They're rods for Air-surveying.
I'll just explain. The Air's, in outline, like
One vast extinguisher; so then, observe,
Applying here my flexible rod, and fixing
My compass there,—you understand?

Peisthetaerus. I don't.

Meton. With the straight rod I measure out, that so

The circle may be squared; and in the center
A market-place; and streets be leading to it
Straight to the very center; just as from
A star, though circular, straight rays flash out
In all directions.

    Peisthetaerus.   Why, the man's a Thales!
Meton!

    Meton.   Yes, what?

    Peisthetaerus.   You know I love you, Meton,
Take my advice, and slip away unnoticed.

    Meton. Why, what's the matter?

    Peisthetaerus.   As in Lacedaemon
There's stranger-hunting; and a great disturbance;
And blows in plenty.

    Meton.   What, a Revolution?

    Peisthetaerus. No, no, not that.

    Meton.   What then?

    Peisthetaerus.   They've all resolved
With one consent to wallop every quack.

    Meton. I'd best be going.

    Peisthetaerus.   Faith, I'm not quite certain
If you're in time; see, see the blows are coming!

                       [*Striking him.*

    Meton. O, murder! help!

    Peisthetaerus.   I told you how 'twould be.
Come, measure off your steps some other way.

    Commissioner. Ho! consuls, ho!

    Peisthetaerus.   Sardanapalus, surely!

    Commissioner. Lo, I to your Cloudcuckooburies come,
By lot Commissioner.

    Peisthetaerus.   Commissioner?
Who sent you hither?

    Commissioner.   Lo, a paltry scroll
Of Teleas.

    Peisthetaerus.   Come now, will you take your pay
And get you gone in peace?

    Commissioner.   By heaven I will.
I ought to be at home on public business,
Some little jobs I've had with Pharnaces.

Peisthetaerus. Then take your pay, and go: your pay's just—
this.

[*Striking him.*

Commissioner. What's that?

Peisthetaerus. A motion about Pharnaces.

Commissioner. Witness! he's striking a Commissioner.

Peisthetaerus. Shoo! shoo! begone; you and your verdict-
urns.
The shame it is! They send Commissioners
Before we've finished our inaugural rites.

Statute-Seller (*reading*). *But if the Cloudcuckooburian
wrong the Athenian–*

Peisthetaerus. Here's some more writing. What new misery's
this?

Statute-Seller. I am a Statute-seller, and I'm come
Bringing new laws to sell you.

Peisthetaerus. Such as what?

*Statute-Seller. Item, the Cloudcuckooburians are to use the
selfsame weights and measures, and the selfsame
coinage as the Olophyxians.*

Peisthetaerus. And you the selfsame as the Oh! Oh! -tyxians.

[*Striking him.*

Statute-Seller. Hi! what are you at?

Peisthetaerus. Take off those laws, you rascal.
Laws you won't like I'll give you in a minute.

Commissioner (*reappearing*). I summon Peisthetaerus for
next Munychion on a charge of outrage.

Peisthetaerus. O that's it, is it? What, are you there still?

Statute-Seller (*reappearing*). *Item, if any man drive away
the magistrates, and do not receive them according to
the pillar—*

Peisthetaerus. O mercy upon us, and are *you* there still?

Commissioner (*reappearing*). I'll ruin you! I claim ten
thousand drachmas!

Peisthetaerus. I'll overturn your verdict-urn, I will.

Statute-Seller (*reappearing*). Think of that evening when
you fouled the pillar.

Peisthetaerus. Ugh! seize him, somebody! Ha, you're off
there, are you?

Let's get away from this, and go within,
And there we'll sacrifice the goat in peace.

   Chorus. Unto me, the All-controlling,
       . All-surveying,
   Now will men, at every altar,
      Prayers be praying;
   Me who watch the land, protecting
      Fruit and flower,
   Slay the myriad-swarming insects
   Who the tender buds devour
  In the earth and on the branches
                    with a never-satiate malice,
Nipping off the blossom as it widens from the chalice.
   And I slay the noisome creatures
      Which consume
  And pollute the garden's freshly scented bloom;
And every little biter, and every creeping thing
Perish in destruction at the onset of my wing.
Listen to the City's notice,
                   specially proclaimed to-day:
Sirs, Diagoras the Melian
                  whosoever of you slay,
Shall receive, reward, one talent;
               and another we'll bestow
If you slay some ancient tyrant,
               dead and buried long ago.
We, the Birds, will give a notice,
             we proclaim with right good will,
Sirs, Philocrates, Sparrovian,
             whosoever of you kill,
Shall receive, reward, one talent,
           if alive you bring him, four;
Him who strings and sells the finches,
          seven an obol, at his store,
Blows the thrushes out and, rudely,
         to the public gaze exposes,
Shamefully entreats the blackbirds,
        thrusting feathers up their noses.
                  [645]

Pigeons too the rascal catches,
keeps and mews them up with care,
Makes them labor as decoy-birds,
tethered underneath a snare.
Such the notice we would give you.
And we wish you all to know,
Who are keeping birds in cages,
you had better let them go.
Else the Birds will surely catch you,
and yourselves in turn employ,
Tied and tethered up securely,
other rascals to decoy.

O the happy clan of birds
Clad in feather;
Needing not a woollen vest in
Wintry weather;
Heeding not the warm far-flashing
Summer ray,
For within the leafy bosoms
Of the flowery meads I stay,
When the Chirruper in ecstasy
is shrilling forth his tune,
Maddened with the sunshine,
and the rapture of the noon.
And I winter in the caverns'
Hollow spaces,
With the happy Oreads playing; and in Spring
I crop the virgin flowers of the myrtles white and tender,
Dainties that are fashioned in the gardens of the Graces.

Now we wish to tell the Judges,
in a friendly sort of way,
All the blessings we shall give them
if we gain the prize to-day.
Ne'er were made to Alexander
lovelier promises or grander.
First, what every Judge amongst you
most of all desires to win,
Little Lauriotic owlets
shall be always flocking in.

Ye shall find them all about you,
>> as the dainty brood increases,
Building nests within your purses,
>> hatching little silver pieces.
Then as if in stately Temples
>> shall your happy lives be spent,
For the birds will top your mansions
>> with the Eagle pediment.
If you hold some petty office,
>> if you wish to steal and pick,
In your hands we'll place a falcon,
>> very keen and small and quick.
If a dinner is in question,
>> crops we'll send you for digestion.
But should you the prize deny us,
>> you had better all prepare,
Like the statues in the open,
>> little copper disks to wear;
Else whene'er abroad ye're walking,
>> clad in raiment white and new,
Angry birds will wreak their vengeance,
>> spattering over it and you.

Peisthetaerus. Dear Birds, our sacrifice is most auspicious.
But strange it is, no messenger has come
From the great wall we are building, with the news.
Hah! here runs one with true Alpheian pantings.
Messenger. Where, where,—O where, where, where,—
>> O where, where, where,
Where, where's our leader Peisthetaerus?
Peisthetaerus. Here.
Messenger. Your building's built! The wall's complete!
Peisthetaerus. Well done.
Messenger. And a most grand, magnificent work it is.
So broad, that on its top the Braggadocian
Proxenides could pass Theagenes
Each driving in his chariot, drawn by horses
As bulky as the Trojan.
Peisthetaerus. Heracles!
Messenger. And then its height, I measured that, is just

Six hundred feet.

    Peisthetaerus.   Poseidon, what a height!
Who built it up to that enormous size?

    Messenger. The birds, none other; no Egyptian, bearing
The bricks, no mason, carpenter was there;
Their own hands wrought it, marvelous to see.
From Libya came some thirty thousand cranes
With great foundation-stones they had swallowed down;
And these the corn-crakes fashioned with their beaks.
Ten thousand storks were carrying up the bricks;
And lapwings helped, and the other water-birds,
To bring the water up into the air.

    Peisthetaerus. Who bare aloft the mortar for them?

    Messenger.   ·   Herons
In hods.

    Peisthetaerus.   But how did they get the mortar in?

    Messenger. O that was most ingeniously contrived.
The geese struck down their feet, and slid them under,
Like shovels, and so heaved it on the hods.

    Peisthetaerus. Then is there anything that FEET can't do!

    Messenger. And then the ducks, with girdles round their
        waists,
Carried the bricks: and up the swallows flew,
Like serving-lads, carrying behind them each
His trowel, and the mortar in their mouths.

    Peisthetaerus. Then why should men hire hirelings any
        more!
Well, well, go on; who was it finished off
The great wall's woodwork?

    Messenger.   Canny Pelicans,
Excellent workmen, hewing with huge beaks
Gate-timber; and the uproar as they hewed
Was like an arsenal when ships are building.
Now every gateway has its gate, fast-barred,
And watched the whole way round; and birds are pacing
Their beats, and carrying bells, and everywhere
The guards are stationed, and the beacons blaze
On every tower. But I must hurry off
And wash myself. You, manage what remains.

    Chorus. O man, what ails you? Do you feel surprised

To hear the building has been built so soon?
Peisthetaerus. By all the Gods I do; and well I may.
In very truth it seems to me like—lies.
But see! a guard, a messenger from thence
Is running towards us with a war-dance look!
 Guard. Hallo! Hallo! Hallo! Hallo! Hallo!
 Peisthetaerus. Why, what's up now?
 Guard.   A terrible thing has happened.
One of the Gods, of Zeus's Gods, has just,
Giving our jackdaw sentinels the slip,
Shot through the gates and flown into the air.
 Peisthetaerus. A dreadful deed! A wicked scandalous deed!
Which of the Gods?
 Guard.   We know not. Wings he had,
So much we know.
 Peisthetaerus.   Ye should have sent at once
The civic guard in hot pursuit.
 Guard.   We sent
The mounted archers, thirty thousand falcons,
All with their talons curved, in fighting trim,
Hawk, buzzard, vulture, eagle, eagle-owl.
Yea, Ether vibrates with the whizz and whirr
Of beating pinions, as they seek the God.
Ay, and he's near methinks; he's very near;
He's somewhere here.
 Peisthetaerus.   A sling, a sling, I say!
Arrows and bows! Fall in, my merrymen all!
Shoot, smite, be resolute. A sling! a sling!
 Chorus. War is begun, inexpressive war,
   War is begun twixt the Gods and me!
   Look out, look out, through the cloud-wrapt air
   Which erst the Darkness of Erebus bare,
   Lest a God slip by, and we fail to see.
   Glance eager-eyed on every side,
  For close at hand the wingèd sound I hear
  Of some Immortal hurtling through the Sky.

 Peisthetaerus. Hoi! whither away there? whither away?
  Stop! stop!
Stop where you are! keep quiet! stay remain!

Who, what, whence are you? where do you come from? Quick!
Iris. Whence do I come? From the Olympian Gods.
Peisthetaerus. Your name! What is it? Sloop or Head-dress?
Iris.   Iris
The fleet.
Peisthetaerus.   The Paralus, or the Salaminian?
Iris. Why, what's all this?
Peisthetaerus.   Fly up, some buzzard there,
Fly up, and seize her.
Iris.   Me! Seize ME, do you say?
What the plague's this?
Peisthetaerus.   You'll find to your cost, directly.
Iris. Well now, this passes!
Peisthetaerus.   Answer! By what gates
Got you within the city wall, Miss Minx?
Iris. I' faith, I know not, fellow, by what gates.
Peisthetaerus. You hear the jade, how she prevaricates!
Saw you the daw-commanders? What, no answer?
Where's your stork-pass?
Iris.   My patience, what do you mean?
Peisthetaerus. You never got one?
Iris.   Have you lost your wits?
Peisthetaerus. Did no bird-captain stick a label on you?
Iris. On ME? None stuck a label, wretch, on ME.
Peisthetaerus. So then you thought in this sly stealthy way
To fly through Chaos and a realm not yours?
Iris. And by what route, then, ought the Gods to fly?
Peisthetaerus. I' faith, I know not. Only not by this.
This is a trespass! If you got your rights,
Of all the Irises that ever were
You'd be most justly seized and put to death.
Iris. But I am deathless.
Peisthetaerus.   All the same for that
You should have died. A pretty thing, forsooth,
If, whilst all else obey us, you the Gods
Run riot, and forget that you in turn
Must learn to yield obedience to your betters.
But tell me, where do you navigate your wings?
Iris. I? From the Father to mankind I'm flying,
To bid them on their bullock-slaughtering hearths

Slay sheep to the Olympian Gods, and steam
The streets with savor.
>   *Peisthetaerus.*   What do you say? What Gods?
>   *Iris.* What Gods? To us, the Gods in Heaven, of course.
>   *Peisthetaerus* (*with supreme contempt*). What, are YOU
>   Gods?
>   *Iris.*   What other Gods exist?
>   *Peisthetaerus.* Birds are now Gods to men; and men must
>   slay

Victims to them; and not, by Zeus, to Zeus.
>   *Iris.* O fool, fool, fool! Stir not the mighty wrath

Of angry Gods, lest Justice, with the spade
Of vengeful Zeus, demolish all thy race,
And fiery vapor, with Licymnian strokes,
Incinerate thy palace and thyself!
>   *Peisthetaerus.* Now listen, girl; have done with that bombast.

(Don't move.) A Lydian or a Phrygian is it,
You think to terrify with words like those?
Look here. If Zeus keep troubling me, I'll soon
Incinerate his great Amphion's domes
And halls of state with eagles carrying fire.
And up against him, to high heaven, I'll send
More than six hundred stout Porphyrion rails
All clad in leopard-skins. Yet I remember
When one Porphyrion gave him toil enough.
And as for you, his waiting-maid, if you
Keep troubling me with your outrageous ways,
I'll outrage *you*, and you'll be quite surprised
To find the strength of an old man like me.
>   *Iris.* O shame upon you, wretch, your words and you.
>   *Peisthetaerus.* Now then begone; shoo, shoo! Eurax patax!
>   *Iris.* My father won't stand this; I vow he won't.
>   *Peisthetaerus.* Now Zeus-a-mercy, maiden; fly you off,

Incinerate some younger man than I.
>   *Chorus.* Never again shall the Zeus-born Gods,
>   Never again shall they pass this way!
>   Never again through this realm of ours
>   Shall men send up to the heavenly Powers
>   The savor of beasts which on earth they slay!

Peisthetaerus. Well but that herald whom we sent to men,
'Tis strange if he should nevermore return.

Herald. O Peisthetaerus, O thou wisest, best,
Thou wisest, deepest, happiest of mankind,
Most glorious, most—O give the word!

Peisthetaerus.   What news?

Herald. Accept this golden crown, wherewith all peoples
Crown and revere thee for thy wisdom's sake!

Peisthetaerus. I do. What makes them all revere me so?

Herald. O thou who hast built the ethereal glorious city,
Dost thou not know how men revere thy name,
And burn with ardor for this realm of thine?
Why, till ye built this city in the air,
All men had gone Laconian-mad; they went
Long-haired, half-starved, unwashed, Socratified,
With scytales in their hands; but O the change!
They are all bird-mad now, and imitate
The birds, and joy to do whate'er birds do.
Soon as they rise from bed at early dawn,
They settle down on laws, as we on lawns,
And then they brood upon their leaves and leaflets,
And feed their fill upon a crop of statutes.
So undisguised their madness, that full oft
The names of birds are fastened on to men.
One limping tradesman now is known as 'Partridge';
They dub Menippus 'Swallow'; and Opuntius
'Blind Raven'; Philocles is 'Crested Lark,'
Theagenes is nicknamed 'Sheldrake' now;
Lycurgus 'Ibis'; Chaerephon the 'Vampire';
And Syracosius 'Jay'; whilst Meidias there
Is called the 'Quail'; aye and he's like a quail
Flipped on the head by some quail-filliper.
So fond they are of birds that all are singing
Songs where a swallow figures in the verse,
Or goose, or may-be widgeon, or ring-dove,
Or wings, or even the scantiest shred of feather.
So much from earth. And let me tell you this;
More than ten thousand men will soon be here,
All wanting wings and taloned modes of life.
Somehow or other you must find them wings.

Peisthetaerus. O then, by Zeus, no time for dallying now;
Quick, run you in; collect the crates and baskets,
And fill them all with wings; that done, let Manes
Bring me them out; whilst I, remaining here,
Receive the wingless travelers as they come.

Chorus. Very soon 'fully-manned' will this City be called,
   If men in such numbers invade us.
Peisthetaerus. So fortune continue to aid us.
Chorus. O, the love of my City the world has enthralled!
Peisthetaerus (*to* MANES). Bring quicker the baskets they're
 packing
Chorus. For in what is it lacking
   That a man for his home can require?
Here is Wisdom, and Wit, and each exquisite Grace,
And here the unruffled, benevolent face
  Of Quiet, and loving Desire.

Peisthetaerus. Why, what a lazy loon are you!
     Come, move a little faster, do.

Chorus. O see that he brings me a basket of wings.
   Rush out in a whirlwind of passion,
   And wallop him, after this fashion.
  For the rogue is as slow as a donkey to go.
Peisthetaerus. No pluck has your Manes, 'tis true.
   But now 'tis for *you*
   The wings in due order to set;
Both the musical wings, and the wings of the seers,
And the wings of the sea, that as each one appears,
  The wings that he wants you can get.

Peisthetaerus. O, by the kestrels, I can't keep my hands
From banging you, you lazy, crazy oaf.

Sire-Striker (*singing*). O that I might as an eagle be,
   Flying, flying, flying, flying
   Over the surge of the untilled sea!
Peisthetaerus. Not false, methinks, the tale our envoy told
 us.

For here comes one whose song is all of eagles.

    Sire-Striker. Fie on it!
There's nothing in this world so sweet as flying;
I've quite a passion for these same bird-laws.
In fact I'm gone bird-mad, and fly, and long
To dwell with you, and hunger for your laws.

    Peisthetaerus. Which of our laws? for birds have many laws.

    Sire-Striker. All! All! but most of all that jolly law
Which lets a youngster throttle and beat his father.

    Peisthetaerus. Aye, if a cockerel beat his father here,
We do indeed account him quite a—Man.

    Sire-Striker. That's why I moved up hither and would fain
Throttle my father and get all he has.

    Peisthetaerus. But there's an ancient law among the birds,
You'll find it in the tablets of the storks;
When the old stork has brought his storklings up,
And all are fully fledged for flight, then they
Must in their turn maintain the stork their father.

    Sire-Striker. A jolly lot of good I've gained by coming,
If now I've got to feed my father too!

    Peisthetaerus. Nay, my poor boy, you came here well-dis-
        posed,
And so I'll rig you like an orphan bird.
And here's a new suggestion, not a bad one,
But what I learnt myself when I was young.
Don't beat your father, lad; but take this wing,
And grasp this spur of battle in your hand,
And think this crest a game-cock's martial comb.
Now march, keep guard, live on your soldier's pay,
And let your father be. If you want fighting,
Fly off to Thraceward regions, and fight there.

    Sire-Striker. By Dionysus, I believe you're right.
I'll do it too.

    Peisthetaerus.   You'll show your sense, by Zeus!

    Cinesias (*singing*). On the lightest of wings I am soaring
        on high,
Lightly from measure to measure I fly;

    Peisthetaerus. Bless me, this creature wants a pack of wings!

    Cinesias (*singing*). And ever the new I am flitting to find,
With timorless body, and timorless mind.

[654]

Peisthetaerus. We clasp Cinesias, man of linden-wyth.
Why in the world have you whirled your splay foot hither?
Cinesias (singing). To be a bird, a bird, I long,
          A nightingale of thrilling song.
Peisthetaerus. O stop that singing; prithee speak in prose.
Cinesias. O give me wings, that I may soar on high,
And pluck poetic fancies from the clouds,
Wild as the whirling winds, and driving snows.
Peisthetaerus. What, do you pluck your fancies from the
    clouds?
Cinesias. Why our whole trade depends upon the clouds;
What are our noblest dithyrambs but things
Of air, and mist, and purple-gleaming depths,
And feathery whirlwings? You shall hear, and judge.
Peisthetaerus. No, no, I won't.
Cinesias.   By Heracles you shall.
I'll go through all the air, dear friend, for you.
    (Singing). Shadowy visions of
        Wing-spreading, air-treading,
           Taper-necked birds.
Peisthetaerus. Steady, there!
Cinesias (singing). Bounding along on the path to the seas,
Fain would I float on the stream of the breeze.
Peisthetaerus. O by the Powers, I'll stop your streams and
    breezes.
Cinesias (singing). First do I stray on a southerly way;
Then to the northward my body I bear,
Cutting a harborless furrow of air.
A nice trick that, a pleasant trick, old man.
Peisthetaerus. O you don't like being feathery-whirl-winged,
   do you?
Cinesias. That's how you treat the Cyclian-chorus-trainer
For whose possession all the tribes compete!
Peisthetaerus. Well, will you stop and train a chorus here
For Leotrophides, all flying birds,
Crake-oppidans?
Cinesias.   You're jeering me, that's plain.
But I won't stop, be sure of that, until
I get me wings, and peragrate the air.

Sycophant (*singing*). Who be these on varied wing,
                        birds who have not anything?
O tell me, swallow, tell me, tell me true,
O long-winged bird, O bird of varied hue!
Peisthetaerus. Come, it's no joke, this plague that's broken
    out;
Here comes another, warbling like the rest.
Sycophant (*singing*). Again I ask thee, tell me, tell me true,
O long-winged bird, O bird of varied hue!
Peisthetaerus. At his own cloak his catch appears to point;
More than one swallow *that* requires, I'm thinking.
Sycophant. Which is the man that wings the visitors?
Peisthetaerus. He stands before you. What do you please
    to want?
Sycophant. Wings, wings I want. You need not ask me twice.
Peisthetaerus. Is it Pellene that you're going to fly to?
Sycophant. No, no: but I'm a sompnour for the Isles,
Informer,—
Peisthetaerus.   O the jolly trade you've got!
Sycophant. And law-suit-hatcher; so I want the wings
To scare the cities, serving writs all round.
Peisthetaerus. You'll summon them more cleverly, I sup-
    pose,
To the tune of wings?
Sycophant.   No, but to dodge the pirates,
I'll then come flying homeward with the cranes,
First swallowing down a lot of suits for ballast.
Peisthetaerus. Is this your business? you, a sturdy youngster,
Live by informing on the stranger-folk?
Sycophant. What can I do? I never learnt to dig.
Peisthetaerus. O, but by Zeus, there's many an honest calling
Whence men like you can earn a livelihood,
By means more suitable than hatching suits.
Sycophant. Come, come, no preaching; wing me, wing me,
    please.
Peisthetaerus. I wing you now by talking.
Sycophant.   What, by talk
Can you wing men?
Peisthetaerus.   Undoubtedly. By talk
All men are winged.

[656]

Sycophant.   All!

Peisthetaerus.   Have you never heard
The way the fathers in the barbers' shops
Talk to the children, saying things like these,
'*Diitrephes has winged my youngster so
By specious talk, he's all for chariot-driving.*'
'*Aye*,' says another, '*and that boy of mine
Flutters his wings at every Tragic Play.*'

Sycophant. So then by talk they are winged.

Peisthetaerus.   Exactly so.
Through talk the mind flutters and soars aloft,
And all the man takes wing. And so even now
I wish to turn you, winging you by talk,
To some more honest trade.

Sycophant.   But I DON'T wish.

Peisthetaerus. How then?

Sycophant.   I'll not disgrace my bringing up.
I'll ply the trade my father's fathers plied.
So wing me, please, with light quick-darting wings
Falcon's or kestrel's, so I'll serve my writs
Abroad on strangers; then accuse them here;
Then dart back there again.

Peisthetaerus.   I understand.
So when they come, they'll find the suit decided,
And payment ordered.

Sycophant.   Right! you understand.

Peisthetaerus. And while they're sailing hither you'll fly
    there,
And seize their goods for payment.

Sycophant.   That's the trick!
Round like a top I'll whizz.

Peisthetaerus.   I understand.
A whipping-top; and here by Zeus I've got
Fine Corcyraean wings to set you whizzing.

Sycophant. O, it's a whip!

Peisthetaerus.   Nay, friend, a pair of wings,
To set you spinning round and round to-day.

                       [*Striking him.*

Sycophant. O! O! O! O!

Peisthetaerus.   Come, wing yourself from hence.

Wobble away, you most confounded rascal!
I'll make you spin! I'll law-perverting-trick you!
Now let us gather up the wings and go.

> *Chorus.* We've been flying, we've been flying
> Over sea and land, espying
>   Many a wonder strange and new.
> First, a tree of monstrous girth,
> Tall and stout, yet nothing worth,
>   For 'tis rotten through and through:
> It has got no heart, and we
> Heard it called 'Cleonymus-tree.'
> In the spring it blooms gigantic,
> Fig-traducing, sycophantic,
> Yet in falling leaf-time yields
> Nothing but a fall of shields.
>
> Next a spot by darkness skirted,
> Spot, by every light deserted,
>   Lone and gloomy, we descried.
> There the human and divine,
> Men with heroes, mix and dine
>   Freely, save at even-tide.
> 'Tis not safe for mortal men
> To encounter heroes then.
> Then the great Orestes, looming
> Vast and awful through the glooming,
> On their right a stroke delivering,
> Leaves them palsied, stript, and shivering.

Prometheus. O dear! O dear! Pray Heaven that Zeus won't
    see me!
Where's Peisthetaerus?
    Peisthetaerus.   Why, whatever is here?
What's this enwrapment?
    Prometheus.   See you any God
Following behind me there?
    Peisthetaerus.   Not I, by Zeus.
But who are you?
    Prometheus.   And what's the time of day?

[658]

Peisthetaerus. The time of day? A little after noon.
(*Shouting*). But WHO ARE YOU?
    Prometheus.   Ox-loosing time, or later?
    Peisthetaerus. Disgusting idiot!
    Prometheus.   What's Zeus doing now?
The clouds collecting or the clouds dispersing?
    Peisthetaerus. Out on you, stupid!
    Prometheus.   Now then, I'll unwrap.
    Peisthetaerus. My dear Prometheus!
    Prometheus.   Hush! don't shout like that.
    Peisthetaerus. Why, what's up now?
    Prometheus.   Don't speak my name so loudly.
'Twould be my ruin, if Zeus see me here.
But now I'll tell you all that's going on
Up in the sky, if you'll just take the umbrella,
And hold it over, that no God may see me.
    Peisthetaerus. Ha! Ha!
The crafty thought! Prometheus-like all over.
Get under then; make haste: and speak out freely.
    Prometheus. Then listen.
    Peisthetaerus.   Speak: I'm listening, never fear.
    Prometheus. All's up with Zeus!
    Peisthetaerus.   Good gracious me! since when?
    Prometheus. Since first you built your city in the air.
For never from that hour does mortal bring
Burnt-offerings to the Gods, or savory steam
Ascend to heaven from flesh of victims slain.
So now we fast a Thesmophorian fast,
No altars burning; 'and the Barbarous Gods
Half-starved, and gibbering like Illyrians, vow
That they'll come marching down on Zeus, unless
He gets the marts reopened, and the bits
Of savory inwards introduced once more.
    Peisthetaerus. What, are there really other Gods, Barbarians,
Up above you?
    Prometheus.   Barbarians? Yes; thence comes
The ancestral God of Execestides.
    Peisthetaerus. And what's the name of these Barbarian
        Gods?
    Prometheus. The name? Triballians.

Peisthetaerus.   Aye, I understand.
'Tis from that quarter Tribulation comes.
Prometheus. Exactly so. And now I tell you this;
Envoys will soon be here to treat for peace,
Sent down by Zeus and those Triballians there.
But make no peace, mind that, unless king Zeus
Restores the scepter to the Birds again,
And gives yourself Miss Sovereignty to wife.
   Peisthetaerus. And who's Miss Sovereignty?
   Prometheus.   The loveliest girl.
'Tis she who keeps the thunderbolts of Zeus,
And all his stores,—good counsels, happy laws,
Sound common sense, dockyards, abusive speech,
All his three-obols, and the man who pays them.
   Peisthetaerus. Then she keeps EVERYTHING!
   Prometheus.   Of course she does.
Win her from Zeus, and *you'll* have EVERYTHING.
I hastened here that I might tell you this,
You know I am always well-disposed to men.
   Peisthetaerus. Aye, but for you we could not fry our fish.
   Prometheus. And I hate every God, you know that, don't
     you?
   Peisthetaerus. Yes, hatred of the Gods; you always felt it.
   Prometheus. A regular Timon! but 'tis time to go;
Let's have the umbrella; then, if Zeus perceives me,
He'll think I'm following the Basket-bearer.
   Peisthetaerus. Here, take the chair, and act the Chair-girl
     too.

   Chorus. Next we saw a sight appalling,
               Socrates, unwashed, was calling
                 Spirits from the lake below,
             ('Twas on that enchanted ground
             Where the Shadow-feet are found).
               There Peisander came to know
             If the spirit cowards lack
             Socrates could conjure back;
             Then a camel-lamb he slew,
             Like Odysseus, but withdrew,

Whilst the camel's blood upon
Pounced the Vampire, Chaerephon.

Poseidon. There, fellow envoys, full in sight, the town
Whereto we are bound, Cloudcuckoobury, stands!
(To the TRIBALLIAN). You, what are you at, wearing your
  cloak left-sided?
Shift it round rightly; so. My goodness, you're
A born Laispodias! O Democracy,
What will you bring us to at last, I wonder,
If voting Gods elect a clown like this!

Triballian. Hands off there, will yer?

Poseidon.   Hang you, you're by far
The uncouthest God I ever came across.
Now, Heracles, what's to be done?

Heracles.   You have heard
What I propose; I'd throttle the man off-hand,
Whoever he is, that dares blockade the Gods.

Poseidon. My dear good fellow, you forget we are sent
To treat for peace.

Heracles.   I'd throttle him all the more.

Peisthetaerus (*to servants*). Hand me the grater; bring the
  silphium, you;
Now then, the cheese; blow up the fire a little.

Poseidon. We three, immortal Gods, with words of greeting
Salute the Man!

Peisthetaerus.   I'm grating silphium now.

Heracles. What's this the flesh of?

Peisthetaerus.   Birds! Birds tried and sentenced
For rising up against the popular party
Amongst the birds.

Heracles.   Then you grate silphium, do you,
Over them first?

Peisthetaerus.   O welcome, Heracles!
What brings you hither?

Poseidon.   We are envoys, sent
Down by the Gods to settle terms of peace.

Servant. There's no more oil remaining in the flask.

Heracles. O dear! and bird's-flesh should be rich and
  glistering.

Poseidon. We Gods gain nothing by the war; and you,

[661]

Think what ye'll get by being friends with us;
Rain-water in the pools, and halcyon days
Shall be your perquisites the whole year through.
We've ample powers to settle on these terms.

    Peisthetaerus. It was not we who ever wished for war,
And now, if even now ye come prepared
With fair proposals, ye will find us ready
To treat for peace. What I call fair is this;
Let Zeus restore the scepter to the birds,
And all make friends. If ye accept this offer,
I ask the envoys in to share our banquet.

    Heracles. I'm altogether satisfied, and vote—
    Poseidon (*interrupting*). What, wretch? A fool and glutton,
        that's what *you* are!
What! would you rob your father of his kingdom?

    Peisthetaerus. Aye, say you so? Why, ye'll be mightier far,
Ye Gods above, if Birds bear rule below.
Now men go skulking underneath the clouds,
And swear false oaths, and call the Gods to witness.
But when ye've got the Birds for your allies,
If a man swear by the Raven and by Zeus,
The Raven will come by, and unawares
Fly up, and swoop, and peck the perjurer's eye out.

    Poseidon. Now by Poseidon there's some sense in that.
    Heracles. And so say I.
    Peisthetaerus (*to* TRIBALLIAN).   And you?
    Triballian.   Persuasitree.
    Peisthetaerus. You see? he quite assents. And now I'll give
    you
Another instance of the good ye'll gain.
If a man vow a victim to a God,
And then would shuffle off with cunning words,
Saying, in greedy lust, *The Gods wait long,*
This too we'll make him pay you.

    Poseidon.   Tell me how?
    Peisthetaerus. Why, when that man is counting out his
    money,
Or sitting in his bath, a kite shall pounce
Down unawares, and carry off the price
Of two fat lambs, and bear it to the God.

Heracles. I say again, I vote we give the scepter
Back to the Birds.

Poseidon.   Ask the Triballian next.

Heracles. You there, do you want a drubbing?

Triballian.   Hideythine
I'se stickybeatums.

Heracles.   There! he's all for me.

Poseidon. Well then, if so you wish it, so we'll have it.

Heracles (*to* PEISTHETAERUS). Hi! we accept your terms
    about the scepter.

Peisthetaerus. By Zeus, there's one thing more I've just
    remembered.
Zeus may retain his Hera, if he will,
But the young girl, Miss Sovereignty, he must
Give me to wife.

Poseidon.   This looks not like a treaty.
Let us be journeying homewards.

Peisthetaerus.   As you will.
Now, cook, be sure you make the gravy rich.

Heracles. Why, man alive, Poseidon, where are you off to?
What, are we going to fight about one woman?

Poseidon. What shall we do?

Heracles.   Do? Come to terms at once.

Poseidon. You oaf, he's gulling you, and you can't see it.
Well, it's yourself you are ruining. If Zeus
Restore the kingdom to the Birds, and die,
You'll be a pauper. You are the one to get
Whatever money Zeus may leave behind him.

Peisthetaerus. O! O! the way he's trying to cozen you!
Hist, step aside, I want to whisper something.
Your uncle's fooling you, poor dupe. By law
No shred of all your father's money falls
To you. Why, you're a bastard, you're not heir.

Heracles. Eh! What? A bastard? I?

Peisthetaerus.   Of course you are.
Your mother was an alien. Bless the fool,
How did you think Athene could be 'Heiress,'
(Being a girl), if she had lawful brethren?

Heracles. Well, but suppose my father leaves me all
As bastard's heritage?

Peisthetaerus.   The law won't let him.
Poseidon here, who now excites you on,
Will be the first to claim the money then,
As lawful brother, and your father's heir.
Why here, I'll read you Solon's law about it.
'A bastard is to have no right of inheritance, if there be lawful
children. And if there be no lawful children, the goods are
to fall to the next of kin.'
    Heracles. What! none of all my father's goods to fall
To me?
    Peisthetaerus.   No, not one farthing! tell me this,
Has he enrolled you ever in the guild?
    Heracles. He never has. I've often wondered why.
    Peisthetaerus. Come, don't look up assault-and-battery-wise.
Join *us*, my boy; I'll make you autocrat,
And feed you all your days on pigeon's milk.
    Heracles. I'm quite convinced you're right about the girl;
I said Restore her; and I say so now.
    Peisthetaerus (to POSEIDON*).* And what say you?
    Poseidon.   I vote the other way.
    Peisthetaerus. All rests with this Triballian. What say you?
    Triballian. Me gulna charmi grati Sovranau
Birdito stori.
    Heracles.   There! he said Restore her.
    Poseidon. O no by Zeus, he never said Restore her;
He said to migrate as the swallows do.
    Heracles. O then he said Restore her to the swallows.
    Poseidon. You two conclude, and settle terms of peace,
Since you both vote it, I will say no more.
    Heracles (to PEISTHETAERUS*).* We're quite prepared to give
        you all you ask,
So come along, come up to heaven yourself,
And take Miss Sovereignty and all that's there.
    Peisthetaerus. So then these birds were slaughtered just in
        time
To grace our wedding banquet.
    Heracles.   Would you like me
To stay, and roast the meat, while you three go?
    Poseidon. To *roast* the meat! To TASTE the meat, you mean.
Come along, do.

Heracles.   I'd have enjoyed it though.
Peisthetaerus. Ho there within! bring out a wedding robe.

Chorus. In the fields of Litigation,
               Near the Water-clock, a nation
                   With its tongue its belly fills;
               With its tongue it sows and reaps,
               Gathers grapes and figs in heaps,
                   With its tongue the soil it tills.
               For a Barbarous tribe it passes,
               Philips all and Gorgiases.
               And from this tongue-bellying band
               Everywhere on Attic land,
               People who a victim slay
               Always cut the tongue away.

Messenger. O all-successful, more than tongue can tell!
O ye, thrice blessèd wingèd race of birds,
Welcome your King returning to his halls!
He comes; no Star has ever gleamed so fair,
Sparkling refulgent in its gold-rayed home.
The full far-flashing splendor of the Sun
Ne'er shone so gloriously as he, who comes
Bringing a bride too beautiful for words,
Wielding the wingèd thunderbolt of Zeus.
Up to Heaven's highest vault, sweet sight, ascends
Fragrance ineffable; while gentlest airs
The fume of incense scatter far and wide.
He comes; he is here! Now let the heavenly Muse
Open her lips with pure auspicious strains.

Chorus. Back with you! out with you!
                              off with you! up with you!
               Flying around
Welcome the Blessèd with blessedness crowned.
   O! O! for the youth and the beauty, O!
Well hast thou wed for the town of the Birds.

Great are the blessings, and mighty, and wonderful,
   Which through his favor our nation possesses.

Welcome them back, both himself and Miss Sovereignty,
  Welcome with nuptial and bridal addresses.

      Mid just such a song hymenaean
      Aforetime the Destinies led
      The King of the thrones empyréan,
      The Ruler of Gods, to the bed
      Of Hera his beautiful bride.
      Hymen, O Hymenaeus!

      And Love, with his pinions of gold,
      Came driving, all blooming and spruce,
      As groomsman and squire to behold
      The wedding of Hera and Zeus,
      Of Zeus and his beautiful bride.
      Hymen, O Hymenaeus!
      Hymen, O Hymenaeus!

Peisthetaerus. I delight in your hymns, I delight in your
    songs;
      Your words I admire.
  Chorus. Now sing of the trophies he brings us from Heaven,
The earth-crashing thunders, deadly and dire,
And the lightning's angry flashes of fire,
And the dread white bolt of the levin.
Blaze of the lightning, so terribly beautiful,
                   Golden and grand!
Fire-flashing javelin, glittering ever in
               Zeus's right hand!
Earth-crashing thunder, the hoarsely resounding, the
              Bringer of showers!
He is your Master, 'tis he that is shaking the
             Earth with your powers!
      All that was Zeus's of old
      Now is our hero's alone;
      Sovereignty, fair to behold,
      Partner of Zeus on his throne,
      Now is for ever his own.
      Hymen, O Hymenaeus!
  Peisthetaerus. Now follow on, dear feathered tribes,

To see us wed, to see us wed;
Mount up to Zeus's golden floor,
And nuptial bed, and nuptial bed.
And O, my darling, reach thine hand,
And take my wing and dance with me,
And I will lightly bear thee up,
And carry thee, and carry thee
    Chorus. Raise the joyous Paean-cry,
Raise the song of Victory.
Io Paean, alalalae,
Mightiest of the Powers, to thee!

ARISTOPHANES
THE FROGS

⫸⫷

TRANSLATED
by
BENJAMIN BICKLEY ROGERS

CHARACTERS IN THE PLAY

The God DIONYSUS.
XANTHIAS, *slave to Dionysus.*
The God HERACLES.
A CORPSE.
CHARON, *the ferryman on the Styx.*
FROGS.
AEACUS, *door-keeper in the hall of Pluto.*
MAID-SERVANT *of Persephone.*
A HOSTESS ⎰
PLATHANE ⎱ *keepers of a cook-shop.*
EURIPIDES, *the tragic poet,* 480-406 B.C.
AESCHYLUS, *the tragic poet,* 525-456 B.C.
PLUTO, *king of Hades.*
CHORUS OF VOTARIES.

ARGUMENT

Dionysus, patron of the drama, is dissatisfied with the tragic poets of the day; he determines to visit the lower regions in order to procure the release and return of Euripides, who had died the year before. He garbs himself as Heracles, and carrying a club is accompanied by Xanthias, his slave, upon an ass.

The wit and gaiety in the incidents the travelers experience on their journey, and the great patriotism evinced by Aristophanes throughout the play, have contributed much to the great success and lasting popularity of the *Frogs.* Of particular interest and importance for modern readers is the literary contest between Aeschylus and Euripides, which Dionysus and Xanthias find in progress in the halls of Pluto. With sound literary criticism Aristophanes displays the aims and merits of the rival poets as well as specific details in their plays. Aeschylus wins the competition, and is released by Pluto to accompany Dionysus on his return; yet Aristophanes also shows a high appreciation of Euripides, whom he evidently studied with care. But he must balance the two opponents in the *agon* of a comedy, where Sophocles, his favorite, cannot be a third.

The Chorus is made up of votaries, who in life had been initiated into the Eleusinian mysteries. When they are first heard behind the scenes, they are chanting the songs of the dead frogs that give the comedy its name.

THE FROGS

Handwritten margin note (top): Slaves frequent characters in O. Comedy

Handwritten margin note: recognizes presence of audience

Handwritten margin note: breaking of dramatic illusion

Handwritten margin note: frequent source of humor

Handwritten margin note (right): dialogue

Xanthias. Shall I crack any of those old jokes, master,
At which the audience never fail to laugh?
   Dionysus. Aye, what you will, except *I'm getting crushed:*
Fight shy of that: I'm sick of that already.
   Xanthias. Nothing else smart?
   Dionysus.   Aye, save *my shoulder's aching.*
   Xanthias. Come now, that comical joke?
   Dionysus.   With all my heart.
Only be careful not to shift your pole,
And—
   Xanthias.   What?
   Dionysus.   And vow that you've a belly-ache.
   Xanthias. May I not say I'm overburdened so
That if none ease me, I must ease myself?
   Dionysus. For mercy's sake, not till I'm going to vomit.
   Xanthias. What! must I bear these burdens, and not make
One of the jokes Ameipsias and Lycis
And Phrynichus, in every play they write, *(handwritten: cracks at rivals)*
Put in the mouths of all their burden-bearers?
   Dionysus. Don't make them; no! I tell you when I see
Their plays, and hear those jokes, I come away
More than a twelvemonth older than I went.
   Xanthias. O thrice unlucky neck of mine, which now
Is *getting crushed,* yet must not crack its joke!
   Dionysus. Now is not this fine pampered insolence
When I myself, Dionysus, son of—Pipkin,
Toil on afoot, and let this fellow ride,
Taking no trouble, and no burden bearing?
   Xanthias. What, don't I bear?
   Dionysus.   How can you when you're riding?
   Xanthias. Why, I bear these.
   Dionysus.   How?

[671]

Xanthias.   Most unwillingly.
Dionysus Does not the donkey bear the load you're bearing?
Xanthias. Not what I bear myself: by Zeus, not he.
Dionysus. How can you bear, when you are borne yourself?
Xanthias. Don't know: but anyhow *my shoulder's aching.*
Dionysus. Then since you say the donkey helps you not,
You lift him up and carry him in turn.
Xanthias. O hang it all! why didn't I fight at sea?
You should have smarted bitterly for this.
Dionysus. Get down, you rascal; I've been trudging on
Till now I've reached the portal, where I'm going
First to turn in. Boy! Boy! I say there, Boy!
Heracles. Who banged the door? How like a prancing
   Centaur
He drove against it! Mercy o' me, what's this?
Dionysus. Boy.
Xanthias.   Yes.
Dionysus.   Did you observe?
Xanthias.   What?
Dionysus.   How alarmed
He is.
Xanthias.   Aye truly, lest you've lost your wits.
Heracles. O by Demeter, I can't choose but laugh.
Biting my lips won't stop me. Ha! ha! ha!
Dionysus. Pray you, come hither, I have need of you.
Heracles. I vow I can't help laughing, I can't help it.
A lion's hide upon a yellow silk,
A club and buskin! What's it all about?
Where were you going?
Dionysus.   I was serving lately
Aboard the—Cleisthenes.
Heracles.   And fought?
Dionysus.   And sank
More than a dozen of the enemy's ships.
Heracles. You two?
Dionysus.   We two.
Heracles.   And then I awoke, and lo!
Dionysus. There as, on deck, I'm reading to myself
The *Andromeda,* a sudden pang of longing
Shoots through my heart, you can't conceive how keenly.

[672]

Heracles. How big a pang?

Dionysus.   A small one, Molon's size.

Heracles. Caused by a woman?

Dionysus.   No.

Heracles.   A boy?

Dionysus.   No, no.

Heracles. A man?

Dionysus.   Ah! ah!

Heracles.   Was it for Cleisthenes?

Dionysus. Don't mock me, brother: on my life I am
In a bad way: such fierce desire consumes me.

Heracles. Aye, little brother? how?

Dionysus.   I can't describe it.
But yet I'll tell you in a riddling way.
Have you e'er felt a sudden lust for soup?

Heracles. Soup! Zeus-a-mercy, yes, ten thousand times.

Dionysus. Is the thing clear, or must I speak again?

Heracles. Not of the soup: I'm clear about the soup.

Dionysus. Well, just that sort of pang devours my heart
For lost Euripides.

Heracles.   A dead man too.

Dionysus. And no one shall persuade me not to go
After the man.

Heracles.   Do you mean below, to Hades?

Dionysus. And lower still, if there's a lower still.

Heracles. What on earth for?

Dionysus.   I want a genuine poet,
'For some are not, and those that are, are bad.'

Heracles. What! does not Iophon live?

Dionysus.   Well, he's the sole
Good thing remaining, if even he is good.
For even of that I'm not exactly certain.

Heracles. If go you must, there's Sophocles—he comes
Before Euripides—why not take *him?*

Dionysus. Not till I've tried if Iophon's coin rings true
When he's alone, apart from Sophocles.
Besides, Euripides, the crafty rogue,
Will find a thousand shifts to get away,
But *he* was easy here, is easy there.

Heracles. But Agathon, where is he?

Dionysus. He has gone and left us.
A genial poet, by his friends much missed.
Heracles. Gone where?
Dionysus. To join the blessed in their banquets.
Heracles. But what of Xenocles?
Dionysus. O he be hanged!
Heracles. Pythangelus?
Xanthias. But never a word of me,
Not though my shoulder's chafed so terribly.
Heracles. But have you not a shoal of little songsters,
Tragedians by the myriad, who can chatter
A furlong faster than Euripides?
Dionysus. Those be mere vintage-leavings, jabberers, choirs
Of swallow-broods, degraders of their art,
Who get one chorus, and are seen no more,
The Muses' love once gained. But O, my friend,
Search where you will, you'll never find a true
Creative genius, uttering startling things.
Heracles. Creative? how do you mean?
Dionysus. I mean a man
Who'll dare some novel venturesome conceit,
Air, Zeus's chamber, or *Time's foot,* or this,
'Twas not my mind that swore: my tongue committed
A little perjury on its own account.
Heracles. You like that style?
Dionysus. Like it? I dote upon it.
Heracles. I vow it's ribald nonsense, and you know it.
Dionysus. 'Rule not my mind': you've got a house to mind.
Heracles. Really and truly though 'tis paltry stuff.
Dionysus. Teach me to dine!
Xanthias. But never a word of me.
Dionysus. But tell me truly—'twas for this I came
Dressed up to mimic you—what friends received
And entertained you when you went below
To bring back Cerberus, in case I need them.
And tell me too the havens, fountains, shops,
Roads, resting-places, stews, refreshment-rooms,
Towns, lodgings, hostesses, with whom were found
The fewest bugs.
Xanthias. But never a word of me.

[674]

Heracles. You are really game to go?

Dionysus.   O drop that, can't you?
And tell me this: of all the roads you know
Which is the quickest way to get to Hades?
I want one not too warm, nor yet too cold.

Heracles. Which shall I tell you first? which shall it be?
There's one by rope and bench: you launch away
And—hang yourself.

Dionysus.   No thank you: that's too stifling.

Heracles. Then there's a track, a short and beaten cut,
By pestle and mortar.

Dionysus.   Hemlock, do you mean?

Heracles. Just so.

Dionysus.   No, that's too deathly cold a way;
You have hardly started ere your shins get numbed.

Heracles. Well, would you like a steep and swift descent?

Dionysus. Aye, that's the style: my walking powers are
        small.

Heracles. Go down to the Cerameicus.

Dionysus.   And do what?

Heracles. Climb to the tower's top pinnacle—

Dionysus.   And then?

Heracles. Observe the torch-race started, and when all
The multitude is shouting *Let them go,*
Let yourself go.

Dionysus.   Go! whither?

Heracles.   To the ground.

Dionysus. And lose, forsooth, two envelopes of brain.
I'll not try that.

Heracles.   Which *will* you try?

Dionysus.   The way
You went yourself.

Heracles.   A parlous voyage that,
For first you'll come to an enormous lake
Of fathomless depth.

Dionysus.   And how am I to cross?

Heracles. An ancient mariner will row you over
In a wee boat, *so* big. The fare's two obols.

Dionysus. Fie! The power two obols have, the whole world
        through!

[675]

How came they thither!

Heracles.   Theseus took them down.
And next you'll see great snakes and savage monsters
In tens of thousands.

Dionysus.   You needn't try to scare me,
I'm going to go.

Heracles.   Then weltering seas of filth
And ever-rippling dung: and plunged therein,
Whoso has wronged the stranger here on earth,
Or robbed his boylove of the promised pay,
Or swinged his mother, or profanely smitten
His father's cheek, or sworn an oath forsworn,
Or copied out a speech of Morsimus.— *contemp playing?*

Dionysus. There too, perdie, should *he* be plunged, whoe'er
Has danced the sword-dance of Cinesias.

Heracles. And next the breath of flutes will float around you,
And glorious sunshine, such as ours, you'll see,
And myrtle groves, and happy bands who clap
Their hands in triumph, men and women too.

Dionysus. And who are they?

Heracles.   The happy mystic bands,

Xanthias. And I'm the donkey in the mystery show.
But I'll not stand it, not one instant longer.

Heracles. Who'll tell you everything you want to know.
You'll find them dwelling close beside the road
You are going to travel, just at Pluto's gate.
And fare thee well, my brother.

Dionysus.   And to you
Good cheer. (*To* XANTHIAS.) Now sirrah, pick you up the
    traps.

Xanthias. Before I've put them down?

Dionysus.   And quickly too.

Xanthias. No, prithee, no: but hire a body, one
They're carrying out, on purpose for the trip.

Dionysus. If I can't find one?

Xanthias.   Then I'll take them.

Dionysus.   Good.
And see! they are carrying out a body now.
Hallo! you there, you deadman, are you willing
To carry down our little traps to Hades?

Corpse. What are they?

Dionysus. These.

Corpse. Two drachmas for the job?

Dionysus. Nay, that's too much.

Corpse. Out of the pathway, you!

Dionysus. Beshrew thee, stop: may-be we'll strike a bargain.

Corpse. Pay me two drachmas, or it's no use talking. *(for carrying bags)*

Dionysus. One and a half.

Corpse. I'd liefer live again!

Xanthias. How absolute the knave is! He be hanged!
I'll go myself.

Dionysus. You're the right sort, my man.
Now to the ferry.

Charon. Yoh, up! lay her to.

Xanthias. Whatever's that? *[Scene change]*

Dionysus. Why, that's the lake, by Zeus,
Whereof he spake, and yon's the ferry-boat.

Xanthias. Poseidon, yes, and that old fellow's Charon.

Dionysus. Charon! O welcome, Charon! welcome, Charon!

Charon. Who's for the Rest from every pain and ill?
Who's for the Lethe's plain? the Donkey-shearings?
Who's for Cerberia? Taenarum? or the Ravens?

Dionysus. I.

Charon. Hurry in.

Dionysus. But where are you going really?
In truth to the Ravens?

Charon. Aye, for your behoof.
Step in.

Dionysus (to XANTHIAS*).* Now, lad.

Charon. A slave? I take no slave,
Unless he has fought for his bodyrights at sea.

Xanthias. I couldn't go. I'd got the eye-disease.

Charon. Then fetch a circuit round about the lake.

Xanthias. Where must I wait?

Charon. Beside the Withering stone,
Hard by the Rest.

Dionysus. You understand?

Xanthias. Too well.
O, what ill omen crossed me as I started!

Charon (*to* DIONYSUS). Sit to the oar. (*Calling.*) Who else
  for the boat? Be quick.
(*To* DIONYSUS.) Hi! what are you doing?
  Dionysus.　　　　　　　　　What am I doing? Sitting
On to the oar. You told me to, yourself.
  Charon. Now sit you there, you little Potgut.
  Dionysus.　　　　　　　　　　So?
  Charon. Now stretch your arms full length before you.
  Dionysus.　　　　　　　　　　So?
  Charon. Come, don't keep fooling; plant your feet, and now
Pull with a will.
  Dionysus.　　　Why, how am *I* to pull?
I'm not an oarsman, seaman, Salaminian.
I can't!
  Charon.　　　You can. Just dip your oar in once,
You'll hear the loveliest timing songs.
  Dionysus.　　　　　　　　What from?
  Charon. Frog-swans, most wonderful.
  Dionysus.　　　　　　　　Then give the word.
  Charon.　　　Heave ahoy! heave ahoy!
  Frogs.　　　Brekekekex, ko-ax, ko-ax,
　　　　　　　Brekekekex, ko-ax, ko-ax!
　　　We children of the fountain and the lake
　　　　　　Let us wake
　　Our full choir-shout, as the flutes are ringing out,
　　　　Our symphony of clear-voiced song.
　　The song we used to love in the Marshland up
　　　　　above,
　　　　　In praise of Dionysus to produce,
　　　　　Of Nysaean Dionysus, son of Zeus,
　　When the revel-tipsy throng, all crapulous and
　　　　　gay,
　　To our precinct reeled along on the holy Pitcher
　　　　　day,
　　　　　Brekekekex, ko-ax, ko-ax.
Dionysus. O, dear! O, dear! now I declare
　　　　　I've got a bump upon my rump,
  Frogs.　　　Brekekekex, ko-ax, ko-ax,
  Dionysus.　　But you, perchance, don't care.
  Frogs.　　　Brekekekex, ko-ax, ko-ax.

Dionysus.	Hang you, and your ko-axing too!
	There's nothing but ko-ax with you.
Frogs.	That is right, Mr. Busybody, right!

For the Muses of the lyre love us well;
And hornfoot Pan who plays
               on the pipe his jocund lays;
And Apollo, Harper bright,
               in our Chorus takes delight;
For the strong reed's sake
               which I grow within my lake
To be girdled in his lyre's deep shell.
     Brekekekex, ko-ax, ko-ax.

Dionysus.	My hands are blistered very sore;

My stern below is sweltering so,
'Twill soon, I know, upturn and roar
Brekekekex, ko-ax, ko-ax.
O tuneful race, O pray give o'er,
O sing no more.

Frogs.	Ah, no! ah, no!

Loud and louder our chant must flow.
Sing if ever ye sang of yore,
When in sunny and glorious days
Through the rushes and marsh-flags springing
On we swept, in the joy of singing
Myriad-diving roundelays.
Or when fleeing the storm, we went
Down to the depths, and our choral song
Wildly raised to a loud and long
Bubble-bursting accompaniment.

Frogs and Dionysus.	Brekekekex, ko-ax, ko-ax.
Dionysus.	This timing song I take from you.
Frogs.	That's a dreadful thing to do.
Dionysus.	Much more dreadful, if I row
	Till I burst myself, I trow.
Frogs and Dionysus.	Brekekekex, ko-ax, ko-ax.
Dionysus.	Go, hang yourselves; for what care I?
Frogs.	All the same we'll shout and cry,
	Stretching all our throats with song,
	Shouting, crying, all day long,
Frogs and Dionysus.	Brekekekex, ko-ax, ko-ax.

Dionysus.   In this you'll never, never win.
Frogs.   This you shall not beat us in.
Dionysus.   No, nor ye prevail o'er me.
                Never! never! I'll my song
                Shout, if need be, all day long,
      Until I've learned to master your ko-ax.
                Brekekekex, ko-ax, ko-ax.
      I thought I'd put a stop to your ko-ax.
Charon. Stop! Easy! Take the oar and push her to.
Now pay your fare and go.
    Dionysus.   Here 'tis: two obols.
Xanthias! where's Xanthias? Is it Xanthias there?
    Xanthias. Hoi, hoi!
    Dionysus.   Come hither.
    Xanthias.   Glad to meet you, master.
    Dionysus. What have you there?
    Xanthias.   Nothing but filth and darkness.
    Dionysus. But tell me, did you see the parricides
And perjured folk he mentioned?
    Xanthias.   Didn't you?
    Dionysus. Poseidon, yes. Why look!
                            [*Pointing to the audience.*
                                  I see them now.
What's the next step?
    Xanthias.   We'd best be moving on.
This is the spot where Heracles declared
Those savage monsters dwell.
    Dionysus.   O hang the fellow.
That's all his bluff: he thought to scare me off,
The jealous dog, knowing my plucky ways.
There's no such swaggerer lives as Heracles.
Why, I'd like nothing better than to achieve
Some bold adventure, worthy of our trip.
    Xanthias. I know you would. Hallo! I hear a noise.
    Dionysus. Where? what?
    Xanthias.   Behind us, there.
    Dionysus.   Get you behind.
    Xanthias. No, it's in front.
    Dionysus.   Get you in front directly.
    Xanthias. And now I see the most ferocious monster.

Dionysus. O, what's it like?

Xanthias.　　　　　　　　Like everything by turns.
Now it's a bull: now it's a mule: and now
The loveliest girl.

　Dionysus.　　　O, where? I'll go and meet her.

　Xanthias. It's ceased to be a girl: it's a dog now.

　Dionysus. It is Empusa!

　Xanthias.　　　　　　Well, its face is all
Ablaze with fire.

　Dionysus.　　　Has it a copper leg?

　Xanthias. A copper leg? yes, one; and one of cow dung.

　Dionysus. O, whither shall I flee?

　Xanthias.　　　　　　　　O, whither I?

　Dionysus. My priest, protect me, and we'll sup together.

　Xanthias. King Heracles, we're done for.

　Dionysus.　　　　　　　　　O, forbear,
Good fellow, call me anything but that.

　Xanthias. Well then, Dionysus.

　Dionysus.　　　　　　O, that's worse again.

　Xanthias (*to the* SPECTER). Aye, go thy way. O master,
　　here, come here.

　Dionysus. O, what's up now?

　Xanthias.　　　　　　Take courage; all's serene.
And, like Hegelochus, we now may say
'Out of the storm there comes a new fine wether.'
Empusa's gone.

　Dionysus.　　Swear it.

　Xanthias.　　　　　By Zeus she is.

　Dionysus. Swear it again.

　Xanthias.　　　　　By Zeus.

　Dionysus.　　　　　　　Again.

　Xanthias.　　　　　　　　By Zeus.
O dear, O dear, how pale I grew to see her,
But *he*, from fright has yellowed me all over.

　Dionysus. Ah me, whence fall these evils on my head?
Who is the god to blame for my destruction?
Air, Zeus's chamber, or the Foot of Time?

　　　　　　　[*A flute is played behind the scenes.*
Hist!

　Xanthias.　　　What's the matter?

[681]

Dionysus. Didn't you hear it?

Xanthias. What?

Dionysus. The breath of flutes.

Xanthias. Aye, and a whiff of torches
Breathed o'er me too; a very mystic whiff.

Dionysus. Then crouch we down, and mark what's going on.

Chorus (in the distance). O Iacchus! O Iacchus! O Iacchus!

Xanthias. I have it, master: 'tis those blessed Mystics,
Of whom he told us, sporting hereabouts.
They sing the Iacchus which Diagoras made.

Dionysus. I think so too: we had better both keep quiet
And so find out exactly what it is.

[*The calling forth of Iacchus.*

Chorus. O Iacchus! power excelling,
here in stately temples dwelling,
O Iacchus! O Iacchus!
Come to tread this verdant level,
Come to dance in mystic revel,
Come whilst round thy forehead hurtles
Many a wreath of fruitful myrtles,
Come with wild and saucy paces
Mingling in our joyous dance,
Pure and holy. which embraces
all the charms of all the Graces,
When the mystic choirs advance.

Xanthias. Holy and sacred queen, Demeter's daughter,
O, what a jolly whiff of pork breathed o'er me!

Dionysus. Hist! and perchance you'll get some tripe yourself.

[*The welcome to* IACCHUS.

Chorus. Come, arise, from sleep awaking,
come the fiery torches shaking,
O Iacchus! O Iacchus!
Morning Star that shinest nightly.
Lo, the mead is blazing brightly,
Age forgets its years and sadness,
Agèd knees curvet for gladness,
Lift thy flashing torches o'er us,
Marshal all thy blameless train,

[682]

Lead, O lead the way before us;
      lead the lovely youthful Chorus
  To the marshy flowery plain.

      [*The warning-off of the profane.*
All evil thoughts and profane be still:
     far hence, far hence from our choirs depart,
Who knows not well what the Mystics tell,
      or is not holy and pure of heart;
Who ne'er has the noble revelry learned,
     or danced the dance of the Muses high;
Or shared in the Bacchic rites which old
      bull-eating Cratinus's words supply;
Who vulgar coarse buffoonery loves,
     though all untimely the jests they make;
Or lives not easy and kind with all,
     or kindling faction forbears to slake,
But fans the fire, from a base desire
     some pitiful gain for himself to reap;
Or takes, in office, his gifts and bribes,
     while the city is tossed on the stormy deep;
Who fort or fleet to the foe betrays;
     or, a vile Thorycion, ships away
Forbidden stores from Aegina's shores,
     to Epidaurus across the Bay
Transmitting oar-pads and sails and tar,
     that curst collector of five per cents;
The knave who tries to procure supplies
     for the use of the enemy's armaments;
The Cyclian singer who dares befoul
     the Lady Hecate's wayside shrine;
The public speaker who once lampooned
     in our Bacchic feasts would, with heart malign,
Keep nibbling away the Comedians' pay;—
     to these I utter my warning cry,
I charge them once, I charge them twice,
     I charge them thrice, that they draw not nigh
To the sacred dance of the Mystic choir.
     But YE, my comrades, awake the song,

The night-long revels of joy and mirth
                    which ever of right to our feast belong.

                              [The start of the procession.
              Advance, true hearts, advance!
              On to the gladsome bowers,
              On to the sward, with flowers
                    Embosomed bright!
              March on with jest, and jeer, and dance,
              Full well ye've supped to-night.
                         [The processional hymn to Persephone.
              March, chanting loud your lays,
              Your hearts and voices raising,
              The Saviour goddess praising
                    Who vows she'll still
              Our city save to endless days,
              Whate'er Thorycion's will.

Break off the measure, and change the time;
                    and now with chanting and hymns adorn
Demeter, goddess mighty and high,
                    the harvest-queen, the giver of corn.

                         [The processional hymn to Demeter.
              O Lady, over our rites presiding,
              Preserve and succor thy choral throng,
              And grant us all, in thy help confiding,
              To dance and revel the whole day long;
              AND MUCH in earnest, and much in jest,
              Worthy thy feast, may we speak therein.
              And when we have bantered and laughed our best,
              The victor's wreath be it ours to win.

Call we now the youthful god,
                    call him hither without delay,
Him who travels amongst his chorus,
                    dancing along on the Sacred Way.

                         [The processional hymn to Iacchus.
              O, come with the joy of thy festival song,

O, come to the goddess, O, mix with our throng
Untired, though the journey be never so long.
    O Lord of the frolic and dance,
    Iacchus, beside me advance!
For fun, and for cheapness, our dress thou hast rent,
Through thee we may dance to the top of our bent,
Reviling, and jeering, and none will resent.
    O Lord of the frolic and dance,
    Iacchus, beside me advance!
A sweet pretty girl I observed in the show,
Her robe had been torn in the scuffle, and lo,
There peeped through the tatters a bosom of snow.
    O Lord of the frolic and dance,
    Iacchus, beside me advance!

Dionysus. Wouldn't I like to follow on, and try
A little sport and dancing?
Xanthias.   Wouldn't I?

               [The banter at the bridge of Cephisus.
Chorus. Shall we all a merry joke
      At Archedemus poke,
Who has not cut his guildsmen yet, though seven years old;
    Yet up among the dead
    He is demagogue and head,
And contrives the topmost place of the rascaldom to hold?
    And Cleisthenes, they say,
    Is among the tombs all day,
Bewailing for his lover with a lamentable whine.
    And Callias, I'm told,
    Has become a sailor bold,
And casts a lion's hide o'er his members feminine.
Dionysus. Can any of you tell
    Where Pluto here may dwell,
For we, sirs, are two strangers who were never here before?
Chorus. O, then no further stray,
    Nor again inquire the way,
For know that ye have journeyed to his very entrance-door.
Dionysus. Take up the wraps, my lad.

Xanthias. Now is not this too bad?
Like 'Zeus's Corinth,' he 'the wraps' keeps saying o'er and o'er.

Chorus. Now wheel your sacred dances through the glade
with flowers bedight,
All ye who are partakers of the holy festa. rite;
And I will with the women and the holy maidens go
Where they keep the nightly vigil, an auspicious light to show.

[*The departure for the Thriasian Plain.*
Now haste we to the roses,
And the meadows full of posies,
Now haste we to the meadows
In our own old way,
In choral dances blending,
In dances never ending,
Which only for the holy
The Destinies array.
O, happy mystic chorus,
The blessed sunshine o'er us
On us alone is smiling,
In its soft sweet light:
On us who strove for ever
With holy, pure endeavor,
Alike by friend and stranger
To guide our steps aright.

Dionysus. What's the right way to knock? I wonder how
The natives here are wont to knock at doors.
Xanthias. No dawdling: taste the door. You've got, re-
member,
The lion-hide and pride of Heracles.
Dionysus. Boy! Boy!
Aeacus. Who's there?
Dionysus. I, Heracles the strong!
Aeacus. O, you most shameless desperate ruffian, you!
O, villain, villain, arrant vilest villain!
Who seized our Cerberus by the throat, and fled,
And ran, and rushed, and bolted, haling off
The dog, my charge! But now I've got thee fast.

[686]

So close the Styx's inky-hearted rock,
The blood-bedabbled peak of Acheron
Shall hem thee in: the hell-hounds of Cocytus
Prowl round thee; whilst the hundred-headed Asp
Shall rive thy heart-strings: the Tartesian Lamprey
Prey on thy lungs: and those Tithrasian Gorgons
Mangle and tear thy kidneys, mauling them,
Entrails and all, into one bloody mash.
I'll speed a running foot to fetch them hither.

Xanthias. Hallo! what now?

Dionysus.   I've done it: call the god.

Xanthias. Get up, you laughing-stock; get up directly,
Before you're seen.

Dionysus.   What, *I* get up? I'm fainting.
Please dab a sponge of water on my heart.

Xanthias. Here! Dab it on.

Dionysus.   Where is it?

Xanthias.   Ye golden gods,
Lies your heart THERE?

Dionysus.   It got so terrified
It fluttered down into my stomach's pit.

Xanthias. Cowardliest of gods and men!

Dionysus.   The cowardliest? I?
What I, who asked you for a sponge, a thing
A coward never would have done!

Xanthias.   What then?

Dionysus. A coward would have lain there wallowing;
But I stood up, and wiped myself withal.

Xanthias. Poseidon! quite heroic.

Dionysus.   'Deed I think so.
But weren't *you* frightened at those dreadful threats
And shoutings?

Xanthias.   Frightened? Not a bit. I cared not.

Dionysus. Come then, if you're so *very* brave a man,
Will you be I, and take the hero's club
And lion's skin, since you're so monstrous plucky?
And I'll be now the slave, and bear the luggage.

Xanthias. Hand them across. I cannot choose but take them.
And now observe the Xanthio-heracles
If I'm a coward and a sneak like you.

[687]

Dionysus. Nay, you're the rogue from Melite's own self.
And I'll pick up and carry on the traps.
Maid. O welcome, Heracles! come in, sweetheart.
My Lady, when they told her, set to work,
Baked mighty loaves, boiled two or three tureens
Of lentil soup, roasted a prime ox whole,
Made rolls and honey-cakes. So come along.
Xanthias (declining). You are too kind.
Maid.   I will not let you go.
I will not LET you! Why, she's stewing slices
Of juicy bird's-flesh, and she's making comfits,
And tempering down her richest wine. Come, dear,
Come along in.
Xanthias (still declining). Pray thank her.
Maid.   O you're jesting,
I shall not let you off: there's such a lovely
Flute-girl all ready, and we're two or three
Dancing-girls also.
Xanthias.   Eh! what! Dancing-girls?
Maid. Young budding virgins, freshly tired and trimmed.
Come, dear, come in. The cook was dishing up
The cutlets, and they are bringing in the tables.
Xanthias. Then go you in, and tell those dancing-girls
Of whom you spake, I'm coming in Myself.
Pick up the traps, my lad, and follow me.
Dionysus. Hi! stop! you're not in earnest, just because
I dressed you up, in fun, as Heracles?
Come, don't keep fooling, Xanthias, but lift
And carry in the traps yourself.
Xanthias.   Why! what!
You are never going to strip me of these togs
You gave me!
Dionysus.   Going to? No, I'm doing it now.
Off with that lion-skin.
Xanthias.   Bear witness all,
The gods shall judge between us.
Dionysus.   Gods, indeed!
Why, how could *you* (the vain and foolish thought!)
A slave, a mortal, act Alcmena's son?

[688]

Xanthias. All right then, take them; maybe, if **God will,**
You'll soon require my services again.

Chorus. This is the part of a dexterous clever
     Man with his wits about him ever,
     One who has traveled the world to see;
     Always to shift, and to keep through all
     Close to the sunny side of the wall;
     Not like a pictured block to be,
     Standing always in one position;
     Nay but to veer, with expedition,
     And ever to catch the favoring breeze,
     This is the part of a shrewd tactician,
     This is to be a—THERAMENES!
Dionysus. Truly an exquisite joke 'twould be,
     Him with a dancing-girl to see,
     Lolling at ease on Milesian rugs;
     Me, like a slave, beside him standing,
     Aught that he wants to his lordship handing;
     Then as the damsel fair he hugs,
     Seeing me all on fire to embrace her,
     He would perchance (for there's no man baser),
     Turning him round like a lazy lout,
     Straight on my mouth deliver a facer,
     Knocking my ivory choirmen out.
Hostess. O Plathane! Plathane! Here's that naughty man,
That's he who got into our tavern once,
And ate up sixteen loaves.
    Plathane.   O, so he is!
The very man.
    Xanthias.   Bad luck for somebody!
    Hostess. O and, besides, those twenty bits of stew,
Half-obol pieces.
    Xanthias.   Somebody's going to catch it!
    Hostess. That garlic too.
    Dionysus.   Woman, you're talking nonsense.
You don't know what you're saying.
    Hostess.   O, you thought
I shouldn't know you with your buskins on!
Ah, and I've not yet mentioned all that fish,

No, nor the new-made cheese: he gulped it down,
Baskets and all, unlucky that we were.
And when I just alluded to the price,
He looked so fierce, and bellowed like a bull.
    Xanthias. Yes, that's his way: that's what he always does.
    Hostess. O, and he drew his sword, and seemed quite mad.
    Plathane. O, that he did.
    Hostess.   And terrified us so
We sprang up to the cockloft, she and I.
Then out he hurled, decamping with the rugs.
    Xanthias. That's his way too; but something must be done.
    Hostess. Quick, run and call my patron Cleon here!
    Plathane. O, if you meet him, call Hyperbolus!
We'll pay you out to-day.
    Hostess.   O filthy throat,
O how I'd like to take a stone, and hack
Those grinders out with which you chawed my wares.
    Plathane. I'd like to pitch you in the deadman's pit.
    Hostess. I'd like to get a reaping-hook and scoop
That gullet out with which you gorged my tripe.
But I'll to Cleon: he'll soon serve his writs;
He'll twist it out of you to-day, he will.
    Dionysus. Perdition seize me, if I don't love Xanthias.
    Xanthias. Aye, aye, I know your drift: stop, stop that talk-
        ing.
I won't be Heracles.
    Dionysus.   O don't say so.
Dear, darling Xanthias.
    Xanthias.   Why, how can I,
A slave, a mortal, act Alcmena's son!
    Dionysus. Aye, aye, I know you are vexed, and I deserve it,
And if you pummel me, I won't complain.
But if I strip you of these togs again,
Perdition seize myself, my wife, my children,
And, most of all, that blear-eyed Archedemus.
    Xanthias. That oath contents me: on those terms I take
        them.
    Chorus. Now that at last you appear once more,
        Wearing the garb that at first you wore,
        Wielding the club and the tawny skin,

Now it is yours to be up and doing.
Glaring like mad, and your youth renewing,
Mindful of him whose guise you are in.
If, when caught in a bit of a scrape, you
Suffer a word of alarm to escape you,
Showing yourself but a feckless knave,
Then will your master at once undrape you,
Then you'll again be the toiling slave.

Xanthias. There, I admit, you have given to me a
Capital hint, and the like idea.
Friends, had occurred to myself before.
Truly if anything good befell
He would be wanting, I know full well,
Wanting to take to the togs once more.
Nevertheless, while in these I'm vested,
Ne'er shall you find me craven-crested,
No, for a dittany look I'll wear,
Aye, and methings it will soon be tested,
Hark! how the portals are rustling there.

Aeacus. Seize the dog-stealer, bind him, pinion him,
Drag him to justice?
   Dionysus.   Somebody's going to catch it.
   Xanthias (*striking out*). Hands off! get away! stand back!
   Aeacus.   Eh? You're for fighting,
Ho! Ditylas, Sceblyas, and Pardocas,
Come hither, quick; fight me this sturdy knave.
   Dionysus. Now isn't it a shame the man should strike
And he a thief besides?
   Aeacus.   A monstrous shame!
   Dionysus. A regular burning shame!
   Xanthias.   By the Lord Zeus,
If ever I was here before, if ever
I stole one hair's-worth from you, let me die!
And now I'll make you a right noble offer,
Arrest my lad: torture him as you will,
And if you find I'm guilty, take and kill me.
   Aeacus. Torture him, how?
   Xanthias.   In any mode you please.
Pile bricks upon him: stuff his nose with acid:
Flay, rack him, hoist him; flog him with a scourge

Of prickly bristles: only not with this,
A soft-leaved onion, or a tender leek.
  Aeacus. A fair proposal. If I strike too hard
And maim the boy, I'll make you compensation.
  Xanthias. I shan't require it. Take him out and flog him.
  Aeacus. Nay, but I'll do it here before your eyes.
Now then, put down the traps, and mind you speak
The truth, young fellow.
  · *Dionysus (in agony).*   Man! don't torture ME!
I am a god. You'll blame yourself hereafter
If you touch ME.
  Aeacus.   Hillo! What's that you are saying?
  Dionysus. I say I'm Bacchus, son of Zeus, a god,
And *he's* the slave.
  Aeacus.   You hear him?
  Xanthias.   Hear him? Yes.
All the more reason you should flog him well.
For if he is a god, he won't perceive it.
  Dionysus. Well, but you say that you're a god yourself.
So why not *you* be flogged as well as I?
  Xanthias. A fair proposal. And be this the test,
Whichever of us two you first behold
Flinching or crying out—he's not the god.
  Aeacus. Upon my word you're quite the gentleman,
You're all for right and justice. Strip then, both.
  Xanthias. How can you test us fairly?
  Aeacus.   Easily,
I'll give you blow for blow.
  Xanthias.   A good idea.
We're ready! Now! (AEACUS *strikes him*) see if you catch me
    flinching.
  Aeacus. I struck you.
  Xanthias (incredulously). No.
  Aeacus.   Well, it seems 'no,' indeed.
Now then I'll strike the other.
                  [*Strikes* DIONYSUS.
  Dionysus.   Tell me when?
  Aeacus. I struck you.
  Dionysus.   Struck me? Then why didn't I sneeze?
  Aeacus. Don't know, I'm sure. I'll try the other again.

[handwritten margin notes:] the flogging jokes are not supposed to feel pain / flogging of slave was very funny

THE FROGS

Xanthias. And quickly too. Good gracious!

Aeacus. Why 'good gracious'?
Not hurt you, did I?

Xanthias. No, I merely thought of
The Diomeian feast of Heracles.

Aeacus. A holy man! 'Tis now the other's turn.

Dionysus. Hi! Hi!

Aeacus. Hallo!

Dionysus. Look at those horsemen, look!

Aeacus. But why these tears?

Dionysus. There's such a smell of onions.

Aeacus. Then you don't mind it?

Dionysus (*cheerfully*). Mind it? not a bit.

Aeacus. Well, I must go to the other one again.

Xanthias. O! O!

Aeacus. Hallo!

Xanthias. Do pray pull out this thorn.

Aeacus. What does it mean? 'Tis this one's turn again.

Dionysus (*shrieking*). Apollo! Lord! (*calmly*) of Delos
and of Pytho.

Xanthias. He flinched! You heard him?

Dionysus. Not at all; a jolly
Verse of Hipponax flashed across my mind.

Xanthias. You don't half do it: cut his flanks to pieces.

Aeacus. By Zeus, well thought on. Turn your belly here.

Dionysus (*screaming*). Poseidon!

Xanthias. There! he's flinching.

Dionysus (*singing*). who dost reign
Amongst the Aegean peaks and creeks
And o'er the deep blue main.

Aeacus. No, by Demeter, still I can't find out
Which is the god, but come ye both indoors;
My lord himself and Persephassa there,
Being gods themselves, will soon find out the truth.

Dionysus. Right! right! I only wish you had thought of that
Before you gave me those tremendous whacks.

Chorus. Come, Muse, to our Mystical Chorus,
O come to the joy of my song,

O see on the benches before us
         that countless and wonderful throng,
Where wits by the thousand abide,
         with more than a Cleophon's pride—
On the lips of that foreigner base,
         of Athens the bane and disgrace,
    There is shrieking, his kinsman by race,
    The garrulous swallow of Thrace;
    From that perch of exotic descent,
    Rejoicing her sorrow to vent,
She pours to her spirit's content,
         a nightingale's woeful lament,
That e'en though the voting be equal,
         his ruin will soon be the sequel.

Well it suits the holy Chorus
         evermore with counsel wise
To exhort and teach the city;
         this we therefore now advise—
End the townsmen's apprehensions;
         equalize the rights of all;
If by Phrynichus's wrestlings
         some perchance sustained a fall,
Yet to these 'tis surely open,
         having put away their sin,
For their slips and vacillations
         pardon at your hands to win.
Give your brethren back their franchise.
         Sin and shame it were that slaves,
Who have once with stern devotion
         fought your battle on the waves,
Should be straightway lords and masters,
         yea Plataeans fully blown—
Not that this deserves our censure;
         there I praise you; there alone
Has the city, in her anguish,
         policy and wisdom shown—
Nay but these, of old accustomed
         on our ships to fight and win,

(They, their fathers too before them),

                these our very kith and kin,

You should likewise, when they ask you,

                pardon for their single sin.

O by nature best and wisest,

                O relax your jealous ire,

Let us all the world as kinsfolk

                and as citizens acquire,

All who on our ships will battle

                well and bravely by our side.

If we cocker up our city,

                narrowing her with senseless pride,

Now when she is rocked and reeling

                in the cradles of the sea,

Here again will after ages deem we acted brainlessly.

And O if I'm able to scan

                the habits and life of a man

Who shall rue his iniquities soon!

                not long shall that little baboon,

That Cleigenes shifty and small,

                the wickedest bathman of all

Who are lords of the earth—which is brought

                from the isle of Cimolus, and wrought

        With nitre and lye into soap—

        Not long shall he vex us, I hope.

        And this the unlucky one knows,

        Yet ventures a peace to oppose,

And being addicted to blows

                he carries a stick as he goes,

Lest while he is tipsy and reeling,

                some robber his cloak should be stealing.

Often has it crossed my fancy,

                that the city loves to deal

With the very best and noblest

                members of her commonweal,

Just as with our ancient coinage,

                and the newly-minted gold.

Yea for these, our sterling pieces,

                all of pure Athenian mould,

All of perfect die and metal,

> all the fairest of the fair,

All of workmanship unequalled,

> proved and valued everywhere

Both amongst our own Hellenes

> and Barbarians far away,

These we use not: but the worthless

> pinchbeck coins of yesterday,

Vilest die and basest metal,

> now we always use instead.

Even so, our sterling townsmen,

> nobly born and nobly bred,

Men of worth and rank and mettle,

> men of honorable fame,

Trained in every liberal science,

> choral dance and manly game,

These we treat with scorn and insult,

> but the strangers newliest come,

Worthless sons of worthless fathers,

> pinchbeck townsmen, yellowy scum,

Whom in earlier days the city

> hardly would have stooped to use

Even for her scapegoat victims,

> these for every task we choose.

O unwise and foolish people,

> yet to mend your ways begin;

Use again the good and useful:

> so hereafter, if ye win

'Twill be due to this your wisdom:

> if ye fall, at least 'twill be

Not a fall that brings dishonor,

> falling from a worthy tree.

Aeacus. By Zeus the Saviour, quite the gentleman
Your master is.

Xanthias.   Gentleman? I believe you.
He's all for wine and women, is my master.

Aeacus. But not to have flogged you, when the truth came out
That you, the slave, were passing off as master!

Xanthias. He'd get the worst of that.

Aeacus.   Bravo! that's spoken
Like a true slave: that's what I love myself.

Xanthias. You love it, do you?

Aeacus.   Love it? I'm entranced
When I can curse my lord behind his back.

Xanthias. How about grumbling, when you have felt the
stick,
And scurry out of doors?

Aeacus.   That's jolly too.

Xanthias. How about prying?

Aeacus.   That beats everything!

Xanthias. Great Kin-god Zeus! And what of overhearing
Your master's secrets?

Aeacus.   What? I'm mad with joy.

Xanthias. And blabbing them abroad?

Aeacus.   O heaven and earth!
When I do that, I can't contain myself.

Xanthias. Phoebus Apollo! clap your hand in mine,
Kiss and be kissed: and prithee tell me this,
Tell me by Zeus, our rascaldom's own god,
What's all that noise within? What means this hubbub
And row?

Aeacus.   That's Aeschylus and Euripides.

Xanthias. Eh?

Aeacus.   Wonderful, wonderful things are going on.
The dead are rioting, taking different sides.

Xanthias. Why, what's the matter?

Aeacus.   There's a custom here
With all the crafts, the good and noble crafts,
That the chief master of his art in each
Shall have his dinner in the assembly hall,
And sit by Pluto's side.

Xanthias.   I understand.

Aeacus. Until another comes, more wise than he
In the same art: then must the first give way.

Xanthias. And how has this disturbed our Aeschylus?

Aeacus. 'Twas he that occupied the tragic chair,
As, in his craft, the noblest.

Xanthias.   Who does now?

Aeacus. But when Euripides came down, he kept

[697]

Flourishing off before the highwaymen,
Thieves, burglars, parricides—these form our mob
In Hades—till with listening to his twists
And turns, and pleas and counterpleas, they went
Mad on the man, and hailed him first and wisest:
Elate with this, he claimed the tragic chair
Where Aeschylus was seated.

 Xanthias.   Wasn't he pelted?
 Aeacus. Not he: the populace clamored out to try
Which of the twain was wiser in his art.
 Xanthias. You mean the rascals?
 Aeacus.   Aye, as high as heaven!
 Xanthias. But were there none to side with Aeschylus?
 Aeacus. Scanty and sparse the good (*regards the audience*),
  the same as here.
 Xanthias. And what does Pluto now propose to do?
 Aeacus. He means to hold a tournament, and bring
Their tragedies to the proof.
 Xanthias.   But Sophocles,
How came not he to claim the tragic chair?
 Aeacus. Claim it? Not he! When *he* came down, he kissed
With reverence Aeschylus, and clasped his hand,
And yielded willingly the chair to him.
But now he's going, says Cleidemides,
To sit third-man: and then if Aeschylus win,
He'll stay content: if not, for his art's sake,
He'll fight to the death against Euripides.
 Xanthias. Will it come off?
 Aeacus.   O yes, by Zeus, directly.
And then, I hear, will wonderful things be done,
The art poetic will be weighed in scales.
 Xanthias. What! weigh out tragedy, like butcher's meat?
 Aeacus. Levels they'll bring, and measuring-tapes for words,
And moulded oblongs,
 Xanthias.   Is it bricks they are making?
 Aeacus. Wedges and compasses: for Euripides
Vows that he'll test the dramas, word by word.
 Xanthias. Aeschylus chafes at this, I fancy.
 Aeacus.   Well,
He lowered his brows, upglaring like a bull.

Xanthias. And who's to be the judge?

Aeacus.   There came the rub.
Skilled men were hard to find: for with the Athenians
Aeschylus, somehow, did not hit it off,

Xanthias. Too many burglars, I expect, he thought.

Aeacus. And all the rest, he said, were trash and nonsense
To judge poetic wits. So then at last
They chose your lord, an expert in the art.
But we go in: for when our lords are bent
On urgent business, that means blows for us.

Chorus. O surely with terrible wrath
                    will the thunder-voiced monarch be filled,
When he sees his opponent beside him,
                    the tonguester, the artifice-skilled,
Stand, whetting his tusks for the fight!
                    O surely, his eyes rolling-fell
        Will with terrible madness be fraught!
O then will be charging of plume-waving words
                    with their wild-floating mane,
And then will be whirling of splinters,
                    and phrases smoothed down with the plane,
When the man would the grand-stepping maxims,
                    the language gigantic, repel
        Of the hero-creator of thought.
There will his shaggy-born crest
                    upbristle for anger and woe,
Horribly frowning and growling,
                    his fury will launch at the foe
Huge-clamped masses of words,
                    with exertion Titanic up-tearing
        Great ship-timber planks for the fray.
But here will the tongue be at work,
                    uncoiling, word-testing, refining,
Sophist-creator of phrases,
                    dissecting, detracting, maligning,
Shaking the envious bits,
                    and with subtle analysis paring
        The lung's large labor away.

[699]

Euripides. Don't talk to me; I won't give up the chair,
I say I am better in the art than he.

Dionysus. You hear him, Aeschylus: why don't you speak?

Euripides. He'll do the grand at first, the juggling trick
He used to play in all his tragedies.

Dionysus. Come, my fine fellow, pray don't talk too big.

Euripides. I know the man, I've scanned him through and
      through,
A savage-creating stubborn-pulling fellow,
Uncurbed, unfettered, uncontrolled of speech,
Unperiphrastic, bombastiloquent.

Aeschylus. Hah! sayest thou so, child of the garden quean!
And this to ME, thou chattery-babble-collector,
Thou pauper-creating rags-and-patches-stitcher?
Thou shalt abye it dearly!

Dionysus.   Pray, be still;
Nor heat thy soul to fury, Aeschylus.

Aeschylus. Not till I've made you see the sort of man
This cripple-maker is who crows so loudly.

Dionysus. Bring out a ewe, a black-fleeced ewe, my boys:
Here's a typhoon about to burst upon us.

Aeschylus. Thou picker-up of Cretan monodies,
Foisting thy tales of incest on the stage—

Dionysus. Forbear, forbear, most honored Aeschylus;
And you, my poor Euripides, begone
If you are wise, out of this pitiless hail,
Lest with some heady word he crack your skull
And batter out your brain—less Telephus.
And not with passion, Aeschylus, but calmly
Test and be tested. 'Tis not meet for poets
To scold each other, like two baking-girls.
But you go roaring like an oak on fire.

Euripides. I'm ready, I! I don't draw back one bit.
I'll lash or, if he will, let him lash first
The talk, the lays, the sinews of a play:
Aye and my Peleus, aye and Aeolus,
And Meleager, aye and Telephus.

Dionysus. And what do *you* propose? Speak, Aeschylus.

Aeschylus. I could have wished to meet him otherwhere.
We fight not here on equal terms.

Dionysus.   Why not?
Aeschylus. My poetry survived me: his died with him:
He's got it here, all handy to recite.
Howbeit, if so you wish it, so we'll have it.
   Dionysus. O bring me fire, and bring me frankincense.
I'll pray, or e'er the clash of wits begin,
To judge the strife with high poetic skill.
Meanwhile (*to the* CHORUS) invoke the Muses with a song.
   Chorus. O Muses, the daughters divine
                              of Zeus, the immaculate Nine,
Who gaze from your mansions serene
                              on intellects subtle and keen,
When down to the tournament lists,
                              in bright-polished wit they descend,
With wrestling and turnings and twists
                              in the battle of words to contend,
O come and behold what the two
                              antagonist poets can do,
Whose mouths are the swiftest to teach
                              grand language and filings of speech:
For now of their wits is the sternest
                              encounter commencing in earnest.
   Dionysus. Ye two, put up your prayers before ye start.
   Aeschylus. Demeter, mistress, nourisher of my soul,
O make me worthy of thy mystic rites!
   Dionysus (*to* EURIPIDES). Now put on incense, you.
   Euripides.   Excuse me, no;
My vows are paid to other gods than these.
   Dionysus. What, a new coinage of your own?
   Euripides.   Precisely.
   Dionysus. Pray then to them, those private gods of yours.
   Euripides. Ether, my pasture, volubly-rolling tongue,
Intelligent wit and critic nostrils keen,
O well and neatly may I trounce his plays!

   Chorus. We also are yearning from these to be learning
         Some stately measure, some majestic grand
         Movement telling of conflicts nigh.
         Now for battle arrayed they stand,
         Tongues embittered, and anger high.

Each has got a venturesome will,
Each an eager and nimble mind;
One will wield, with artistic skill,
Clearcut phrases, and wit refined;
Then the other, with words defiant,
Stern and strong, like an angry giant
Laying on with uprooted trees,
Soon will scatter a world of these
Superscholastic subtleties.

Dionysus. Now then, commence your arguments,
                              and mind you both display
True wit, not metaphors, nor things
                              which any fool could say.
    Euripides. As for myself, good people all,
                              I'll tell you by-and-by
My own poetic worth and claims;
                              but first of all I'll try
To show how this portentous quack
                              beguiled the silly fools
Whose tastes were nurtured, ere he came,
                              in Phrynichus's schools.
He'd bring some single mourner on,
                              seated and veiled, 'twould be
Achilles, say, or Niobe
                              —the face you could not see—
An empty show of tragic woe,
                              who uttered not one thing
    Dionysus. 'Tis true.
    Euripides.   Then in the Chorus came,
                              and rattled off a string
Of four continuous lyric odes:
                              the mourner never stirred.
    Dionysus. I liked it too. I sometimes think
                              that I those mutes preferred
To all your chatterers now-a-days.
    Euripides.   Because, if you must know,
You were an ass.
    Dionysus.   An ass, no doubt;
                              what made him do it though?

Euripides. That was his quackery, don't you see,
                        to set the audience guessing
When Niobe would speak; meanwhile,
                        the drama was progressing.
Dionysus. The rascal, how he took me in!
                        'Twas shameful, was it not?
(*To* AESCHYLUS.) What makes you stamp and fidget so?
   Euripides.   He's catching it so hot.
So when he had humbugged thus awhile,
                        and now his wretched play
Was halfway through, a dozen words,
                        great wild-bull words, he'd say,
Fierce Bugaboos, with bristling crests,
                        and shaggy eyebrows too,
Which not a soul could understand.
   Aeschylus.   O heavens!
   Dionysus.   Be quiet, do.
Euripides. But not one single word was clear.
Dionysus.   St! don't your teeth be gnashing.
Euripides. 'Twas all Scamanders, moated camps,
                        and griffin-eagles flashing
In burnished copper on the shields,
                        chivalric-precipice-high
Expressions, hard to comprehend.
   Dionysus.   Aye, by the Powers, and I
Full many a sleepless night have spent
                        in anxious thought, because
I'd find the tawny cock-horse out,
                        what sort of bird it was!
Aeschylus. It was a sign, you stupid dolt,
                        engraved the ships upon.
Dionysus. Eryxis I supposed it was,
                        Philoxenus's son.
Euripides. Now really should a cock be brought
                        into a tragic play?
Aeschylus. You enemy of gods and men,
                        what was *your* practice, pray?
Euripides. No cock-horse in *my* plays, by Zeus,
                        no goat-stag there you'll see,

[703]

Such figures as are blazoned forth

                in Median tapestry.

When first I took the art from you,

                bloated and swoln, poor thing,

With turgid gasconading words

                and heavy dieting,

First I reduced and toned her down,

                and made her slim and neat

With wordlets and with exercise

                and poultices of beet,

And next a dose of chatterjuice,

                distilled from books, I gave her,

And monodies she took, with sharp

                Cephisophon for flavor.

I never used haphazard words,

                or plunged abruptly in;

Who entered first explained at large

                the drama's origin

And source.

    Aeschylus.   Its source, I really trust,

                was better than your own.

    Euripides. Then from the very opening lines

                no idleness was shown;

The mistress talked with all her might,

                the servant talked as much,

The master talked, the maiden talked,

                the beldame talked.

    Aeschylus.   For such

An outrage was not death your due?

    Euripides.   No, by Apollo, no:

That was my democratic way.

    Dionysus.   Ah, let that topic go.

Your record is not there, my friend,

                particularly good.

    Euripides. Then next I taught all these to speak.

    Aeschylus.   You did so, and I would

That ere such mischief you had wrought,

                your very lungs had split.

    Euripides. Canons of verse I introduced,

                and neatly chiseled wit;

To look, to scan: to plot, to plan: *model audience*
                                         sceptical of everything.
                                  to twist, to turn, to woo:

On all to spy; in all to pry.
    Aeschylus.   You did: I say so too.
    Euripides. I showed them scenes of common life,
               the things we know and see,
Where any blunder would at once
               by all detected be.
I never blustered on, or took
               their breath and wits away
By Cycnuses or Memnons clad
               in terrible array,
With bells upon their horses' heads,
               the audience to dismay.
Look at *his* pupils, look at mine:
               and there the contrast view.
Uncouth Megaenetus is his,
               and rough Phormisius too;
Great long-beard-lance-and-trumpet-men,
               flesh-tearers with the pine:
But natty smart Theramenes,
               and Cleitophon are mine.
    Dionysus. Theramenes? a clever man
               and wonderfully sly:
Immerse him in a flood of ills,
               he'll soon be high and dry,
'A Kian with a kappa, sir,
               not Chian with a chi.'
    Euripides. I taught them all these knowing ways
      By chopping logic in my plays,
      And making all my speakers try
      To reason out the How and Why.
      So now the people trace the springs,
      The sources and the roots of things,
      And manage all their households too
      Far better than they used to do,
      Scanning and searching *What's amiss?*
      And, *Why was that?* And, *How is this?*
    Dionysus. Ay, truly, never now a man
      Comes home, but he begins to scan;

And to his household loudly cries,
Why, where's my pitcher? What's the matter?
'Tis dead and gone my last year's platter.
Who gnawed these olives? Bless the sprat,
Who nibbled off the head of that?
And where's the garlic vanished, pray,
I purchased only yesterday?
—Whereas, of old, our stupid youths
Would sit, with open mouths and eyes,
Like any dull-brained Mammacouths.

Chorus. 'All this thou beholdest, Achilles our boldest.'
And what wilt thou reply? Draw tight the rein
Lest that fiery soul of thine
Whirl thee out of the listed plain,
Past the olives, and o'er the line.
Dire and grievous the charge he brings.
See thou answer him, noble heart,
Not with passionate bickerings.
Shape thy course with a sailor's art,
Reef the canvas, shorten the sails,
Shift them edgewise to shun the gales.
When the breezes are soft and low,
Then, well under control, you'll go
Quick and quicker to strike the foe.
O first of all the Hellenic bards
           high loftily-towering verse to rear,
And tragic phrase from the dust to raise,
       pour forth thy fountain with right good cheer.

Aeschylus. My wrath is hot at this vile mischance,
      and my spirit revolts at the thought that I
Must bandy words with a fellow like *him:*
      but lest he should vaunt that I can't reply—
Come, tell me what are the points for which
      a noble poet our praise obtains.
Euripides. For his ready wit, and his counsels sage,
      and because the citizen folk he trains
To be better townsmen and worthier men.
Aeschylus.   If then you have done the very reverse,

Found noble-hearted and virtuous men,
   and altered them, each and all, for the worse,
Pray what is the meed you deserve to get?
 Dionysus.   Nay, ask not *him.* He deserves to die.
 Aeschylus. For just consider what style of men
   he received from me, great six-foot-high
Heroical souls, who never would blench
   from a townsman's duties in peace or war;
Not idle loafers, or low buffoons,
   or rascally scamps such as now they are.
But men who were breathing spears and helms,
   and the snow-white plume in its crested pride,
The greave, and the dart, and the warrior's heart
   in its sevenfold casing of tough bull-hide.
 Dionysus. He'll stun me, I know, with his armory-work;
   this business is going from bad to worse.
 Euripides. And how did you manage to make them so grand,
   exalted, and brave with your wonderful verse?
 Dionysus. Come, Aeschylus, answer, and don't stand mute
   in your self-willed pride and arrogant spleen.
 Aeschylus. A drama I wrote with the War-god filled.
 Dionysus. Its name?
 Aeschylus. 'Tis the *Seven against Thebes* that I mean.
Which whoso beheld, with eagerness swelled
   to rush to the battlefield there and then.
 Dionysus. O that was a scandalous thing you did!
   You have made the Thebans mightier men,
More eager by far for the business of war.
   Now, therefore, receive this punch on the head.
 Aeschylus. Ah, *ye* might have practised the same yourselves,
   but ye turned to other pursuits instead.
Then next the *Persians* I wrote, in praise
   of the noblest deed that the world can show,
And each man longed for the victor's wreath,
   to fight and to vanquish his country's foe.
 Dionysus. I was pleased, I own, when I heard their moan
   for old Darius, their great king, dead;
When they smote together their hands, like this,
   and *Evir alake* the Chorus said.

[707]

Aeschylus. Aye, such are the poet's appropriate works:
                      and just consider how all along
From the very first they have wrought you good,
                    the noble bards, the masters of song.
First, Orpheus taught you religious rites,
              and from bloody murder to stay your hands:
Musaeus healing and oracle lore;
                and Hesiod all the culture of lands,
The time to gather, the time to plow.
              And gat not Homer his glory divine
By singing of valor, and honor, and right,
            and the sheen of the battle-extended line,
The ranging of troops and the arming of men?
    Dionysus.   O ay, but he didn't teach *that,* I opine,
To Pantacles; when he was leading the show
             I couldn't imagine what he was at,
He had fastened his helm on the top of his head,
          he was trying to fasten his plume upon that.
    Aeschylus. But others, many and brave, he taught,
           of whom was Lamachus, hero true;
And thence my spirit the impress took,
          and many a lion-heart chief I drew,
Patrocluses, Teucers, illustrious names;
          for I fain the citizen-folk would spur
To stretch themselves to *their* measure and height,
         whenever the trumpet of war they hear.
But Phaedras and Stheneboeas? No!
         no harlotry business deformed my plays.
And none can say that ever I drew
         a love-sick woman in all my days.
    Euripides. For *you* no lot or portion had got
           in Queen Aphrodite.
    Aeschylus.   Thank Heaven for that.
But ever on you and yours, my friend,
         the mighty goddess mightily sat;
Yourself she cast to the ground at last.
    Dionysus.   O ay, that came uncommonly pat.
You showed how cuckolds are made, and lo,
        you were struck yourself by the very same fate.

Euripides. But say, you cross-grained censor of mine,
                         how *my* Stheneboeas could harm the state.
Aeschylus. Full many a noble dame, the wife
                                of a noble citizen, hemlock took,
And died, unable the shame and sin
                         of your Bellerophon-scenes to brook.
Euripides. Was then, I wonder, the tale I told
                         of Phaedra's passionate love untrue?
Aeschylus. Not so: but tales of incestuous vice
                         the sacred poet should hide from view,
Nor ever exhibit and blazon forth
                         on the public stage to the public ken.
For boys a teacher at school is found,
                         but we, the poets, are teachers of men.
We are BOUND things honest and pure to speak.
  Euripides.   And to speak great Lycabettuses, pray,
And massive blocks of Parnassian rocks,
                         is *that* things honest and pure to say?
In human fashion we ought to speak.
  Aeschylus.   Alas, poor witling, and can't you see
That for mighty thoughts and heroic aims,
                         the words themselves must appropriate be?
And grander belike on the ear should strike
                         the speech of heroes and godlike powers,
Since even the robes that invest their limbs
                         are statelier, grander robes than ours.
Such was *my* plan: but when *you* began,
                         you spoilt and degraded it all.
  Euripides.   How so?
  Aeschylus. Your kings in tatters and rags you dressed,
                         and brought them on, a beggarly show,
To move, forsooth, our pity and ruth.
  Euripides.   And what was the harm, I should like to know.
  Aeschylus. No more will a wealthy citizen now
                         equip for the state a galley of war.
He wraps his limbs in tatters and rags,
                         and whines *he is poor, too poor by far.*
  Dionysus. But under his rags he is wearing a vest,
                         as woolly and soft as a man could wish.

[709]

Let him gull the state, and he's off to the mart;
                      an eager, extravagant buyer of fish.
    Aeschylus. Moreover to prate, to harangue, to debate,
                is now the ambition of all in the state.
Each exercise-ground is in consequence found
                   deserted and empty: to evil repute
Your lessons have brought our youngsters, and taught
              our sailors to challenge, discuss, and refute
The orders they get from their captains and yet,
           when *I* was alive, I protest that the knaves
Knew nothing at all, save for rations to call,
        and to sing 'Rhyppapae' as they pulled
                      through the waves.
    Dionysus. And bedad to let fly from their sterns in the eye
           of the fellow who tugged at the undermost oar,
And a jolly young messmate with filth to besmirch,
            and to land for a filching adventure ashore;
But now they harangue, and dispute, and won't row
And idly and aimlessly float to and fro.
    Aeschylus. Of what ills is he NOT the creator and cause?
Consider the scandalous scenes that he draws,
His bawds, and his panders, his women who give,
    Give birth in the sacredest shrine,
Whilst others with brothers are wedded and bedded,
    And others opine
That 'not to be living' is truly 'to live.'
And therefore our city is swarming to-day
With clerks and with demagogue-monkeys, who play
Their jackanape tricks at all times, in all places,
Deluding the people of Athens; but none
Has training enough in athletics to run
    With the torch in his hand at the races.
    Dionysus. By the Powers, you are right! At the Panathenaea
I laughed till I felt like a potsherd to see a
Pale, paunchy young gentleman pounding along,
With his head butting forward, the last of the throng,
In the direst of straits; and behold at the gates,
The Ceramites flapped him, and smacked him, and slapped
    him,
In the ribs, and the loin, and the flank, and the groin,

And still, as they spanked him, he puffed and he panted,
Till at one mighty cuff, he discharged such a puff
    That he blew out his torch and levanted. ✓

Chorus. Dread the battle, and stout the combat,
                  mighty and manifold looms the war.
    Hard to decide is the fight they're waging,
    One like a stormy tempest raging,
One alert in the rally and skirmish,
                clever to parry and foin and spar.
    Nay but don't be content to sit
Always in one position only:
              many the fields for your keen-edged wit.
    On then, wrangle in every way,
    Argue, battle, be flayed and flay,
    Old and new from your stores display,
Yea, and strive with venturesome daring
             something subtle and neat to say.
Fear ye this, that to-day's spectators
             Lack the grace of artistic lore,
    Lack the knowledge they need for taking
    All the points ye will soon be making?
Fear it not: the alarm is groundless:
           that, be sure, is the case no more.
    All have fought the campaign ere this:
Each a book of the words is holding;
          never a single point they'll miss.
    Bright their natures, and now, I ween,
    Newly whetted, and sharp, and keen.
    Dread not any defect of wit,
Battle away without misgiving,
        sure that the audience, at least, are fit.

Euripides. Well then I'll turn me to your prologues now,
Beginning first to test the first beginning
Of this fine poet's plays. Why he's obscure
Even in the enunciation of the facts.
    Dionysus. Which of them will you test?
    Euripides.   Many: but first
Give us that famous one from the Oresteia.

Dionysus. St! Silence all! Now, Aeschylus, begin.

Aeschylus. Grave Hermes, witnessing a father's power,
Be thou my saviour and mine aid to-day,
For here I come and hither I return.

Dionysus. Any fault there?

Euripides. A dozen faults and more.

Dionysus. Eh! why the lines are only three in all.

Euripides. But every one contains a score of faults.

Dionysus. Now Aeschylus, keep silent; if you don't
You won't get off with three iambic lines.

Aeschylus. Silent for *him!*

Dionysus. If *my* advice you'll take.

Euripides. Why, at first starting here's a fault skyhigh.

Aeschylus (*to* DIONYSUS). You see your folly?

Dionysus. Have your way; I care not.

Aeschylus (*to* EURIPIDES). What is my fault?

Euripides. Begin the lines again.

Aeschylus. Grave Hermes, witnessing a father's power—

Euripides. And this beside his murdered father's grave
Orestes speaks?

Aeschylus. I say not otherwise.

Euripides. Then does he mean that when his father fell
By craft and violence at a woman's hand,
The god of craft was witnessing the deed?

Aeschylus. It was not he: it was the Helper Hermes
He called the grave: and this he showed by adding
It was his sire's prerogative he held.

Euripides. Why this is worse than all. If from his father
He held this office grave, why then—

Dionysus. He was
A graveyard rifler on his father's side.

Aeschylus. Bacchus, the wine you drink is stale and fusty.

Dionysus. Give him another: (*to* EURIPIDES) you, look out
for faults.

Aeschylus. Be thou my saviour and mine aid to-day,
For here I come, and hither I return.

Euripides. The same thing twice says clever Aeschylus.

Dionysus. How twice?

Euripides. Why, just consider: I'll explain
'I come,' says he; and 'I return,' says he:

[712]

It's the same thing, to 'come' and to 'return.'
   Dionysus. Aye, just as if you said, 'Good fellow, lend me
A kneading trough: likewise, a trough to knead in.'
   Aeschylus. It is not so, you everlasting talker,
They're not the same, the words are right enough.
   Dionysus. How so? inform me how you use the words.
   Aeschylus. A man, not banished from his home, may 'come'
To any land, with no especial chance.
A home-bound exile both 'returns' and 'comes.
   Dionysus. O good, by Apollo!
What do you say, Euripides, to that?
   Euripides. I say Orestes never did 'return.'
He came in secret: nobody recalled him.
   Dionysus. O good, by Hermes!
(*Aside*) I've not the least suspicion what he means.
   Euripides. Repeat another line.
   Dionysus.   Ay, Aeschylus.
Repeat one instantly: *you,* mark what's wrong.
   Aeschylus. *Now on this funeral mound I call my father*
To hear, to hearken.
   Euripides.   There he is again.
To 'hear,' to 'hearken'; the same thing, exactly.
   Dionysus. Aye, but he's speaking to the dead, you knave,
Who cannot hear us though we call them thrice.
   Aeschylus. And how do you make *your* prologues?
   Euripides.   You shall hear;
And if you find one single thing said twice,
Or any useless padding, spit upon me.
   Dionysus. Well, fire away: I'm all agog to hear
Your very accurate and faultless prologues.
   Euripides. A happy man was Oedipus at first—
   Aeschylus. Not so, by Zeus; a most unhappy man.
Who, not yet born nor yet conceived, Apollo
Foretold would be his father's murderer.
How could *he* be a happy man at first?
   Euripides. Then he became the wretchedest of men.
   Aeschylus. Not so, by Zeus; he never ceased to be.
No sooner born, than they exposed the babe,
(And that in winter), in an earthen crock,
Lest he should grow a man, and slay his father.

[handwritten: Battle of the prologues]

Then with both ankles pierced and swoln, he limped
Away to Polybus: still young, he married
An ancient crone, and her his mother too.
Then scratched out both his eyes.
    Dionysus.   **Happy indeed**
Had he been Erasinides's colleague!
    Euripides. Nonsense; I say my prologues are first-rate.
    Aeschylus. Nay then, by Zeus, no longer line by line
I'll maul your phrases: but with heaven to aid
I'll smash your prologues with a bottle of oil.
    Euripides. You mine with a bottle of oil?
    Aeschylus.   **With only one.**
You frame your prologues so that each and all
Fit in with a 'bottle of oil,' or 'coverlet-skin,'
Or 'reticule-bag.' I'll prove it here, and now.
    Euripides. You'll prove it? You?
    Aeschylus.   **I will.**
    Dionysus.   **Well then, begin.**
    Euripides. Aegyptus, sailing with his fifty sons,
As ancient legends mostly tell the tale,
Touching at Argos
  Aeschylus.   Lost his bottle of oil.
    Euripides. Hang it, what's that? Confound that bottle of oil!
    Dionysus. Give him another: let him try again.
    Euripides. Bacchus, who, clad in fawnskins, leaps and
      bounds
With torch and thyrsus in the choral dance
Along Parnassus
  Aeschylus.   Lost his bottle of oil.
  Dionysus. Ah me, we are stricken—with that bottle again!
    Euripides. Pooh, pooh, that's nothing. I've a prologue here,
He'll never tack his bottle of oil to this:
No man is blest in every single thing.
One is of noble birth, but lacking means.
Another, baseborn,
    Aeschylus.   Lost his bottle of oil.
    Dionysus. Euripides!
    Euripides.   **Well?**
    Dionysus.   **Lower your sails, my boy;**
This bottle of oil is going to blow a gale.

Euripides. O, by Demeter, I don't care one bit;
Now from his hands I'll strike that bottle of oil.
    Dionysus. Go on then, go: but ware the bottle of oil.
    Euripides. Once Cadmus, quitting the Sidonian town,
Agenor's offspring
    Aeschylus.   Lost his bottle of oil.
    Dionysus. O pray, my man, buy off that bottle of oil,
Or else he'll smash our prologues all to bits.
    Euripides. I buy of *him?*
    Dionysus.   If *my* advice you'll take.
    Euripides. No, no, I've many a prologue yet to say,
To which he can't tack on his bottle of oil.
Pelops, the son of Tantalus, while driving
His mares to Pisa
    Aeschylus.   Lost his bottle of oil.
    Dionysus. There! he tacked on the bottle of oil again.
O for heaven's sake, pay him its price, dear boy;
You'll get it for an obol, spick and span.
    Euripides. Not yet, by Zeus; I've plenty of prologues left.
Oeneus once reaping
    Aeschylus.   Lost his bottle of oil.
    Euripides. Pray let me finish one entire line first.
Oeneus once reaping an abundant harvest,
Offering the firstfruits
    Aeschylus.   Lost his bottle of oil.
    Dionysus. What, in the act of offering? Fie! Who stole it?
    Euripides. O don't keep bothering! Let him try with this!
Zeus, as by Truth's own voice the tale is told,
    Dionysus. No, he'll cut in with 'Lost his bottle of oil!'
Those bottles of oil on all your prologues seem
To gather and grow, like styes upon the eye.
Turn to his melodies now for goodness' sake.
    Euripides. O I can easily show that he's a poor
Melody-maker; makes them all alike.

    Chorus. What, O what will be done!
                 Strange to think that he dare
                 Blame the bard who has won,
                 More than all in our days,
                 Fame and praise for his lays,

Lays so many and fair.
Much I marvel to hear
What the charge he will bring
'Gainst our tragedy king;
Yea for himself do I fear.

Euripides. Wonderful lays! O yes, you'll see directly.
I'll cut down all his metrical strains to one.
    Dionysus. And I, I'll take some pebbles, and keep count.
        [*A slight pause, during which the music of a flute
        is heard.*
    Euripides. Lord of Phthia, Achilles, *why hearing the voice
        of the hero-dividing*
    Hah! smiting! approachest thou not to the rescue?
We, by the lake who *abide, are adoring our ancestor Hermes.*
    Hah! smiting! approachest thou not to the rescue?
Dionysus.   O Aeschylus, twice art thou smitten!
Euripides. Hearken to me, great king; yea, hearken *Atreides,
    thou noblest of all the Achaeans.*
    Hah! smiting! approachest thou not to the rescue?
Dionysus.   Thrice, Aeschylus, thrice art thou smitten!
Euripides. Hush! the bee-wardens are here: they *will
    quickly the Temple of Artemis open.*
    Hah! smiting! approachest thou not to the rescue?
I will expound (for *I know it*) *the omen the chieftains en-
    countered.*
    Hah! smiting! approachest thou not to the rescue?
Dionysus. O Zeus and King, the terrible lot of smitings!
I'll to the bath: I'm very sure my kidneys
Are quite inflamed and swoln with all these smitings.
    Euripides. Wait till you've heard another batch of lays
Culled from his lyre-accompanied melodies.
    Dionysus. Go on then, go: but no more smitings, please.
    Euripides. How the twin-throned powers of *Achaea, the
    lords of the mighty Hellenes.*
    O phlattothrattophlattothrat!
Sendeth *the Sphinx, the unchancy, the chieftainness blood-
    hound.*
    O phlattothrattophlattothrat!

[716]

Launcheth fierce with brand *and hand the avengers the terrible
        eagle.*
    O phlattothrattophlattothrat!
So for the swift-*winged hounds of the air he provided a booty.*
    O phlattothrattophlattothrat!
    The throng down-bearing on Aias.
    O phlattothrattophlattothrat!
    Dionysus. Whence comes that phlattothrat? From Marathon,
    or
Where picked you up these cable-twister's strains?
    Aeschylus. From noblest source for noblest ends I brought
        them,
Unwilling in the Muses' holy field
The self-same flowers as Phrynichus to cull.
But *he* from all things rotten draws his lays,
From Carian flutings, catches of Meletus,
Dance-music, dirges. You shall hear directly.
Bring me the lyre. Yet wherefore need a lyre
For songs like these? Where's she that bangs and jangles
Her castanets? Euripides's Muse,
Present yourself: fit goddess for fit verse.
    Dionysus. The Muse herself can't be a wanton? No!
    Aeschylus. Halcyons, who by the ever-rippling
        Waves of the sea are babbling,
        Dewing your plumes with the drops that fall
        From wings in the salt spray dabbling.

    Spiders, ever with twir-r-r-r-rling fingers
    Weaving the warp and the woof,
    Little, brittle, network, fretwork,
    Under the coigns of the roof.

The minstrel shuttle's care.

    Where in the front of the dark-prowed ships
    Yarely the flute-loving dolphin skips.

Races here and oracles there.

    And the joy of the young vines smiling,
    And the tendril of grapes, care-beguiling.

O embrace me, my child, O embrace me.
(*To* Dionysus.) You see this foot?
   Dionysus.   I do.
   Aeschylus. And this?
   Dionysus.   And that one too.
   Aeschylus (*to* Euripides). You, such stuff who compile,
     Dare my songs to upbraid;
     You, whose songs in the style
     Of Cyrene's embraces are made.
So much for them: but still I'd like to show
The way in which your monodies are framed:
    'O darkly-light mysterious Night,
    What may this Vision mean,
    Sent from the world unseen
    With baleful omens rife;
    A thing of lifeless life,
    A child of sable night,
    A ghastly curdling sight,
    In black funereal veils,
  With murder, murder in its eyes,
    And great enormous nails?
Light ye the lanterns, my maidens,
         and dipping your jugs in the stream,
Draw me the dew of the water,
         and heat it to boiling and steam;
So will I wash me away the ill effects of my dream.
    God of the sea!
    My dream's come true.
    Ho, lodgers, ho,
    This portent view.
   Glyce has vanished, carrying off my cock,
    My cock that crew!
  O Mania, help! O Oreads of the rock
  Pursue! pursue!
  For I, poor girl, was working within,
  Holding my distaff heavy and full,
  Twir-r-r-r-rling my hand as the threads I spin,
  Weaving an excellent bobbin of wool;
  Thinking "To-morrow I'll go to the fair,
  In the dusk of the morn, and be selling it there."

[718]

But he to the blue upflew, upflew,
On the lightliest tips of his wings outspread;
To me he bequeathed but woe, but woe,
And tears, sad tears, from my eyes o'erflow,
Which I, the bereaved, must shed, must shed.
O children of Ida, sons of Crete,
Grasping your bows to the rescue come;
Twinkle about on your restless feet,
Stand in a circle around her home.
O Artemis, thou maid divine,
Dictynna, huntress, fair to see,
O bring that keen-nosed pack of thine,
And hunt through all the house with me.
O Hecate, with flameful brands,
O Zeus's daughter, arm thine hands,
Those swiftliest hands, both right and left;
Thy rays on Glyce's cottage throw
That I serenely there may go,
And search by moonlight for the theft.'

Dionysus. Enough of both your odes.
Aeschylus.   Enough for me.
Now would I bring the fellow to the scales.
That, that alone, shall test our poetry now,
And prove whose words are weightiest, his or mine.
    Dionysus. Then both come hither, since I needs must weigh
The art poetic like a pound of cheese.

    Chorus. O the labor these wits go through!
        O the wild, extravagant, new,
        Wonderful things they are going to do!
        Who but they would ever have thought of it?
        Why, if a man had happened to meet me
        Out in the street, and intelligence brought of it,
        I should have thought he was trying to cheat me;
        Thought that his story was false and deceiving.
        That were a tale I could never believe in.

    Dionysus. Each of you stand beside his scale.
Aeschylus and Euripides.   We're here.
    Dionysus. And grasp it firmly whilst ye speak your lines,

And don't let go until I cry 'Cuckoo.'
Aeschylus and Euripides. Ready!
Dionysus. Now speak your lines into the scale.
Euripides. O that the Argo had not winged her way—
Aeschylus. River Spercheius, cattle-grazing haunts—
Dionysus. Cuckoo! let go. O look, by far the lowest
His scale sinks down.
Euripides. Why, how came that about?
Dionysus. He threw a river in, like some wool-seller
Wetting his wool, to make it weigh the more.
But *you* threw in a light and wingèd word.
Euripides. Come, let him match another verse with mine.
Dionysus. Each to his scale.
Aeschylus and Euripides. We're ready.
Dionysus. Speak your lines.
Euripides. Persuasion's only shrine is eloquent speech.
Aeschylus. Death loves not gifts, alone amongst the gods.
Dionysus. Let go, let go. Down goes his scale again.
He threw in Death, the heaviest ill of all.
Euripides. And I Persuasion, the most lovely word.
Dionysus. A vain and empty sound, devoid of sense.
Think of some heavier-weighted line of yours,
To drag your scale down: something strong and big.
Euripides. Where have I got one? Where? Let's see.
Dionysus. I'll tell you.
'Achilles threw two singles and a four.'
Come, speak your lines: this is your last set-to.
Euripides. In his right hand he grasped an iron-clamped
mace.
Aeschylus. Chariot on chariot, corpse on corpse was hurled.
Dionysus. There now! again he has done you.
Euripides. Done me? How?
Dionysus. He threw two chariots and two corpses in;
Five-score Egyptians could not lift that weight.
Aeschylus. No more of 'line for line'; let him—himself,
His children, wife, Cephisophon—get in,
With all his books collected in his arms,
Two lines of mine shall overweigh the lot.
Dionysus. Both are my friends; I can't decide between them:
I don't desire to be at odds with either:

[720]

One is so clever, one delights me so.

 Pluto. Then you'll effect nothing for which you came?

 Dionysus. And how, if I decide?

 Pluto.   Then take the winner;

So will your journey not be made in vain.

 Dionysus. Heaven bless your Highness! Listen, I came down

After a poet.

 Euripides.   To what end?

 Dionysus.   That so

The city, saved, may keep her choral games.

Now then, whichever of you two shall best

Advise the city, *he* shall come with me.

And first of Alcibiades, let each

Say what he thinks; the city travails sore.

 Euripides. What does she think herself about him?

 Dionysus.   What?

She loves, and hates, and longs to have him back.

But give me *your* advice about the man.

 Euripides. I loathe a townsman who is slow to aid,

And swift to hurt, his town: who ways and means

Finds for himself, but finds not for the state.

 Dionysus. Poseidon, but that's smart! (*To* AESCHYLUS.) And

  what say *you?*

 Aeschylus. 'Twere best to rear no lion in the state:

But having reared, 'tis best to humor him.

 Dionysus. By Zeus the Saviour, still I can't decide.

One is so clever, and so clear the other.

But once again. Let each in turn declare

What plan of safety for the state ye've got.

 Euripides. [First with Cinesias wing Cleocritus,

Then zephyrs waft them o'er the watery plain.

 Dionysus. A funny sight, I own: but where's the sense?

 Euripides. If, when the fleets engage, they holding cruets

Should rain down vinegar in the foemen's eyes,]

I know, and I can tell you.

 Dionysus.   Tell away.

 Euripides. When things, mistrusted now, shall trusted be,

And trusted things, mistrusted.

 Dionysus.   How! I don't

Quite comprehend. Be clear, and not so clever.

Euripides. If we mistrust those citizens of ours
Whom now we trust, and those employ whom now
We don't employ, the city will be saved.
If on our present tack we fail, we surely
Shall find salvation in the opposite course.
    Dionysus. Good, O Palamedes! Good, you genius you.
[Is this *your* cleverness or Cephisophon's?
    Euripides. This is my own: the cruet-plan was his.]
    Dionysus (to AESCHYLUS). Now, you.
    Aeschylus.   But tell me whom the city uses.
The good and useful?
    Dionysus.   What are you dreaming of?
She hates and loathes them.
    Aeschylus.   Does she love the bad?
    Dionysus. Not love them, no: she uses them perforce.
    Aeschylus. How can one save a city such as this,
Whom neither frieze nor woolen tunic suits?
    Dionysus. O, if to earth you rise, find out some way.
    Aeschylus. There will I speak: I cannot answer here.
    Dionysus. Nay, nay; send up your guerdon from below.
    Aeschylus. When they shall count the enemy's soil their
        own,
And theirs the enemy's: when they know that ships
Are their true wealth, their so-called wealth delusion.
    Dionysus. Aye, but the justices suck that down, you know.
    Pluto. Now then, decide.
    Dionysus.   I will; and thus I'll do it.
I'll choose the man in whom my soul delights.
    Euripides. O, recollect the gods by whom you swore
You'd take me home again; and choose your friends.
    Dionysus. 'Twas my tongue swore; my choice is—Aeschylus.
    Euripides. Hah! what have you done?
    Dionysus.   Done? Given the victor's prize
To Aeschylus; why not?
    Euripides.   And do you dare
Look in my face, after that shameful deed?
    Dionysus. What's shameful, if the audience think not so?
    Euripides. Have you no heart? Wretch, would you leave me
        dead?
    Dionysus. Who knows if death be life, and life be death,

And breath be mutton broth, and sleep a sheepskin?
  Pluto. Now, Dionysus, come ye in,
  Dionysus.   What for?
  Pluto. And sup before ye go.
  Dionysus.   A bright idea.
I'faith, I'm nowise indisposed for that.

  Chorus. Blest the man who possesses a
              Keen intelligent mind.
              This full often we find.
              He, the bard of renown,
              Now to earth reascends,
              Goes, a joy to his town,
              Goes, a joy to his friends,
              Just because he possesses a
              Keen intelligent mind.
              RIGHT it is and befitting,
              Not, by Socrates sitting,
              Idle talk to pursue,
              Stripping tragedy-art of
              All things noble and true.
              Surely the mind to school
              Fine-drawn quibbles to seek,
              Fine-set phrases to speak,
              Is but the part of a fool!

  Pluto. Farewell then, Aeschylus, great and wise,
Go, save our state by the maxims rare
Of thy noble thought; and the fools chastise,
  For many a fool dwells there.
And *this* to Cleophon give, my friend,
And *this* to the revenue-raising crew,
Nicomachus, Myrmex, next I send,
  And *this* to Archenomus too.
And bid them all that without delay,
To my realm of the dead they hasten away.
For if they loiter above, I swear
I'll come myself and arrest them there.
And branded and fettered the slaves shall go
With the vilest rascal in all the town,

Adeimantus, son of Leucolophus, down,
> Down, down to the darkness below.

Aeschylus. I take the mission. This chair of mine
Meanwhile to Sophocles here commit,
(For I count him next in our craft divine,)
> Till I come once more by thy side to sit.

But as for that rascally scoundrel there,
That low buffoon, that worker of ill,
O let him not sit in my vacant chair,
> Not even against his will.

Pluto (*to the* CHORUS). Escort him up with your mystic
> throngs,
While the holy torches quiver and blaze.
Escort him up with his own sweet songs,
> And his noble festival lays.

Chorus. First, as the poet triumphant
> is passing away to the light,
Grant him success on his journey,
> ye powers that are ruling below.
Grant that he find for the city
> good counsels to guide her aright;
So we at last shall be freed
> from the anguish, the fear, and the woe,
Freed from the onsets of war.
> Let Cleophon now and his band
Battle, if battle they must,
> far away in their own fatherland.

SUPPLEMENT FROM THE 'POETICS' OF ARISTOTLE

SUPPLEMENT FROM THE 'POETICS' OF ARISTOTLE

Principles of Aristotle, and the Greek Dramas We Possess

THE principles or art of poetry which we find in the *Poetics* of Aristotle, supplemented, doubtless, by the De Coislin tract on comedy, come down to us from a larger body of critical writings. Before the time of Aristotle Homer had been critically studied, as we infer from the Platonic dialogue *Ion*, and from Chapters 23-6 of the *Poetics* itself, which deal with problems in criticism and their solutions. In the *Poetics*, Aristotle refers to a dozen or more treatises on poetry; he doubtless knew a work of Sophocles on the Chorus, possibly also some writing on the relation of Art to Nature by Agathon; and the writers of comedy, as Aristophanes in the *Frogs*, dealt in their way with literary and artistic themes. There is much to be learnt about art from the *Frogs*. Aristotle must have profited also from discussions in the Academy of questions which Plato had raised in the *Republic, Phaedrus,* and *Symposium;* the problem, for instance, of artistic imitation with which we find Plato still engaged while leading the Academy, to the end of his life, as witness the *Laws.*

In the following paraphrase or adaptation of the *Poetics*, an attempt has been made to add examples from plays in this volume. Added explanatory matter, as far as is feasible, is enclosed in square brackets.

I

Artistic Imitation

[Chapter 1.] [Assuming the presence of genius in the poet, and without discussing the education that poetic genius needs for its growth, Aristotle in the *Poetics* deals with the art of poetry in general, with the relations of this art to other imitative arts, and, above all, with the effect of poetry on the audience or reader. Poetry as a genus has its effect; each kind of poetry, as tragedy, epic poetry, or comedy, has its own effect, its special pleasure or satisfaction; and each element in a poem—the plot—the bias of the agents—their fashion of speaking—the diction, metrical, cadenced only, or un-adorned—the music or singing, tragic or comic—and the play as a visible thing, a spectacle—each element contributes its share to the effect of the whole. The effect of the whole is that delight or satisfaction which Sophocles' *Oedipus the King*, or Aeschylus' *Prometheus Bound* or *Agamemnon*, or Euripides' *Bacchae* produces in a qualified spectator, not an expert, but a 'judicious' person, as Shakespeare's Hamlet calls him; the person Aristotle styles *phronimos*. Such a judge will also receive the proper satisfaction from the *Iliad* or *Odyssey*, which have much in common with the drama, but lack the singing chorus, and are not acted out before our eyes.]

[Chapter 2.] [A tragedy about Prometheus, about Oedipus, or about Orestes and Iphigenia among the Taurians, is, like a statue or a painting, an imitation. Aeschylus, Sophocles, or Euripides has in mind a story, an action which he purposes to imitate in words, and with actors on the stage; this action performed by agents is his 'object,' and words are his medium. As a tragic poet he will tend to represent the agents as better than most human beings are, or if his men and women come from myths of the heroic age, as superior to men and women now, in the time of the poet. A comic poet, Aristophanes, will worsen his agents, making Aeschylus and Euripides, and even Dionysus and Plutus, god of wealth, inferior to what they actually were, or were commonly thought to be. Arts differ, again, in their manner of representation. Thus tragedy, as Sophocles' *Antigone*, directly presents the actions of men and women, whereas epic poetry, the *Iliad* or the *Odyssey*, narrates such actions.]

The objects of tragedy and comedy are men and women in action, doing or undergoing something. Aeschylus' Agamemnon undergoes, 'suffers'; his Clytemnestra 'does.' The objects of poetry, generally considered, are human beings doing or undergoing; [that is true of Homer or Dante as it is of Sophocles. As for the gods and goddesses, apart from the arbitrary device of the 'god from the machine,' they are, in the plays of Aeschylus and Sophocles, to all intents and purposes men. In the *Bacchae* of Euripides, Dionysus, cousin of Pentheus, acts more like a man throughout much of the play, and more like the *deus ex machina* towards the end.]

The agents, we have seen, will be of a higher or lower type. The line between better and worse divides mankind; virtually all other distinctions in human character are derived from this primary distinction between good and bad. In the imitation the agents must be represented as better or worse than the general run, or some such men as we. [It is so in the drama—Sophocles represents Antigone and Creon as tending towards the better type; Aristophanes represents Euelpides and Peisthetaerus as tending towards the worse. The tendency of Euripidean agents is to be like most of us. The distinction is seen in other arts. Polygnotus and Raphael depicted persons better than the average, Pauson and Hogarth worse, Dionysius and Rembrandt persons like ourselves. So far as the objects of the imitation are concerned, the nobility or inferiority of the agents is what distinguishes tragedy from comedy. Aristophanes tends to represent the agents as worse, and Sophocles tends to represent them as better, than the people we commonly meet.]

Arts differ, then, with respect to the objects they represent, that is, in taking a worse object or a better for the imitation; with respect to the manner of imitation, whether, for example, the action (the object) is directly presented, or is narrated; and with respect to the means.

Thus the painter uses line and color for his means. The sculptor uses metal, marble, clay, and so on. The imitative dancer uses the human body with its attitudes and motions. The composer of music uses notes. [The architect uses many materials or means, as wood and stone, in which to embody his plan or structure. The landscape gardener uses earth, vegetation, water, and air-spaces.[1]

The art of poetry has language for its means, words rhythmically arranged, or more strictly arranged in metres. But Greek tragedy had means in addition to language; for Sophocles in his plays was not merely poet in our sense; he was also a musical composer, using notes, was the trainer of a chorus, using the motions of the dancers, and was a painter, and in his scenery used line and color. He made use of costume too; the robes, the masks, the shoes of the players were a part of his media. His lyre-players and flute-players made use of melody and rhythm combined; see the lament of Oedipus above, p. 203. It is perhaps easier for readers now to imagine the effect of a Greek drama in its use of embellished language, of song, and of instrumental music, along with visible media, if we turn to Aristophanes' *Birds;* see, for example, the song of the Nightingale, p. 612; cf. pp. 631-5.

While discussing the means of poetry we may, with Aristotle, glance at the Dialogues of Plato, in which the medium is language without melody or metre in the technical sense; the language is rhythmical or cadenced, and closer to the diction of Aristophanes than to that of any other poet. But in so far as Plato is a poet, for Aristotle he will be so through his imitative faculty, and his power of constructing plots, rather than because of his skill in diction. A Poet is by etymology a Maker, and Sophocles, like Aristophanes and Plato, is first of all a maker of plots, a representer of actions. People call Sophocles a poet because he makes verses; but the principle of imitation is, for thinking readers, the distinguishing mark of the literary artist.]

[Chapter 3.] A third difference in the imitative arts that include epic poetry, drama, and the dialogue, concerns the manner in which their objects are imitated. The author may imitate his object—say, men in action—(1) by speaking now

---

[1] Aristotle does not give the last two examples, but the student will make the point of artistic media clear to himself if he persistently seeks to differentiate the arts by the media they employ. Finally, the art of human life has portions of time for its means, minutes, hours, days, years; compare Wordsworth on the arch of life ('My heart leaps up when I behold') as built of days.

in narrative, and now in an assumed rôle; this is the manner
of the epic poet. Or (2) he may continue speaking throughout
in his own person, without change. Or (3) the whole story
may be represented as an action, or a debate, carried on by
several persons as in real life; [this is the method employed
by Sophocles in a tragedy, as *Antigone*, by Aristophanes in
his *Frogs*, and by Plato in *Phaedrus* and *Crito*.]

Thus the difference with respect to the medium, the objects,
and the manner of imitation, lets us see points of similarity
in the arts. The art of Sophocles is akin to that of Homer, in
that both poets represent agents of a higher type; [Plato, too,
in his Dialogues represents speakers mostly of a higher type,
as, for example, Socrates and Phaedrus in *Phaedrus*, and the
Athenian, Megillus, and Clinias in the *Laws*.] In the manner
of imitation, the tragedies of Sophocles are like the comedies
of Aristophanes; [in *Antigone* and the *Frogs* both poets represent the agents directly as experiencing and doing in person.
Such, too, is in general the manner of the dialogue; the
author, Plato, does not appear; he lets us listen to his speakers
argue.]

[Chapter 4.] Poetry springs from two sources in human
nature, first, the impulse to imitate, which leads Sophocles to
represent the tragic tale of Oedipus, and, next, the pleasure
we all take in contemplating the imitations, in a Greek theatre
or elsewhere. [So, according to Hebrew and Christian tradition, Divine Love for the space of six days created after the
model of eternal ideas, and on the seventh day with pleasure
contemplated the results of this imitation.] Even when the
objects which an artist takes for imitation are painful or
repulsive, it gives us pleasure to see them well imitated. [The
story of Oedipus is painful, all tragic stories are so; but the
skilful imitation of them gives us pleasure. Likewise in comedy,
while frogs and wasps in themselves may be unpleasing, yet
they give us pleasure as Aristophanes represents them. So a
dead body may be unpleasing, but the representation in the
Frogs of the carrier on his way to Hades is amusing.[2] Our
pleasure in such pictures comes from the human appetite for
learning; for among the pleasures of mankind that of learning
is the keenest, a delight not alone to the scholarly, but to all

---

[2] Note that Aristophanes avoids any depiction of death or its agony.

men, however limited their capacity. The reason why men like a picture is that when they look at it they are acquiring knowledge and drawing inferences; [compare the pictures, doubtless stage-properties painted by Sophocles, at the opening of his *Electra*, where the Paedagogus asks Orestes to look at 'the ancient Argos,' 'the Lycean Agora,' 'Hera's . . . temple,' and so on (see above, p. 305).]

To imitate, then, is natural to man, just as our sense for harmony and our sense for rhythm are natural to us.

In its history, the poetic art broke up into two varieties; the graver spirits would represent noble actions, while the meaner would represent the doings of the ignoble. Of the early poets, then, some became writers of iambic verse, and composed lampoons, and others of heroic. Homer, indeed, shared in both tendencies, and was superior to the other early poets of either class. In the serious style he stands alone, for general excellence, and in the dramatic quality as well, for he makes his personages live before us. He was superior too in the comic vein, since he marked out the general lines of Comedy, by rendering the ludicrous (and not personal satire) dramatic.

When tragedy and comedy came into existence, poets with a bent towards lower subjects no longer took up lampooning, but became writers of comedy; and the graver spirits no longer became epic poets, but producers of tragedy; for these newer forms were grander, and were held in greater esteem.

The question whether tragedy has by Aristotle's day reached the end of its development would, he says, demand a separate investigation; he does not go into it. He considers the development thus far. Tragedy certainly originated in improvisations, as did comedy also. Tragedy goes back to the improvising poet-leaders in the dithyrambic chorus of satyrs; and comedy to the *comus*, the joyous song and dance, the performance of which is still to be found as a custom in many towns. From this beginning, tragedy progressed little by little, as the successive authors gradually improved upon what went before. Finally tragedy, through a long series of changes, attained to its natural form. The principal changes were three. (1) From the single spokesman of the original form, Aeschylus increased the number of actors to two. [Be it understood that one actor might take more than one part in a play.] He reduced the part taken by the chorus [—reduced the number of them, and the amount of choral chanting]. And he made the spoken dialogue the chief element in the play. (2) Sophocles introduced a third actor, and was the first to use painted scenery. [In competing with Sophocles, Aeschylus seems to have followed him in both innovations.] (3) Further the action changed to a greater magnitude; the little plots arising from the old satyr-dance gave way, and with its development out of that, tragedy also abandoned the grotesque early diction. Thus at length it assumed its characteristic elevation of tone, and at the same time the trochaic tetrameter gave way to an iambic measure. The trochaic measure is the measure of dancing; when tragedy lost its close relation to the satyr-dance, and as the element of spoken discourse entered in, the iambic measure came with it, for this is the readiest measure in speaking; observe our ordinary conversation, where we tend to fall into an iambic measure. [Much the same thing may be observed in English as in Greek, as one may discover by listening for an iambic beat in everyday speech.]

[Chapter 5.] Comedy, as aforesaid, is an imitation of persons of inferior moral bent; faulty, however, not in any or every way, but only so far as their shortcomings are ludicrous, and not painful or injurious. The ludicrous is a species or part, not all, of the ugly; we may call it that kind of shortcoming or deformity which does not strike us as painful, and does no harm to others. The comic mask, for example, is ludicrous; it is ugly and distorted, but without any suggestion of pain. [Similarly the agents in Aristophanes' *Birds* and *Frogs*, both the human agents and the creatures of a lower sort. A fuller treatment of comedy will be given later (below, pp. 785-92).]

The successive changes which tragedy underwent have been recorded, but we have no early record of the sort for comedy, since not until late did comedy become a matter of public concern. But we know that the framing of comic plots was due to Epicharmus and Phormis, and hence originated in Sicily; and that, of Athenian poets, Crates was the first to discard personal satire, and to construct, instead, plots of an impersonal nature and general comic value. [In this advance, Crates was followed by Aristophanes; in the *Birds*, for example, and in the *Frogs* and *Plutus*.]

We saw that epic poetry has thus much in common with tragedy: it is an imitation, in a lofty kind of verse, of serious events. But there are differences.

Epic poetry employs one metre throughout; tragedy employs more than one metre. And epic poetry is in the manner of a tale that is told, and is not, like tragedy, in the manner of an action directly presented. Further, an epic poem is longer than a drama; [the *Odyssey* contains about eight times as many lines as Sophocles' *Oedipus the King*;] for the epic poem is not restricted to any fixed limit of time. Nor was tragedy in former days so restricted; but now [in Aristotle's own day] writers of tragedy aim to represent the action as taking place within the limit of one revolution of the sun, or at all events try to avoid exceeding this limit by very much. This difference in respect to time exists at present; at first, however, tragic and epic poets were alike in not restricting themselves to any special limits. Finally, epic poetry and tragedy differ in respect to their constituent parts. Four parts are common to both forms. [These are plot, moral bent (*ethos*), thought (*dianoia*, way of arguing), and diction (*lexis*).] All the parts of an epic poem are to be found in tragedy; but two parts of tragedy [music (*melos*) and spectacle (*opsis*)] are not found in an epic poem. It follows that a person who can tell what is good art or bad in the composition of a tragedy can do the same for epic poetry as well.

[We see that with respect to time Aristotle notes a difference between the tragic poets of his own day (seventy years after the death of Euripides and Sophocles) and the practice of an earlier day; his contemporaries aim to confine the action as represented on the stage to certain limits of time; the time which is supposed to elapse before us would not be much more than twenty-four hours, and could include evening, night, or early morning, as well as daylight. What Aristotle here observes as a customary practice with respect to time he neither censures nor commends; at this point he is observing, and not advising either poets or critics. And hence the supposed law or rule of 'the unity of time' finds slender justification in the present treatise, though there has been much talk of it since the Italian critics and commentators of the sixteenth century, from whom French writers such as Corneille and Racine derived their notion of the 'unities.' As for 'the unity of place,' there is no mention of any such thing in the *Poetics* of Aristotle; he does say (see p. 774) that whereas the narrative poet may tell us successively about simultaneous events, the dramatist is confined to the one thing occurring before us on the stage. This observation, however, offers no argument for a *unity* of place. And whatever Aristotle's contemporaries may have done, the elder tragic poets did not invariably confine the action to one place. In the *Eumenides* of Aeschylus, for example, the scene shifts from the temple of Apollo at Delphi to the court of the Areopagus at Athens; and there is an obvious change of place in his *Agamemnon* as also in Sophocles' *Ajax*. Some stories, as the *Iliad,* represent an action in a more limited space; others, as the *Odyssey,* represent an action that moves from one place to another. In comedy, Aristophanes in the *Clouds* keeps his action in one place; the *Frogs* by its very nature goes from this world to another, and is a wandering or procession. 'Unity of place' seems to have developed out of the later, domestic, comedy, where the scene so often is a house, or two houses, with a section of a street; this unity, found in Roman comedy, doubtless had its origin in the New Greek Comedy of Menander and his age. It seems to have been first associated with the 'unity of time' by the aforesaid sixteenth-century Italian critics. Aristotle lays stress upon but one unity, that of action, organic unity. He mentions two other unities, first, the unity or continuity of a speech; a speech (*logos*) of one word may have unity, as *amo;* or the whole *Iliad* may be regarded as one continuous *logos* or speech. Secondly, having one person for your story does not produce a unified action (see p. 743). There is less of an approach to unity when you tell all the things that happened to one man than in the story of what happened in common to the members of one household; witness the return of Agamemnon or Odysseus to his wife and offspring. A dramatic action requires more than one person for agents, and presumably must have at least two, one to suffer, and one to do.]

II

Tragedy. The Principles of its Construction.

[Chapter 6.] First, let us gather up a definition of tragedy
from what has been thus far said.

A tragedy is an artistic imitation of an action that is serious,
complete in itself, and of an adequate magnitude; so much for
the object that is imitated. As to medium, the imitation is produced in language embellished in more than one way; one
kind of embellishment being introduced in one part, and another in another part of the play. And as to the function of
the whole, it is to arouse our emotions of pity and fear, and
by arousing to purge them away.

By language embellished in more than one way, we mean
(1) language that is simply rhythmical or metrical, (2) language that is delivered in recitative (intoned), and (3) language that is sung. [A whole tragedy, as *Oedipus the King,*
is composed in metre; the opening is metrical without being
sung or intoned. The lyrical parts, as Oedipus' lament (above,
p. 203), were, in a Greek tragedy, nearly always sung. Other
passages might be intoned to the accompaniment of the flute.]

[It is assumed that each several art has its own special
pleasure for the observer or audience. But the effects of tragedy
and epic poetry are alike in that the *Iliad,* for example, and
Sophocles' *Oedipus the King,* arouse and purge away the emotions of pity and fear. What Aristotle means by the catharsis
of these emotions has been the subject of much discussion. His
meaning probably was simple enough. The word catharsis
was familiar to the Greeks in a general sense, as the same
notion of cleansing, physical and spiritual, was to the He-
brews; witness their constant reference to purification, and
their rites, among these the rite of baptism, now characteristic
also of Christianity. We need not speculate whether Aristotle
used catharsis as a medical term, or as a term familiar in
the usage of religion. He knew it as a medical term; as a
philosophic term used by the Platonic Socrates in *Phaedo;*
as a concept in the worship of Dionysus, the cult out of which
he is sure that comedy as well as tragedy sprang. He knew
it too in other associations with tragic story, and not merely

in the Dionysiac Theban cycle. If the need of cleansing is stressed in the tale of Oedipus, at the opening of *Oedipus the King*, and also in Sophocles' *Antigone*, so is it also found at the beginning of the *Iliad* and throughout the Orestean trilogy. Likewise in Euripides' *Iphigenia among the Taurians*, Orestes comes with the aim of being finally cleansed for his murder of Clytemnestra. For the *Poetics*, the historical and traditional associations of catharsis with the drama are more important than its associations with medicine in a technical sense. But a note on the medical catharsis may help us to understand the *Poetics*, and may explain why the term is not defined in our treatise. In medicine a discussion of catharsis, the effecting of an intestinal purge, would hardly be expected to include a definition of purging. For practice, no definition would be needed. Rather, a practical treatise on medicine would go into detail on the means by which the catharsis should be effected. The parallel is obvious. The extant *Poetics* does go into detail on the proper means of effecting the tragic catharsis. One way and another, a very large part of the treatise is concerned with this problem, not What is the catharsis, but What are the right means of producing it. Aristotle does, however, remark on the physical signs of fear and pity (see p. 752), namely shivers and tears. Beyond that, if we wish to ask, What does Aristotle mean by the effect of tragedy, we may say that he must have in mind the effect which the *Iliad* or Sophocles' *Oedipus the King* has on a person of refinement and good sense; some such person as Shakespeare alludes to as 'judicious.' Aristotle calls such a man *phronimos*. What, then, is the pleasure of tragedy? It is the effect which an actual tragedy, the best, has upon the best part of an audience. That must be what Aristotle means by tragic catharsis, and what he himself experienced when he saw or read good tragedy. And the comic catharsis must be the effect of the best comedy on a similar person or group (see below, pp. 786-7, 791).]

From the synthetic definition of tragedy, we proceed to analyse the elements of a drama that separately demand attention from its author. [These constitutive, qualitative, elements are six in number.] (1) First, everything appertaining to the appearance of the agents, the actors, who carry on the action on the stage—costume, scenery, stage-properties—all this will constitute an element in dramatic technique. [This first element is spectacle or *opsis;* the whole play taken as something seen may be regarded under this head.] (2) The composition of the music (*melos*), and (3) the composition in words (*lexis*), will constitute two further elements; melody and diction are the medium in which the action is imitated. By diction, *lexis,* is here meant the fitting together of the words in metre. [*Lexis,* properly considered, means the component parts of language, beginning with the letter, syllable, word, phrase, sentence, taken into combination to produce the whole verbal expression of a drama or an epic poem.] As for melody (song, *melos*), the meaning is obvious.

Further, the object which is to be imitated is an action of men. In the production, then, the imitation, which is likewise an action, must be carried on by agents, the persons of the drama. And these agents must necessarily be endowed by the poet with distinctive qualities of (4) moral character (*ethos*) and (5) intellect (*dianoia,* thought, way of reasoning and arguing). [One might say, 'qualities of heart and head';] for it is from a man's moral bent, and from the way in which he reasons, that we are led to ascribe goodness or badness, success or failure, to his acts. Accordingly, as there are two natural causes, moral bent and thought, of the particular deeds of men, so there are the same two natural causes of their success or failure in life. And the poet must take cognizance of this point.

Finally, the action which the poet imitates is represented in a drama by (6) the fable or plot (*muthos*). Here plot means that synthesis of the incidents which gives form or being to the play as a whole; whereas moral bent (*ethos*) is that which leads us to characterize the agents as right or wrong in what they do, and intellect (*dianoia*) is that which shows itself whenever they try to prove a particular point, or when they avouch a general truth.

In every play, therefore, there are six constitutive elements, according to the quality of which we judge the excellence of the work as a whole. [Considered from within outward—from the centre, so to speak, to the surface, these are:] Plot (*muthos,* 6); moral bent (*ethos,* 5); intellect (*dianoia,* 4); diction (*lexis,* 3); melody (*melos,* 2); spectacle (*opsis,* 1). Two of them, *melos* and *lexis,* concern the medium of imitation; one, *opsis,* concerns the manner (that is, direct presentation); and three, *muthos, ethos,* and *dianoia,* concern the objects. There can be no other constituents of a play. [The six elements are an exhaustive list of the qualitative parts into which a play may be resolved. It is important to note that what we often call the 'characters' of a drama are by Aristotle resolved into two elements, namely the bent or bias of an agent, and his way of thinking and reasoning, above all as displayed in the way he argues in the speeches. It is therefore desirable not to call the persons of a Greek drama 'characters' but rather 'agents,' and to regard these agents, first as tending to choose and refuse in accord with their *ethos,* and then as arguing and speaking in favor of their choices. Thus the vacillating side of Hamlet's *ethos* is seen when he says: 'To be, or not to be, that is the question.' Whereupon he proceeds to speak and argue about this question; compare the *ethos* and *dianoia* of the Guard in *Antigone* (pp. 223-4). In what follows, Aristotle does not say that plot or action, the most important of the six elements, is more important than the agents who carry on the action; he does not say that *muthos* is more important than *ethos* and *dianoia* combined, but that it is more important than *ethos* taken alone; he might equally well have said that *ethos* is more important than *dianoia, dianoia* more important than *lexis,* and so on. Of course he holds that all six elements are indispensable to a Greek tragedy on the stage. The same thing would be true of a modern opera, whether tragic or comic, as Gluck's *Orpheus* and *Eurydice,* or the *Mikado* of Gilbert and Sullivan. A modern stage-play may lack the element of music.]

Most important of the six elements is plot or action; for tragedy is in essence an imitation, not of men in themselves, but of action and life, of happiness and misery—of what they do, and how they fare. And happiness and misery are not states of being, but forms of activity; the end for which we live is some activity, not the realization of a moral quality. Men are better or worse according to their moral bent, but they become happy or miserable in their actual deeds. Consequently in a play the agents do not perform for the sake of exhibiting their individuality; rather, the revelation of character is subsidiary to what is done. Thus the incidents of the action, and the ordering of these incidents, constitute the end and purpose of the play. Here, as in all else, the final purpose is the main thing. [The plot, above all else, effects that catharsis of pity and fear which gives the distinctive pleasure of tragedy. The form is the end or function.]

Such is the importance of this element that, we may say, whereas tragedy cannot exist without action, it is possible to construct a tragedy in which the agents lack a distinct moral bent. In fact, the works of the later tragic poets, from the time of Euripides on, are lacking in the element of character. The defect is common among poets of all sorts, and may be seen in painters as well. [The *ethos* of Clytemnestra, Cassandra, Agamemnon, and Aegisthus, is in each case made clear and distinct by Aeschylus in *Agamemnon;* similarly the *ethos* of Creon, Haemon, Ismene, Antigone, and Eurydice is carefully worked out for each of them by Sophocles. Aristotle counts Sophocles with Aeschylus among the elder poets. Euripides is classed with Agathon among the later poets, who fail in depicting *ethos,* and fail to make the action grow out of it.]

Again, one may string together a series of speeches in which the *ethos* is well delineated and the *dianoia* well worked out, and yet fail to produce the right effect. One is far more likely to produce this effect with a tragedy, deficient in other respects, if it has a well-constructed plot. Further, the most vital features of a play, by which the interest and emotions of the audience are most powerfully aroused, are reversals of fortune and discoveries of identity; and these are parts of the plot. [The same may be said of the *pathos,* an incident of a painful or destructive sort, which stirs our emotions; it is a part of the plot.] Note, too, that beginners in dramatic art succeed in versification and in delineating personal traits before they succeed in constructing good plots. Herein the progress of the individual author repeats the history of the art; for almost all the early poets succeeded better with these two elements than in the construction of plots.

(1) Plot (*muthos*), then, is the first principle, and as it were the very soul of tragedy.

(2) And *ethos* comes next in importance. So in painting:

the most beautiful colors, laid on with no order, will not give as much pleasure as the simplest figure done in outline. Tragedy is an imitation of an action; mainly on account of this action does it become, in the second place, an imitation of personal agents.

(3) Third in importance comes *diánoia*, the power of the agent to say what can be said, or is suitable, in a given situation. It is that element in the speeches of a drama which is supplied by the study of Politics and the art of Rhetoric; for the elder poets [as Sophocles in *Oedipus the King* (p. 163— opening speech)] make their agents speak like statesmen, whereas the modern [as Euripides in the opening of the *Bacchae*] make their agents use the devices of the rhetoricians [Sophists]. *Dianoia* [way of arguing] must be clearly distinguished from *ethos* in the drama; for *ethos* comprises only such things as reveal the moral bias of the agents, their choices in taking or avoiding a line of action, where the motive is not otherwise clear. And hence there is no call for employing *ethos* where an agent is neither choosing nor avoiding any action. But *dianoia* is manifest in all that the agents say to prove or disprove any point, and in all their generalization. [There is the reason why for the treatment of *dianoia* Aristotle refers us to his *Rhetoric,* since this work deals in detail with the construction of speeches. A dramatist, in fact, from beginning to end in a play is faced with the task of devising speeches for his persons; each speaker must argue in accordance with his *ethos*. The *Rhetoric* thus becomes, as it were, a section of the *Poetics* more extended than the *Poetics* taken by itself. Types of argument used by the poets, as Homer and Sophocles, are freely cited in the *Rhetoric;* the references there to *Antigone* have a special value for readers of Sophocles' play.]

(4) Next in importance comes the element of diction (*lexis*), the representation of the *ethos* and *dianoia* of the agents in words and combinations thereof. This element is in essence the same whether the diction is metrical or not.

(5) Of the two remaining elements, melody (*melos*) is the more important, since it holds first place among the accessory pleasures of the drama.

(6) The element of spectacle (*opsis*), though it stirs the

[741]

interest of the audience, is last in importance; it demands the lowest order of artistic skill, and has least to do with the art of poetry. A tragedy (as *Oedipus the King*) can produce its effect independently of a stage-performance and actors, when it is read. Further, the business of preparing the stage and actors is the office of the costumer rather than of poets.

[Chapter 7.] We turn to consider the plot, the organization of the incidents that will produce the ideal dramatic effect. As we have seen (p. 740), a tragedy is an imitation of an action that is complete in itself, forming a whole of adequate magnitude or extent; for a thing may be a whole and yet wanting in magnitude.

A whole is that which has a beginning, a middle, and an end. A beginning is that which does not come after anything else in a necessary sequence, but after which some other thing [a middle] does naturally exist or come to pass. An end, on the contrary, is that which naturally comes after something else in either a necessary or a usual sequence, but has nothing following it. A middle is that which naturally follows something else, and is followed by a third thing.

A well-constructed plot, then, can neither begin nor end where and when the poet happens to like, but must conform to the principles we have just laid down. Further, with respect to magnitude, to be beautiful, a living organism, or any other individual thing made up of parts, must have not only order in these parts, but a proper magnitude as well; for beauty depends upon these two qualities, size and order. And hence a minute creature cannot be beautiful, for we see the whole in a moment, and lose the pleasure arising from a perception of order in the parts. Nor could a creature of vast dimensions be beautiful to us, one a thousand miles long; the eye could not take in all the object at once; we should see the parts, but not the unity of the whole. Accordingly, as an inanimate object made up of parts, or a living creature, must be of such size that the parts and the whole may be easily taken in by the eye, so must the parts of a drama have a proper length, so that the parts and the whole may be readily embraced by the memory. The artificial limits of stage-presentation, and depending on the attention of the audience, do not concern the art of poetry. The artistic limit, set by the nature of the thing itself, is this. So long as the plot is perspicuous, the greater the length, the more beautiful will the story be on account of its magnitude. But to define in a simple way, an adequate limit is this. Let the length be such that there may be a passage from bad to good fortune, or from good to bad, through a series of incidents linked together in a probable or inevitable sequence.

[Chapter 8.] The unity of a plot does not consist, as some suppose, in having a story about one person; for the number of accidents that befall the individual is endless, and some of them cannot be reduced to unity. So, too, in a lifetime any one man will perform many acts which cannot be brought together into the form of a unified action. Thus we see the faulty choice of subject by such poets as have written a *Heracleid* or a *Theseid*, or the like; they suppose that, since Heracles or Theseus was a single person, the story of Heracles or Theseus must have unity. [The fault is exemplified in many novels; so the *Old Wives' Tale* of Arnold Bennett.] Homer, on the contrary, whether by conscious art or native insight, evidently understood the correct method; for he excels the rest of the epic poets in this as in all other respects. Thus, in composing a story of Odysseus, he did not make his plot include all that ever happened to Odysseus. For example, it befell him to be gashed by a boar on Mount Parnassus; and it befell him also to feign madness at the time of the mustering against Troy; but what he suffered in the first case and what he did in the second are incidents between which there was no necessary or probable connection. [And hence the poet did not join them; the first has a minor place in the *Odyssey* (Book 19), and the second has none.] Instead of joining disconnected incidents, Homer took for the subject of the *Odyssey* an action with the kind of unity here described. [The action calls for many agents, and a union of the reactions between them. Likewise for the drama of *Oedipus the King*, Sophocles took an action having the requisite unity; he took some incidents, and omitted others, that were found in the traditions about Oedipus; and the drama has unity, not because it concerns one man, but through the interaction of all the agents in the play.] And the subject chosen for the *Iliad* is likewise unified. As in the other imitative arts, painting and the rest, so in poetry, the object of the imitation in each case is a unit; therefore in an epic poem or a drama, the plot, which is an imitation of an action, must represent an action that is unified; the order of the incidents must be such that transposing or removing any one of them will dislocate and disorganize the whole. Every part must be necessary, and in its place; for a thing the presence or absence of which makes no perceptible difference is not an organic part of the whole.

[Chapter 9.] From what has been said, it is clear that the office of the poet consists in displaying not what actually has happened, but what in a given situation might well happen—a sequence of events that is possible in the sense of being either likely or inevitable. That is, the poet is not a historian. They differ not in that one writes in metrical, and the other in non-metrical, language. For example, you might turn the work of Herodotus into verse, and it would still be a species of history, with metre no less than without it. The real distinction is this: the historian relates what has happened, and the poet represents what might well happen. Poetry, therefore, is something more philosophic and of a higher seriousness than history; for poetry tends rather to express what is universal, whereas history relates particular events. [The historian does not neglect the chronological order of events when there is no necessary or seeming connection between them; his first concern is the actual events of the past and their actual sequence. The poet must use time in his own way. Thus in the *Odyssey* Homer begins at a point that is right for the opening of a poem. In the middle it is natural that Odysseus should relate antecedent events to Alcinous. Similarly in *Oedipus the King* Sophocles begins at the point where Oedipus addresses the suppliants; in a natural sequence he makes Oedipus relate what is needed from the past at a later point in the play.] By an exhibition of what is universal is meant the representation of what a certain type of person is likely or is bound to say or do in a given situation. That is the aim of the poet, though at the same time he attaches the names of persons to the types. As distinguished from the universal, the particular, which is the matter of history, consists of what an actual person, Alcibiades or the like, actually did or underwent. That poetry represents the universal has become clear enough in the present stage of comedy; for the comic poets first combine plots out of probable incidents, and then supply such names for the agents as chance to fit the types; in contrast to the old iambic lampooners, whose method was to begin with particular individuals. [The change from the old to the new is illustrated perhaps in the difference between the *Clouds* of Aristophanes, where 'Socrates' appears as a main agent, and Aristophanes' *Plutus;* though one may argue that in the *Clouds* Aristophanes began with a sequence of not improbable incidents, and attached the name 'Socrates' to a type, that of Sophist. But the reference of Aristotle to a later stage of comedy is better illustrated by the New Greek Comedy and Roman imitations of it, as *The Self-Tormentor* (*Heautontimorumenos*) of Terence.]

In tragedy, however, the poets still keep to the names of persons [Agamemnon, Oedipus, and the like] who are said to have existed. The reason is that what we accept as true we regard as possible. That which never has come to pass we do not necessarily take to be possible; but what we believe to have happened is manifestly possible; if it were impossible, it would not have occurred. Still, even in tragedy there are cases where only one or two of the personages are familiar, the rest having names invented by the poet; and there are yet other plays where none of the names are familiar. Such is the *Antheus* of Agathon, in which both the incidents and the names were devised by the poet; nor do they give less pleasure on that account. Accordingly, in his choice of subjects no poet is rigorously bound to adhere to the traditional stories upon which tragedies have been written. Indeed, it would be absurd to feel so constrained, since even such stories as are traditional are familiar to relatively few, yet give pleasure to any one.

From all this it is evident that the poet [*poietes,* 'maker'] is a maker of plots more than a maker of verses; he is a poet by virtue of imitating some object, and the objects he imitates are actions. And even if he happens to take a subject from history, he is not the less a poet for that; since there is nothing to keep certain actual events from having a probable sequence; and by representing this quality in such events he is their poet. [So Aeschylus treats the historical subject of *The Persians.*]

Of imperfect plots and actions, the purely episodic are the worst, a plot being called 'episodic' when there is neither probability nor necessity in the sequence of incident. A bad poet will construct this kind of plot through his own want of insight; a good poet, in order to meet the demands of the players. Since his work must be performed on the stage, and occupy a certain length of time, a good poet often stretches out the plot beyond its inherent capacity, and by the insertion of unnecessary matter is forced to distort the sequence.

Tragedy, however, is an imitation not only of a complete action, but of incidents that arouse pity and fear; and such incidents affect us most powerfully when we are not expecting them, if at the same time they are caused by one another. We are struck with more wonder if we find a causal relation in them than if they came about of themselves and by chance; since even pure coincidences seem most marvelous if there is something in them that looks like design. For example, when the man who had caused the death of Mitys was looking at the statue of Mitys in Argos, the statue fell over and killed him; such things strike us as not the result of mere chance. So plots that illustrate the principle of necessity or probability in their sequence are finer than others.

[Chapter 10.] But plots are either uninvolved or involved, since the actions which are imitated in the plots readily fall into the same two classes. We call an action uninvolved when the incidents, as we have explained, follow one another in a single continuous movement; that is, when the change of fortune [for one or more persons] comes about without a reversal of situation [*peripetia*] and without a discovery [*anagnorisis*, recognition, identification of some person or fact hitherto unrecognized. Such an action is represented in Aeschylus' *Prometheus Bound;* and, for epic poetry, in the *Iliad.*] An involved action is one in which the change of fortune is attended by such reversal, or by such discovery, or by both. [Examples are Sophocles' *Oedipus the King* and *Antigone;* Euripides' *Bacchae* and *Iphigenia among the Taurians;* and, for epic poetry, the *Odyssey.*] And each of these two incidents, reversal and discovery, should arise from the structure of the plot itself; that is, each should be the necessary or probable result of the incidents that have gone before, and not merely follow them in point of time; for in the sequence of events there is a vast difference between *post hoc* and *propter hoc.*

[Chapter 11.] A reversal of situation [*peripetia*] is a change in some part of the action from one state of affairs to its precise opposite—as we said, from good fortune to ill, or from ill to good. For example, in Sophocles' *Oedipus the King* the Messenger comes to cheer Oedipus by removing his fears about marrying his mother, but, by disclosing whose son Oedipus really is, brings about the opposite state of affairs for him—brings about the change from happiness to misery. [The episode (see pp. 190-94) is here described as Sophocles intends it and the audience takes it, rather than according to the intent of the Messenger in the play as we have it.—A reversal may constitute the main turning-point in a drama, as in the case of Oedipus, or in that of Euripides' *Electra* (p. 376); or it may be a subsidiary episode, as are many of the reversals in the *Iliad* and *Odyssey*. Main reversals in the *Odyssey* occur in the meeting of Odysseus and the Cyclops, and after Odysseus is made known to the suitors of Penelope.] Of the opposite change, from ill fortune to good, there is an example in the *Lynceus* of Theodectes; when Lynceus is led away to die, and Danaus follows to be his executioner, it comes about, from the previous incidents of the drama, that Lynceus is saved and Danaus executed. [The play also illustrates the twofold reversal in opposite directions. The plot of the *Odyssey* is likewise of this dual type. Compare also the reversal of fortune, from misery to happiness, in Euripides' *Iphigenia among the Taurians* (pp. 444-6).]

A discovery [recognition, *anagnorisis*], as the word itself implies, is a transition from ignorance to knowledge, and hence a passing into love or hate by those who are marked for happiness or misfortune. Discovery is at its best when it is attended by a reversal of fortune—such a reversal as attends the discovery in Sophocles' *Oedipus the King* (p. 199). There are, of course, other kinds of discovery besides this; some such transition from ignorance to knowledge may come about with reference to inanimate, even casual things. It is also possible to discover whether some person has, or has not, done a particular deed; [for example, whether it was Oedipus who killed Laius (p. 186).] But the type of discovery that is most intimately connected with the plot, and with the action imitated, is the one we have especially mentioned; for the discovery bringing love or hate, and the reversal bringing happiness or misery, will occasion either pity or fear; and by definition it is these emotions that the tragic imitation is to arouse. Further, this kind of discovery will be instrumental in bringing about the happy or unhappy ending of the action as a whole. Now since discovery here means a recognition of persons [rather than things or deeds], there are two possibilities: (1) X may learn the identity of Y, when Y already knows the identity of X; or (2) X and Y may each have to learn the identity of the other. [Thus (1) in the *Odyssey* Odysseus, knowing the identity of Polyphemus, while Polyphemus does not know him, foolishly reveals his identity to Polyphemus.] (2) An example of the second possibility is in Euripides' *Iphigenia among the Taurians,* where Iphigenia is made known to her brother Orestes through her desire to send a letter in her own name to 'Orestes, son of Agamemnon,' and another discovery is required to reveal her brother Orestes to her. [The interest in a double discovery is double; another example is found in Sophocles' *Oedipus the King,* where Oedipus is revealed to his wife as her son, and Jocasta is revealed to Oedipus as his mother.]

Two parts of the plot then, reversal [*peripetia*] and discovery [*anagnorisis*], represent these things in the action, and have been sufficiently explained. A third part of the plot is suffering [*pathos*]; this may be defined as an incident of a destructive or painful sort, such as violent death, physical agony, woundings, and the like. [This third part, *pathos* or suffering, should not be taken to include mental anguish, such as the grief of Oedipus when he finds that he has married his mother. The technical *pathos,* this third part of the plot, is for Aristotle strictly physical. True examples are, in *Oedipus the King,* the suicide of Jocasta and the self-inflicted blinding of Oedipus; in *Antigone,* the suicide of Antigone, the suicide of Haemon, and the suicide of Eurydice. The grief of Creon over the death of Haemon is not an example of *pathos* in this technical sense; rather, it is a display of *ethos*.]

[Chapter 12.] Mention has been made above (pp. 737-42) of the six formative [qualitative] elements of tragedy which are to be used by the poet. We come now to the division of a play into its quantitative parts, the members that may be separated in the text. They are: (1) prologue; (2) episode; (3) exode; (4) choral song; this choral portion being divided into (a) parode and (b) stasimon. These two are common to all tragedies; whereas only in some are there (c) songs from the stage by one or more actors (not by the chorus) and commoi, or songs by actors and chorus together.

(1) The prologue is the entire part of the tragedy from the beginning to the parode of the chorus. (2) An episode is one of those entire parts of a tragedy, each of which intervenes between two choral songs. (3) The exode is that entire part of a tragedy which follows after the last choral song, and reaches to the end. (4) Of the choral portion, (a) the parode is the first undivided utterance of the chorus; (b) a stasimon is a song of the chorus, not in anapaestic or trochaic metre; and (c) a commos [lament, threnody] is a song of lamentation in which the chorus and one or more actors unite. [Though Aristotle's definitions here refer rather to the drama of his own age, the kind of thing he has in mind, for example under the lament, may be illustrated by the utterance of Creon and the Chorus in Sophocles' *Antigone* (p. 246), and by those of Oedipus and the Chorus in Sophocles' *Oedipus the King* (pp. 199-203).] . . .

[Chapter 13.] Following what has been said up to this point, we must next discuss that ideal structure of the plot which will bring about the fullest measure of tragic effect. (1) What is the poet to aim at, and what is he to avoid, in the construction of his plots? In other words, (2) what are the specific sources of the tragic catharsis?

In the finest kind of tragedy, as we have seen (p. 740; pp. 746-8), the synthesis of incidents must be not uninvolved, but involved, and this plot must be imitative of events that arouse pity and fear; for therein lies the distinctive function of this kind of imitation. It immediately follows that there are three forms of plot to be avoided. (1) Good and just men are not to be represented as passing from happiness into misfortune, for such a spectacle does not arouse pity or fear in us; it is simply revolting. (2) Nor must evil men be represented as passing from ill fortune to prosperity; for this is the most untragic situation of all; it does not stir our general human sympathy [*to philanthropon,* the human feeling in us], or arouse tragic pity or tragic fear. (3) Nor, again, may excessively wicked men be represented as falling from prosperity into misfortune. Such a course of events may arouse in us some measure of human sympathy, but not the emotions of pity and fear. Pity is what we feel at a misfortune that is out of proportion to the faults of a man; and fear is what we feel when misfortune comes upon one like ourselves. Now the excessively wicked man deserves misery in proportion; and since his wickedness exceeds the average, he is not like one of ourselves. Accordingly, in this third situation there is nothing to arouse either pity or fear. There remains, then, (4) the case of the man intermediate between these extremes; a man not superlatively good and just, nor yet one whose misfortune comes about through vice and depravity; but a man who is brought low through some shortcoming [*hamartia,* mistake, mistaken way, missing the mark]; such a person as Oedipus [of the line of Thebes], Thyestes [of Pelops' line], and the eminent men of other noted families. [*Hamartia* is the inward flaw, or the outward mistake that comes from it, or the inward flaw seen in the outward error. In the *Odyssey,* Book 1, Zeus calls the human frailty which is said to bring sufferings beyond the ordinary lot of man (in the translation by Butcher and Lang) 'blindness of heart.' In like manner, Sophocles makes Creon, in *Antigone* (p. 246), attribute the woes that have come upon his household to 'the wretched blindness of my counsels'; and the Sophoclean story of Oedipus turns upon a blindness of impulse which at length is recognized by Oedipus himself, who thereupon rashly puts out his own eyes. In tragedy we have to do with a moral bent in the chief agent or agents, towards goodness in the main, and hence with a shortcoming which will show itself at critical points in the action. If right action is the result of sympathetic insight in the poet, faulty action in an agent may be described as the result of the opposite quality, a quality having a dual

[750]

nature, compounded of something in the 'head' and something in the 'heart,' or, in other words, 'blindness of heart.' This flaw makes the action of an Oedipus or a Hamlet at critical junctures sometimes too slow and sometimes too hasty. The concept in the *Poetics* of the ideal tragic agent with his imperfect insight, proper for tragedy, may be contrasted with the ideal man of the *Nicomachean Ethics,* whose natural bent has been corrected, whose clarity of judgment enables him to perform the right action at the right time, and whose career, as a result, is likely to be prosperous. Finally, we may note again that Aristotle does not take *ethos* to be unimportant; it gains its importance because action springs from it. Nor does the action spring from the *ethos* of one agent; in *Oedipus the King* it springs from the choices of many.]

To be perfectly tragic, then, the plot must not, as some hold, have a double issue, fortunate for the good, unfortunate for the bad, but a single one. And the change of fortune must be not a passage from misery to happiness, but a passage from happiness to misery; and this change must come about not through depravity, but through a great shortcoming [*hamartia*] in a person such as we have described [as good as the average man], or better than that rather than worse. In support of this view the history of the drama itself is significant. In early days the poets were content with any stories that came their way; but now the practice has narrowed down to traditions about a few houses, and the best tragedies are founded on the legends of Alcmeon, Oedipus, Orestes, Meleager, Thyestes, and similar persons who have been either the movers or the victims in some signal overthrow of fortune. From practice as well as theory, then, we argue that the ideal tragedy will have a plot of this type. Those critics, therefore, are in error who blame Euripides for adhering to this plan in his tragedies, since many of them have the unhappy ending. It is, as we have said, the correct procedure. And the best proof of its correctness is that in the public contests, when they are acted, such plays, if they have been properly worked out, are seen to have the most tragic effect; and Euripides, even if his procedure be faulty in every other respect [as some maintain], is yet, through the unhappy ending, certainly the most tragic of poets on the stage.

Second in excellence comes the form of construction which some rank first, where the thread of the plot is double, as in the *Odyssey*, and there is a happy and an unhappy ending, respectively, for the better agents and the worse. It is rated first, however, only through the weakness of the audience [the inability of the general run to endure the highest tragic tension]; for the poets follow the general taste, and cater to the wishes of the spectator. But the pleasure arising from this double structure is not the distinctive pleasure of tragedy. It is rather one that belongs to comedy; where the deadliest of legendary enemies, like Orestes and Aegisthus, become friends, and quit the stage without any one slaying or being slain.

[Chapter 14.] The effect of fear and pity may be produced by means that appertain simply to stage-presentation [such as the dreadful costume and masks and menacing attitudes of the Furies (pp. 128-38), or the wretched appearance of Orestes (p. 134) or Electra (p. 310)]; but the tragic effect may also arise from the very structure and incidents of the play, which is the preferable way, and is the mark of a better poet. The plot, in truth, should be so constructed that, even without help from the eye, one who simply hears the play recited must feel the chill of fear, and be stirred with pity, at what occurs. In fact, these are just the emotions one would feel in listening to the story of Oedipus away from the stage. To bring about this emotional effect by spectacular means is less a matter of the poetic art, and depends upon adventitious aid. But those who employ the means of the stage to produce what strikes us as merely monstrous, without being terrible, are absolute strangers to the art of tragedy; for not every kind of pleasure is to be sought from a tragedy, but only that specific pleasure which is characteristic of this art.

[We are passing from the question, What is the poet to aim at, and what to avoid, in the general construction of his plots? We are coming to the question, What are the specific sources of the tragic catharsis? The two questions are interdependent, yet obviously may be distinguished.]

Since the characteristic pleasure of tragedy comes from the arousal of pity and fear, and since the poet must produce this pleasure through an imitation of some action, it is clear that the tragic quality must be impressed upon the incidents

that make up the story. Let us see, then, what kinds of occur·
rence strike us as terrible, or rather what kinds of terrible
occurrence strike us as piteous. When persons are involved
in some deed of horror, they must be either (1) friends, or (2)
enemies, or (3) indifferent to one another. Now when (2) an
enemy injures, or wishes to injure, an enemy, there is nothing
to arouse our pity either in his deed or his intent, except in
so far as concerns the suffering of the one who is injured.
And the same is true when (3) the persons are indifferent to
one another. But when the tragic incident [*pathos*, suffering
(see p. 748)] occurs within the circle of those who are bound
by natural ties—when murder or the like is done or intended
by brother upon brother, son upon father, mother upon son,
or son upon mother—pity is aroused; and such are the situations the poet must look for in the traditional stories. The
general framework of these stories, then, the poet must not
disturb; Clytemnestra must be slain by her son Orestes, and
Eriphyle by her son Alcmeon. At the same time, the poet must
select for himself from the materials of tradition, and he must
employ the given materials with skill.

Let us explain more clearly what is meant by the skilful use
of material; for example, the tale of a deed of violence among
friends. The deed may be done, as the early poets manage it,
(1) by a person aware of what he is doing, to another who
knows the identity of the doer, as is the case also with Euripides; for he makes Medea kill her children with premeditation,
while they recognize her as their slayer (pp. 488-90). [The
'early poets' here include Aeschylus and Sophocles. Aeschylus
makes Clytemnestra kill her husband Agamemnon, and Orestes
kill his mother Clytemnestra, in situations where murderers
and victims alike recognize each other (pp. 75, 118).] Or the
deed may be done (2) by persons ignorant of the terrible
nature of what they are doing, who afterwards discover their
relationship with the victims; as Oedipus, in Sophocles' version
of the tale, kills a man who he subsequently learns was his
father. In this case, however, the deed lies outside of the drama
proper (see p. 186). But it may be included in the drama; as
Alcmeon unwittingly kills his mother Eriphyle in the version
of that story by Astydamas; or as Telegonus injures his unrecognized father in the *Odysseus Wounded* of (?)Sophocles.

SUPPLEMENT

Yet a third possibility of treatment is that where (3) a person
meditating some irreparable injury to another, unaware of
their relationship, may discover the identity of his victim in
time to avoid the deed. [A variation of the first possibility is
to intend some injury to a near relation whose identity is
known, and then to draw back from the deed.] This list ex-
hausts the possibilities; for the deed must either be done, or
not done; and the persons must either be aware, or not aware,
of what they are doing.

Of all the possibilities, the worst is the situation in which
some one, aware of the relationship, is about to do another a
deadly injury, and does not do it. The situation is revolting to
our sense of natural affection; and it is not tragic—pity is not
aroused—because the intended victim does not suffer. Accordingly, the persons of tragedy do not act in this way save in
rare instances; as when Haemon, in Sophocles' *Antigone*,
pursues his father with intent to kill, and then desists (p.
245). [Aristotle no doubt would distinguish between the
artistic handling of the incident, and the wrong choice of such
incidents to begin with. Haemon turns the violence against
himself, and pitifully commits suicide. The suicide, then, arises
from probable antecedents, and fits in with the suicide of
Antigone and the suicide of Eurydice.] A second situation,
not so bad, is that in which the victim is known, as in the
first case, but the act which is intended is also performed [as
in *The Libation-Pourers* of Aeschylus (p. 118), where Orestes
fulfils his purpose of killing his mother, Clytemnestra.] Better
yet is the situation where the deed is done by a person who
does not recognize his victim, and discovers the relationship
afterwards; for this is not revolting to our sense of natural
affection, and the discovery will have the proper effect of
astounding us. [Such is the situation in *Oedipus the King*.] But
best of all is the third of the possible methods of treatment.
This is exemplified in the *Cresphontes* of Euripides, where
Merope is about to slay her son, and does not slay him, but
discovers his identity; in Euripides' *Iphigenia among the
Taurians* (p. 425), where the sister, Iphigenia, is about to
sacrifice her brother, Orestes, but discovers who he is before
it is too late; and in [? Euripides'] *Helle*, where the son is
on the point of giving up his mother [? to the enemy], and

[754]

recognizes her just in time. [It is hard to explain the prefer-ence of an imminent horror with a happy issue and the prefer-ence above (pp. 749, 751) of a plot with an unhappy ending. To have an imminent horror with a happy issue as the crucial incident seems incompatible with an unhappy ending of a tragedy as a whole. When Aristotle wishes to sketch an ideal plot, he outlines Euripides' *Iphigenia among the Taurians,* where the happy issue is delayed as long as may be. In the most nearly perfect tragedy he knows, *Oedipus the King,* the basic incident of horror is treated in such fashion that the deed is done in ignorance, and the discovery comes later. Since the murder of Laius by Oedipus is also anterior to the action on the stage, the shock to our sense of natural affection is dimin-ished, yet the play can end unhappily.]

These considerations will explain why tragedies, as we noted (p. 751), have come to be restricted to the tales of a few families only. In searching for themes, it was through fortune rather than art that the poets came to embody inci-dents of this tragic kind in their plots. And for want of inven-tion they are still obliged to have recourse to the tales of those families in which such deeds of horror occurred.

With respect to tragic effect, enough has now been said on the proper synthesis of the incidents in the plot, and the kind of stories to be used as materials.

[Chapter 15.] We turn to the moral dispositions of the agents. With respect to *ethos,* there are four things which the poet must aim at. First and foremost, the agents must be (1) good. The ethical element will be present in a play if, as was said (pp. 738, 740-41), by speech or act the agents mani-fest a certain bent in what they choose to do or avoid; and the *ethos* will be good if the habit of choice is good. ['Good' means tending ordinarily to be just and kind, and implies some firmness and decision, and being good for something, but the goodness does not exclude the possibility of erroneous action involving on occasion harsh and unjust words and acts.] Such goodness is possible in all types of mankind, even in a woman or a slave, though woman is perhaps an inferior type, and the slave quite worthless. (2) The agents must be true to type. There is, for example, a type of manly valor and eloquence; but it would be inappropriate for the poet to represent a woman as valorous in this way, or masterly in argument. (3) Thirdly, they must be true to life, which is something different from making them good or true to type, as these terms have just been defined. [In general, they must express themselves as people do, in terms that will strike us as natural. Similarly with motions and attitudes of the body. Retiring, or hiding the face, when one is moved to weep, would be true to life.] (4) Fourthly, they must be consistent, true to their own nature throughout the play. Even if the person whom the poet is representing [? as Dionysus in the *Bacchae* of Euripides, or Achilles in the *Iliad*] should happen to be inconsistent, and should be taken as an example of that type, still the representation should be consistent (consistently inconsistent).

There is an instance of baseness, a baseness not required by the plot, in the Menelaus of Euripides' *Orestes;* an instance of what is unsuitable and untrue to type [here the manly type] in the lament of Odysseus in the *Scylla* of (?) Timotheus; and another [here the feminine type] in the too masterly speech of Euripides' Melanippe the Wise; and an example of inconsistency in his *Iphigenia at Aulis.* In this, the Iphigenia who at first pleads for her life is not at all the same sort of person as the Iphigenia who later is ready to meet death. [Examples are given of the second and fourth cases, untruth to type, and inconsistency of *ethos,* but not of the third, unlikeness, untruth to life or reality. Goodness is discussed or touched on, and so adequately treated, elsewhere. Truth to life finds its explanation in the next paragraph, and also in Aristotle's *Rhetoric* 3.16.1417[b]. A baseness beyond what is needed for the plot is found in the Edmund and Regan of *King Lear;* the badness of Clytemnestra in Aeschylus' *Agamemnon* is needed, and she appears to better advantage in *The Libation-Pourers,* while the base Aegisthus is in both plays, so far as may be, kept off-stage. The Richard of *King Richard the Second* is unmanly, and the clever speech of Portia in *The Merchant of Venice* might in Aristotle's view be untrue to the womanly type. The personages of Shelley's *Cenci* throughout seem untrue to life.]

As in combining the incidents of the plot, so also in representing the *ethos* of the agents, the poet must seek after a necessary or probable relation between one thing and another. That is, a certain kind of person must speak or act in a certain fashion as the necessary or probable outcome of his inward nature; and thus one thing will follow another in a necessary or probable sequence. From this it is clear that the solution of dramatic situations should arise from the progress of the story itself; the solution should not be brought about by a mechanical device [like the *deus ex machina*], as when Euripides' *Medea* (p. 491) is concluded by the escape of Medea in an aerial chariot drawn by dragons, or as in the *Iliad* (Book 2), where the Greeks are withheld from a premature return home through the intervention of the goddess. These arbitrary devices must be reserved for matters lying outside of the drama proper, to explain past occurrences that are beyond the range of human knowledge (for example, in a prologue by a god), or future events that need to be foretold and announced; for we credit the gods with seeing all things, both past and future. In the events of the drama itself there should be nothing that does not square with our reason; but if an irrational element cannot be avoided, it must lie outside of the tragedy proper, as in the case of Sophocles' *Oedipus the King*. [Long before the opening of this play, Oedipus unwittingly slew his father Laius, King of Thebes, and then unwittingly married his mother the queen. For years he reigned as king, his ignorance meanwhile of the facts being essential to the plot. Aristotle thinks it 'improbable' that Oedipus never should have learned the circumstances under which his predecessor died; but, lying among the events preceding the drama, the irrational element escapes our notice. Further, Sophocles represents Oedipus as an astute man with a sluggish mind till something external plunges him into hasty investigation.]

Since tragedy is an imitation of persons better than the ordinary, our tragic poet must observe the method of good portrait-painters; for they reproduce the distinctive features of the original, and yet, while preserving the likeness of a man, ennoble him in the picture. So too the poet, in imitating men who are quick to anger, or easy-going [slack, lax], or have other comparable infirmities, must represent them as such, and yet kind and honorable. Thus Homer represents Achilles as a marvel of hard-heartedness, and at the same time good.

[Achilles is a signal instance of obstinate anger, yet when not aroused or when placated, tending to be generous and just. Aristotle's first demand with respect to *ethos* (p. 755), that it must be good, does not mean possessed of every virtue, but, in a simple ethics suited to the art of poetry, that, when the tragic flaw is not operating at a critical point in the drama, the agents should be kindly and desirous of what is right. We may put the matter either way. The poet must represent the flaw (*hamartia*), a flaw adequate to the tragic plot, and then balance the flaw with better traits, or must represent the agents as good, and then display the *hamartia* (flaw, error, tendency to miss the mark). A similar task confronts the comic poet, who must represent his agents as worse than the average, and yet not offensive; the badness must not be destructive or in a high degree morally harmful. As we see, even when the story requires a bad agent, the poet must do what he can to redeem the character of that agent; or at least the badness must not be greater than the story demands.]

These principles, accordingly, one must constantly bear in mind, and such principles of stage-effect as are necessarily dependent upon the art of the poet [as contrasted with the art of the costumer, or the like], since here also it is often possible to make mistakes . . .

[Chapter 16.] The general nature of discovery [recognition, *anagnorisis*] has been explained above (p. 747). We may now examine the several species. (1) The first and least artistic kind is at the same time the one that is most frequently employed, because of a lack of invention in the poets; this is recognition by marks or tokens. Of these, some are congenital, such as 'the spear-head which the Earth-born have on them,' or stars [as a birth-mark on the shoulder] like those that Carcinus employs in his *Thyestes*. Others, again, are acquired after birth; and of this class some are marks on the body, as scars, and some are external tokens, necklaces, et cetera, and things like the ark in which the sons of Tyro were exposed, that brings about the discovery in Sophocles' *Tyro*. [Compare the cloak employed in *The Libation-Pourers* of Aeschylus (p. 96) to convince Electra that it is Orestes who wears it.] Even these marks or tokens, however, may be used in a better way or a worse. Thus in the *Odyssey* Odysseus is made known, through his scar, in one way to the nurse [that is, in the natural course of things, when in the Bath-Scene she comes to wash the limb], and in another way to the herdsmen [that is, in a worse, a more arbitrary, fashion, since Odysseus displays the scar in order to convince the men of his identity]. Those discoveries are less artistic in which signs are used as a final means of convincement, and so are all such as require a formal proof of identity; those are better in which the recognition comes by a natural turn of events, as in the Bath-Scene.

(2) The second kind are discoveries arbitrarily introduced by the poet, and for that reason inartistic. Thus in *Iphigenia among the Taurians,* Euripides simply makes Orestes disclose his own identity (p. 424); and whereas the sister reveals who she is in a natural way, by trying to send the letter to Orestes, Orestes is made to say what the poet wishes, and not what the sequence of events might demand. Accordingly, this fault is not far removed from the one just mentioned, since Orestes could easily have been made to establish his identity with tokens also. [The arguments he uses (pp. 424-5) in the play as we have it are, in Aristotle's view, arbitrary means of convincement.] . . .

(3) The third kind is discovery through the memory, when the inward man, stirred by hearing or seeing something familiar, is led to display his feelings. For example, in the *Cypria* of Dicaeogenes Teucer bursts into tears when he sees the portrait of his father. And in the *Lay of Alcinous* in the *Odyssey,* when Odysseus hears the harper chant the adventure of the wooden horse, he is reminded of the past, and weeps; and thus, in both cases, there comes about a recognition. [The discovery of Orestes by the Herdsman in Euripides' *Iphigenia among the Taurians* (p. 409) is of this third kind.]

(4) The fourth kind is discovery by a process of reasoning [by inference]. One example is in *The Libation-Pourers* of Aeschylus (pp. 94-5), where Electra in effect argues thus: 'Some one with hair like mine has come; no one has hair like mine but Orestes; therefore it is he that has come.' Another is the discovery devised by Polyidus the Sophist with reference to Iphigenia; it would be natural for Orestes to argue: 'My sister was sacrificed at Aulis, and now it is my lot to be sacri-

ficed also'; whereupon Iphigenia would recognize him as her
brother . . .

(5) Related to discovery by inference is a kind of 'fictitious
discovery' where the poet causes A to be recognized by B
through the false inference of B [or through a logical deception practised upon B by A]. There is a case of this in
Odysseus with the False Tidings [? Odysseus disguised as a
beggar, bringing false tidings of himself, but now revealing
his identity, and saying:] 'I shall know [? or string] the
bow' which [as yet] he has not seen; but to depict the
other person [or persons] as recognizing Odysseus [? from
his stringing the bow] is, for the poet, to represent a false
inference. [Compare what is said (pp. 775-6) on the right
poetical way of representing a lie. The 'fictitious' recognition,
characterized by a false inference, is illustrated in the *Odyssey*,
Book 23, where Odysseus reveals his identity to the doubtful
Penelope. Odysseus says in effect: 'I shall so describe our
nuptial bed,' which as Beggar he had not seen, 'that you will
know it is Odysseus who is speaking.' His circumstantial account of the bed, which he could give if he were her husband,
leads Penelope not to the legitimate inference that he *might*
be her husband, but to the unwarranted inference that he
must be. The episode has both a serious and a comic aspect;
mistaken discoveries by false inference are very frequent in
comedy.]

(6) But of all discoveries, the best is the kind that grows
out of the very nature of the incidents, when an astounding
revelation comes about from probable antecedents, as in
Sophocles' *Oedipus the King*. And there is an example in
Iphigenia among the Taurians (when his sister is revealed to
Orestes), since it is natural that she should wish to dispatch
a letter home. Among the discoveries in this class are the
only ones that dispense with arbitrary indications of identity,
and necklaces, et cetera. Next best are those (No. 4) that come
about through a process of reasoning.

[Chapter 17.] When actually constructing his plots and
working them out [composing] in the diction, the poet should
do his best to visualize what he is representing. In this way,
seeing everything with the utmost vividness, as if he were a
spectator of the events he is depicting, he will devise what is

suitable, and run the least danger of overlooking inconsist-
encies. The need of this practice is shown by the flaw that
brought down censure upon Carcinus, when he made Amphi-
araus come out of the shrine; an inconsistency that escaped
the notice of one who was not visualizing. On the stage, however, the play was a fiasco, for the audience took offense at
the oversight.

So far as he can, the poet should also assume the very
attitudes and gestures appropriate to the agents; for among
authors of the same natural ability, they will be most convincing who themselves experience the feelings they represent.
The poet who himself feels distress or anger will represent
distress or anger with the most lifelike reality. And hence
the art of poetry calls rather for a man with a natural gift
than for one with a touch of madness. Of the gifted, some
readily assume one personality after another, and some pass
out of themselves into various states of emotion.

As for the story, whether it be traditional or of his own invention, the poet should first make a general brief or outline
of the whole, and then extend this by the insertion of episodes.
How one may take a bird's-eye view of the whole may be illustrated from Euripides' *Iphigenia among the Taurians:*

A maiden has been offered in sacrifice; has mysteriously
vanished from the sight of those who were sacrificing her; and
has been transported to a foreign land where it is the custom
to offer up all strangers to the goddess. Here she is appointed
priestess of this rite. Some time later it chances that the brother
of this priestess arrives.—The fact, however, that the oracle
for a certain reason bade him go thither does not lie within
the general plan of the story, and his aim in coming lies outside of the drama proper.—Upon his arrival he is seized, and,
on the point of being sacrificed, reveals his identity; either
as Euripides arbitrarily makes him disclose it himself, or, as
Polyidus proceeds, by the not unnatural utterance: 'As my
sister was offered in sacrifice, so must I be also'; and thus
the discovery leads to his preservation.

When the general outline has been settled, and the right
names have been supplied for the agents, the next thing is to
fill in the scheme with particular episodes. And care must be
taken that the episodes are appropriate to the action and the

agents. In *Iphigenia among the Taurians,* for example, Orestes' fit of madness, leading to his capture (p. 410), is an appropriate episode; and so is the ruse (p. 435) that he must be cleansed of his madness before he can be sacrificed. The episodes must also be of an appropriate length. In dramas, they are short; in epic poetry, it is they that serve to extend the poem. The main plan of the *Odyssey* is not long:

A man has been absent from home for many years; he is dogged by Poseidon; and he is left companionless. Meanwhile, affairs at home are in evil case; his substance is being wasted by suitors to his wife, who have also formed a conspiracy to kill his son. Tempest-tossed, the man himself at length arrives, reveals who he is to certain persons, and attacks his enemies, the outcome being that he is preserved, and they perish.

That is the essence of the *Odyssey;* all the rest is in the nature of episode.

[Chapter 18.] To every tragedy there appertain a complication [*desis,* tying] and an unraveling [*lusis,* untying, dénouement]; the incidents that lie outside of the drama [before the opening of it], and often some of the incidents within it, form the complication [*desis*]; the rest of the play is the dénouement [*lusis*]. Specifically, by complication is meant everything from the beginning of the story up to the point, last in a series, out of which comes the change of fortune. . . . [Thus in *Iphigenia among the Taurians,* the critical point, after which the dénouement begins, is the recognition of Orestes by his sister. The dividing-line between *desis* and *lusis* may preferably be called the 'crisis,' rather than 'climax.' The 'crisis' in *Oedipus the King* occurs in the meeting between Oedipus, the Herdsman, and the Messenger; the words of the Herdsman to Oedipus in line 1181 (p. 199), 'Know, to affliction thou art born' (Jebb translates: 'Know that thou wast born to misery'), mark the transition precisely.]

There are four kinds of tragedy, in accordance with the number of parts we have described [from which the tragic catharsis can arise:] (1) The involved kind, where the whole play is a recognition with reversal; [this is substantially true of Sophocles' *Electra.*] (2) The tragedy of suffering [characterized by death, dire physical injury, *pathos* in the technical sense (see p. 748)]; for example, plays on the story of Ajax or Ixion. (3) The tragedy in which the *ethos* of the agents is paramount; as Sophocles' *Women of Phthia* and the *Peleus* of (?) the same author. (4) The fourth kind is the simple [with an uninvolved plot]; as Aeschylus' *Daughters of Phorcys* and his *Prometheus,* and all plays having their scene laid in Hades. In the light of all this, one concludes that the poet must do his best to combine every element of interest in a tragedy, or, failing that, the most effective elements, and as many as possible. The effort is especially desirable at present, because of unfair contemporary criticism. Just because in the past there have been authors who were successful, each of them, in the use of some one source of interest, it is expected that the individual poet of to-day will surpass them all in their several lines of excellence. But in comparing one tragedy with another, that is, in pointing out similarities and differences in the handling of material, the fairest way is to take the plots as a basis of comparison. And this, of course, amounts to comparing complication [*desis*] with complication and dénouement [*lusis*] with dénouement. Many dramatists succeed in the complication, and then fail in the unraveling [*lusis*]. But the poet must show his mastery of construction in both.

The poet must likewise remember what has more than once been said, and not employ an entire epical scheme, that is, a multiple story, for the subject of a tragedy. One should not, for example, try to dramatize the whole story of the *Iliad.* In an epic poem, owing to its scale, every part assumes its proper magnitude; but when the entire thing is reduced to the scale of a drama, the result is far below one's expectations. Witness the ill success of those dramatists who have taken everything in the fall of Ilium as the subject of one tragedy, and not, like Euripides, a single phase to a play, or the entire legend of Thebes, instead of a portion, like Aeschylus; for they have all either utterly failed, or at best made a poor showing on the stage. Even Agathon failed simply in this respect.

Contemporary poets, however, show marvelous skill in constructing reversals, and also uninvolved situations, with a view to producing the effects they desire, their aim being to arouse the tragic emotions and a human feeling. This feeling is aroused when a man combining intelligence with villainy, like Sisyphus, is outwitted, or when one is brought low who is brave and unjust. The outcome is probable, however only in Agathon's sense; it is likely, he says, that many unlikely things will occur.

The chorus should be regarded as one of the persons of the drama; it should be an integral part of the whole, and take its share in the action. The model is the practice of Sophocles, and not that of Euripides. In subsequent poets the choral songs in a tragedy have no more connection with the plot than with that of any other play. Accordingly, at the present day, the chorus sing mere interludes, a practice that goes back to Agathon. And yet what real difference is there between introducing a song that is foreign to the action and attempting to fit a whole speech, or a whole episode, from one drama into another? [The correct use of the chorus may be seen (pp. 146-58) in the *Eumenides* of Aeschylus, and (pp. 228-35) the *Antigone* of Sophocles.]

[Chapter 19.] The other formative elements of tragedy (pp. 737-42) have now been discussed [especially plot and *ethos*], and it remains to speak of diction [*lexis*] and thought [*dianoia*]. As for *dianoia*, we may assume what is said of it in the treatise on Rhetoric, to which inquiry the subject more properly belongs. *Dianoia* includes everything that is to be effected by the arguments of the agents, in their efforts to prove and to refute; to arouse one another's emotions, such as pity, or fear, or anger, and all the like; and to magnify or minimize the importance of things. [To illustrate: Sophocles makes Jocasta (p. 187) try to prove that Laius was killed by a band of robbers, and not by one man, and thus to refute the argument of Oedipus that he had done the deed. Tiresias is made (p. 174) to arouse the anger of Oedipus, and then tries to arouse his fear. Sophocles also makes Jocasta (p. 184) minimize the importance of oracles, and (p. 185) of summoning the Herdsman. Since the composition of a play, so far as concerns the words, means the construction of speeches, Aristotle naturally refers to his *Rhetoric* for a detailed study of the method of composing a speech. We can hardly lay too much stress upon the *Rhetoric* as a work to be consulted by the poet and the student of poetry.] It is evident, too, that the same underlying forms of thought must be in operation whenever the poet makes the agents try by their acts to arouse pity or alarm in one another, or to give these acts an air of importance or naturalness. The only difference is that the act must produce its effect on the other persons without verbal explanation, whereas if a speech be employed, the author must see to it that the effect is produced by the agent's speaking, and that it comes from the particular language the agent uses; for what point would there be in having A make a speech if B already saw things in the desired light, quite apart from anything that might be said?

Among the subjects of inquiry concerning diction, one is the modes of oral utterance, including such matters as the difference between a command and a prayer, a simple statement and a threat, a question and a reply, and so forth. A knowledge of such distinctions, however, falls within the province of the interpreter, not of the poet, and is the concern of the general theorist on some art like Elocution. Whether the poet knows these things, or is ignorant of them, they do not directly touch his art, nor do they offer any ground for objections that are worth considering. For example, why should any one find fault with the opening of the *Iliad*, 'Sing, Goddess, of the wrath,' et cetera?—to which Protagoras objected on the ground that, whereas Homer thinks he is uttering a prayer, actually he is giving a command; since to bid one do or not do a thing, says Protagoras, is an order. We may pass over this inquiry, therefore, as appertaining to another art, and not to the art of poetry.

[Chapter 20.] The diction [*lexis*], taken as a whole, is made up of the following [eight] parts: (1) The ultimate element [individual letter or sound]; (2) the primary combination of ultimate elements [approximately a 'syllable']; (3) the connective particle; (4) the separative particle; (5) the noun ['name'= adjective as well as noun]; (6) the verb; (7) the inflection; (8) the speech. [A 'speech' is a unified utterance, from a phrase or single statement to an entire poem. Aristotle's remarks on *lexis* constitute the first extant scientific grammar. They naturally belong to a systematic art of poetry, and are found here rather than in the *Rhetoric* as a basic discussion for the poet; the treatment of *lexis* in the *Rhetoric* is more specific and subordinate, but the two treatments are complementary, and must be taken together. For the most part, yet with some notable exceptions, they do not concern the student of Greek dramas in an English dress. Aristotle passes from the indivisible elements of spoken sounds, and the primary combinations of these in syllables, to higher combinations, the elements of the phrase or sentence, and finally, as we have noted, to the single speech (*logos*), which may be taken as anything from the simplest statement to a literary composition regarded as one connected whole. The elements of a phrase or sentence are either particles which (as 'and,' 'or,' 'but') have no significance when taken by themselves, or elements, such as nouns and verbs (as 'man,' 'woman,' 'Agamemnon,' 'walks,' 'strikes,' 'falls'), which have a significance of their own.] . . .

A speech [*logos*, unified utterance] is a composite significant sound, of which at least some of the parts [as nouns and verbs] are significant in themselves. Such a composite utterance is not always made up of nouns and verbs; it may, for example, be without a verb, as in the definition of Man: 'A biped land-animal.' [Compare some of the phrases in the Sophoclean Chorus in *Antigone* (p. 222).] However, there will always be a part that stands for some person or thing, as 'Cleon' in the sentence, 'Cleon is walking.' A speech [*logos*] may be a unit in either of two ways: it may signify one thing; or the unity may be brought about through the linking together of more than one utterance. Thus the *Iliad* is one utterance through the binding together of a number; and the definition of Man is a unit because it signifies one thing.

[Chapter 21.] Nouns [name-words, including adjectives] are of two kinds, simple and compound. By simple are meant those that are formed of non-significant elements, as the word *ge* ['earth']. A compound noun may be made up of a significant and a non-significant part—though the distinction is lost when the parts are united; or it may be made up of two parts, both of which, taken by themselves, are significant. A compound noun may also be triple or quadruple, or multiple, in form, as, for example, the Massiliot composite name 'Hermo-Caico-Xanthos.'

Whatever the formation, a term must always be either (1) the current word; or (2) a strange [rare, not the usual] word;

or (3) a metaphor; or (4) an ornamental term; or (5) a newly-coined word; or a word that is (6) lengthened, or (7) curtailed, or (8) altered.

(1) By a current term is meant the word that is used for a thing by the people we know; by a (2) strange (or rare) word, one that is used in another region. It is obvious that the same word may be both strange and current, though not with respect to the same region. The word *sigynon* ('lance'), for example, is current in Cyprus, but rare at Athens. [For poets in general, 'rare' words are more likely to be 'old' words, that is, words from another time, than dialectal words from another place.]

(3) Metaphor consists in the application to one thing of the term that belongs to another: (a) the term for the genus may be applied to a subordinate species; (b) the term for the species may be applied to the inclusive genus; (c) the term for one species may be applied to another; or (d) there may be a transfer of terms on grounds of analogy [or proportion].

(a) The transfer of a term from genus to species is illustrated in 'Here *stands* my ship'; for *to be at anchor* is one of the species of the genus *standing*.

(b) The transfer from species to genus, in 'Of a truth, *ten thousand* noble deeds hath Odysseus wrought'; where *ten thousand*, a specific large number, is used instead of *a large number* in general.

(c) The transfer from species to species, in 'With a knife of bronze *drawing* away the life-blood,' and in '*Cutting* with the unwearing bronze'; where the poet [? Empedocles] uses *drawing* for *cutting*, and *cutting* for *drawing*, when both terms are species of the genus *removing*.

(d) By metaphor formed on the basis of analogy [or proportion] is meant the case when a second term, B, is to a first, A, as a fourth, D, is to a third, C; whereupon the fourth term, D, may be substituted for the second, B, or the second, B, for the fourth, D. Sometimes, too, the poet will qualify the metaphorical word by adding to it the term ($+$ A or $+$ C) to which the non-figurative term is relative. To illustrate: the drinking-bowl (B) is to Dionysus (A) as the shield (D) is to Ares (C). Accordingly, the bowl (B) may be called the *shield* (D) of

Dionysus, and the shield (D) the *bowl* (B) of Ares: Or another illustration: Old Age (B) is to life (A) as evening (D) is to the day (C). And hence one will speak of *the evening* (D) as the *old age* (B) of the day—or as Empedocles does; and of *old age* (B) as *the evening* of life—or as 'the sunset of life.' In certain cases, the language may not have any word corresponding to one of the terms in the proportion, but the figure nevertheless will be employed. For example, when a fruit casts forth its seed, the action is called 'sowing,' but the action of the sun in casting forth its flame has no special name. Yet this nameless action (B) is to the sun (A) as *sowing* (D) is to the fruit (C); and hence we have the expression of the poet, '*sowing* a god-created flame.' There is yet another way in which this kind of metaphor may be used. We may substitute one term, B, for another, D, and then subtract some attribute of B. For example, you might call *the shield*, not *the bowl* (B) of Ares, but 'the *wineless* bowl.'

[(4) The ornamental term is not discussed or illustrated by Aristotle in the *Poetics*. It is illustrated in the *Rhetoric*. The word used in the *Poetics* for this element of diction, *kosmos*, no doubt illustrates itself, as in English *adorn, adorning*, may serve for verbal ornaments. The names of ornamental objects often fall under this head, as *jewel, chalice, coral*. Note that a given term may illustrate more than one of the eight categories of diction; a metaphor, for example, might also be the current term, or a rare, or an ornamental term, or a curtailed or lengthened, or otherwise altered word or term. Similarly an ornamental term might be a metaphor, a rare word, a lengthened word, and so on. Even the current term on occasion might serve better for ornament than one less usual.[3]]

(5) A newly-coined term is one that is wholly unknown to any region, and is applied to something by an individual poet; for there seem to be certain words of this origin—as *ernyges* for 'horns,' and *areter* for 'priest.'

(6) A lengthened word is one in which a customary short vowel is made long, or in which an extra syllable is inserted. . . . [Compare Milton's use of *mee* and *hee* for metre

[3] See Lane Cooper's article, 'The Verbal "Ornament" in Aristotle's Art of Poetry,' pp. 61-77 in *Studies in Honor of E. K. Rand*, New York, 1938.

and stress, instead of *me* and *he;* and Wordsworth's use of *thorough* for *through.*]

(7) A curtailed word is one from which some part has been removed. . . . [Compare Milton's shortening of *adventurous* to *adventrous.*]

(8) An altered word is one in which the poet, having left some part unchanged, remodels the rest. . . .

[Chapter 22.] In respect to diction, the ideal for the poet is to be clear without being mean. The clearest diction is that which is wholly made up of current terms [the ordinary words and expressions]. But a style so composed is mean; witness the poetry of Cleophon or Sthenelus. [Compare Kipling in 'The female of the species,' et cetera.] But the language attains majesty and distinction when the poet makes use of terms that are less familiar: rare words, metaphors, lengthened forms—everything that deviates from the ordinary usage. Yet if one composes in a diction of such terms alone, the result will be either a riddle or an unnatural jargon; a riddle if the language be nothing but metaphors, and a jargon if it be nothing but words that are strange [dialect words and the like]. Indeed, the very essence of a riddle consists in describing an actual occurrence in an impossible combination of words. Now this cannot be done through any arrangement of words in their primary meanings, but it can be through their metaphorical substitutes. For example: 'A man I saw gluing bronze on a man with fire' [an enigmatical description of blood-letting with a vacuum caused by heat in a cup of bronze], and the like. [Compare the celebrated riddle propounded by the Sphinx to Oedipus: 'What is it that goes on four legs in the morning, on two at noon, and on three at night?'—the answer being 'Man,' or in particular, Oedipus himself, since he crawled as infant, walked proudly as king, and as a blind old man traveled with a staff in his age.] A similar combination of strange words would be a jargon. [For example, the cry of Dante's Nimrod, 'Pape Satan, Pape Satan, aleppe!' Compare the 'Brek ek ek kex' of Aristophanes' *Frogs* (p. 678), and the jargon of the Triballian deity in his *Birds* (p. 663).

The poet, then, should employ a certain admixture of these

expressions that deviate from the ordinary usage; for distinction and elevation of style will result from the use of such means as the strange word, the metaphor, the ornamental word, and the rest; and clearness will arise from such part of the language as is in common use. Very important in helping to make the style clear without loss of distinction are the lengthened, curtailed, and altered forms of words. Their deviation from the customary forms will lend the quality of distinction; and the element they have in common with the ordinary usage will give clearness. Those critics are wrong, therefore, who censure such a modification of usage, and ridicule the poet for resorting to it; as when the elder Euclid said it was easy enough to make poetry if they would let you lengthen out words as you pleased. So he caricatured the practice by reading

I saw Epichares a-walking Marathon-wards . . .

as verse. An obtrusive employment of the device of lengthening words becomes, of course, ridiculous, but the same holds true of any similar stylistic procedure. The principle of moderation should govern the use of every element of diction; for with metaphors also, and strange words, and the rest, a like effect will ensue if they are used without propriety and with the aim of causing laughter.

The proper use of lengthened forms is a different thing; as may be seen in epic poetry, if we take a verse and substitute therein the common forms of the words. And a similar test should be made with the strange [rare] word, and with metaphors and the rest. One has only to replace them by the terms in ordinary use, and the truth of our remarks will be obvious. For example, the same iambic line occurs in Aeschylus and Euripides, though in Aeschylus it is commonplace; but Euripides, by the substitution of just one word—a rare word in place of the ordinary—has rendered the line beautiful. Aeschylus in his *Philoctetes* makes Philoctetes say:

The cancer that *is eating* the flesh of my foot;

Euripides replaces 'is eating' by 'feasts on.' Or take the line uttered by the Cyclops in the *Odyssey:*

Lo, now, a dwarf, a man of no worth and a weakling;

and fancy some one reciting it in the terms of ordinary usage:

See, now, a small man, feeble, and unprepossessing.

Or take the line:

And placed for him [Odysseus] an unseemly seat and a
meagre table;

and suppose it to be read thus:

And brought for him a sorry chair and a small table.

Or substitute for 'the sea-beach bellows,' in the *Iliad,* 'the
beach is roaring.' Again, Ariphrades used to ridicule the
tragedians for locutions which no one would employ in ordinary conversation; for example, 'from the house away,' instead
of 'away from the house'; 'of thee,' instead of 'yours'; . . .
'Achilles about,' instead of 'about Achilles'; and so on. [Com-
pare Wordsworth: 'That glides the dark hills under.'] It is
just because these expressions are not ordinary that they give
distinction to the language; and that is the point Ariphrades
failed to catch.

It is, indeed, important to make the right use of each of the
elements mentioned—lengthened, curtailed, and altered words
—as well as of compounds and rare words. But most important by far is it to have a command of metaphor. That is the
one thing the poet cannot learn from others. It is the mark of
genius; for to coin good metaphors involves an insight into
the resemblances between objects that are superficially unlike.
Of the several kinds we have noted, compound words are
best adapted to the dithyramb, strange words to heroic metre
[to epic poetry], and metaphors to iambic metre [to the
tragic dialogue]. In heroic poetry, it is true, all the special
forms may be used. But iambic verse, as far as may be, represents the spoken language, and hence employs only the kinds
of words one would use in oratory; that is, the current term,
the metaphor, and the ornamental term.

Herewith we close the discussion of tragedy, or the art of
imitation in the form of action.

[771]

III

Epic Poetry. The Principles of Its Construction

[Chapter 23.] And now for the species of poetry which is purely narrative, the art which imitates in a single metre.

In an epic poem, as in tragedy, the story should be constructed on dramatic principles; everything should turn about a single action, one that is a whole, and is organically perfect, with a beginning, and a middle, and an end. In this way, just as a living animal, individual and perfect, has its own beauty, so the poem will arouse in us its own characteristic pleasure. So much is obvious from what has gone before. Putting the thing negatively, we may say that the plot of an epic poem must be unlike what we commonly find in histories, which perforce represent, not a single action, but some one period, with all that happened therein to one or more persons, however unrelated the several occurrences may have been. For example, the battle of Salamis took place at the same time as the defeat of the Carthaginians in Sicily; but the two events did not converge to the same end. And similarly, one event may directly follow another in point of time, and yet there may be no sequence leading to one issue. Nevertheless, we may venture to say, most of the epic poets commit this very fault of making their plots like chronicles.

In precisely this respect, therefore, Homer, as we already have said (p. 743), manifestly transcends the other epic poets. Far from taking all the legend of Ilium for his theme, he did not attempt to deal even with the war in its entirety, although this had a definite beginning and end. Very likely he thought that the story would be too long to be easily grasped as a whole; or, if it were not too long, that it would be too complicated from the variety of the incidents. As it is, he has selected a single phase of the war for his main action, and employs a number of the other incidents by way of episode; for example, he diversifies his narrative with the *Catalogue of the Ships,* and so forth. Of the other epic poets, some take for their subject all the deeds of one person; others all the events of one period; and others a single action, but one with a multiplicity of parts. This last is what was done by the author

of the *Cypria*, and by the author of the *Little Iliad*. Consequently, the *Iliad* and the *Odyssey* each furnish materials for
but a single tragedy, or at most for two; while the *Cypria*
supplies subjects for several; and the *Little Iliad* for eight
or more: an *Award of the Arms*, a *Philoctetes*, a *Neoptolemus*,
a *Eurypylus*, a *Mendicant Odysseus*, a *Spartan Women*, a
Sack of Ilium, a *Sailing of the Fleet*—one might add a *Sinon*
and a *Trojan Women*.

[Chapter 24.] Furthermore, there must be the same varieties
of epic poetry as of tragedy (cf. pp. 762-3). That is, an epic
plot must be (1) uninvolved or (2) involved, or the story
must be one (3) of suffering [*pathos*] or (4) of character
[*ethos*]. The constituent parts, also, of the epic poem must
be the same as in tragedy, save that the epic poet does not use
the elements of music [*melos*] and spectacle [*opsis*]; for
there necessarily are reversals, discoveries, and sufferings in
this form of poetry as in that. And the intellectual processes
[*dianoia*] and the diction must be artistically worked out.
Forerunner in the use of all these elements was Homer, who
laid the proper emphasis on them severally; for each of his
poems is a model of construction—the *Iliad* of an uninvolved
plot and a story of tragic suffering [*pathos*, violence], the
Odyssey of an involved plot (since there are discoveries
throughout) and a story of character. And in addition to these
excellences, each of the poems surpasses all others in point
of diction and thought. [The excellence in 'thought' is seen,
for example, in the structure of the speeches; the speakers
argue each in accordance with his *ethos*. So much for similarities between epic poetry and tragedy.]

But epic poetry differs from tragedy (1) in the length of the
composition, and (2) in respect to metre. As for the length,
an adequate limit has already been suggested (pp. 742-3):
it must be possible for us to embrace the beginning and end
of the story in one view. Now this condition would be met
if the work were shorter than the old epic poems; if it were
about as long as one of the groups of tragedies that are presented for a single hearing. [Say 3500-4000 lines in all; the
Orestean Trilogy of Aeschylus runs to 3795.] But through its
capacity for extension, epic poetry has a great and peculiar
advantage; for in a tragedy it is not possible to represent a

number of incidents in the action as carried on simultaneously; the poet is limited to the one thing done on the stage by the actors who are there. But in an epic poem, because of the narrative form, he may represent a number of incidents as simultaneous occurrences; and these, if they are relevant to the action, materially add to the poem. The increase in bulk tends to the advantage of the epic poem in grandeur, and in variety of interest for the hearer through diversity of incident in the episodes. Uniformity of incident quickly satiates the audience, and makes tragedies fail on the stage.

As for the metre, epic poetry has appropriated the heroic [hexameter verse] as a result of experience. And the fitness of this measure might be critically tested; for if any one were to produce a narrative poem in another metre, or in several others, the incongruity would be obvious. Of all metres, in fact, the heroic is the stateliest and most impressive. On this account, it most readily admits the use of strange [rare] words and metaphors (see p. 771) ; for in its tolerance of forms that are out of the ordinary range, narrative poetry goes beyond the other kinds. The iambic and trochaic measures, on the other hand, are the concomitants of motion, the trochaic being appropriate to dancing, and the iambic expressive of life and action. [Thus neither is suited to the stately epic poem.] Still more unfitting would it be to compose an epic poem in a hotchpotch of metres after the fashion of Chaeremon's rhapsody. And hence no one ever has written a long story in any other metre than the heroic. Rather, nature herself, as we have said (cf. p. 733), teaches us to select the proper kind of verse for such a story.

Homer, so worthy of praise in other respects, is especially admirable in that he alone among epic poets is not unaware of the part to be taken by the author himself in his work. The poet should, in fact, say as little as may be in his own person. Now the rest of the epic poets constantly appear in their own works, and their snatches of artistic imitation are few and far between. But Homer, after a brief preliminary, straightway brings in a man, or a woman, or some other type; no one of them vague, but each sharply differentiated.

Some element of the marvelous unquestionably has a place in tragedy; but the irrational [illogical, unnatural], which is the chief factor in the marvelous, and which must as far as possible be excluded from tragedy, is more freely admitted in epic poetry, since the persons of the story are not actually before our eyes. Take the account of the pursuit of Hector in the *Iliad*. On the stage, the scene would be ridiculous: Achilles running after Hector all alone, beneath the walls of Troy; the Grecian warriors halting instead of following, and Achilles shaking his head to warn them not to throw darts at their foe. In the narrative, however, since we do not combine the circumstances into one picture, the absurdity of the situation is not perceived.

That the marvelous is a source of pleasure may be seen by the way people add to a story; for they always embellish the facts with striking details, in the belief that it will gratify the listeners. Yet it is Homer above all who has shown the rest of us how a lie ought to be told. The essence of the method is the use of a fallacy in reasoning, as follows. Suppose that whenever A exists or comes to pass, B must exist or occur; men think, if the consequent B exists, the antecedent A must also; but the inference is illegitimate. For the poet, accordingly, the right method is this: if the antecedent A is untrue, and if there is something else, B, which would necessarily exist or occur if A were true, one must add on the B; for, knowing the added detail to be true, we ourselves mentally proceed to the fallacious inference that the antecedent A is likewise true. We may take an instance from the *Bath-Scene* in the *Odyssey*. [Here Odysseus, disguised in rags, wishes to convince Penelope that he, the Beggar, has seen the real Odysseus alive; that is A, the falsehood. Accordingly, he adds an accurate description of the warrior's clothing, etc.; that is B, the true details. Penelope knows B to be true, since the garments came from her. If A were true, that is, if the Beggar had seen Odysseus, the natural consequence, B, would be a true description of the clothing. From the truth of B, Penelope mistakenly infers the occurrence of A, and believes the Beggar. The illusion, which is partly shared by any one who hears the story, witnesses to the artistic method of the poet. Compare the method of Aeschylus in Clytemnestra's detailed account of the signal-fires which, she says, have announced the fall of Troy (*Agamemnon*, pp. 43-4).]

A sequence of events which, though actually impossible, looks reasonable should be preferred by the poet to what, though really possible, seems incredible. The story [whether of an epic poem or a tragedy] should not be made up of incidents which are severally improbable; one should rather aim to include no irrational element whatever. At any rate, if an irrational element is unavoidable, it should lie outside of the story proper; as Oedipus' ignorance in Sophocles' *Oedipus the King* (p. 166) of the way in which Laius met his death. It should not lie within the story; so the anachronism in Sophocles' *Electra* (p. 325), where the legendary Orestes is described as being killed at the modern, historical, Pythian games; similarly the silence of (?)Telephus in *The Mysians* of (?)Aeschylus, where the man comes all the way from Tegea to Mysia without speaking. Accordingly, it is ridiculous for a poet to say that his story would be ruined if such incidents were left out; he has no business to construct such a plot to begin with. But if he does set out to represent an irrational incident, and if he obviously could have treated it in a way less offensive to our notions of probability, his fault is worse than ridiculous; lying, not in his choice of an object to imitate, but in his art as an imitator. In the hands of an inferior poet, how manifest and intolerable would the improbabilities become which we find even in the *Odyssey*, at the point where Odysseus is set ashore. [Earnestly desiring to see his native land, Odysseus nevertheless sleeps from the time he leaves the land of the Phaeacians until after they have disembarked him on his own island, and gone away; although 'the vessel in full course ran ashore, half her keel's length high.'] As it is, Homer conceals the absurdity, and renders the incident charming, by means of his other excellences [in particular by his elaborate description of the nocturnal voyage, and of the haven and cave at Ithaca].

Elaborate diction, however, is to be used only when the action pauses, and no purposes and arguments of the agents are to be displayed. [The incident just mentioned, in the *Odyssey*, is a good example.] Conversely, where the purposes and reasonings of the agents are to be revealed, a too ornate diction will obscure them.

IV

Problems in Criticism. The Principles of Their Solution

[Chapter 25.] As to problems in criticism, and the respective solutions of them: they rest upon certain basic principles, and the number and nature of these will be clear if we take account of the following considerations.

(1) The poet, as we have seen, is an imitator, just like a painter or any other maker of likenesses; of necessity, then, he must, in all instances, represent one of three objects (cf. pp. 728, 731): (a) things as they once were, or are now; (b) things as they are said or thought to be; (c) things as they ought to be. (2) The poet's medium of expression is the diction, unadorned, or with an admixture of strange words and metaphors; indeed, there are various modifications of ordinary usage that we concede to the poets. (3) Further, the standard of correctness is not the same in Poetry as in Politics; the standard is different in Poetry from that in any other art. [A citizen who fulfilled his duty to the State and in private life would meet the standard of correctness in Politics and Ethics; but to satisfy the standard of correctness in tragedy, the agents, while they must be represented as 'good' (by nature aiming ordinarily to be kind and just), must yet through some *hamartia* come short of real justice and constant goodness. And the persons of comedy must have comic flaws and failings; to be comic they must as a rule be 'worse than the average.' (See pp. 729, 733.)] Within the limits of poetry there can be two kinds of errors, the one (a) directly involving the art, the other (b) adventitious. If the poet has chosen something for the object of his imitation, and through want of capacity fails properly to represent what he has in mind, this is (a) a fault in his art itself. But let us suppose that he has made an incorrect choice in the object he wishes to represent; suppose, for example, that he wishes to represent a moving horse with both right legs thrown forward; or suppose that he makes a mistake in any other special branch of knowledge, as medicine or the like; or let the impossible objects be what they may. If he succeeds in duly imitating the object which he has in mind, his mistake is not (a) one that con-

cerns the Poetic Art itself. It is (b) adventitious. These, then, are the considerations from which one must proceed in answering the strictures of the critics.

Let us first consider the strictures relating to the Poetic Art itself. If impossibilities have been represented, the poet is guilty of a fault. Yet such impossibilities may be justified, if their representation serves the purpose of the art itself—for we must remember what has been said of the end of poetry; that is, they are justified if they give the passage they are in, or some other passage, a more astounding effect. The pursuit of Hector (see p. 775) is a case in point, being justified by the poetic effect. [Compare also Clytemnestra's account of the signal-fires in *Agamemnon* (pp. 43-4), and the sudden appearance of her husband thereafter. And with this compare the arrival of the Magi, after the appearance of the star, in the mediaeval plays on the Nativity.] But if the ends of poetry could have been as well or better subserved by scientific accuracy, the error is not justified; for the poet ought if possible to make no mistakes whatever.

Again, when an error is found, one must always ask: Is the mistake adventitious, arising from ignorance in some special field of knowledge, or does it concern the art of imitation as such? If a painter thinks that a doe has horns, for example, it is less of an error than to fail in representing his actual conception. [Compare the adventitious mistake of Keats in placing 'stout Cortez' (instead of Balboa) upon 'a peak in Darien.']

Further, it may be objected that the representation of the poet is not true [to things as they are or have been]. Here the answer may be that they are represented as they ought to be [that they are typical]; just as Sophocles affirmed that he drew men as they ought to be, and Euripides men as they are. But if the representation be true neither to the fact nor to the ideal, the answer may be that it accords with current legends and popular belief: 'People say so.' The unedifying poetical tales about the gods, for instance, are, very possibly, neither true nor the preferable thing to relate; in fact, they may be as false and immoral as Xenophanes maintains. But they certainly are in keeping with popular belief. Of still other things which are objected to in poetry, one may possibly say, not that they are better than the fact here and now, but that the fact was so at the time [historical truth]. Such is the case with the description of the arms of Diomed and his companions in the *Iliad:* 'Their spears were driven into the ground, erect upon the spikes of the butts' [the practice described by Homer is not better than the method familiar to his critics, but it accords with historical truth]; for that was the custom then, as it is in Illyria even now.

As for the question whether something said or done by some one in a poem is proper or not; to answer this question we must not merely consider the intrinsic quality of the act or utterance, to see whether it is noble or base in itself; we must also consider (a) the person who does or says the thing, (b) the person to whom it is done or said, or (c) when, or (d) in whose interest, or (e) with what motive, it is done or said. Thus we must examine any questionable word or act, to see whether the motive of the agent is to secure some greater good or to avert a greater evil. [The sentiments of persons in a drama such as *Oedipus the King,* or *Antigone,* are to be 'in character'; the speeches they make are not to be taken at their face value, ethically better or worse, whether in tragic poetry or comic. Thus the speeches of Satan in *Paradise Lost* are not morally good in themselves, having, as Milton says, 'semblance of worth, not substance'; the poet intends to represent a sophistical and deceptive speaker. Similarly in the *Odyssey* Homer must supply Odysseus with deceptive speeches. The dispute of Clytemnestra and her husband in *Agamemnon* over the carpet (p. 62) well illustrates all the points of Aristotle regarding this problem. The faithless wife in fear and hate wishes Agamemnon to enter the house where she can safely slay him; the unfaithful husband wishes to be at home, and to have Cassandra with him. Husband and wife keep talking about the carpet, and how the gods will view his manner of entrance, and not how they view the crimes of adultery and murder.]

The justice or injustice of other criticisms must be decided by the principles of poetic diction. For example, objection may be raised to a passage because the poet is using (a) a strange word. . . .

Other difficulties may be explained under this head, if we

regard the language as (b) metaphorical. Homer says: 'Now *all* gods and men were sleeping through the night'; and at the same time he tells us: 'And whenever he looked at the Trojan plain, he marveled at the sound of flutes and pipes.' [That is, some men were awake.] The difficulty may be resolved if we regard *all* as used metaphorically for *many*, since *all* is a species of the genus *many*. So also we may explain, 'And she *alone* hath no part in the baths of Ocean'; for the other Northern constellations that do not set are not familiar like the Great Bear, and the one which is very familiar may be figuratively called the only one.

Again, a passage that is censured may be defended after a study of (c) the pronunciation. . . .

Other difficulties one may solve by considering (d) the punctuation, as in the sentence of Empedocles: 'Suddenly things became mortal that before had learnt to be immortal and things unmixed before mixed.' [If the passage is censured when a comma follows 'unmixed,' perhaps the comma ought to precede 'mixed'; thus: 'and things unmixed before, mixed.']

Or we may have to consider (e) the grammatical ambiguity of an expression, as in the passage: 'Of the night *pleon* two watches are spent'; if *pleon* means *'more than'* two watches, the phrase contradicts 'but a third part still remains.' But the solution may be that the expression means 'full two watches.'

Or we may have to appeal to (f) the custom of language. Just as we now call wine and water 'wine,' so Homer in speaking of 'the greave of new-wrought *tin*,' from which the spear rebounded, may mean a metallic alloy of tin. And as we call workers in iron *chalkeas* ['braziers'], so Homer may call Ganymede the *'wine*-pourer to Zeus,' although the gods drink, not wine, but nectar. This difficulty, however, may be resolved as an instance of (b) metaphor.

Finally, a passage in dispute may be defended through an appeal to (g) the several possibilities of meaning in a single word—as distinguished from (e) ambiguities in grammar. When a word seems to involve some inconsistency, one should consider the different senses it may bear in the context. For example: 'There' [at or in the third and golden layer of the shield] *'scheto'* ['stuck' or 'stayed'] 'the spear of bronze.' One should ask in how many ways we may take *scheto*.

[Homer says that the spear pierced two layers, and implies that the next remained unpierced; but if the spear *stuck* in the third layer, it must have pierced that also. The alleged inconsistency disappears if we reflect that *scheto* may also mean *stayed:* 'There stayed the spear of bronze.']

In other words, the right procedure is just the opposite of the method condemned by Glaucon, who says of certain critics: 'They begin with some unwarranted assumption, and having pronounced judgment in a matter, they go on to argue from this; and if what the poet says does not agree with what they happen to think, they censure his supposed misstatement.' Such is the fashion in which the question about Icarius, in the *Odyssey*, has been handled. The critics begin by imagining that he was a Lacedaemonian, and accordingly think it strange that his grandson, Telemachus, did not meet him on his journey to Lacedaemon. But perhaps the case may be as the Cephallenians say; for their story is that Odysseus took a wife from Cephallenia, and that her father's name was not Icarius, but Icadius. It is doubtless a mistake of the critics that has given rise to the problem.

In general, questions as to the poet's use of impossibilities must be decided by an appeal either to (a) the end of poetry, or to (b) ideal truth, or to (c) what is commonly believed. For the ends of poetry, (a) a thing really impossible, yet on the face of it convincing, is preferable to one that, though possible, does not win belief. And if such men as Zeuxis painted be called too beautiful, the pictures may be defended as (b) true to the ideal; for the type necessarily excels the average and actual.

What the critics term improbable one must judge by (c) an appeal to popular belief, and by an attempt to show that on occasion the thing may not be improbable; for [as Agathon suggested (see p. 764)] it is likely that something improbable will now and then occur.

As for alleged contradictions in the poet's language, these we must scrutinize as one deals with sophistical refutations in an argument; that is, as is done in dialectic. Then we can see whether the poet in his several statements refers to the same thing, in the same relation, and in the same sense, and can judge whether or not he has contradicted what he himself says, or what a person of intelligence normally assumes as true.

The censure of the critic is just, however, when it is directed against improbability in the plot, and, similarly, against depravity in the agents; that is, when there is no inner necessity for a base agent, and when the irrational element serves no artistic purpose. Thus there is no adequate reason for Aegeus' appearing (p. 470) in Euripides' *Medea*, and none for the baseness of Menelaus in his *Orestes*.

We see, accordingly, that all the strictures of critics are reducible to five species. Objections are raised against poetry on the ground that something is either (1) impossible, (2) irrational [improbable], (3) morally hurtful, (4) contradictory, or (5) contrary to artistic correctness. The answers to these objections must be sought under one or another of the heads enumerated above (pp. 777-8). And these answers are twelve in number. [The twelve problems and answers apparently correspond to criticisms that touch the poetic art (1) directly, (2) indirectly; or that touch the poet as an imitator of things (3) as they were or are, (4) as they are said or thought to be, (5) as they ought to be; or that bear on (6) strange words, (7) metaphors, (8) pronunciation, (9) punctuation, (10) grammatical ambiguity, (11) custom of language, (12) different meanings of the same word.]

[Chapter 26.] The question finally suggests itself: Which is the higher form of art, epic poetry or tragedy? Those who favor the epic poem may argue thus: The less vulgar form is the higher; and that which addresses the better audience is always the less vulgar. If this be so, it is obvious that a pantomimic art like tragedy is exceedingly vulgar; for [so the argument runs] the performers suppose that unless they throw in something of their own, the audience will not understand what is meant, and hence they indulge in all sorts of bodily motions. An inferior flute-player, for instance, when throwing the discus is to be represented, will twist and twirl like the athlete himself; or if he is playing the *Scylla*, he will clutch at the leader of the chorus. Tragedy, then, is said to be an art of this kind, and to lie under the same condemnation as the earlier actors passed upon the next generation. Thus Mynniscus used to call Callipides 'the Ape,' for overacting his parts; and the actor Pindarus got a similar reputation. And as the later generation is held to be worse than the earlier among the actors, so the whole art of tragedy, which is later than epic poetry, is considered inferior to it. So we are told that the epic poem is addressed to a cultivated audience, which does not need gestures and postures, and tragedy to an audience that is inferior and does. Accordingly, if tragedy is a vulgar art, it evidently is the lower form.

The reply to this argument is twofold. (1) First, then, as to gesture and movement. (a) The censure attaches, not to the art of the poet as such, but to the art of his interpreter. And it touches the interpreter of epic as well as tragic poetry; for the epic reciter likewise may overdo the gesticulation, as did Sosistratus; and it may be overdone in a singing-contest, as by Mnasitheus of Opus.

(b) In artistic representation, we are not to condemn all bodily movement; otherwise we should have to condemn outright the art of dancing. What we must object to is the attitudes and gestures of the ignoble; the very objection that was brought against Callippides. The same criticism is passed on certain actors of to-day, who in assuming the rôle of women are said to lack the bearing of ladies.

(c) It is quite possible for tragedy to produce its characteristic effect without any movement or gesture, in just the same way as epic poetry; for if we merely read a play, its quality becomes evident. Accordingly, if it be true that tragedy is superior in all other respects, this alleged weakness need not be present.

(2) Secondly, one must argue in favor of tragedy (a) that it contains every element to be found in epic poetry—since it may have a use even for the epic metre; and that in addition (see pp. 738, 773) it has no inconsiderable elements of its own in spectacular effects and in music, and through the music the characteristic pleasure is distinctly heightened.

Next, (b) the greater vividness of tragedy is felt when we read the play as well as when we see it acted.

Further, (c) the tragic imitation attains its end in less space. And this may be deemed an advantage, since the concentrated effect is more delightful than one which is long drawn out, and so diluted. Consider the result, for example, if one were to lengthen out *Oedipus the King* into the number of lines in the *Iliad*.

And again, (d) the unity of action is less strict in the work of the epic poets, as is shown by the number of subjects for tragedies to be derived from any one of their poems. Consequently, if an epic poet takes a strictly unified story, either he will tell it briefly, and it will seem abrupt, or he will make it conform to the usual heroic scale, and it will seem thin and watery. By a less strict unity in an epic poem is meant a case in which the story is made up of a plurality of actions. Thus the *Iliad* has many such parts, and the *Odyssey* also; and each of these parts is of some magnitude. Nevertheless these two poems are as perfect in structure as the nature of the epic poem will permit; and the action represented is as nearly as may be a unit.

If, now, tragedy is superior to epic poetry in all these respects, and particularly in fulfilling its special function as a form of art; and if we recall, as we must [see pp. 751-2], that the two forms of serious poetry are to give us not any chance pleasure, but the definite pleasure we have mentioned; then it is clear that tragedy, since it attains the right end more effectively than the epic poem, is the higher form of the two. . . .

ARISTOTLE ON COMEDY

MANY principles of Aristotle concerning tragedy and epic poetry can with justice be applied to comedy, or modified in ways that will help to explain it. In studying a comedy such as the *Birds* or the *Frogs*, one does well to go through the *Poetics*, noting, first, the direct reference in it to Aristophanes, to the comic side of Homer, to the Dionysiac origin of comedy, to the nature of the agents in comedy (worse men instead of better), to their flaws (of a ridiculous sort, neither painful nor repellent), to the comic mask as an example of amusing distortion, to a comedy dealing with Orestes and Aegisthus, to the *Odyssey* as partly offering the satisfaction of comedy, and so on—all told, a good deal of direct reference by Aristotle to the comic drama. And then one should study the *Poetics* in order to see how much of the discussion in it can be taken over from tragedy and directly applied to comedy; for example, what is said of imitation, of the constituent elements of a drama, *plot, ethos, dianoia, lexis, melos, opsis*, all of which could be found in the *Birds* and *Frogs*. So also we can illustrate the kinds of discovery (in particular perhaps the fifth, yet the others as well), and the reversal. Finally, with a proper shift, we can see what in the *Poetics* must be modified in its application to comedy. Obviously the law of probability or necessity in the relation of one thing to another does not operate in the same way for tragedy and comedy. Comedy admits the marvelous more freely; it makes more use of the incredible. Nevertheless the comic poet must study the law of probability in order to deviate from it in the right way. Aristophanes is very careful in what he does and what he avoids. He leads us adroitly from the world about us by stages, sure if rapid, to another world, and multiplies the phenomena that would be true if his primary assumption, as in the *Frogs*, were true. It is the method which Aristotle says

is the right one when the poet is to represent a lie. If A is untrue, but B would follow if A were true, amplify B (see p.
775).

For the pleasure of comedy, corresponding to the pleasure
arising from the catharsis of pity and fear in tragedy, we must
say that whatever the effect of comedy has upon a normal
person of taste and experience, upon a qualified audience, that
doubtless would be for Aristotle the proper effect, that pleasure the right pleasure. We may assume that it is not a catharsis
of pity and fear. According to a tradition of English writers
on comedy, this kind of art relieves us of 'spleen'; obviously
that is a notion derived from the old medical theory of the
'humors.' Aristotle's catharsis of pity and fear in tragedy is
related to the same medical theory. Comedy does certainly
put us into good humor. Its plots and scenes and characters
evincing palpable disproportions do relieve us of a sense of
disproportion, and of emotions, such as anger and envy, which
we have when we feel that our personal situation is unfair,
that we are not treated according to our deserts.

Besides representing what is ludicrous because ugly and
out of proportion (but not painful or repulsive), comedy, as
in the *Birds,* the *Frogs,* the *Tempest,* also delights us with
beauty, in the song of the Nightingale, of the Votaries, of
Ariel, the beauty of beautiful women, a beauty of *melos* and
opsis, not like that of tragedy, not grave, and yet it may be
noble. Sometimes it is hard to find the precise line dividing
the ludicrous element of comedy from the beauty. But the
extremes are easy to see. Perhaps we may say that the basic
pleasure of comedy is negative, so to speak, namely the relief
through the ludicrous of our sense of disproportion; and that
the embellishment of the play through our pleasure in seeing
and hearing beautiful faces, forms, and music, is a positive
addition. Let us add that the basic concepts of Aristophanes
which he works out in the *Birds* and *Frogs* are noble concepts
and beautiful; and that the beauty of his diction and metre,
when he aims at beauty more than comic ugliness, are unsur-
passed. We are tempted to say that he is the most accomplished
metrist of all time.

Subordinate to the *Poetics* and its main positions is the outline of a theory of Greek comic drama which was first printed

in 1839, and is called the *Tractatus Coislinianus*. We shall here call it the Tractate,[1] and regard it as a sketch in the main representing an otherwise lost section of the *Poetics* which followed the last chapter (26) of this work as it now stands.

The Tractate contains a definition of comedy which we may thus paraphrase and amend: Comedy is an imitation of an action that is ludicrous, but complete, of adequate length, in embellished language, the several kinds of embellishment being separately found in the several parts of the play; the action being directly presented, and not given in narrative; through pleasure and laughter effecting a catharsis of disturbing emotions.

Laughter arises (1) from the diction (*lexis*), and (2) from the things (objects, persons, incidents, content).

(1) From the diction, through the use of:

(a) Homonyms (*equivoca,* ambiguities). So in the *Plutus* of Aristophanes, the changes are rung on *Wealth,* the god, and *wealth,* riches; or take the remark of the tramp: 'Speaking of famous springs, I bathed in the spring of 1912.' See also the various turns on the word *polos* in *Birds* 179-84, and on *ornis* in *Birds* 719-21.

Diction (b). Synonyms. Thus one may call the same act *stealing* or *conveying:* ' "Convey" the wise it call. "Steal"! foh! a fico for the phrase' (*Merry Wives of Windsor* 1.3.30).

Diction (c). Garrulity. See, for example, *Frogs* 1331-63.

Diction (d). Paronyms. A paronym is a name lying at the side of another. Two words are concerned, one derived from the other, as, for example, by a change of termination. So in the popular derivation of *Middleton* from *Moses:* you take away the termination -*oses* and add the termination -*iddleton.* Or note the error of the Parisian, 'You cockroach,' corrected by the Londoner, 'You mean *hen*croach.'

Diction (e). Diminutives. Thus: *Socratidion,* 'dear little Socrates' (*Clouds* 233) ; *Euripidion,* 'Euripides, Euripidarling' (*Acharnians* 404).

Diction (f). Perversion (i) by the voice, (ii) by other means of the same sort. So Bottom: 'Thisby, the flowers have

---

[1] For a detailed study of it, and for extended applications of it and of Aristotelian principles to comedy, see Lane Cooper, *An Aristotelian Theory of Comedy*, New York, Harcourt, Brace and Company, 1922.

odious savors sweet.' Quince: 'Odorous, odorous!' (*MND.* 3.1.79).

Diction (g). Grammar and syntax (including rhythm and cadence). Compare the quotations by Aeschylus and Euripides in the *Frogs* (pp. 714-20).

Laughter arises (2) from the things (acts and objects, including persons, as distinct from their names and from diction, or *lexis,* as a whole). Things done include the acts and experiences of the mind. But it is hard to dissociate a thing from its name. If a garrulous person repeats a word, as 'prunes,' he will refer repeatedly to the thing. Thus an example of the ludicrous may sometimes be classified under more than one head. If the humor does not disappear when a joke is translated, we have to do with laughter arising from the 'things.'

(a) Assimilation (i) from the better to the worse. Thus men may be assimilated to birds, frogs, and wasps. Comedy in general tends to represent men and other things by assimilating them to what is worse. In the 'thinking-house' of Socrates are they who 'teach . . . us that heaven is a muffle enveloping us, and we are the charcoal within' (*Clouds* 94-7). Euelpides looks like a gander done by a penny-artist (*Birds* 803-6). But the assimilation may be (ii) of the worse to the better. As in the *Frogs* the god Dionysus may be assimilated to the slave Xanthias, so the slave may be assimilated to the god. The effeminate and froglike Dionysus is also assimilated to the warrior Heracles. In comedy the worse does not tend to gain from its assimilation to the better, but what is low or painful may be raised or softened to the right degree for comic pleasure.

Things (b). Deception. This category overlaps with (e) the unexpected. Every ludicrous accident to which an author leads us for laughter through surprise has the nature of deception. Deception governs the plot of the *Birds,* which is an elaborate lie (Men are birds); see the *Poetics* on the right way of representing a lie (pp. 760, 775). Impostors, pretenders, quacks, men and women in disguise, are to be considered under this head of laughter arising from deception.

Things (c). The impossible. Compare Socrates: 'I tread the air, and look down on the sun' (*Clouds* 225; p. 553).

Things (d). The possible but inconsequent (irrelevant). See Dionysus' test of literary value when he weighs the lines of Aeschylus and Euripides in the scales—to find Aeschylus too heavy, Euripides too light (*Frogs* 1365-1410; see pp. 719-20).

Things (e). The unexpected. Deception and surprise are the two primary sources of laughter, and underlie the others. Thus the irrelevant is unexpected, and likewise the impossible, since things normally follow one another in a 'probable' or a 'necessary' sequence. Still we may have a category of the unexpected including simpler forms, and also the strange, the marvelous, the astounding, as in the *Birds* and *Frogs,* comedies having the scene laid outside the world of everyday experience. Verbal jokes often arise from an unexpected sequence: 'There is plenty of spirit in women, if—the wine-shop is handy' (*Lysistrata* 465-6).

Things (f). From worsening the personages. So Aristophanes makes the Socrates of the *Clouds* worse than the Socrates of reality. Compare Aristotle on the difference between comedy and tragedy in their treatment of the agents (pp. 728, 733).

Things (g). Comic (pantomimic) dancing. Aristophanes prides himself on the absence of the indecent dance from the *Clouds* (cf. line 540), but makes free use of jocose dancing. Comic dancing may be beautiful as well as ludicrous.

Things (h). Choice of what is inferior and trivial when you could take the best. Thus Dionysus intends to bring back Euripides, when Heracles reminds him (*Frogs* 76-7) that he might have Sophocles. So Bottom. Will he have fairy music? 'I have a reasonable good ear in music: let us have the tongs and the bones' (MND. 3.161 ff.). In the *Birds* (1683 ff.) Heracles gives up his right to the Lady Sovereignty for a dish of thrushes.

Things (i). When the sequence of the *logos* is disjointed. A *logos* may be a single speech, or may be the whole comedy regarded as one telling or reduced to a story in one outline. In the comedy as a whole the poet should rather aim at a seeming than at a real lack of coherence. The *Frogs* has a stricter sequence than at first appears, though, as the representation of the incidents of a journey, it is mainly episodic.

As for individual comic agents, their speeches often lack

sequence. Examples of garrulity depend much on this lack for their effect; they are easy to find.

Comedy differs from low abuse. Abuse openly censures the bad qualities in men, whereas comedy employs 'emphasis' (innuendo). 'Emphasis' doubtless characterized the last two plays of Aristophanes, which are lost, forerunners of the New Greek Comedy, that of Menander and his fellows. But 'abuse' belonged rather to the earliest type of Attic comedy, and to the iambic invective of its predecessors.

The joker will make game of defects in the soul and in the body. In the *Birds* the ridiculous bulk of Heracles is represented, as well as his simplicity and gross appetite. Perhaps the propriety of laughter at bodily defects was questioned in Greek treatises on poetry. Certain blemishes, however, such as baldness, strabismus, bandy-legs, like the comic mask, do not strike us as painful. The poet will not go beyond a certain limit in representing bodily defects; so there are degrees of vice which a comic poet will avoid.

As in tragedies there should be a due proportion of fear, so in comedies there should be a due proportion of laughter. The element of laughter, based upon ugliness, should not be in excess; with the birds that are ridiculous there must be a sufficient admixture of beautiful birds, for example, or beauty in the chorus of Frogs or Clouds, along with other embellishments.

The constituent elements of a comedy are (1) plot, (2) *ethos*, (3) *dianoia*, (4) *lexis*, (5) *melos*, (6) *opsis* (compare pp. 738-42).

(1) The comic plot is the structure (synthesis) that binds together the ludicrous incidents.

(2) The characters (*ethe*) of comedy are (a) the buffoonish, (b) the ironical, and (c) those of the impostors. Dionysus in the *Frogs*, Strepsiades in the *Clouds*, and Euelpides in the *Birds*, are buffoons. Polonius, Dogberry, and Bottom are buffoons, and Monsieur Jourdain in the *Bourgeois Gentilhomme*. Monsieur Jourdain leans also towards the type of 'impostor.' Impostors in comedy are legion. The great example of the 'ironical man' is the Socrates of Plato. The unmixed ironical type is not so common as are the buffoons and impostors.

Witness the crew of impostors in the *Birds*, would-be citizens in the new republic of Cloudcuckootown.

(3) The parts of *dianoia* are two: (a) opinion, and (b) proof. Proofs (means of persuasion) are of five sorts: (i) oaths, (ii) compacts (contracts), (iii) testimonies, (iv) tortures (tests, ordeals), (v) laws.[2]

(4) The *lexis* (diction) of comedy is the common, popular language. The comic poet must endow the personages with his own native idiom, but an alien speaker with the alien idiom.

(5) *Melos* is the province of the art of music; so here comedy must take its basic rules from that art.

(6) Spectacle is of great service to dramas in supplying what is in accord with them. So, for example, the *Frogs* gains much from the dress of Dionysus, which approximates the colors of the frog; we may also imagine the costumer working upon the actors who took the parts of Euripides and Aeschylus so as to make the first look like a smaller, and the second like a larger, frog.

Plot, *lexis*, and *melos* are found in all comedies; *dianoia*, *ethos*, and *opsis* in few. . . .

The kinds of comedy are (1) Old, with a superabundance of the laughable; (2) New, which disregards laughter, tends toward the serious; and (3) Middle, which is a mixture of the two. The three kinds represent periods of time, but also tendencies which were all present in Greek comedy from an early time, before Aristophanes. His plays exemplify all three tendencies. The *Clouds* has a leaning to the type of Old, the *Plutus* to the type of New, and the *Birds* is intermediate. It may be thought that the intermediate type, exemplified also by Shakespeare's *Tempest* gives the most, and the most varied, pleasure. All three types are found in the comedies of Molière. The New Comedy, derived in part by Aristophanes from Euripides, was partly taken from the last plays of Aristophanes by writers between him and Menander, passed from Menander and his fellows to Plautus and Terence, and so to the comic poets of the Middle Ages and the Renaissance.

[2] For a study of comic *dianoia*, with its divisions and subdivisions, one should consult the Tractate and Aristotle's *Rhetoric*; see above, and see my translation of the *Rhetoric*, New York, 1932.

The influence of the New Comedy has thus been dominant in modern times. A direct influence from Aristophanes began to exert itself again in Europe when the Renaissance ceased to be almost exclusively Latin, and the study of Greek was more freely promoted.

A LIST OF USEFUL BOOKS

(The list includes a number of prose translations; other books listed, as Allen's, contain bibliographies.)

AESCHYLUS.—With an English Translation by Herbert Weir Smyth. 2 vols. New York, G. P. Putnam's Sons, 1922 (Loeb Classical Library)

AESCHYLUS.—*Plays,* translated by Walter Headlam and C. E. S. Headlam. London, George Bell and Sons, 1909 (Bohn's Classical Library)

ALLEN, JAMES TURNEY.—*The Stage Antiquities of the Greeks and Romans and Their Influence.* New York, Longmans, Green and Company, 1927. (*Our Debt to Greece and Rome,* No. 28)

ARISTOPHANES.—With the English Translation of Benjamin Bickley Rogers. 3 vols. New York, G. P. Putnam's Sons, 1924 (Loeb Classical Library)

ARISTOTLE.—*On the Art of Poetry;* a Revised Text, with Critical Introduction, Translation, and Commentary, by Ingram Bywater. Oxford, At The Clarendon Press, 1909

ARISTOTLE.—*On the Art of Poetry;* an Amplified Version . . . for Students of English, by Lane Cooper. Boston, 1913; New York, Harcourt, Brace and Company

BIEBER, MARGARETE.—*Die Denkmäler zum Theaterwesen im Altertum.* Berlin, De Gruyter, 1920 (with 142 illustrations in the text, and 109 tabular illustrations)

COOPER, LANE.—*An Aristotelian Theory of Comedy* (etc.). New York, Harcourt, Brace and Company, 1922

CROISET, ALFRED AND MAURICE.—*An Abridged History of Greek Literature,* translated by George F. Heffelbower. New York, The Macmillan Company, 1904

CROISET, ALFRED AND MAURICE.—*Histoire de la Littérature Grecque.* Vol. 3 by Maurice Croiset. Paris, Fontemoing, 1914

EURIPIDES.—*The Plays* . . . translated into English Prose . . . by Edward P. Coleridge. 2 vols. London, George Bell and Sons, 1891 (Bohn's Classical Library)

FLICKINGER, ROY C.—*The Greek Theater and Its Drama.* Chicago, University of Chicago Press, 1926

HAIGH, A. E.—*The Attic Theatre.* Third edition . . . by A. W. Pickard-Cambridge. Oxford, At The Clarendon Press, 1907

HAIGH, A. E.—*The Tragic Drama of the Greeks.* Oxford, At The Clarendon Press, 1896

KITTO, H. D. F.—*Greek Tragedy;* a Literary Study. London, Methuen and Company, 1939

MENANDER.—*The Principal Fragments,* with an English Translation by Francis G. Allinson. New York, G. P. Putnam's Sons, 1921 (Loeb Classical Library)

NICOLL, ALLARDYCE.—*The Development of the Theatre;* a Study of Theatrical Art from the Beginnings to the Present Day. New York, Harcourt, Brace and Company, 1927 (with 271 illustrations)

PICKARD-CAMBRIDGE, A. W.—*Dithyramb, Tragedy, and Comedy.* Oxford, At The Clarendon Press, 1927

SOPHOCLES.—*The Ichneutae* ('Trackers'), with . . . a Translation into English (etc.) by Richard Johnson Walker. London, Burns and Oates, 1919

SOPHOCLES.—*The Tragedies,* translated into English Prose by Sir Richard C. Jebb. Cambridge, At the University Press, 1904 (The translations are taken from Jebb's edition of Sophocles; this also should be consulted.)